Clement B. Stone
from Uncle Charles
Christmas 1855

I0836591

SELF-MADE MEN.

BY

CHAS. C. B. SEYMOUR.

NEW YORK:
HARPER & BROTHERS, PUBLISHERS,
FRANKLIN SQUARE.
1858.

Entered, according to Act of Congress, in the year one thousand eight hundred and fifty-eight, by

HARPER & BROTHERS,

In the Clerk's Office of the District Court for the Southern District of New York.

PREFACE.

In this volume will be found the lives of more than sixty distinguished persons who have attained eminence in spite of adverse circumstances of birth and fortune. They are presented in the usual biographical form, and with as much fullness as the object in view and the space at command would permit.

It has not been deemed necessary to append to each sketch a little sermon to point out its moral tendencies. The real moral of a man's life is found in his actions. These have been related faithfully, and they will, it is believed, convey their lesson without any laborious essay on the part of the writer.

For the omissions that occur, the writer has only to say that the extent and variety of material which every where rewarded his search rendered the task of selection an embarrassing one. The sixty biographies that are given have their value, and those that are omitted have theirs also. A book, unfortunately, will but contain a certain quantity, and that quantity is here supplied.

New York, March, 1858.

CONTENTS.

SELF-MADE MEN.

ANDREW JACKSON.

Andrew Jackson was descended from a Scotch family which emigrated to the North of Ireland at a very early period. The troubled state of that country induced Andrew's father to seek a new home in the land of promise, America. In 1765 he arrived at the port of Charleston, South Carolina, bringing with him a wife and two sons, Hugh and Robert. He settled on a tract of land then called "Waxhaw Settlement," near the boundary-line of North Carolina. Here, two years subsequently, the subject of this memoir was born (15th March, 1767).

Soon after the birth of Andrew, his father died, leaving him and his two brothers to the sole care and guardianship of Mrs. Jackson, an excellent woman, famed for her heroic resolution, and admirable qualities of head and heart. In early life she had witnessed the tyranny of British rule in Ireland, and the still more tyrannous exactions of the Irish nobility. These reminiscences she recounted to her sons, and their influence was observable in after-life in a sturdy opposition to tyranny and exaction.

The education which the lads received was necessarily of a limited character. The two eldest were simply taught the rudiments of the English language, but Andrew, being intended for the ministry, enjoyed some additional advantages. He was sent to a flourishing academy at the Waxhaw Meeting-house, where he studied the classics and the higher branches of a superior education, until the Revolutionary War had extended itself to the immediate vicinity. South Carolina was invaded by the British in 1779, and in the following year it became necessary for the neighborhood in which Jackson resided to declare itself for or against the enemy. The struggles of the patriot army during five long years of trial were perfectly familiar to Andrew and his little home circle, and the spirit of resistance was strong within them. On the 29th of May, 1780, an engagement took place at Waxhaw Settlement between the British and American forces, in which the latter were defeated, suffering a loss in killed and wounded of nearly three hundred men.

It became necessary to retire before the invading army into North Carolina. Mrs. Jackson, with her two remaining sons (she had lost one at the battle of Stono, from the excessive heat of the weather), abandoned the homestead for a short time, but returned in time to allow the boys to take part in the battle of Hanging Rock (6th of August, 1780), where the corps to which they were attached greatly distinguished itself. They were again compelled to retire to North Carolina, but returned in a few months, when it was known that Lord Cornwallis had crossed the Yadkin.

It was during the trying scenes of this period that Andrew Jackson gave the first illustration of that quickness of thought and instant decision which afterward placed him in the front rank of military commanders. A captain of the American forces named Sands, who had been absent from home for some time, desired to spend a night with his family. Robert and Andrew Jackson, with seven others, consented to act as his body-guard. They numbered seven muskets, and, when night came on, lay down to sleep with their weapons handy in case of need. The precaution was well taken. During the night the Tories made their appearance. The moment the alarm was given, Andrew ran out of the house, and, putting his gun through the fork of an apple-tree, hailed the advancing column. No answer was given, and Jackson fired. A volley was the return, which killed Andrew's companion. It now became apparent that the Tories had divided their party into two sections, so as to attack the building at either end. Young Andrew returned to the house, and, with two others, commenced a fire from the door. In the mean time the enemy's second division came up, and, mistaking the firing in front, actually commenced fighting with its own men. They kept up the fire upon each other, as well as upon the house, until, startled by the sound of a cavalry bugle in the distance, they beat a hasty retreat. The charge sounded on the bugle was nothing but an ingenious *ruse* of a Major Isbel. He had not a single man with him; but, knowing that stratagem often accomplishes more than actual force, he blew the blast, and trusted to fortune. But for the decision of Jackson in firing the first shot, every man of the little party would have been captured.

The patriots were not so fortunate at a subsequent rencounter which took place at Waxhaw Meeting-house. It was with the greatest difficulty that a portion of their number, including Andrew and his brother, obtained safety by flight. The two brothers remained together until the following morning. Pressed by hunger, they ventured from the woods, and fell into the hands of the enemy before they were well aware of their presence. To escape was impossible, and both were made prisoners. Being placed under guard, Andrew was ordered in a very imperious tone by a British officer to clean his boots, which had become muddied. This order he positively and peremptorily refused to obey, alleging that he was entitled to the treatment of a prisoner of war, and not that of a menial. Incensed at this refusal, the British officer aimed a blow at his head with a drawn sword. Throwing up his arm, he sheltered himself from what would have probably proved a fatal wound, but in doing so was badly cut. The mark of this cowardly assault Andrew Jackson bore with him to the grave. Turning to Robert Jackson, the British bully repeated his order, and received a reply similar to that made by Andrew. Additionally furious at being foiled twice, he struck Robert on the head, and inflicted an injury from which the poor young fellow never recovered. The prisoners were then taken to jail, and confined in separate cells. They were treated with great harshness until after the battle of Camden, when, owing to an exchange of prisoners (brought about in a great measure by the exertions of Mrs. Jackson), they were set at liberty. Robert died a few days after his release from the effects of his wound. Bowed down by affliction and an overwrought mind, Mrs. Jackson was taken sick, and in a few days lay beside the two sons she had already consecrated to the cause of liberty.

Notwithstanding the hopeful buoyancy of youth, it was sometime before Andrew recovered from the severe shock of these calamities. He sought forgetfulness in the easy pleasures of the neighboring town, mixed with the gay and frivolous, and for a time seemed to imbibe their tastes and fancies with satisfaction. He accompanied some of his new-found companions to Charleston, and soon dissipated the small patrimony which was his all. He found himself at last with nothing left but a fine horse. Even this he staked against a sum of money in a game called "rattle and snap." Jackson won the game, recovered possession of his horse and his senses, bade adieu to a life of foolish dissipation, and returned home.

It was now his determination to become a lawyer (1784), and, devoting himself with assiduity to this object, he obtained a license to practice in the winter of 1786. He continued in the State of North Carolina until the spring of 1788, following his profession, with only moderate patronage. He was now twenty-one, and eager to find a field for the liberal exercise of his talents. The western district of the state was spoken of as presenting flattering prospects to adventurers, and, at the solicitation of Judge M'Nairy, who was going out to hold the first Supreme Court that had ever sat in that section of the country, Andrew Jackson determined to accompany him. In the month of October, 1789, they reached Nashville, Jackson bearing with him an appointment from the governor to act as solicitor for the western district of the state, embracing the present State of Tennessee.

The condition in which he found things at Nashville was extraordinary, and in the highest degree promising to a young lawyer. Most of the young men of the place were in debt to the merchants, who were unable to help themselves for the simple reason that there was but one lawyer in the country, and he had been judiciously retained by the scapegraces. The merchants were consequently unable to recover their debts, or to bring actions for the purpose of doing so. The arrival of Jackson was most opportune. He commenced business the following morning by issuing no fewer than seventy writs. The consternation which this decided action threw into the camp of the enemy was prodigious. The first feeling was one of common safety. Jackson must be got rid of. He must be bullied or browbeaten out the town. The experiment was made, but it was a miserable failure. The youngsters found that they had a man of iron to deal with, and that it would be better for their own safety to leave him alone; and they did so. They learned this lesson from two incidents which occurred. A flax-breaker of considerable strength and courage set upon Jackson without any pretense of provocation. Jackson reduced him to submission with his own winding blades. His next encounter was at a court in Sumner County. While he was conversing with a gentleman a noted bully approached, and, without saying a word, placed his heels on Jackson's feet. Pushing him off, Jackson seized a slab which happened to be handy, and, with a forward thrust upon the breast, brought him to the ground. The interference of the crowd put an end to the conflict; but the baffled bully, snatching a stake from the fence, again approached with dreadful imprecations. At the earnest entreaty of Jackson, the crowd retired from between them. Poising his slab, he then advanced, with a firm step and steady eye, upon his antagonist, who dropped his stake at his approach, scaled the fence, and ran into the woods.

During his sojourn at Nashville he became acquainted with and married Mrs. Robards. The circumstances of this marriage were extremely curious. Jackson boarded in the same house with Mr. and Mrs. Robards, a couple that lived unhappily together, and had only recently been reconciled. Mr. Robards became jealous of Jackson, and went away to Virginia, where he quietly obtained a divorce. Unconscious of this fact, Mrs. Robards followed, in company with Colonel Stark and Jackson, the latter acting as pilot through the Indian country. On arriving at Natchez they learned what steps had been taken. Jackson was naturally indignant, and immediately went to expostulate with the blind and jealous husband. No good came of it. The divorce was granted, and Mrs. Robards was a free woman. Acting on the quick impulses of a generous mind, Jackson hastened to offer his hand and his heart to the innocent and amiable woman who had been sacrificed without a shadow of pretext. It was a manly step, and showed to the world that he, at least, thought her innocent. From reasons of discretion as well as of delicacy, the offer was at first declined, but after the lapse of a few months the wedding took place. Jackson soon became devotedly attached to his wife, and after her decease cherished her memory with an almost holy reverence.

On the formation of the State Government of Tennessee in 1796, Andrew Jackson was appointed one of the members of the Convention to frame a State Constitution. The same year he was elected to represent Tennessee in the House of Representatives in Congress. The following year he was chosen senator in Congress, and took his seat on the 22d of November, 1797. Business at home compelled him to resign his seat before the next session. On returning to Tennessee, he was surprised to find that the Legislature had quite unexpectedly conferred on him the appointment of Judge of the Supreme Court. He entered on the duties of this office with some reluctance, but the firmness, justice, and courage he displayed were soon the themes of general admiration. These characteristics, however, were not always acceptable, especially to those who had held the law in their own hands. Jackson had plenty of enemies of this sort.

On the admission of Tennessee into the Union it comprised one military division. The death of Major General Conway, which occurred about this time, created a vacancy in the office, which was filled by the election of Jackson. In 1804 he resigned the judgeship, and confined his attention exclusively to his own affairs and this commission. Accordingly, he purchased an excellent farm ten miles from Nashville, on the Columbia River, where for several years he devoted himself to agricultural pursuits and the agreeable duties of a social and hospitable home.

In this comparative retirement General Jackson remained, with few exceptions, until the declaration of war with Great Britain in June, 1812. Without seeking a command in the regular army, he issued a special address to the citizens of his division, calling upon them to unite with him in protecting the rights and the honor of the republic. Twenty-five hundred volunteers flocked to his banner in a few days, ready to follow him in any direction and on any expedition against the enemy. In November, 1812, he placed himself at their head, and in the following month found a rendezvous at Nashville. The general's ardor inspired the men with the greatest devotion; and their cheerful spirits were proof against privation and hardship. At the opening of the new year (1813) Jackson and his companions descended to Natchez, where they were to remain until they received further orders. He selected the most healthful spot he could find for his encampment, and devoted all his attention to the training of his volunteers, many of whom were, of course, quite green. The speck of war, however, disappeared for a time, and an order was received from the Secretary of War directing the disbanding of the volunteers and the delivering up of the property of the corps to General Wilkinson. When this order reached the camp there were one hundred and fifty on the sick-list, fifty-six of whom were completely prostrated, and the remainder so feeble and destitute that they were entirely unable to reach their homes, or defray the expenses of the journey, even if it could be undertaken. If the order had been complied with, numbers would have perished, and others of necessity been compelled to enter the regular army under General Wilkinson.

Jackson felt himself compromised by this order. His men were volunteers, not recruits. They had left their homes for the sake of their country, and it was but fair that when the danger which had brought them out was at an end, the nation should enable them to return to their homes to enjoy the peaceful result. At present, it looked very much like a trick to fill the ranks of the regular army. Under these convictions, Jackson determined to disobey the orders of the secretary.

The officers seemed to be satisfied with his determination, but were, in reality, alarmed at its consequences. After holding a secret meeting among themselves, they presented a recommendation to the general to adhere to the secretary's instructions. Disgusted at their pusillanimity, the general replied that it was the men he thought of, and not the officers, who had means at their disposal, and could go whither they pleased. He concluded by telling them that, as his resolution was not hastily formed, so it would not be easily changed. During these negotiations the officers of General Wilkinson arrived in the camp, with the object of recruiting from the volunteer army. So soon as Jackson was apprised of this, he gave orders that any officer found recruiting from among his troops, that were already in the service of the United States, should be arrested and confined. All sorts of mean stratagems were now resorted to to frustrate Jackson's purpose, but his iron will and indomitable energy overcame every obstacle, and he had the satisfaction of marching the whole of his division to the section of country whence they had been drawn. He then dismissed them, and awaited the consequences of his bold action. It is almost unnecessary to add that when the matter was presented in its proper light to the President, he entirely approved the course adopted by the general.

The repose of General Jackson and his volunteers was of short duration. They had scarcely reached their homes when the Indian nations scattered over the territory comprising the States of Alabama and Mississippi made incursions into Tennessee and Kentucky, and committed the most savage murders and cruelties. The Creek Indians, residing in the vicinity of the Coosa and Tallapoosa Rivers, were the most implacable and hostile. On the 30th of August, 1813, these dusky rascals made a successful attack on Fort Mimms. A most dreadful slaughter took place. Mercy was shown to none. Men, women, and children fell beneath the fatal tomahawk and scalping-knife. The fort was occupied by Major Beasley, with a force of one hundred and fifty men, and a large number of women and children who had sought shelter and protection. Of this number seventeen only made their escape; the rest were mercilessly massacred.

The atrocity of this outrage was in some respects advantageous. It roused the people, and gave them a timely insight into the danger which lay at their very doors. It nerved them for one great retaliatory effort, and paved the way for a subsequent peace. The war was entered into with enthusiasm. It was prosecuted in the face of great difficulties, hardships, and reverses, but it was triumphant. The qualities displayed by General Jackson in this hazardous, energetic, and remarkable campaign proved beyond doubt that he possessed military gifts of the highest order, and in a well-balanced combination rarely found save in the greatest heroes of the world. The difficulties he had to encounter were of the most disheartening kind; discontents were everlastingly rising up in his army; the Governor of Tennessee recommended him to abandon his enterprise; a general deserted him with his entire brigade; opposition after opposition he encountered from different officers, yet he proceeded to assault the bloodthirsty enemy in spite of every impediment. In this campaign he had to imprison officers, to hang a militia soldier, and to do other things which, from their daring, almost require credulity unbounded to believe to be true. Finally, however, he succeeded, subdued the savage tribes, and scattered them before him like chaff in the wind. They were glad to sue for peace, and to enter into a treaty securing it to them. The warriors returned to their homes in the early part of 1814.

In the spring of the same year Jackson received the appointment of major general in the service of the United States. The protection of the coast near the mouth of the Mississippi was intrusted to him. In pursuing the duties of this appointment, General Jackson became convinced that the Indians received assistance from the Spanish authorities at Pensacola, and from the British. He was persuaded, also, that it was the intention of the latter to make a descent on New Orleans so soon as they had perfected their arrangements at Pensacola. The general endeavored to treat with the Spanish authorities, and to point out to them the impropriety of the course they were pursuing; but the Spanish authorities prevaricated, falsified, and even flatly denied the truth of what was charged against them. Jackson dispatched Captain Gordon to see what was passing in the month of August (1814), and ascertained that from fifty to two hundred British officers and soldiers were in the garrison, with a park of artillery, and about five hundred savages under drill. A proclamation dated from "Head-quarters at Pensacola," and signed by Colonel Nicholls, of the British expedition, placed the matter beyond doubt.

General Jackson was never remarkable for being caught asleep, and he was determined not to be somnolent on this occasion. He resolved at once to march against Pensacola, and break up that rendezvous. On the 6th of November, 1814, he carried out this intention, demolished the Spanish defenses and protections, and drove out what remained of the English, Spaniards, and savages. He then made the best of his way to New Orleans, whither the English expedition had already departed. His repulse of the British on that occasion is one of the most brilliant achievements recorded in American history, and is familiar to every schoolboy. It is unnecessary to repeat a story so perfectly well known. General Jackson covered himself and his country with imperishable fame.

Peace having been declared at Ghent, the remainder of the British forces sailed away, after making a stay of about ten days in Jackson's vicinity.

Though honored and respected by the greater part of the citizens of New Orleans, General Jackson was not without his opponents, who saw in some of his actions the worst features of despotism. The decision which he was so fond of exercising, and which was perhaps necessary to a certain extent, was undoubtedly calculated, in its exaggerated form, to produce the worst apprehensions in the minds of the timid and moderate. The general's enemies made the most of this circumstance. Before the departure of the British, an anonymous article appeared in one of the newspapers, commenting on the state of things. Jackson forced the editor of the paper to divulge the name of the writer, who turned out to be a member of the State Legislature. He was flung into prison. Application was made to one of the judges for a writ of *habeas corpus*, which was immediately granted and issued. Jackson then imprisoned the judge for issuing the writ, and the lawyer for drawing it out. These proceedings were undoubtedly despotic and tyrannous, but we must remember that at the time they occurred the city was under the edict of martial law. When military rule was at an end, Jackson had to answer for his interference with the civil courts. He did not attempt to defend himself, but paid the penalty imposed (a fine of one thousand dollars), with the consciousness that he had done his duty thoroughly, if a little sternly.

In the month of March General Jackson returned once more to his home in Tennessee, carrying with him a larger amount of popularity than had ever been borne by any man except Washington. For two years he remained on his farm, prepared for service, if need be, but occupied with rural pleasures and labors. In 1817 fresh difficulties were experienced from the Indians, and General Jackson received orders to repair to Fort Scott, and take the command of the forces in that quarter, with authority, in case he should deem it necessary, to call upon the executives of the adjoining states for additional troops. They also authorized him to cross the Florida line, if necessary to the execution of his orders. Florida was then a Spanish possession. The power vested in Jackson shows the confidence in which he was held by the government.

The campaign against the Seminoles was prosecuted with great vigor, and without any special delicacy concerning Spanish rights, or squeamishness about hanging and shooting British prisoners. It was brought to a successful termination, but did not contribute to the general's permanent fame.

In June, 1818, Jackson was once more at the Hermitage, but, as his conduct in the Seminole war was arraigned by the House of Representatives and by the press, he determined on visiting Washington for the purpose of defending himself. He made a kind of triumphal journey, receiving honors in every city through which he passed. No man could be more popular with the masses than the gallant defender of New Orleans. If he had been a little harsh, and a trifle unmindful of the law of nations, people were disposed to be lenient with a man whose integrity and sincere patriotism were beyond the breath of suspicion. It is almost unnecessary to add that he succeeded in clearing himself before the country.

When the Floridas were ceded by Spain to America, the President appointed General Jackson to act in the first place as commissioner for receiving the provinces, and then to assume the government of them. It was intended and expressed that the American governor should exercise all the functions belonging to the Spanish governors, captain-general, and intendants, until Congress should provide a deliberate system of administration, as in the instances of the other territories.

On the 1st of July, 1821, General Jackson entered upon his delicate office, and at once published a declaration announcing that the authority of the United States thereafter existed in the Territory. He had some difficulties to encounter with the Spanish governors, who did not cheerfully surrender the records and state papers in their possession. Jackson had to resort to arbitrary measures, and did so with success, but not without again provoking bitter complaints at Washington.

On the 7th of October Jackson delegated his power to two gentlemen, his secretaries, and returned to Nashville. The condition of his health was one of the reasons which induced him to take this step. On the 4th of July, 1822, the Governor of Tennessee, acting for the Legislature, presented him with a sword, as a testimonial "of the high respect" entertained by the state for his public services; and on the 20th of August of the same year, the members of the General Assembly of Tennessee recommended him to the Union for the office of President, a recommendation which was repeated by the Legislature of Alabama, and various assemblages of private citizens in other parts of the country. In the autumn of 1823 he was elected to the Senate of the United States, and in the following year was put in regular nomination for the presidency. The election had to be decided by the House of Representatives, and Adams, who stood next to Jackson in popularity at the polls, was declared to be President.

After the expiration of four years Jackson was once more entered for the grand presidential race. He distanced his rival, and was elected President (1828), and re-elected (1832), thus serving his country in the highest office within her gift for a term of eight years. The same decision which characterized his military career gave strength and vigor to his presidency. It exposed him, however, to the severest red-tape criticism, and it is not yet conceded that some of the individual actions of President Jackson were those which can be safely handed down as wholesome precedents for the future administration of the country.

On retiring from the presidency in 1836, General Jackson returned to his home in Tennessee, where he remained in honorable retirement for the residue of his life, largely respected by all classes of men, and looked up to by a great party as the oracle of its destinies. He died on the 8th of June, 1845. The heart of the nation was profoundly moved by the calamity, and some of her most eminent sons pronounced eulogiums on the departed warrior. From one of these—the splendid effort of Daniel Webster—we reproduce the following estimate of the general's character:

"The character of General Jackson while he lived was presented in two relations to his country. He was a soldier, and had commanded the armies of the republic, and he has filled the office of chief magistrate. So far as regards his military reputation and merits, I partake fully in the general estimate. He was a soldier of dauntless courage, vigor, and perseverance, an officer of skill and sagacity, of quickness of perception, and of prompt and resolute execution of his purposes. There is probably no division, at home or abroad, as to his merits in these particulars.

"During the whole of his civil administration it happened that I was a member of the Senate of the United States, and it was my misfortune to be obliged to differ with him in regard to most of his leading measures. To me this was painful, because it much better suits my temper and feelings tó be able to support the measures of government than to find myself called upon by duty to oppose them.

"There were occasions, however, in the course of his administration, in which no duty of opposition devolved upon me. Some of these were not unimportant. There were times which appeared to me to be critical, calling for wisdom and energy on the part of the government, and in which measures proposed and opinions expressed by him seemed to me to be highly suitable to the exigency. On these occasions I supported those measures with the same sincerity and zeal as if I had never differed from him before, or never expected to differ from him again.

"There is no doubt that he sought to distinguish himself by exalting the character and honor of his country, and the occasion on which it was uttered rendered somewhat remarkable his celebrated sentiment in favor of the preservation of the Union. I believe he felt the sentiment with the utmost sincerity, and this can not be denied to be one strong proof of his devotion to the true interests of his country.

"He has now ceased from his earthly labors, and affects the public interests of the state only by his example and the influence of his opinions. We may well suppose that in the last days, and hours, and moments of his life, and with the full consciousness of the change then before him and so near, one of his warmest wishes would be, that whatever errors he might have committed should be passing and transitory in their effect upon the Constitution and institutions of his country; and while we may well ascribe this praiseworthy and benign sentiment to him, let us, with equal ingenuousness, cherish the feeling, that whatever he has accomplished for the real good of the country, its true character and real glory, may remain a just inheritance attached to his memory."

"In person," says one of his biographers, "General Jackson was tall, and remarkably erect and thin. His weight bore no proportion to his height, and his frame in general did not appear fitted for trials such as it had borne. His features were large; his eyes dark blue, with a keen and strong glance; his eyebrows arched and prominent, and his complexion that of the war-worn soldier. His demeanor was easy and gentle: in every station he was open and accessible to all. The irritability of his temper, which was not denied by his friends, produced contrasts in his manner and countenance leading to very different conceptions and representations as to both; but those who have lived and acted with him bear unanimous testimony to the general mildness of his carriage and the kindness of his disposition. It is certain that he inspired his soldiers, his military household, his domestic circle, and his neighbors with the most affectionate sentiments. The impetuosity of his nature, his impatience of wrong and encroachment, his contempt for meanness, and his tenaciousness of just authority, involved him in bitter altercations and sanguinary duels: his resentments were fiercely executed, and his censures rashly uttered; yet he can not be accused of wanton or malicious violence; the sallies which may be deemed intemperate can be traced to strong provocation, operating, in most instances, upon his patriotic zeal, and the very generosity and loftiness of his spirit."

JACOB LEISLER.

THE downfall of Popery in England, occasioned by the flight of King James and the accession of William of Orange, produced a revolution and a hero in New York both of a remarkable nature. It is a fragment of history belonging exclusively to the times, and having no kind of bearing on subsequent events, except that its lesson has been too soon forgot. But it ended in bloodshed, and in the martyrdom of a man whose name will be imperishably recorded in the annals of the country.

When the news of the change of dynasty in England reached New York, it was greeted with approbation by the majority of the inhabitants. Papists who held offices were at once suspended. By this action, and by the common cause of misfortune, they became banded together, and formed a formidable party, all the more dangerous from the fact that the administration under the new government had not yet made its appearance. Fearful rumors were circulated that the Jacobites (as they were called) intended to take summary vengeance on the triumphant Protestants; that they were marching in great force to destroy the city, and generally that they were going to avenge the cause of their fallen master in a savage manner, and regain the authority which had been hastily wrested from them.

In a community not abundantly protected, these rumors and apprehensions were very fearful. The desire for safety suggested to the citizens the propriety of delegating the entire authority of the city to one man, until such time as the new governor appointed by WILLIAM should arrive. The choice fell upon Jacob Leisler, the subject of the present brief sketch.

Of Leisler's early history very little is known. He came before the public at a time when the hard work of his life—the building of a fortune—had been nearly accomplished. Previous to this he had resided in Albany, probably engaged in the fur trade, and where also he discharged the duties of a magistrate. He was known for his opposition to Popery, and for the exercise of all his power to prevent its spread. From Albany he came to

New York, and at once obtained popularity by benevolently purchasing the freedom of a family of French Huguenots, who were so poverty-stricken on landing that a public tribunal decided they should be sold into slavery in order to pay the expenses of their voyage. By these and similar acts Leisler became known, and favorably known, to the little community.

At that time there were five military companies in the city, and a sergeant's guard of royal troops. These were the only organized protectors of the town, and were under the command of Nicholas Bayard, a man who was believed to be favorable to the cause of the late king. Jacob Leisler was captain of one of the companies, and was eminently popular with the men and with his brother officers, excepting, of course, the colonel.

On the 2d of June, 1689, the people of New York, supported by the military companies aforesaid, proceeded to the residence of Leisler, and invited him to place himself at their head. At first he refused, but finally consented. Immediately afterward the keys of the fort were placed in his hands. Alarmed at these proceedings, Lieutenant Governor Nicholson convened his council, and, calling upon all public magistrates to unite with him, he demanded the government money, which, being kept in the fort, was now in possession of Leisler. No attention was of course paid to the demand. The colonel of the military companies also tried what effect his influence would have, but found out in a very short time that the most prudent thing he could do was to look after his own safety. On Leisler's side, four hundred of his companions in arms signed an agreement to hold the fort "for the present Protestant power that reigns in England," while a committee of safety, composed of ten freeholders of the city, whose names, as they have come down to us, represent in equal ratio the Dutch, the French, and the English population of that early period, assumed the powers of a provisionary government, of which they declared Jacob Leisler to be the head. They appointed him "captain of the fort or citadel," gave him power "to suppress external and internal enemies of the peace, and preserve the order of the Province of New York," to "use the power of authority of commander-in-chief until orders shall have come from their majesties," and to "do all such acts as were requisite for the good of the province, taking council with the militia and civil authority as occasion might require."

Leisler's first act was one of loyalty. He proclaimed King William by sound of trumpet to the rejoicing people. This step provoked immediate action from the other side. The deposed Jacobins appointed three commissioners to receive the revenues until orders should arrive from the king. Leisler proceeded to the Custom-house, where the commissioners held their meetings, and demanded by what right they pretended to act. The only reply they condescended to make was an attempt to forcibly eject Leisler from their presence. Nothing could have been more ill advised. The adherents of the popular cause were naturally incensed at the treatment of their captain. The preparatory demonstrations of a riot began to show themselves. Captain Bayard was set upon, and would have been the first victim of vengeance but for the intercession of Leisler. It became apparent that it would not do to trifle with the people, so Bayard fled to Albany, rather the worse for handling, and Nicholson, the lieutenant governor, obtained safety on shipboard, and, as soon as possible, sailed for England.

When quiet was restored, Leisler made active preparations for the defense of the city, not only against the Papists, but against the French. He established a six-gunned battery commanding the harbor, and thereby secured for the city one of the most pleasant promenades it can boast (the Battery). Having thus attended to the most important duties of his station, he sat down and honestly wrote an account of what he had done to the King of England. He was not much of a scholar, and there were some defects in the style and spelling of his dispatch, but it was straightforward and manly, and told the truth—qualities that are not too often combined in official documents.

To provide against an invasion of French and Indians from Canada, Leisler dispatched his secretary, Colonel Milbourne (who had recently arrived from England), to Albany, with a body of followers. They took their departure in three ships, and arrived in due course. At this time most of the officials at Albany held their commissions from the deposed monarch, and were consequently violently opposed to the administration of Leisler, whom they denounced as a *boor*, and looked upon as a usurper. The most active among these was Robert Livingston, and by his instigation the citizens of Albany were made to believe that Milbourne and the troops under his command came to invade their rights, and not to protect them. Bloodshed would have resulted but for the discretion and cool bravery of Milbourne.

When these things were made known to Leisler, he immediately issued a warrant against Livingston as a rebel, and against Colonel Bayard, who had also contributed his influence to excite the Albanians. Livingston fled to New England, and was not heard of afterward, except in a very tragical way, which will be related hereafter. Bayard sneaked into New York, and tried to obtain possession, in a surreptitious way, of a dispatch from the king. He was denounced to Leisler by the bearer of the dispatch in question; was forthwith arrested and put in jail "upon the charge of high misdemeanors against his majesty's authority."

These events gave a decided character to the administration of Jacob Leisler, and his opponents saw that nothing but an extensive and unscrupulous organization could overthrow its power. Parties were now distinctly defined: for the people's governor—for the Jacobites.

In midwinter the threatened attack of the French took place. On the 9th of February, 1690, after a remarkable march, about two hundred French and Indians made a sudden descent upon Schenectady, and massacred sixty-three men, women, and children, besides making twenty-seven prisoners and destroying the village. The atrocity and boldness of this crime threw the province into a state of the most intense agony. For their own safety, the Albanians were now ready to co-operate with the executive of New York. Leisler concluded, and wisely, that the success of this attack would lead to others of a more horrible character, and that the only remedy was to carry the war into the enemy's own country, and conquer Canada itself. He at once addressed letters to the governors of the other provinces, and Jersey, Maryland, and Connecticut favored the enterprise. Thus encouraged, he straightway armed and equipped the first man-of-war ever fitted out in the harbor of New-York; and in a short time a fleet of three vessels sailed from the bay, with orders to proceed immediately to Quebec, and co-operate with the land forces that would join them there from the other provinces. This decision and activity met with a poor return. A number of disasters befell the expedition, and no good was done at all. There is no reason to doubt that Leisler's enemies threw all the impediments they could in his way, and were perhaps more pleased with the failure of the expedition than they would have been with its success. Certain it is that the land forces (upon whom every thing depended) under General Winthrop made an ignominious retreat, without having even reached the shores of Lake Champlain.

When the news became known to Leisler, he hurried in person to Albany, and ordered the general to be placed under arrest—a very proper measure, but extremely hazardous for one whose power was not yet consolidated. The Jacobites attributed the failure of the expedition to Leisler, and this decided action was a good opportunity for raising the cry of tyranny. All the malcontents united themselves to oppose the power of the governor and to effect his overthrow. The people, who had exhausted themselves in equipping the unsuccessful expedition, were impatient and dissatisfied. It was not difficult to persuade the thoughtless and unreasonable masses. The Jacobites had their opportunity, and made the best use of it.

In England a new governor had been appointed by William as early as 1689, but, until two years later, Leisler knew nothing of the circumstance. The first notice of Governor Sloughter's appointment was brought to this country by Captain Ingoldsby, who, with his company, arrived in advance. This weak creature fell into the hands of the anti-Leislerians, and was immediately used by them. With an impudence that was remarkable even for a captain of foot, he demanded that Leisler should immediately surrender his authority into his hands. Leisler replied that he would do so the moment he saw an order from the British ministry requiring him to do so, or from Colonel Sloughter, the newly-appointed governor. Ingoldsby being destitute of the authority that Leisler required, the latter simply issued a proclamation announcing that Colonel Sloughter had been appointed governor of the Province of New York, and that on his arrival the fort and government would be cheerfully surrendered to him. In the mean time he desired that Ingoldsby and his companions might receive all proper entertainment and kindness.

This discreet policy did not satisfy the enemies of Leisler. The willing tool, Ingoldsby, was once more used to make another demand for the surrender of the fort, and, being again unsuccessful, to end by besieging it. Leisler was not to be intimidated, and retained possession, protesting most vehemently against the conduct of Ingoldsby. He had the mayor and common council on his side, but against him were wealth, fanaticism, and unscrupulousness. The royal authority, too, was held in dread, and people were afraid of opposing it even in a right cause. Desertions became frequent from the popular ranks. Every day Ingoldsby's position became stronger. He saw his advantage, and freely used the terrible word *rebel* against Leisler and those who sided with him.

The noble little band were not to be daunted by words. They simply replied that they would not be turned from their duty to God and the king by fear of the term rebels, and resolved that they would protect their liberty at the hazard of their lives. Ingoldsby and his backers were somewhat daunted by this courageous action; but, while they were deliberating as to what should be the next step, the long absent Sloughter made his appearance (19th of March, 1691). Before he had touched land, Ingoldsby, as the mouthpiece of the Jacobin party, had poisoned his ear with an *ex parte* statement.

Leisler's first act was to satisfy himself as to the identity of Sloughter. He then dispatched his son-in-law, Col. Milbourne, and Mr. De la Noye, the mayor, to consult with him as to the proper form of making a transfer of the government, and also to procure some guarantee for the safety of himself and his friends. These peaceful embassadors were immediately handed over to the guard. Thus brutally outraged, Leisler determined that he would not surrender the fort until the governor and his full council had taken the customary oath of allegiance to the Protestant king and government. This ceremony was gone through on the day following, and Leisler immediately handed over his authority to the new official. He felt that he had protected the province in a critical period; that he had acted firmly and conscientiously for the common good. It was with a sense of relief, therefore, that he wrote to Sloughter "that he would give his excellency an exact account of all his actions and conduct."

The ink with which he wrote was scarcely dry when he and nine of his friends were dragged off to prison as common rebels. A special commission of Oyer and Terminer was issued to try the prisoners, and the governor named eight judges for the purpose. The task of making a selection was an easy one. He selected four of his own friends and four others who were known enemies of Leisler. When the trial came on, Leisler refused to acknowledge the authority of the court, but it was of no avail. An iniquitous verdict was returned, and Leisler and Milbourne were condemned to death.

By this time Sloughter seems to have awakened to a slight sense of justice, as clear, perhaps, as his fuddled faculties would allow him to see it. He hesitated to sign the death-warrant. This did not satisfy the bloodhounds who were seeking Leisler's life. Unfortunately, they were acquainted with Sloughter's weaknesses. They invited him to a supper, plied him with wine, and in the midst of the orgy the drunken idiot scrawled his name to the fatal document. Without a moment's delay it was conveyed to the sheriff, and the two unfortunate men were led forth to execution.

The scaffold stood at the lower end of what is now called the Park. A company of soldiers under the command of Ingoldsby surrounded it, and kept off the populace, already pressing forward to obtain a last look of a noble martyr and his brave companion; some, perhaps, to triumph over their downfall. They stood together, unawed by the occasion. Milbourne spoke first. He had but little to say, but it was awful: "Robert Livingston, I will implead thee at the bar of heaven for this deed!" Leisler, touched by the untimely fate of his son-in-law, turned to him and said, "Why must you die? You have been but as a servant doing my will, and, as a dying man, I declare before God that what I have done was for King William and Queen Mary, the defense of the Protestant religion, and the good of the country." Commending his soul to the Savior, and praying for his enemies, "Father, forgive them; they know not what they do," this strong man, upright and noble to the last, suffered the final penalty of the law, if the word law can be used in such a base connection. A fierce tempest raged in the heavens, as if Nature were indignant at the outrage. "The shrieks of the people," says a writer of the time, "were dreadful; some were carried away lifeless, and some, rushing forward, almost ere the life of their beloved ruler was extinct, cut off pieces of his garments as precious relics, and his hair was divided, out of great veneration, as for a martyr."

These measures were subsequently disapproved by the English king, and the attainders against the murdered heroes reversed; but the shame of the transaction will last to the end of history. Well might Dr. Increase Mather write to Governor Dudley, "I am afraid that the guilt of innocent blood is still crying in the ears of the Lord against you: I mean the blood of Leisler and Milbourne. My Lord Bellamont said to me that he was one of the committee of Parliament who examined the matter, and that those men were not only murdered, but barbarously murdered."

DANIEL WEBSTER.

This renowned statesman and eloquently intellectual man was born at Salisbury, Merrimac County, New Hampshire, on the 18th of January, 1782. In the immediate vicinity his ancestors (who were of Scotch descent) had lived from the earliest times. The house in which he was born was the centre of a tract of one hundred and sixty acres of land, on the produce of which the family depended. His father was a man of large and stalwart form, of swarthy complexion, and of remarkable features; of clear intellect, strong convictions, and indomitable will. Many of these traits, especially the last, survived in his illustrious son.

From his mother Daniel Webster received the first rudiments of an education. Mrs. Webster is described as an unusually beautiful woman, of superior intellect and of the warmest affections. She prophesied that her son would become eminent, and lived to see a portion of the prophecy fulfilled. He was a member of Congress when she died.

About half a mile from the farm was a log school-house kept by Master Tappan. To this primitive academy the little Daniel repaired when he could be spared from home. "He was the brightest boy in the school," wrote the master many years afterward, "and Ezekiel next; but Daniel was much quicker at his studies than his brother. He would learn more in five minutes than another boy in five hours. One Saturday, I remember, I held up a handsome new jack-knife to the scholars, and said, the boy who would commit to memory the greatest number of verses in the Bible by Monday morning should have it. Many of the boys did well; but when it came to Daniel's turn to recite, I found that he had committed so much, that, after hearing him repeat some sixty or seventy verses, I was obliged to give up, he telling me that there were several chapters yet that he had learned. Daniel got that jack-knife." Mr. Webster never forgot his early tutor, and only a few months before his death wrote him a kind note inclosing a remittance. In the busy time of the year Daniel Webster assisted his father. He was a "handy" lad, and could learn how to do a thing with much quickness. He was particularly useful in assisting his father to saw logs at a little mill which he worked. Here, while waiting for the saw to pass through the logs (an operation which consumed about ten minutes), he economized his time by carefully studying some author whose prized volume he had brought with him. So tenacious was his memory, that, in the last year of his life, he was able to recite large portions of the works he had committed in this strange manner. It was at this period of his life that he first became acquainted with the Constitution of the United States, the first copy of which he perused on a cotton pocket-handkerchief imported from England.

When Mr. Webster had attained his fourteenth year, he had an opportunity of spending a few months at the Phillips Academy, Exeter, where he enjoyed the tuition and kindly counsels of Dr. Benjamin Abbot. He mastered the principles and philosophy of the English grammar in less than four months, and immediately commenced the study of the Latin. In his fifteenth year he was privileged to spend some months with the Rev. Samuel Woods, a popular divine who lived at Boscawen, and prepared boys for college at one dollar a week for tuition and board. Daniel was unmindful of the routine of the establishment, although he studied his lessons attentively and well. He seemed to be too fond of hunting in the neighborhood, and Mr. Woods reprimanded him, giving him, as a punishment, a hundred lines of Virgil to commit to memory. Daniel made up his mind that he would be revenged. He knew that on the next day Mr. Woods wanted to get away from the school as early as possible, in order to pay a visit to a neighboring town; before going, however, he was to hear the hundred lines. On the following morning Daniel presented himself, book in hand, and without the slightest hesitation recited the hundred lines in a way which drew forth the commendation of his instructor. "I have a few more lines that I can recite," said the malicious Daniel, as he observed Mr. Woods about to close the book and take his departure. An additional hundred lines were reeled off with the greatest ease. "You are a smart boy," said Mr. Woods, making another start for the door. "I have a few more I can recite, sir," said Daniel, adding, by way of last feather to break the camel's back, "about five hundred, I think." This was more than the doctor had bargained for. He was behind time with his engagement, and was really the only one of the twain who received punishment. "That is enough, Dan; you may have the whole day for pigeon-shooting."

The extraordinary promise which Daniel Webster displayed induced his father, though ill able to bear the expense, to send him to Dartmouth, where he graduated in 1801. His progress in the college had been so rapid that it was fully expected he would have received the valedictory, but that was reserved for some more fortunate scholar. All that he received was a diploma, which he deliberately tore up in the presence of a few companions. "My industry may make me a great man," he said, "but this miserable parchment can not." It must not be supposed from this circumstance that Mr. Webster was indifferent to the advantages of a college education. On the contrary, the moment he returned home it became the object of his life to secure to his brother Ezekiel similar advantages. He felt probably a little indignant that he had received merely the common honors of the collegiate, when he had worked for something more praiseworthy. It was his determination now to become a schoolmaster, in order that he might have the funds to assist his brother. In a short time he established himself in Fryeburg, Maine, with a friend of his father. He received a salary of $350, and by devoting his evenings to the laborious occupation of copying deeds for the county recorder at twenty-five cents each, was able to make a considerable increase to this sum. The latter occupation directed his attention to the study of the law, and while pursuing it he carefully read Blackstone's Commentaries and other substantial works, which contributed in a large measure to the solid foundation of his after-fame. Mr. Webster described himself at this time as "long, slender, pale, and all eyes." He was known round the country by the nickname of *All Eyes.* In his habits he was remarkably steady, his only recreation being trout-fishing, the solitary enjoyment of which he greatly enhanced by usually taking with him a volume of Shakspeare.

Mr. Webster studied the law with Mr. Christopher Gore, and was admitted to practice in Boston in 1805. Two years later he was admitted to practice in the courts of New Hampshire, and soon after took up his residence at Portsmouth, where he remained about nine years. He enjoyed a fair share of practice, and was able to assist his father in a pecuniary way, so as to relieve him of a burden of debts which pressed heavily on his spirits.

In 1817 Mr. Webster took up his permanent residence in the city of Boston. This step was rendered necessary by the condition of his finances, which had suffered greatly by his election to Congress (in 1812), and by a fire in which all his property was destroyed. In Boston he was well known and highly appreciated, but it was a dangerous experiment for a young man to thrust himself into an arena where the best forensic talent of the country struggled for pre-eminence. He had the friendship of a number of opulent merchants, and in a few months his name was known as the senior counsel in many important trials. His powers were soon recognized, and the sharpness of his invective, free, however, from narrowness or personality, became a matter of complaint with his brethren of the bar. The people appreciated this kind of oratory, and he soon became famous. "As were his manners at the bar some thirty years ago," says Mr. Knapp, "so were they through his life, whenever he appeared in a deliberative assembly. He began to state his points in a low voice, and in a slow, cool, cautious, and philosophical manner. If the case was of importance, he went on hammering out, link by link, the chain of argument with ponderous blows leisurely inflicted; and while thus at labor, you rather saw the sinews of the arm than the skill of the artist. It was in reply, however, that he came out in the majesty of intellectual grandeur, and poured forth the opulence of his mind;

it was when the arrows of the enemy had hit him that he was all might and soul, and showered his words of weight and fire. His style of oratory was founded on no model, but was entirely his own. He dealt not with the fantastical and poetical, but with the matter-of-fact every-day world, and the multifarious affairs of his fellow-men, extricating them from difficulties, and teaching them how to become happy. He never strove to dazzle, astonish, or confuse, but went on to convince and conquer by great but legitimate means. When he went out to battle he went alone, trusting to no earthly arm but his own. He asked for no trophies but his own conquests; he looked not for the laurel of victory, but it was proffered to him by all, and bound his brow until he went out on some new exploit."

Mr. Webster's public career belongs to the history of the country. In this place it is only necessary to say that he occupied a prominent position in its councils for upward of forty years—for a good portion of the time being nearest to the President in position, and seldom falling beneath him in absolute power. "It was before he had attained his thirtieth year," says Mr. Lanman, in his interesting "Private Life of Daniel Webster," quoting from Knapp, "when the times were stormy, and party spirit ran high in view of a war with Great Britain, that he entered the field of politics, like one who had made up his mind to be decided and straightforward in all his actions. No politician was ever more direct and bold, and he had nothing of the demagogue about him. Fully persuaded of the true course, he followed it with so much firmness and principle that sometimes his serenity was taken by the furious and headstrong as apathy; but when a fair and legitimate opportunity offered, he came out with such strength and manliness that the doubting were satisfied and the complaining silenced. In the worst of times and the darkest hour, he had faith in the redeeming qualities of the people. They might be wrong, but he saw into their true character sufficiently to believe that they would never remain permanently in error. In some of his conversations upon the subject, he compared the people, in the management of the national affairs, to that of the sagacious and indefatigable raftsmen on his native Merrimac, who had falls and shoals to contend with in their course to the ocean, guiding fearlessly and skillfully over the former, between rocks and through breakers; and, when reaching the sand-banks, jumping off into the water with lever, axe, and oar; and then, with pushing, cutting, and directing, made all rub and go, to the astonishment of those looking on. The first political glory that hung around his brow was at a convention of the great spirits in the county of Rockingham, where he then resided, and such representatives from other counties as were sent to this convention, to take into consideration the state of the nation, and to mark out such a course for themselves as should be deemed advisable by the collected wisdom of those assembled. On this occasion, an address, with a string of resolutions, were proposed for adoption, of which he was the author. They exhibited uncommon powers of intellect, and a profound knowledge of our national interests. He made a most powerful speech in support of these resolutions, portions of which were printed at the time, and much admired throughout the Union. From this time he belonged to the United States, and not to New Hampshire exclusively. Massachusetts also took as great an interest in his career as his native state. After the above *débût*, crowds gathered around him on every occasion that he appeared, and his speeches were invariably received with the most sincere and heartfelt applause." The preparation of these speeches was a matter of serious solicitude to Mr. Webster. He obtained the material for them with great care and industry, and wrought them with considerable labor. They were, on all important occasions, finished productions, which will endure as long as the language is read and understood. Mr. Webster was not a believer in extemporaneous oratory. The position he occupied before the world was undoubtedly one reason why he bestowed unusual care on all his efforts; another is to be found in the fact that he had never "gone through the mill" in State Legislatures. In alluding to this circumstance at Syracuse, Mr. Webster made the following humorous remarks: "It has so happened that all the public services which I have rendered in the world, in my day and generation, have been connected with the general government. I think I ought to make an exception. I was ten days a member of the Massachusetts Legislature, and I turned my thoughts to the search of some good object in which I could be useful in that position; and, after much reflection, I introduced a bill, which, with the general consent of both houses of the Massachusetts Legislature, passed into a law, and is now a law of the state, which enacts that no man in the state shall catch trout in any other manner than in the old way with an ordinary hook and line. (Great laughter.) With that exception, I never was connected for an hour with any state government in my life. I never held office, high or low, under any state government. Perhaps that was my misfortune.

"At the age of thirty I was in New Hampshire practicing law, and had some clients. John Taylor Gilman, who for fourteen years was governor of the state, thought that, a young man as I was, I might be fit to be an attorney general of the State of New Hampshire, and he nominated me to the council; and the council, taking it into their deep consideration, and not happening to be of the same politics as the governor and myself, voted, three out of five, that I was not competent, and very likely they were right. (Laughter.) So you see, gentlemen, I never gained promotion in any state government."

In 1807 Mr. Webster found himself in a position to settle in life, and was united in marriage to Grace Fletcher, a young lady of his own age, with whom he had long had a satisfactory understanding. Mrs. Webster died in 1827, leaving a husband who never ceased to remember her with affection. Mr. Webster delighted to speak of her as the "mother of his children"—a title fraught with exalted love. In April, 1816, Mrs. Webster, the mother of the statesman, died, at the advanced age of seventy-six. Among the specimens of art which adorned Mr. Webster's library at Marshfield was a quaint old profile, cut in black paper, as was the fashion some years back. Under the portrait were the words, "My excellent mother," in the handwriting of the statesman. Following close on this event was another which threw him into deep affliction. His first-born, and, at that time, only daughter, sickened and died. Throughout her illness Mr. Webster remained by her bedside, watching her with a tenderness almost feminine. He was detained from his place in Washington for two months of the session of 1816–17 by this calamity.

When Mr. Webster settled in Boston it was his intention to decline all political nominations, and devote himself exclusively to the pursuit of his profession. For a time he succeeded in doing so, but occupying as he did a most prominent place in the public regard, the task was a difficult one. In 1822 a committee called upon him and read to him the vote of the Convention by which he had been nominated a representative to the Congress of the United States, and informed him that they were instructed to listen to no answer. Mr. Webster thus found himself almost a compulsory candidate. He was elected by a thousand majority, and re-elected in 1824, receiving four thousand and ninety out of five thousand votes. In 1826 he was re-elected for the third time, but, before taking his seat, a vacancy occurring in the senatorial delegation, he was sent to the Senate of the United States by the Legislature of Massachusetts. It was while on his way to Washington that his wife died in the city of New York.

Mr. Webster visited Europe in 1839. In England he was received with gratifying enthusiasm. On his return he was called to the cabinet, and in relations equally near to the highest continued during the remainder of his political career.

Mr. Webster was a man of enormous mental capacity, and from the earliest was a hard worker. He had the genius and the inclination to do things perfectly; to do every thing as well as it could be done. He was methodical, and "an early riser." "What little I have accomplished," he used to say, "has been done early in the morning." He rose with the lark, and even in Washington found time to do the marketing for his own table, or to cast a fly on the Potomac before the business of the day commenced. Mr. Webster was passionately fond of out-door recreations; he was a farmer in feeling and in fact. "You can not mention the fee which I value half as much as I do a morning walk over my farm, the sight of a dozen yoke of my oxen furrowing one of my fields, or the breath of my cows, and the pure ocean air." With in-door amusements, such as chess, billiards, etc., he was unfamiliar. Every one has heard of Mr. Webster's piscatorial predilections. Nothing gave him greater satisfaction than a quiet day's fishing.

In his domestic habits he was remarkable for a graceful playfulness and a complete unbending to the sportive impulse of the moment. When he arose in the morning he might be heard singing a scrap of discordant melody, much to his own amusement. He generally wound up on such occasions with the remark that if there was any thing he understood well it was singing. He had a fondness, too, for spelling out, in the most unheard-of manner, the various familiar remarks which he had occasion to utter. The lowing of a cow or the cawing of a crow has sometimes started him not only to imitate those creatures with his own voice, but nearly all the other animals that were ever heard. He was also in the habit, when in a certain mood, of grotesquely employing the Greek, Latin, and French languages, with a sprinkling of Yankee and Western phrases, in familiar conversation; and he had an amusing way of conjugating certain proper names, and of describing the characters of unknown persons by the meaning of their names. He was, withal, one of the best story-tellers in the world, and every thing he related in that line had a good climax. When fishing, he used to round off sentences for futnre use, and many a trout has been apostrophized in imperishable prose. A couple of fine fish were passed into his basket with the following rhetorical flourish, which was subsequently heard in the Bunker Hill Oration: "Venerable men! you have come down to us from a former generation. Heaven has bounteously lengthened out your lives that you might behold this day."

It remains for us now to transfer to these pages a record of the last moments of this truly great man. In doing so we shall use the language of Mr. Lanman, his private secretary and friend, who was with him to the last, and who describes the last moments of Mr. Webster with such grace and simple loveliness that no excuse would justify the omission.

"The more rapid decline of Mr. Webster commenced while at Marshfield, about one week before his death, which occurred just before three o'clock on Sunday morning, the twenty-fourth of October (1852). He was in the seventy-first year of his age, and had, therefore, just passed the allotted period of human life. He looked upon his coming fate with composure and entire resignation. On the afternoon of the twenty-third he conversed freely, and with great clearness and detail, in relation to the disposal of his affairs. His last autograph letter was addressed to the President; and among the directions that he gave respecting his monument was that it should be no larger than those erected to the mother of his children, and to Julia and Edward. He dictated an epitaph, which will in due time be published.

"At five o'clock he was seized with a violent nausea, and raised considerable dark matter tinged with blood, which left him in a state of great exhaustion and debility. The physician in attendance, Dr. John Jeffries, then announced to Mr. Webster that his last hour was rapidly approaching. He received the announcement calmly, and directed all the females of the family to be called into the room, and addressed to each of them individually a few affectionate parting words, and bade them a final farewell. He then took leave of his male relatives and personal friends, including his farmers and servants, addressing each individually in reference to their past relations, and bade each an affectionate adieu. The last of his family that he parted with was Peter Harvey Webster, a grandson, the child of Fletcher Webster, for whom he invoked the richest blessings of Heaven. He then said, as if speaking to himself, 'On the twenty-fourth of October all that is mortal of Daniel Webster will be no more.' In a full and clear voice he then prayed most fervently, and impressively concluded as follows: 'Heavenly Father, forgive my sins, and welcome me to thyself, through Christ Jesus.' Dr. Jeffries then conversed with him, and told him that medical skill could do nothing more, to which he replied, 'Then I am to lie here patiently to the end. If it be so, may it come soon.' His last words were, '*I still live;*' and, coming from such lips, it seems to me they can not but fully convince the most hardened skeptic of the immortality of the soul. They seem to fall upon the ear from beyond the tomb, and to be the language of a disembodied spirit passing into Paradise. During his last hour he was entirely calm, and breathed his life away so peacefully that it was difficult to fix the precise moment that he expired."

Mr. Webster was buried without form or parade at Marshfield, on the 29th of October, 1852, the simple and unpretending ceremonies of the grave being performed by the village pastor. Throughout the length and breadth of the nation the memory of the departed was solemnly honored. In the heart of every American, on that day and forever, Daniel Webster "*still lives.*"

ELIHU BURRITT.

It was remarked by Coleridge that the shoemaker's trade nurtured a greater number of eminent men than any other. Sir Edward Bulwer Lytton quaintly theorizes on this assertion. In his novel of "What will he do with it?" he introduces a worthy son of St. Crispin, who, after touching on the mental peculiarities of butchers, bakers, and tallow-chandlers, establishes an agreeable comparison between his own trade and that of a tailor. "A tailor sits on a board with others, and is always a talking with 'em, and a reading the news; therefore he thinks as his fellows do, smart and sharp, bang up to the day, but nothing 'riginal, and all his own like. But a cobbler," continued the man of leather, with a majestic air, "sits by hisself, and talks with hisself, and what he thinks gets into his head without being put there by another man's tongue." A reason sufficiently philosophical for human purposes.

The subject of this memoir was the son of a shoemaker of Bridgeport, Connecticut, and was born at New Britain, in the same state, on the 11th of December, 1811. Both his parents were of English descent; Elihu being the youngest of five brothers, who, with five sisters, comprised his father's family. This extensive home circle was swayed with upright firmness and paternal attention. The children were educated by their parents, and brought up in the fear of God, and love of liberty, so essential to the well-being of Republican youth.

During the winter months Elihu and his brothers enjoyed the privilege of attending the district school, where, until he was sixteen years of age, he studied with avidity. It must be remembered, however, that it was only for three or four months in the year that he could be spared for these congenial pursuits. At other times he bore his share of the general labor.

The death of Mr. Burritt occurred when Elihu was sixteen. It became necessary to strike out a path for himself in the world; and, with this object in view, Elihu apprenticed himself to a blacksmith, with whom he remained until his twenty-first year. Long before this period he had displayed a fervent thirst for knowledge. All the incidents of the Revolutionary war were securely stored in his mind; he was familiar with the Bible, and now obtained access to the town library. At the age of sixteen he had read every book of history contained in it. He next proceeded to poetry. Thomson's "Seasons" took his earliest attention in this department. From the paucity of books, and his love of this kind of reading, he limited himself to a page a day, lest he should get through the luxury too soon. His memory was tenacious, and he committed astonishing quantities of "Young's Night Thoughts," "Pollok's Course of Time," "Shakspeare," and "Milton." Notwithstanding his literary tastes, he became a most excellent blacksmith. He seemed to possess the faculty of making extremes meet in the most powerful way; of welding sentences and cartwheels with equal facility.

Having digested all that he could attack in the library, and mastered his trade, he began to look fondly at those authors who were yet beyond his reach. The idea of becoming a scholar now illuminated his mind. It grew with his growth, and became irresistible. He determined that he would make an effort to accomplish his desires, and, on the expiration of his indentures, placed himself under the tuition of his brother, a lawyer and man of education. With the assistance which this gentleman afforded him Elihu pursued the study of the Mathematics, took up Latin, and commenced French. After spending the winter, and exhausting his scanty resources in this way, he returned to the forge, and voluntarily undertook the work of two men in order that he might make up for lost time. Physically laborious as was his occupation, he wrought hard for fourteen hours a day.

After he could read French with pleasure, says the Reverend R. W. Bailey, to whom we are indebted for the materials of this sketch, he took up Spanish. After reading the Spanish with ease he commenced the Greek, carried his grammar in his hat while he worked, and studied at the anvil and the forge. He pursued this course until the fall of the year (1833). He then made his arrangements to devote himself to study for another winter. He went to New Haven, not so much, as he said, to find a teacher, as under a conviction that there was the proper place to *study*. As soon as he arrived he sat down to the reading of Homer's Iliad alone, without notes, or translation, or any other help. At the close of the first day, after intense application, he had read fifteen lines, much to his own satisfaction. After this successful effort, he determined to go on without a teacher; he accordingly made a systematic distribution of his time and studies. He rose at four, and studied German until breakfast, then studied Greek until noon, then spent an hour at Italian. In the afternoon he studied Greek until night, and then studied Spanish until bedtime. This course he continued until he could read two hundred lines a day of Homer, besides carrying forward the other studies in their order. During the winter he read twenty books of Homer's Iliad, besides studying with equal success the other languages in the hours assigned to them.

In the spring he returned to the anvil, but an invitation to teach a grammar-school soon after induced him to cast aside his apron and assume the ferule of the pedagogue. In this occupation he continued for a year, and then, as agent for a manufacturing company, traveled extensively through the country. During this period his studies were of course entirely interrupted. He returned to the anvil once more, and resumed his mental and physical labors with renewed enthusiasm.

Having become proficient in the ancient and European languages, this indefatigable scholar turned his attention to the Oriental tongues. The means for acquiring a competent knowledge of these were limited, and Burritt conceived the idea of enlisting as a sailor, in order that he might travel to places more available for his purposes. Acting on the impulse, he abandoned his forge, and proceeded to Boston to obtain a ship. Unsuccessful in this, he began to look around, and heard accidentally of the American Antiquarian Society at Worcester. He immediately proceeded thither, and found, as he says, to his infinite gratification, such a collection of books on ancient, modern, and Oriental languages as he never before conceived to be collected together in one place. The free use of the library was cordially tendered to him, and, in order that he might enjoy it at his leisure, he made arrangements to study three hours a day, and follow his business of blacksmith at other times. In this manner he made the acquaintance of a number of Oriental tongues, and before he left Worcester was able to read "Hebrew, Greek, Latin, Gaelic, English, Welsh, Irish, Celtic, French, Spanish, Portuguese, Italian, German, Flemish, Saxon, Gothic, Icelandic, Polish, Bohemian, Russian, Sclavonic, Armenian, Turkish, Chaldaic, Syriac, Samaritan, Arabic, Ethiopic, Indian, Sanscrit, and Tamul."

Mr. Bailey publishes an interesting account of a visit to Mr. Burritt's *smithy*. "On my first arrival at Worcester, I proceeded directly from the cars to inquire out Mr. Burritt. After two or three directions I arrived at an extensive iron foundry. In a long line of workshops I was directed to that in which Mr. Burritt was employed. I entered, and, seeing several forges, sought for the object of my visit. 'He has just left, and is probably in his study,' said a son of Vulcan, resting his hammer on his shoulder meanwhile; 'there is his forge,' pointing to one that was silent. I had but a moment to study it. Its entire structure and apparatus resembled ordinary forges, except that it was neater and in better order. Mr. Burritt is a bachelor and a journeyman, and earns a shilling an hour by contract with the proprietor of this foundry. He lives and furnishes himself with books by this laborious application to his trade. Seeing on his table what appeared to be a diary, I read as follows: 'August 18. Forged 16 hours—read Celtic 3 hours—translated 2 pages of Icelandic, and three pages of German.' This was a single item of similar records which run through the book. To abate my surprise, he told me that this was a correct memorandum of the labors of every day; but the sixteen hours of labor was that which he performed in a *job*, and for which he was paid by the estimate of its value, but that he performed it in eight hours, thus gaining both time and money by double labor. Eight hours a day is his ordinary habit of labor at the forge." The same writer describes Mr. Burritt (1843) as a person of middle stature, rather slender proportions, high, receding forehead, deeply set, steady, grayish eye, thin visage, fair complexion, thin, compressed upper lip, a hectic glow, and hair bordering on the brown or auburn. There is nothing in his frame to indicate a habit of hard labor except the round shoulder, and an arm and hand disproportioned in size and muscle to the other parts of the body, and resulting, of course, from the practice of his trade.

In 1844 Mr. Burritt commenced the publication of a newspaper called "The Christian Citizen," and from that time to the present has been best known for his advocacy of peace doctrines, in connection with the "League of Universal Brotherhood." The earnestness with which he disseminates his views, and his enthusiasm on the subject of brotherhood have doubtless had their effect on the temper of the times. Mr. Burritt is also a strenuous advocate of an ocean penny postage. As the gifted advocate of these matters, he has visited Europe, and delivered animated and popular lectures in most of the principal cities. In the peace conferences of London, Paris, Brussels, and Frankfort he took a conspicuous part. In the publications of the League Mr. Burritt exercises his pen with eminent ability. His other literary productions include "Sparks from the Anvil," "A Voice from the Forge," and "Peace Papers for the People," besides some translations from the northern classics.

Mr. Burritt furnishes a remarkable instance of what may be accomplished by perseverance in spite of the most unfavorable circumstances. A forge, of all places in the world, would seem the least favorable for the prosecution of studies demanding an unusual concentration of mind; yet, by a contented exercise of the will, Mr. Burritt was deaf to the tumult which surrounded him, and was able to accomplish an amount of study which places him in the front rank of great scholars. The other phase of his character, in which he has manifested decided originality and philanthropy, will be better appreciated when the beneficence of his efforts are reviewed by the historian. In every respect Mr. Burritt is great and noble, and his name will descend to future generations as a bright example of a self-made man.

DR. ALEXANDER MURRAY.

This eminent man was born in a little parish called Minnigaff, Scotland, on the 22d of October, 1775. His father deserves some fame, for at the time of Alexander's birth he was nearly seventy years of age; a mature, but hale and hearty parent. He had been a shepherd all his life, and to the unrestrained and healthful freedom of that ancient occupation may be ascribed the continued vigor of his physical being to such an advanced period.

To this patriarch Alexander was indebted for the rudiments of an education. A Catechism, with an alphabet in it, was the text-book used, and esteemed as a treasure of such price that it was never delivered into the hands of the pupil. "As it was too good a book for me to handle at all times," says the doctor, "it was generally locked up, and he, throughout the winter, drew the figures of the letters to me, in his *written* hand, on the board of an old *wool-card*, with the black end of an extinguished heather stem, or root snatched from the fire. I soon learned all the alphabet in this form, and became *writer* as well as *reader*." In a little while Alexander had mastered the Catechism and a book of Psalms. The family Bible was out of his reach, but he secured a loose copy of the holy book, and read it so attentively that he was able to astonish every one with the capacity of his memory and the extent of his research.

Among the lowly it is at all times difficult to step beyond the narrow limits of their occupation. All Mr. Murray's sons were shepherds, and at the age of seven or eight Alexander became one as a matter of course. He was not destined to succeed, however, in this calling, and was often blamed by his father as lazy and useless. He was too much given to books, and writing on boards with charcoal, to pay particular attention to the flocks. He became a very remarkable peasant boy, and a very bad shepherd.

His prospects in life were considered decidedly gloomy by his parents and brothers. But in May, 1784, an uncle came to the cottage, and, struck with the remarkable brightness of the youth, offered to take him to New Galloway for a short time, and put him to school there. The advantages which might have accrued from this act of liberality were cut short by the ill health of Alexander. He was in the school but two months, when it became actually necessary that he should return home. Here he became once more a shepherd, with a literary turn for boards and charcoal pencils. Whenever by good fortune he obtained a sixpence, he disbursed it instantly on ballads and penny histories, with which his pockets and his head were constantly filled. These established his reputation as a prodigy in the neighborhood. "My fame," he says, "for reading and memory was loud, and several said that I was a living miracle." Serious elders of the Church, even, were astonished at his remarkable acquaintance with Holy Writ.

In 1787 Alexander was able to greatly extend his course of reading. A friend loaned him a translation of "Josephus" and "Salmon's Geographical Grammar," works that he perused with such avidity that he remembered their contents to the end of his life. He was now twelve years of age, very clever at every thing except taking care of sheep, and, consequently, a source of very great perplexity to his parents. It was necessary that he should maintain himself; and, with this object in view, he became private teacher in the families of two neighboring farmers. For his labors in this new field of enterprise he received as compensation, for an entire winter, the magnificent sum of sixteen shillings! With this sum he unsealed the sources of human knowledge. He procured an edition of the veritable Cocker, and studied arithmetic up to the rule of three; he obtained other books, and read them with a purpose. "My memory now," he says, "contained a very large mass of historical facts and ballad poetry, which I repeated with pleasure to myself, and the astonished approbation of the peasants around me."

Much to the delight of Alexander, circumstances permitted him once more to become a student at the school at Minnigaff to the extent of three days' attendance per week. He made the most of his opportunity, but it was a brief one, for in six weeks he had to look after his own living again—that is to say, to teach what he knew to the children of the neighboring farmers.

In 1790 he again attended school for about three months and a half of the summer, and it was during this brief term that he conceived the ambitious idea of becoming a scholar. His first impulse he attributes to the curiosity awakened by perusing, in

"Salmon's Geography" a transcript of the Lord's Prayer, translated into a variety of living and dead languages. About the same time he resolved to fit himself, if possible, for the duties of a clerk. To make his studies contribute to both results was now his endeavor. During the few weeks he remained at school, he obtained a grammatical knowledge of the English language, and commenced the study of French. While pursuing the latter, his attention was directed to the Latin by the circumstance of a boy complaining that he had once been set to learn it. Young Alexander Murray thus describes the circumstance: "About the 15th of June, Kerr (one of his classmates) told me that he had once learned Latin for a fortnight, but had not liked it, and still had the Rudiments beside him. I said, 'Do lend me them; I wish to see what the nouns and verbs are like, and whether they resemble our French.' He gave me the book. I examined it for four or five days, and found that the nouns had changes on the last syllables, and looked very singular. I used to repeat a lesson from the French Rudiments every forenoon in school. On the morning of the midsummer fair of Newton Stewart I set out for school, and accidentally put into my pocket the Latin Grammar instead of the French Rudiments. On an ordinary day Mr. Cramond would have chid me for this; but on that festive morning he was in excellent spirits, and very communicative. With great glee he replied, when I told him my mistake and showed him the Rudiments, 'Gad, Sandy, I shall try thee with Latin;' and accordingly read over to me no less than two of the declensions. It was his custom with me to permit me to get as long lessons as I pleased, and never to fetter me by joining me to a class. There was at that time in the school a class of four boys advanced as far as the pronouns in Latin Grammar. They ridiculed my separated condition. But before the vacation in August I had reached the end of the Rudiments, knew a good deal more than they by reading at home the notes on the foot of each page, and was so greatly improved in French that I could read almost any French book at opening of it. I compared French and Latin, and riveted the words of both in my memory by this practice. When proceeding with the Latin verbs, I often sat in the school all midday, and pored on the first page of Robert Cooper's (another schoolmate) Greek Grammar, the only one I had ever seen. He was then reading Livy and learning Greek. By help of his book

I mastered the letters, but I saw the sense of the Latin rules in a very indistinct manner. Some boy lent me an old Corderius, and a friend made me a present of Eutropius. I got a common vocabulary from my companion Kerr. I read to my teacher a number of colloquies, and before the end of July was permitted to take lessons in Eutropius. There was a copy of Eutropius in the school that had a literal translation. I studied this last with great attention, and compared the English and Latin. When my lesson was prepared, I always made an excursion into the rest of every book; and my books were not, like those of other school-boys, opened only in one place, and where the lesson lay."

A boy of young Murray's tastes only needed to be placed on the right track. He would pursue it of his own enthusiasm. After leaving school he purchased an old copy of Ainsworth's Latin Dictionary, and "literally read it through," he says. His method of studying was remarkable, and was probably as dry as any that could be conceived by the mind of man. He studied the dictionary backward and forward, and took relaxation in the Grammar, in Cæsar, or (by way of dissipation) in Ovid. During the following summer (1791) he continued this course; and when he went to school again for another course of three months' instruction, he was able to pass all the other scholars, and to read whatever came in his way in English, Latin, or Greek. In the latter languages he addressed Mr. Maitland, the clergyman of the parish, who, struck with the proficiency of the boy, extended to him the freedom of a small classical library, the contents of which Alexander Murray eagerly devoured. He arose from the repast with a fresh appetite, namely, for Hebrew. To appease this, he procured a copy of Robertson's Hebrew Grammar, and got through it in a month, notwithstanding its many intricacies; next followed a dictionary, which he subjugated in his usual way. Before the end of the summer he was able to read the Bible in Hebrew. Thus, in something less than eighteen months, he had mastered the principal difficulties of four languages, the French, Latin, Greek, and Hebrew, and had read several of the best authors in each. All this, too, in spite of innumerable and discouraging interruptions.

The winter of 1791 he passed in teaching, and earned thirty-five or forty shillings, so that he was able to return to school for the last time in the summer of 1792, remaining three months and a half. The different periods of school attendance added together, says one of his biographers, make about thirteen months, scattered over a period of nearly eight years. From November, 1792, till March of the following spring, he was once more employed in teaching, at a salary of thirty shillings. During this time he prosecuted his studies vigorously, and made the acquaintance of an Anglo-Saxon alphabet, which was his introduction to the northern languages. He obtained also a treatise in Welsh, and, without dictionary or grammar, set about making it out. "I mused a good deal on the quotations of Scripture that abound in it," he says, "and got acquainted with many Welsh words and sentences. If I had a copy of the Bible in any language of which I knew the alphabet, I could make considerable progress in learning it, without grammar or dictionary. This is done by minute observation and comparison of words, terminations, and phrases."

In the autumn of 1792 Murray's ambition took a new direction. His imagination had become inflamed by reading the classic poets and Milton, and he believed himself capable of writing an epic poem. After perpetrating several thousand lines, he had the good sense to feel and acknowledge that he was not yet fitted for the task, and the firmness, remarkable in a young poet, to commit his crude verses to the flames. Far more practical was his next literary effort, which consisted of a translation from the Latin of a series of lectures by a German professor. With this work under his arm, he repaired to Dumfries in 1794, but neither of the two publishers in the place would undertake the risk of publication. He then prepared a small volume of poems in the Scottish dialect; but Burns, to whom he showed them, advised him not to publish them. The object that young Murray had in view was to raise the means, in some way or other, of defraying his expenses at college. It was natural that he should feel downhearted and dispirited at these reverses.

To a very humble admirer Murray was indebted for his first step in the world. This was a peddler by the name of M'Harg, who knew Murray well, and who was in the habit of sounding his fame as a genius wherever he went. Among others to whom he spoke on the subject was Mr. James Kinnear, of Edinburgh, then a journeyman printer in the King's Printing-office. Mr. Kinnear, with a zeal in behalf of unfriended merit which does him infinite honor, immediately suggested that Murray should transmit an account of himself and some evidences of his attainments to Edinburgh, which he undertook to lay before some of the literary characters of that city. Murray was of course too happy to act on this suggestion, and the result exceeded his most sanguine expectations. The professors of the University were astonished at his attainments, and at once threw open their classes, and provided for his maintenance while attending them. Assistance he did not long need. In the city he found plenty of employment for his pen, and good remuneration for the exercise of his acquirements.

The struggles of this remarkable youth were now at an end. He remained in Edinburgh until 1806, having in the interval passed through the course of studies necessary to qualify him for the Scottish Church. His fondness for languages remained unabated; one by one he mastered the Oriental and northern languages, and of the Ethiopic and Abyssinian dialects he had a more critical knowledge than any other European of his day. This circumstance led him to undertake a new edition of Bruce's Travels (1802), a work which at once placed him in the foremost rank of Oriental scholars.

In 1806 he left Edinburgh to assume the duties of the pulpit, and for six years officiated as clergyman of the parish of Urr in Dumfriesshire. From this honored field of labor he was recalled to the University, to fill the professor's chair of Oriental languages. The degree of doctor of divinity was now conferred upon him, and he entered on the discharge of his duties with an ardor which led to the most untimely result. The preparation of his lectures, the supervision of philological works, the rendering of new translations, the prosecution of fresh studies, were undertaken and accomplished at the price of health. Dr. Murray could not be persuaded that he was sick and failing, nor indeed did he know it, until it was too late. He kept his bed for one day only, and died in the thirty-eighth year of his age, at a time when all that could gratify a scholar was within his grasp. He left behind him a reputation and an example which may be imitated by the hard-pressed and humble in this world.

LIEUT. MATTHEW F. MAURY.

It seems to be the fate of the most ancient and honorable of professions to lag tardily in the rear of the spirit of the age. Agriculture and navigation have been peculiarly open to this charge, and it is only of late years that either has made any progress indicating a high degree of philosophical observation. So far as this relates to navigation, the credit is almost entirely due to Lieut. Maury, a gentleman whose persevering efforts, continued through a course of years, have enabled him to furnish results which are of the highest importance to the marine of the world.

Matthew F. Maury was born near Fredericksburg, Spottsylvania County, Virginia, on the 14th of January, 1806. He was the seventh of nine children. His parents were in humble circumstances, and Matthew's early years partook of the rough characteristics that are inseparable from the experience of the pioneer families of our country. When he was only four years of age his parents migrated to the State of Tennessee, then a wild, uncultivated region, full of delightful scenery and hardy promise to the adventurer. The Maury family established themselves near the little village of Franklin, where, on the outskirts of civilization, young Maury grew up to the verge of manhood. Under such circumstances, his educational advantages were necessarily slight, and wholly due to the exertions of a clergyman, the Rev. Mr. Otey, now bishop of a southern diocese.

Young Maury's first and most enduring passion was for the sea, and when his parents found it was unconquerable, they wisely abandoned their opposition, and permitted him to follow it as a profession. He was nineteen years of age (1825) when he joined the United States Navy in the frigate *Brandywine*, then a new and splendid vessel, commissioned for the honorable duty of conveying General Lafayette from this country to France, and with orders to undertake a subsequent cruise in the Mediterranean. Maury was midshipman on board this ship-of-war, and soon became remarkable for the quiet skill and courage with which he discharged his duties, and the enthusiasm with which he applied himself to all that was theoretical or scientific in his profession. It is said that during the voyage across the Atlantic the *Brandywine* was overtaken by a severe storm. A scene of general excitement prevailed on board; but in the midst of the fury of the elements and the vociferous bustle of his companions, Maury was discovered quietly working away at a nautical problem, and entirely unconscious of aught else.

After carrying out her instructions in the Mediterranean the *Brandywine* was ordered home, to be placed under the broad pennant of Commodore Jones. Maury returned with her, and was retained in active service under the new commander. The frigate soon sailed for the Pacific. The little midshipman was still bent on his nautical studies. Some curious stories of his devotion, says Mr. Augustus Maverick, to whom we are largely indebted, are rife among the seamen who knew Maury at this time. It was one of his rules, to which he adhered inflexibly, that he would never allow himself to be idle, but, on duty or off, keep his mind actively employed in some way or other. A man-of-war is not the best place in the world for the indulgence of contemplative ways, or for the prosecution of studies demanding much thought and some practical demonstration. The only chance he had of being perfectly quiet and unmolested was while he was on watch. It became now a question how to use this time to the most advantage. He hit upon a plan which drove the old gunner of the frigate to the verge of despair. It was this. He provided himself with a bit of chalk, and quietly drew on the cannon balls the problem he wanted to work out. Then pacing backward and forward with his mind intent on it, he added figure to figure until the demonstration was complete. In this way he learned with rapidity, and laid the foundation of his future fame. The old gunner often raved at the troublesome "middy," who covered his shot with chalk-marks; but it was not held to be a heinous crime, and no hindrance followed. Two and a half years passed away in this manner, the young student applying himself closely, and gaining experience and wisdom with years. At the end of this period, while still cruising in the Pacific, he was, at his own request, transferred to the U. S. sloop-of-war *Vincennes*, then under orders for the East Indies.

This was Mr. Maury's third cruise; it proved of immense service to him. It enlarged his field of observation, and enabled him so far to verify his theories of navigation that he felt justified, upon his return home, in putting to press a volume comprising the results of the investigations he had already undertaken. The entire volume was written on shipboard.

The *Vincennes* arrived at New York in the summer of 1830, after an absence of four years. During the period of his service on board Mr. Maury had found time to visit the South Sea Islands, China, the Cape of Good Hope, St. Helena, and other points of interest, omitting no opportunity of adding to his stock of information. A fourth cruise was undertaken soon after the return of the *Vincennes*, and again Mr. Maury found himself in the Pacific Ocean, attached as acting master to the sloop-of-war *Falmouth*. Having been examined for promotion before leaving port, his qualifications as an officer were admitted and subsequently fully proved during his term of service on board this vessel. Promotion speedily followed. The appointment of acting lieutenant of the *Falmouth* was tendered to and accepted by him, and he continued to fill this post until transferred by Commodore Downes to the *Dolphin*, in the Pacific, two and a half years later. Of the *Dolphin*, Mr. Maury was made first lieutenant. The commodore presently transferred him to the flag-ship *Potomac*, on board of which he served as acting lieutenant until her return to the United States. This cruise occupied three and a half years. The opportunities it afforded Mr. Maury he was not slow in embracing. A mass of marine statistics was collected which afterward proved of signal service to him, and the compilation of a series of nautical tables occupied with profit a considerable period. The journals of experienced navigators whom he met in the Pacific were carefully examined and compared, and facts deduced from these sources of information and his own observations took the form of a record of reliable results. Mr. Maury's knowledge of astronomical science also led him to a series of investigations in that department of research, with a view to correct the prevailing methods of observing solar, lunar, and stellar distances. He contrived an instrument which was calculated to give the true measurement of distance, and completed a model of it, but, on applying to the Board of Navy Commissioners for assistance in carrying out the experiment, was repulsed. His own resources being inadequate to meet the necessary expenditure, the project failed, and the instrument never saw the light.

In the year 1836, when thirty years of age, Mr. Maury received his full commission as lieutenant in the navy. The appointment of astronomer and assistant hydrographer of the United States Exploring Expedition was soon afterward tendered to him, and was at first accepted, but subsequently declined. About this period Lieutenant Maury became interested in literary pursuits. An interesting and valuable essay on the Navigation of the Pacific and the Doubling of Cape Horn appeared from his pen in the pages of *Silliman's Journal;* and an article published soon after, on the interests of Southern Commerce, attracted attention. In this latter production Mr. Maury displayed accurate knowledge of mercantile regulations and observances, and, by means of an elaborate array of statistical facts, demonstrated the means which were to impart to the port of New York its commercial supremacy. He showed that the wealth of that great city lay chiefly in her lines of packets, which, by bringing her into active connection and competition with the commercial emporiums of other nations, insured at once her rapid growth, and a financial standing second to no other city. Taking this stand-point as representative of the argument he wished to enforce, Mr. Maury proceeded to discuss with great elaboration the commercial advantages of the South, which was the material point of his article. Mr. Maury's sympathies have generally been with the South in all its enterprises, and he has striven with voice and pen to encourage the interests and develop the resources of that section of the Union. This apparent partiality has called down a measure of condemnation upon Mr. Maury, but his convictions have been honest, sincere, and are still earnestly pressed when opportunity offers. In his writings upon these subjects Mr. Maury has given expression to his belief that the energies of the southern portion of the United States, if directed with enterprise, prudence, and skill, are competent to rival the business capacities of the North; and while he has not failed to press the advantages of the South upon the people of that district of the country, he has not forgotten to preserve throughout a tone of courtesy and consideration that has added a fresh charm to the native grace and polish of his diction. For a number of years, down to the present moment, the question of the development of southern interests has been a favorite one with him, a marked share of his attentions having been devoted to that branch of commerce which contemplates the establishment of a permanent and speedy means of communication between the South and the principal ports of Europe.

Turning for a time from literary avocations, Mr. Maury was again in active naval service until the early part of 1839. He was assigned the command of a government survey steamer, and was detailed to prosecute investigations along the southern coast. The sickly season approaching, this labor was suspended. Being comparatively free, Mr. Maury determined to avail himself of the opportunity to visit his aged parents, still residing in Tennessee.

This journey was destined to affect the entire course of his life in a melancholy way. The stage-coach in which he was traveling through Ohio met with an accident and was overturned. Among the passengers who received serious injuries was Mr. Maury. His knee was fractured, and he became a cripple for several months; indeed, it was nearly three years before he could dispense with the use of crutches. The injury was a permanent one, and sufficient to disable him for active service in his profession.

The resources of a man of thought and study are never entirely dependent on a single accident of life. To be torn from a profession which he loved so fervently was in the highest degree unhappy, but, by directing his thoughts into a new channel, it opened the path to a greatness which probably could not have been accomplished amid the hardships and turmoil of a sailor's life. No man in the country knew more of maritime subjects than Mr. Maury. He determined to use this knowledge for the benefit of the public; to work out his experience and observations with the pen and the press.

His first attempt was to effect a reform in the navy of the United States, by pointing out the evils of which he had been an attentive observer. A series of articles published in the *Southern Literary Messenger* drew public attention to the defects of the service, and the facts which Mr. Maury adduced as occurring under his own observation led to an animated warfare on paper. We have not space to recapitulate the arguments which were employed in the course of this controversy; it is sufficient to know that the attacks of Mr. Maury upon naval abuses have not been unattended by useful results. The title he gave them was the unique one of "Scraps from the Lucky Bag."

The peculiar channel into which Mr. Maury's thoughts have been almost exclusively directed of late years was suggested to him as long since as the year 1831. While going out in the capacity of sailing-master on his cruise of that year, he was struck with the fact that all information concerning the routes from the United States to Cape Horn was derived chiefly from tradition, sailors having their individual theories, and captains conglomerating the scraps of nautical wisdom which years of experience at sea had developed. Mr. Maury saw in this a field for the display of his peculiar characteristics. His observations upon the tides and currents of the ocean had already suggested to his mind the expediency of preparing a series of instructions for navigators; and the manifest ignorance on these subjects which prevailed at the time, even among seamen the most celebrated for their skill, led him to put his thoughts in shape for the benefit of the service. The "Wind and Current Charts" were the result of this resolution. Beginning at once, he presently brought his scheme into useful activity. He commenced by collecting from all practicable sources the log-books of vessels which had accomplished the passage around Cape Horn. The preparation of a series of charts was the object of a labored and minute comparison of results. This work is yet in progress (1858), and, when completed, will no doubt contribute largely to the high fame of the author.

In the year 1842 Mr. Maury was placed in charge of the hydrographical department of the American Navy, and was furnished with a great amount of valuable data taken from the old log-books of the government vessels. No one can apply such material to better purpose. In 1844 he became the superintendent of the National Observatory at Washington, and holds that office at the present time. He has not been slow to improve his opportunities. From time to time new charts have been issued, and, under instructions from this department, officers of the naval and merchant service regularly transmit to the Observatory the log of each of their outward and inward voyages. The publication of the "Wind and Current Charts" is now sanctioned by the American government, and new editions of Mr. Maury's "Instructions to Navigators" are issued at short intervals, embodying the latest results of the investigations which he is always actively prosecuting.

The practical utility of Mr. Maury's system having been fully established in Europe, a maritime conference was, at Mr. Maury's suggestion, held at Brussels in 1853, for the purpose of devising a uniform series of meteorological observations at sea. At this conference formulæ were prepared, which are now generally used by vessels under all flags.

A kindred subject to which Mr. Maury's attention has been directed is the establishment of a series of deep-sea soundings. Growing out of this subject, he has given to the world one of its most remarkable books, "The Physical Geography of the Sea." Mr. Maury claims to have demonstrated the much-talked-of sub-Atlantic Plateau, which is said to be available for the use of a trans-Atlantic telegraph. This position has not been allowed to pass without incurring severe criticism. Mr. Maury contends for the existence of an elevation or ridge at the bottom of the Atlantic, extending from the shore of Newfoundland to the coast of Ireland, and maintains, of course, the practicability of the same for the purposes mentioned.

Mr. Maury has led and still leads an active life. His leisure moments have been devoted to the popular exposition of science in the lecture-room. As a lecturer, he possesses every requisite to enchain an audience, and a rare faculty of imparting information in a ready and communicative way. He is looked upon with respect and admiration by a larger public than most scientific men can call their own, especially on a speciality such as that which Mr. Maury has made his peculiar study. Foreign governments have acknowledged the value and importance of his contributions to nautical science, but, in conformity with the regulations of the navy, which forbid the officers of the service to accept complimentary awards from other powers, Mr. Maury has declined all offers of the kind. The last tender was a knighthood offered by the King of Denmark, with expressions of the most flattering regard. This honor, like its predecessors, was declined, and Mr. Maury yet continues a simple lieutenant in the American Navy, debarred by his physical incapacity from active service, but occupying, with undiminished honor and usefulness, his post as the superintendent of the National Observatory.

CHRISTIAN GOTTLOB HEYNE.

Men of great learning are common to all ages, the thirst for knowledge being insatiable. The few who rise to pre-eminence have this fact to contend with, and, ere they can rise to distinction, have to pass a critical ordeal which can not be over-estimated. An author by an inward gift reaches the goal at once, like Burns. All the learning he needs, if he have genius, is that which teaches him to express his thoughts in the most fluent and natural way. A scholar, however, needs the patient talent to become learned, and when he has achieved this, he must possess force to carry him past the great learning of his greatest contemporaries, or he gains but a share of their general reputation. One who did this was Christian Gottlob Heyne, the greatest classical scholar of his age. Mr. Heyne was the son of a poor linen-weaver of Silesia, a district long and chronically affected with poverty. He was born at Chemnitz, in Saxony, on the 25th of September, 1729, in the midst of the saddest indigence. A large family were dependent on the exertions of the father, and, in spite of his exertions, often needed food. Want was the earliest companion of his childhood. "I well remember," he says, in the Memoirs of his own Life, "the painful impression made on my mind by witnessing the distress of my mother when without food for her children. How often have I seen her on a Saturday evening weeping and wringing her hands, as she returned home from an unsuccessful effort to sell the goods which the daily and nightly toil of my father had manufactured."

Notwithstanding this lowly condition, young Christian was sent to school, and with unusual rapidity acquired the little learning within his reach. Before his tenth year he had made himself master of all that could be taught, and was able to pay a portion of his school-fees in teaching younger members of the seminary. He displayed his passion for the classics at this time by a craving desire to learn Latin, and made an arrangement with the schoolmaster's son, who had studied at Leipsic, to do so, at the rate of fourpence a week. This enormous remuneration was the subject of much agitation to him. At first it seemed an impossible sum to raise, and he almost gave up in despair. One day he was sent to procure a loaf of bread from his godfather, who was a baker. As he trudged along, he thought sadly of the great project, and he wept at the disappointment which seemed inevitable. The baker was a good-tempered man, and he was quite affected by the tears of the boy. He inquired the cause of his distress, and when poor little Heyne sobbed out that it was because he could not afford fourpence a week to take lessons in Latin, his godfather patted him on the head, and made him glad and happy by promising to defray the ruinous fee. Heyne tells us that he was perfectly intoxicated with joy; and as he ran, all ragged and barefoot, through the streets, tossing the loaf in the air, it slipped from his hands and rolled into the gutter. This accident was attended with a sharp reprimand at home, and brought the young enthusiast to his senses. He immediately commenced taking lessons, however, and in less than two years had completely exhausted the classic resources of his instructor.

It seemed probable at this time that Heyne must abandon his studies for the more irksome duties of the world. His father had already made arrangements for placing him at a trade, when, fortunately, another godfather of the boy, a clergyman, agreed to bear the expense of continuing his education at the principal seminary of his native town of Chemnitz. His new patron, although a plethoric churchman, was decidedly stingy, and doled out his bounty with such an unwilling hand, that Heyne was frequently put to great straits to obtain the necessary books for study. After a little while, however, he obtained the situation of private tutor in the family of a citizen, and the stipend he received for this addition to his labors enabled him to become less dependent on his godfather.

Heyne was determined to continue his studies at the University, and for this purpose resolved to go to Leipsic. He arrived in that city of learning and literature, having his whole fortune, consisting of two florins, in his waistcoat pocket, and nothing else to depend upon except the small assistance he might receive from his godfather, who had reluctantly promised to continue his bounty. He had to wait so long, however, for his expected supplies from this source, which were accompanied with much grudging and reproach when they did make their appearance, that, destitute of both money and books, he would even have been without bread too, had it not been for the compassion of the maid-servant of the house where he lodged. What sustained his courage in these circumstances was neither ambition nor presumption, nor even the hope of one day taking his place among the learned. The stimulus that incessantly spurred him on was the feeling of the humiliation of his condition; the shame with which he shrank from the thought of that degradation which the want of a good education would impose upon him; above all, the determined resolution of battling courageously with Fortune. He was resolved to try, he said, whether, although she had thrown him among the dust, he should not be able to rise up by his own efforts. With an ambition so worthy, the difficulties that sprung up in his path were unheeded, or served but to increase his natural ardor and determination. The unremitting application to study which characterized his life at this epoch may be judged from the fact that for six months he only allowed himself two nights' sleep in the week; yet, while he was bending all energies to the great purpose of his life, he received nothing but reproaches from his godfather, who often directed his letters to "*Mr. Heyne, Idler, at Leipsic.*"

While at Leipsic he had an opportunity to escape the intolerable and oppressive poverty of his position. A situation was offered him as private tutor in a family in Magdeburg. It was in every way an enviable offer, but its acceptance involved one immense sacrifice: he must leave Leipsic and abandon his studies. He soon determined not to do so, and decided in favor of poverty and Leipsic. It was a noble self-sacrifice, and met with its reward. In a few weeks he obtained a situation, similar to the one he had refused, in the University town. For a time he enjoyed comparative prosperity, and studied and labored without his most-time companion, Want. But he worked too hard, and brought on a dangerous illness. He had to resign his situation, and what little funds he had were scattered in doctors' potions and nurses' fees. When he recovered he found himself poor, and destitute, and weak, with few friends, and no influence to thrust him forward in the world. There is a Divine eye which never sleeps on the deserving. A copy of Latin verses which Heyne had written accidentally fell into the hands of one of the ministers of the court of Saxony, who advised the author to repair to the court at Dresden. The advice, coming from a minister in power, was considered highly promising, and almost certain to lead to fortune. Heyne borrowed a small sum to defray his expenses, and started for the land of promise. Arrived at Dresden, he made the most of his introduction, but soon discovered that ministers' promises were not to be relied on. He received a few unproductive compliments, and was graciously permitted to starve. He subsisted on his books as long as they lasted, and was then obliged to accept the place of copyist in the library of the Count de Bruhl, at the miserable annual salary of eighty dollars; a sum which, even in that cheap country, was scarcely sufficient to keep him from perishing of hunger. After he had held this situation for above two years, his salary was doubled; but, before he derived any benefit from the augmentation, the Seven Years' War had commenced. Saxony was overrun with the forces of Frederick the Great, and Heyne's place, and the library itself, to which it was attached, were swept away at the same time. He was obliged to fly from Dresden, and wandered about for a long time without any employment. At last he was received into a family at Wittenberg; but in a short time the progress of the war drove him from this asylum also, and he returned to Dresden, where he still had a few articles of furniture, purchased with the little money saved while he held his place in the library. He arrived just in time to witness the bombardment of that capital, in the conflagration of which his furniture perished, as well as some property which he had brought with him from Wittenberg, belonging to a lady, one of the family in whose house he lived, and for whom he had formed an attachment during his residence there. Two young people were thus thrown on the world without a dollar to save them from want. At a moment so critical, they determined to unite their fortunes, on the Irish principle which advises that, when you are very poor, the best thing you can do is to marry. They were married, and, by the exertions of some common friends, a retreat was procured for Heyne and his wife in the establishment of a M. de Leoben, where he spent some years, during which time he was principally occupied in the management of that gentleman's property.

When peace was declared (1763) Heyne returned to Dresden. His hard fortunes were soon to be brought to an end. During his absence, the Professorship of Eloquence in the University of

Göttingen had become vacant by the death of John Mathias Gesner. Heyne was proposed for the chair by Ruhnken, a Greek critic of distinction, and a man who knew thoroughly the value of Heyne's acquirements. He received the appointment (1763), and held the professorship until the day of his death, which happened by apoplexy in 1812. No man living ever threw a brighter lustre on an institution of learning than Heyne on the University of Göttingen. He maintained its reputation with his pen and with his eloquence. The department to which he specially applied himself was the critical interpretation of classic literature and the illustration of the writing of the ancients, by showing how they ought to be studied with reference to the manners and characters of their respective ages. Heyne published his views on these subjects in his notes to the "Bibliotheca" of Apollodorus, and afterward in the "Transactions" of the University. He has many disciples of great eminence.

Heyne was an extremely industrious man, and edited a great variety of classic works, all of which are extremely valuable for the erudition and just criticism displayed in the notes and commentaries. An interesting and lengthy memoir of the early life of this celebrated man has been written by his son-in-law.

ROBERT BURNS.

Robert Burns, the pride of Scotland, and one of the most extraordinary poets the world has ever produced, was born in a rickety little hovel on the banks of the Doon, near Ayr, Scotland, on the 25th of January, 1759. His father was a man of superior abilities, of marked piety, and of some acquaintance with literature. His skill, however, did not extend to architecture, for the building in which they lived, erected by his hands, tumbled down two or three days after Robert was born. The mother and child were conveyed, through a fierce snow-storm, to a neighbor's cottage. Burns, in after-life, described his mother as "a very sagacious woman, without forwardness or awkwardness of manner." Unlike most men of eminence, he owed more to his father than his mother in the elements of his character. Especially did he inherit "the headlong, ungovernable irascibility and ungainly integrity" of Mr. Burns.

When about six years of age, the poet and his family removed to the parish of Ayr, hoping that they would be able to improve their circumstances by the change. But the new farm was no less sterile than the old one. After struggling with the most destitute circumstances until 1772, Mr. Burns and his family were driven from the place, and found refuge at Lochlea. Better times awaited them here, and for a while things went on prosperously. Mr. Burns's two sons, Gilbert and Robert, were sent to school. The schoolmaster thus describes his pupils at this time: "Gilbert," he says, "always appeared to me to possess a more lively imagination, and to be more the wit than Robert. I attempted to teach them a little church music: here they were left far behind by all the rest of the school. Robert's ear, in particular, was remarkably dull, and his voice untunable. It was long before I could get them to distinguish one tune from another. Robert's countenance was generally grave, and expressive of a serious, contemplative, and thoughtful mind. Gilbert's face said, 'Mirth, with thee I mean to live;' and certainly, if any person who knew the two boys had been asked which of them was the most likely to court the Muses, he would never have guessed that Robert had a propensity of that kind." The worthy schoolmaster entertained the popular idea that a man of a literary turn of mind ought to look books and speak books from his earliest infancy.

At the grammar-school of Ayr Robert and his brother studied "week about," and in the winter evenings their father gave them what instruction he had at his disposal. Both boys assisted on the farm, and Robert describes himself as a dexterous plowman. The most rigid economy had to be exercised in the little homestead. Butcher's meat was unknown at the table, and all the members of the family exerted themselves to the utmost of their strength, and sometimes a little beyond it, in the labors of the farm. There were an aged couple and seven children to be supported off its ungenerous soil.

Robert studied easily, and read with avidity all the books that came within his reach. "In my seventeenth year," says Burns, "to give my manners a brush, I went to a country dancing-school. My father had an unaccountable antipathy against these meetings, and my going was, what to this moment I repent, in opposition to his wishes. My father was subject to strong passions. From that instance of disobedience in me he took a sort of dislike to me, which I believe was one cause of the dissipation which marked my succeeding years. I say dissipation, comparatively with the strictness, and sobriety, and regularity of Presbyterian country life; for, though the will-o'-wisp meteors of thoughtless whim were almost the sole lights of my path, yet early ingrained piety and virtue kept me for several years afterward within the line of innocence. The great misfortune of my life was to want an aim. I saw my father's situation entailed on me perpetual labor. The only two openings by which I could enter the temple of Fortune were the gates of niggardly economy, or the path of little chicaning bargain-making. The first is so contracted an aperture I could never squeeze myself into it. The last I always hated—there was contamination in the very entrance! Thus, abandoned of aim or view in life, with a strong appetite for sociability, as well from native hilarity as from a pride of observation and remark; a constitutional melancholy or hypochondriacism that made me fly solitude; add to these incentives to social life my reputation for bookish knowledge, a certain wild logical talent, and a strength of thought something like the rudiments of good sense, and it will not seem surprising that I was generally a welcome guest where I visited, or any great wonder that always, where two or three met together, there was I among them. But far beyond all other impulses of my heart was *un penchant pour l'adorable moitié du genre humain.* My heart was completely tinder, and was eternally lighted up by some goddess or other; and, as in every other warfare in the world, my fortune was various: sometimes I was received with favor, and sometimes I was mortified with a repulse. At the plow, scythe, or reap-hook I feared no competitor, and thus I set absolute want at defiance; and as I never cared farther for my labors than while I was in actual exercise, I spent the evenings in the way after my own heart. A country lad seldom carries on a love adventure without an assisting confidant. I possessed a curiosity, zeal, and intrepid dexterity that recommended me as a proper second on these occasions, and I dare say I felt as much pleasure in being in the secret of half the loves of the parish of Tarbolton as ever did statesman in knowing the intrigues of half the courts of Europe."

When in his nineteenth year Burns spent some months in learning mensuration and surveying at a school at Kirkoswald, with the object of following the profession of land surveyor. The society in which he found himself was not calculated to improve the tendency of his mind to dissipation. The smugglers of the neighborhood found a boon companion, and Burns, as he expressed himself, observed "a new phase of life." He found time, however, to pursue his study of English literature, and to commence a literary correspondence with some of his schoolfellows. In this manner his life glided away until he had reached his twenty-third year. He had already composed one or two poetical pieces, occasioned by some circumstance of local importanec. Now he began to feel a necessity for verse. His passions, which were always strong, raged furiously until they found vent in rhyme.

In 1781 Burns went to Irvine to learn the trade of a flax-dresser. A fire broke out in the shop, and destroyed every thing, including Burns's little all. This event put an end to a matrimonial engagement into which the poet had entered, and exercised a depressing influence on his mind. His visit to Irvine was in other respects unfortunate. It threw him into the society of men who did not scruple to applaud the budding viciousness of the young man. His father died at a time when he could be least spared, and Burns, with very wild and uncertain ideas, repaired to the farm at Mossgiel, to assume, with his brother Gilbert, its cultivation. The fame he acquired in the neighborhood about this time was due to his poetic achievements rather than those of agriculture. Some additional notoriety was obtained in a less creditable way, arising from the laxity of morals which resulted from his sojourn at Irvine. The bad odor in which he found himself suggested to his mind the advisability of leaving the country. He had for some time expressed a desire to go to the West Indies, and would undoubtedly have taken his departure if the state of his finances had allowed him to do so. In this dilemma he resolved to try his luck with a volume of poems. His friends encouraged the idea, and a number of subscribers were readily obtained. In a letter to one of his friends, dated the 12th of June, 1786, he says: "You will have heard that I am going to commence a poet in print, and to-morrow my works go to press. I expect it will be a volume of about two hundred pages. It is just the last foolish action I intend to do, and then turn a wise man *as fast as possible.*" The poet also describes his feelings in another place. "Before leaving my native land, I resolved to publish my poems. I weighed my productions as impartially as was in my power: I thought they had merit; and it was a delicious idea that I should be called a clever fellow, even though it should never reach my ears, a poor negro-driver, or perhaps a victim to that inhospitable clime, and gone to the world of spirits. I can truly say that, *pauvre inconnu* as I then was, I had pretty nearly as high an idea of myself and of my works as I have at this moment, when the public has decided in their favor. It ever was my opinion that the mistakes and blunders, both in a rational and religious point of view, of which we see thousands daily guilty, are owing to their ignorance of themselves. To know myself had been all along my constant study. I weighed myself alone; I balanced myself with others: I watched every means of information, to see how much ground I occupied as a man and as a poet; I studied assiduously Nature's design in my formation—where the lights and shades in character were intended. I was pretty confident my poems would meet with some applause; but, at the worst, the roar of the Atlantic would deafen the voice of censure, and the novelty of West Indian scenes make me forget neglect. I threw off six hundred copies, for which I got a subscription for about three hundred and fifty. My vanity was highly gratified by the reception I met with from the public; and besides, I pocketed, all expenses deducted, nearly twenty pounds. This sum came very seasonably, as I was thinking of indenting myself, for want of money to procure my passage. As soon as I was master of nine guineas, the price of wafting me to the torrid zone, I took a steerage passage in the first ship that was to sail from the Clyde; for

"'Hungry ruin had me in the wind.'

I had been for some days skulking from covert to covert, under all the terrors of a jail, as some ill-advised people had uncoupled the merciless pack of the law at my heels. I had taken the last farewell of my few friends; my chest was on the way to Greenock; I had composed the last song I should ever measure in Caledonia, 'The gloomy night is gathering fast,' when a letter from Dr. Blacklock to a friend of mine overthrew all my schemes by opening new prospects to my poetic ambition."

The history of literature does not afford another instance of such extraordinary popularity as was obtained by Burns immediately on the appearance of this volume. All thoughts of the West Indies were immediately abandoned in the necessary preparations for a second edition. This, on its appearance, had an enormous sale, and realized quite a little fortune to the author. It was read extensively by all classes of the community, and was as heartily commended by the learned as by the illiterate. In Edinburgh he was received in the most enthusiastic manner by persons of eminence in the social and literary worlds. He passed at one step from the cottage to the palace. The peasant-boy became the associate of noblemen, and the "lion" of the fashionable world.

The profits arising from this second edition of his works amounted to upward of £500. After assisting his brother with £200 to get him out of some difficulties, he bade farewell to the Scottish capital, the brilliant society of which did not agree with his rude notions of jollity, and took a series of tours through Scotland as a professed "rustic bard" and man of genius, writing diaries and letters, scratching impromptu verses on the windows of inns and taverns, and inditing passionate love-strains to ladies and damsels of every degree with whom he had the slightest possible acquaintance. After spending three months in this erratic way, he married Jean Armour, a peasant-girl whom he had wronged, and leased a farm on the banks of the Nith, near Dumfries, with the intention of once more following agriculture as a profession.

In August, 1789, he entered the excise, with the object of eking out an insufficient income. It was an unfortunate step, for he, of all men, was least able to resist temptation. The farm was more and more neglected. At last he relinquished it altogether, and became a regular exciseman, with an income of £70 per year. To this profession he remained faithful for about five years, residing in Dumfries until the time of his death, which happened on the 21st of July, 1796. He was never in actual want, but his circumstances were often of the narrowest, arising in a great measure from his extravagance, and unpardonable habits of dissipation. Subscriptions were entered into for the benefit of Burns's widow, and for the erection of monuments in various localities to the poet's memory.

The life of Robert Burns does not furnish an example, but a warning. A man of the most unquestionable genius, he lived and died in an obscurity which might, without doubt, have been averted, if his habits and inclinations had been different to what they were. By study and patient effort he succeeded in raising himself far above the station in which nature had placed him. He asserted to the world, and the world recognized, his genius. Without waiting wearisome years for the tardy verdict of the public, it was pronounced instantly, and in his favor. In a few months he became the idol of a large community. Men of vast acquirements in the realms of knowledge, and men of rank, wealth, and refinement, instantly recognized him as an equal, and even more than an equal. He went among them for a short time, but confirmed habits of inebriety and coarse enjoyment rendered him incapable of appreciating their society. Conscious of his weaknesses, although unable to combat them, he became suspicious of courtesy, and willfully stubborn. Dragged down to the lowest level of his boon companions, he forgot the respect that was due to himself and to the genius with which God had intrusted him. He fancied that every one saw his defects, and, in consequence, became irritable, imagining that it was poverty that gave him irritation, and not viciousness. He hated patronage with a manliness that was worthy of all admiration, but he blundered constantly in always imagining that kindness and appreciation were intended as patronage. Incensed with these mistaken ideas, he plunged once more into idle dissipation—into the society of men who revered him, perhaps, but who were incapable of estimating his real worth. Thrust back into the sorry habits of his old life, he lost his opportunity, and squandered his best days in an unheroic struggle with poverty. Had he pursued a different policy he would have lived in affluent ease, and produced works worthy of the extraordinary genius he possessed.

GEORGE FOX.

A REMARKABLE man, thoroughly antagonistic to the age in which he lived, and bestowing on it an enduring virtue, was George Fox, founder of the society of Friends, commonly called the "Quakers." He was the son of a weaver, and first saw the light (July, 1624) in the town of Drayton, Leicestershire, England, where his father was widely known and respected for his uprightness and integrity. These traits were so willingly recognized that he was known in the neighborhood as "righteous Christer." His mother was a woman of unusual intelligence, simple and pious in her habits, and tenderly good in all her actions.

The paternal Fox was a man well read in the Scriptures, and delighted to instill into the youthful mind of his son the truths of revealed religion. Under this pious instructor, the lad grew up in physical and moral strength. Of regular education he had but little—not more than could be readily obtained at the adjacent schools—nor in after-life did he display any eager thirst for knowledge. Of a remarkably vigorous mind, he found ample employment in digesting the information which lay within his immediate reach.

For several years young Fox followed the business of a grazier, and found much consolation in the solitude which it afforded. It is said that he passed days in the hollow of an old tree meditating on religious subjects, and revolving with enthusiasm a life of moral purity. According to Neal, he afterward became a shoemaker—a business also fitted for his contemplative habits. He was remarkably steady and exact, had no relish for the sports and gayeties of youth, and resisted pleasure with a firmness which was curious as it was sincere. The wickedness of the times troubled him by night and by day. So convinced was he of its perniciousness, that, when only nineteen years of age, he resolved to break off all commerce with the world and its vanities. In simple pilgrim costume he started from home, and traveled through various portions of the country seeking out persons who were most famous for devotion, that he might gain consolation for his perturbed spirit. Such a pilgrim, in such times, was not likely to be understood, and his journey was in vain; but in all disappointments he was sustained by a belief, which he cherished to the end of his life, that he had received a special call from above to become a minister of reformation to the world. Whenever he met with a difficulty, he had an "opening" which revealed to him the course he should pursue. "When I had openings," he says, "they answered one another, and answered the Scriptures; for I had great openings of the Scriptures."

Although he claims to have received the revelation to which we have referred in his youth, he did not essay the active duties of his ministry until the twenty-third year of his life. "I was sent to turn the people from darkness to light—to the grace of God, and to the truth in the heart which came by Jesus, that all might come to know their salvation nigh. I saw that Christ died for all men, and that the manifestations of the Spirit were given to every man to profit withal. These things I did not see by the help of man, nor by the letter, though they are written in the letter; but I saw them in the light of the Lord Jesus Christ, and by his immediate spirit and power, as did the holy men of God by whom the Scriptures were written."

It is conceded that Fox had a wonderful power of preaching; that his enthusiasm was overpowering; that his sincerity was unquestionable, and that his boldness and courage were equal to any emergency. Acting as he did under an impression which gave tone and importance to his words rather than to his thoughts, it is not remarkable that he possessed and exercised extreme fascination over masses, who listened eagerly to the words he uttered. Moreover, the absolute matter of his harangues was sound, wholesome, and elevating. In precept and in practice he was alike sincere. The people listened to his discourses, and found them strange; they watched his actions, and found them strange; for there was depravity in neither.

He traveled extensively, and made converts every where. In 1648 several meeting-houses were in operation. "He fasted much," says Neal, "and walked often abroad in retired places, with no other companion but his Bible." A man of peace, he excited war. The authorities tried to crush him. He was thrown into prison; put in the stocks; hooted from the house of meeting; stoned from the city. This, and more, he bore with patience. At the first opportunity he preached again, and made more converts. Not content with this, he exercised himself with "going to courts to cry for justice—in speaking and writing to judges to do justly—in warning such as kept houses for public entertainment that they should not let the people have more drink than would do them good—in testifying against wakes, feasts, May-games, sports, plays, and shows, which train people up to vanity, and lead them from the fear of God. In fairs, also, and markets, he was made to declare against their deceitful merchandise and cheating; warning all to do justly, to speak the truth, to let their yea be yea, and their nay nay, and to do unto others as they would have others do unto them. He was moved also to cry against all sorts of music, and against mountebanks playing tricks on their stages, for they burdened the pure life, and stirred up the minds of the people to vanity." A man moved with so many internal admonitions, and ostentatious of pronouncing them, was not likely to escape the wrath of those whose sympathies were in an opposite direction.

In the present day it is a matter of mirth even to right-minded people to see with what tenacity a Quaker's hat sticks to his head. Nothing was more irritating to Fox's opponents than the positive scorn of authority which the covered head implied. At times it was difficult to decide whether it was Fox or his hat that gave most offense. "Oh!" exclaimed Fox, "the blows, the punchings, the beatings, and imprisonments we underwent for not pulling off the hat! The bad language and evil usage we received on this account is hard to be expressed, besides the danger we were sometimes in of losing our lives for this matter, and that, too, by the great professors of Christianity."

The authorities were never very severe with him, although he was frequently arrested and thrown into prison on frivolous charges. He was detained sometimes for days, sometimes for months, and then set at liberty. It was difficult to fabricate a grave charge against him, for, with all his enthusiasm, he was circumspect and well meaning; it was still more difficult to sustain a charge, for he had an exact and logical mind which confounded the lawyers. Frequently he prayed for his tormentors in open court, and invariably bade them "tremble at the word of the Lord." From this circumstance, the sect which he founded obtained the nickname of "Quakers."

Cromwell, with his austere regard for every thing moral, recognized all that was good in Fox and his tenets. He helped him out of some difficulties, and, it is said, invited him to dine at the palace, which, however, Fox declined. On a subsequent occasion he had an interview with the Protector, and laid all his grievances before him, not without result, for he was a man who possessed the power of persuasion in an eminent degree. Some curious anecdotes are related of this power. On one occasion, as he was traveling through Wales, he was overtaken by a man of some distinction, who had maliciously determined to arrest him on some unjust pretense. They entered into conversation, and Fox said so many things that were good, pure, and lofty, that his would-be-persecutor forgot his first intention, and invited Fox to his house, where he was treated with the greatest respect and hospitality. The result was that the man and his wife became converts to Quakerism. On another occasion, while undergoing a term of imprisonment, he was subjected to many unnecessary cruelties by the jailer, who seemed to take a special pleasure in trying the patience of his prisoner. He was unable to disturb the placidity of Fox's temper. All he could obtain was an earnest lesson of Christian forbearance, not unmixed with instruction, which was wholesome as it was strange in such a place. By these means Fox so won upon the better feelings of the jailer, that after his liberation the latter wrote to him in language humble and affectionate, begging that he might be admitted into the society of Friends. Many similar instances are recorded.

In 1660, members of the society of Friends were to be found in all parts of the United Kingdom. The rapid increase in their numbers became a subject of serious alarm to the bigoted and the foolish. Quakers became the objects of peculiar aversion to country magistrates. The jails were filled with them. Persecution strengthened their cause, and their numbers continued to increase. A number of country bigots resolved to put a stop to the evil by boldly striking at its head. Accordingly, Fox was arrested as a seditious and dangerous person, and as one who had committed a very long list of offenses, which were carefully enumerated in the indictment. The matter might have proved serious if Fox's friends had not procured an examination before the Court of King's Bench. The judges in that high court were amazed at the stupidity of the charges brought against the prisoner, and ordered him to be immediately discharged. On this occasion and on others he was set at liberty the moment he gave his word that he would appear for trial at an appointed day. This fact alone speaks volumes for the reputation he enjoyed even among his enemies.

The oath of Allegiance and Supremacy, which was revived in 1661, became a sore stumbling-block to Fox and his disciples, who, of course, refused to take it. For this refusal Fox was brought to trial, and subjected to an inhuman imprisonment of six years' duration. On his release (1669) he married his wife Margaret, a highly-gifted and influential preacher among the Quakers. It was a mature wedding: Fox being in his forty-fifth year, and his wife ten years older. They lived together but little, but labored assiduously in the cause. When one happened to get into prison, the other endeavored to obtain a release. Sometimes it happened that both were in prison at the same time.

The immense energy which Fox brought to bear on his loved task may be estimated by the fact that during his career he preached in all the principal towns of England, Scotland, Ireland, and Wales. He twice visited Holland and some parts of Germany, where multitudes joined the society. The years 1671–1672 he spent in the British West Indies and the colonies of America, where he traveled extensively, making some stay in New England, Pennsylvania, and Maryland. For more than forty years this remarkable man devoted the best energies of an unusual mind to the interests of a society which, under his guidance, grew to be, and still is, a model of Christian organization. Death found him busy in his ministrations, the 13th of November, 1699, aged 67 years. Had he lived six years longer he would have seen all the claims of his society fully recognized by the English Parliament.

George Fox is described as a man above the ordinary size, of graceful and engaging manners, and with an eye of piercing brilliancy. In his habits he was temperate, ate sparingly, and avoided all intoxicating drinks as a beverage. That he was a man of unusual force of character is amply demonstrated by his career. "His presence expressed a religious majesty," said William Penn. He was sincere in his belief that he had received his commission directly from Heaven, and his actions were not likely to be injured by that belief. He discharged his mission on earth bravely, and with wisdom, forbearance, and Christian hopefulness. His name will live.

AMOS LAWRENCE.

Amos Lawrence—one of the most pure and lovely of all self-made men—was born at Groton, Massachusetts, on the 22d of April, 1786. His ancestors were English, and probably migrated to this country in 1630. His father served in the Revolutionary war, and was wounded at the battle of Bunker Hill. His mother was a woman of the best affections, and of strongly-marked character, capable and willing in the discharge of all those duties that make home delightful.

Young Amos, a weakly child, was often detained from school in consequence of ill health; but, being a lad of quick parts, he made considerable progress in the rudiments of a solid English education, despite this drawback. The master of the district school was frequently a visitor at his father's house, a house famed for its hospitality, and young Amos delightedly listened to the patriotic sentiments which were uttered in those times that tried men's souls.

In 1799, being still too weak to assist on the farm, he was placed at a small store in the town of Dunstable, where he remained a few months. He was then transferred to the counting-house of James Brazer, Esq., of Groton, an enterprising and thrifty country merchant. Several clerks were employed, and as Mr. Brazer, after a few years, ceased to take an active part in the business, much of the responsibility of the establishment rested on young Lawrence. By attention, probity, and fairness, he had justly entitled himself to this confidence. An instance may be given of the self-control which, even at this early day, he was capable of exercising. Mr. Brazer's store contained all sorts of merchandise. It was intended to, and really did, supply the wants of a small neighborhood. In those days temperance was little understood, and total abstinence scarcely thought of. Huge quantities of liquors were retailed daily, and imbibed with the regularity of clock-work. The clerks were accustomed to take their morning draught, and Amos, falling into the habit without thought, joined them. At first he had no appetite for the thing, and merely took it because it appeared to be the fashion; but after a while he began to look forward to the hour for imbibing with pleasure. Alarmed at this circumstance, he immediately resolved that he would break off. The task was an easy one so far as his mere palate was concerned, but delicacy in the matter of drinking was a thing that was looked on as supremely ridiculous by his companions, and his determination excited their laughter and contempt. Unmindful of these, he resolved on total abstinence, and adhered to his resolution in spite of the natural sensitiveness of youth and the unmerciful ridicule of his companions. "My first resolution," he says, "was to abstain for a week, and, when the week was out, for a month, and then for a year. Finally, I resolved to abstain for the rest of my apprenticeship, which was for five years longer. During that whole period I never drank a spoonful, though I mixed gallons daily for my old master and his customers. I decided not to be a slave to tobacco in any form, though I loved the odor of it then, and even now have in my drawer a superior Havana cigar—given me, not long since, by a friend—but only to smell of. I have never in my life smoked a cigar; never chewed but one quid, and that was before I was fifteen; and never took an ounce of snuff, though the scented rappee of forty years ago had great charms for me."

During the term of his apprenticeship he met with an accident which was near proving fatal. In assisting an acquaintance to unload a gun, by some accident the charge exploded, and passed directly through the middle of his hand, making a round hole like a bullet. Sixty-three shot were picked out of the floor after the accident, and it seemed almost a miracle that he ever again had the use of his hand.

After the expiration of his apprenticeship (which lasted seven years), Mr. Lawrence, now in his twenty-first year, made a journey to Boston for the purpose of establishing a credit which might enable him to commence business in Groton on his own account. He had not been many days in Boston when he received the offer of a clerkship from a respectable house. Wishing to familiarize himself with the metropolitan way of doing business, he accepted the offer. His employers were so well satisfied with the capacities of their new clerk, that in a few months they proposed to receive him as a partner. For reasons of his own, Mr. Lawrence declined the honor, but soon after started in business for himself (Boston, December 17th, 1807). He was then, in the matter of property, not worth a dollar, but his character was so well known and appreciated that he had little difficulty in obtaining a sufficient credit. For the rest he was indebted to his father, who mortgaged his farm in order to assist his son with a thousand dollars. In the conduct of his business he adopted a rigid code of principles, beginning with the maxim, "Business before friends." Writing of this period, he says: "I adopted the plan of keeping an accurate account of merchandise bought and sold each day, with the profit, as far as practicable. This plan was pursued for a number of years, and I never found my merchandise fall short in taking an account of stock, which I did as often at least as once in each year. I was thus enabled to form an opinion of my actual state as a business man. I adopted also the rule always to have property, after my second year's business, to represent forty per cent. at least more than I owed; that is, never to be in debt more than two and a half times my capital. This caution saved me from ever getting embarrassed. If it were more generally adopted we should see fewer failures in business. Excessive credit is the rock on which so many business men are broken. * * I made about fifteen hundred dollars the first year, and more than four thousand the second. Probably, had I made four thousand the first year, I should have failed the second or third year. I practiced a system of rigid economy, and never allowed myself to spend a fourpence for unnecessary objects until I had acquired it."

Having become firmly established in Boston, he resolved to take his brother Abbott (afterward minister to the court of St. James) as an apprentice (October, 1808). Abbott was in his fifteenth year, and made his appearance in Boston with a bundle under his arm, and less than three dollars in his pocket. He was a bright lad, but needed the watchful eye of his brother to keep him from the snares and pitfalls with which a large city abounds. In 1814 he was taken into partnership by Amos. Previous to this the latter had taken unto himself the great comfort of the world, a wife (1811). With this estimable lady he lived a life of domestic bliss, cut short by her untimely death in January, 1819. The character of Mrs. Lawrence is touchingly expressed in an incident which occurred a few hours before her dissolution. She called for paper, and with a pencil traced in a trembling hand some directions respecting small memorials to friends, and then added, "Feeling that I must soon depart from this, I trust, to a better world, I resign my very dear friends to God, who has done so much for me. I am in ecstasies of love. How can I praise him enough!"

The loss of his wife (by whom he had three children) was an affliction so severe that Mr. Lawrence became utterly prostrated by it. A gloomy despondency settled on his mind, his health failed, and it became necessary, to avert dire consequences, that he should obtain a change of scene. Under the advice of his physician, he made a tour through Virginia, and paid a visit to Washington, where he had the good fortune to hear Daniel Webster. On his return he was able to resume his usual avocations with greater composure.

Conducted on the surest basis of commercial prosperity, it is not remarkable that the business of the Lawrence establishment prospered. At a time when credit was shaken in every leading city of the Union by the wild and heedless thirst for speculation; when houses that were considered the most secure tottered and fell in the general crash, Lawrence and his brother pursued their quiet, unpretending way, unseduced by the hope of sudden wealth, unterrified by the dread of prospective ruin. By well-directed prudence and easily contented expectations, they weathered the storm that destroyed their neighbors, and possibly derived some benefit from the superior wisdom which enabled them to do so.

In April, 1821, Mr. Lawrence married his second wife, and in the same year was elected a representative from Boston to the Legislature for the session of 1821–1822. This was the only occasion on which he ever served in a public legislative body. He attended faithfully to the duties of his office, although with much sacrifice to his own personal interests.

From this point it is unnecessary to pursue the history of Mr. Lawrence's career. The "Diary and Correspondence" given to the world by his son, Dr. Lawrence, supply all the information that the student may require, and to that work we cheerfully direct the attention of young men, who, on entering life through one of the many channels of trade, desire, and to a great extent need, the encouragement of a successful model. By carefully and earnestly applying himself to the duties of life, Mr. Lawrence became rich, but he did not allow himself to be engrossed by the cares of wealth. On more than one occasion, when he found that he was making too much money, he limited the extent of his trade, so that he might not be tempted. When at length he found himself in the receipt of an income more than sufficient for the frugal wants of his own home, he extended his generous hand, and, with a wise philanthropy, relieved the destitute, assisted the needy, succored the weak, and built up charities with the strong faith of an enlightened Christian. No man knows the extent of his bounties, for it was one of the glories of his life that he seldom spoke of what he did. Throughout all his career he was governed by the pious hope that he would be rewarded with the "Well done!" of his heavenly Master.

With the object of knowing the amount of his expenditures for purposes other than the support of his family, he commenced, in 1829, to keep a particular account of charities and appropriations for others. This was kept up perpetually until the year of his death, a period of twenty-three years. During that time this good man expended in the most wise and beneficent ways no less than six hundred and thirty-nine thousand dollars. "Many persons have done more," says his son, modestly, "but few, perhaps, have done as much in proportion to the means which they had to bestow." The passion for accumulation was entirely unknown to Mr. Lawrence. If he made twenty thousand dollars more in one year than another, he rejoiced simply because it enabled him to expend twenty thousand dollars more for charitable objects. His philanthropy extended to all classes, all sects, all purposes. He was absolutely without a prejudice. Nor did he give merely to charities, and persons in want of charitable assistance. To others who derived nothing but gratification from the approach of a good man, he made suitable gifts, stimulating them to kindred exertions in the good cause of brotherly love. "And in so doing, and in witnessing the results, and in the atmosphere of sympathy and love thus created, there was a test, and a discipline, and an enjoyment, as well as a benefit to others, that could have been reached in no other way." Another peculiarity of the bounty of Mr. Lawrence, and in which he was pre-eminent, was the personal attention and sympathy which he bestowed with it. "He had in his house," says Professor Hopkins, "a room where he kept stores of useful articles for distribution. *He* made up the bundle; *he* directed the package. No detail was overlooked. He remembered the children, and designated for each the toy, the book, the elegant gift. He thought of every want, and was ingenious and happy in devising appropriate gifts. In this attention to the minutest token of regard, while, at the same time, he could give away thousands like a prince, he was unequaled; and if the gift was appropriate, the manner of giving was not less so. There was in this the nicest appreciation of the feeling of others, and an intuitive perception of delicacy and propriety. These were the characteristics that gave him a hold upon the hearts of many, and made his death really felt as that of few other men in Boston could have been. In this we find not a little of the utility, and much of the beauty of charity. Even in his human life man does not live by bread alone, but by sympathy and the play of reciprocal affection, and is often more touched by the kindness than by the relief. Only this sympathy it is that can establish the right relation between the rich and the poor, and the necessity for this can be superseded by no legal provision. This only can neutralize the repellent and aggressive tendencies of individuals and of classes, and make society a brotherhood, where the various inequalities shall work out moral good, and where acts of mutual kindness and helpfulness may pass and repass, as upon a golden chain, during a brief pilgrimage and scene of probation. It is a great and a good thing for a rich man to set the stream of charity in motion; to employ an agent, to send a check, to found an asylum, to endow a professorship, to open a fountain that shall flow for ages; but it is as different from sympathy with present suffering, and the relief of immediate want, as the building of a dam to turn a factory by one great sluiceway is from the irrigation of the fields. By Mr. Lawrence both were done. He gave as a Christian man, from a sense of religious obligation. Not that all his gifts had a religious aspect: he gave gifts of friendship and affection. There was a large inclosure where the affections walked foremost, and where, though they asked leave of Duty, they yet received no prompting from her."

From the eloquent address of President Hopkins we also quote the following estimate of Mr. Lawrence's religious character: "He was a deeply religious man. His trust in God and his hope of salvation through Christ were the basis of his character. He believed in the providence of God as concerned in all events, and as discriminating and retributive in this world. He felt that he could trust God in his providence where he could not see. 'The events of my life,' he says, 'have been so far ordered in a way to make me feel that I know nothing at the time except that a Father rules; and his discipline, however severe, is never more so than is required.' He believed in the Bible, and saw rightly its relation to all our blessings. 'What,' he writes again, 'should we do if the Bible were not the foundation of our self-government? and what will become of us when we willfully and wickedly cast it behind us?' He read the Bible morning and evening in his family, and prayed with them; and it may aid those who are acquainted with the prayers of Thornton, in forming a conception of his religious character, to know that he used them. Family religion he esteemed as above all price; and when he first learned that a beloved relative had established family worship, he wept for joy. He distributed religious books very extensively, chiefly those of the American Tract Society and of the American Sunday School Union. * * * * Of creeds held in the understanding, but not influencing the life, he thought little, and the tendency of his mind was to practical rather than doctrinal views. He believed in our Lord Jesus Christ as a Savior, and trusted in him for salvation. He was a man of habitual prayer. The last time I visited him, he said to me that he had been restless during the night, and that the only way in which he could get 'quieted was by getting near to God,' and that he went to sleep repeating a prayer. During the same visit, he spoke strongly of his readiness, and even of his desire to depart. He viewed death with tranquillity, and hope, and preparation, for it was habitual with him. What need I say more? At midnight the summons came, and his work was done."

At midnight on the 30–31st of December, 1852, this admirable man breathed his last, without having awakened to consciousness from the slumber into which he had fallen. On the morning of his death was found upon his table the following lines, copied by him from a favorite hymn:

> "Vital spark of heavenly flame,
> Quit, oh quit this mortal frame!
> Trembling, hoping, lingering, flying—
> Oh the pain, the bliss of dying!
> Cease, fond nature, cease thy strife,
> And let me languish into life.
> Hark!—"

The abrupt termination, as if called away by the Angel of Death, is most singular.

The memoranda and letters of Mr. Lawrence are voluminous, and display a simple felicity of language rarely surpassed. They have been incorporated to an extent in the "Diary and Correspondence" edited by Dr. Lawrence. To that work we once more direct the attention of the reader.

HANS CHRISTIAN ANDERSEN.

THE story of a thankful man, told in a delightful manner, is the "True Story of My Life," by Mr. Andersen. From this volume we shall condense a narrative of one of the most remarkable literary characters of the age—a man whose delightful fancies are known in every country, whose genial humor is a source of gratification to millions of the rising generation, and whose individual history is full of happy incident and instruction.

Hans Christian Andersen is a native of Denmark—a poetical land, full of popular traditions, old songs, and eventful history. He was born at Odense in the year 1805 (April 2d). His father was a shoemaker, and a man of richly-gifted and truly poetical mind; his mother, a few years older, was a simple peasant-woman, ignorant of life and the world, but possessed of a heart full of love. They were in extremely humble circumstances, and the bedstead on which the little Hans made his first appearance in the world was nearly the only article of furniture in the room, and had been constructed by Mr. Andersen out of the wooden frame which, only a short time before, had borne the coffin of a deceased count. The remnants of the black cloth on the woodwork kept the fact still in remembrance. Being the only child, Hans was, of course, extremely spoiled. His father gratified him in all his wishes. As soon as he could understand the meaning of language, he read to him from Holberg and the "Arabian Nights' Entertainments." On Sundays he went out into the woods, not to talk with him, for he was silent and moody on such occasions, but to give him an opportunity of playing among the wild flowers and plucking the fragrant strawberry.

Young Hans was from the earliest of a warm, genial imagination, and every thing around him tended to excite it. Odense itself, in those days, was a totally different city to what it is now; a person might have fancied himself living hundreds of years ago, so many strange customs prevailed which belonged to an earlier period. The guilds walked in procession through the town, with their harlequin before them, and mace and bells; on Shrove Tuesday the butchers led the fattest ox through the streets adorned with garlands, while a boy in a white shirt, and with great wings on his shoulders, rode upon it; the sailors paraded through the city with music and all their flags flying, and then two of the boldest among them stood and wrestled upon a plank placed between two boats, and the one who was not thrown into the water was the victor. Every event which occurred in or around his home printed itself in vivid colors on his memory. He noticed every thing, seldom played with other boys, and even at school took little interest in their games. He was a singularly dreamy child, and so constantly went about with his eyes shut as at last to give the impression of having weak sight. Like most people who observe a great deal, he seemed to observe nothing.

In the summer months he used to accompany his mother to the harvest-fields, and assist in the operation of gleaning. One day they went to a place, the bailiff of which was well known for being a man of a rude and savage disposition. They had not been engaged long when they saw him coming with a huge whip in his hand. The gleaners hurried away with the greatest precipitation, but poor little Hans lost his wooden shoes, and the thorns pricked him so that he could not run as fast as the others. The bailiff came up and lifted his whip to strike him. Hans looked in his face, and involuntarily exclaimed,

"How dare you strike me, when God can see it?"

The strong, stern man looked at him, and at once became mild; he patted the little fellow on his cheek, and gave him money.

At an early age Hans Christian lost his father, who was a strange man, superior to his station, and unwisely dissatisfied with it. One morning he awoke in a state of the wildest excitement, and Hans was dispatched in all haste to a wise woman, who lived some miles from Odense, to obtain medical relief. She questioned him, measured his arm with a woolen thread, made extraordinary signs, and at last laid a green twig upon his breast, saying that it was a piece of the same kind of tree upon which the Savior was crucified. "Go, now," she said, "by the river's side toward home. If your father will die this time, then you will meet his ghost." Hans obeyed the injunction, but, as he did not meet any one, he congratulated himself that his father was safe. He died the third day after that. His corpse lay on the bed, and Hans slept with his mother. A cricket chirped the whole night through.

"He is dead," said Mrs. Andersen, addressing the insect; "thou needest not call him. The ice maiden has fetched him."

The allusion was to an incident which occurred the winter before, when the window-panes were frozen. Mr. Andersen pointed to them, and showed to his son a figure as of a maiden with outstretched arms. "She is come to fetch me," said he, in jest. And now, when he lay dead on the bed, mother and son remembered it with sorrow.

After his father's death Hans was left entirely to himself. His mother went out washing, and he amused himself as best he could with books and playthings. There dwelt in the neighborhood the widow of a clergyman, Madame Bunkeflod, with the sister of her deceased husband. This lady opened her doors to the boy, and hers was the first house belonging to the educated classes into which he was kindly received. The deceased husband had written poems, and had gained a reputation in Danish literature. His spinning songs were at that time in the mouths of the people. Here it was that Hans heard for the first time the word *poet* spoken, and that with so much reverence as proved it to be something sacred. "My brother the poet," said Bunkeflod's sister, and her eyes sparkled as she said it. From her he learned that it was something glorious and something fortunate to be a poet. Here, too, for the first time, he read Shakspeare, in a bad translation, to be sure; but the bold descriptions, the heroic incidents, witches, and ghosts were exactly to his taste. The more persons died in a play, the more interesting he thought it; and when, soon after, he himself wrote a play, he killed every body at the end, and thought it very fine. After this he commenced a new piece, in which a king and queen were among the *dramatis personæ.* He did not agree with Shakspeare that these dignified personages should speak like other men and women. He asked his mother and different people how a king ought properly to speak, but no one knew exactly. They said it was many years since a king had been in Odense, but he certainly spoke in a foreign language. Acting on this suggestion, Hans procured a sort of lexicon, in which were German, French, and English words with Danish meanings. He took a word out of each language, and inserted them in the speeches of his king and queen. It was a regular

Babel-like language, suitable, he thought, for such elevated personages.

Hans was now a tall lad, remarkable for a splendid voice, a passion for reading and acting, and for making fancy costumes for the puppets which he used on a little stage to enact his plays. He was sent to the charity-school, but he learned little there, and could scarcely spell or count when he left. His mother, in the mean time, had married again, and determined that Hans should be confirmed, in order that he might be apprenticed to the tailoring trade, and thus do something rational. An old female tailor altered his deceased father's great-coat into a suit for the occasion, and never before had he worn so good a coat. He had also, for the first time in his life, a pair of boots. His delight was only equaled by his fear that every body would not see them. To avert this latter calamity, he drew them up over his trowsers, and thus marched through the church. The boots creaked, and that inwardly pleased him, for thus the congregation were informed of the fact that they were new. "My whole devotion," says Mr. Andersen, "was disturbed; I was aware of it; and it caused me a horrible pang of conscience that my thoughts should be as much with my new boots as with God. I prayed him earnestly from my heart to forgive me, and then again I thought about my new boots."

Hans had contrived to save a small sum of money, amounting to about six dollars. With this he begged that he might be allowed to go to Copenhagen before he entered on the unwelcome business of tailoring. He was anxious to see what he then considered the greatest city in the world. He wept and prayed until his mother consented. She packed up his clothes in a small bundle, and made a bargain with the driver of a post-carriage to take him back to Copenhagen for three rix-dollars. On the 5th of September, 1819, he arrived there in safety. It was his ambition to become in some way connected with the theatre, for his tastes and his talents alike seemed to indicate that sphere as one in which he might win distinction. On the following day he dressed himself in his confirmation suit, not forgetting the boots, although this time they were worn under the pantaloons; and thus, in his best attire, with a hat which fell half over his eyes, he hastened to present a letter of introduction to the celebrated dancer, Madame Schall, who was the reigning attraction of the theatre. "Before I rung the bell, I fell on my knees before the door, and prayed God that I here might find help and support. A maid-servant came down the steps with her basket in her hand. She smiled kindly at me, gave me a shilling (Danish), and tripped on. Astonished, I looked at her and the money. I had on my confirmation suit, and thought I must look very smart. How, then, could she think that I wanted to beg? I called after her.

"'Keep it! keep it!' said she to me in return, and was gone.

"At length I was admitted to the dancer. She looked at me in great amazement, and then heard what I had to say. She had not the slightest knowledge of him from whom the letter came, and my whole appearance and behavior seemed very strange to her. I confessed to her my heartfelt inclination for the theatre; and upon her asking me what characters I thought I could represent, I replied, Cinderella. This piece had been performed in Odense by the royal company, and the principal character had so greatly taken my fancy, that I could play the part perfectly from memory. In the mean time, I asked her permission to take off my boots, otherwise I was not light enough for this character; and then, taking up my broad hat for a tambourine, I began to dance and sing. My strange gestures and my great activity caused the lady to think me out of my mind, and she lost no time in getting rid of me."

From the dancer Hans went to the manager of the theatre. This functionary looked at him, and said he was too thin. "Oh," replied the boy, "if you will only engage me with one hundred rix-dollars banco salary, then I shall soon get fat!" The manager was not persuaded, and bade him go on his way, saying that they only engaged people of education. Deeply mortified, he did so. The next morning he discovered that his funds had dwindled down to a solitary rix-dollar. It became necessary, therefore, either to return home or obtain work with some handicraftsman. He determined on the latter course, and soon obtained a trial at a cabinet-maker's, where he was placed in a workshop with a number of men. Their conversation was so repulsive and coarse that young Andersen was unable to stand it. He rushed from the place, forlorn and destitute.

He now bethought him of having read of an Italian, Siboni, who was the director of the Academy of Music in Copenhagen.

Every one had praised the lad's voice: perhaps something might be done for its sake, if not for the owner's. Hans hurried to the *maestro's* house, and discovered that there was a large dinner-party within. Nothing dismayed, he unbosomed himself to the housekeeper, and so worked on her sympathies that she faced the company up stairs, and repeated the boy's story. At length the door opened, and all the guests came out and looked at him. "They would have me to sing, and Siboni heard me attentively. I gave some scenes out of Holberg, and repeated a few poems; and then all at once the sense of my unhappy condition so overcame me that I burst into tears. The whole company applauded. 'I prophesy,' said one of the guests, 'that something will come out of him; but do not be vain when, some day, the whole public shall applaud thee;' and then he added something about pure, true nature, and that this is too often destroyed by years and by intercourse with mankind. I did not understand it at all.

"Siboni promised to cultivate my voice, and that I therefore should succeed as singer at the Theatre Royal. It made me very happy; I laughed and wept; and as the housekeeper led me out, and saw the excitement under which I labored, she stroked my cheeks, and said that on the following day I should go to Professor Weyse, who meant to do something for me, and upon whom I could depend.

"I went to Weyse, who himself had risen from poverty; he had deeply felt and fully comprehended my unhappy condition, and had raised by a subscription seventy-six rix-dollars banco for me. I then wrote my first letter to my mother, a letter full of rejoicing for the good fortune the whole world seemed to pour on me. My mother, in her joy, showed my letter to all her friends; many heard of it with astonishment; others laughed at it; for what was to be the end of it? In order to understand Siboni, it was necessary for me to learn something of German. A woman of Copenhagen, with whom I traveled from Odense to this city, and who gladly, according to her means, would have supported me, obtained, through one of her acquaintance, a language-master, who gratuitously gave me some German lessons, and thus I learned a few phrases in that language. Siboni received me into his house, and gave me food and instruction; but half a year afterward my voice broke, or was injured, in consequence of my being compelled to wear bad shoes through the winter, and having, besides, no warm under-clothing. There was no longer any prospect that I should become a fine singer. Siboni told me candidly, and counseled me to go to Odense, and there learn a trade.

"I, who, in the rich colors of fancy, had described to my mother the happiness which I actually felt, must now return home, and become an object of derision! Agonized with this thought, I stood as if crushed to the earth."

He found two good friends in this dark moment of his life. Professor Weyse and the poet Guldberg stepped forward, and undertook to support and educate the young fellow. For more than two years he devoted himself to the study of the German and Danish languages, under their auspices. At the end of that time he had partly regained the use of his voice, and the singing-master of the choir-school offered him a situation. He remained here until May, 1823, and was then dismissed on account of limited education. Once more he felt himself cast on the wide world without support or help. In this emergency, he determined on restoring his fallen fortunes by writing a tragedy, from the proceeds of which he hoped to be able to perfect his education. It was founded on a passage in history, and rejoiced in the title of "Alfsol." He was delighted with the first act, and immediately hurried off with it to a literary gentleman, who heard it read good-humoredly, and did all he could to secure its reception by a manager. The play was returned, but the director of the Theatre Royal accompanied the rejection with a letter, in which he said some kind words to the author, and "expressed a hope that by study, after going to school, and the previous knowledge of all that is requisite, he might some time be able to write a work which should be worthy of being acted on the Danish stage." In order, therefore, to obtain the means for his support, Collin, the director referred to, recommended young Andersen to King Frederick the Sixth, who granted to him a certain sum annually for some years; and by means of Collin, also, the directors of the High Schools allowed him to receive free instruction in the grammar-school at Slagelse, where a new and active rector had just been appointed. Dumb with astonishment, he was unable to sufficiently thank the generous man who had thus interested himself in his welfare. He has done it subsequently by grateful and touching remembrances in his works.

He was a student until September, 1828. Immediately after the examination he published his first work, "A Journey on Foot to Amack," a sportive, fantastic work, crowded with strange fancies and whims. It achieved an immediate success, and passed through several editions in a very short time. With the proceeds of this work he made a tour through Jutland and Fünen in 1830, and in North Germany the year following. On the latter occasion he left Denmark for the first time, and saw much that astonished his simple nature. The journey had great influence on his mind, which, by criticism and other causes, had been brought into a condition of morbid excitability. His second work, containing his impressions of this tour, was called "Shadow Pictures." It elicited some petty criticism. On one occasion a stuck-up pedagogue asked him whether he wrote Dog with a little d, having discovered such an error in the press. Andersen jestingly replied, "Yes, because I here spoke of a little dog."

From the end of the year 1828 to the beginning of 1839 he maintained himself solely by his writings. Denmark is a small country; but few books at that time went to Sweden and Norway, and on that account the profit could not be great. He found it difficult to support the appearance necessary for his calling and the circles in which he moved. To produce and always to be producing was destructive, nay, impossible. He translated a few pieces for the theatre, and wrote the text of an opera, which Hartmann set to music. He also worked up Sir Walter Scott's novel of the "Bride of Lammermoor" for another young composer. These necessary productions—necessary, because they secured the means and leisure for better works—were mercilessly treated by the reviewers. They denied him all talent, and hailed these works as an indication of inevitable decay. So prejudiced were people by these attacks, that when, soon after, he printed a new collection of poetry, called "The Twelve Months of the Year," they could detect no merit in the volume, although subsequently they found out that it contained some of the author's best poems. He experienced much unkindness from his contemporaries, and heaped burning coals on their heads by publishing a little volume called "Vignettes to the Danish Poets," in which he characterized the dead and the living authors in a few lines each, but only spoke of that which was good in them. The book excited attention; it was regarded as one of his best works; it was imitated, but the critics did not meddle with it.

Shortly after this, Andersen obtained a traveling stipend from government, and once more set out on his travels, praying to God that he might die far away from Denmark, or return strengthened for activity, and in a condition to produce works which should win for him and his beloved friends joy and honor. During his sojourn in France and Switzerland he composed his poem "Agnete and the Merman," a work which possesses merit, but which met with a cold reception. In August, 1834, Andersen returned to Denmark, bearing with him the manuscript, nearly completed, of his best known work, the "Improvisatore." It was with difficulty that he found a publisher. At length it appeared. Every one was delighted; the critics were silent, his sunken fortunes raised, and his position as an author of decided originality and power fully recognized. Other tales and stories followed in quick succession, and his name became known beyond the boundaries of his own country. In 1840 he traveled into the East, and on his return gave to the world, as the fruit of his journey, the "Poets' Bazar." In 1845 he received from his old friend and patron, the King of Denmark, a pension, which placed him beyond the reach of want or pecuniary need. In the next year he traveled through Rome, Naples, and the Pyrenees, and wrote his "True Story of My Life." The following year he visited England, and met with a hearty reception, which he has remembered in subsequent works.

Mr. Andersen is a prolific author. A collected edition of his works, published at Leipsic in 1847, numbered no fewer than thirty-five volumes, and since that time there have been several additions. He is undoubtedly a man of genius, but his genius is more quaint than comprehensive. In fairy tales and brief stories he shines to best advantage. The brightness and genial fervor of his imagination, his poetical spirit and quaint humor, combined with unvarying kindliness, render these little works peculiarly delightful. They rank among the very best of their class, and are unquestionably of enduring value. In his longer works he is too descriptive, and too fond of elaboration. The wholeness of the art production is lost in the exaggeration of its details. In his books of travel there is a strong current of personal vanity, which, under Andersen's treatment, becomes a modest virtue. At first it is pleasant, but constant iteration makes it tedious. There is so much, however, that is excellent in every thing Mr. Andersen has written, that no one should deny himself the luxury of reading his smallest or his greatest work.

We will conclude this sketch of a thankful man with a tranquil and beautiful quotation from the "True Story of My Life:"

"The story of my life, up to the present hour, lies unrolled before me, so rich and beautiful that I could not have invented it. I feel that I am a child of good fortune; almost every one meets me full of love and candor, and seldom has my confidence in human nature been deceived. From the prince to the poorest peasant, I have felt the noble human heart beat. It is a joy to live, and to believe in God and man. Openly and full of confidence, as if I sat among dear friends, I have here related the story of my life, have spoken both of my sorrows and joys, and have expressed my pleasure at each mark of applause and recognition, as I believe I might even express it before God himself. But, then, whether this may be vanity? I know not; my heart was affected and humble at the same time; my thought was gratitude to God. * * * * When the Christmas tree is lighted—when, as people say, the white bees swarm—I shall be, God willing, again in Denmark with my dear ones, my heart filled with the flowers of travel, and strengthened both in body and mind. Then will new works grow upon paper; may God lay his blessing on them! He will do so. A star of good fortune shines upon me; there are thousands who deserve it far more than I. I often myself can not conceive why I, in preference to numberless others, should receive so much joy: may it continue to shine! But should it set, perhaps while I conclude these lines, still it has shone; I have received my rich portion; let it set! From this, also, the best will spring. To God and men my thanks—my love!"

ANTHONY WAYNE.

This illustrious warrior and eccentric man was born in the county of Chester, Pennsylvania, on the 1st of January, 1745. His parents were of English descent, and owned a farm which the first immigrant had purchased on his arrival. Of Anthony's youth we have but little knowledge. A letter written by his uncle informs us that he was not particularly smart in a literary point of view, but that he would make a good soldier, having already distracted the brains of two thirds of his schoolmates with rehearsals of battles, sieges, etc. A reprimand from his father, accompanied with a threat that he should be taken from school and placed on the farm, turned Anthony's attention more seriously to his studies; he applied himself with diligence, and in a few months left the academy prepared for a higher place of instruction. He was removed to the Philadelphia Academy, where he remained until his eighteenth year. Shortly after this he returned to his native county, and opened an office as a land surveyor. In his twenty-first year, Mr. Wayne was appointed agent to inspect the American settlements in Nova Scotia: the threatening aspect of the relations between the two countries brought the undertaking to an end in 1767. In this year Mr. Wayne returned once more to Chester County, bearing with him a young and newly-married wife. He continued to pursue the business of land surveyor until duties of national importance drew him from his office to a sphere of greater usefulness.

At the earliest period of the Revolutionary struggle, Mr. Wayne gave the whole of his attention to the formation and instruction of military associations. In a very short space of time he succeeded in organizing a volunteer corps in his native county, which soon became remarkable for its efficiency. Early in January, 1776, Congress conferred on Mr. Wayne the rank of colonel, and the command of one of the four regiments required from Pennsylvania to re-enforce the northern army. The regiment was soon raised, and, under Colonel Wayne, proceeded to Canada, where it speedily became a part of Thompson's brigade. In an unfortunate expedition against the enemy, conducted by General Thompson, Wayne distinguished himself by effecting a difficult but successful retreat for that portion of the troops which devolved to his command. Subsequently, when a retreat was ordered to Lake Champlain, Wayne was assigned the duty of covering the movement with the Pennsylvania troops. The retreat had to be conducted with great expedition, and Wayne's troops were scarcely in the boats when the enemy came up. Owing, however, to the excellence of the arrangements, Ticonderoga was reached in safety on the 17th of July.

The British general advanced to Crown Point, where he commenced a series of careful reconnoitrings. The result was unfavorable to an immediate assault, and the British general concluded to defer it until the following spring, withdrawing his army to Canada for the winter months. So soon as this was found to be actually the fact, the American general repaired to the assistance of Washington, leaving Ticonderoga in charge of Wayne, with a garrison of two thousand five hundred men. Congress soon after confirmed the trust by making Wayne a brigadier general. He remained at Ticonderoga during the winter, and in spring, at his own earnest solicitation, joined the main army. He arrived at head-quarters on the 15th of May, and was immediately placed at the head of a brigade, concerning the operations of which Washington expressed the liveliest expectations. The position of the American commander-in-chief at Middlebrook interfered with the operations of the English so severely that it was determined to expulse him, if possible (1777). Several military stratagems were resorted to to draw Washington into an engagement, but he denied the enemy the opportunity it sought, and remained carefully on the defensive. At length the British feigned a retreat, and Washington, unwilling to lose what for a moment seemed to be an advantage, ordered a pursuit, under the commands of Sullivan, Maxwell, Wayne, and Morgan, while he, with the main army, was to follow in person, in case of engagements. Owing to various causes, two, only, out of the four corps arrived in time for the pursuit—those commanded by Wayne and Morgan. They displayed great bravery and good conduct, but when it was discovered that the English general's retreat was merely a feint, Washington recovered his position at Middlebrook, and the pursuit was, of course, abandoned. The English general retired to New York, and thence made preparations for a descent on Philadelphia. This brings us to the period of the famous battle of Brandywine.

The defense of Chad's Ford, the most accessible point on the line of English march, was intrusted to Wayne, who on this occasion had a second brigade and a portion of Proctor's artillery added to his command. It is not necessary for the purpose of this sketch to narrate the accidents of the day, or recount how the American army was driven from its position by the British. Wayne was the last to leave the field; in fact, he did not know that the American columns were broken and scattered until after sunset, when, being apprised of the fact, he withdrew his division. On the 16th an engagement took place at Warren Tavern, but a violent shower of rain separated the combatants. The ammunition of the Americans having become seriously injured, an immediate retreat became necessary to Parker's Ferry, where a fresh supply could be obtained. A change of positions now took place, and Wayne was appointed to watch the enemy, and cut off baggage and hospital trains. On the 20th of September, at night, Wayne was attacked by the British forces, and, owing to the negligence or misapprehension of an officer, lost one hundred and fifty men. For this mishap he was subsequently tried by court-martial. After a full and patient hearing of all the testimony adduced, the court decided unanimously that "General Wayne was not guilty of the charge exhibited against him, but that on the night of the 20th of September he did every thing that could be expected from an active, brave, and vigilant officer, under the orders that he then had, and do therefore acquit him with the highest honor."

The British established themselves at Germantown, and Washington conceived the bold project of routing their camp by a surprise movement. For this purpose, the American army marched from Skippack Creek in two columns (3d of October); that of the right composed of the divisions of Sullivan and Wayne, with Conway's brigade; the column of the left composed of the divisions of Greene and Stephens, with M'Dougall's brigade, and fourteen hundred Maryland and Jersey militia. On reaching the summit of Chestnut Hill a brisk engagement took place. The enemy sought refuge in a large stone house, and established a galling fire on the advancing columns, but without impeding the progress of Sullivan and Wayne, who pressed forward and met the enemy at every point with prowess and success. The columns under the command of Greene were equally successful, and for a time every thing seemed to promise favorable to the American arms. On the following day, however, a serious reverse was experienced. We give the account of it in the words of Sullivan: "My division, with the North Carolina regiment, commanded by Colonel Armstrong, and a part of Conway's brigade, having driven the enemy a mile and a half below Chew's house, and finding themselves unsupported by any other troops, their cartridges all expended, the force of the enemy on the right collecting on the left to oppose them, being alarmed by the firing at Chew's house, so far in their rear, and by the cry of a light horseman on the right that the enemy had got round us, and at the same time discovering some troops flying on the right, retired with as much precipitation as they had before advanced, against every effort of their officers to rally them. When the retreat took place, we had been engaged near three hours, which, with the march of the preceding night, rendered them almost unfit for fighting or retreating. We, however, made a safe retreat, though not a regular one. We brought off all our cannon and wounded." Washington, writing on the same subject, says: "In justice to the right wing of the army (composed of the divisions of Sullivan and Wayne), whose conduct I had an opportunity of observing, as they acted immediately under my eye, I have the greatest pleasure to inform you that both the officers and men behaved with a degree of gallantry which did them the highest honor."

After this lamentable defeat, Wayne was detached on a foraging expedition, and by coolness and determination succeeded in making valuable contributions to the scanty commissariat of the American army. We hasten now to that celebrated event in American history which owes all its lustre to the bravery of Wayne—we refer to the capture of Stony Point. This was one of the strongest positions of the enemy, and, fully aware of the fact, no precautions had been spared to make it impregnable. On two sides it was protected by the Hudson; on the third by a marsh; the remaining approach was strongly fortified, and garrisoned with six hundred soldiers. Wayne surveyed the place with a determination to find an opening, and soon took up his position within a mile and a half of his object. We quote the following account of the attack from Mr. Armstrong's sketch of the hero: "By the organization given to the attack, the regiments of Ferbiger and Meigs, with Hull's detachment, formed the column of the right, and the regiment of Butler and Murfey's detachment that of the left. A party of twenty men, furnished with axes for pioneer duty, and followed by a sustaining corps of one hundred and fifty men with unloaded arms, preceded each column, while a small detachment was assigned to purposes merely of demonstration. At half past eleven o'clock, the hour fixed on for the assault, the columns were in motion; but, from delays made inevitable by the nature of the ground, it was twenty minutes after twelve before this commenced; when neither the morass, now overflowed by the tide, nor the formidable and double row of *abatis*, nor the high and strong works on the summit of the hill, could for a moment damp the ardor or stop the career of the assailants, who, in the face of an incessant fire of musketry, and a shower of shells and grape-shot, forced their way through every obstacle, and with so much concert of movement that both columns entered the fort and reached its centre nearly at the same moment. Nor was the conduct of the victors less conspicuous for humanity than for valor. Not a man of the garrison was injured after the surrender, and during the conflict of battle all were spared who ceased to make resistance.

"The entire American loss in this enterprise, so formidable in prospect, did not exceed one hundred men. The pioneer parties, necessarily the most exposed, suffered most. Of the twenty men led by Lieutenant Gibbons, of the sixth Pennsylvania regiment, seventeen were killed or wounded. Wayne's own escape on this occasion was of the hair-breadth kind. Struck on the head by a musket ball, he fell; but, immediately rising on one knee, he exclaimed, 'March on! carry me into the fort; for, should the wound be mortal, I will die at the head of the column.'"

In commemoration of this brilliant exploit, regarded by military writers as the most gallant and remarkable of the campaign, Congress directed a gold medal to be struck emblematical of the action. From the commander-in-chief, and from all quarters, Wayne received the most flattering testimonials of esteem and admiration. He was the most renowned chieftain of the day.

In 1781, Wayne accompanied La Fayette to the South, in order to put an end to the ravages of the British in that section of the country. They followed closely on the tracks of Cornwallis, and at length heard that the main body of the British army had succeeded in crossing Jamestown Ferry, but that a rear guard of ordinary force remained behind. La Fayette determined that this should be cut off, if possible, and directed Wayne to advance with seven hundred men to effect the object. Wayne did so with his usual coolness and dispatch, and succeeded in driving in the enemy's pickets, but, very unexpectedly, he found that he had fallen into a trap, and, instead of being in the neighborhood of the rear guard of the army, was within fifty yards of the main body. At this critical moment Wayne's daring came to his rescue. Instead of retreating in confusion, he made a bold charge, and so perplexed the enemy with the manœuvre that he succeeded in escaping with a much smaller loss than would otherwise have been the case. Subsequently Wayne was employed in Georgia, where he succeeded in bringing the enemy into a state of comparative harmlessness in spite of very insufficient means. The treaty of peace which followed the evacuation of Charleston enabled Wayne to return to his own fireside in Pennsylvania, after an absence of seven years. Soon after he was elected a member of the Council of Censors, and subsequently to a seat in the Convention to revise and amend the Constitution of the State. He was not, however, destined to a long civil career. Although the war with England was at an end, the Indians still continued their depredations and hostilities. Two unsuccessful attempts had been made to subdue them. It was now determined to organize an army sufficiently powerful to act with vigor, and leave the rest with General Wayne, to whom the command was intrusted.

Wayne began his march from a camp near the site of the present town of Cincinnati, and on the 8th of August, 1794, reached the Indian settlements, the destruction of which formed the first object of the enterprise. On the 19th, after repeated attempts to bring the savages peaceably to terms, the army marched on to the position taken by the Indians, a strong one naturally and artificially, and protected with two thousand of their best fighting men. Wayne's advanced guard was briskly attacked from a thicket, made up of tall grass and underwood, and in a few minutes the action commenced. The Indians and Canadians were routed with great loss. "We remained," says General Wayne, in his dispatch, "three days and nights on the banks of the Miami, in front of the field of battle, during which time all the houses and corn were consumed, or otherwise destroyed for a considerable distance both above and below Fort Miami; and we were within pistol-shot of the garrison of that place, who were compelled to remain quiet spectators of this general devastation and conflagration." This severe but necessary treatment was pursued until the enemy sued for peace. A treaty was at once drawn up, and the war brought to a satisfactory termination. Complimentary resolutions were unanimously passed by the Congress then in session, and President and people alike vied in the cordial expression of their gratitude to a noble old warrior newly returned from the wars.

The last mark of confidence which General Wayne received from the government was his appointment as commissioner for treating with the Northwestern Indians, and as receiver of the military posts given up by the British government. The duties attached to these offices he discharged in his usual punctual manner, and proceeded from the West on his way homeward. While descending Lake Erie from Detroit, he was attacked by the gout with such severity that in a few days his life and his labors were brought to a sudden termination. His remains were temporarily buried on the shore of the lake, but in 1809 they were removed to the cemetery of St. David's Church, in Chester County, Pennsylvania. A monument recalling the patriotic achievements of his life was placed over the grave, and still marks the spot where lie the remains of a true warrior patriot.

EMMANUEL KANT.

EMMANUEL KANT, the illustrious founder of the philosophical school which succeeded that of Liebnitz, was a native of Königsberg, in Prussia, where he was born on the 22d of April, 1724. His father was a saddler, and of Scotch descent. The elder Kant is described as a man of superior intelligence and inflexible moral character. His wife was an estimable woman, pious and devoted in her ministrations. "I never," said Emmanuel Kant, "saw or heard in my father's family any thing inconsistent with honor, propriety, or truth." From his earliest days he was thus placed on the right path. Bred in the love of truth, and with such examples of moral worth before him, it is not remarkable that he became eminent for his good life as for his great mind.

At the proper age he received the usual instruction of the common schools, and as he displayed diligence and capacity, it was determined that his studies should be continued in the higher seminaries. Here he pursued a peaceful course of severe, systematic, and persevering study. He learned all that could be learned in the circle of language, history, and science. He carried into each department of this extensive field that scrutinizing spirit and that avidity for knowledge which afford no rest to the mind until it has explored the whole surface of the ground and examined its nature, sounded its depth, ascertained the limits of the portion already cultivated, and determined what yet remains to be accomplished.

Kant's life was purely scholastic. His intellectual career began and ended at the University. For his offices and his fortune he was indebted solely to the usual course of academic advancement. He supported himself first as a teacher in private families; in 1755 he became doctor of philosophy, and for fifteen years was only one of the *privatim docentes* without salary, although his lectures were much frequented; in 1766 he was made under-librarian, with a miserable support, and obtained at last, in 1770, the chair of professor of logic and metaphysics. In 1786–88 he was rector of the University; in 1787 inscribed among the members of the Academy of Berlin, and died without seeing any dignity added to his title of professor, excepting that of Senior of the Philosophical Faculty. This was his worldly career, and concerning it Madame de Stäel has remarked that there is scarcely another example, except among the Greeks, of a life so rigorously philosophical. He lived to a great age, and never once quitted the snows of murky Königsberg. There he passed a calm and happy existence, meditating, professing, and writing. He had mastered all the sciences; he had studied languages, and cultivated literature. He lived and died a type of the German professor: he rose, smoked, took his coffee, wrote, lectured, and took his daily walk at precisely the same hour. The Cathedral clock, it was said, was not more punctual in its movements than Emmanuel Kant. Mathematics and physics principally occupied his attention at first, and the success with which he pursued these studies was soon made manifest in various publications. He became renowned as a profound logician and natural philosopher. An instance of his wonderful powers of speculative reasoning and deduction was the prediction of the existence of the planet Uranus long before it was known by astronomers. He argued that it should be in a certain position, and Herschel, whose attention was thus directed to the subject, found it there. Other conjectures on the system of the world, the Milky Way, the nebulæ, the ring of Saturn, were also confirmed by the same eminent astronomer thirty years after they had been uttered by the illustrious subject of this sketch.

Kant's fame as the greatest philosopher and metaphysician of the age dates from the publication of his "Critique of Pure Reason" (1781), an examination of the faculty of knowledge, of the powers which concur in its exercise, of their laws, of the play of their operations, and of the effects thence resulting for man, relatively to the impressions which he receives, to the judgments which he makes, to the conceptions which he forms, and to the ideas to which reason elevates itself. This work was the product of twelve years' meditation, although written in five months. The novelty of its views, the toughness of its terminology and style, for some time obscured its real value. When it became known, all Germany went wild with the new philosophy. Almost every "chair" was filled by a Kantist. Endless books and pamphlets came from the press, defending or attacking the principles of the critical philosophy. Kant had likened himself to Copernicus; his disciples likened him both to Copernicus and Newton. He had not only changed the whole science of metaphysics, as Copernicus had changed the science of astronomy, but had also consummated the science he had originated. Kant published many other works, in the smallest of which the profoundest meditations are to be found.

He became famous, and had to endure the penalty of popularity. Bores from all parts of the world broke in upon his privacy. It was with the greatest reluctance that he satisfied the curiosity of his visitors, for he was modest and simple to a fault. In the latter part of his life he would only show himself for a few minutes at the door of his study, and express to his visitors his astonishment at their curiosity. He would then return to his private friends and say, "I have seen to-day some noble virtuosi." He never spoke of his philosophy; and while it was the subject of conversation among the most enlightened men in all the countries where the language and literature of Germany prevail, from his house it was entirely banished. It is said that he hardly ever read any of the works in which, during twenty years, his principles (we have refrained from referring to them on account of the utter impossibility of merely indicating their scope in a brief article) were attacked, defended, developed, and applied to all the branches of human knowledge.

The greatest enjoyment of the latter years of his life was to invite to his table a few intimate friends, and discuss with them the events of the French Revolution, in which he took great interest. His gay and instructive conversation was in the highest degree delightful. His manners were simple and pure. Owing to the smallness of his income, he was unable to take upon himself the responsibilities of a wife and family, although he was far from being indifferent to the charms and graces of the opposite sex.

On the 24th of February, 1804, this intellectual giant passed to the land of shadows. He was fully conscious of the approaching dissolution, and nearly the last words he uttered were these: "I do not fear death; I know how to die. I assure you, before God, that if I knew that this night was to be my last, I would raise my hands and say, God be praised. The case would be far different if I had ever caused the misery of any one of his creatures."

Kant was of small stature, and fine, delicate complexion. He was distinguished by the strictest veracity, and by an extreme attention to avoid every thing which could give pain, if the interests of truth did not require it. He was affable, benevolent without ostentation, and thankful for any attentions which he received. During his last illness he was frequently so much moved by the attentions of an old male servant, that it was with the greatest difficulty the latter could prevent his master from kissing his hand. It was discovered after his death that, although a poor man all his life, he had been in the habit of dispensing more than eleven hundred florins annually out of his small earnings to poor relations and indigent families.

"Such," says Professor Stapfer (to whom we are indebted for the materials of this sketch), "was the extraordinary man who has agitated the human mind to a greater depth than any of the philosophers of the same rank before him. The opinions on the permanent result of his analysis of the human faculties are naturally exceedingly diverse. His faithful disciples—of whom the number, it is true, is much diminished—regard him as the Newton, or, at least, the Kepler of the intellectual world. Beyond his own school, many ascribe to his principles that revival of patriotic and generous sentiments, that return of vigor of mind, and that disinterested zeal, which have of late years manifested themselves in Germany, so much to the honor of the nation, to the success of her independence, and advantage of the moral sciences. A numerous party accuse him of having created a barbarous terminology, making unnecessary innovations for the purpose of enveloping himself in an obscurity almost impenetrable—of having produced systems absurd and dangerous, and increased the uncertainty respecting the most important interests of man; of having, by the illusion of talent, turned the attention of youth from positive studies to consume their time in vain speculations; of having, by his transcendental idealism, conducted his rigidly consequent disciples, some to absolute idealism, others to skepticism, others, again, to a new species of Spinosism, and all to systems equally absurd and dangerous. They farther accuse his doctrine of being in itself a tissue of extravagant hypothesis and contradictory theories, of which the result is to make us regard man as a creature discordant and fantastic. They accuse him, finally, of having, by his demanding more than stoical efforts, produced in the mind discouragement and uncertainty, much more than the germs of active virtue, confidence, and security. There is, undoubtedly, exaggeration in both these extreme opinions. The disciples of Socrates departed still farther from his doctrines than those of Kant have from the principles of criticism; yet who will deny the merit of Socrates, or his salutary influence?"

JOHANN GOTTLIEB FICHTE.

JOHANN GOTTLIEB FICHTE was the son of a poor peasant couple who resided at Rammeneau, in Upper Lusatia, Prussia, where he was born on the 19th of May, 1762. From his earliest infancy he gave indications of unusual mental capacity and great moral energy, for both of which he was afterward famous. He was a precocious child, and long before he was old enough to be sent to school had learned many things from his father, who taught him to read and to remember the pious songs and proverbs which formed his own simple stock of erudition. He was not much beyond his simple station, but he had traveled in Saxony and Franconia, and had observed the manners and customs of the people, and was especially well informed in their fables and romances. These he would recite to the little Johann as he sat in the warm sunshine listening with eagerness to all that was wonderful and strange. When left to himself he would wander in the fields, leaving his boisterous companions in order that he might turn over in his own mind all that he had heard. Probably he dreamed of unspeakable joys in roaming free and happy through the world, and seeing and remembering every thing. Whatever were his meditations, he loved solitude, and would stand for hours gazing into the far distance, and dreaming methodically, like a young philosopher, of what might be. At home he read the family prayers with so much feeling and propriety, that his father fondly hoped he might one day see him in the pulpit. An event curious in itself, and very important in its influence on his subsequent career, soon occurred, which favored that hope, and went far to realize it. But, before we relate it, we must give a touching anecdote, which exhibits Fichte's heroic self-command in a very interesting light.

The first book which fell into his hands after the Bible and Catechism was the renowned history of "Siegfried the Horned," and it seized so powerfully on his imagination that he lost all pleasure in any other employment, became careless and neglectful, and for the first time in his life was punished. Then, in the spirit of the injunction which tells us to cut off our right hand if it cause us to offend, Fichte resolved to sacrifice the beloved book, and, taking it in his hand, walked slowly to a stream flowing past the house, with the intention of throwing it in. Long he lingered on the bank ere he could muster courage for this first self-conquest of his life; but at length, summoning all his resolution, he flung it into the water. His fortitude gave way as he saw the treasure, too dearly loved, floating away forever, and he burst into a passionate flood of tears. Just at this moment the father arrived on the spot, and the weeping child told what he had done, but, either from timidity or incapacity to explain his feelings, was silent as to his true motive. Irritated at this treatment of his present, Fichte's father inflicted upon him an unusually severe punishment; and this occurrence formed a fitting prelude to his after-life, in which he was so often misunderstood, and the actions springing from the purest convictions of duty were exactly those for which he had most to suffer. When a sufficient time had elapsed for the offense to be in some measure forgotten, the father brought home another of these seducing books; but Fichte dreaded being again exposed to the temptation, and begged that it might rather be given to some of the other children.

It was about this time that the other event before alluded to occurred. The clergyman of the village, who had taken a fancy to Gottlieb, and had often assisted in his instruction, happened one day to ask him how much he thought he could remember of the sermon of the preceding day. Fichte made the attempt, and, to the astonishment of the pastor, succeeded in giving a very tolerable account of the course of argument, as well as the texts quoted in its illustration. The circumstance was mentioned to the Count von Hoffmansegg, the lord of the village; and when one day another nobleman, the Baron von Mittie, who was on a visit to the castle, happened to express his regret at having been too late for the sermon on the Sunday morning, he was told, half in jest, that it was of little consequence, for that there was a boy in the village who could repeat it all from memory. Little Gottlieb was sent for, and soon arrived in a clean smock frock, and bearing a large nosegay, such as his mother was accustomed to send to the castle occasionally as a token of respect. He answered the first questions put to him with his accustomed quiet simplicity; but when asked to repeat as much as he could recollect of the morning's sermon, his voice and manner became more animated, and, as he proceeded, entirely forgetting the presence of the formidable company, he became so fervid and abundant in his eloquence that the count thought it necessary to interrupt him, lest the playful tone of the circle should be destroyed by the serious subjects of the sermon. The young preacher had, however, made some impression on his auditory; the baron made inquiries concerning him; and the clergyman, wishing for nothing more than an opportunity to serve his favorite, gave such an account that the baron determined to undertake the charge of his education. The next day the young Gottlieb was on his way to the Castle of Siebeneichen, in Saxony, near Meissen, on the Elbe. One of his most ardent desires, namely, to travel, was about to be gratified. Like many other pleasures in this world, it was more of the imagination than experience. Visions of his own peaceful home, and of the kind friends he had left there, crowded upon him, and his heart sunk within him as the distance lengthened. The melancholy grandeur of the baronial halls to which he was transported did not add to his peace of mind. He became thoroughly wretched—so deeply dejected that his health began to fail. Fortunately, his noble patron was a man of sense and delicacy. He traced the cause of the boy's ailings to the right source, and in a kindly and liberal spirit removed him from the cold shadow of the castle to the domestic circle of a neighboring clergyman. Once more within the influence of moral precept and support, his spirits revived rapidly. Some of the happiest years of his life were passed beneath the roof of this estimable man and his admirable spouse, toward whom Fichte always preserved the warmest affection and gratitude. They treated him as if he were their son, and as such he remembered them.

It was here that he received his first instruction in the learned languages. When his kind preceptor could teach him no more, he was transferred to the High School at Meissen, and afterward to the seminary at Schulpforte. The monastic gloom of the latter establishment, added to many unpleasant customs which prevailed among the pupils, filled him once more with melancholy. He shed tears plentifully, and was jeered at contemptuously by his companions. Sensibility is not an ordinary weakness of schoolboys, and in a large public establishment where flogging prevails, it is brought down to its lowest standard. Fichte, who was yet but thirteen years of age, felt every unkind word most acutely. It was in vain that he looked for a kindred spirit to pour balmy consolation into his bleeding wounds. It was natural, therefore, that the idea of escape should occur to his mind. The dread, however, of being retaken and brought back again in disgrace made him pause. While brooding over this project, it happened that he met with a copy of "Robinson Crusoe"—that thing of beauty, that joy forever to the youthful world. His enthusiasm was now unbounded. No longer would he hesitate. He would flee to the desert, and make it his dwelling-place—selecting the desert, probably, on account of the advantages it offered of seeing any one who might happen to be in pursuit. The manner in which he carried this curious idea into execution was remarkable. Nothing could have been easier than for him to have taken his departure unperceived on one of the days when the scholars were allowed to go to the playground, but he scorned to steal away in secret; he would have the matter appear as the result of necessity and calm determination. He therefore made a formal declaration to his superior, a tyrannous lad who had much abused his brief authority, that he would no longer endure the treatment he received, but would leave the place at the first opportunity. The announcement was of course received with jeers and laughter, which only added to Fichte's determination. He then procured a map, and carefully studied the route which he proposed to take. Having made himself master of this, he found his opportunity, and set off on foot in the direction of the town of Naumburg. As he walked, however, he bethought himself of a saying of his dear old pastor, that one should never begin an important undertaking without asking the blessing of Heaven. He dropped on his knees by the road side, and implored the Divine assistance with tears in his eyes. While thus engaged, the thought flashed across his mind that his absence would occasion much grief to his parents—that he might never, perhaps, see them more. He was so overcome with this terrible thought that he resolved to retrace his steps, and meet all the punishments that might be in store for him, "that he might look once more on the face of his mother." God had hearkened to the prayer of the innocent, and guided his footsteps.

The school was already in an uproar, and scouts were out in every direction in pursuit of the runaway. He was immediately carried before the rector, and at once confessed that he had intended to escape. With child-like simplicity and frankness he related the whole story, his hesitation, and the cause of his return. The rector not only remitted his punishment, but became his friend, and placed him under another master, who treated him with extreme kindness.

He continued his studies until he was sufficiently advanced to become a candidate for holy orders. Unfortunately, at this critical epoch, his generous patron, the baron, died, and all hopes of becoming a clergyman were at an end. It became necessary that he should go out in the world and seek his own way in it. Fortunately, he was offered the situation of private tutor to a family in Switzerland. He at once closed with the parties, and for two years discharged the irksome duties incidental to the position he had taken. He then proceeded to Leipsic, where he gave lessons in Greek and philosophy, and for the first time became acquainted with the writings of Kant. This was an important event in his life, and threw him into raptures. "I have been living," he writes, "for the last four or five months in Leipsic the happiest life I can remember. I came here with my head full of grand projects, which all burst one after another, like so many soap-bubbles, without leaving me so much as the froth. At first this troubled me a little, and, half in despair, I took a step which I ought to have taken long before. Since I could not alter what was without me, I resolved to alter what was within. I threw myself into philosophy —the Kantian, videlicet—and here I found the true antidote for all my evils, and joy enough into the bargain. The influence which this philosophy, particularly the ethical part of it (which, however, is unintelligible without a previous study of the "Critique of Pure Reason"), has had upon my whole system of thought, the revolution which it has effected in my mind, is not to be described. To you, especially, I owe the declaration that I now believe with my whole heart in free-will, and that I see that under this supposition alone can duty, virtue, and morality have any existence. From the opposite proposition, of the necessity of all human actions, must flow the most injurious consequences to society, and it may, in fact, be in part the source of the corrupt morals of the higher classes which we hear so much of. Should any one adopting it remain virtuous, we must look for the cause of this purity elsewhere than in the innocuousness of the doctrine. With many it is their want of logical consequence in their actions.

"I am, furthermore, well convinced that this life is not the land of enjoyment, but of labor and toil, and that every joy is granted to us but to strengthen us for further exertion; that the management of our own fate is by no means required of us, but only self-culture. I trouble myself, therefore, not at all concerning the things that are without; I endeavor not to appear, but to *be*. And to this, perhaps, I owe the deep tranquillity I enjoy. My external position, however, is well enough suited to such a frame of mind: I am no man's master, and no man's slave. As to prospects, I have none at all, for the constitution of the Church here does not suit me, nor, to say the truth, that of the people either. As long as I can maintain my present independence, I shall certainly do so."

Fichte's enthusiasm for Kant induced him to pay a visit to the eminent philosopher at Königsberg. Instead of a letter of introduction, he presented Kant with a work written in eight days, called "A Critique of every possible Revelation." Kant immediately recognized the merits of the production, and became his friend. He was too poor to assist him in a material point of view—and Fichte sorely needed assistance—but he promised to obtain him a publisher for his "Critique," and otherwise treated him hospitably and kindly.

In due time the "Critique" made its appearance. There was no name on the title-page, and every one said it was the production of Kant. When it became known that Fichte was the author, he was at once placed in the highest ranks of philosophy. The celebrity he acquired was the means of procuring him the chair of philosophy at Jena (1793), the leading university of Germany.

Fichte now fondly believed that his wanderings and his privations were at an end, and that henceforth he could devote himself to philosophy without interruption from the external world. He was mistaken. Even at Jena he found himself soon opposing and opposed. His endeavors to instill a higher moral feeling into the students, his anxiety for their better culture, were misunderstood. A cry of Atheism was raised against the professor—an unjust cry, but not without its effects. The government required some kind of explanation from the philosopher. He refused to give it, tendered his resignation, and recommenced his wanderings. He found an asylum in Prussia, where he occupied the chair at Erlangen, and afterward at Berlin. From his career in the latter place the following incident is related by one of his biographers (Mr. Lewes):

"It is 1813. The students are assembled in crowds to hear their favorite professor, who is to lecture that day upon duty—on that duty whose ideal grandeur his impassioned eloquence has revealed to them. Fichte arrives, calm and modest. He lectures with his usual dignified calmness, rising into fiery bursts of eloquence, but governed by the same marvelous rigor of logic as before. He leads them from the topic to the present state of affairs. On them he grows still more animated, the rolling of drums without frequently drowning his voice, and giving him fresh spirit. He points to the bleeding wounds of his country; he warms with hatred against oppressors; and enforces it as the duty of every one to lend his single arm to save his country.

"'This course of lectures,' he exclaims, 'will be suspended till the end of the campaign. We will resume them in a free country, or die in the attempt to recover her freedom.' Loud shouts respondent ring through the hall; clapping of hands and stamping of feet make answer to the rolling drums without; every German heart there present is moved as at the sound of a trumpet. Fichte descends, passes through the crowd, and places himself in the ranks of a corps of volunteers then departing for the army. It is the commencement of the memorable campaign of 1813."

Throughout this struggle for liberty Fichte took an active part, and was nobly assisted by his wife. The hospitals of the city were filled with the sick and the wounded; they became at length unequal to the demands made upon them, and the authorities, through the public journals, called on the inhabitants to come to their assistance with money, and with women to take charge of the sick. Fichte's wife was one of the earliest to volunteer in the good cause. She devoted her days to the distribution of clothes, food, and medicine, and to pious cares around the beds of the unknown sick and dying; and after she returned late on a winter's evening to her home, often again went out to collect contributions from her friends and acquaintances.

For five months she devoted herself in this noble way to the service of the helpless and wretched. In January, 1814, from want of sleep or other causes, alarming symptoms began to manifest themselves, and soon after she was attacked with a dangerous nervous fever. It soon attained such a height as to leave scarce a hope of recovery; and on the very day when she was in the greatest peril, Fichte, who had been engaged in close and anxious attendance upon her during her illness, was compelled to leave her, to deliver the first of a course of philosophical lectures, which he had now recommenced. With wonderful self-command, he continued to speak for two hours on the most abstract subjects, scarcely hoping to find, on his return, his beloved companion still alive. This was, however, the crisis of her illness, and those who witnessed the transports of joy and gratitude with which he hailed the symptoms of recovery were able to estimate the power of self-control he had exercised. It was probably at that moment that, innocently and unconsciously, she communicated to him the fatal infection. On the following day the commencement of a serious indisposition was evident, but Fichte could not be induced to relax any of his customary exertions. The continued sleeplessness, however, soon produced its usual effect on his mental faculties, and in the course of fourteen days the attack terminated fatally.

Thus passed away the amiable spirit of one of the great thinkers of the age—a man who shed on the country of his birth not only intellectual splendor, but rays of moral worth that will burn and glow on the nation's brow when much that is purely philosophical shall be forgotten.

"So robust an intellect," says Mr. Thomas Carlyle, in one of his tempestuous bursts of enthusiasm, "a soul so calm, so lofty, massive, and immovable, has not mingled in philosophical discussion since the time of Luther; for the man rises before us, amid contradiction and debate, like a granite mountain amid clouds and winds. Ridicule of the best that could be commanded has been already tried against him, but it could not avail. What was the wit of a thousand wits to him. The cry of a thousand choughs assaulting that old cliff of granite. Seen from the summit, these, as they winged the midway air, showed scarce so gross as beetles, and their cry was seldom even audible. Fichte's opinions may be true or false, but his character as a thinker can be slightly valued only by those who know it ill; and as a man approved by action and suffering in his life and in his death, he ranks with a class of men who were common only in better ages than ours."

DAVID RITTENHOUSE.

DAVID RITTENHOUSE, whose scientific eminence characterized a period of our history when such eminence was uncommon in the most advanced circles of the world, was born at Germantown, Pennsylvania, on the 8th of April, 1732. His parents were of Dutch descent, and emigrated to the New World at an early period of its history. Concerning David's education and youth we have no satisfactory information. It has been supposed that he received some tuition from a humble relative, a joiner by trade, who lived in the house of Rittenhouse, and died there. This relative appears to have been a superior man, for among his papers were discovered some elementary treatises on mathematics and astronomy, and numerous manuscripts containing calculations and investigations. When he died David was in his twelfth year, and the books and papers were treasures to him, which, even then, he appreciated. The barns and fences about the farm, and even the implements of industry, were covered with diagrams and figures by the young mathematician.

When David was nineteen years of age (1751), he made the

acquaintance of the Rev. Thomas Barton, a well-informed clergyman of the Episcopal Church. This gentleman was astonished at the intelligence and natural aptitude of young Rittenhouse, and, being but a few years older, a strong intimacy sprung up between them, cemented subsequently by the marriage of Mr. Barton to a sister of David's. Under the auspices of this gentleman, Rittenhouse obtained a satisfactory knowledge of the Latin language, and a rudimental acquaintance with the Greek. In addition to these valuable acquirements, Mr. Barton assisted David in his mathematical studies, and added to his knowledge by judicious loans of books.

Rittenhouse had no inclination toward agriculture, and chose the profession of clock-maker, as more in accordance with his tastes and predilections. His first store was erected on his father's farm (1751), where he turned out some unusually good work, and made some important improvements in the rude timepieces of that day. For seven years he devoted himself to the philosophical pursuit of this business, but was compelled for a time to abandon it on account of ill health. A short period of relaxation restored him, but the intense and unremitting attention he paid to every thing laid the foundation of a complaint which compelled him later in life to abandon the business to which he had so enthusiastically devoted himself. He became noted for the excellence of his workmanship, and the philosophical accuracy with which he examined and perfected his instruments and pieces. He made many acquaintances, and some friends; among the latter were Dr. Smith, provost of the College of Philadelphia, and John Lukens, surveyor general of the province. The unusual capacity of Rittenhouse's mind became known to them, and on the first opportunity they availed themselves of his high philosophical and astronomical attainments. The boundary-lines of Pennsylvania, Delaware, and Maryland were at that time subjects of much discussion and litigation. They existed merely on paper, and had never been determined by actual survey. The governor of the province of Pennsylvania was therefore directed to seek out a competent person to trace the lines on the ground, and thus settle all causes of complaint and dispute. For this important and extremely difficult task Mr. Rittenhouse was selected (1763), and he performed it so much to the satisfaction of his employers, that he was proffered and received more than the stipulated compensation. What was even a greater compliment was the fact that the British commissioners—two eminent astronomers, Messrs. Mason and Dixon—corroborated the accuracy of Mr. Rittenhouse's calculations. Subsequently he was employed in defining the limits of nearly all the thirteen original states. He was probably the only American capable of doing so in those days.

In 1767, the College of Philadelphia conferred on Mr. Rittenhouse the honorary degree of Master of Arts as a reward for a number of ingenious inventions which he introduced in the construction of time-pieces, and which were intended to counteract the atmospheric influence on the metals composing their works. His clocks were celebrated not only for unusual accuracy, but for great elegance. They were supplied with apparatus for striking the hours and the chimes, and sometimes musical pieces. Among other embellishments, he adapted to one of his time-keepers a small planetary machine, in which the mean motions of the bodies of the solar system were made to keep their proper rate with the time marked by the instrument. While perfecting this toy, his attention was directed to a more perfect instrument, and he projected an orrery, differing in many important respects from the machines commonly designated by that name, and much more philosophical and ingenious.

The year 1769 was famous among astronomers by the recurrence of that rare phenomenon, the transit of the planet Venus over the sun's disk. (A similar event will take place, it is calculated, in 1874.) In all parts of the world, men of eminence in the sciences were on the alert, and more than usual on account of the failure of the observations of 1761, when a similar event took place, and gave rise to a vast number of contradictions. The anxiety was enhanced by the fact that but a small part of the transit of 1769 was to be visible at any of the great observatories of Europe. At Stockholm, London, Paris, Lisbon, and Madrid, the immersion might be seen just before sunset, and the emersion at St. Petersburg soon after sunrise on the following morning, but at no other European capital. In the northern frozen zone, beyond the latitude of sixty-seven and a half degrees, the sun was not to set on the day of the transit; the whole of the phenomenon would therefore be visible; and at Wardhuys, in Lapland, where the observation would be included between the hours of half past nine in the afternoon and three in the morning, the circumstances would be the most favorable possible. In less high northern latitudes, near the same meridian, the beginning might occur before sunset, and the end take place after sunrise. The British astronomers were perfectly aware of these facts, and dispatched their expeditions to all quarters of the globe. But they overlooked one very important circumstance, namely, that a much better position for making observations could be found in Pennsylvania. Rittenhouse, alive ot this fact, communicated to the Philosophical Society of Philadelphia a calculation of the anticipated times and phenomena of the transit, as likely to be visible at Norriton, and set about preparing instruments for his own observations. The society was fully sensible of the importance of the occasion, and appointed a large and well-informed committee to attend to it, of which Rittenhouse was of course one. Three places of observation were selected—the State House Square of Philadelphia; Cape Henlopen, at the mouth of the Delaware; and Norriton, the residence of Rittenhouse. At the latter station, Provost Smith and Mr. Lukens were detailed to assist Mr. Rittenhouse. Liberal aid was extended to the operators, and the best instruments that could be obtained supplied. Rittenhouse, however, was left to prepare and furnish his own observatory—probably out of deference to his own mechanical and philosophical skill. He erected a suitable building, and furnished it with an apparatus from his own hands, with the exceptions of an instrument for determining the latitude, which was supplied by an associate, and a micrometer and telescope sent out by Mr. Penn. All the preliminary arrangements were intrusted to Rittenhouse; and so assiduously did he apply himself to the task, that, when the morning arrived, his anxiety and exhaustion were so great that he could scarcely apply himself to the close and serious matter of observation. The morning of the expected day, however, says Dr. Renwick, in his excellent sketch, broke without a cloud, and not even a floating wreath of vapor appeared to interfere with the observations. Exhilarated by the favorable state of the atmosphere, and stimulated by the near approach of the time when he was to reap the fruit of his long and patient labors, excitement supplied the place of strength. But when the contact had been observed, and the planet had entered fairly upon the disk of the sun, his bodily strength was exhausted, and he sunk fainting to the ground, unable to bear the intense feelings of delight which attended the accomplishment of his wishes. He, however, speedily recovered, and proceeded to perform the measures of the distances between the centres of the two bodies at proper intervals during the continuance of the transit.

The calculations which were the necessary results of these observations were made by Rittenhouse, and published by the Philosophical Society of Philadelphia. When they reached Europe, they corroborated the calculations of the most famous astronomers, and upset the theory of the old school that the sun was but eighty millions of miles from the earth, placing the distance at ninety-six millions. The learned men of the Old World did not hesitate to award to Rittenhouse the highest meed of praise, and one accomplished judge declared that no learned society in Europe "could at the moment boast of a member possessing the various merits of Rittenhouse, who united, in his own person, tact as an observer, theoretic skill as a calculator, and practical talent as a constructer of instruments."

During the same year Rittenhouse was engaged in observing the transit of Mercury, and his calculations were again so perfect that the longitude of places on the American continent were for fifty years determined by them.

These elevated occupations did not entirely divert his attention from his workshop; he still dwelt on the subject of a perfect orrery with devotion, and occupied all his leisure moments in finishing one on a new plan. It was at length completed, and became the property of the institution at Princeton, in whose cabinet it may still be found. Rittenhouse refers to it in the following words: "I did not design a machine which should give to the ignorant in astronomy a first view of the solar system, but would rather astonish the skillful and curious examiner by a most accurate correspondence between the situations and motions of our little representatives of the heavenly bodies and the situations and motions of those bodies themselves. I would have my orrery really useful, by making it capable of informing us truly of the astronomic phenomena for any particular point of time, which I do not find that any orrery yet made can do." The mechanism by which this is accomplished is described by competent judges as truly wonderful. A duplicate of this machine was subsequently executed for the College of Philadelphia.

In 1770, Rittenhouse took up his residence in the city of Philadelphia, having been invited to make that capital his home. In the following year he was elected one of the secretaries of the American Philosophical Society. In 1775, a scheme was set on foot to establish a public observatory in Philadelphia, under the direction of Rittenhouse, but, owing to the political agitations of the time, it was abandoned. The contest for freedom was now at hand, and Rittenhouse enrolled himself on the popular side, although he did not immediately take any part in the public meetings and deliberations. The modest integrity and wisdom of his life, however, pointed him out as a fitting object of public trust, and in 1775, when Franklin was called to the Provincial Assembly of Pennsylvania, Rittenhouse was elected to fill his seat in the General Congress. When the old government was dissolved, he was chosen a member of the Convention called for the purpose of framing a Constitution, and also of the Committee of Public Safety. In 1776 he was unanimously elected to the responsible and laborious office of State Treasurer, and was annually re-elected, until he declined any longer to hold office. When the city fell into the hands of the British, the responsibilities and dangers of this appointment were of the most oppressive kind, but by activity and firmness Rittenhouse discharged them to the satisfaction of every one. One cause of very great anxiety to him was the rumor that his two orreries had been destroyed by the enemy. This proved to be unfounded. The British commanders respected the work of art, and took effectual means to preserve its safety.

After the close of hostilities against Great Britain, Mr. Rittenhouse was engaged in settling the boundaries of Pennsylvania and Virginia by astronomical observations of the longitudinal lines; also in establishing a division line between the States of New York and Pennsylvania; and the limits of a territory, the right of soil of which the State of Massachusetts had accepted in lieu of a contested claim both to the land and the jurisdiction of a large part of the State of New York. These arduous operations engaged Mr. Rittenhouse until 1787, and, with the duties of the State Treasury and Loan Office, of which he was a trustee, kept him fully employed. During a part of the time the emoluments of his offices were so small that he was unable to afford the necessary assistance of a clerk, and had to call in the aid of his wife. Mr. Rittenhouse surrendered his trusts in 1790.

Under the federal government he was appointed a commissioner to receive subscriptions to the Bank of the United States; and when the law establishing a national mint was passed, he was named by Washington as its first director. The machinery of that establishment was put up under his direction, and the workmen instructed beneath his eye. The first coinage of the United States bore the impress of his practical skill, and sufficed for many years. Mr. Rittenhouse applied himself so laboriously to the duties of his office that his health became seriously impaired, and he was compelled, in June, 1795, to retire. His resignation was accepted by the government with great unwillingness.

He did not afterward take any active part in politics, or hold office except as president of a Democratic society. So seriously had his constitution been impaired by his labors, that he survived his resignation little more than one year, his death occurring on the 26th of June, 1796, in the sixty-fifth year of his age. Mr. Rittenhouse was a distinguished member of all the learned societies of his own country, and was elected a foreign member of the Royal Society of London—an honor greatly esteemed and never hastily conferred.

CARSTEN NIEBUHR.

CARSTEN NIEBUHR, the Oriental traveler, was a native of a Friesland province called Hadeln, where he was born a free peasant, among a free people, on the 17th of March, 1733. In those days all the peasants owned their own farms, and were, consequently, in good circumstances, without belonging to the wealthy. The little Carsten lost his mother before he was six weeks old, and was brought up by a stepmother in the house of his father, where his mode of living and occupations, as well as his education, were distinguished by nothing from those of other peasant-boys. Probably it was his own longing for information that occasioned his father to send him to the Latin school in Otterndorf, and, somewhat later, to that of Altenbruch; merely, however, that he might acquire a little more knowledge than an ordinary farmer. But the dismissal of the schoolmaster at Altenbruch, and the prejudices of his guardian (for his father had died meantime), put an early end to his studies, before he was far enough advanced to experience any profit from this first beginning.

The paternal property was divided among the children, producing but a small sum to each. Carsten had now to look out for himself in the cold world. Having a natural taste for music, he studied various instruments, hoping that he might eventually succeed in obtaining a situation as organist. His guardians, however, were averse to this hazardous experiment, and his uncle took him into his house, where he followed for four years the business of farming. It was distasteful to him, and he longed for a more intellectual life. The trifling circumstances which often determine the vital issues of life were very curious in the case of Carsten Niebuhr. A lawsuit in regard to the superficial contents of a farm could only be decided by a geometrical survey. A surveyor was consequently needed, but the country of Hadeln could not produce one. Niebuhr was a patriotic man, and felt a kind of humiliation at this circumstance. It became a duty to supply this want. He determined to study practical geometry, and suit himself for the office. With this object, he proceeded to

Bremen to take lessons from a professor there. This plan, however, did not succeed. The professor on whom he had depended was dead. He would not have declined the instruction of an inferior practical surveyor; but this man wished to take him as a boarder in his house; and the young countryman, diffident, bashful, and of the severest principles, found the obliging manners of the two sisters of his intended teacher so questionable that he left Bremen on the spot. It was this circumstance which made him a traveler. He now set his face toward Hamburg, where he arrived in the summer of the year 1755. In this city it was his intention to take lessons of the celebrated Succow, and, indeed, to begin his school studies anew. Eight months were entirely devoted to preparatory studies before he could become a student in the gymnasium; and twelve months more were wholly insufficient, notwithstanding all his exertions, and his perfect health of body and mind, to acquire what every youth more favored by circumstances carries with him to the University without difficulty. Succow being absent, he commenced his mathematical studies under Büsch, whose friendship and esteem he secured for the remainder of his life. In 1757 he went to Göttingen, still in pursuit of his mathematical studies, and with the hope, too, of finding some kind of employment which would enable him to eke out his scanty means. For more than a year he continued his studies with the greatest possible assiduity and devotion, but without securing any appointment to contribute to his means.

In 1756, Michaelis's celebrated philological expedition to Arabia was proposed to the government of Denmark, and accepted by the minister, Baron Bernstorf, who lent to it all his influence and aid. Michaelis was commissioned to name a philologian, a mathematician, and a natural philosopher. To obtain the mathematician he addressed himself to Kästner, of the Academy of Sciences at Göttingen. Carsten was a pupil of this gentleman, and, when the moment arrived, he proposed him as the mathematician of the expedition. Niebuhr was, of course, delighted, but he had misgivings of his own ability. Kästner, however, set his mind at rest about it by promising him a long term for preparation, especially for the study of astronomy under Mayer.

For eighteen months—the term allowed by the king for the necessary preparations of the expedition—Niebuhr devoted himself to the closest study. He continued the study of pure mathematics, perfected himself in drawing, and endeavored to acquire as much historical knowledge as he could with his imperfect preliminary studies, without leaving his main purpose too much out of view. He also exercised himself in practical mechanics, that he might learn to handle his instruments; and also in all those points of mechanical skill, the acquirement and practice of which would be a waste of time for every one in Europe who does not make them his business. But he was principally occupied with two courses of private lessons, viz., in the Arabic language with Michaelis, and in astronomy with Mayer. Of these he preserved a very different remembrance. The slow, methodical method of Michaelis discouraged him, and he acquired the conviction that the professor by no means possessed any special treasure of Arabic knowledge and philology. He therefore gave up this study, and Michaelis never forgave him. With Mayer he got on excellently. The teacher's zeal was only exceeded by the pupil's enthusiasm. A mutual friendship sprang up between them, which lasted, under the most happy and gratifying circumstances, to the day of Mayer's death. It was Niebuhr's delight in later days to acknowledge that he owed every thing to this eminent astronomer and excellent man.

In the autumn of 1760, every thing being in readiness, Niebuhr left Göttingen. His companions were Von Haven and Forskaal—the latter a man of undoubted ability, the former a supercilious and querulous person; Dr. Cramer, a physician of mean capacity, and Bauernfeind, a painter, "not unskilled in drawing." The voyage commenced under the most unfavorable auspices, the vessel being three times driven back into port before she was able to make her way to the Mediterranean. A stay of a few weeks at Marseilles, and a shorter one at Malta, afforded a very pleasing recreation to the travelers. Their scientific enterprise being known, they were every where treated with great consideration and courtesy. From Malta the travelers proceeded to the Dardanelles. In the Archipelago Niebuhr was seized with the dysentery, which brought him near the grave. At Constantinople his health returned, though very slowly; so that at the end of two months from the commencement of the attack, he was only so far recovered as to be able, with evident hazard of relapse, to embark for Alexandria. On this voyage they encountered a fresh danger. The plague broke out among the crowded mass of Oriental passengers. The Europeans, however, escaped.

From September, 1761, until October, 1762, the travelers remained in Egypt, without going higher up than Cairo. During their sojourn Niebuhr determined the longitude of Alexandria, Cairo, Rosetta, and Damietta, by numerous lunar observations, and with an exactness which was subsequently justified by the astronomers in Bonaparte's expedition. He also executed a chart of the two arms of the Nile, and a plan of Cairo. He likewise took the altitude of the pyramids, and copied many hieroglyphic inscriptions on obelisks and sarcophagi.

In October the travelers embarked at Suez on board of a Turkish ship; they landed at Djidda, and reached Loheia, the first point of their proper destination—the land of Yemen—in the last days of the year 1762. After some stay in this friendly city, the company, and more especially Forskaal and Niebuhr, traveled over the western part of Yemen in various directions; the former for botanical purposes, and the latter in order to determine the geographical positions of the various places. They afterward proceeded to Mocha, where Von Haven died toward the end of May, 1763. About the same time, Niebuhr was again attacked by dysentery, but was saved by prudent foresight and extreme temperance. His health was not fully restored when the party moved on to Saná, the capital of Yemen. On the way Forskaal was seized with a bilious disorder, of which he died at Yerim, July 11th, 1763. With but two remaining companions Niebuhr pursued the journey. His own health was feeble, and for the only time in his life he gave way to despondency. His anxiety was not so much for the safety of his own life as for the preservation of the papers of the expedition. The surviving members of the expedition were thoroughly disheartened, and, in consequence, declined a friendly invitation to remain a full year in Saná and Upper Yemen. They hastily descended once more to the coast in the hope that the ships might not yet have taken their departure, and made so much haste that they had more than a month to remain at Mocha before the ship in which they were to return to Malta was ready. It was in the height of summer, and the surviving travelers, with their servant, were all attacked by the fever of the climate. Bauernfeind and the servant died at sea. Cramer reached Bombay, remained ill several months, and died. Of the entire expedition, Niebuhr was now the sole survivor.

Niebuhr remained in Bombay until his health was completely

re-established. He used his time advantageously in studying the English language. He collected also all the information which was to be obtained respecting the Parsees and Hindoos; visited the pagodas hewn in the rocks of Elephanta, and made drawings of their sculptures. He occupied himself further in reducing all his journals into proper order, and forwarded a copy to Denmark.

After a sojourn of fourteen months he left Bombay; visited Muscat; proceeded to Shiraz and Persepolis, and spent nearly four weeks in drawing and measuring the ruins in the latter place, of which he always preserved the most vivid recollection. From Shiraz he crossed the Persian Gulf to Bassora, and thence through Bagdad and Mosul to Haleb. An opportunity of going to Jaffa tempted him to visit Palestine. After that he explored Asia Minor, and reached Constantinople on the 20th of February, 1767. After having spent five months in that city, he passed over Turkey in Europe to Poland, and in November reached Copenhagen. He was received with great distinction by the court, the ministers, and all the learned men. When the expenses of the expedition were calculated, they were found not to exceed $17,000—a remarkably small sum, considering the magnitude of the original arrangements, and the unusual outlays to which they were necessarily exposed. It was a point of conscience with Niebuhr to settle up his accounts with the greatest expedition, having been appointed treasurer from the commencement. His next solicitude was to arrange his voluminous notes, and arrange for the speedy publication of his travels. The materials contained in his journals were in the highest degree rich and profuse, and that he wrought them up with a degree of perfection, to which the entire artlessness and simplicity of his manner contributed not a little, every one will now acknowledge. His first design was to publish two separate works before his Travels; first, answers to the questions which had been directed to the travelers, out of his own and Forskaal's papers; and, secondly, the whole of his astronomical observations. The difficulties and hostilities he had to encounter from a variety of causes and persons interfered with this arrangement. Some years elapsed before even the Travels made their appearance, and then they were published slowly, and mainly at his own expense. The engravings, however, were made at the expense of the Danish government, the plates being presented to him. The Description of Arabia appeared in 1772.

In 1773 Mr. Niebuhr was married to the daughter of Blumenberg, the physician. Two children were the fruits of this union, a daughter, and B. G. Niebuhr, the eminent historian of Rome, and author of the Memoir from which this sketch is compiled. After his marriage Mr. Niebuhr took up his residence at Melford, of which district he was appointed secretary by the government (1778). He had a large house and garden, and much of his time was occupied in attending to them and educating his children; the rest to preparing his works for the press.

The first volume of his Travels appeared in 1774; the second in 1778. Both volumes were attended with loss. The political agitations of the times were unfavorable to works which, although eminently instructive, did not appeal to a large class of readers, and required much calm and serious study. The third volume was not published. Niebuhr felt the indifference of his countrymen keenly, and was, moreover, seriously inconvenienced by it in a pecuniary point of view. It was not until after his death that the great merits of this excellent traveler were fully recognized. In 1795 a sad misfortune befell him. The engraved plates, both of his published works and also for the still unpublished part, were destroyed in the great conflagration at Copenhagen. This new calamity removed the opportunity and even the inclination to supply the deficient volume. For the remainder of his life Mr. Niebuhr devoted himself to purely domestic pursuits.

His son relates some pleasing anecdotes of the green old age of this worthy man. "I have a very lively recollection," he says, "of many stories out of my boyish years about the system of the universe, and about the East; when he used to take me upon his knee at evening before going to bed, and feed me with such food, instead of children's fables. The history of Mohammed, of the first califs, and especially of Omar and Ali, for whom he felt the profoundest veneration; that of the conquests and extension of Islamism, of the virtues of the early heroes of the new faith, the history of the Turks—all these impressed themselves early and in the most pleasing colors on my mind. The historical works which treat of these subjects were also almost the first books which came into my hands. I recollect also, about my tenth year, how at Christmas, in order to give the festival still more importance in my eyes, he brought out and read with me the manuscripts which contained the accounts collected by him respecting Africa. These and his other manuscripts were kept in an ornamental coffer, which was venerated by the children and inmates of the house like a second ark."

In November, 1792, Mr. Niebuhr was brought near to the grave by pleurisy, and recovered only by slow degrees. In consequence of his full habit of body, his fixed and almost sedentary life for so many years had prepared the way for severe sickness and a long interruption of his health. In the following year he spat blood. He was not positively ill, but without energy, low-spirited, out of humor, breathed with difficulty, and walked only with great effort. Another complaint also increased his anxiety. Several years before, there had appeared under his right eye a small excrescence like a wart, which continued to spread slowly but constantly, and was only made worse by all the means employed to remove it. The physicians regarded it with the more solicitude because they durst not venture upon its extirpation. After many years of anxiety and trouble, a remedy was at length found in 1796 by which it was loosened and removed, roots and all. After this, on the completion of his sixty-sixth year, his health, and with it his frame of mind, took a more happy turn. Circumstances induced him to purchase some marsh lands about an hour's distance from his house, and to undertake the reclamation of them for tillage. It was refreshing to him thus to return to the employment of his youth; he sketched plans for making these lands productive, prosecuted them with youthful ardor, and promised himself the best success—planted trees, dug drains and ditches, and so purchased by degrees a great estate. The result disappointed his hopes, and a large sum was lost. Still, in this case, it is not to be regretted; for, says Mr. Niebuhr's son, "not only does much remain in a state of improvement and tillage, but the old age of my father was, without doubt, by this means prolonged and rendered more serene. He took much and active exercise, visited the newly-planned farm now on foot and now on horseback, and inspected indefatigably every spot where any thing was to be done or directions to be given. As the fields were separated by broad ditches, in order to shorten the distances he often made use of a leaping-staff, to the use of which he had been accustomed from childhood. He had now so renewed his strength that, with the aid of such a staff, *Kluvstaaken*, he was able, in his seventieth year, to spring over ditches ten feet wide."

Mr. Niebuhr was a man of a full-blooded, stout, and phlegmatic temperament. For a number of years he had accustomed himself to periodical bloodlettings, imagining that his health required them. Unhappily, he took it into his head that he ought to omit this on account of his great age, and could not be induced, by any warnings or representations, to give up this idea, until dizziness, apoplectic stupor, and spitting of blood had brought him into the most imminent danger. In October, 1813, he was seized with a violent hemorrhage through the nose. With no weariness of life, but yet satiated with it, he often expressed himself anxious to depart and join his wife, if God should call him. In March, 1814, his symptoms were aggravated by a fall, in which his right leg received a permanent injury. He was never able afterward to place his foot upon the ground; he could move only with pain by the help of others; he was taken out of bed only in the afternoon, and placed in a chair with rollers. A numerous and still unbroken family circle were gathered around him; and he himself, except, perhaps, when some day of particular illness occurred, was full of heartfelt joy over the change of times, and ever ready to converse. "We succeeded," says his son, "in drawing from him continued recitals of his travels, which he at this time gave us with peculiar fullness and sprightliness. Thus he once spoke for a long time and much in detail of Persepolis, and described the walls on which the inscriptions and bas-reliefs of which he spoke were found, just as one would describe a building which he had recently visited. We could not conceal our astonishment. He said to us that as he lay thus blind upon his bed, the images of all that he had seen in the East were ever present to his soul, and it was therefore no wonder that he should speak of them as of yesterday. In like manner, there was vividly reflected to him in the hours of stillness the nocturnal view of the deep Asiatic heavens, with their brilliant host of stars, which he had so often contemplated, or else their blue and lofty vault by day; and this was his greatest enjoyment."

In this condition Mr. Niebuhr lingered until April, 1815. Toward evening of the 26th he desired some one to read to him, and asked several questions with entire consciousness. He fell again into a slumber, and died without a struggle, in the eighty-third year of his age.

His funeral was attended by a multitude of people from every part of the district. In the memory of the oldest inhabitant, no one had died there so universally lamented.

Mr. Niebuhr was a man of extremely frugal habits; until late in life he drank nothing but water and milk. He had no favorite dishes except the peasant food of his native place. It was his greatest pride that he was a child of free Friesland. His character was without a spot; his morals in the highest degree severe and pure. As a traveler, he was remarkable for keen observation; every thing he saw remained firmly fixed in his mind, and he remembered it with astonishing tenacity. "To this day," says his son, "no traveler returns from the East without admiration and gratitude for this teacher and guide, the most distinguished of Oriental travelers. None of those who have hitherto followed him can be compared with him;* and we may well inquire whether he will ever find a successor who will complete the description of Arabia, and be named along with him."

* This, it must be remembered, was written in 1816.

HENRY CLAY.

THE readers of this brief memoir of one of America's greatest politicians need not expect to find an important political biography. The character, principles, and policy of the acts of Henry Clay belong to the history of the country, which can not fail to do him justice. In this and similar instances, all we shall attempt will be to trace the footsteps of our illustrious personage from the first round on the ladder of fame to the last on its giddy eminence. With the aid of patient courage, devotion, and talent (which God so often gives to the lowly), great men have thus struggled upward, and obtained the suffrage of the world. It is our pleasant task to record the instances.

Henry Clay was a native of Hanover County, Virginia, where, in a low, swampy neighborhood, called the *Slashes*, he was born, on the 12th of April, 1777. Henry was the fifth of a family of seven children, which, at an early age, were left to the care of a widowed mother. The limited means at the disposal of this lady did not allow her to bestow on her sons the advantages of a classical education. All the schooling that Henry enjoyed at this period of his life was received at the log cabin schoolhouse of Peter Deacon, an establishment consisting of one room, with no floor but the earth, and no window but the door. At this primitive institution of learning Henry Clay was instructed in the important mysteries of reading, writing, and arithmetic, progressing in the latter "as far as practice." The circumstances of his early life did not allow him to devote all his time to study. He had to assist in the serious business of providing for a large family, and in his humble way did all he could. He plowed in the fields, and, when the grain was garnered, carried it to the mill to be converted into meal or flour. On such occasions he generally rode a horse without a saddle, and with a rope for a bridle. From this circumstance he became known as the "Mill-boy of the Slashes"—a name which will be handed down to posterity. In the political pageants of the Whig party in later days, it was a common thing to have a living personification of the future statesman. The horse, the meal-bag, the rope bridle, were there to convey a healthy sentiment to American minds, but the man who crossed the back of the steed was probably a *little* different to the original.

When Henry had reached his fourteenth year (1791), he was placed in a retail store at Richmond, Virginia. In the mean time, Mrs. Clay had changed her condition for the second time, and united her fortunes to a gentleman—Captain Henry Watkins—not unworthy of her. Mr. Watkins entertained a fatherly regard for the children, and was especially attached to Henry. At his suggestion, Henry was removed from the store, and, by his influence, placed at a desk in the office of the clerk of the High Court of Chancery, Peter Tinsley, Esq. There were several other clerks in the same office, and, when Henry made his appearance, they promised themselves no small amount of fun at his expense. His appearance was certainly eccentric. His mother had dressed him up in a new suit of Figginy (Virginia) cloth, cotton and silk mixed, of the complexion of pepper and salt, with clean linen well starched, and the tail of his coat standing out from his legs at a fearful angle. So long as the other clerks only laughed at his comical appearance, Henry had nothing to say; but when they proceeded farther, they discovered that Master Clay had a tongue of his own, and a sharp intellect to tip it with venom. In a very short time he gained complete ascendency over them. They were the first to look up to the "Mill-boy of the Slashes."

A frequent visitor at Mr. Tinsley's office was the venerable Chancellor Wythe. There was something about Henry's appearance which attracted the chancellor's attention, and induced him to make inquiries about him. The chancellor needed an amanuensis, and proposed to Mr. Tinsley that Henry's services should be loaned to him. As they were not of much importance in an office where he was merely a supernumerary, the proposition was readily acceded to.

Henry Clay found a sincere friend and adviser in the chancellor, and the latter soon discovered that he had a willing and capable assistant. One of the fruits of this fortunate connection may be seen to the present day in a folio volume of the Supreme Court of the United States at Washington. It is an eminently profound work, abounding in quotations from Latin and Greek authors. These quotations were copied by Clay in a neat and legible hand. Not understanding a single Greek character, the young copyist had to transcribe each letter by imitation.

In the latter part of 1796, Henry Clay left the office of Mr. Tinsley, and became a regular student of law in the office of Attorney General Brooke. In the following year he was admitted to practice by the Virginia Court of Appeals, and soon after removed to Lexington, Kentucky, to establish himself in the profession he had adopted with so much devotion. It must not be supposed that his studies were confined to the one year spent in the office of the attorney general. Under the chancellor he acquired the surest basis of legal knowledge, and all that he needed for the practice of the law was a methodical arrangement of what he knew.

He was now in his twenty-first year, and, to use his own words, found himself in Lexington without patrons, without the favor or countenance of the great or opulent, without the means of paying his weekly board, and in the midst of a bar uncommonly distinguished by eminent members. "I remember," he adds, "how comfortable I thought I should be if I could make one hundred pounds, Virginia money, per year, and with what delight I received the first fifteen shillings fee." He devoted himself with assiduity to his profession, and seized every moment to improve himself in learning. He became known for his brilliant talents and for his masterly oratory, and, much sooner than he anticipated or had a right to expect, rushed into a lucrative practice. His subtle appreciation of character, knowledge of human nature, and faculties of persuasion, rendered him peculiarly successful in his appeals to a jury, and he obtained great celebrity for his adroit and careful management of criminal cases.

Finding himself in a position to act with regard to the future, he took on himself the responsibilities of domestic life, and in April, 1799—eighteen months after his removal to Kentucky—married Lucretia Hart, daughter of Colonel Thomas Hart, a gentleman of high standing in Lexington, and famed for his enterprise, public spirit, and hospitality. By this lady he had a numerous family, several of whom were married during Mr. Clay's lifetime, and became parents of a numerous progeny, who were privileged to call the great statesman grandfather.

Mr. Clay's practice was destined to be interrupted by calls to a higher field of labor. The power he exercised over masses of human beings rendered him an invaluable speaker on political subjects. It is unnecessary to dwell on the many criminal cases in which he was engaged. They were conducted with a skill which made his services of the highest value to defendants in danger of their necks. Men in such a position generally contrive to get a counsel who can most successfully influence a jury, and Henry Clay was seldom without a retaining-fee. The success of his efforts may be estimated by the fact that, during his long career, he never lost a client by capital punishment, although it is to be feared many of them deserved it. We will now briefly refer to the case that first placed Henry Clay on that extended field which he was destined to fill so nobly. His entrance on the theatre of public life was as early as 1798, the year after he removed to Kentucky. A series of articles were written by his pen, and published in the Kentucky Gazette, advocating emancipation doctrines with much earnestness and power. Soon afterward he took the field more openly, and headed a party of emancipationists during the agitation for remodeling the State Constitution, proposing and advocating the introduction of an article for the gradual and ultimate abolition of slavery in the commonwealth. This decided step in the cause of human liberty was not calculated to increase his popularity, and, indeed, in later times, gave his enemies many opportunities of heaping obloquy on the conscientious statesman. Notwithstanding the immediate failure of his exertions, Mr. Clay never shrunk from the avowal of his sentiments on the subject, nor from practically acting on them whenever the opportunity occurred. For several years, whenever a slave brought an action to recover his liberty, Mr. Clay volunteered as his advocate, and he always succeeded in obtaining a decision in the slave's favor.

During the administration of John Adams in 1798–1799, the notorious alien and sedition laws were passed, measures which were destined to arouse the fiercest political indignation. By the "Alien Law" the President was authorized to order any alien "whom he should judge dangerous to the peace and safety" of the country "to depart out of the territory within such a time" as he should judge proper, upon penalty of being "imprisoned for a term not exceeding three years." The Sedition Law was intended to curb the freedom of the press. The apology for these outrageous measures was that there were many thousand Frenchmen and Englishmen in the country who were banded together in private societies for no good purpose; and that there were two hundred newspapers published in the United States, some of which were under the control of aliens. The "Sedition Law" imposed a heavy fine, and imprisonment for a term of years, "upon such as should combine or conspire together to oppose any measure of government, and upon such as should write, print, utter, publish, etc., any false, scandalous, and malicious writing against the government of the United States or the President."

Mr. Clay was one of the first to express his abhorrence of these extreme measures, and in doing so he gave expression to the common voice of the state. The Legislature declared the law to be unconstitutional, and for the part Mr. Clay had taken in this happy decision he received the title of THE GREAT COMMONER. From a Life of Henry Clay we quote the following anecdote of the time: "A gentleman who was present at a meeting where these obnoxious laws were discussed describes the effect produced by Mr. Clay's eloquence as difficult adequately to describe. The populace had assembled in the fields in the vicinity of Lexington, and were first addressed by Mr. George Nicholas, a distinguished man and a powerful speaker. The speech of Mr. Nicholas was long and eloquent, and he was greeted by the most enthusiastic cheers as he concluded. Clay, being called for, promptly appeared, and made one of the most extraordinary and impressive harangues ever addressed to a popular assembly. A striking evidence of its thrilling and effective character may be found in the fact that when he ceased *there was no shout, no applause.* So eloquently had he interpreted the deep feelings of the multitude, that they forgot the orator in the absorbing emotions he had produced. A higher compliment can hardly be conceived. The theme was a glorious one for a young and generous mind filled with ardor in behalf of human liberty, and he did it justice. The people took Clay and Nicholas upon their shoulders, and, forcing them into a carriage, drew them through the streets amid shouts of applause. What an incident for an orator who had not yet completed his twenty-second year!"

Four years after this Mr. Clay was elected to the General Assembly of Kentucky (1803). He had now fairly entered upon his political career, and all that remains for us is to indicate it in the briefest manner possible. His first election to Congress was in 1806, but it was only for the remaining portion of a term; and in 1807 he was again elected to the General Assembly of Kentucky, of which he was chosen Speaker. In 1809 he was elected for an unexpired term of two years to the Senate of the United States. On the expiration of this term he was elected a representative to Congress, where he was chosen Speaker of the House of Representatives. He was five times re-elected to this honorable post. In all the prominent measures of the day he took an active part, and especially distinguished himself by his earnest denunciations of the English claims to right of search and other maritime prerogatives; and as he was one of the prime instigators of the war with England, so during its continuance he remained one of its strongest advocates. In consequence of the active part he took in all matters relating to this war, he was appointed in 1814 one of the commissioners to negotiate the treaty of peace. In France, whither he repaired, he was treated with much distinction, and on his return to America was re-elected to Congress. In 1819 Mr. Clay resigned his seat, and, with the object of improving his pecuniary position, returned to the practice of his profession. In a short time he regained a highly remunerative practice. Four years later (1823) he was again returned to the House of Representatives, and at once restored to his place as Speaker. Under the administration of President Adams Mr. Clay was appointed Secretary of State, which office he held until 1827. On the election of General Jackson in 1829, Clay retired for a while into private life, but in 1831 he was elected to the United States Senate. In 1833 he was an unsuccessful candidate for the presidency, and was equally unsuccessful in the two subsequent campaigns. Henry Clay remained a member of the Senate till 1842, when, finding that his strength was insufficient to undergo the arduous tasks he imposed on it, he took a formal leave of the scene of his long labors in a speech which thrilled the heart of the nation, and which moved it, also, with shame that a servant so faithful and gifted had been neglected. "Justice to Clay" became a rallying cry, and in 1844 he was once more nominated for the highest office in the gift of the people. This time the majority belonged to the opposite party, and President Polk was elected. Clay remained in retirement until 1849, when he was again returned to the Senate. The severe labors which he imposed on himself in the patriotic endeavor to reconcile the interests of the North and South on the subject of slavery seriously impaired his already feeble health. He tendered his resignation as senator, but before the day named for it to take effect he had breathed his last. He died on the 29th of June, 1852, still a GREAT COMMONER, at the age of seventy-five. He was buried with great pomp, and the people throughout the length and breadth of the land recognized his death as a national calamity.

Mr. Clay, in his domestic relations, sustained an enviable reputation as a husband, father, and master. It was his good fortune to be united to a lady of great excellence, and the homely and happy influence of her sway made Ashland a retreat of the most tranquil delight. She was a noticeable housewife, and superintended not only the house, but the farm of her husband, containing upward of six hundred acres, and populated with a small army of negroes. Mr. Clay was universally respected, and in the immediate neighborhood of his home received a meed of respect almost amounting to adoration. The following anecdote is related in Colton's Life. Some few days after the result of the presidential election of 1844 was known, Mr. Clay met a woman on horseback as he was walking in the public road near Ashland, who stopped to salute him, but immediately burst into tears. "Madam," inquired Mr. Clay, "pray what is the matter?" "Sir," said she, in broken accents, "you do not know me, but my father, once your neighbor, always taught me to revere you. I have lost my father, my husband, and my children, and passed through other painful trials; but all of them together have not given me so much sorrow as the late disappointment of your friends."

Mr. Clay was a tall man, six feet one inch high, spare in body, with long arms and small hands. His carriage was remarkably erect, and became additionally so in debate. Of his facial appearance we need say nothing. There is scarcely an American family in the country that does not possess a bust or a portrait of the famous "Mill-boy of the Slashes." His temper was quick and easily excited, but, like most quick-tempered persons, he permitted nothing to linger behind. In his valedictory to the Senate of the United States, the following touching and manly passage occurs, with which we close this brief sketch of a great man:

"That my nature is warm, my temper ardent, my disposition —especially in relation to the public service—enthusiastic, I am fully ready to own. During a long and arduous career of service in the public councils of my country—especially during the last eleven years I have held a seat in the Senate—from the same ardor and enthusiasm of character, I have no doubt, in the heat of debate, and in an honest endeavor to maintain my opinions against adverse opinions equally honestly entertained, as to the best course to be adopted for the public welfare, I may have often, inadvertently or unintentionally, in moments of excited debate, made use of language that has been offensive and susceptible of injurious interpretation toward my brother senators. If there be any here who retain wounded feelings of injury or dissatisfaction produced on such occasions, I beg to assure them that I now offer the amplest apology for any departure on my part from the established rules of parliamentary decorum and courtesy. On the other hand, I assure the senators, one and all, without exception and without reserve, that I retire from this Senate-chamber without carrying with me a single feeling of resentment or dissatisfaction to the Senate or any one of its members."

JOHN LEDYARD.

In America, every man, more or less, is a traveler. It is not remarkable, therefore, that America has produced some of the most enterprising of the class. The constant pioneering which every man undertakes in search of fortune has given to our citizens a natural aptitude for the perils, excitements, and rude pleasures of the traveler's lot. In a country so vast as this, geographical ideas of distance are forgotten. We pay a winter visit to our relatives in New Orleans, as if that tropical city lay somewhere on the North River. Thus accustomed to travel an immense continent, it is not remarkable that our citizens penetrate all parts of Europe with great rapidity and energy, or that some few, who have a special talent for the vocation, become great and world-known travelers.

One of our earliest distinguished men in this way was John Ledyard, whose romantic story we are now about to condense. Ledyard was born in the year 1751, at Groton, in Connecticut. His parents were in easy circumstances, but, on the death of his father, the family were thrown into difficulties, owing to a fraud which was practiced on the widow, depriving her of a small estate which of right was hers. Young Ledyard received an ordinary grammar-school education, and at an early day was placed in a lawyer's office. From this irksome imprisonment he was released by Dr. Wheelock, the amiable and pious founder of Dartmouth College, who invited Ledyard to enter his institution recently established at Hanover, New Hampshire, and qualify himself to become a missionary among the Indians. This plan was so much in accordance with his mother's wishes, that Ledyard —who probably had an eye to its romantic bearings—assented to it. In due time he started for Hanover, performing the journey in a broken-down sulky, and bearing with him, in addition to his clothes and books, a queer assortment of calico curtains and "properties" for dramatic entertainments. Ledyard had a passion for plays, and burdened himself with these accessories of the stage in order that he might be able to get up some private theatricals during the winter months. It is to be feared that he thought more of this matter than of his studies; for in a short time he fitted up a stage, and, assisted by the other students, produced the tragedy of *Cato*, himself playing the character of Syphax in a long gray beard, and a dress of a pantomimical character supposed to bear some resemblance to the national costume of a Numidian prince. With a head full of these idle fancies, it is not remarkable that he neglected his studies, and longed to escape from the irksome routine of a student's life. He had only been in the college four months, when one day he was missed, and for nearly four months nothing whatever was heard of him. When he returned he explained that he had been taking an excursion among the Six Nations on the borders of Canada, reviewing the missionary ground, and picking up some knowledge of the manners and language of the Indians. The impressions he received on this tour were not favorable to the missionary project. He abandoned it in his own mind, and only waited for an opportunity to cut loose from the college and its associations. Every day this determination received new strength, inasmuch as every day he received some fresh hint from Dr. Wheelock concerning the value of time and necessity for well-disciplined study.

It was not an easy thing to escape from Dartmouth College in those days, and Ledyard had to exercise all his ingenuity to do so. To go away on foot was out of the question; of public conveyances there were none, and the use of a private one could not be obtained without exciting suspicion. In this state of things, he directed all his attention to the Connecticut River, which flowed past the college grounds. Along its margin he observed a number of glorious old trees, monarchs of the forest, which had stood there for centuries. One of these Ledyard contrived to cut down, and then wrought its huge trunk into a canoe. When the work was finished, he bade adieu to the home of the Muses, and set off alone to explore a river with the navigation of which he was entirely ignorant. The distance to Hartford was not less than one hundred and forty miles, much of the way being through dark, primeval forests, and in several places there were dangerous falls and rapids. He had a bearskin for a covering, and his canoe was liberally provisioned, so that he had little to apprehend save from these dangers. Of books he took but two: a Greek

Testament and a copy of Ovid. With these he amused himself while the canoe dropped leisurely down the stream. One day he was deeply absorbed in his reading when his canoe approached Bellows' Falls, where he was suddenly aroused by the dashing of the waters among the rocks as they passed through the narrow passage. With difficulty he gained the shore, and thus escaped inevitable destruction. With the exception of this adventure, we hear of no other incident in his voyage worth recording. He arrived in safety at Hartford, much to the astonishment of his relatives.

Ledyard, after this, appears to have conceived a violent desire to become a clergyman, and he applied to the clergy for approval as a candidate with his usual impetuosity, but with no success. He was greatly disappointed at the moment, but, a few weeks later, he cheerfully abandoned all ideas of the Church, and took to the very opposite profession of the sea. He entered himself as a common sailor for a voyage to the Mediterranean, but was treated by the captain rather as a friend and associate than as one of the crew. The voyage was first to Gibraltar, next to a port on the Barbary coast, for taking in a cargo of mules, and thence homeward by way of the West Indies. While the vessel was lying at Gibraltar, Ledyard was suddenly missed. Inquiries were made in the town without success. At length a messenger was dispatched to the barracks. There he was discovered in the full costume of a British soldier. He explained the circumstance by stating that he had a fondness for the profession of arms, and had therefore enlisted in the king's service. The captain of the vessel remonstrated with him, and, with his consent, fortunately secured a discharge.

The voyage took about a year to complete, and at the end of that time he found himself once more in America, with nothing in his pocket, and no prospect before him for the future. He was now in his twenty-second year, and began to realize the necessity of striking out a course of action for himself. His erratic conduct had wearied his friends. He had no one to depend on but himself, and no one to look to, unless, indeed, it were some relatives of his grandfather, who was an Englishman of good family, and had many connections in Britain. The idea of hunting up these lost relatives was pleasing to his adventurous mind, and he determined to do so. For this purpose, he started out once more; took ship at New York, and in due time arrived at Plymouth, England. Being entirely without means, he was compelled to travel on foot from this port to London. Arrived in the English metropolis, he made a single effort to discover his lost relatives, but, finding that his story was doubted, he abandoned the undertaking in disgust. With beggary staring him in the face, he had now to determine quickly his future plans.

In a crowded city like London, there was little chance of employment for a stranger who knew nothing of business, and was not master of a trade. His hopes lay in the maritime profession. He knew how to handle a rope as well as any other Jack Tar, and perhaps had some other and more valuable nautical lore. At the time of his visit a great deal of attention was directed to seafaring matters. The celebrated circumnavigator, Captain Cook, was on the eve of departure for his third and last great voyage round the world, and was, of course, the especial object of conversation. Ledyard's enterprising spirit thirsted for such a cruise, and he made up his mind to use every endeavor to accompany the famous captain. As a preliminary step, he enlisted in the marines. Then he applied to the captain, and, by dint of persuasion and assiduity, succeeded in obtaining an appointment. Cook's great knowledge of men enabled him to form an instant estimate of Ledyard's character, and that it was no mean estimate was immediately proved by his promoting him to be corporal of marines. In this manner did Ledyard commence the career for which nature had evidently intended him, and which was destined to give renown to his name for ages afterward.

The expedition, consisting of two ships, the *Resolution* and the *Discovery*, left England on the 12th of July, 1776, and proceeded at once to the Cape of Good Hope, where the final arrangements for the voyage were completed. The men of science made short incursions into the interior to test the accuracy of their instruments; the sailors busied themselves in making all taut and comfortable; and the stewards interested themselves in the riches of the larder. Last of all were taken on board a heterogeneous collection of animals, designed to be left at islands where they did not exist, and consisting of horses, cattle, sheep, goats, hogs, dogs, cats, hares, rabbits, monkeys, ducks, geese, turkeys, and peacocks. "Thus," says Ledyard, "did we resemble the ark, and appear as though we were going as well to stock, as to discover, a new world."

The events of this voyage are known to most readers. Ledyard, on his return, wrote a book describing what he had seen in a picturesque and attractive style. We lack the necessary space for following the narrative, although it would be found extremely interesting. It must suffice that Ledyard enjoyed the confidence of Captain Cook, and was frequently employed to execute little tasks apart from his regular duties. One of these was so characteristic of the daring of the man, that we shall transcribe it in his own words. It happened at the island of Onalaska. "I have before observed that we had noticed many appearances to the eastward of this, as far almost as Sandwich Sound, of a European intercourse, and that we had, at this island in particular, met with circumstances that did not only indicate such an intercourse, but seemed strongly to intimate that some Europeans were actually somewhere on the spot. The appearances that led to these conjectures were such as these. We found among the inhabitants of this island two different kinds of people ; the one we knew to be the aborigines of America, while we supposed the others to have come from the opposite coasts of Asia. There were two different dialects also observed, and we found them fond of tobacco, rum, and snuff. Tobacco we even found them possessed of, and we observed several blue linen shirts and drawers among them.

"But the most remarkable circumstance was a cake of rye meal newly baked, with a piece of salmon in it, seasoned with pepper and salt, which was brought and presented to Cook by a comely young chief, attended by two of those Indians whom we supposed to be Asiatics. The chief seemed anxious to explain to Cook the meaning of the present and the purport of his visit; and he was so far successful as to persuade him that there were some strangers in the country, who were white, and had come over the great waters in a vessel somewhat like ours, and, though not so large, was yet much larger than theirs.

"In consequence of this, Cook was determined to explore the island. It was difficult, however, to fix upon a plan that would at once answer the purpose of safety and expedition. An armed body would proceed slowly, and, if they should be cut off by the Indians, the loss in our present circumstances would be irreparable; and a single person would entirely risk his life, though he would be much more expeditious if unmolested, and if he should be killed, the loss would be only one. The latter seemed the best, but it was extremely hard to single out an individual, and command him to go upon such an expedition. It was therefore thought proper to send a volunteer, or none.

"I was at this time, and indeed ever after, an intimate friend of John Gore, first lieutenant of the *Resolution*, a native of America as well as myself, and superior to me in command. He recommended me to Captain Cook to undertake the expedition, with which I immediately acquiesced. Captain Cook assured me that he was happy I had undertaken it, as he was convinced I should persevere; and after giving me some instructions how to proceed, he wished me well, and desired I would not be longer absent than a week, if possible, at the expiration of which he should expect me to return. If I did not return by that time, he should wait another week for me, and no longer. The young chief before mentioned and his two attendants were to be my guides. I took with me some presents adapted to the taste of the Indians, brandy in bottles, and bread, but no other provisions. I went entirely unarmed, by the advice of Captain Cook.

"The first day we proceeded about fifteen miles into the interior part of the island, without any remarkable occurrence, until we approached a village just before night. This village consisted of about thirty huts, some of them large and spacious, though not very high. The huts were composed of a kind of slight frame, erected over a square hole sunk about four feet into the ground; the frame is covered at the bottom with turf, and upward it is thatched with coarse grass. The whole village was out to see us, and men, women, and children crowded about me. I was conducted by the young chief who was my guide, and seemed proud and assiduous to serve me, into one of the largest huts.

"I was surprised at the behavior of the Indians, for, though they were curious to see me, yet they did not express that extraordinary curiosity that would be expected had they never seen a European before; and I was glad to perceive it, as it was an evidence in favor of what I wished to find true, namely, that there were Europeans now among them. The women of the house, which were almost the only ones that I had seen at this island, were much more tolerable than I expected to find them; one, in particular, seemed very busy to please me; to her, therefore, I made several presents, with which she was extremely well pleased. As it was now dark, my young chief intimated to me that we must tarry where we were that night, and proceed further the next day, to which I very readily consented, being much fatigued. Our entertainment, the subsequent part of the evening, did not consist of delicacies, or much variety; they had dried fish, and I had bread and spirits, of which we all participated. Ceremony was not invited to the feast, and Nature presided over the entertainment.

"At daylight, Perpheela (which was the name of the young chief that was my guide) let me know that he was ready to go on, upon which I flung off the skins I had slept in, put on my shoes and outside vest, and arose to accompany him, repeating my presents to my friendly hosts. We had hitherto traveled in a northerly direction, but now went to the westward and southward. I was now so much relieved from the apprehension of any insult or injury from the Indians, that my journey would have been even agreeable had I not been taken lame with a swelling in the feet, which rendered it extremely painful to walk; the country was also rough and hilly, and the weather wet and cold. About three hours before dark we came to a large bay, which appeared to be four leagues over.

"Here my guide, Perpheela, took a canoe and all our baggage, and set off, seemingly to cross the bay. He appeared to leave me in an abrupt manner, and told me to follow the two attendants. This gave me some uneasiness. I now followed Perpheela's two attendants, keeping the bay in view; but we had not gone above six miles before we saw a canoe approaching us from the opposite side of the bay, in which were two Indians. As soon as my guides saw the canoe, we ran to the shore from the hills and hailed them, and finding they did not hear us, we got some bushes and waved them in the air, which they saw, and stood directly for us. This canoe was sent by Perpheela to bring me across the bay, and shorten the distance of the journey.

"It was beginning to be dark when the canoe came to us. It was a skin canoe, after the Esquimaux plan, with two holes to accommodate two sitters. The Indians that came in the canoe talked a little with my two guides, and then came to me and desired I would get into the canoe. This I did not very readily agree to, however, as there was no other place for me but to be thrust into the space between the holes, extended at length upon my back, and wholly excluded from seeing the way I went, or the power of extricating myself upon any emergency; but, as there was no alternative, I submitted thus to be stowed away in bulk, and went head foremost very swift through the water about an hour, when I felt the canoe strike a beach, and afterward lifted up and carried some distance, and then set down again; after which I was drawn out by the shoulders by three or four men, for it was now so dark that I could not tell who they were, though I was conscious I heard a language that was new.

"I was conducted by two of these persons, who appeared to be strangers, about fifty rods, when I saw lights, and a number of huts like those I saw in the morning. As we approached one of them a door opened, and discovered a lamp, by which, to my joy and surprise, I discovered that the two men who held me by each arm were Europeans, fair and comely, and concluded from their appearance they were Russians, which I soon after found to be true. As we entered the hut, which was particularly long, I saw, arranged on each side, on a platform of plank, a number of Indians, who all bowed to me; and as I advanced to the further end of the hut, there were other Russians. When I reached the end of the room, I was seated on a bench covered with fur skins, and as I was much fatigued, wet, and cold, I had a change of garments brought me, consisting of a blue silk shirt and drawers, a fur cap, boots, and gown, all which I put on with the same cheerfulness they were presented with. Hospitality is a virtue peculiar to man, and the obligation is as great to receive as to confer.

"As soon as I was rendered warm and comfortable, a table was set before me with a lamp upon it; all the Russians in the house sat down round me, and the bottles of spirits, tobacco, snuff, and whatever Perpheela had, were brought and set upon it. These I presented to the company, intimating that they were presents from Commodore Cook, who was an Englishman. One of the company then gave me to understand that all the white people I saw there were subjects of the Empress Catharine of Russia, and rose and kissed my hand, the rest uncovering their heads. I then informed them, as well as I could, that Commodore Cook wanted to see some of them, and had sent me there to conduct them to our ships.

"These preliminaries over, we had supper, which consisted of boiled whale, halibut fried in oil, and broiled salmon. The latter I ate, and they gave me rye bread, but would eat none of it themselves. They were very fond of the rum, which they drank without any mixture or measure. I had a very comfortable bed, composed of different fur skins both under and over me, and, being harassed the preceding day, I went soon to rest. After I had lain down, the Russians assembled the Indians in a very silent manner, and said prayers after the manner of the Greek Church, which is much like the Roman.

"I could not but observe with what particular satisfaction the Indians performed their devoirs to God through the medium of their little crucifixes, and with what pleasure they went through the multitude of ceremonies attendant on that sort of worship. I think it a religion the best calculated in the world to gain proselytes, when the people are either unwilling or unable to speculate, or when they can not be made acquainted with the history and principles of Christianity without a formal education.

"I had a very comfortable night's rest, and did not wake the next morning until late. As soon as I was up, I was conducted to a hut at a little distance from the one I had slept in, where I saw a number of platforms raised about three feet from the ground, and covered with dry coarse grass and some small green bushes. There were several of the Russians already here besides those that conducted me, and several Indians, who were heating water in a large copper caldron over a furnace, the heat of which, and the steam which evaporated from the hot water, rendered the hut, which was very tight, extremely hot and suffocating.

"I soon understood this was a hot bath, of which I was asked to make use in a friendly manner. The apparatus being a little curious, I consented to it; but, before I had finished undressing myself, I was overcome by the sudden change of the air, fainted away, and fell back on the platform I was sitting on. I was, however, soon relieved by having cold and lukewarm water administered to my face and different parts of my body. I finished undressing, and proceeded as I saw the rest do, who were now all undressed. The Indians, who served us, brought us, as we sat or extended ourselves on the platforms, water of different temperatures, from that which was as hot as we could bear, to quite cold. The hot water was accompanied with some hard soap and a flesh-brush. It was not, however, thrown on the body from the dish, but sprinkled on with the green bushes. After this, the water made use of was less warm, and by several gradations became at last quite cold, which concluded the ceremony.

"We again dressed and returned to our lodgings, where our breakfast was smoking on the table; but the flavor of our feast, as well as its appearance, had nearly produced a relapse in my spirits, and no doubt would, if I had not had recourse to some of the brandy I had brought, which happily served me. I was a good deal uneasy lest the cause of my discomposure should disoblige my friends, who meant to treat me in the best manner they could. I therefore attributed my illness to the bath, which might possibly have partly occasioned it, for I am not very subject to fainting. I could eat none of the breakfast, however, though far from wanting an appetite. It was mostly of whale, sea-horse, and bear, which, though smoked, dried, and boiled, produced a composition of smells very offensive at nine or ten in the morning. I therefore desired I might have a piece of smoked salmon broiled dry, which I ate with some of my own biscuit.

"After breakfast I intended to set off on my return to the ships, though there came on a disagreeable snow-storm; but my new-found friends objected to it, and gave me to understand that I should go the next day, and, if I chose, three of them would accompany me. This I immediately agreed to, as it anticipated a favor I intended to ask them, though I before much doubted whether they would comply with it. I amused myself within doors while it snowed without, by writing down a few words of the original languages of the American Indians and of the Asiatics, who came over to this coast with these Russians from Kamtschatka.

"In the afternoon the weather cleared up, and I went out to see how those Russian adventurers were situated. I found the whole village to contain about thirty huts, all of which were built partly under ground, and covered with turf at the bottom and coarse grass at the top. The only circumstance that can recommend them is their warmth, which is occasioned partly by their manner of construction, and partly by a kind of oven, in which they constantly keep a fire night and day. They sleep on platforms built on each side of the hut, on which they have a number of bear and other skins, which render them comfortable; and as they have been educated in a hardy manner, they need little or no other support than what they procure from the sea and from hunting.

"The number of Russians were about thirty, and they had with them about seventy Kamtschatdales, or Indians from Kamtschatka. These, with some of the American Indians whom they had entered into friendship with, occupied the village, enjoyed every benefit in common with the Russians, and were converts to their religion. Such other of the aborigines of the island as had not become converts to their sentiments in religious and civil matters were excluded from such privileges, and were prohibited from wearing certain arms.

"I also found a small sloop of about thirty tons' burden lying in a cove behind the village, and a hut near her containing her sails, cordage, and other sea equipage, and one old iron three pounder. It is natural to an ingenuous mind, when it enters a town, a house, or ship that has been rendered famous by any particular event, to feel the full force of that pleasure which results from gratifying a noble curiosity. I was no sooner informed that this sloop was the same in which the famous Behring had performed those discoveries which did him so much honor and his country such great service, than I was determined to go on board of her and indulge the generous feelings the occasion inspired.

"I intimated my wishes to the man that accompanied me, who went back to the village and brought a canoe, in which we went on board, where I remained about an hour, and then returned. This little bark belonged to Kamtschatka, and came from thence with the Asiatics already mentioned to this island, which they call Onalaska, in order to establish a pelt and fur factory. They had been here about five years, and go over to Kamtschatka once a year to deliver their merchandise and get a recruit of such supplies as they need from the chief factory there.

"The next day I set off from this village, well satisfied with the happy issue of a tour which was now as agreeable as it was at first undesirable. I was accompanied by three of the principal Russians and some attendants. We embarked at the village in a large skin boat, much like our large whale-boats, rowing with twelve oars; and, as we struck directly across the bay, we shortened our distance several miles, and the next day, passing the same village I had before been at, we arrived by sunset at the bay where the ships lay, and before dark I got on board with our new acquaintances. The satisfaction this discovery gave Cook, and the honor that redounded to me, may be easily imagined, and the several conjectures respecting the appearance of a foreign intercourse were rectified and confirmed."

It will be seen that Ledyard's pen was extremely minute, and capable of jotting down impressions with much vividness. The book from which the above extract is made was written from memory, and with the object of allaying the public appetite, which had been greatly excited by rumors of the varied incidents of Cook's last, sad voyage. We have not the requisite space for following the author in his narrative of the cruise, but as Ledyard was present at the death of Captain Cook, his description of that event will be read with interest. The expedition returned to the Society Islands, and remained there for some days refitting and making all needful preparations for the voyage to the north pole. During their sojourn they were constantly annoyed by the thievish propensities of the natives. To put a stop to this, Cook, in accordance with his invariable custom, seized some conspicuous chief, and held him as hostage until the missing properties were returned. Owing to this, a coldness sprung up between the natives and the English, and it was with the greatest difficulty that the latter could obtain a supply of provisions. The events which follow occurred in Kearakekua Bay:

"Our return to this bay," says Mr. Ledyard, "was as disagreeable to us as it was to the inhabitants, for we were reciprocally tired of each other. They had been oppressed, and we were weary of our prostituted alliance, and we were aggrieved by the consideration of wanting the provisions and refreshments of the country, which we had every reason to suppose, from their behavior antecedent to our departure, would now be withheld from us, or brought in such small quantities as to be worse than none. What we anticipated was true. When we entered the bay, where before we had the shouts of thousands to welcome our arrival, we had the mortification not to see a single canoe, and hardly any inhabitants in the towns. Cook was chagrined, and his people were soured.

"Toward night, however, the canoes came in, but the provisions, both in quantity and quality, plainly informed us that times were altered; and what was very remarkable was the exorbitant price they asked, and the particular fancy they all at once took to iron daggers or dirks, which were the only articles that were any ways current, with the chiefs at least. It was also equally evident from the looks of the natives, as well as every other appearance, that our former friendship was at an end, and that we had nothing to do but to hasten our departure to some different island where our vices were not known, and where our extrinsic virtues might gain us another short space of being wondered at, and doing as we pleased, or, as our tars expressed it, of being happy by the month.

"Nor was their passive appearance of disgust all we had to fear, nor did it continue long. Before dark a canoe, with a number of armed chiefs, came alongside of us without provisions, and, indeed, without any perceptible design. After staying a short time only, they went to the *Discovery*, where a part of them went on board. Here they affected great friendship, and, unfortunately overacting it, Clerke was suspicious, and ordered two sentinels on the gangways. These men were purposely sent by the chief, who had formerly been so very intimate with Clerke, and afterward so ill treated by him, with the charge of stealing his jolly-boat. They came with a determination of mischief, and effected it.

"After they were all returned to the canoe but one, they got their paddles and every thing ready for a start. Those in the canoes, observing the sentinel to be watchful, took off his attention by some conversation that they knew would be pleasing to him, and by this means favored the designs of the man on board, who, watching his opportunity, snatched two pairs of tongs, and other iron tools that then lay close by the armorers at work at the forge, and, mounting the gangway-rail, with one leap threw himself and his goods into the canoe, that was then upon the move, and, taking up his paddle, joined the others; and, standing directly for the shore, they were out of our reach almost instantaneously, even before a musket could be had from the arms'-chest to fire at them. The sentries had only hangers.

"This was the boldest exploit that had yet been attempted, and had a bad aspect. Clerke immediately sent to the commodore, who advised him to send a boat on shore to endeavor to regain the goods, if they could not the men who obtained them; but the errand was as ill executed as contrived, and the master of the *Discovery* was glad to return with a severe drubbing from the very chief who had been so maltreated by Clerke. The crew were also pelted with stones, and had all their oars broken, and they had not a single weapon in the boat, not even a cutlass, to defend themselves. When Cook heard of this, he went armed himself in person to the guard on shore, took a file of marines, and went through the whole town demanding restitution, and threatening the delinquents and their abettors with the severest punishments; but, not being able to effect any thing, he came off just at sunset, highly displeased, and not a little concerned at the bad appearance of things. But even this was nothing to what followed.

"On the 13th, at night, the *Discovery's* large cutter, which was at her usual moorings at the lower buoy, was taken away. On the 14th, the captains met to consult what should be done on this alarming occasion; and the issue of their opinions was, that one of the two captains should land with armed boats and a guard of marines at Kiverua, and attempt to persuade Teraiobu, who was then at his house in that town, to come on board upon a visit, and that when he was on board he should be kept prisoner until his subjects should release him by a restitution of the cutter; and if it was afterward thought proper, he, or some of the family who might accompany him, should be kept as perpetual hostages for the good behavior of the people during the remaining part of our continuance at Kearakekua.

"This plan was the more approved of by Cook, as he had so repeatedly, on former occasions to the southward, employed it with success. Clerke was then in a deep decline of his health, and too feeble to undertake the affair, though it naturally devolved upon him as a point of duty not well transferable; he therefore begged Cook to oblige him so much as to take that part of the business of the day upon himself in his stead. This Cook agreed to do; but, previous to his landing, made some additional arrangements respecting the possible want of things, though it is certain, from the appearance of the subsequent arrangements, that he guarded more against the flight of Teraiobu, or those he could wish to see, than from an attack, or even much insult.

"The disposition of our guards when the movement began was thus: Cook in his pinnace, with six private marines, a corporal, sergeant, and two lieutenants of marines, went ahead, followed by the launch, with other marines and seamen, on one quarter, and the small cutter on the other, with only the crew on board. This part of the guard rowed for Kearakekua. Our large cutter and two boats from the *Discovery* had orders to proceed to the mouth of the bay, form at equal distances across, and prevent any communication by water from any other part of the island to the towns within the bay, or from those without. Cook landed at Kiverua about nine o'clock in the morning, with the marines in the pinnace, and went by a circuitous march to the house of Teraiobu, in order to evade the suspicion of any design. This route led through a considerable part of the town, which discovered every symptom of mischief, though Cook, blinded by some fatal cause, could not perceive it, or, too self-confident, would not regard it.

"The town was evacuated by the women and children, who had retired to the circumjacent hills, and appeared almost destitute of men; but there were at that time two hundred chiefs, and more than twice that number of other men, detached and secreted in different parts of the houses nearest to Teraiobu, exclusive of unknown numbers without the skirts of the town; and those that were seen were dressed, many of them, in black. When the guard reached Teraiobu's house, Cook ordered the lieutenant of marines to go in and see if he was at home, and if he was, to bring him out. The lieutenant went in, and found the old man sitting with two or three old women of distinction; and when he gave Teraiobu to understand that Cook was without and wanted to see him, he discovered the greatest marks of uneasiness, but arose and accompanied the lieutenant out, holding his hand. When he came before Cook, he squatted down upon his hams as a mark of humiliation, and Cook took him by the hand from the lieutenant, and conversed with him.

"The appearance of our parade, both by water and on shore, though conducted with the utmost silence, and with as little ostentation as possible, had alarmed the towns on both sides of the bay, but particularly Kiverua, where the people were in complete order for an onset; otherwise it would have been a matter of surprise that, though Cook did not see twenty men in passing through the town, yet, before he had conversed ten minutes with Teraiobu, he was surrounded by three or four hundred people, and above half of them chiefs.

"Cook grew uneasy when he observed this, and was the more urgent in his persuasions with Teraiobu to go on board, and actually persuaded the old man to go at length, and led him within a rod or two of the shore; but the just fears and conjectures of the chiefs at last interposed. They held the old man back, and one of the chiefs threatened Cook when he attempted to make them quit Teraiobu. Some of the crowd now cried out that Cook was going to take their king from them and kill him, and there was one in particular that advanced toward Cook in an attitude that alarmed one of the guard, who presented his bayonet and opposed him, acquainting Cook, in the mean time, of the danger of his situation, and that the Indians in a few minutes would attack him; that he had overheard the man whom he had just stopped from rushing in upon him say that our boats which were out in the harbor had just killed his brother, and he would be revenged.

"Cook attended to what this man said, and desired him to show him the Indian that had dared to attempt a combat with him, and, as soon as he was pointed out, Cook fired at him with a blank. The Indian, perceiving he received no damage from the fire, rushed from without the crowd a second time, and threatened any one that should oppose him. Cook, perceiving this, fired a ball, which entering the Indian's groin, he fell, and was drawn off by the rest.

"Cook, perceiving the people determined to oppose his designs, and that he should not succeed without further bloodshed, ordered the lieutenant of marines, Mr. Phillips, to withdraw his men, and get them into the boats, which were then lying ready to receive them. This was effected by the sergeant; but, the instant they began to retreat, Cook was hit with a stone, and, perceiving the man who threw it, shot him dead. The officer in the boats, observing the guard retreat, and hearing this third discharge, ordered the boats to fire. This occasioned the guard to face about and fire, and then the attack became general.

"Cook and Mr. Phillips were together a few paces in the rear of the guard, and, perceiving a general fire without orders, quitted Teraiobu and ran to the shore to put a stop to it; but, not being able to make themselves heard, and being close pressed upon by the chiefs, they joined the guard, who fired as they retreated. Cook, having at length reached the margin of the water, between the fire of the boats, waved with his hat for them to cease firing and come in; and while he was doing this, a chief from behind stabbed him with one of our iron daggers just under the shoulder-blade, and it passed quite through his body. Cook fell with his face in the water, and immediately expired. Mr. Phillips, not being able any longer to use his fusee, drew his sword, and, engaging the chief whom he saw kill Cook, soon dispatched him. His guard, in the mean time, were all killed but two, and they had plunged into the water and were swimming to the boats. He stood thus for some time the butt of all their force; and being as complete in the use of his sword as he was accomplished, his noble achievements struck the barbarians with awe; but, being wounded, and growing faint from loss of blood and excessive action, he plunged into the sea with his sword in his hand and swam to the boats, where, however, he was scarcely taken on board before somebody saw one of the marines that had swum from the shore lying flat upon the bottom. Phillips, hearing this, ran aft, threw himself in after him, and brought him up with him to the surface of the water, and both were taken in.

"The boats had hitherto kept up a very hot fire, and, lying off without reach of any weapon but stones, had received no damage, and being fully at leisure to keep up an unremitted and uniform action, made great havoc among the Indians, particularly among the chiefs, who stood foremost in the crowd and were most exposed; but whether it was from their bravery, or ignorance of the real cause that deprived so many of them of life that they made such a stand, may be questioned, since it is certain that they in general, if not universally, understood heretofore that it was the fire only of our arms that destroyed them. This opinion seems to be strengthened by the circumstance of the large, thick mats they were observed to wear, which were also constantly kept wet; and furthermore, the Indian that Cook fired at with a blank discovered no fear when he found his mat unburnt, saying in their language, when he showed it to the by-standers, that no fire had touched it. This may be supposed to have had at least some influence. It is, however, certain, whether from one or both these causes, that the numbers that fell made no apparent impression on those who survived; they were immediately taken off, and had their places supplied in a constant succession. Lieutenant Gore, who commanded as first lieutenant under Cook in the *Resolution*, which lay opposite the place where this attack was made, perceiving with his glass that the guard on shore was cut off, and that Cook had fallen, immediately passed a spring upon one of the cables, and, bringing the ship's starboard guns to bear, fired two round shot over the boats into the middle of the crowd; and both the thunder of the cannon and the effects of the shot operated so powerfully, that it produced a most precipitate retreat from the shore to the town."

With as much expedition as possible, the ships retreated from a neighborhood fraught with so much calamity; proceeded to the polar regions in search of the northwest passage, touched at Kamtschatka, passed through Behring's Straits, and visited many islands in a high latitude, but with no success. The expedition then returned home by way of China and the Cape of Good Hope, reaching England after an absence of four years and three months.

For two years after this we find no mention of Ledyard, except that he remained in the navy, but refused to serve in any of the expeditions which were fitted out against his native country. The desire of returning, however, induced him in 1782 to obtain a transfer to a British man-of-war bound for an American station. Fortunately, the destination of the ship was Huntingdon Bay, Long Island Sound. Immediately on his arrival he obtained leave of absence to visit his mother, who still resided at Southold, where she kept a boarding-house, chiefly supported by British officers—New York at that time being in possession of the British. He had so much changed during his eight years' absence that the poor old lady did not know him. It is said that she passed and repassed him many times, as if uncertain whether she had seen him before. At length she put on her spectacles, and, apologizing for the liberty she took in scrutinizing a stranger so closely, said that he resembled a son of hers who had been long absent, and concerning whose fate nothing was known. The scene that followed must have been affecting, for Ledyard, although a rover, was dearly attached to his mother.

Ledyard's leave of absence was for seven days, but, before the expiration of that brief term, he had fully made up his mind to return no more to the British service. "I made my escape from the British at Huntingdon Bay," he wrote. "I am now at Mr. Seymour's, and as happy as need be. I have a little cash, two coats, three waistcoats, six pair of stockings, and half a dozen ruffled shirts. I am a violent Whig and a violent Tory. Many are my acquaintances. I eat and drink when I am asked, and visit when I am invited; in short, I generally do as I am bid. All I want of my friends is friendship; possessed of that, I am happy." During this period he wrote his Journal of Cook's Voyage, from which our extracts have been taken.

Early in the following spring he began to agitate a subject on which his heart was fully set—namely, a trading voyage to the Northwest Coast of the Pacific—a traffic entirely unknown in those days, and which, as subsequent events have proved, is eminently profitable. In turn he applied to all the merchants and ship-owners of New York, Boston, and Philadelphia, sometimes with apparent success. In this heart-chilling way he spent two seasons, and then, satisfied that nothing could be done in America, he started once more for Europe. He took with him some excellent letters of introduction, and, on presenting them to the merchants of L'Orient, received immediate encouragement. He was requested to remain until the approaching summer, and employ himself, in the mean time, in making the necessary preparation for the cruise. When the spring came they procured him a ship, and every thing promised an immediate consummation of his wishes; but, for some reason which has never been explained, all these preparations were in vain. The expedition was abandoned, and Ledyard repaired to Paris to look out for men of more energy and speculation. In the latter city he made the acquaintance of Jefferson, who was the minister from the United States, and also of Paul Jones. With each of these he discussed the project he had in view, and received much encouragement, especially from the latter. He submitted the enterprise, also, to the mercantile community of Paris, and some progress was made in the organization of a public company. Several months were passed in these efforts, which were destined, after all, to prove unavailing. From inability, unwillingness, or distrust, every one made some kind of excuse when the moment arrived for action. At length Ledyard crossed the Channel to the English metropolis. While in France he had been fortunate enough to make the acquaintance of an eccentric Englishman, Sir James Hall by name, and it was at his invitation that he now repaired to London. Much to his astonishment, he there found an English ship in complete readiness to sail for the Pacific Ocean. Sir James Hall introduced him to the owners, who immediately offered him a free passage in the vessel, with the promise that he should be set on shore at any point he chose in the Pacific Ocean—their recompense being the advantage of having a man so experienced on board the vessel. "Sir James Hall," says Mr. Ledyard, "presented me with twenty pounds *pro bono publico.* I bought two great dogs, an Indian pipe, and a hatchet. My want of time, as well as of money, will prevent my going any otherwise than indifferently equipped for such an enterprise." What a queer outfit for the Pacific Ocean—two great dogs, an Indian pipe, and a hatchet! His intention was now to proceed to Nootka Sound, and then strike across the American continent to the Atlantic States, thus traversing the land from one side to the other. The propitious day arrived. Ledyard embarked, and the vessel floated down the Thames on her long voyage. There did not seem to be the faintest prospect of a fresh disappointment, when suddenly a terrific one loomed up in the distance. An order from government arrested the progress of the vessel; she was seized by the custom-house, and eventually exchequered. Thus the expedition was at once permanently crushed. One would suppose that after so many disappointments, so many evidences that Dame Fortune was against him, Ledyard would abandon his projects, and sink into a helpless condition of wretchedness and despair. Not at all. He was now so used to these disappointments that they had even ceased to surprise him. The only effect this last blow had was to lead him to trust for the future entirely to himself. In a letter to his brother he says, "I am going in a few days to make the tour of the globe, from London east, on foot." There was no possibility of disappointment in this arrangement. Ledyard's project interested the scientific world of London, who saw in his contemplated overland journey the opportunity of obtaining valuable geographical information concerning regions comparatively unknown. They were willing to assist him too, and for this purpose a subscription was put on foot, which, whatever its amount, was sufficient to start him on his journey.

On the 1st of January, 1789, he arrived at Copenhagen, from thence crossed over into Sweden, and reached Stockholm by the end of the month. His destination was St. Petersburg, for which purpose it was necessary that he should cross the Gulf of Bothnia. In the winter this is usually effected in sledges, but occasionally it happens that the water is not sufficiently frozen for this kind of passage, although too thickly covered with floating ice to admit of vessels crossing in safety. Under these perplexing circumstances it became necessary to travel round the Gulf, a distance of twelve hundred miles, through Lapland and the Arctic Circle, in order to reach the opposite point, which, under favorable circumstances, is only fifty miles distant. Such was the state of things when Ledyard arrived at the usual place of crossing. The only alternative was to stay in Stockholm till the spring should open, or to go around the Gulf into Lapland, and so reach St. Petersburg. With very little deliberation, he arrived at the latter determination, and at once started on foot to perform the perilous journey. Unfortunately, we have no record of this remarkable act of pedestrianism, or of the innumerable adventures that must have attended it. On the 20th of March Ledyard reached Petersburg—that is, within seven weeks of the time of leaving Stockholm—making the average distance traveled about two hundred miles per week. "I can not tell you," he says, in one of his letters, "by what means I came to Petersburg, and hardly know by what means I shall quit it in the further prosecution of my tour round the world by land. If I have any merit in the affair, it is perseverance, for most severely have I been buffeted; and yet still am even more obstinate than before; and Fate, as obstinate, continues her assaults. How the matter will terminate I know not. The most probable conjecture is that I shall succeed, and be buffeted around the world as I have hitherto been from England through Denmark, through Sweden, Swedish Lapland, Swedish Finland, and the most unfrequented parts of Russian Finland, to this aurora borealis of a city."

After remaining a short time in St. Petersburg, Ledyard started once more, in company with a Scotch physician, who was traveling on state business, and who accompanied our hero for a distance of upward of three thousand miles. It is probable that he defrayed his expenses too, for Ledyard's funds were wretchedly low, consisting, in fact, of the remains of twenty pounds which he had raised in St. Petersburg. How he succeeded in getting from place to place, mixing wherever he went in the best society, is indeed always a mystery. He was, unquestionably, a presentable, courteous, and charming man, one of those whose blandness and decision of character pass them into the ranks of the wealthy and educated as a matter of course. At Barnaoul, Ledyard parted company with Dr. Brown. "How I have come thus far," he writes to his favorite correspondent, Mr. Jefferson, "and how I am to go still farther, is an enigma that I must disclose to you on some happier occasion. I shall never be able, without seeing you in person, and perhaps not then, to tell you how universally and circumstantially the Tartars resemble the aborigines of America. They are the same people, the most ancient and the most numerous of any other, and, had not a small sea divided them, they would all have been still known by the same name. The cloak of civilization sits as ill upon them as upon our American Tartars. They have been a long time Tartars, and it will be a long time before they will be any other kind of people."

From Barnaoul to Irkutsk he traveled post, a distance of 1155 miles; from the latter place to Yakutsk, a distance of 1500 miles, in a vessel down the River Lena, traveling at the rate of eighty or a hundred miles per day. On the 18th of September he arrived at Yakutsk in safety. Lodgings were provided for him by order of the commandant, but, to his dismay, he was informed that the season was too far advanced to admit of his going farther north until the spring. "What, alas! shall I do?" he exclaims, piteously, in his journal, "for I am miserably prepared for this unlooked-for delay. By remaining here through the winter I can not expect to resume my march until May, which will be eight months. My funds! I have but two long frozen stages more, and I shall be beyond the want or aid of money, until, emerging from the deep deserts, I gain the American Atlantic States; and then, thy glowing climates, Africa, explored, I will lay me down, and claim my little portion of the globe I have viewed. May it not be before? How many of the noble minded have been subsidiary to me or to my enterprises! yet that meagre demon, Poverty, has traveled with me hand in hand over half the globe, and witnessed what—the tale I will not unfold. * * * This is the third time I have been overtaken and arrested by winter, and both the others, by giving time for my evil genius to rally his hosts about me, have defeated the enterprise. Fortune, thou hast humbled me at last, for I am this moment the slave of cowardly solicitude, lest in the heart of this dread winter there lurk the seeds of disappointment to my ardent desire of gaining the opposite continent. But I submit."

The commandant, who seems to have been a very good fellow, invited Ledyard to the hospitalities of his house, but, unfortunately, Ledyard was badly off for clothes, and had but thirty shillings in his pocket to get a fresh stock with. Even in Siberia, where hospitality is the fashion, this state of things was disheartening. However, he seems to have cheered up and made the best of it. During his forced stay he employed his time profitably in making inquiries concerning the country, and especially concerning the various Tartar tribes which he had met in Russia and Siberia. The results of his investigations were summed up in a letter to Mr. Jefferson, from which we extract. "I am certain that all the people you call *red* people on the continent of America, and on the continents of Europe and Asia, as far south as the southern parts of China, are all one people, by whatever names distinguished, and that the best general name would be *Tartar*. I suspect that all red people are of the same family. I am satisfied that America was peopled from Asia, and some, if not all, its animals from thence. I am satisfied that the great general analogy in the customs of men can only be accounted for by supposing them all to compose one family; and, by excluding the idea and uniting customs, traditions, and history, I am satisfied that this common origin was such, or nearly, as related by Moses, and commonly believed among the nations of the earth. There is also a transposition of things on the globe that must have been produced by some cause equal to the effect, which is vast and curious. Whether I repose on arguments drawn from facts observed by myself, or send imagination forth to find a cause, they both declare to me a general deluge." His journal, written here, contains a great deal of observant critical matter, jotted down hastily, with no view to direct publication. We have but room for the following eulogy on woman, and then must hurry on: "I have observed among all nations that the women ornament themselves more than the men; that, wherever found, they are the same kind, civil, obliging, humane, tender beings; that they are ever inclined to be gay and cheerful, timorous and modest. They do not hesitate, like man, to perform a hospitable or generous action; not haughty, nor arrogant, nor supercilious, but full of courtesy and fond of society; industrious, economical, ingenuous; more liable in general to err than man, but in general, also, more virtuous, and performing more good actions than he. I never addressed myself in the language of decency and friendship to a woman, whether civilized or savage, without receiving a decent and friendly answer. With man it has often been otherwise. In wandering over the barren plains of inhospitable Denmark, through honest Sweden, frozen Lapland, rude and churlish Finland, unprincipled Russia, and the wide-spread regions of the wandering Tartar, if hungry, dry, cold, wet, or sick, woman has ever been friendly to me, and uniformly so; and to add to this virtue, so worthy of the appellation of benevolence, these actions have been performed in so free and so kind a manner, that if I was dry, I drank the sweet draught, and if hungry, ate the coarse morsel with a double relish."

The weariness of his winter captivity in Yakutsk was thus relieved by the exercises of composition, hasty and imperfect to be sure, but exciting to an imagination alive with the freshness of the things described. An unexpected surprise was in store for him while in the midst of these employments. He had not been quite two months in his winter quarters when the town was aroused from its usual lethargy by the arrival of Captain Billings, who was employed by the Empress of Russia on a mission for exploring the northeastern regions of her territory, and who came now from his expedition to superintend the construction of certain boats necessary for farther explorations. Billings was an old acquaintance of Ledyard's; they had served together on Cook's voyage, and were mutually astonished to meet thus unexpectedly in the heart of Siberia. He was now on his way to Irkutsk, and, needing a companion, invited Ledyard to accompany him back to that town. The latter was of course glad of any opportunity of killing time, and at once cheerfully assented, intending to return in the spring and prosecute his journey northward. They started on the 29th of December, and traveled in sledges up the River Lena, on the ice, with such rapidity that in seventeen days they covered the distance, fifteen hundred miles.

Having leisure and companions, Ledyard enjoyed himself in society, and made the most of the long, dreary evenings, now that he could do so. The following extract from Sauer's "Account of a Geographical and Astronomical Expedition to the Northern parts of Russia" will explain how this period of repose was brought to a sudden close: "In the evening of the 24th of February," says Sauer, "while I was playing at cards with the brigadier and some company of his, a secretary belonging to one of the courts of justice came in, and told us, with great concern, that the governor general had received positive orders from the empress immediately to send one of the expedition, an Englishman, under guard, to the private inquisition at Moscow, but that he did not know the name of the person, and that Captain Billings was with a private party at the governor general's. Now, as Ledyard and I were the only Englishmen here, I could not help smiling at the news, when two hussars came into the room, and told me that the commandant wished to speak to me immediately. The consternation into which the visitors were thrown is not to be described. I assured them that it must be a mistake, and went with the guards to the commandant.

"There I found Mr. Ledyard under arrest. He told me that he had sent to Captain Billings, but he would not come to him. He then began to explain his situation, and said he was taken up as a French spy, whereas Captain Billings could prove the contrary, but he supposed that he knew nothing of the matter, and requested that I would inform him. I did so, but the captain assured me that it was an absolute order from the empress, and that he could not help him. He, however, sent him a few rubles, and gave him a pelisse; and I procured him his linen quite wet from the wash-tub. Ledyard took a friendly leave of me, desired his remembrance to his friends, and, with astonishing composure, leaped into the kibitka, and drove off, with two guards, one on each side. I wished to travel with him a little way, but was not permitted. I therefore returned to my company, and explained the matter to them."

In this cruel manner were all his schemes once more frustrated. He was hurried to Moscow, and then, without any investigation of the ridiculous charge of being a French spy, ordered to quit the Russian dominions, and informed that if he returned he would assuredly be hanged. The actual cause of his arrest appears to be shrouded in much mystery. It is probable, however, that it arose from the jealous unwillingness of Russia to have her new possessions on the western coast of America examined by a foreigner, especially when she had an expedition on the spot for the purpose of examining them herself for her own private advantage.

We hear little of Ledyard after this severe rebuff until we find him once more in London, after an absence of one year and five months. Here he found his old friend, Sir Joseph Banks, ready to receive him with open arms. All the incidents of his eventful journey were listened to with eagerness, and Ledyard received the sympathy of one man of science for another. Sir Joseph questioned him about his future movements, and recommended to his attention an expedition to Central Africa, which the African Association were anxious to have undertaken. Nothing could have given Ledyard greater satisfaction than this project. It was with a light and elastic step that he left Sir Joseph, and made his way to the rooms of the association. The secretary was struck with the manliness of his person, the breadth of his chest, the openness of his countenance, and the inquietude of his eye. He spread the map of Africa before him, and, tracing a line from Cairo to Sennaar, and from thence westward in the latitude and supposed direction of the Niger, told him that was the route by which the association were anxious that Africa might, if possible, be explored. Ledyard replied that he should consider himself singularly fortunate to be trusted with the venture. The secretary then asked him when he would be ready to set out. Ledyard replied, "To-morrow morning." The association immediately closed with a man who displayed such fearless promptitude and eagerness, but they were, of course, unable to dispatch him on the following morning. On the 30th of June he left London, and proceeded through France to the Mediterranean, thence to Alexandria, where he passed ten days, and then up the Nile to Cairo, where he arrived on the 19th of August. Having letters of introduction to the British consul, he found no difficulty in procuring such information as he needed for the prosecution of his journey. His intention was to join a caravan bound to the interior, and continue with it to the end of its route. After that he would have to be guided entirely by circumstances. He passed three months in Cairo studying the habits of the people he was about to associate with, and in otherwise preparing himself.

His zeal in these respects was attended with the most melancholy end. Exposure to the action of the sun produced a bilious complaint, and he treated it, with no apprehensions of its result, in the usual way, with vitriolic acid. The quantity he took was excessive, and produced burning pains, that threatened to be fatal unless immediate relief could be procured. A powerful dose of tartar emetic was administered, but in vain. The principal doctors of Cairo were called in, but their advice was impracticable and too late. In the thirty-eighth year of his age, he was doomed to end his strange career in this unfortunate and miserable way. The precise day of his death is not known, but it was toward the end of November, 1788. He was decently interred, and his remains were followed to the grave by many European residents in the capital of Egypt.

It is impossible to read the history of John Ledyard without experiencing the keenest sensation of regret that a career so energetic and promising was thus abruptly terminated. A more unfortunate man it would be hard to find in the world. His life was one constant struggle against poverty, but the cheerfulness of his disposition made him underrate the actual hardships beneath which he was constantly groaning. He was so accustomed to disappointments that they ceased to excite his indignation. With a steadiness of purpose which can not be too largely imitated, he entered upon the execution of his plans, totally indifferent to the obstacles which surrounded him. The one great object of his life he may be said to have accomplished, namely, to travel through the Russian possessions to the coast of America. A desire nearly as strong as this was to penetrate into the central parts of Africa. Under circumstances of peculiar good luck he started on this enterprise. For the first time in his life he was backed by liberal patrons, and discomfort arising from scanty means seemed impossible. With natural gayety and ardor he started for the burning land of the African, when death, as if dissatisfied with his triumph, smote him, and he fell in the pride of manhood and strength.

The following description of Mr. Ledyard is from the pen of Mr. Beaufoy, Secretary of the African Society. "To those who have never seen Mr. Ledyard, it may not, perhaps, be uninteresting to know that his person, though scarcely exceeding the middle size, was remarkably expressive of activity and strength; and that his manners, though unpolished, were neither uncivil nor unpleasing. Little attentive to difference of rank, he seemed to consider all men as his equals, and as such he respected them. His genius, though uncultivated and irregular, was original and comprehensive. Ardent in his wishes, yet calm in his deliberations; daring in his purposes, but guarded in his measures; impatient of control, yet capable of strong endurance; adventurous beyond the conception of ordinary men, yet wary and considerate, and attentive to all precautions, he appeared to be formed by nature for achievements of hardihood and peril."

STEPHEN GIRARD.

CONCERNING the early history of this eccentric and remarkable man we know but little, except that he was a native of France, and born in the environs of Bordeaux, on the 24th of May, 1750. His parents were in very humble circumstances, and Girard does not appear to have been indebted to them for any advantage beyond the essential one of birth. It is probable that his early years were passed in much misery, for he never desired to return to the scene of them. Gratitude, which is certainly a feature in the character of most self-made men, did not infuse warmth into Girard's heart, and even his parents were not remembered with the usual prompt affection of nature. Of education he had but little, being barely able to read his own language. The knowledge of this deficiency weighed heavily on his mind through life, and was undoubtedly one cause of that munificence which has given lasting interest to his name.

He is supposed to have left France at the early age of ten or twelve years, in the capacity of a cabin-boy, bound for the West Indies. Many causes have been assigned for this step; among others, soreness at being ridiculed for a blind eye, and ill-treatment from his parents. The most probable reason is, that he left France because he thought he could do better elsewhere. He did not remain in the West Indies for any length of time, but proceeded in his vessel to New York, from which port he afterward sailed as an apprentice. When the term of his indenture had expired, he abandoned the sea as a profession, and embarked his small savings in little semi-mercantile, semi-nautical ventures. The sound judgment he displayed in these matters was not without its result. Every day he made an addition to his capital, until finally it had swollen to proportions ample enough to purchase an interest in a small vessel which plied between New York and New Orleans, of which he took command.

In 1769 he removed to Philadelphia, and in the following year married Miss Polly Lum, a young lady remarkable for her beauty. It is said that Girard "fell in love" with Miss Lum under very peculiar, if not romantic circumstances. The fascinating creature was a servant in the family of Colonel Walter Shee, and Girard's first interview was in the open street, where he beheld the damsel, destitute of shoes and stockings, and operating on a pump. She was a beautiful brunette of sixteen, with a wide reputation for modesty and charms—a reputation which was fully sustained by her subsequent but short elevation in society. The match was an unfortunate one, and productive of much wretchedness to both parties. After his marriage he rented a small house in Water Street, and continued his business in the mercantile and seafaring way. In 1771 he entered into partnership with Mr. Hazelhurst, of Philadelphia, for the purpose of carrying on trade with the island of St. Domingo. Two brigs were purchased, and of one of these Girard took the command. On the passage both were captured and sent to Jamaica, thereby breaking up the adventure, dissolving the partnership, and sadly dissappointing the owners. Much censure was thrown upon Girard for not defending his vessel, as it had been expressly furnished with an armament to make resistance if attacked. It can not now be ascertained, and, indeed, is no longer interesting, whether this censure be just or not. It may be remarked, however, that Girard was not the kind of man to lose his property cheerfully. If he had seen a way of preserving it, we may safely conclude that he would have done so. From 1772 to 1776 there is no distinct trace of his movements. He followed the profession of sea-captain, and voyaged to those places where the most money could be made; but the extreme danger of maritime property, owing to the incessant watchfulness of British cruisers, induced him to seek his fortunes in the store rather than on the deep. Consequently, he opened a small grocery in Water Street, to which he attached a bottling establishment for claret and cider. Here he contrived to drive a profitable trade until the approach of the British army in 1777, when, with five hundred dollars which he had saved, he purchased a small farm at *Mount Holly*, and removed his store and business, so as to be out of harm's way. Here he continued his bottling business, and by supplying the American army, which was in the neighborhood, managed to turn an honest penny. In 1779 he returned to Philadelphia, and we find him occupying a range of frame stores on the east side of Water Street. A gentleman who at this period saw him nearly every day describes him as a plain and simply-attired man—so much so that even then he went by the general appellation of *Old Girard*, and was an object of curiosity in his junk-shop as much as any other article there. He made a few maritime adventures to the south with moderate success, but the depressed state of the country was unfavorable to the immediate accumulation of wealth. The St. Domingo trade, however, proved highly remunerative, and enabled him, in 1782, to brave the dullness of the times, and secure upon lease a range of frame and brick stores and dwellings. The terms were extremely moderate, the trade and commerce of the city being then at its lowest ebb. Girard, with the penetration of a man destined to become a millionaire, knew that a reaction must soon take place, and that these buildings would then be of inestimable value. His lease was for ten years, and contained a proviso that if, at the expiration of that period, Girard was willing to continue the occupancy, it might be renewed for ten years more. From the rent of these stores and dwellings Girard realized enormous profits. On the day of the expiration of the term of his first lease, he waited on Mr. Stiles, his landlord, for the stipulated renewal. Mr. Stiles, anticipating his object, observed, "Well, Mr. Girard, you have made out so well by your bargain that I suppose you will hardly hold me to the renewal of the lease for ten years more." "I have come," replied Mr. Girard, "to secure the ten years more; I shall not let you off."

After this, his brother, Captain John Girard, arriving in this country, the two brothers entered into copartnership, under the firm of Stephen & John Girard, in connection with a firm at Cape Française, under the name of Girard, Bernard & Lacrampe, who were then prosecuting a highly lucrative commerce to the West Indies. The brothers were not at all fraternal in temper, and for a long time were merely united by pecuniary interests. Stephen was grasping, parsimonious, and authoritative, while John had some little sentiment in his composition, which made him yearn for something beside the unscrupulous accumulation of wealth. A rupture took place, the firm was dissolved, and it was agreed to call in an umpire to adjust and settle their concerns (1790). At that period Stephen had fallen behind his brother either in the acquisition of money or the disparity of his capital invested in the concern; for, upon the settlement of the respective portions, John was found to be worth *sixty thousand dollars*, while Stephen, with all his closeness, possessed but *thirty thousand*. Several years after the dissolution, John (who had a family) died in the West Indies, leaving Stephen executor of his will. For some eccentric reason, the latter never informed his nieces of the fortune they inherited, but reared them in total ignorance of the fact. It was not until the marriage of Antoinette to Mr. Hemphill that he rendered an account of his brother John's estate, and astonished his nieces with a knowledge of their good fortune.

Immediately after the dissolution of partnership he recommenced his career as a ship-owner, and in a short time built four vessels, and dispatched them on voyages to China and the East Indies. His mind was now bent on the accumulation of riches, and the only enjoyment he permitted himself was the pursuit of this object. His biographer says that his sympathies were not with the common race of merchants or the every-day order of men. His ambition was to be rich, not that he might enjoy riches, but that he might die a millionaire, and so leave his name to posterity. It is scarcely probable that he possessed the faculty of enjoying himself, or, if he did, it was so intimately mixed up with making money that it assumed all the appearance of intense business application. Of domestic bliss he knew little or nothing. His wife had long been an inmate of a lunatic asylum, where she was destined to pass the remainder of her days in wretched captivity. Possibly her lot had not been of the happiest. Men of

Girard's temperament do not make good husbands, and we look in vain for the first indication of kindliness in his domestic rule. A daughter was born to him, but the poor weakly thing died, in spite of all the promise of Girard's wealth. At the period of which we are writing, Girard was unquestionably a crusty, plodding, penurious man, singularly repulsive in his appearance, and awkward and vulgar in his address. It was with the greatest difficulty that he could express himself in broken English, and never did so if there was an opportunity of speaking French. "Sympathy, feeling, friendship, pity, love, or commiseration," says his biographer, who is also his apologist and eulogist, "were emotions that never ruffled the equanimity of his mind, at least to such a degree as to relax his energy of accumulation, or impair the mass of money that rose like mountains round about him. Friends, relations, old companions, confidential agents, or the general family of mankind, might sicken and die around him, and he would not part with his money to relieve and save one among them." The dark coloring of this picture leaves us but little to expect from a man so hopelessly abandoned to Mammon; yet a bright and extraordinary trait of goodness manifested itself. In 1793, Philadelphia was desolated with the plague. The horrors of that frightful visitation have been so often described that it is unnecessary to rehearse them now. Husbands deserted their wives; children their parents; every one, in fact, who could rush from the scene of destruction, did so. The instinct of preservation rose paramount above all other considerations, and scenes of the most revolting and unnatural character were the inevitable result of a general panic. Among the poorer classes the mortality and suffering were of course greatest. The impossibility of getting proper attendance and medical skill pressed with fatal weight upon them. Many of these evils the rich could avoid. If they were attacked, their money obtained for them the best physicians in the city; if they were well, it carried them into the country, beyond the reach of infection. It would have been excusable if Stephen Girard, like thousands of his fellow-townsmen, had thus consulted his personal safety by flight. To the surprise of every one, however, he not only staid, but volunteered his services to nurse the sick. We quote from Mr. Carey's pamphlet: "At a meeting on Sunday, September 15th, a circumstance occurred to which the most glowing pencil could hardly do justice.

Stephen Girard, a wealthy merchant, a native of France, and one of the members of the committee, sympathizing with the wretched situation of the sufferers at Bush Hill, voluntarily and unexpectedly offered himself as a manager to superintend that hospital. The surprise and satisfaction excited by this extraordinary spirit of humanity can be better conceived than expressed. Peter Helm, a native of Pennsylvania, also a member, actuated by the like benevolent motives, offered his services in the same department. Their offers were accepted; and the same afternoon they entered on the execution of their dangerous and praiseworthy office. To form a just estimate of the value of the offer of these citizens, it is necessary to take into consideration the general consternation which at that period pervaded every quarter of the city, and which caused attendance on the sick to be regarded as little less than a certain sacrifice. Uninfluenced by any reflections of this kind, without any possible inducement but the purest motives of humanity, they magnanimously offered themselves as the forlorn hope of the committee." An anecdote is related by Mr. Simpson, which illustrates in an astonishing way the remarkable fortitude and courage of Girard at this dreadful crisis.

A Mr. T—— had been induced, like most other citizens, to move with his family out of Philadelphia, to avoid the ravages of the yellow fever, which was then making fearful havoc. Previous engagements, however, rendered it necessary for him to visit the city almost every day, and, unfortunately, his presence was demanded in Walnut Street, a few doors below Second. This was a fearful neighborhood, as the fever was raging in a shocking degree in "Farmer's Row," leading from Dock Street, only a few doors from his place of resort. For several days Mr. T—— felt that he was earning the name of a man of courage at a fearful risk, to venture into such a vicinity; but his business was imperative, and he continued to yield to its demands, of course with all those precautions which science or kindness suggested. One day Mr. T—— turned the corner of Walnut and Second Street, and went a few steps down the latter street until he came opposite the avenue called Farmer's Row. There pestilence had chased away every vestige of business; there was nothing to break the almost unearthly silence of the place, or give an idea that motion was an attribute of any object within view. He stood gazing at the buildings that contained the victims, living and dead, of the appalling disease, when suddenly the approach of a carriage, driven rapidly by a black man, broke the silence of the place. The carriage was driven up in front of one of the frame buildings on the Row. The driver laid his whip back upon its top, bound his handkerchief close to his mouth, opened the door of his vehicle, and resumed his seat. A short, thick-set man stepped from the coach, and went into one of the abodes of wretchedness. Interested in the result of such a movement, involving such imminent danger, Mr. T—— pressed his camphorated handkerchief closer to his face, and withdrew as far as he could without losing sight of the carriage and the house. His movement enabled him to look, though from a distance, into the door of the tenement. Shortly afterward he saw a slow movement on the stairs, as if some person was descending with difficulty. No noise, however, was heard, nor did there appear to be any other movement in the house. In a few minutes he distinguished the object of his solicitude approaching the outer door; at length he stood full in his view on the pavement. The man who had left the carriage had been into one of the chambers of the house, and had taken thence a human being, who had probably been left without the least attendance, suffering with the yellow fever. The size of the sufferer did not allow the visitor to take him up in the best mode for conveying him. As they were on the pavement, the right arm of the man partly supported the sick person, while the left arm was pressed close to his emaciated body, so as to prevent his falling; the feet of the sick man touched the ground, and his yellow, cadaverous face rested against the cheek of his conductor. Every breath he exhaled poured over the nostrils and mouth of his supporter a volume of putrid effluvium, while his hair, long from neglect, and knotted and matted with filth, added to the disgusting and fearful spectacle. In this situation the well man partly carried and partly dragged the sufferer to the carriage, in which, with great exertion and after much time, he succeeded in placing him; the driver, of course, refusing to aid in such a dangerous enterprise. The door of the carriage was drawn to by the person inside, and then they were driven slowly off, the sick man lying in the arms of the person who had brought him from his wretched abode. Who the sick man was Mr. T—— did not inquire; but HE who risked so much to help a human being that had no claims of consanguinity or friendship upon his services—

he who thus did good to others at such an imminent hazard to himself, was STEPHEN GIRARD.

What a remarkable compound of mean selfishness and noble philanthropy is found in the character of this strange man! Unwilling to give a dollar to save his dearest friend from destruction, yet voluntarily jeopardizing his life to assuage the sufferings of strangers. His office in the hospital was of the most alarming kind; he had to encourage and comfort the sick, to hand them necessaries and medicines, to wipe the sweat of their brows, and to perform many disgusting offices of kindness for them, which nothing could render tolerable but the exalted motives that impelled him to this heroic conduct.

We dwell on this incident with peculiar pleasure, because it is the only one worth recording in the life of Girard—at all events, the only one which seems to have been dictated by purely disinterested motives. His philanthropy was too often the result of keen, calculating, selfish motives. He would give money for the erection of churches (dealing out hundreds and thousands with unsparing hand), but it was always necessary that the church should be in some location likely to benefit his property. Of individual wants he was totally indifferent; the moans of the suffering, the hollow cry of the famished, the lamentations of the widowed and fatherless, never reached his ears. If he gave to benevolent institutions, it was that he might be remembered in the blazoned subscription list, and not that he conceived the necessity of such institutions. In a word, he was a thoroughly wretched being, utterly unworthy of imitation or even remembrance. The Giver of all things sometimes selects an unworthy instrument to perform His behests, and Girard was sent into the world to do good, although with a repulsiveness that did not suggest beneficence. It was, as we have before remarked, his ambition to be remembered and respected after death. For the living he cared nothing. The good opinion of his fellow-man (a worldly prize that the poorest may possess) he treated with contempt, and at any moment would sacrifice it for a cent. Overbearing, grasping, tyrannous, and mean, he looked on those around him as so many tools. If they were sharp and expeditious, he was willing to use them; but the moment they had been applied in the right way, he cast them from him. Gratitude for their services (which were sometimes of inestimable value to him) never entered his mind. His career was one of horrible closeness. He gave the smallest wage for the largest amount of work, and if there was an opportunity of pulling down a poor fellow's salary, after many years of devoted labor, he pulled it down without a moment's hesitation. In a country where the pursuit of riches is conducted in the most liberal spirit, and where paltry meanness is utterly unknown, the character of Girard naturally excited disgust. His wealth gave him a certain influence which had to be respected, but his acts were viewed with contempt by every American with whom he came in contact.

If a man start in life with the determination to eschew all its social obligations, he is at once in a position of advantage toward his neighbor which must lead to his own aggrandizement. By dint of indefatigable industry and unscrupulous stinginess, Girard found his hoards increasing daily, until he was in a position to become proprietor of a public bank, and to take government loans to any amount. One step on the ladder of riches secures another. The command of a bank enabled Girard to extend his commercial transactions, and to enter on fields of commerce which were closed to smaller capitalists. With such advantages, it was no unusual stroke of luck that netted him half a million of dollars at a single venture. Thus he amassed the immense fortune which it was his mission to leave behind for the public good. It would be tedious and unprofitable to follow his career more minutely.

For some time previous to the illness which terminated his career, Mr. Girard underwent the gradual breaking up of constitution common to men of great age, but he never relaxed in his business application. In 1826 he was violently attacked with the erysipelas in his head and legs, which confined him to his house for several weeks, and finally left him much debilitated. Unable to attend *at* the bank, he transacted its business at home. Every day his cashier visited him with the bills offered for discount, and took his views concerning them. On partly recovering, he altered his mode of living (he was fond of good dinners), and adopted a vegetable diet, which he persisted in to the day of his death. He continued, as might be expected, to grow weaker, his eyesight became more dim, and he found it difficult to walk the streets with safety. "In the year 1830," says Mr. Simpson, "I have often discovered him groping in the vestibule of his bank, and feeling about for the door without success. Still he would suffer no one to attend on or assist him." The result of this proud obstinacy was an accident. In crossing a street he was knocked down by a wagon, the wheel of which struck the side of his face, lacerating the flesh, and tearing off the greater part of his right ear. He walked home, but an examination of the wound showed that it was more serious and extensive than was at first imagined, and he suffered a long confinement. He lost nearly the whole of his right ear, and the eye, before but slightly open, was now entirely closed. The pain occasioned by the wound and the necessary operations of the doctor seriously affected his constitution, and left it exposed to the prey of other diseases. In the following year (1831) he was attacked with bronchitis. Fitful insanity or partial derangement quickly succeeded, which, increasing from day to day, terminated in unconsciousness and utter prostration. He refused to take medicine, and on the 26th of December, 1831, departed this life, in the 82d year of his age. The only emotion excited by the event was one of curiosity to know how old Girard had disposed of his property, amounting to *ten millions of dollars.* "The moment the true character of his bequests was known," says Mr. Simpson, "a loud shout of applause and admiration filled the public press, and flowed from every tongue, succeeded by a profound sentiment of gratitude and esteem for the man, the citizen, and the philanthropist. Surprise and incredulity for a time divided the minds of men. His friends were disappointed, and his enemies disarmed; Prejudice confessed she had done him injustice, and Charity wept that she had ever deemed him hard of heart. Perhaps the anxiety as well as depth of the emotions excited by his unique will in the public mind were never before equaled."

It is melancholy to reflect that the only gratitude excited by the life-efforts of an individual should be confined to that brief period allotted to the formation of his will; that the only admirable act of his life was the one which was consummated by death. Yet this was the case with Girard. It is charitable to believe that the extreme parsimony of his life was a part of a large plan of philanthropy which it was his ambition to perfect, and which, requiring millions, demanded economy. Whether a man discharge the obligations of wealth by thus penuriously grinding the last penny out of those around him, thus shutting out the sympathies, the fellowship, and good opinion of the world, may well admit of doubt. The test of a man's life is the example he presents for the imitation of others. Judged by this standard, Girard certainly falls short. There is nothing whatever in his life worthy of hearty commendation save his disinterested conduct during the yellow fever crisis. He was mean, tyrannous, ignorant, and utterly destitute of religious sentiment. Even the credit of having devoted his enormous wealth to worthy objects is mitigated by the fact that, after all, a man must do something with the money he has accumulated; he can not carry it with him to the grave.

The following is a list of the public bequests under the testamentary documents of Stephen Girard. His desire to be remembered "forever" is very observable:

1. To the "Contributors of the Pennsylvania Hospital" the sum of $30,000, to remain part of their capital "forever."

2. To the "Pennsylvania Institution for the Deaf and Dumb" the sum of $20,000.

3. To "the Orphan Asylum of Philadelphia" the sum of $10,000.

4. To the "Controllers of the Public Schools for the City and County of Philadelphia" the sum of $10,000, for the use of the schools "upon the Lancaster system."

5. To the "Mayor, Aldermen, and Citizens of Philadelphia" the sum of $10,000, in trust, to safely invest the same in some productive fund, and with the interest and dividends arising therefrom, to purchase fuel between the months of March and August in every year "forever," and in the month of January in every year "forever," distribute the same among poor white housekeepers and room-keepers of good character residing in the city of Philadelphia.

6. To the "Society for the Relief of Poor and Distressed Masters of Ships, their Widows and Children," the sum of $10,000.

7. To the trustees of the "Masonic Loan" the sum of $20,000, to remain "forever" a permanent fund or capital.

8. To "Trustees of Passyunk Township" the sum of $6000, to erect a schoolhouse.

9. To the "Corporation of the City of New Orleans" real estate, consisting of a thousand acres of land, appurtenances, and thirty slaves, in trust, after twenty years' inheritance by Judge Bree, to be applied to such uses and purposes as they shall con-

sider most likely to promote the health and general prosperity of the inhabitants of the city of New Orleans.

10. To the "Mayor, Aldermen, and Citizens of Philadelphia," their successors and assigns, in trust, all the residue and remainder of his real and personal estate, to and for the several uses, intents, and purposes hereinafter mentioned and declared of and concerning the same. So far as regarded his real estate in Pennsylvania, in trust, that no part should be sold, but should "forever" be let, from time to time, to good tenants at yearly or other rents, the profits arising therefrom to be applied toward keeping that part of said real estate constantly in good repair, and toward improving the same whenever necessary by erecting new buildings, and that the nett residue be applied to the same uses and purposes as are herein declared of and concerning the residue of his personal estate. And so far as regards his real estate in Kentucky, to sell and dispose of the same, whenever it may be expedient to do so, and to apply the proceeds of such sale to the same uses and purposes as are herein declared of and concerning the residue of his personal estate. And so far as regards the residue of his personal estate, in trust, as to two millions of dollars part thereof, to apply and expend so much of that sum as may be necessary in erecting on his square of ground, between High and Chesnut Streets, and Eleventh and Twelfth Streets, Philadelphia (which square of ground he devotes to the purpose forever), a permanent college, with suitable out-buildings, sufficiently spacious for the residence and accommodation of at least three hundred scholars, and the requisite teachers and other persons necessary in such an institution, and in supplying the said college and out-buildings with decent and suitable furniture, as well as books and all things needful to carry into effect his general design. Concerning the construction of the building he gives explicit directions, which it is only necessary to say have been carried out. He directs that a room in this building most suitable for the purpose shall be set apart for the reception and preservation of his books and papers, and carefully preserved therein. His plate and furniture of every sort he directs his executors to place in one of the out-buildings of the college. When the college and appurtenances shall have been constructed, and supplied with plain and suitable furniture and books, philosophical and experimental instruments and apparatus, and all other matters needful to carry his general design into execution, the income,

issues, and profits of so much of the said sum of two millions of dollars as shall remain unexpended shall be applied to maintain the said college according to his directions, which are as follows:

1. The institution shall be organized as soon as practicable, and to accomplish that purpose more effectually, due public notice of the intended opening of the college shall be given, so that there may be an opportunity to make selections of competent instructors and other agents, and those who may have the charge of orphans may be aware of the provisions intended for them.

2. A competent number of instructors, teachers, assistants, and other necessary agents shall be selected, and, when needful, their places from time to time supplied. They shall receive adequate compensation for their services; but no person shall be employed who shall not be of tried skill in his or her proper department, of established moral character, *and in all cases persons shall be chosen on account of their merit, and not through favor or intrigue.*

3. As many poor white male orphans, between the ages of six and ten years, as the said income shall be adequate to maintain, shall be introduced into the college as soon as possible; and from time to time, as there may be vacancies, or as increased ability from income may warrant, others shall be introduced.

4. On the application for admission, an accurate statement should be taken, in a book prepared for the purpose, of the name, birth-place, age, health, condition as to relatives, and other particulars useful to be known of each orphan.

5. No orphan should be admitted until the guardians or directors of the poor, or a proper guardian, or other competent authority, shall have given, by indenture, relinquishment, or otherwise, adequate power to the mayor, aldermen, and citizens of Philadelphia, or to directors or others by them appointed, to enforce, in relation to each orphan, every proper restraint, and to prevent relatives or others from interfering with or withdrawing such orphans from the institution.

6. Those orphans for whose admission application shall first be made shall be first introduced, all other things concurring; and at all future times, priority of application shall entitle the applicant to preference in admission, all other things concurring; but if there shall be at any time more applicants than vacancies, and the applying orphans shall have been born in different places, a preference shall be given, *first*, to orphans born in the city of

Philadelphia; *secondly*, to those born in any other part of Pennsylvania; *thirdly*, to those born in the city of New York (that being the first port on the continent of North America at which Girard first arrived); and, *lastly*, to those born in the city of New Orleans (being the first port of the said continent at which he first traded, in the first instance as first officer, and subsequently as master and owner of a vessel and cargo).

7. The orphans admitted into the college shall be there fed with plain but wholesome food, clothed with plain but decent apparel (no distinctive dress ever to be worn), and lodged in a plain but safe manner. Due regard shall be paid to their health, and to this end their persons and clothes shall be kept clean, and they shall have suitable and rational exercise and recreation. They shall be instructed in the various branches of a sound education, comprehending reading, writing, grammar, arithmetic, geography, navigation, surveying, practical mathematics, astronomy, natural, chemical, and experimental philosophy, the French and Spanish languages (he does not forbid, nor does he recommend, the Greek and Latin languages), and such other learning and science as the capacities of the several scholars may merit or warrant: he would rather have them taught facts and things than words or signs. And especially he desires that, by every proper means, a pure attachment to our republican institutions, and to the sacred rights of conscience as guaranteed by our happy Constitutions, shall be formed and fostered in the minds of the scholars.

8. Should it unfortunately happen that any of the orphans admitted into the college shall, from malconduct, have become unfit companions for the rest, and mild means of reformation prove abortive, they should no longer remain therein.

9. Those scholars who shall merit it shall remain in the college until they shall respectively arrive at between fourteen and eighteen years of age; they shall then be bound out by the mayor, aldermen, and citizens of Philadelphia, or under their direction, to suitable occupations, as those of agriculture, navigation, arts, mechanical trades, and manufactures, according to the capacities and acquirements of the scholars respectively, consulting, as far as prudence shall justify it, the inclinations of the several scholars as to the occupation, art, or trade to be learned.

In relation to the organization of the college and its appendages, he leaves, necessarily, many details to the mayor, aldermen, and citizens of Philadelphia, and their successors; and he does so with the more confidence, as, from the nature of his bequests and the benefits to result from them, he trusts that his fellow-citizens of Philadelphia *will observe and evince special care and anxiety in selecting members for their city councils, and other agents.*

There were, however, some restrictions, which he considered it his duty to prescribe, and to be, among others, conditions on which his bequest for said college is made and enjoyed: *first,* he enjoins and requires that if, at the close of any year, the income of the fund devoted to the purposes of the said college shall be more than sufficient for the maintenance of the institution during that year, then the balance of the said income, after defraying such maintenance, shall be forthwith invested in good securities, thereafter to be and remain a part of the capital; but in no event shall any part of the capital be sold, disposed of, or pledged to meet the current expenses of the said institution, to which he devotes the interest, income, and dividends thereof exclusively; *secondly,* he enjoins and requires that no *ecclesiastic, missionary, or minister of any sect whatsoever, shall ever hold or exercise any station or duty whatever in the said college; nor shall any such person ever be admitted for any purpose, or as a visitor, within the premises appropriated to the purposes of the said college.* In making this restriction, he says, he does not mean to cast any reflection upon any sect or person whatsoever; but as there is such a multitude of sects, and such a diversity of opinion among them, he desires to keep the minds of the orphans who are to derive advantage from this bequest free from the excitement which clashing doctrines and sectarian controversy are so apt to produce. His desire is, that all the instructors and teachers in the college shall take pains to instill into the minds of the scholars the *purest principles of morality,* so that, on their entrance into active life, they may from *inclination and habit* evince *benevolence toward their fellow-creatures,* and a *love of truth, sobriety, and industry,* adopting, at the same time, such religious tenets as their *matured reason* may enable them to prefer.

If the income arising from that part of the said sum of two millions of dollars remaining after the construction and furnishing of the college and out-buildings shall, owing to the increase of the number of orphans applying for admission, or other cause, be inadequate to the construction of new buildings, or the maintenance and education of as many orphans as may apply for admission, then such farther sum as may be necessary for the construction of new buildings and the maintenance and education of such farther number of orphans as can be maintained and instructed within such buildings as the said square of ground shall be adequate to, shall be taken from the final residuary fund hereinafter expressly referred to for the purpose, comprehending the income of his real estate in the city and county of Philadelphia, and the dividends of his stock in the Schuylkill Navigation Company; his design and desire being that the benefits of said institution should be extended to as great a number of orphans as the limits of the said square and buildings therein can accommodate.

For the improvement of various parts of the city of Philadelphia Mr. Girard bequeaths the sum of five hundred thousand dollars in trusts for the purposes specified; also the sum of three hundred thousand dollars for the purpose of internal improvement by canal navigation. The residue of his property he bequeaths in trust to be invested in good securities, and the income thereof applied,

1st. To the farther improvement and maintenance of the aforesaid college.

2d. To enable the corporation of the city of Philadelphia to provide more effectually for the security of the persons and property of the said city, by a competent police, including a sufficient number of watchmen really suited to the purpose.

3d. To enable the said corporation to improve the city property and the general appearance of the city itself, and in effect to diminish the burden of taxation. To all of which objects he directs the income arising from the fund aforesaid to be devoted "forever."

The will from which the above abstract is taken was executed on the 16th of February, 1830. Four months later Mr. Girard published a codicil, declaring it to be his intention, and directing that the orphan establishment provided for in his will, instead of being built, as therein directed, upon his square of ground between High and Chestnut Streets and Eleventh and Twelfth Streets in the city of Philadelphia, should be built upon the estate then recently purchased from Mr. Parker, and consisting of the mansion-house, out-buildings, and forty-five acres and some perches of land, called Peel Hill, on the Ridge Road, in Penn Township. The square of ground originally intended for the site he constitutes and declares to be a part of the residue and remainder of his real and personal estate.

SIR WILLIAM PHIPS.

When the early history of America shall be shrouded in the dim traditions of the past, the life-story of Sir William Phips will seem like a legend built of men's fancies, and not based upon the realities of the day. There is nothing more romantic in our volume.

Phips was born on the 2d of February, 1651, at Woolwich, in Maine, a small settlement near the mouth of the River Kennebec. His father was a robust Englishman, a gunsmith by trade, and the parent of no fewer than twenty-six children, all by one mother. At an early age, William (who was one of the youngest) had to look out for himself. The death of his father placed him in the responsible position of head of the family. Until his eighteenth year he gained a scanty income by tending sheep, but his adventurous disposition was not content with the primeval simplicity of this occupation. He longed to become a sailor, and roam through the world. At first he was unable to change occupations with the facility he expected. He could not get a situation as a sailor, so he apprenticed himself to a ship-builder. It is probable that he learned this lucrative trade in a very thorough manner, for we find him afterward in Boston pursuing it with success, and devoting his leisure hours to reading and writing. In addition to these accomplishments, he found time to make love to a rich widow, and with such success that he married her, in spite of some disparity in age. Immediately after this he went into business as a ship-builder, and constructed a vessel on Sheepscot River. Having in due time launched the craft, he engaged to procure a lading of lumber, and return to Boston. He consoled his wife with the assurance that he would some day get the command of a king's ship, and become the owner "of a fair brick house in the Green Lane of North Boston." In those days, brick houses were as aristocratic as marble palaces in our time.

These magnificent visions were not to be immediately realized. Phips and his ship appear to have lived an industrious, plodding sort of life for at least ten years, and without any particularly golden results. He did little jobs at his ship-yard, and performed short coasting voyages, all the while dreaming of better times, and sighing that they were still so distant. One day, as he strolled through the crooked streets of Boston, he heard the sombre-looking merchants talking to each other about a shipwreck that had occurred near the Bahamas. It was a Spanish vessel, and was known to have money on board. Phips walked straight down to his vessel, shipped a few hands, and sailed for the Bahamas without farther delay. It was exactly the sort of enterprise for his ardent nature. He succeeded in finding the wreck, and in recovering a great deal of its cargo, but the value of it scarcely defrayed the expenses of the voyage. He was told, however, of another and more richly-laden vessel which had been wrecked near Port de la Plata more than half a century before, and which was known to contain treasure to an enormous amount. Phips immediately conceived the idea of fishing up this wealth; but, as he was too poor to undertake the operation without assistance, he proceeded to England, while the fame of his recent expedition was new in people's mouths, and succeeded in persuading the government to go into the matter. He arrived in London in 1684, and, before the expiration of the year, was appointed to the command of the Rose-Algier, a ship of eighteen guns and ninety-five men. The first part of the destiny he had marked out for himself was now fulfilled—he was the commander of a king's ship.

When you want to find a thing that has been lost, some knowledge of the locality where the loss occurred is certainly useful; but Phips started with very vague ideas on the subject, extending merely to a general indication of the coast on which the ship had foundered. He was light of heart, however, and full of hope. Perhaps he thought it was all right so long as he had ship and crew. The latter, however, began to grow dissatisfied, and, when they had fished in the depths of old ocean for some time without bringing up any thing but sea-weed, and gravel, and bits of rock, they mutinied outright, and demanded that the immediate object of the voyage should be relinquished. They rushed upon the quarter-deck and bullied the commander, but they could not intimidate him. He got the better of them every time they attempted it. On one occasion the ship had been brought to anchor at a small and uninhabited island for the purpose of undergoing some repairs. It was found necessary to lighten the vessel by removing some of her stores to the shore. The ship was then brought down by the side of a rock stretching out from the land, and a bridgeway constructed, so that an easy communication from the shore was established. The crew had a good deal of time to spare while the carpenters were at work, and, like all idle boys, they got into mischief. They plotted to overthrow Phips and the few men he had with him on board, seize the vessel, and start on a piratical cruise against Spanish vessels in the South Sea. Phips and his adherents, if they objected to this arrangement, were to be put to death. Only one man did they care about saving, and that was the principal ship-carpenter. They thought his services might be useful. To this worthy they imparted their design, informing him, moreover, that if he did not join in its execution, they would put him to instant death. The ship-carpenter was an honest fellow, and in his heart despised these mean traitors. It was necessary to be prudent, however, so he told them that he would give them an answer in half an hour, and, in the mean time, collect his tools. He returned to the ship, and, by pretending to be suddenly sick, found an opportunity of telling the captain what was brewing, in spite of the watchfulness of those around him. Phips was perfectly cool; bade him return with the others, and leave the rest to him. In a brief address, he told the few men who were on board what was about to take place, and, finding them loyal, immediately commenced adopting measures of precaution and defense. A few of the ship's guns had been removed with the stores to the land, and planted in such a manner as to defend them. He caused the charges to be drawn from these, and their position reversed, and then he removed all the ammunition to the frigate. The bridge communicating with the land was taken up, and the ship's guns loaded and trained so as to command all approaches to the encampment. When the mutineers made their appearance, they were hailed by Phips, and warned that if they approached the stores they would be fired upon. Knowing the man, they respected this intimation, and kept at a respectful distance, while Phips and the few faithful fellows he could spare for the purpose removed the stores from the island to the ship under cover of the guns. The prospect of being left on the island with nothing to eat and drink soon brought the mutineers to terms, and they threw down their arms, and begged for permission to return to their duty. This request was granted when suitable precautions had been taken to deprive them of any future ability to do mischief. When Phips touched port, he thought it best for his own safety and for the welfare of the expedition to get rid of his troublesome crew, and ship another less disposed to piracy.

Soon after this, Phips gained precise information of the spot where the Spanish treasure-ship had sunk. He proceeded to it, but, before his explorations were any way complete, he had to return to England for repairs. The English Admiralty pretended to be immensely pleased with his exertions, but would not again intrust him with the command of a national vessel. He had, therefore, to appeal to private individuals. In a short time he had secured the interest of the Duke of Albemarle, who, with a few other gentlemen, fitted out a vessel and gave him the command. A patent was obtained from the king giving to the company an exclusive right to all the wrecks that might be discovered for a number of years. A tender was also provided for navigating shallow water where the ship could not venture. Having manned and equipped his vessel, he started once more for Port de la Plata, and arrived in safety at the reef of rocks where the Spanish vessel was supposed to lie. A number of Indian divers were employed to go down to the bottom, and the ship's crew dredged in every direction, but with no success. Just as they were leaving the reef one day in despair, a sailor observed a curious sea-plant growing in what appeared to be a crevice of the rock. He told a diver to fetch it for him, and, when the red gentleman came up again, he said that there were a number of ships' guns in the same place. The news was received with incredulity, but in a very little time it was ascertained to be substantially correct. Presently a diver returned with a bar of solid silver in his arms worth two or three hundred pounds sterling, and every one knew that the wreck had been discovered. "Thanks be to God, we are all made!" was all that Phips could say. In the course of a few days treasure was recovered to the amount of a million and a half of dollars.

In 1687 Phips reached England, surrendered his treasure to his employers, paid the seamen their promised gratuity, and took for his own share a nice little fortune of eighty thousand dollars. In consideration of his integrity, King James made the New England sea-captain a knight, and thenceforward he was known as Sir William Phips. He was desired, also, to remain in England, but his heart was on the other side of the Atlantic; so he shipped his fortune, and packed up a golden cup, worth five thousand dollars, which the Duke of Albemarle sent to his wife, and once more returned to his native land. Prior to his departure, he interested himself with the king to obtain a restitution of rights to his fellow-countrymen, but without success. He succeeded, however, in gaining a commission as high sheriff of New England, and returned with the patriotic object of exercising any power he might possess to the advantage of his fellow-countrymen.

The first thing he did on his return was to gratify his wife's ambition, and fulfill the other condition of his youthful prediction, namely, to build "a fair brick house in Green Lane." After this he tried to exercise his powers as sheriff, but the governor of the colony opposed him, and, in spite of all his efforts, he was unable to enter upon a discharge of the duties intrusted to him by King James. Naturally indignant at this slight of a royal patent, he determined on undertaking another voyage to England, and in 1687 arrived in that country. He found things much changed. His old patron, King James, had been driven from the throne by an indignant people, and William and Mary reigned in his place. From politic motives, the latter were friendly to Phips, sympathized with him, and offered him the governorship of New England; but this he declined. Seeing that there was no other immediate prospect for him, and unwilling to sacrifice his time in unavailing attendance at court, he returned to America in the summer of 1689. An Indian war, fomented by the French, was waging, and, although unfamiliar with military life, Phips volunteered his services. He was not immediately employed, but his patriotism was understood and appreciated. It became necessary to deal the French a severe blow, in order to put a stop to the encouragement they were constantly giving the Indians. For this purpose, the General Court, in January, 1690, issued the following order: "For the encouragement of such gentlemen and merchants of this colony as shall undertake to reduce Penobscot, St. John's, and Port Royal, it is ordered that they shall have two sloops of war for three or four months at free cost, and all the profits which they can make from our French enemies, and the trade of the places which they may take, till there be other orders given from their majesties." This offer was too tempting for Sir William; once more he offered himself, and was invested with the command of all the forces raised for the expedition, and of the shipping and seamen employed therein. Sir William's instructions were too curious to be omitted in this place. He was ordered "to take care that the worship of God be maintained and duly observed on board all the vessels; to offer the enemy fair terms upon summons, which if they obey, the said terms are to be duly observed; if not, you are to gain the best advantage you may, to assault, kill, and utterly extirpate the common enemy, and to burn and demolish their fortifications and shipping; having reduced that place, to proceed along the coast, for the reducing of the other places and plantations in the possession of the French to the obedience of the crown of England." One would scarcely suppose that the worship of God was compatible with the killing and utterly extirpating His creatures.

Phips reached Port Royal on the 11th of May, and achieved an easy victory over the surprised and unprepared garrison. He took possession in the name of the English government, demolished the fort, and administered the oath of allegiance to those who were prepared to take it. He then appointed a governor, left a small garrison, and set sail on his return, heavily laden with public and private spoils. On his way home he landed at the various settlements, and took formal possession of the sea-coast from Port Royal to Penobscot. The entire province of Acadia was thus subdued, and remained in possession of the English until its restitution in 1697. On his return Sir William was elected to the Board of Assistants.

The extremely successful issue of this first undertaking against the French encouraged the colonists to pitch into their neighbors on a still larger scale; and, accordingly, an expedition against Quebec was fitted out, the command of which was intrusted to Sir William Phips. The fleet sailed on the 9th of August, 1690. It was divided into three squadrons, one of thirteen vessels, and two of nine each. They proceeded to the mouth of the St. Lawrence, and arrived there in safety, but, owing to ignorance of the stream, their progress was very slow, and calculated to afford the enemy every opportunity for preparing elaborate defenses. At length Phips arrived before Quebec, and a messenger was sent on shore with a summons to the governor to surrender. The messenger barely returned with his life. The governor, Frontenac, indignant at the request, flung the letter in his face, and shouted out fiercely that "Sir William Phips and those with him were heretics and traitors, and had taken up with that usurper, the Prince of Orange, and had made a revolution, which, if it had not been made, New England and the French had all been one; and that no other answer was to be expected from him but what should be from the mouth of his cannon."

To attack a fortified city requires something more than mere physical bravery; it demands a high amount of military knowledge, and a thorough perception of accidental advantage. Phips was entirely ignorant of military tactics, and therefore gave the command of the land forces to an officer who boasted of greater knowledge, himself retaining command of the fleet. After innumerable delays a landing was effected, but the troops were badly supplied with ammunition and provisions, and were hemmed in and starved from the moment they first set foot on the soil. The French, assisted by their Indian allies, harassed them on every side, and decimated their numbers by drawing them into skirmishes which led to no result. Phips carried his ships up to the town, and blazed away at the stone walls; but the stone walls refused to tumble down, and all his powder was expended in vain. The enemy, on the contrary, poured in torrents of effective shot. For five days a state of confusion prevailed, every day making matters worse. The men were exhausted and dispirited, for they saw that both their commanders were incapable. The cold weather began to freeze their limbs, and wound them more cruelly than the sword. Provisions and ammunitions were growing scarcer and scarcer, and every thing save the enemy seemed to wear a look of despair. At length a violent storm arose; many of the vessels were driven from their anchorage, and the remainder availed themselves of the opportunity of getting out of the river as speedily as possible. Thus ended the expedition against Quebec. Misfortunes pursued the fleet even at sea. The weather was so stormy that the vessels could not be kept together. One ship was never heard of after the separation; another was wrecked; and another—a fire-ship—was burned at sea. Four other vessels were blown so far out of their course that they did not reach Boston for five or six weeks after the arrival of Phips.

The failure of the expedition was a great blow to the colonial government. They had fitted it out on credit, depending on plunder for the payment of the soldiers and a nice little profit for themselves. To get out of the difficulty with the best grace possible, they issued paper notes on the faith of the colony. It was all they could do, for there was no money in the treasury. At first it was supposed this ingenious expedient would be successful; but every day the bills sank lower and lower in public credit, and the poor soldiers who had been paid with them could only get fourteen shillings for every pound on their face.

The defeat before Quebec rankled in Phips's mind, and, as there seemed to be no immediate prospect of employment in the colony, he determined on another voyage to England, with the view of inducing the king to fit out a fresh expedition against the French. In this he was disappointed, but his voyage was not without a result. Increase Mather was at that time eagerly agitating the matter of a new charter for the colony, the old one having been taken away in consequence of royal displeasure, and the colony being thus without any legal guaranty of its rights. After much vexatious delay, the king consented to the issuing of another charter on condition that the delegates should name a governor known to the crown, and yet popular with the people of Massachusetts. If he had wished to nominate Phips, he could not have more accurately described the man. Notwithstanding his Canadian failure, he was still eminently popular at home, and his curious history was well known abroad. Increase Mather, on behalf of the other agents, consequently nominated Phips, and a commission was accordingly prepared under the great seal, by which Sir William Phips was appointed captain general and governor-in-chief of the province of Massachusetts Bay in New England. With this document in his pocket, he returned to his native country in May, 1692. On the following Monday he was conducted from his own house to the town-house by a large escort of military and a number of the principal gentlemen of Boston and the vicinity.

Sir William Phips was a very unhappy governor. With every disposition in the world to be lenient, kind, and just, he found that he could not avoid making enemies. The new charter was not considered satisfactory, and Sir William Phips, the principal officer under it, had to bear all the odium it excited. His authority was disputed in the most vexatious way, and an opposition sprung up which daily gained strength. There were other men, too, who wanted to be governor, and their hostility, having a direct object, was of the most active kind. Sir William became cross with the world, and broke out into wild fits of passion, all of which increased his unpopularity. At length the discontents went so far as to petition the crown that he might be removed, and another governor appointed in his stead. Beside this, two gentlemen, whom Phips had thrashed for disputing his authority, preferred their complaints to the king, and the Lords of the Treasury, together with the Board of Trade, united in the request that the governor might be displaced. The king refused to condemn the governor unheard, but invited him to visit England and defend himself. Sir William accordingly left Boston on the 17th of November, 1694, and proceeded to London. It was the last time he ever crossed the Atlantic.

On his arrival he was subjected to fresh annoyances, such as being arrested by the assaulted gentlemen before mentioned, and held to heavy bail; but, in spite of these, we are assured by Cotton Mather that he was triumphant in his vindication, and received assurances of being restored to office. While these things were going on, he amused himself with two new schemes: one for supplying the English navy with timber and naval stores from the eastern parts of New England, the other for going into the shipwreck-fishing business again. The prosecution of these designs was, however, brought to an unexpected termination. About the middle of February, 1695, he took cold, and was immediately confined to his chamber. Fever ensued, and on the 18th of the month he died. Few men in the world have had more experience than Sir William Phips; yet he was but forty-five years of age. In that brief period he had raised himself from the condition of a plowboy to the highest office recognized in his country, from poverty to wealth, from insignificance to esteem. In the words of his best biographer,* "Fortune befriended him only when he had earned her favors by ceaseless industry and the most indomitable perseverance. He succeeded in enterprises so hopeless at first sight that men of sober judgment would never have engaged in them, and after failures and discouragements which would have caused persons of ordinary prudence to give up the attempt in despair. He enjoyed a large fortune, acquired solely by his own exertions; but he was neither purse-proud, parsimonious, nor extravagant. Far from concealing the lowness of his origin, he

* Francis Bowen.

made it a matter of honest pride that he had risen from the business of a ship-carpenter to the honors of knighthood and the government of a province. Soon after he was appointed to the chief magistracy, he gave a handsome entertainment to all the ship-carpenters of Boston; and, when perplexed with the public business, he would often declare that it would be easier for him to go back to his broad-axe again. He was naturally of a hasty temper, and was frequently betrayed into improper sallies of passion, but never harbored resentment long. Though not rigidly pious, he reverenced the offices of religion, and respected its ministers. He was credulous, but no more so than most of his better-educated contemporaries. The mistakes which he committed as a public officer were palliated by perfect uprightness of intention, and by an irreproachable character in private life; for even his warmest opponents never denied him the title of a kind husband, a sincere patriot, and an honest man."

DANIEL BOONE.

Daniel Boone, the mighty hunter of the West, and pioneer of Kentucky, was born in Bucks County, Pennsylvania, in the month of February, 1735. His parents were of English birth, and Daniel was the sixth of a family of eleven children. Of education he received but little, at least of the kind then taught in the hedge schools of the frontier settlements. Perhaps book-knowledge was of less value to him than that other knowledge which he seems to have picked up from his earliest youth, namely, the knowledge of directing the rifle with unerring precision, of observing the habits of wild beasts, and of noting the least indication of the approach or presence of an Indian. At a time when the only guaranty of a man's life was his ability to keep it, these points of a practical education were all important.

When Daniel was in his eighteenth year he removed with his parents to North Carolina, and settled on the waters of the Yadkin, where he had ample opportunities for indulging his favorite pastime, and found plenty of game to reward his expertness. Here, also, he married. There is a pretty little story which says that Boone was out hunting one day, and saw in a thicket before him what he supposed to be the large beautiful eyes of a deer. In an instant the rifle was at his shoulder, and in another the trigger would have been drawn but for a terrified little scream, which admonished the hunter that he was wrong in his game this time. Presently a charming girl, with large, flashing hazel eyes, started from the bush. Boone spoke to her, and found that her name was Rebecca Bryan. This was the lady whom he subsequently married; but the story (which is very delightful) is only a story, and has, we are sorry to say, no foundation in exact truth.

When a man gets married he wants to stay at home, and make himself comfortable in the society of his wife, if not for good, certainly for a time; so Boone adopted the calling of a farmer for several years, and only used his gun around the farm. Occasionally, however, he made an excursion with a party of hunters into the wilderness, where the abundance of game made it profitable to do so. These excursions afforded him the keenest enjoyment. Apart from the pleasure which every man must feel in the exercise of unusual skill, and which is especially keen in a sportsman, Boone possessed a genuine love of nature, and delighted in viewing her in her primeval splendor. Such natures require space; they can not breathe in crowded settlements; the approach of a mixed population with its class distinctions is horrible to them.

In 1767, John Finley, a famous backwoods hunter, made an excursion along the waters of the Kentucky River, and returned with glowing accounts of what he had seen. These were sufficient for Boone, who already began to feel that he was crowded in North Carolina. He determined to explore the new country, and settle there if it equaled the vivid picture he had drawn in his mind. A party of six was formed, but much time elapsed before the hunters were ready to start, and it was not until June, 1769, that they reached the waters of the Red River, and encamped somewhere within the boundaries of the present Morgan County. In this vicinity the party hunted with much success until December, and without encountering any Indians. Feeling more at ease from this circumstance, it was now proposed to divide the members of the party, so that they might cover a greater expanse of ground. Boone and a companion started in the direction of the main Kentucky River, and had nearly reached its banks, when they were suddenly set upon by a band of Indians, who rushed out of a cane-brake and made them prisoners. This was the penalty of the over-security they had permitted themselves to feel.

The Indians robbed them of all they possessed, and detained them for seven days, but treated them with hospitality, evidently intending to receive them into their tribe; but Boone and his companion were not eager for this distinction, and they availed themselves of the first opportunity to make their escape. One night, when the Indians were quietly slumbering round their fires, Boone signaled to Stewart, his companion, that the moment had arrived. They crept stealthily into the darkness of the forest, and never paused or rested until they had reached their old hunting-camp. Here they expected to find their companions, but, to their amazement and distress, they were nowhere to be seen, and the spot furnished abundant indications of having been visited by the Indians and plundered. Of the fate of this party nothing is known. It was never heard of more.

Now that they knew they were in the country of enemies, they had to proceed with the greatest caution. One day, while they were looking around for game, they discerned the figures of two men coming toward them. Both parties were immediately on their guard. Boone shouted, "Hilloa, strangers, who are you?" "White men and friends," was the reply. The next moment, to his extreme surprise and joy, he recognized the well-known features of his brother and another adventurer from North Carolina. They were on an exploring expedition, and had been following Boone with news from his family and a supply of powder and lead. The accession to the strength of the little party was particularly acceptable at the present moment, but, unhappily, it did not afford them any additional protection. Boone and Stewart, on a second excursion from the camp, were again set upon by a party of Indians. Boone succeeded in effecting his escape, but Stewart was shot in the attempt, and scalped. Shortly afterward, the hunter whom Boone's brother had brought with him from North Carolina was missing. Nothing was heard of his fate for some time. At length a decayed skeleton and some fragments of clothing were discovered near a swamp. They were supposed to be his remains, but the cause of his death has ever remained a mystery. The two brothers were now alone in the forest, and lived and hunted in safety through the winter. They found abundance of game, and consequently plenty of occupation for their guns and their knives. When the warm breezes of spring unlocked the earth, Daniel determined on sending his brother, Squire Boone, to North Carolina for supplies, while he remained to protect the peltry and increase the stock. The journey was over five hundred miles, and it was not until the end of July that Squire returned, bringing with him good news from home, a couple of horses, and an ample supply of all necessaries. In the mean time, Daniel had made an exploring tour to the southwest, and he ascertained on his return that the Indians had paid him a visit. The brothers were convinced that if they remained they would assuredly fall into the hands of some straggling party of hunters, and perhaps perish beneath their brutal scalping-knives. To avert such an unpleasant fate, they made up their minds to vacate their present quarters, and seek a more secure spot on the Cumberland River. They placed all their possessions upon the backs of horses, and took their departure; but, after traversing most of the Cumberland region (which they found hilly and indifferently stocked with game), they returned in a northeastern direction to the Kentucky River, and selected a site where they determined to establish a settlement. From the first it had been Daniel's intention to bring on his wife and family so soon as he felt justified in doing so. The moment had now arrived. After an absence of two years, he turned homeward, heavily laden with peltry, and accompanied by his brother. During that time he had neither tasted bread nor salt, and had seen no human faces except those of his brother and companions, and of the Indians who made him prisoner. He arrived in safety at Yadkin, and made preparations for speedy return to the forest; but, in spite of all his exertions, two years elapsed before he was in a position to make a start. "On the 25th of September, 1773," says Mr. Peck, in his biography of Daniel Boone, "the two brothers bade adieu to their friends and neighbors on the Yadkin, and entered on the perilous task of traversing the wilderness to the banks of the Kentucky. A drove of pack-horses carried their bedding, clothing, provisions, and other necessaries; a number of milch cows, with some young cattle and swine, were intended to constitute the herd of the western wilderness. At Powell's Valley, through which their route lay, they were joined by forty families and forty men, all well armed. This accession of strength gave them courage, and the party advanced full of hope and confident of success. At night they encamped, as is still the custom of emigrating parties throughout the vast West. The camping-place is near some spring or water-course; temporary shelters are made by placing poles in a sloping position, with one end resting on the ground, the other elevated on forks. On these, tent-cloth, prepared for the purpose, or, as in the case of these pioneers, articles of bed-covering, are stretched. The fire is kindled in front against a fallen tree or log, toward which the feet are placed while sleeping. If the ground is wet, twigs or small branches, with leaves and dry grass, are laid under the beds. Each family reposes under a separate cover, and the clothing worn by day is seldom removed at night."

In this way the train proceeded without an incident until the 6th of October. The pioneers were then approaching the romantic mountain opening called the Cumberland Gap. Seven young men who had charge of the cattle were lagging behind some six or seven miles, when suddenly they were attacked by the Indians; six of the number were instantly killed, and the seventh, who was wounded, barely succeeded in making good his escape. In the noise and confusion of the struggle the cattle dispersed in the forest. Such a calamity at such a moment was irreparable. It struck dismay into the hearts of the pioneers, and, in spite of Boone's entreaties, they refused to go on for the present. The expedition was consequently abandoned, and the party retired to the settlements of Clinch River, Virginia, to recruit. The following summer, Boone received a message from Governor Dunmore, requesting him to proceed to the wilderness of Kentucky in search of some surveyors who were believed to be either lost or in danger of being so. In company with another hunter, he undertook this task, and accomplished it successfully. He was absent sixty-two days, and traveled eight hundred miles on foot.

In the spring of the year 1775, Boone was employed by a company of land speculators (who imagined they had secured a valid title to the land in Kentucky by virtue of a deed of purchase from the Cherokees) to survey and lay out roads in Kentucky. He was placed at the head of a body of well-armed men, and proceeded to his work with great willingness. The party had arrived within fifteen miles of Boonesborough, when they were fired on by Indians, and suffered a loss of two killed and two wounded. Three days later they were again attacked, and had two killed and three wounded. Boone was not the sort of man to be deterred by a calamity even of this severe kind. He pressed forward, and on a favorable site erected a fort (called Boonesborough), sufficiently strong and large to afford protection against any further attack. He was so well satisfied with its security, that, shortly afterward, he returned to Clinch River for his wife and family. They arrived safely, his "wife and daughters being the first white women that ever stood on the banks of the Kentucky River." A number of families followed their example, and the little place soon became cheerful and populated. The Indians did not venture to attack the settlers so long as they remained within sight of the fort, but it was very well known that they hovered about the outskirts, ready for a descent on any unhappy wight who might expose himself unguardedly to their vengeance. The men were suspicious and careful, and never went out without their rifles. In spite of these precautions, a most thrilling and tragic incident occurred. On the 14th of July, 1776, three young girls belonging to the fort (one of them was Boone's daughter) heedlessly crossed the river in a canoe late in the afternoon. When they got to the other side they commenced playing and splashing with the paddles, as gay young girls, unconscious of danger, might naturally do, until the canoe, floating with the current, drifted close to the shore, which at this part was thickly covered with trees and shrubs. Concealed in this natural ambuscade lay three savage Indians. They had been watching every motion of the girls, and were prepared now to seize their opportunity. One of the coppery rascals dropped stealthily into the stream, caught hold of the rope that hung from the bow of the canoe, and drew it out of view of the fort. The girls, aroused to a sense of their danger, screamed as loud as they could, and were heard at the fort; but, before assistance could come, their captors hurried them on shore and bore them to the interior. "Next morning by daylight," says Colonel Floyd, who was one of the actors in what he describes, "we were on the track, but found they had totally prevented our following them by walking some distance apart through the thickest canes they could find. We observed their course, and on which side they had left their sign, and traveled upward of thirty miles. We then imagined that they would be less cautious in traveling, and made a turn in order to cross their trace, and had gone but a few miles before we found their tracks in a buffalo path; pursued and overtook them on going about ten miles, just as they were kindling a fire to cook. Our study had been more to get the prisoners, without giving the Indians time to murder them, after they discovered us, than to kill them.

"We discovered each other nearly at the same time. Four of us fired, and all rushed on them, which prevented them from carrying away any thing except one shot-gun without ammunition. Mr. Boone and myself had a pretty fair shoot just as they began to move off. I am well convinced I shot one through, and the one he shot dropped his gun; mine had none. The place was very thick with canes, and being so much elated on recovering the three little broken-hearted girls prevented our making farther search. We sent them off without their moccasins, and not one of them with so much as a knife or a tomahawk." The simplicity of this narrative exceeds its clearness, but, with all its involutions, is it not graphic, and does it not convey an excellent idea of the rough indifference to danger so characteristic of true pioneer life?

After this it was necessary to be doubly watchful, for the Indians became more aggressive, and apprehensions were felt that a general attack would be made on the fort and stations. These fears appeared to be so well founded, that it was only the oldest and bravest of the pioneers who could withstand their influence. The land speculators and other adventurers, to the number of nearly three hundred, left the country, and new-comers, although prepared for danger, were with difficulty prevailed upon to remain. The year 1777 passed in this gloomy way, marked only by frequent attacks on the various stations by the Indians. Two attempts were made on the fort, but each time the besiegers were beaten off. The brave little garrison lost two men killed and five wounded. With all means of transit cut off by their wary foes, great privations were necessarily suffered by the little band. The immediate necessaries of life they could of course procure, but some articles which were essential to the preservation of health they were without. This was especially the case with regard to salt. Boone, while in the wilderness, could do without this article of luxury, but the families in the fort sorely felt its need, and all kinds of efforts were made to obtain a supply. At length it was determined to fit out an expedition, consisting of thirty men, with Boone at its head, to effect this desirable object. It was necessary to proceed to the Lower Blue Licks, on Licking River, and there manufacture the article, which, in due course, was to be forwarded by pack-horses to the fort. The enterprise, which seemed at first to promise success, cost Boone and his companions their liberty. One day, while hunting a short distance from his comrades, he was surprised by a party of Indians, one hundred and two in number. He attempted to escape, but their swiftest runners were put on his trail, and he soon abandoned all idea of doing so. The sagacity and presence of mind of the old hunter had now to be exercised. He parleyed with the Indians, professed all sorts of friendship for them, succeeded in gaining their confidence, and finally made honorable terms for the surrender of his men, who became prisoners of war. Boone has been blamed for not offering resistance, but a moment's reflection will demonstrate that the course he pursued was the wisest and safest. Had he offered resistance, his little band would have been overpowered, and the next point of attack would have been the fort, which, from the absence of the garrison, would have been entirely at the mercy of the savages. To avert a certain massacre, he surrendered his men, after having made excellent conditions for the safety of their lives. "The generous usage the Indians had promised before, in my capitulation," says Boone, "was afterward fully complied with, and we proceeded with them as prisoners to Old Chilicothe, the principal Indian town on Little Miami, where we arrived, after an uncomfortable journey in very severe weather, on the 18th of February, and received as good treatment as prisoners could expect from savages. On the 10th day of March following, I and ten of my men were conducted by forty Indians to Detroit, where we arrived on the 30th day, and were treated by Governor Hamilton, the British commander at that post, with great humanity." The governor endeavored to obtain Boone's liberation by purchase, but his captors were not willing to part with him. He had so ingratiated himself in their good graces that they were determined to have him for a chief, and insisted on carrying him back to their town for the purpose of adoption. He bade farewell to his friends in Detroit, and, under the friendly escort of his pertinacious admirers, returned to Chilicothe, where he was adopted by an illustrious individual of the name of Blackfish, to supply the place of a deceased son and warrior. He was treated with great kindness, and in a short time became universally popular. He was careful to avoid all cause for suspicion, and to appear constantly happy, although, of course, he was forever dreaming of his wife and family, and praying for the happy day that should enable him to escape to them. Early in the following June he was taken to the Salt Springs, on the Scioto, to assist in making salt. On his return, he was alarmed to see a fearful array of four hundred and fifty warriors, and still more so when he discovered that they were bound on an expedition against Boonesborough. He determined to effect his escape, and, on the following morning, the 16th of June, 1778, he arose and went forth as usual without exciting suspicion. He never returned, and Blackfish had to adopt another son. Boone succeeded in reaching the fort in safety. His sudden appearance greatly astonished the people there, for they had given him up, and his wife, with some of the children, had actually departed for North Carolina. Not a moment was to be lost in making the necessary preparations for the defense of the settlement. The fort, which had fallen into a very rickety condition, was put in thorough repair, and the garrison mustered and drilled so as to be in perfect readiness. The Indians, however, changed their minds. Alarmed, probably, at the escape of Boone, they postponed their expedition for three weeks, but, in the mean time, they made some additions to their strength in the shape of French and Canadian officers. On the 7th of September, the Indian army, numbering four hundred and forty-four, with Captain Duquesne and eleven other Canadians, appeared before Boonesborough. The Indians were commanded by Boone's would-be father-in-law, Mr. Blackfish, and the Canadians by Captain Duquesne. When this alarming force had assembled before the unhappy little fort, a summons was issued to "surrender, in the name of his Britannic majesty." The garrison consisted of between sixty and seventy men, and a large number of women and children. If they *had* surrendered it would have been nothing remarkable, but they did not even think of doing such a thing. Boone expected re-enforcements from Holston, and it became necessary, therefore, to procure as much delay as possible. For this purpose, he desired that he might have two days to consider the proposition of his Britannic majesty. Strange as it may appear, this proposition was acceded to. About five minutes were sufficient for the garrison to arrive at a determination, and this was that they would fight it out to the last. All the cows and horses were collected within the fort, and every vessel filled with water from the spring, the latter task being performed by the ladies. When the hour arrived for giving an answer to bold Captain Duquesne, it was done in this wise by Boone: "We laugh at your formidable preparations, but thank you for giving notice and time to prepare for defense." Captain Duquesne was not incensed at this reply, but still insisted on a capitulation. "He declared his orders from Colonel Hamilton were to take the garrison captives, to treat them as prisoners of war, and not to injure, much less to murder them; and that they had horses to take the women and children, and all others who could not bear the fatigue of traveling on foot. He then proposed that, if the garrison would depute nine persons to come out of the fort and hold a treaty, the terms should be liberal. It is impossible at this time, after the demise of every person concerned in the affair, to account for the singular course of Captain Duquesne and his Indian allies."*

Although Duquesne's affectionate course savored of treachery, Boone thought it desirable to accede to his proposition, as it would at least secure a little more delay. Nine commissioners were selected for the purpose of discussing the treaty, Boone being one of the number. A plot of ground in front of the fort was selected for the conference, all parties to go unarmed. Before leaving for this hazardous interview, Boone took the precaution to place a number of experienced riflemen in advantageous positions, so that, if the commissioners retreated hastily, they might be protected. The parties met, and the treaty proposed was of the most liberal kind. It simply demanded that the residents and garrison of the fort should acknowledge the British authorities, and take the oath of allegiance to the king; in return for which they were to remain unmolested. After these points had been settled, the Indians proposed that, as a commemoration of the joyous occasion, they should revive an ancient custom of their tribe, which consisted in two Indians shaking hands with one white man at the same moment. Boone and his companions knew exactly what this meant, but they did not betray any uneasiness. Eighteen stalwart, muscular Indians now advanced, and, in the way prescribed by the very ancient custom before mentioned, endeavored to drag off the white men. But the iron frames of the pioneers were braced for a struggle. Being without weapons, they appealed to their Anglo-Saxon knowledge of fisticuffs, and in a very little while had tumbled the red villains in the dust. In the excitement which followed they made good their retreat to the fort, and the riflemen imme-

* Peck's Life of Daniel Boone.

diately opened a murderous fire to keep off the pursuers. Hostilities now commenced on both sides. The Indians kept up a brisk fire at the fort, but, owing to its favorable situation, could not effect much mischief. The garrison, on the contrary, never fired a charge without an especial object. A regular siege, conducted in the usual Indian style, was kept up for nine days, but with no result. The Kentuckians never flinched for a moment. Even the women assisted in the defense, for they loaded the rifles, moulded bullets, and supplied refreshments. On one occasion the fort was fired by the enemy, but a heroic young man extinguished the flames, in spite of a shower of bullets which greeted his appearance with the buckets on the roof. Foiled in this, the Indians, under the direction of the Canadians, commenced digging a mine; but Boone was equal to this emergency. He began a countermine, and threw all the dirt into their works, so that they had the pleasure of shoveling it away before they could make the slightest progress. On the 20th of September they raised the siege and took their departure, after having suffered a loss of thirty-seven killed and many more wounded. The loss on the pioneer side was two killed and four wounded: it would not have been so great but for the desertion of a vagabond negro who went over to the enemy, carrying with him an excellent rifle. During the siege, this rascal placed himself in a tree on the other side of the river, and was able, owing to the excellence of his weapon, to fire into the fort. He had killed one and wounded another, when Boone caught a glimpse of his woolly head. It was sufficient; the next moment Sambo rolled from the tree. After the retreat his body was found, and in the centre of his forehead an explanatory hole told the story of his death. The old hunter brought him down at a distance of one hundred and seventy-five yards.

During the autumn of this year Boone rejoined his wife and family in North Carolina. "The history of my going home and returning with my family forms a series of difficulties, an account of which would swell a volume." The principal difficulty to which he here refers was the loss of all his property by robbery. With the view to purchase land in Kentucky, he converted every thing he possessed into cash, amounting in all to about twenty thousand dollars paper money. With this he started for Richmond, where the Court of Commissioners was held (1779), and on the road was robbed of the whole. The event was additionally distressing to him from the fact that, in addition to his own money, he had various sums belonging to other people, who had intrusted it to him for the same purpose.

After this misfortune, Boone returned to Boonesborough in 1780. In October of this year, he and his brother had occasion to visit the Blue Licks, and on their return were fired upon by Indians. His brother fell a victim, and was scalped. Boone, with the greatest difficulty, escaped. Outrages of this kind were frequent, and it became daily more apparent that a strong blow had to be struck ere the security of the settlers could in the least degree be insured. The Legislature of Virginia took the matter in hand soon after; divided Kentucky into three counties, and effected a civil and military organization. John Todd was made colonel, and Daniel Boone lieutenant colonel of Lincoln County. Each county was expected to raise a regiment, and the whole force of the three counties was placed under the command of Brigadier General Clark.

It was not long before this force was brought into active service. The attack on Bryant's Station called all the settlers to arms. A large number of Indians had made an unsuccessful attack on that point, and it was now determined to follow up the advantage by pursuing the Indian army, and, if possible, destroying it. Colonel Boone, with his son Israel and his brother Samuel, headed a strong party from Boonesborough, and Colonel Todd commanded the militia from Lexington. A council of war was held, and Boone opposed the scheme of pursuit, but was overruled. Consequently, the forces started, and were soon on the trail; but no Indians were to be seen until they reached the Lower Blue Licks. A few were then discovered marching over a ridge on the opposite side. Before crossing the river, Colonel Todd ordered a halt, and another conference was held, at which Boone's views were especially solicited. They were now at the spot where, some years before, Boone and his companions had been surprised while making salt, and he was thoroughly familiar with every crevice and rock in the neighborhood. He gave it as his opinion that an ambuscade was prepared for them, and, if they crossed the ridge where they saw the Indians, they would inevitably fall into it and be destroyed. If they *were* determined to proceed, he gave them some sound advice about the division of the troops, so that the enemy might be attacked at two points simultaneously.

Boone's calmness (the result of a remarkable knowledge of the Indian character) appears to have been misconstrued into timidity. In the midst of his deliberations, an officer named Major M'Gary raised the war-whoop, and, addressing the troops, said, "Those who are not cowards, follow me; I will show you where the Indians are." In the excitement of the moment, two thirds of the men followed this dashing but indiscreet leader, and the remainder soon after crossed the river. Another halt was ordered, and scouts were sent out to examine the ravine. Not an Indian was to be seen. Boone still persisted that they were in ambush, but the order was given to march, and the troops went on to within forty yards of the ravine. Here they received the first intimation of the presence of an enemy. A withering volley of musketry poured down upon them from every side; Colonel Trigg and a number of the Harrodsburg troops fell like leaves before the autumn wind. Major Harlan then advanced with his company, and was swept away in like manner. Only three of the entire force remained to tell the story. Colonel Todd shared the unhappy fate of his comrades. The Indians now rushed upon the remaining military with their tomahawks, and a precipitate and disorderly retreat commenced. Those who reached the river endeavored to cross, but were still pursued by the Indians. The slaughter was terrible. The Kentuckians, escaping over a bleak rock, were most palpable marks, and in the river, as they strove to make the opposite shore, they were scarcely to be missed by an Indian eye. The nearest place to retreat to was Bryan's Station, thirty-six miles distant, and for this they made with all possible expedition. Although the Indians pursued them for twenty miles, they did but little execution after the ford had been crossed. The men were no longer exposed to their unerring aim. Boone had command of the left, and maintained his ground until the panic became general. All he could then effect was to preserve as many lives as possible by indicating the safest means of retreat. He knew every inch of ground, and, bearing his son (who was mortally wounded) across his breast, he made for a part of the river where he knew he could cross easily. He struck into the current, but before he could reach the opposite bank his son had expired. No pen can describe the emotions of the wretched parent as he lay panting on the shore with the dead and dripping body of his child before him, and a pack of fierce savages swimming toward him for his life. They were so quick that he had to leave the body to their mercies in order to effect his own escape. Exhausted with fatigue, and alone, he made his way through the wilderness to Bryan's Station. Here he discovered that Colonel Logan, with a re-enforcement of four hundred and fifty men, had arrived, and he became bitterly conscious of the unnecessary horrors that had attended the rash daring of his companions. Had they listened to his advice, and waited for this re-enforcement, they would now have had a victory to triumph over instead of a defeat to lament. At a late hour at night, Colonel Logan and his troops, accompanied by Boone, started once more for the battle-field. The enemy had fled, but a terrible scene presented itself. "Dead and mutilated bodies were strewn through the scattering timber, submerged in the river, and spread over the rocky ridge. Immense flocks of vultures were perched in the trees, hovering in the air, or moving over the field among the slain, gorged with the horrid repast. The savages had mangled and scalped many; the wolves had torn others; and the oppressive heat of August had so disfigured their remains that the persons of but few could be distinguished by their friends." They were interred with as much haste as possible, for Boone was still apprehensive that the Indians might not be quite off.

The intelligence of this defeat spread rapidly through the country, and produced the greatest consternation and alarm. Convinced of the necessity for an immediate blow, General George R. Clark made arrangements for a formidable expedition into the Indian country. In a short time a thousand mounted riflemen —all volunteers—were in the saddle, and eager to avenge the slaughter of their neighbors. There were hundreds of others who were too old, or otherwise unable to go, who sent all sorts of supplies, to testify how cordially they sympathized with the cause. Bryan's Station was selected as the place of rendezvous for the upper country, and the Falls of the Ohio for the lower. The troops marched with immense celerity and secrecy. As an evidence of the latter, it may be mentioned that, although they were passing through a country densely stocked with game, they suffered from hunger rather than pull a trigger to give the alarm. So rapid were they in their movements that they actually overtook a portion of the Indian army on its way home from the Kentucky scene of blood. A couple of Indians gave the alarm, however, and empty cabins and deserted villages were all the volunteers could find. "The savages fled in the utmost disorder," writes Boone, who was simply a volunteer on this occasion, and held no kind of commission, "evacuated their towns, and reluctantly left their territory to our mercy." Of the latter they received but little; Old Chilicothe and four other towns were razed to the ground, the Indian crops ruined, and the country rendered desolate. But no enemy could be found. "In this expedition we took seven prisoners and five scalps, with the loss of only four men, two of whom were accidentally killed by our own army." The blow was decisive, however. It taught the Indians that to defeat the whites in an ambuscade was not to gain a victory, but rather to insure a speedy and terrible revenge. No more formidable invasions of Kentucky occurred after this demonstration, although attacks on isolated individuals were common enough. It was the last, too, in which Boone was engaged for the defense of Kentucky.

A period of peace now smiled on the harassed settlers, and they were at liberty once more to return to their farms and enjoy the comforts of home. Colonel Boone, from the proceeds of his military pay, purchased several locations of land, on one of which he constructed a comfortable log house and cleared a farm. For several years he devoted himself to this peaceful occupation, and, by industry and thrift, secured all the necessaries and many of the luxuries of frontier life. One day, while he was looking after a small crop of tobacco which he had raised for the accommodation of his friends, four Indians, with guns in their hands, surprised him. He was standing on the top of a little building which had been erected for the purpose of drying the tobacco, when he heard the foremost Indian shout out, "Now, Boone, we got you. You no get away more. We carry you you off to Chilicothe this time. You no cheat us any more." Boone looked down, and saw their ugly-looking guns and still more ugly-looking faces without losing a particle of his presence of mind. He recognized four of the men who had made him prisoner at the Blue Licks in 1778, and to whose tribe he was inducted by the late lamented Mr. Blackfish. He greeted them as friends, and expressed himself delighted at the interview. They were impatient at his cool politeness, and desired him to come down. He replied that he would do so with the utmost dispatch, but begged that they would give him a few moments to remove his tobacco, so that it might not be spoiled.

To divert their attention, he entered into minute inquiries concerning the health of his former Indian comrades, and in this way gained sufficient time to gather up an armful of dry tobacco. When he had done this, he dropped it carefully in their faces, and followed up the playfulness by leaping bodily on them. The rascals began to sneeze and choke with the dust, and in their confusion Boone managed to escape to his cabin. After this incident he appears to have led a tranquil life, farming with great industry, and sporting with great enthusiasm at the proper times.

In 1792, Kentucky came into the Federal Union as a sovereign state. Its population was rapidly on the increase, and much eagerness was displayed to obtain lands by immigrants. Lawsuits were the inevitable consequence. Titles were scrutinized with the greatest severity, and the slightest defect led to speedy ejectment. Unfortunately, many of the titles granted by the Virginia commissioners were entirely worthless, and this, we are sorry to add, was found to be the case with regard to the land held by Boone. The home he had defended so bravely against the savages fell beneath the more subtle warfare of the lawyer. He was ejected. In his old age he found himself without an acre of ground that he could call his own, and this in a country he had explored and populated. A harder case can not be imagined. Deeply grieved, he made up his mind to leave the state, and seek peace and plenty elsewhere. With this intention, he removed to the Kenhawa, in Virginia, and settled on that river, not far from Point Pleasant. During his short residence here he met with some hunters who were just returned from Upper Louisiana, and were full of tales of the vast game products of the prairies. The old hunter fired at their narratives, and determined to emigrate thither without any farther delay. It is said that he made particular inquiries concerning the lawyers of the Far West before he came to this determination. In 1795 he took his departure, and proceeded to the district of St. Charles, about forty-five miles west of St. Louis, where he settled, having received assurances from the Spanish lieutenant governor that ample portions of land should be given to him and his family. In 1800, the lieutenant governor, as a mark of distinction and friendship, appointed Boone commandant of the Femme Osage District, in which capacity he acted until the transfer of the government to the United States. He appears to have been very much delighted with the simple habits of the people of his new home. Prior to the transfer we have mentioned, a grant of land was made to Boone, in return for his official services, but, owing to some informality, the grant was once more repudiated, and Boone left landless.

In 1812, by the advice of his friends, he petitioned Congress to obtain a confirmation of his claim, and, at the same time, sent a memorial to the General Assembly of Kentucky, begging them to use their influence in the matter. "This memorial," says Mr. Peck, "contained a sketch of his labors in the wilderness, and 'of his claims to the remembrance of his country in general.' He spoke of 'his struggles in the fatal fields which were dyed with the blood of the early settlers, among whom were his two eldest sons, and others of his dearest connections. The history of the settlement of the Western country,' he said, 'was his history.' He alluded to the love of discovery and adventure which had induced him to expatriate himself, 'under the assurance of the governor of St. Louis that ample portions of land should be given to him and to his family.' He mentioned the allotment of land, his failure to consummate the title, and his unsuccessful application to the commissioners of the United States. Of the vast extent of country which he had discovered and explored, 'he was unable to call a single acre his own,' and 'he had laid his case before Congress. Your memorialist,' he added, 'can not but feel, so long as feeling remains, that he has a just claim upon his country for land to live on, and to transmit to his children after him. He can not help, on an occasion like this, to look toward Kentucky. From a small acorn she has become a mighty oak, furnishing shelter to upward of four hundred thousand souls. Very different is her appearance now from the time when your memorialist, with his little band, began to fell the forest, and construct the rude fortifications at Boonesborough.'" The memorial of the worthy old pioneer was received favorably by the Legislature, who reported in both houses without a division. The application to Congress was equally successful, and one thousand arpents of land (more than eight hundred acres) were confirmed to him in the Femme Osage District, as originally granted to him by the Spanish government.

In March, 1813, Mrs. Boone, the partner and sharer of all his joys and dangers, died at the advanced age of seventy-six. Daniel was still a hale, hearty old man when this occurred, but he viewed with perfect tranquillity the approaching close of his own earthly career. A singular fact is related of him. Soon after his wife's demise, he gave directions to a cabinet-maker to make a coffin of black walnut for himself. This was done, and it remained in his possession for some time; but, fancying that it was not a good fit, he gave it away, and procured another of cherry wood, which he kept under his bed to the day of his death. He was very anxious to be placed beside his wife, and entered into a written contract with a companion, who usually accompanied him on his hunting tours, that, should he die in the wilderness, he would convey the body to the cemetery in which she lay, and there inter him. His passion for hunting never deserted him, and to the day of his death he made excursions into the wilderness, seldom visiting the same place twice, or, when this was impossible, amused himself with repairing rifles, making powder-horns, etc. In his domestic relations he was perfectly happy, surrounded with a large family of grandchildren, all of whom doted on the hero, and vied with each other in tendering him every attention and kindness. On the 26th of September, 1820, he departed this life, in the eighty-sixth year of his age. His remains were disposed in the way he had desired, but, a quarter of a century later, they were removed, together with those of his wife, to the cemetery at Frankfort, where they were reinterred with appropriate ceremonies.

"The life of Daniel Boone," says Governor Morehead, "is a forcible example of the powerful influence which a single absorbing passion exerts over the destiny of an individual. Born with no endowments of intellect to distinguish him from the crowd of ordinary men, and possessing no other acquirements than a very common education bestowed, he was enabled, nevertheless, to maintain a long and useful career, a conspicuous rank among the most distinguished of his contemporaries; and the testimonials of the public gratitude and respect with which he was honored after his death were such as were never awarded by an intelligent people to the undeserving."

JOSEPH BRAMAH.

One of the most talented and ingenious artisans that England has ever produced was the late Mr. Joseph Bramah, a man whose useful inventions are to be found in every nook and corner of the United Kingdom, and who has given to the world an almost unlimited power in the apparatus known as the hydrostatic press.

Joseph Bramah was the son of a small farmer, and was born at Stainsborough, Yorkshire, on the 13th of April, 1749. He was the eldest of the family, and was intended to follow the avocation of an agriculturist; but at a very early age he exhibited remarkable mechanical aptness, and seemed to fancy tools rather than implements. At the age of sixteen he met with an accident which incapacitated him for the laborious duties of the farm, and gave a direction to his future life. Being badly lamed, it became necessary that he should choose a business in which walking was not essential. Most farmers' boys know something of carpentering, and Bramah, who delighted in it, could handle tools with decided skill. It was determined, therefore, that this should be his future business. He was apprenticed to a carpenter and joiner, and, at the expiration of his time, proceeded to London, where he worked journeyman for some years. By the exercise of industry and prudence, he was soon in a position to start in business on his own account. With more leisure and extended means, he was now able to indulge his mechanical inclinations, and soon was widely known as a skillful and ingenious workman, and a mechanic of fine inventive powers. A few years later he adopted the profession of engineer or machinist, having, in the mean time, invented some important improvements in water-closets, which article he manufactured. But what gave him most reputation was an ingenious lock, still universally used in England, and known by his name. The construction of this lock is remarkably ingenious. Its security depends on the nice adjustment of a number of levers or sliders, which preserve, when at rest, a uniform situation. The key presses down these levers to a certain extent, and no more; and so exact is its operations, that the lock was considered impregnable until Mr. Hobbs, an American mechanic of great talent, succeeded in picking it, after many hours' labor, at the Crystal Palace. On another occasion, this lock was opened before a committee of the House of Commons by means of a common quill. The object of the experiment was to show the extreme delicacy of the works, the quill having been cut into the required shape from the true key. This lock obtained a patent in 1784.

Among other inventions by Mr. Bramah were improvements in water-cocks, pumps, and fire-engines; but the most important of all, and the one for which he will be always remembered, is the hydraulic press. The principle of this machine is thus described: A given pressure, as that given by a plug forced inward upon a square inch of the surface of a fluid confined in a vessel, is suddenly communicated to every square inch of the vessel's surface, however large, and to every inch of the surface of any body immersed in it: thus, if we attempt to force a cork into a vessel full of water, the pressure will not merely be felt by the portion of the water directly in the range of the cork, but by all parts of the mass alike; and the liability of the bottle to break, supposing it to be of uniform strength throughout, will be as great in one place as another; and a bottle will break at the point wherever it is the weakest, however that point may be situated relatively to the place where the cork is applied; and the effect will be the same, whether the stopper be inserted at the top, bottom, or side of the vessel. It is this power which operates with such astonishing effect in the hydrostatic press. The application of the hand at the handle with a force of only ten pounds produces an actual power of two thousand five hundred pounds, and so in proportion to the size, strength, and capacity of the machine. A man can easily exert ten times the force supposed, and thus command a power of twenty-five thousand pounds. These stupendous effects seem almost magical when it is remembered that they are produced by two small pipes, each fitted with a piston and a little water, which for years needs no replenishing. This invaluable machine was patented in 1796. In the following year Bramah patented the beer-machine now so common in hotels, and in private houses where water is not easily obtained. By the aid of this elegant little contrivance, fluids may be drawn from remote places with the greatest ease. He was also the inventor of improvements in steam-engines, especially in boilers; in machinery for producing smooth and accurate surfaces on wood or metal; in paper-making machinery; in making pens by a mechanical process, by which several nibs resembling steel pens were cut out of one quill and fixed in a holder for use; and in the construction of carriages. In 1806 he contrived an exceedingly ingenious mode of printing, which was shortly afterward applied to the consecutive numbering of bank-notes, and by the introduction of which, during the issue of one pound notes by the Bank of England, the labor of 100 clerks out of 120 was dispensed with.

In 1812 Mr. Bramah patented an elaborate scheme for laying mains or large water-pipes through the principal streets of London, of sufficient strength to withstand great pressure applied by force-pumps. The object was to provide the means of extinguishing fires by throwing water without the aid of a fire-engine, and also to supply a lifting power applicable to the raising of great weights, by forcing water or air into an apparatus consisting of a series of tubes, sliding into one another like the tubes of a telescope, and capable of being projected when necessary. He declared that he was able to make a series of five hundred such tubes, each five feet long, capable of sliding within each other, and of being extended in a few seconds by the pressure of air to the length of 2500 feet. With this apparatus he proposed to raise wrecks, and regulate the descent of weights. The last patent secured by Mr. Bramah was for a mode of preventing dry-rot in timber by covering it with a thin coat of Roman cement.

Mr. Bramah died on the 9th of December, 1814. He was superintending the uprooting of trees in Holt forest by his hydraulic press at the time, and contracted a severe cold, from which he never recovered. Mr. Bramah was a sincere Christian and an excellent man; in his disposition he was cheerful, benevolent, and affectionate; in his habits, staid, soberly, and tidy; in his relations with his fellow-man, liberal and upright. He never forgot his humble origin, and always treated the mechanics who were employed in his workshops with kindness and consideration—so much so, indeed, that, during times of commercial stagnation, he would carry on his works, although without a market for the goods that were produced. Mr. Bramah was not an author, but two articles from his pen were published, "A Dissertation on the Construction of Locks," and a "Letter to the Right Honorable Sir James Eyre, Lord Chief Justice of the Common Pleas, on the subject of the cause of Boulton & Watt *versus* Hornblower & Maberley."

JAMES HARGREAVES.

THE spinning-jenny, one of the most important items in the improved machinery now used for weaving, was the invention of James Hargreaves, a poor weaver of Stand Hill, near Blackburn, England. The machine is said to have received its name from a fair damsel, probably the sweetheart of the inventor. Its object is to spin the loose threads (called a roving or slubbin) into yarn. This operation was performed by hand up to Hargreaves's time, and was slowly and imperfectly done. Being a weaver himself, he was aware of the importance of the machine he invented, but nevertheless he owed its invention to accident. It is said that he received the original idea from seeing a one-thread wheel overturned on the floor (an accident that had occurred hundreds of times before, and passed unnoticed), and observing that the wheel and spindle continued to revolve. The spindle was thrown from a horizontal into an upright position; and the thought immediately struck him that, if a number of spindles were placed upright, and side by side, several threads might be spun at once. Acting on this suggestion, he constructed a frame, in which he placed eight rovings and eight spindles. The rovings, when extended to the spindles, passed between two horizontal bars of wood, forming a clasp, which opened and shut somewhat like a parallel ruler; when pressed together, the clasp held the threads fast. A certain portion of roving being extended from the spindles to the wooden clasp, the latter was closed, and then drawn along the horizontal frame to a considerable distance from the spindles, thus lengthening the threads and reducing them to their proper thinness. The spinner's left hand performed this operation; with his right he turned a wheel which caused the spindles to revolve rapidly, and thus the roving was spun into yarn. By returning the clasp to its first position, and letting down a presser wire, the yarn was wound upon the spindle.

This machine was rudely constructed, but it was practicable, and Hargreaves put it into operation for the benefit of himself and family. He endeavored to keep it a secret, and spun weft merely for his own weaving; but such an important piece of machinery was not likely to remain unknown for a great length of time. First his intimate friends became acquainted with its rapid operations, and then they spread the rumor among their fellow-workmen. An excitement was the consequence. The weavers began to complain, in the usual way, that the bread was being taken from their mouths, and that, if the machines came into use, multitudes would be thrown out of employment and reduced to a state of starvation. So virulent did these complaints become at length, that a mob broke into Hargreaves's house and destroyed his jenny—imagining, possibly, that it was not within the compass of human ingenuity to construct another. Not alone did he thus suffer in his property; his person was exposed to the greatest danger, and he was compelled to flee to Nottingham (1768), where he hoped to be safe. Here he entered into partnership with Mr. Thomas James, a joiner, who raised sufficient capital to start a small mill, and to secure a patent for the invention (1770). The specification describes "a method of making a wheel or an engine of an entire new construction, and never before made use of, in order for spinning, drawing, and twisting of cotton, and to be managed by one person only; and that the wheel or engine will spin, draw, and twist *sixteen* or more threads at one time, by a turn or motion of one hand and a draw of the other." The operations of the machine are thus described by Hargreaves: "One person with his or her right hand turns the wheel, and with the left hand takes hold of the clasps, and therewith draws out the cotton from the slubbin box; and being twisted by the turn of the wheel in the drawing out, then a piece of wood is lifted by the toe, which lets down a presser wire, so as to press the threads so drawn out and twisted, in order to wind or put the same regularly upon bobbins which are placed on the spindles."

The advantages of the invention were soon recognized by the manufacturers, and some few machines of Hargreaves's manufacture found a ready market in Blackburn; but the opposition of the mob was still an alarming contingency. A desperate effort was made in 1779—when the machines had obtained a decided footing in that town—to put a stop to their operations. A series of disgraceful riots ensued; a mob scoured the country for miles and miles round, and every manufacturer or weaver who was suspected of possessing one of the obnoxious machines had his premises searched, and, if evidence of the fact were found, destroyed. It was a war of extermination against machinery in general, and an immense deal of valuable property was destroyed.

It is said that the rioters spared the jennies that had only twenty spindles (in the present day they are constructed with as many as one hundred and fifty), and only destroyed those with a greater number. The lamentable ignorance which provoked this futile hostility did not belong merely to the lower classes. There were thousands of others who viewed the introduction of machinery with alarm. The idea that an increased and consequently cheaper supply would occasion an increased demand never entered their minds. All they thought about were the poor's rates.

The effect of these riots on the thriving town of Blackburn was immediate. Many of the most wealthy and influential weavers removed to Manchester and other large places, where the municipal authorities guaranteed them more security. It was many years before cotton-spinning was resumed in Blackburn with the old energy.

At Nottingham, Mr. Hargreaves and his partner carried on the spinning business with moderate success. Their means were too limited to enable them to go into it in a manner calculated to secure a large return. From his patent Hargreaves received little or nothing. A number of Lancashire manufacturers used his jenny without paying any thing for the privilege. He gave notice of action against them, and they sent a delegation to Nottingham to treat with him on the subject. Hargreaves demanded the sum of seven thousand pounds for the exclusive privileges they required. Subsequently he came down to four thousand pounds; but the delegation refused to pay more than three thousand. Here the negotiation was broken off, very unfortunately for Hargreaves. The actions went on, but were relinquished before the day of trial, Hargreaves's attorney having discovered that his client, compelled by necessity, before leaving Lancashire had sold some jennies to obtain clothing for his children, of whom he had six or seven. The lawyer despaired of getting a verdict in the face of such evidence.

In April, 1778, Mr. Hargreaves departed this life, leaving a widow and a large family. He had succeeded in obtaining a comfortable living from the fruits of his ingenuity and industry, but for his invention he got nothing beyond what it produced him as a labor-saving machine for his own use. His widow received four hundred pounds from Mr. James for her husband's share in the business. The profits must have been rather small to leave such a poor residue.

ALEXANDER WILSON.

Alexander Wilson, the world-known ornithologist, was a native of Scotland, born at Paisley on the 6th of July, 1766. His father, although in humble circumstances, was ambitious to see his son in the ministry, but inability to afford the necessary education for such a position rendered it impossible for this ambition to be gratified. Beyond the plain rudiments of an English education, Wilson had no advantage over the other boys of his native town. Like them, he had to contribute to the income of the household, and at the age of thirteen was bound apprentice to his brother-in-law, Mr. William Duncan, to learn the business of a weaver. The employment was not acceptable to him, but he prosecuted it industriously for three years, amusing himself in the intervals of labor with the composition of verses. During the subsequent four years he worked as a journeyman weaver, and labored hard as a poet. He was particularly anxious to excel in the latter character, and believed in his own mind that he was destined to excel the poet Burns, the lustre of whose genius was then suffusing the bleak mountains of Scotland. He produced many pieces, some of which appeared in the poet's corner of the papers. It is said they possessed much merit, but were mechanically defective. Beyond this it is unnecessary to refer to them except as indications of a refined mind struggling for expression in spite of local difficulties. When he was in his twenty-first year, he joined his brother-in-law in a peddling campaign through the eastern districts of Scotland. Wilson was rejoiced at the opportunity of escaping from the wearisome captivity of the loom, and went forth with his pack on his back in the gayest mood. He made it not only a tour of profit, but of pleasure; he not only sought customers, but wooed the Muses. It seldom happens that a man can do two things at the same time with even moderate success. Wilson soon discovered that poetry and peddling were incompatible, and being, like most poets, a little impractical, he made up his mind to devote himself wholly to poetry. After a great deal of trouble, and an enormous amount of patience, he succeeded in getting some small pieces published in book form, and the work went through two tiny editions with credit to the author. It is extremely difficult to live on any kind of credit, and poetic credit is perhaps the shortest in the world. Wilson found it necessary to descend from his Pegasus and return to the ignoble loom, and shortly afterward became involved in a dispute between the manufacturers and the weavers. He sided, of course, with the latter, and revenged himself on the former by launching fearfully fierce pieces of poetic satire at their heads. In this way he contributed largely to the hot temper of the struggle, doing good service to his party, and carrying dismay into the ranks of the enemy. The most sagacious generals sometimes take a false step in the heat and excitement of the battle. This was the case with Wilson. There was one man in the town who had rendered himself singularly obnoxious to the weavers, and this man Wilson was determined to annihilate. He wrote a severe personal satire, in which the individual referred to was held up to the execration of the world as a spectacle of all that was bad, and depraved, and vicious, and profligate. The article was, of course, libelous, but as it was published anonymously, there was some difficulty in fastening it upon Wilson. One night, as he was going home, some spies in the employ of the libeled one seized him, and in the search which followed discovered some papers which settled the question of authorship. He was immediately prosecuted before the sheriff, sentenced to a short imprisonment, and compelled to burn the offensive effusion at the public cross of Paisley. After this he determined on leaving Scotland, and at the first opportunity sailed for America, where he arrived on the 14th of July, 1794. He staid in Philadelphia for a short time, pursuing his old trade, and then removed to Sheppardstown, in Virginia, in the hope of getting rid of the loom forever. Finding that this was impossible, he returned once more to Pennsylvania. He was still subject to violent attacks of poetic phrensy, and perpetrated huge quantities of verse, which, although they did not yield any profit, procured him some consideration. Gratified with this, he abandoned weaving, and set up as village schoolmaster. In this arduous profession he continued for several years, and prospered. The defects of an imperfect education had always weighed upon his mind, and, now that he had the opportunity, he used every exertion to repair them. He was himself the most indefatigable student of the establishment, and made considerable progress in many departments of human knowledge hitherto sealed to him. The emoluments from his school were not enormously great, nor sufficient to deter him from accepting a situation as teacher from the trustees of Union School, in the township of Kingsessing, a short distance from Gray's Ferry, on the Schuylkill, and a few miles from the city of Philadelphia.

The school-house was pleasantly situated near the botanical garden of William Bartram, and to this circumstance, more than any other, may be traced the after-career of Wilson. Bartram was a man unusually versed in natural history, and knew more about birds than any other man in the state. From the day of his arrival in America, Wilson had been struck with the beauty of the birds he saw, and now that he had an opportunity of conversing with a man who knew so much of their habits, the subject of ornithology became one of great interest to him. In a short time he devoted himself to it with an enthusiasm which denoted a natural aptitude for the study. From Bartram he extracted all that the experience of that remarkable man had gathered, but without accepting the information as correctly philosophical. When the one stated that such and such were the habits of such and such birds, the other placed the birds referred to under strict surveillance; surprised them in their homes, interrupted them in their domestic felicities, robbed them of their suppers, and otherwise behaved in an inquisitorial manner. Thus, by making experience and observation his only guides, he became an ornithologist. A few books in Mr. Bartram's library supplied him with the necessary technical tools; for the rest, he trusted to himself. Circumstances often converge to the point we hope to reach, and especially is this the case with men of genius. In the ordinary course of life they learn many things that are apparently useless, when suddenly a new idea, a new passion, a new pursuit demands the very knowledge that has been thus casually acquired. So was it with Wilson. As a relaxation from severer duties, he studied drawing. At first he did not meet with extraordinary success, and was barely able to satisfy himself; but later, when he wanted to depict the form and plumage of a rare bird, he found his hand, although imperfectly tutored, skillful and true.

Before embracing ornithology as a specialty, he made natural history, in all its beautiful comprehensiveness, a study. His little apartment was crowded with specimens of the familiar animals, birds, and reptiles of the neighborhood; and all the boys of the country for miles round knew that they were certain of a few coppers if they could secure some scarce specimen of the animal creation. His own scholars, aware of his passion, rendered good service in the cause. Their eagerness in this respect is illustrated in the following beautiful little incident, described in the most beautiful way by Wilson himself. "One of my boys caught a mouse in school a few days ago, and directly marched up to me with his prisoner. I set about drawing it the same evening, and all the while the pantings of its little heart showed that it was in the most extreme agonies of fear. I had intended to kill it, in order to fix it in the claws of a stuffed owl; but, happening to spill a few drops of water where it was tied, it lapped it up with such eagerness, and looked up in my face with such an expression of supplicating terror as perfectly overcame me. I immediately untied it, and restored it to life and liberty. The agonies of a prisoner at the stake, while the fire and instruments of torture are preparing, could not be more severe than the sufferings of that poor mouse; and, insignificant as the object was, I felt at that moment the sweet sensation that mercy leaves on the mind when she triumphs over cruelty." Is it not a pleasure to sympathize with a mind like this, so keenly sensitive, so poetically kind?

In 1803 Wilson wrote to a friend in Scotland that he found the confinement of the school-room injurious to his health, and that, for the purpose of gaining a little healthful recreation, he was engaged in making a collection of American birds. This appears to be the first indication of his direct application to a science, his connection with which was destined to cover his name with world-wide fame. The real scheme which he had in view when he wrote this letter was to prepare an American Ornithology for the press. He mentioned it to Mr. Bartram, who, while he approved the idea, doubted whether it could be profitably carried into execution. He also broached the matter to Mr. Lawson, an engraver, and eminently practical man, who recapitulated the objections which had been previously urged. But Wilson was now excited, and not easily turned from a subject which had taken firm hold of his imagination. He determined that he would travel through the United States, obtain specimens of all the birds that he could discover, make drawings of them, and then trust to the future for some happy opportunity of placing his labors before the public. It is characteristic of the man that, when he came to this determination, he was in possession of the enormous fortune of *seventy-five cents.* Three years elapsed before he was able to take any farther step, but during this period he neglected no opportunity of improving and educating himself for the vocation he had selected. Among other things, he made an essay at etching, under the friendly tuition of Mr. Lawson, but, as might have been expected, the result was not astonishingly gratifying. Whenever he could snatch a few days from his scholastic duties, he made tours into the woods, and never came home empty-handed. On one occasion he went on foot to Niagara, the results of which trip he incorporated in a lengthy poem called the "Foresters," which, with many other of his effusions, appeared in a periodical of the day, and enjoyed a brief popularity. As a draughtsman, he made rapid progress. Mr. Jefferson, to whom he sent one of his drawings, wrote him an extremely friendly letter, and even begged his assistance in discovering a strange bird which he, Mr. Jefferson, had often heard, but never seen closely. Wilson had the profoundest veneration for the great statesman, and was immensely gratified at this compliment, coming as it did from one who was not meanly versed in ornithology. In 1806 the newspapers announced that Mr. Jefferson had it in contemplation to send an expedition, composed of men of science, to explore the country of the Mississippi. This was an opportunity not to be neglected. Wilson consulted with his friends Bartram and Lawson, and, with their approval, dispatched a memorial to the President, begging that he might be included in the expedition as a practical ornithologist. It is probable that this memorial never reached its destination, for no reply was made to it. Notwithstanding this disheartening rebuff (if it may so be termed), better fortunes were in store for him. Mr. Samuel F. Bradford, a bookseller of Boston, being about to publish an edition of Rees' new Cyclopædia, Wilson was introduced to him as qualified to superintend the work, and was engaged at a liberal salary as assistant editor. This unexpected, and, therefore, doubly welcome promotion did not divert his mind from the scheme it had so long and ardently nourished. Two days after he signed the contract, and when his exultation may be supposed to have been at its height, he wrote to Mr. Bartram: "This engagement will, I hope, enable me, in more ways than one, to proceed in my intended Ornithology, to which all my leisure moments will be devoted." He little thought, when he penned these lines, how soon his fondest hopes were to be realized. Not long after his engagement with Mr. Bradford, he communicated his plans to that gentleman, who, without any hesitation, approved them. He agreed to be the publisher of the work, and felt so much confidence in its success, that he volunteered to furnish the funds necessary for its completion. If there was a happy man in the world, it was Wilson.

Much of the material for the first two volumes was already completed. In various pedestrian tours, he had made himself thoroughly familiar with all the birds of the Northern and Eastern States, had noted their habits, peculiarities, and organization, and had transferred their forms to paper. It was proposed now to publish the first volume with all possible dispatch, after which Wilson might start on his travels, and, by making them both commercial and scientific, kill two birds with one stone. In other words, he was to take a copy under his arm as a sample, and obtain subscribers through the country. In September, 1808, the first volume made its appearance, and immediately Wilson set out in search of "birds and subscribers," as he says. It is unnecessary to add that he obtained a much greater proportion of the former than the latter. The work was expensive, though beautiful, and was scientifically and artistically a novelty in advance of the age. But, although subscribers did not rush upon him with the violence he anticipated, he found in every important city some few cultivated and wealthy men who cheerfully placed their names on his list, and every where the work created unbounded admiration. In other respects the journey was invaluable to him. Wherever he could find the proper kind of man, he cultivated him, and begged a correspondence on all ornithological matters. In this way he placed the entire feathered tribe under severe espionage. Not a strange wing could be raised without his knowledge. In a commercial point of view the journey could not have been considered a failure, for, in spite of the enormous sum at which the work was published (one hundred and twenty dollars), he succeeded in getting forty-one subscribers. This number would be ridiculously small in the present day, when we are accustomed to expensive works of art, and know better how to appreciate the genius that produces them; but we must remember that it was different in Wilson's time. People knew nothing of the subject, and naturally hesitated at purchasing a book at what must have appeared a fabulous price.

After his Eastern tour he remained a few days at home, and then started for the South, where his success was scarcely equal to his expectations. In the mean time the second volume of the Ornithology had made its appearance (January, 1810), and the remaining volumes were put in hand. He has left ample details of this tour, and, as they are extremely interesting, we shall make no apology for drawing largely from them.

Wilson's first point was Lancaster, where he was introduced to the governor, who subscribed, and to many members of both houses, whom he describes as "a pitiful, squabbling, political mob; so split up, and justling about the mere formalities of legislation, without knowing any thing of its realities," that he abandoned them with disgust. From Lancaster he proceeded to Columbia, and thence crossed the Susquehanna, cutting his way through the ice for several hundred yards. Passing on to York, he heard of an extraordinary character, between eighty and ninety years of age, who had lived by trapping birds and quadrupeds for upward of thirty years. Of course he paid a visit to this worthy, taking with him half a pound of snuff by way of peace-offering. Wilson showed him the Ornithology, and was much diverted with the astonishment he expressed on looking at the plates. He could tell anecdotes of the greater part of the subjects of the first volume, and some of the second. We may suppose that the scientific and the practical ornithologists were immensely amused with each other. At Hanover, Wilson discovered a more singular being in the person of a learned judge, who took upon himself to say that such a book ought not to be encouraged, as it was not within the reach of the commonalty, and therefore inconsistent with republican institutions. Wilson did not dispute this proposition, but combated it with another, namely, that the judge was a greater culprit than himself, in erecting a large, elegant, three-story brick house, so much beyond the reach of the commonalty, and, consequently, grossly contrary to republican institutions. He harangued the Solon more seriously, until, to use his own words, "he began to show symptoms of *intellect.*" He proceeded quickly from place to place until he reached Pittsburg, where he made a diligent search for subscribers. He was successful beyond his fondest hopes, having obtained nineteen subscribers in three days. The road to Chilicothe being impassable, owing to the freshets, Wilson determined to navigate himself down to Cincinnati, a distance of five hundred and twenty-eight miles, in a small skiff, which he named the ORNITHOLOGIST. The expense of hiring a rower being considerable, he dispensed with that luxury, and, in spite of the opposition of his friends, embarked alone. The Alleghany River was one wide torrent of broken ice, and he calculated on experiencing considerable difficulty on this score. His stock of provisions consisted of some biscuit and cheese, and a bottle of cordial presented to him by a gentleman of Pittsburg. His gun, trunk, and greatcoat occupied one end of the boat, and conveniently at hand was a tin measure, with which he bailed the boat and took his beverage from the Ohio. Thus prepared, he bade adieu to the smoky confines of Pitt, launched into the stream, and was soon winding away among the hills which every where inclose the noble river. The weather was warm and serene, and the stream like a mirror, except where floating masses of ice spotted its surface; but these soon disappeared. Far from being concerned at his novel situation, he felt his heart expand with joy at the novelties which surrounded him. He listened with pleasure to the whistling of the redbird on the banks as he passed, and contemplated the forest scenery as it receded with increasing delight. Dissatisfied with the slow speed of the stream, which flowed at the rate of two and a half miles an hour only, he stripped to the oars, and added three and a half miles more to its velocity. He passed a number of arks, or Kentucky boats, and was much struck with their peculiarities. Several of these floating caravans were laden with store-goods for the supply of the towns and villages through which they passed, having a counter erected, shawls, muslins, etc., displayed, and every thing ready for transacting business. On approaching a settlement, they blow a horn or a tin trumpet, to announce to the inhabitants that they have arrived and commenced business.

The first day he rowed twenty miles, and, experiencing no evil effects, made up his mind that he could "stand it." About an hour after dark he put up at a miserable cabin, about fifty-two miles from Pittsburg, where he slept on what he supposed to be corn-stalks, or something worse. He was so uncomfortable that he preferred the smooth bosom of the Ohio, and long before day resumed his journey. The landscape on each side lay in one mass of shade, but the grandeur of the projecting headlands and vanishing points or lines was charmingly reflected in the smooth, glassy surface below. He could only discover when he was passing a clearing by the crowing of the cocks; and now and then, in more solitary places, the big-horned owl made a most hideous hallooing, that echoed among the mountains. In this lonesome manner, with full leisure for observation and reflection, exposed to hardships all day and hard berths all night, to storms of rain, hail, and snow—for it froze severely almost every night—he persevered from the 24th of February (1810) to Sunday evening, March the 17th, when he moored his skiff safely in Bear-Grass Creek, at the Rapids of the Ohio. His hands had suffered, and it was some weeks before they resumed their former flexibility and feeling.

At Marietta, Wilson visited the celebrated remains of Indian fortifications, as they are called, and also at Big-Grave Creek, seventy miles above. The Big Grave is three hundred paces round at the base, seventy feet perpendicular, and the top, which is about fifty feet over, has sunk in, forming a regular concavity three or four feet deep. This tumulus is in the form of a cone, and the whole, as well as its immediate neighborhood, is covered with a venerable growth of forest four or five hundred years old, which gives it a most singular appearance. In clambering round its steep sides, Wilson found a place where a large white oak had been blown down, and had torn up the earth to the depth of five or six feet. In this place he commenced digging, but with no result. A person of the neighborhood, however, presented him with some beads, fashioned out of a kind of white stone, which were found in digging on the opposite side of the mound. Wilson met the owner of the Big Grave, a placid individual, who was perfectly unconscious of the antiquarian treasures he possessed, and who, Wilson asserts, would not expend three cents to see the whole sifted before his face. He endeavored to work on his avarice by representing the probability that it might contain valuable matters, and suggested to him a mode by which a passage might be cut into it level with the bottom, and by excavating and arching a most noble cellar might be formed for keeping his turnips and potatoes. "All the turnips and potatoes I shall raise this dozen years," said he, "would not pay the expense."

On the 5th of March he was overtaken by a severe storm of wind and rain, which changed to hail and snow, blowing down trees and limbs in all directions. For immediate preservation he was obliged to steer out into the river, which rolled and foamed like a sea, and filled his boat nearly half full of water. It was with the greatest difficulty that he could resist its fury, and it was not until dusk that he succeeded in making a landing at a place on the Kentucky shore. Here he spent the evening in learning the accomplishments of bear-treeing, wolf-trapping, and wild-cat-hunting from an old professor, but he was surprised to find that, notwithstanding the skill of this great master, the country abounded with wolves and wild-cats, black and brown. According to this distinguished hunter's own confession, he had lost sixty dogs since Christmas; and all night long the distant howling of the wolves kept the dogs in a perfect uproar of barking. This man, says Wilson, was one of those people called squatters, who neither pay rent nor own land, but keep roving on the frontiers, retreating as the tide of civilization approaches. They are the immediate successors of the savages, and far below them in good sense and good manners, as well as comfortable accommodations. Nothing, however, adds more to the savage grandeur and picturesque effect of the scenery along the Ohio than their miserable huts lurking at the bottom of a gigantic growth of timber. It is amusing to observe how dear and how familiar habit has rendered those privations, which must have first been the offspring of necessity. Yet none pride themselves more on their possessions. The inhabitants of these forlorn sheds will talk to you with pride of the richness of their soil, of the excellence and abundance of their country, of the healthiness of their climate, and the purity of their waters, while the only bread you find among them is of Indian corn coarsely ground in a horse-mill, with half the grains unbroken; even their cattle are destitute of stables and hay, and look like moving skeletons; their own houses are worse than pig-styes; their clothes an assemblage of rags; their faces yellow, and lank with disease; and their persons covered with filth, and frequently garnished with the humors of the Scotch "fiddle"—a disease which Wilson escaped with much thankfulness. Their condition he attributes to laziness. The corn is thrown into the ground in spring, and the pigs turned into the woods, where they multiply like rabbits. The labor of the squatter is now over till autumn, and he spends his winter in eating pork, cabbage, and hoe-cakes.

Amid very tempestuous weather he reached Cincinnati, which city he describes with minuteness. From this point he made various excursions. He entered Big-Bone Creek, which being passable only about a quarter of a mile, he had to leave his boat and baggage in charge of a family hard by, and set out for Big-Bone Lick, a distance of five miles, through the woods on foot. This place, which lies "far in the windings of a sheltered vale," afforded him a fund of amusement in shooting ducks and paroquets (of which last he skinned twelve, and brought off two slightly wounded), and in examining the ancient buffalo roads to this great licking-place. Mr. Colquhoun, the proprietor, was not at home, but his agent and manager entertained him as well as he was able, and was much amused with his enthusiasm. This place is a low valley, every where surrounded by high hills; in the centre, by the side of the creek, is a quagmire of near an acre; from which, and another smaller one below, the chief part of the big bones which give the place its name have been taken; at the latter places he found numerous fragments of large bones lying scattered about. In pursuing a wounded duck across this quagmire, he nearly made a human contribution to the grand congregation of mammoths below. He sunk up to the middle, and had hard struggling to get out. On leaving, he laid the strongest injunctions on the manager to be on the look-out, and to preserve every thing that might be turned up. To make assurance doubly sure, he left a note for the proprietor, impressing on him the same important matter. In the afternoon of the next day he returned to his boat, replaced his baggage, and once more floated out with the stream. It rained hard all the day, and he had to row hard and drink hard (he had purchased a solitary bottle of native wine at a Swiss settlement) to keep himself comfortable. The pockets of his great-coat were filled with bird-skins, and the garment itself covered others which he wished to preserve; consequently, there was no room for the owner, who got a complete drenching for his disinterestedness. In the evening he lodged at a wretched hovel, owned by a diminutive wretch, who did nothing but tell falsehoods concerning his former greatness. According to this worthy's own account, he had gone through all the war with General Washington, had become one of his *Life Guards*, and had sent many a British soldier to his long home. As Wilson answered with indifference, he attempted to stimulate his curiosity by still stronger doses, administered in the shape of anecdotes. "One day," he said, "a grenadier had the impudence to get up on the works, and to wave his cap in defiance; my commander (General Washington) says to me, 'Dick,' says he, 'can't you pepper that there fellow for me?' says he. 'Please your honor,' says I, 'I'll try at it;' so I took a fair, cool, and steady aim, and touched my trigger. Up went his heels like a turkey; down he tumbled; one buckshot had entered *here*, and another *there* (laying a finger on each breast), and the bullet found the way to his brains right through his forehead. By God, he was a noble-looking fellow!" Though Wilson believed every word of this to be a lie, yet he could not but look with disgust on the being who uttered it. This same miscreant pronounced a long prayer before supper, and immediately after called out, in a splutter of oaths, for the pine splinters to be held to let the gentleman see. Such a farrago of lies, oaths, prayers, and politeness put him in a good humor in spite of himself. The whole herd of this filthy kennel were in perpetual motion with the itch; so, having procured a large fire to be made, under pretense of habit, he sought for the softest plank, placed his trunk and great-coat at his head, and stretched himself there till morning. He set out early, and passed several arks. A number of turkeys, which he observed from time to time on the Indiana shore, caused him to lose half the morning in search of them. On the Kentucky shore he was also decoyed by the same temptations, but could never approach near enough to shoot one of them. These affairs led to so much delay, that he became dubious whether he should be able to reach Louisville that night. Night came on, and he could hear nothing of the Falls; about eight o'clock he first heard the roaring of the rapids, and as it increased he was every moment in hopes of seeing the lights of Louisville; but no lights appeared, and the noise seemed now within less than half a mile's distance. Seriously alarmed lest he might be drawn into the suction of the Falls, he cautiously coasted along shore, which was full of snags and sawyers, and at length, with great satisfaction, reached Bear-Grass Creek, where he secured his skiff to a Kentucky boat, and, loading himself with his baggage, groped his way through a swamp up to the town. The next day Wilson sold his skiff for exactly half what it cost him. The man who bought it expressed his surprise at its droll Indian name (the Ornithologist): "Some old chief or warrior, I suppose," said he.

From Kentucky Wilson proceeded to Tennessee. On his way he passed through a pigeon-roost, or rather breeding-place, which continued for three miles, and, he was informed, extended in length for more than forty miles. The timber was chiefly beech; every tree was laden with nests, and he counted in different places more than ninety nests on a single tree. Shortly after this he fell in with a poor unfortunate soldier, who had been robbed and plundered by the Choctaws while passing through their nation. "Thirteen or fourteen Indians," he said, "surrounded me before I was aware, cut away my canteen, tore off my hat, took the handkerchief from my neck and the shoes from my feet, and all the money I had from me, which was about forty-five dollars." Wilson says that the poor fellow looked pretty much "*done up*." The caves and sink-holes in Kentucky were objects of great curiosity to Wilson, and he never missed an opportunity of exploring them. One of these remarkable places belonged to a man who had a notoriously bad character, and was strongly suspected, even by his neighbors, of having committed a foul murder, and made use of this identical cave as a place of concealment for the body. As this man's house stood by the road side, Wilson was induced by motives of curiosity to stop and take a peep at him. On his arrival he found two persons in conversation under the piazza, one of whom informed him that he was the landlord. He was a dark mulatto, rather above the common size, inclining to corpulency, with legs small in proportion to the other parts of his body, and a limp in his gait. His countenance bespoke a soul capable of deeds of darkness. Wilson had not been three minutes in his company when the landlord invited the other man and Wilson to walk back and see his cave, to which all parties assented. The entrance was in the perpendicular front of a rock behind the house, and had a door with a lock and key to it. It was used as a cellar, and pots of milk and other dairy arrangements were crowded near the running stream which passed through it. The roof and sides were dripping with water. Desiring the landlord to walk before him with the light, Wilson followed, with his hand on his pistol, reconnoitring on every side, and listening to his description of its length and extent. After examining this horrible vault for forty or fifty yards, the mulatto declined to go any farther, complaining of rheumatism in his black legs. Wilson now perceived, for the first time, that the landlord's friend had not accompanied them, and that they were alone. Confident in his means of defense, whatever mischief the devil might suggest to his companion, he fixed his eye steadily on the landlord, and observed to him that he could not be ignorant of the reports circulated about the country relative to that cave. "I suppose," said he, "you know what I mean." "Yes, I understand you," returned the mulatto, without appearing the least embarrassed—"that I killed somebody, and threw them into this cave. I can tell you the whole beginning of that damned lie;" and, without moving from the spot, he entered into the details of a long story. When this labored exculpation came to an end, Wilson asked him why he did not get the cave examined by three or four reputable neighbors, whose report might rescue his character from the suspicion of having committed so horrid a crime. He acknowledged it would be well enough to do so, but did not seem to think it worth the trouble.

At Nashville, Tennessee, Wilson remained for some days, busily engaged in making a set of drawings of all the birds he had seen. These were forwarded to Mr. Lawson, being, of course, intended for the American Ornithology. Unfortunately, they were never received. The post-office in those days was even worse than it is now. When he had completed his arrangements, Wilson made preparations for a visit to St. Louis; but, being detained a week by constant and heavy rains, and considering that it would add four hundred miles to his journey, and detain him at least a month, without even the expectation of obtainin, many subscribers, he abandoned the idea, and prepared instead for a journey through the wilderness. He was advised by many not to attempt it alone; that the Indians were dangerous, the swamps and rivers almost impassable without assistance. All sorts of arguments were used to dissuade him from going *alone*. He weighed all these matters in his own mind, and, attributing a great deal to vulgar fear and exaggerated reports, he equipped himself for the attempt. He had an excellent horse, on which he could depend; a loaded pistol in each pocket, a loaded fowling-piece belted across his shoulder, a pound of gunpowder in his flask, and five pounds of shot in his belt. He next procured some dried beef and biscuit, and on the 4th of May left Nashville. Eleven miles from this city he came to the Great Harpath, a stream of about fifty yards wide, which was running with great violence. He could not discover the entrance to the ford owing to the rains and inundations. There was no time to be lost, so he plunged in, and almost immediately his horse was swimming. He arrived on the other side in safety, and had the pleasure of riding in his wet clothes until the sun made them dry. He repeated this experiment several times, and, thanks to the strength of his horse, always with success, although at times he was nearly knocked from his seat by coming in contact with drift-wood.

On the borders of the Indian country stands the house where the unfortunate traveler, Lewis, committed suicide. Wilson took down from the landlady the particulars of that event. Governor Lewis, she said, came thither about sunset, alone, and inquired if he could stay for the night, and, alighting, brought his saddle into the house. He was dressed in a loose gown, white, striped with blue. On being asked if he came alone, he replied that there were two servants behind, who would soon be up. He called for some spirits, and drank a very little. When the servants arrived, one of whom was a negro, he inquired for his powder, saying he was sure he had some powder in a canister. The servant gave no distinct reply, and Lewis, in the mean while, walked backward and forward before the door, talking to himself.

Sometimes, she said, he would seem as if he were walking up to her, and would suddenly wheel round, and walk back as fast as he could. Supper being ready, he sat down, but had eaten only a few mouthfuls when he started up, speaking to himself in a violent manner. At these times, she said, she observed his face to flush, as if it had come on him in a fit. He lighted his pipe, and, drawing a chair to the door, sat down, saying to Mrs. Grinder (the landlady), in a kind voice, "Madam, this is a very pleasant evening." He smoked his pipe for some time, but quitted his seat and traversed the yard as before. He said he would sleep on the floor, and his servant brought bearskins and a buffalo-robe, which were immediately spread out for him. The landlady then retired to the kitchen, which was in the adjoining apartment. She experienced some alarm at the strange behavior of her guest, and could not sleep. He was still pacing his apartment in an agitated manner, and talking loud, as she said, "like a lawyer." Suddenly she heard the report of a pistol, and simultaneously the fall of a heavy body on the floor, accompanied with the agonized exclamation, "*Oh Lord!*" Immediately afterward she heard the report of another pistol, and in a few minutes she heard him at her door calling out, "*Oh, madam, give me some water and heal my wounds.*" The logs being open and unplastered, she saw him stagger back and fall against a stump that stands between the kitchen and room. He crawled for some distance, and raised himself by the side of a tree, where he sat for about a minute. He once more got to the room; afterward he went to the kitchen door, but did not speak. She then heard him scraping the bucket with a gourd for water, but this cooling element was denied the dying man. The woman was so completely paralyzed by the terrible tragedy that she did not move for two hours. Servants were then aroused, and on entering the room they found the poor fellow on the bed, still alive. He uncovered his side, and showed them where the bullet had entered. A piece of his forehead was blown off, and had exposed the brains without having bled much. He begged they would take his rifle and dispatch him, and he would give them all the money he had in his trunk, exclaiming, "I am no coward; but I am *so* strong—*so hard to die.*" He begged the servant not to be afraid of him, for he would not hurt him. In this dreadful condition he remained for two hours. Just as the sun rose above the trees his mortal sufferings terminated. Few men can read this heart-rending story of a gallant officer without deep emotion. It made a deep and sad impression on Wilson, who gazed now upon his grave close by the common path. He gave Grinder money to put a post-fence round it, to shelter it from the hogs and from the wolves, and left the place in a very melancholy mood. The remaining incidents of his journey through the wilderness were not remarkable, except toward the end, when he was attacked by a dysentery, and cured himself, as he supposed, by eating raw eggs. He was assailed, also, by a tremendous storm of rain, wind, and lightning, until he and his horse were both blinded, and unable to go on. Aware of his danger, he sought the first open space, and, dismounting, stood for half an hour under the most profuse shower-bath he had ever experienced from above. The roaring of the storm was terrible; several trees around him were broken off and torn up by the roots, and those that stood were bent almost to the ground. Limbs of trees, weighing several hundred pounds, whisked past him like feathers. He was astonished how he escaped, and said afterward that he would rather take his chance in a field of battle than in such a storm.

On the fourteenth day of his journey he arrived at Natchez, having overcome every obstacle alone, and without being acquainted with the country. What astonished the boatmen even more than this was the fact that the journey was performed *without whisky*. From Natchez Wilson proceeded to New Orleans, where he arrived on the 6th of June. The approach of the sickly season warned him not to tarry long in this city, and accordingly, on the 24th he embarked in a ship bound for New York, where he arrived on the 30th of July, and soon reached Philadelphia, laden with a light cargo of subscribers, and a much more valuable one of ornithological specimens, many of which were entirely unknown to naturalists.

In the early part of 1812, Wilson published the fifth volume of his Ornithology, and the following volumes, up to the seventh, appeared as rapidly as the nature of the work would admit. The difficulty of obtaining efficient assistance became very embarrassing, and exposed Wilson to a vast amount of annoyance. He was compelled to color many of the plates himself, and the closeness with which he applied himself to this task was no doubt prejudicial to his health. As soon as the seventh volume made its appearance, its author and Mr. Ord (his biographer) set out on an expedition to Great Egg Harbor, New Jersey, where they remained for nearly four weeks, collecting materials for the eighth volume. Immediately on his return to Philadelphia he applied himself with fresh enthusiasm to his task, and by August had completed the letter-press for the eighth volume, though the whole of the plates were not finished. The confinement and intense application which this demanded were more than his frame could sustain. He was seized with a fresh attack of dysentery, and after suffering under it for ten days, died on the 23d of August, 1813, in the forty-seventh year of his age. His remains were deposited in the cemetery of the Swedish Church, in the District of Southwark, Philadelphia. A plain marble tomb marks the spot, bearing an appropriate inscription.

That the industry of Wilson was equal to his natural talents is proved by the fact that in little more than seven years, "without patron, fortune, or recompense," he accomplished more than the combined body of European naturalists had achieved in a century. We need no further evidence of his unparalleled industry than the fact that of two hundred and seventy-five species which were figured and described in his American Ornithology, *fifty-six* had not been taken notice of by any former naturalist. In estimating this devotion to science, we must bear in mind the disadvantages under which he labored. By the terms of his contract with his publishers, he bound himself to supply all the drawings and letter-press necessary for the work; notwithstanding which, we find him, immediately after the publication of the first volume, undertaking all the hardships and annoyances of a canvasser. On his journey, to be sure, he gained valuable specimens, and contributed to his general ornithological knowledge, but he was unable to proceed in the literary portion of the work. Long before the seventh volume was issued the publishers felt disheartened. The success of the work did not satisfy their expectations, and to continue its publication became merely a matter of professional pride with them. Wilson could not be unmindful of this fact, and it must have pained him sadly. It is, indeed, remarkable that, in spite of these drawbacks, he persevered; but they account for the willingness with which he undertook more than his share of the work. He was anxious to get through with it as rapidly as possible, dreading, perhaps, that the enthusiasm of the publishers might wane at any moment, or, at all events, desiring to relieve them of an unwelcome burden.

"Independent of that part of his work which was Wilson's particular province, viz., the drawing and describing of his subjects, he was necessitated," says Mr. Ord, "to occupy much of his time in coloring the plates; his sole resource for support being in this employment, as he had been compelled to relinquish the superintendence of the Cyclopædia. This drudgery of coloring the plates is a circumstance much to be regretted, as the work would have proceeded more rapidly if he could have avoided it. One of his principal difficulties, in effect, and that which caused him no small uneasiness, was the process of coloring. If this could have been done solely by himself, or—as he was obliged to seek assistance therein—if it could have been performed immediately under his eye, he would have been relieved of much anxiety, and would have better maintained a due equanimity, his mind being daily ruffled by the negligence of his assistants, who too often, through a deplorable want of skill and taste, made disgusting caricatures of what were intended to be modest imitations of simple nature. Hence much of his precious time was spent in the irksome employment of inspecting and correcting the imperfections of others. This waste of his stated periods of labor he felt himself constrained to compensate by encroachments on those hours which nature, conscious of her rights, claims as her own—hours which she consecrates to rest—which she will not forego without a struggle, and which all those who would preserve unimpaired the vigor of their mind and body must respect. Of this intense and destructive application his friends failed not to admonish him, but to their kind remonstrances he would reply that 'life is short, and without exertion nothing can be performed.' But *the true cause of this extraordinary toil was his poverty.*"

And thus Alexander Wilson died from over-exertion in trying to gain a living by coloring the plates of that work which was destined to make his name illustrious.

EDMUND CARTWRIGHT.

AMONG the names of those eminent inventors who have given to the useful arts and to manufactures their present importance—who have in the most direct and perceptible way benefited the civilization of the world—the name of Edmund Cartwright, the inventor of the power-loom, deserves to be borne in warm and grateful remembrance. Although not strictly a self-made man, he owes his reputation entirely to himself, and as he obtained this at an advanced period of life, his story furnishes the instructive lesson that it is never too late to exert the highest faculties of the mind, even when they have been occupied in utterly different pursuits to those to which they are now newly called.

Edmund Cartwright was born in the year 1743, at Marnham, in the county of Nottingham, England. His family was ancient and respectable, although in somewhat reduced circumstances. Being intended for the Church, Edmund had more than ordinary care bestowed on his education. After leaving the school at Wakefield, he was sent to University College, Oxford, and subsequently was elected a fellow of Magdalen College. When the time arrived for taking holy orders, he was appointed to the living of Brampton, near Chesterfield, and afterward of Goadby-Marwood in Leicestershire. At an early age he displayed some literary ability, and published, anonymously, a collection of poetical pieces. In 1770 he published, in his own name, a legendary poem entitled "Armida and Elvira," which was received with much favor, and passed through several editions in a short time. He wrote, also, the "Prince of Peace," and sonnets to "Eminent Men." After this he became a regular contributor to the "Monthly Review," and a literary correspondent with many eminent persons.

In these congenial and tranquil callings Cartwright's life passed away peacefully and profitably until his fortieth year. Happening to be at Matlock in the summer of 1784, he fell in company with some Manchester gentlemen, whose conversation was destined to change the whole tenor of his life. They talked of manufacturing, and especially of Arkwright's spinning machinery. One of the company observed that, as soon as Arkwright's patent expired, so many mills would be erected, and so much cotton spun, that hands would never be found to weave it. To this the listener replied that Arkwright must then set his wits to work to invent a weaving-mill. This led to a conversation on the subject, in which the Manchester gentlemen unanimously agreed that the thing was impracticable, and in defense of their opinion they adduced arguments which Cartwright was certainly incompetent to answer, or even to comprehend, being totally ignorant of the subject, having never, at the time, seen a person weave. He controverted, however, the impracticability of the thing by remarking that there had been lately exhibited in London an automaton figure which played at chess. "Now you will not assert, gentlemen," said Cartwright, "that it is more difficult to construct a machine that shall weave, than one that shall make all the variety of moves that are required in that complicated game." Some time afterward, a particular conversation recalled this conversation to his mind. It struck him that, as in plain weaving, according to the conception he then had of the business, there could only be three movements, which were to follow each other in succession, there could be little difficulty in producing and repeating them. Full of these ideas, he immediately employed a carpenter and smith to carry them into effect. As soon as the rough model was finished, he got a weaver to put in the warp, which was of such materials as sailcloth is usually made of. To his great delight, a piece of rough cloth was the result. His delight was unbounded, for it proved that his theory was correct. As he had never before turned his thoughts to mechanism, either in theory or practice, nor had seen a loom at work, nor knew any thing of its construction, it will be readily supposed that his machine was a rough one. The warp was laid perpendicularly, the reed fell with a force of at least half a hundred weight, and the springs which threw the shuttle were strong enough to have thrown a Congreve rocket. It required the strength of two powerful men to work the machine at a slow rate and only for a short time. "Conceiving, in my simplicity," says Cartwright, "that I had accomplished all that was required, I then secured what I thought a most valuable property by a patent, dated 4th of April, 1785. This being done, I then condescended to see how other people wove, and you will guess my astonishment when I compared their easy modes of operation with mine. Availing myself, however, of what I then saw, I made a loom, in its general principles nearly as they are now made; but it was not till the year 1787 that I completed my invention, when I took out my last weaving patent, August the 1st of that year." Mr. Cartwright made an improvement in this loom subsequently, by which patterns in checks could be executed with beautiful precision.

Notwithstanding the obvious advantages of Mr. Cartwright's machinery, there was great difficulty in introducing it, mainly owing to the opposition of the laboring classes, who imagined that their simple lives would be ground out by the iron monster. A factory was erected at Doncaster by some of Cartwright's friends, in which he had an interest, but it was unsuccessful. Another establishment, fitted up with five hundred looms on the new principle, was set upon by an exasperated mob and utterly destroyed. The inventors of labor-saving machines have always these massive difficulties to deal with and to overcome. In Cartwright's case it took some years, but he lived to see his machines in full favor, and to know that they performed the labor of two hundred thousand men.

Cartwright's next invention was to *comb wool by machinery.* Here, again, he was met by popular opposition, and not only this, but by fraudulent attempts to evade his rights. The machines, however, triumphed, and came into general use. Dr. Cartwright now exercised his ingenuity in a variety of ways, giving himself up entirely to the pleasant excitement of invention. He took out more patents, and received several premiums from the Society for the Encouragement of Arts and the Board of Agriculture. The steam-engine engaged much attention, and he used to tell his son (how prophetically time has proved) that, if he lived to be a man, he would see both ships and land-carriages impelled by steam. "It is also certain," says Mr. Craik, "that at that early period he had constructed a model of a steam-engine attached to a barge, which he explained, about the year 1793, in the presence of his family, to Robert Fulton, then a student of painting under West. Later in life, Cartwright engaged himself in the construction of a steam-carriage to run on common roads, but death prevented the completion of his plans. This event took place in October, 1823. He continued his mechanical and philosophical experiments up to the last with unabated vigor, and enjoyed excellent health, mental and physical. On the anniversary of his 77th year, he wrote to his brother, "I this day entered into my 77th year in as good health and spirits, thank God, as I have done on any one birthday for the last half century. I am moving about my farm from eight o'clock in the morning till four in the afternoon, without suffering the least fatigue."

Some curious things are related of Cartwright, which tend to prove that he was a very absorbed or a very forgetful man. He would sometimes lose all memory of his own inventions and other productions of an early date, even when his attention was particularly called to them. On one occasion a daughter repeated some lines from a poem. "They are beautiful, child; where did you meet with them?" he asked; and it was with the greatest astonishment he heard they were from his own poem of the "Prince of Peace." At another time, being shown the model of a machine, he examined it with great attention, and at last observed that the inventor must have been a man of great ingenuity, and that he himself should feel very proud if he had been the author of the contrivance; nor could he be immediately convinced that such was actually the fact. We give these anecdotes for what they are worth, merely remarking that they are curious.

Defective specifications, loose patents, and greedy imitators all combined to rob Cartwright of the just reward of his ingenuity. From his power-loom—the most important of all his inventions—he received little or nothing in the way of remuneration, certainly nothing to compensate him for the loss he sustained at the fire where five hundred of these machines were destroyed. After the expiration of the patent, however, a number of manufacturers and merchants, who recognized his claim to the invention, presented a memorial to the Lords of the Treasury setting forth the merits of his improvements, and begging that the national bounty might be bestowed upon him. In consequence of this and other applications in his favor, the sum of fifty thousand dollars was soon after granted to him by Parliament, "in consideration of the good service he had rendered the public by his invention of weaving." This sum, large as it appears, was smaller than he had expended on his products, but it enabled him to pass the remainder of his life in comfortable retirement, and in a manner suited to his tastes and education. He was eighty-one years of age at the time of his death.

COUNT RUMFORD.

BENJAMIN THOMPSON, more widely known by his title of Count Rumford, was born at Woburn, in the colony of Massachusetts, on the 26th of March, 1753. At an early age he was sent to the public school of his native town, where he speedily acquired a knowledge of reading, writing, and arithmetic, so that in a little time the worthy pedagogue of the establishment had no more knowledge to impart to his greedy scholar. It became necessary, therefore, to remove him to a private establishment, where a more exclusive kind of tuition could be obtained. He is said to have made rapid progress in the study of astronomy, and also in the mathematics.

At the age of sixteen young Thompson took his place on the high stool of a counting-room, and became a punctual and observant clerk; but the routine of the occupation was not in accordance with his tastes, and he diversified it by continuing his studies in astronomy and the physical sciences. He was an extremely ingenious lad—a natural mechanic, to whom tools were as so many additional hands. Among his early achievements, his biographers dwell on an engraved label which he executed for his books, and which they assert was the first work of the kind ever done in America. The design was extremely luxuriant, and must have cost young Thompson an immense amount of trouble and patience. When the Stamp Act was repealed—this is another story related of our hero—Thompson undertook to manufacture a quantity of fireworks to fire off in honor of the American triumph. He knew all about the proper mixtures for producing the gay display, but he seems to have been strangely ignorant of the great danger of packing and preparing them. An apothecaries' shop was selected as the most handy laboratory, and Thompson set about his task with his usual earnestness. As might be expected, an explosion took place; the unfortunate operator was seriously injured, and had to be removed to his mother's house, where he remained several weeks in a critical state. The town of Salem (where he was employed) had to go without its pyrotechnical display.

When he had recovered from the effects of this accident, he returned to his desk; but, in consequence of the commercial stagnation which followed the non-importation agreement, his employer had no farther need of a clerk, and Thompson had to seek his fortunes in a new sphere of action. During the winter of 1769, therefore, he taught a school at Wilmington, and did not resume commercial pursuits until the following year, when he received an engagement in a dry goods store in Boston. This was of short duration, and for some time he was without employment. He made the most of his spare time, however. A course of lectures were being delivered at Harvard College on experimental philosophy, and, although not a student of that establishment, he obtained permission to hear the course, and derived much benefit from the experiments which he saw performed, and which he repeated the moment he returned to his lodgings.

In the autumn of 1770 he was intrusted with the charge of the academy at Rumford (now called Concord), and was received with great favor in that town. Besides being accomplished, he was handsome and manly, and had an open, frank way with him which won all hearts. He became, in consequence, a great pet with the ladies, and especially so with Mrs. Rolfe, the widow of a colonel, who possessed an estate of some magnitude for those days. She was considerably Thompson's senior, but, in spite of this drawback, retained much of the winning way of youth, and was eminently a charming person. The result was a perfectly natural one. On the closing of the school in 1772 Thompson and the widow proceeded together to Boston, where he invested his limbs in a magnificent suit of garments. From this city he proceeded to astonish the little world of Woburn, and, on presenting himself before his mother, won from her the reproachful exclamation, "Why, Ben, my child! how could you spend your whole winter's wages in this way?" Having obtained the assent of his parent, he returned to Rumford, and was immediately wedded. By right of fortune as well as right of intellect, he now became one of the aristocracy of the colonies. At that time all parties were more or less convulsed with the angry strife occasioned by the tyrannic claims of England, but Thompson does not appear to have been in the slightest degree affected with them. He abandoned himself apparently to the enjoyment of his wealth, and freely attended all the places of amusement and fashionable resort. He had worked hard, and now felt disposed to enjoy a little recreation. His affable manners and cultivated mind enabled him to make acquaintance with the most prominent men. Among those who became greatly attached to him was Governor Wentworth. On the first opportunity, he proved his preference by bestowing on Thompson the commission of major in a regiment of New Hampshire militia, thus raising him at once directly over the heads of all the captains and subalterns of the corps. It may have been Governor Wentworth's wish to enlist the sympathies of his young friend in the cause of the mother country, and, although it is certain he did not entirely succeed, it is probable his liberal and appreciative policy was not without a result. We may safely conclude that Thompson would not have accepted the commission if his views had been very hostile to the English government. At a time when every man is supposed to be arrayed on one side or the other of a great question, moderation and neutrality are certain to excite suspicion. His brother officers in the corps, dissatisfied with the favoritism of his promotion, spread all sorts of rumors about him, and endeavored to injure his popularity. They were successful in playing on the excited feelings of the mob, and in November, 1774, Thompson received an intimation that his life was in danger, and that he would assuredly be tarred and feathered. There was no resource to avert the danger and indignity but to escape with the greatest precipitation. At Woburn he sought his first refuge, but the rumor of his Tory predilections had preceded him, and that quiet town was no longer safe. From

Woburn he removed to Charlestown, where he remained for some months, after which he removed to Boston, which was at the time garrisoned by the British army under Gage. He made a fresh attempt to return to Woburn in the following year, under the impression that the excitement against him had subsided; but he was not long in discovering his mistake. The house in which he lived was surrounded by an armed mob, savage with the fiercest hatred against Tories, who demanded that he might be brought forth. Fortunately, a conspicuous patriot resided in the same building, and, owing to his timely intervention, the major was saved from the tender mercies of his enemies. That he deeply felt the indignities to which he was exposed, to say nothing of the danger, is proved by the course he subsequently adopted. Feeling his own innocence, he demanded from the provisional government of the colonies a trial. He was placed in arrest, and advertisements were inserted in the papers inviting all who knew any thing against him to appear. The necessity for this bold step was increased by the eagerness Thompson felt to join the cause of his country at the head of his regiment.

The day of trial arrived, and the meeting-house was crowded. No specific charges were made against him, but his hostility to the American cause was argued by implication. Thus it was asserted that he had hired two British soldiers, who had deserted, to work on his farm; that, when he was in Boston, these men being desirous to return to their allegiance, he had interceded with the British general to avert the punishment which the army awarded to deserters, in consequence of which intercession the men did return. Thompson defended himself on broad philanthropic grounds, and the court declared that it could not condemn him, but, as a concession to the popular excitement, it refused to exonerate him entirely from blame, or give him a full acquittal. This course he denounced upon the spot, and immediately petitioned the Committee of Safety, by whom the matter was referred to the Provincial Congress. The latter refused to grant the petition.

It is creditable to Thompson that, instead of seeking safety within the lines of the enemy, he retired to the camp of his own countrymen, who were by this time engaged in the siege of Boston. Here he employed himself in drilling the undisciplined recruits, and in making himself generally useful; but the obloquy which attached to his name could not be removed even by this devotion. He soon discovered that there was no hope of promotion for him; that he was an object of suspicion; and that he could not move from place to place within the lines of the army. Dispirited and wounded in his susceptibilities, it is not remarkable that he wearied of this hopeless struggle against prejudice, and resolved to leave an army which would not even look on him as a friend. His preparations for departure were conducted without the slightest attempt at secrecy. He converted into money all the property he could dispose of, paid off his debts, and about the 10th of October, 1775, left Cambridge. From that time to the close of the Revolutionary struggle his friends and relatives were without any positive tidings of his fate.

After leaving Cambridge, Thompson proceeded to Newport, probably with the intention of escaping by sea. Here he found a boat belonging to the British ship *Scarborough*, on board of which he was received. He appears to have remained in this vessel for several days, and then took passage in her to Boston. It is incredible that he went to this city of his own free will; we must rather suppose that he shipped himself on board the Scarborough under the impression that she was bound for some foreign port, and that he only discovered his mistake when it was too late to correct it. Certain it is that he went to Boston; was landed there, and remained in the city during all the operations of the American army, even to the moment of their triumphal entry. So securely was he hidden, however, that his nearest friends were unconscious of his whereabouts. During his stay in Boston he renewed his acquaintance with the English commander-in-chief (who was himself married to an American lady), and appears to have won the confidence of that officer. We have no evidence that Thompson was employed against his countrymen. If he harbored some resentment against them for the cruel way in which he had been treated, it is scarcely probable that it went to the extent of hostility to their interests, or of unnatural hatred to the country of his birth. Much as we must regret the situation in which we now find him, we can not think that there was any vengeful triumph in it.

When it became necessary to evacuate Boston, it became also necessary to send dispatches to England, informing the government of that necessity. Few officers were anxious to have this unpleasant commission intrusted to them, and the commanding general was unwilling to part with men who might be serviceable to him and the royal cause. In this emergency he had recourse to Major Thompson, to whom he intrusted his dispatches, and who immediately sailed for England in the ship that had conveyed him from Newport.

In due time Thompson was introduced to Lord George Germaine, Secretary of State for the Colonies, and delivered his dispatches. Lord George was struck with the personal appearance of Thompson, and, finding him well informed, offered him employment in the department over which he presided, probably with the view of obtaining exact information concerning the resources and temper of the colonies. The offer was too flattering to be rejected by Thompson in his present hapless state, and he closed with it without hesitation. No part of a man's experience is useless. Thompson soon found that his business knowledge, picked up in the counting-room and store, were of inestimable value in a sphere which seldom employed business men. He was able to get through a vast amount of work in a very short time, and became so eminently useful and reliable, that in less than four years he was promoted to the highest place in the department. Thrown in this way among the best-informed circles of the country, with ample means to maintain his position, he found opportunity once more to return to his philosophical pursuits. He became a regular attendant at the Royal Society's meetings, and soon afterward contributed to their "Transactions."

When Lord Germaine retired from the administration, he did not forget the services of Thompson, but obtained for him a commission as major in a regiment which had been lately formed, composed mostly of American Tories who had sought refuge in England, or been employed under English colors in America. In a short time he was promoted to the rank of lieutenant colonel. He embarked for America, but, we are happy to say, returned when there was no longer an occasion to lift his hand against the land of his birth. There being no employment for his regiment, he obtained leave of absence, and made a tour into Germany, with the intention, it is said, of offering his services to the Emperor of Austria. On the journey he was fortunate enough to make the acquaintance of Prince Maximilian of Deux-Ponts, afterward King of Bavaria, who, learning his design to enter the Austrian army, recommended him to visit Munich and inquire whether, in the employ of Bavaria, he might not find a quicker and better scope for his talents.

He gave him a letter of introduction to the Elector, and, armed with this, Thompson proceeded to Munich. His serene highness received him with favor, and offered him an instant appointment, holding out many inducements for him to remain; but Thompson seems to have been more strongly inclined toward Austria than he at first supposed, and determined, under any circumstances, to visit Vienna. In this city he remained some time, receiving frequent communications from the Elector urging him to return to Munich. At length Thompson consented to do so on condition that he could obtain permission of the King of England to accept service under a foreign potentate. The permission was at once granted, and the fortunate lieutenant colonel was allowed to retire on half pay. The English government, to mark its sense of the services he had rendered, also conferred on him the honor of knighthood. Thus provided with an income for life and a title, he returned to Munich toward the close of the year 1784. He was at once appointed aid-de-camp and chamberlain to the reigning prince.

Thompson's first exertions for the good of his new prince was to regenerate the army, which had, through neglect and abuse, sunk to a very low condition. In a short time he succeeded in introducing a system of discipline which was at once thorough and radically effective. He then turned his attention to the artillery force of the army, and by introducing a new system of tactics, and new contrivances for moving the carriages, etc., made it the finest corps in Europe. These labors were so successful, and so entirely in accordance with the wishes of the Elector, that he at once promoted Thompson to the Council of State, and made him also major general in the army. The scientific men of the electorate honored him also by admitting him as a member of the two academies of Munich and Manheim. A brief recapitulation of other honors bestowed on him during his stay in Germany may not here be out of place. In 1787 he was elected a member of the Academy of Sciences at Berlin; he was (in Bavaria) elevated to the rank of commander-in-chief of the general staff, minister of war, and superintendent of the police of the electorate; he was for a time chief of the regency that exercised sovereignty during the absence of the Elector, and was created Count of the Holy Roman Empire by Leopold. At his own solicitation, he selected as his title the name of the residence of his wife, and became Count of Rumford.

We now turn to Thompson's curious philanthropic and philosophical career. In Bavaria, at that time, begging was one of the principal conditions of life. It was a trade assiduously cultivated by a large portion of the population. So eager and pertinacious were the beggars, that they followed the citizen into his house, his store, his church. It was impossible to shake them off; they had gained courage by impunity, and actually looked on their profession as a legitimate one. Having made the army a respectable and industrious body of men, Thompson now determined to reform all the sturdy beggars, and win them to ways of industry. For this purpose, he organized a general descent on the mendicant community. New-Year's day was selected for the demonstration—a day on which they came out in strong force. Before night every beggar in the city was under arrest. They were conducted to the town hall, where their names were taken down. They were then dismissed, with instructions to present themselves the next day at the "Military Work-house," a building in the suburbs, which Thompson had had fitted up for the purpose, where they would find well-heated rooms, a warm dinner, and a supply of work provided for them. They were told that they would not be allowed to beg in the streets or elsewhere; that persons were appointed who would inquire into their circumstances, and afford them what relief they needed. To insure the utter annihilation of the begging system, the military guards stationed throughout the city were instructed to arrest all mendicants found in the streets, and to seek for those who failed to attend at the appointed place. The next day not a beggar was to be seen in all Munich; but at the military work-shop a motley crew presented itself, ragged, hungry, fierce, and dirty. Great confusion prevailed until the various cases were classified. Some were set to work immediately; others were placed under the charge of the physician; others were exempted from labor, and supplied with the necessary means of existence; but no one was allowed to go out into the world again to beg. The great object of all Thompson's measures was to elevate the poor wretches in their own opinion. Although arrested in the first instance, they were not locked up like criminals, and were simply dismissed on their promise to return the next day. In the work-shop they were not detained if they could obtain employment elsewhere. They wore, to be sure, a distinctive dress, but it was one of honor. According to the rules of the establishment, all new-comers were compelled to wear their old ragged clothes until, by good conduct, they had earned the privileged uniform. It became necessary, in the first instance, for the purpose of instruction, to separate husband from wife, and parents from children; but, so soon as the parents were found worthy of being trusted, the children were placed under their direction, and thus the halls of the establishment were speedily occupied with family groups.

In this manner begging was eradicated, and from a wretched community of mendicants hundreds of valuable workmen were produced. When the establishment commenced operations it had twenty-six hundred residents; in less than five years the number had decreased to fourteen hundred. In the same period, the finances were elevated from a loss of about twenty-five thousand dollars, to a profit, after paying wages to such as had shown themselves worthy, of forty thousand dollars. These praiseworthy and successful efforts were properly appreciated by the objects for whom they were made. When the inmates of the work-house had thrown off the dirt and sloth of their former habits, they began to perceive the great good that had been done to them, and to recognize in Thompson a benefactor sent for their especial deliverance. He became the object of the sincerest affection. When he was seized with sickness, all the inmates of the work-house went in procession to the Cathedral, where, at their request, divine service was performed, and public prayers offered for his recovery. Four years later, when the news of his being ill at Naples reached Munich, they voluntarily set apart an hour each evening to join in prayerful supplications for his recovery. It is pleasant to read of these things, and to believe they were sincere, so often does it happen in the world that those whom we would benefit are the first to turn round on us with unjust reproaches.

Thompson's career in Bavaria was that of a beneficent prince, eager alike for the dignity of his country and the happiness of his subjects. All his plans were based on broad and comprehensive principles, the justice of which only needed illustration on a scale of sufficient magnitude to be at once appreciated. We must deny ourselves the pleasure of following his career, and will barely mention that, during the remainder of his stay in Bavaria, he established a military academy at Munich, and conducted it under his own immediate auspices for six years. He endeavored to improve the breed of horses (which at that time was very shaggy and queer), for which purpose he imported a number of fine mares and loaned them to the farmers. He attempted, in like manner, to improve the breed of cattle, and with decided success. In carrying into effect these various schemes, he was often met by the interested opposition of men who envied his popularity and position. Having the entire confidence of the prince, he was able to beat down this factitious opposition, but it added the ingredient of trouble to his many labors. He overtasked himself, and his constitution began to show signs of decay. In 1794 he obtained leave of absence, and visited Italy to recruit his shattered system; the following year he paid a visit to England. The fame of his career had preceded him, and he became popular, especially with committees for improving the condition of the poor, who were constantly appealing to him for advice. To gratify them, and render a service to the indigent classes, he published the particulars of his system in Bavaria. During his stay he enlightened the Londoners on the proper way of curing smoky chimneys, and gave them some new and correct notions concerning the radiation of heat, by which their fire-places were made more comfortable and economical. At this time, too, he introduced his cooking-stove, and, according to his plans, the first of this now familiar article was set up in America (1798).

In 1796, Thompson accepted an invitation of the Secretary of State of Ireland to visit that country, for the purpose of giving his advice to various charitable institutions. A philanthropist of such a practical turn of mind was not only a rarity, but a blessing. In Dublin and other cities he superintended the erection of various establishments for benevolent purposes. The now common method of heating by steam was first employed by him in a laundry, where the apparatus heated the irons, warmed the water, aired the clothes, and cooked the dinners of the laundresses.

After his visit to Dublin, Thompson returned suddenly to Bavaria, in consequence of the critical position in which that country was placed by the war. Standing midway between the operating points of Austria and France, it seemed by no means improbable that Bavaria would be the field of battle for the contending forces. The Elector, alarmed at the state of things, was on the point of abandoning his capital when Thompson arrived in Munich; in deference to the latter, he deferred his departure for eight days, and then ran away in spite of all persuasion. Having, however, some kind of respect for Thompson's courage and discretion, he appointed a Council of Regency, at the head of which Thompson was placed. Within a few days the Austrian army arrived, but, to its astonishment, found the gates of the city shut. Batteries were immediately constructed and threats uttered; but Thompson was firm, and the neutrality of the Bavarian capital was maintained. The citizens were delighted, and the Elector heaped new honors on his favorite when he came back, which was after all the danger was over. Thopmson remained two years longer in Bavaria; but, finding that his health once more failed him, he concluded to return to England, the genial climate of which country had proved so beneficial in his previous sickness. As an expression of his esteem, the Elector furnished him with credentials as minister plenipotentiary and envoy extraordinary near the court of St. James. The intention was kindly, but, owing to the laws of England, which will not recognize a change of allegiance in an individual, he was not recognized in his diplomatic capacity, and therefore failed to obtain the position the Elector had hoped to secure for him within the exclusive circle of the court.

Instead, therefore, of wasting his time in the close and lazy atmosphere of palaces, he devoted himself once more to scientific pursuits. At this time the Royal Institution was not in existence, and the idea of founding it had been but just promulgated. Thompson was precisely the man to give practical importance to such a scheme. To his exertions and influence England is largely indebted for the honor which this institution—made illustrious by the names of so many men of genius—has shed on her scientific annals. While he was busily engaged in carrying out this project, he received intelligence of the death of his old friend and patron, the Elector Charles Theodore of Bavaria. His successor was the same Maximilian Joseph of Deux-ponts who had originally furnished him with a letter of introduction to the Bavarian court. This prince, having belonged to the opposition, did not view the popularity of Thompson with any especial favor. He was easily influenced by the representations of the latter's enemies. Thompson saw, therefore, that any farther residence in Bavaria would only tend to angry feeling and discomfort. These views were confirmed during a visit which he made after the peace. Although received with every politeness and consideration, he soon learned that it was not the intention of the administration to give him employment. After assisting in the reorganization of the Bavarian Academy of Sciences, he bade a final adieu to the electorate, and made a tour through Germany, Italy, Switzerland, and France. Unfortunately, there is no record of his adventures in these countries. It is scarcely probable that a man so widely known could have passed from place to place without some kind of valuable experience, or without coming in contact with leading men of similar views, philanthropic and philosophical, with himself.

In Paris Thompson found a city where his reputation and scientific attainments gave him at once a position of importance. He appears to have been delighted with it, and with reason. In addition to the fascinations of cultivated intercourse, he discovered on the borders of the scientific world a lady who was destined to become the partner of his joys and sorrows, and the companion of his journey down the valley of life. He had lost his first wife during his absence in Europe; Madame Lavoisier was the only woman he had met who seemed destined to fill her place in his affections. The lady was well to do, and, by virtue of her deceased husband's great reputation, occupied an elevated position in the best circles of Parisian society. A mutual attachment sprung up between them, which resulted in an indissoluble union. The date of the wedding is not known. In 1804 Thompson wrote to his mother to inform her of the event, and saying, "The lady I am to espouse is four years younger than myself, and is of a most amiable and respectable character." Immediately after his marriage he took up his residence at madame's country-seat at Auteuil, where he was destined to pass the remainder of his days.

We turn now to the record of his philosophical investigations and discoveries. Unfortunately, many of Thompson's papers (which would doubtless have thrown considerable light on these subjects) were stolen from him during a visit to London. "On my return to England," he says, "from Germany in October, 1795, after an absence of eleven years, I was stopped in my post-chaise, in St. Paul's Church-yard in London, at six o'clock in the evening, and robbed of a trunk which was behind my carriage, containing all my private papers, and my original notes and observations on philosophical subjects. By this cruel accident I have been deprived of the fruits of the labors of my whole life, and have lost all that I held most valuable. This most severe blow has left an impression on my mind which I feel that nothing will ever be able entirely to remove."

It will be remembered that Thompson's first experiment with gunpowder was of a kind to impress the force of that combustible on his mind in an extremely unpleasant manner. To this accident we may undoubtedly attribute his subsequent curiosity on the subject. From an early day down to the period of his military career in Bavaria, he was engaged in a series of philosophical investigations, having in view the projectile force of gunpowder, and how to economize it. One of his first papers, published in the "Transactions of the Royal Society," was on this subject, and the conclusions he arrived at were highly important to artillerymen, miners, and others who use gunpowder as a means of obtaining quick and remarkable force. These conclusions were new, and immediately became the basis of practical calculations which are acted upon to the present day.

A series of experiments were also performed by him in relation to the capabilities of various fabrics to absorb moisture, especially with regard to clothing. He demonstrated, what experience had already taught, that woolen goods were by far the most desirable for persons exposed to damp climates, or, when used next to the skin, for persons who were subject to profuse perspiration from heat. Experiments on light (a favorite subject with all philosophers, but treated practically by Thompson) followed. His investigations were confined to, 1. The relative quantities of light given by oil and tallow in lamps and candles; and, 2. The comparative cost of the substances giving equal quantities of light. In the course of these experiments he obtained many curious results then unknown to science, rendered all the more valuable by their adaptation to the ordinary purposes of life. He showed that light is not sensibly diminished by passing through moderate distances in the air; he determined the quantities of light lost in passing through plates of glass, and by reflection from mirrors; and determined the relative quantities of different substances consumed in the production of a certain quantity of light. The result of his experiments was that he considered the Argand lamp the most economical. While conducting these experiments he constructed a lamp of a novel kind, the light from which was so intense that the workman who illuminated it for the first time could not find his way home at night, in consequence of the blindness produced by its extreme brilliancy. This lamp has since become famous, but bears the name of Bude instead of Thompson, who was its inventor. Proceeding farther in his experiments, he examined the action of light in reducing the oxides of silver and gold, phenomena to which daguerreotypists are entirely indebted for their art. He also discovered that these metals, when in solution, may be reduced by charcoal, ether, the essential oils, and gum. It is barely probable that the nature of these experiments and their value will be appreciated by the general reader, but they were sufficient at the time to raise Thompson's name to the highest pinnacle of scientific fame. We have already referred to his experiments on the subject of heat, first instituted with a view to practical utility. Subsequently he continued them on philosophical principles, and obtained explanations of "the more important and extensive operations of nature upon the surface of the globe, and in some cases, as in that of the submarine polar currents, predicted what fifty years of subsequent observation have hardly yet exhibited in its full extent."

To the prosecution of his various occupations Thompson brought to bear a well-disciplined and perfectly methodical mind. He had a time for every thing, and was, in consequence, never hurried. So confirmed was he in habits of industry and method, that it was impossible to tear him from his accustomed task. His death took place on the 21st of August, 1814, at his villa in Auteuil, in the sixty-second year of his age. It was occasioned by a fever, and accelerated by his habits of method, which would not allow him, on this occasion, to desert his favorite occupations for the quiet and regimen of the sick-chamber.

By marriage and otherwise he was the possessor of an ample fortune, and before and after his death made several public dispositions of his money. He instituted prizes, liberally endowed, to be adjudged by the Royal Society of London and the American Academy of Sciences, for the most important discoveries of which light and heat should be the subject; he bequeathed an annual sum of one thousand dollars, together with the reversion of other property, to Harvard University, for the purpose of founding a professorship to teach "the utility of the physical and mathematical sciences, for the improvement of the useful arts, and for the extension of the industry, prosperity, happiness and well-being of society." Although Thompson proved by these liberal bequests that he remembered and was attached to his native country, he never saw it from the time of his first departure. At one time he was on the eve of returning, but circumstances occurred which prevented his fulfilling the intention. He had one daughter by his first wife, who visited him in England.

In the immediate vicinity of Munich is a beautiful ornamental park, with artificial lakes and mountains, and a great variety of splendid trees and flowers. It is a place of recreation, and free to the public, who roam there, and enjoy the fresh breeze and the fine scenery. Thompson caused this park to be laid out and dedicated in the way it is. The people were so thankful for the boon that they caused a monument to be erected in commemoration of Thompson's services in securing it. It has two principal fronts opposite to each other, ornamented with *basso-relievos* and inscriptions. On one side is an inscription in the German language, of which the following is a literal translation:

"Stay, Wanderer.
At the creative fiat of Charles Theodore,
Rumford, the friend of Mankind,
By Genius, Taste, and Love inspired,
Changed this once desert place
Into what thou now beholdest."

On the opposite side of the monument there is a bust of Count Rumford, and the inscription:

"To him
Who rooted out the greatest of Public Evils,
Idleness and Mendacity,
Relieved and instructed the Poor,
And founded many Institutions
For the education of our youth.
Go, Wanderer,
And strive to equal him
In genius and activity,
And us
In gratitude."

THOMAS POSEY.

THOMAS POSEY, whose life furnishes us with another instance of the undeviating integrity and enduring patriotism of the men who struggled for liberty in our Revolution and gained it, was born on the banks of the Potomac, in Virginia, on the 9th of July, 1750. He was in humble circumstances, and received but a scanty education. When he was nineteen years of age he removed to the western part of Virginia, near the frontiers, where he expected to engage in some profitable employment. A few years after his removal to this locality the country became involved in a general war with the Indians. In 1774, an expedition was undertaken against them by the British colonial governor, Lord Dunmore, and General Andrew Lewis. Mr. Posey received an appointment in the quarter-master's department, and marched with General Lewis's division of the army. The course of the army lay through a primitive wilderness, the fastnesses of which were yet unbroken by the foot of man. Difficulties of the most perplexing character were constantly occurring to obstruct the horses, baggage, munitions, and provisions which were under Posey's charge, but the coolness, perseverance, and industry which he displayed enabled him to reach the place of rendezvous in safety. Mr. Hall justly remarks that there was more merit and brilliancy in such an achievement than in the daring and the triumph of a successful battle, for the performance required more labor, more patient courage, more active patriotism than is usually called forth by the excitement of a battle.

On the 10th of October the Indians made their appearance in great force, and an obstinate and bloody engagement immediately ensued (Point Pleasant). They were led by the famous chief Corn-stalk, a chief who, unlike most of his contemporaries, had no fear of open warfare, and attacked Lewis's position with the skill of an experienced general. The battle lasted the entire day, and was at last decided in favor of the Virginians, who lost seventy-five men killed, and one hundred and forty wounded. The Indian loss was of course much greater, but, in accordance with their invariable custom, they carried off their dead, and left it impossible to discover what loss they had sustained. Shortly after this engagement, Lord Dunmore succeeded in effecting a treaty of peace with the Indians.

The battle of Point Pleasant was the first engagement in which Posey took part, although it is probable that at various times he had a hand in the frontier skirmishes which were incessantly waged between the settlers and the savages. He was a minute observer of all the operations of battle, and his imagination, being eminently of a military order, was fired with hot excitement. It is not remarkable, therefore, that when the war of Independence broke out, he was one of the first to enroll his name on the scroll of patriotism. At an early day he was appointed a captain in the regular service, and raised a company, which was incorporated with the seventh Virginia regiment, and afterward put upon the Continental establishment. The seventh regiment distinguished itself in a campaign against Lord Dunmore, and was subsequently ordered to join the army under the immediate command of General Washington. In the spring of 1777 it reached headquarters at Middlebrook, New Jersey—a large force of the enemy then lying at New Brunswick, a few miles distant, under the command of Lord Cornwallis. About this time General Washington authorized the formation of a picked rifle regiment, to be commanded by Colonel Daniel Morgan. The latter distinguished officer availed himself of the opportunity placed in his hand to select from all the army none but the best men. Among others, his choice fell upon Posey, who was at once honored with a captaincy. In this regiment, surrounded by master-spirits who looked on danger as their comrade, Posey distinguished himself equally with his gallant companions. It would be unfair to say more, for every man in that regiment was a patriot. One of the principal uses of a rifle corps is to harass an enemy rather than fight him; to engage the picket-guards, cut off the supplies, and surprise detached parties. Detected in such dangerous tactics, the rifleman receives no quarter, and, indeed, expects none; but the great importance of the service renders it vitally important to have none but the most reliable men in the corps. Morgan's regiment was essentially the "crack" one of the day, and by the daring rapidity of its movements performed inestimable service in the American cause.

In the spring of 1778, Colonel Morgan being on furlough, Lieutenant Colonel Butler having joined his regiment, and Major Morris having been killed, Captain Posey succeeded to the command of the rifle corps, now much reduced by the many actions in which it had taken part, and the hardships and privations it had endured. He continued to perform active duties until the British evacuated Philadelphia, when his detachment joined the army. Posey was promoted to the rank of major, and in 1779 was intrusted with the eleventh Virginia regiment of infantry, from which he was shortly after transferred to the command of a battalion, composing part of Febiger's regiment, under the orders of General Wayne. Under this illustrious commander he distinguished himself at the assault on Stony Point (15th July, 1779), and was the first to enter the main work of the enemy. Marshall, in his history, says that "Colonel Fleury was the first to enter the fort and strike the British standard. Major Posey mounted the works at the same instant, and was the first to give the watchword, '*The fort is ours.*'" In 1780, Posey was employed in the recruiting service, but assisted at the siege of Yorktown, where once more he witnessed the triumph of American arms. He returned to his recruiting station and organized a regiment, of which he obtained the command, having already been promoted to the rank of lieutenant colonel. With this regiment he repaired to Georgetown (1781–2), and served under General Wayne until the evacuation of Savannah by the British. When this event took place, Wayne, with his troops, was ordered to join General Greene in South Carolina. Charleston was evacuated a few months afterward, and Posey was ordered, with his battalion of light infantry, to follow the enemy as they marched out. This was his last employment in the Revolutionary war, as it was, indeed, the last occasion for his services. During the whole period in which the country was struggling for its liberties, Posey was at his post, ever foremost in the time of danger; ever prepared for the privations, disappointments, and misfortunes of that time which truly "tried men's souls." It is nothing for a man to be a patriot now. He has a country and a nationality to fight for; but in those times, a man, if he failed, was a rebel, and suffered an ignominious death, which, to a vast number of recruits, did not carry pity with it.

After the peace, Colonel Posey (who had lost his first wife) was married again (1783) to Mrs. Thornton, a young widow of considerable beauty and accomplishment, and immediately afterward settled in Spottsylvania county, Virginia. A family of ten children were the fruit of this marriage. In 1785 he was appointed captain of militia, and in the following year county lieutenant. He fulfilled the arduous duties of the latter appointment until 1793, when once more he entered, under the banner of General Wayne, as brigadier general, on a decisive campaign against the Indians. The expedition was successful, and much of its honor was reflected on Posey.

On quitting the regular service he settled in Kentucky, where his military reputation had preceded him, and paved the way to new honors. He was immediately elected to the Senate of the State, and was speaker of that body for four years, by virtue of his appointment of lieutenant governor. In 1809, apprehensions of war with England induced the Congress of the United States to provide for the contingency by raising an army of one hundred thousand men. The quota of Kentucky was five thousand men, and this large number was raised with the greatest possible ease. The command was intrusted to General Posey, with the rank of major general. It was an honor that any man might be proud of, for the troops were selected from the flower of the state, and represented some of the best and most patriotic families. The call, however, was premature; and, although Posey set about his duties with the celerity and discipline of earlier days, his exertions were, for the moment, of no avail. The army was disbanded. Governor Scott, of Kentucky, complimented Posey on the occasion. "While I felicitate my fellow-citizens on the prospect of our affairs," says that gentleman, "which has led to this event, permit me particularly to assure you that I entertain a high sense of the promptitude and zeal with which you undertook to discharge the duties of commander-in-chief of this corps. You have set an example of military spirit, at the expense of private convenience, which I hope ever to see imitated by the militia of this state, when the interest of their country is at stake. I beg leave to renew to you my sentiments of regard, and am sincerely your friend and obedient servant."

The purchase of Louisiana from the French opened a new field of enterprise for the South, and among those who determined to settle there was General Posey. Although sixty years of age, he made an exploration into the interior, and finally purchased land in Attakapas, and removed thither with part of his family. When, in 1812, hostilities were about to commence with Great Britain, he gave a fresh illustration of his patriotism by raising a volunteer company at Baton Rouge, of which he condescended to accept the captaincy. In the same year General Posey was elected senator in the Congress of the United States. He repaired to Washington, and served there until March, 1813, when he was appointed governor and commander-in-chief of the Territory of Indiana. This territory was one of the most exposed in the country; infested by hostile Indians, and threatened by the British. Its management required military firmness and experience, which were certainly secured in the appointment of General Posey. He fulfilled the duties of his responsible office until 1816, when the territory became a state.

On relinquishing the government of Indiana, General Posey was appointed Agent for Indian Affairs, the important duties of which office he continued to perform to the day of his death. It was the last position in which he was permitted to serve his country. On the 19th of March, 1818, General Posey departed this life, after a violent attack of typhus fever. The event took place at Shawneetown, Illinois, and was occasioned by a severe cold, which terminated fatally in the way we have mentioned at the end of eight days. The consolations of religion had prepared his spirit for the final change, and when the moment arrived he was ready. Among his papers were found (in his own handwriting) a brief sketch of his life, a letter of advice to his children and grandchildren, and a letter to his wife, to be delivered after his death.

"In the prime of his life," says Mr. Hall, to whom we are indebted for some of the facts in this sketch, "General Posey was remarkable for his personal appearance; tall, athletic, and finely formed, with singularly handsome features, his exterior was very prepossessing. His figure was dignified and graceful, and in his manners the bearing of the soldier was harmoniously blended with the ease of the refined gentleman."

ISRAEL PUTNAM.

THE rich and glorious military history of America is studded with bright names gathered from the dark masses of the time—men who abandoned their humble homes for the tented field, and after a while returned to their homesteads clothed in victory, amid rejoicings and patriotic ovations. Many of these names, of the richer sort too, belong of right to the biography of self-made men. Accident may make a man famous, but it does not make him patriotic. This he owes to a native principle, the product of the soil to which he belongs, and his own large and generous nature. To be more than thousands of his neighbors, to be illustrious in the annals of his country, he must call into play all the self-denial, all the firmness, all the clear-visioned determination of the self-made. Nothing in the world is more natural than patriotism, but nothing in the world is more difficult than being a patriot.

We all know something of Israel Putnam. The romantic story of his life is one of the earliest that attaches us to our daring history, and impresses it vividly on our mind. He was born at Salem, in Massachusetts, on the 7th of January, 1718, his father being a farmer. Education in those days was not, as now, within the easy grasp of the aspiring. People in moderate circumstances were unable to command more than the scantiest smattering of knowledge. Life was physical rather than intellectual; men looked to their hands more than their heads. Young Israel learned a few English branches, and then turned his attention to farming. He was blessed with a good constitution, and strengthened it by a hearty participation in all the manly sports of the time. When only twelve years of age he gave an indication of that strength and courage which were his distinguishing characteristics later in life. It happened that he went to the city of Boston on a visit, and, while quietly trudging through the streets with his hands in his pockets and his eyes wide open, attracted the attention of an impudent city boy, much his superior in age and size. This youth thought it would be capital fun to ridicule the rustic appearance and gait of Israel, and for this purpose followed him through the streets. Israel submitted to his sneers for a short time, and then turned on his tormentor. In a very short time he gave him a complete drubbing.

In the twenty-first year of his age Israel was united in marriage to a Miss Pope, of Salem, and immediately afterward removed to Pomfret, in Connecticut, where he purchased a considerable tract of land, and applied himself closely to cultivation. In the enjoyment of home comfort, and in the pursuit of an honest and healthy independence, there is but little in his life during this period which need be recalled in a biography. One little story, however, must be preserved. In those days the neighborhood of Pomfret was greatly infested by wolves. So great were their depredations, that, in a single night, Putnam lost no fewer than twenty sheep and goats, besides having a number of lambs wounded. All sorts of possible means were employed to destroy these voracious robbers, and generally with success; but there was an old she-wolf who defied all the ingenuity of the farmers. She paid her visits every night to the sheepfold, and, after partaking of a hearty supper, retired to her den in a neighboring cavern. On one occasion she had been caught in a trap, and had left a part of her foot behind in order to effect her escape. The mark of the injured foot could be traced after her nocturnal visits, especially if there had been a slight fall of snow, so that every one knew it was this defiant old lady that caused so much mischief every night, and perhaps initiated younger and more timid depredators. Putnam and a few of his neighbors determined to pursue the robber. Without much difficulty they discovered her den. Dogs were sent in, but they soon came forth wounded and howling; no amount of persuasion could induce them to go in again. Straw and brimstone were lighted at the mouth of the cave, but the stifling fumes had no effect on the hearty constitution of the old she-wolf. After continuing their efforts until late at night, they were about abandoning their game, when Putnam proposed that his negro man should descend into the cavern and shoot the wolf. All things considered, it was not at all remarkable that the negro man declined the honor; it is more remarkable that Putnam should have thought it necessary to reproach him with cowardice. Perfectly resolved not to be foiled, Putnam now undertook the dangerous task, against the wish of his friends and neighbors, who remembered how the dogs had been used, and could scarcely expect a better fate for Israel. Stripping off his coat and waistcoat, and placing a rope round his body, so that he might be drawn back at a concerted signal, he entered the cavern head foremost, holding in his hand a torch of lighted birch bark.

The aperture of the den, on the east side of a very high ledge of rocks, was about two feet square; thence it descended obliquely fifteen feet, and, running horizontally about ten more, gradually ascended sixteen feet, toward its termination. The sides of the cavern were of smooth solid rocks, apparently divided by some violent convulsion of nature. Its floor and top were also of stone, and when covered with ice in winter, its entrance was extremely slippery. In no place was it three feet wide, or high enough for a man to stand upright. Through this long and perilous cavern Putnam groped his way, creeping cautiously on all fours, and waving his torch, until he was arrested by a sullen and fierce growl. Peering into the darkness, he detected the glaring eyeballs of the wolf, flashing defiance on him from the extreme end of the den. Having thus explored the hunting-ground, he gave the signal, and was dragged out so precipitately by his friends (who, hearing the growl, were quite certain that something very dreadful had happened) that his clothes were torn to rags, and his body sadly lacerated. Undeterred by this little accident, he proceeded to load his musket with nine buck-shot, and then for the second time entered the cave. He approached the animal nearer than before, in spite of her fierce and threatening aspect; still nearer and nearer he crept up to her, until she seemed in the very act of springing; then, with a steady hand and true eye, he discharged the musket full at her head. Stunned by the repercussion, and almost suffocated by the smoke, he was again drawn forth. He was too anxious to wait long for the result. In a few moments he descended into the cave for the third time, seized the wolf by the mane, and dragged her out. To the delight and exultation of every one, she was quite dead.

Putnam was thirty-seven years of age when the war which preceded the American Revolution broke out between France and England. As a farmer, he had distinguished himself by great industry and prudence, resulting necessarily in easy circumstances; it was now that he appeared for the first time on the stage of public life. In 1755 he was appointed captain of a company in Lyman's regiment of provincials, which were among the first troops raised in Connecticut on that occasion. With Major Rogers and his company Putnam traversed the wilderness, to gain information, reconnoitre the enemy's line, capture straggling parties, cut off supplies, and generally do all the mischief in their power. Their immediate object was to obtain a correct knowledge of the situation and condition of the fortifications at Crown Point. A delicate task of this kind required more than mere bravery; it demanded prudence and coolness. Putnam soon perceived that it was impossible to approach the fortifications with his company without great danger of detection by stragglers from the garrison. He proposed, therefore, that he and Rogers should go alone, leaving their troops in some safe shelter until their return. During the evening, they advanced so near the fort that they were able to gain all the information their general needed. Once they were nearly detected; a Frenchman caught hold of Rogers, and, after vainly trying to stab him, shouted out to the guard for assistance. Putnam rushed to the rescue of his companion, and, with a single blow from the butt-end of his musket, silenced his captor forever. They made their escape before the guard came up. It was probably owing to the successful issue of this reconnoitring party that Putnam, assisted by Lieutenant Durkee, was intrusted with a similar delicate operation. They were to reconnoitre the enemy's camp at the

Ovens, near Ticonderoga. The French were lodged round their fires, instead of the fires being placed round the men, as in the English camp; their sentinels were, consequently, secreted in the surrounding darkness. Ignorant of this disposition, Putnam and the lieutenant crept cautiously on their hands and knees toward the camp, when, to their great surprise, they found themselves entirely encircled by the enemy. They were quickly observed and fired upon, Lieutenant Durkee receiving a slight wound. In their hurry to escape, Putnam fell into a clay-pit, and Durkee followed. Imagining that the latter was an enemy, Putnam had raised his arm to stab him, when he recognized Durkee's voice. Springing from the pit with fresh activity, they made good their retreat, followed by a perfect storm of bullets. When Putnam loosened his canteen to give a little rum to his wounded companion, he was astonished to find that it had been perforated with bullets, and all the treasured liquor gone. His blanket, too, was pierced with fourteen holes, so that he had had even a narrower escape than with the wolf. In this and similar hazardous undertakings he continued to be employed, always displaying undaunted bravery, and great judgment and presence of mind. The reputation which he gained by these exploits won for him the appreciation of the Provincial Legislature of Connecticut, who, as a recognition of his merits, promoted him to the rank of major in 1757.

At the siege of Fort William Henry, Putnam distinguished himself by obtaining much valuable information concerning the movements of the enemy, which, had it been acted on with promptness and courage, would have averted the sad fate of that fort, and the subsequent massacre by the Indians, which has made it odious. Putnam reached the scene of carnage just as the rear guard of the French were embarking on the lake. The bodies of brutally-murdered human beings lay around him in every direction; hundreds of women and of children were heaped on the smouldering ruins of the barracks and fort. We can imagine the emotions of Putnam as he gazed on the scene, knowing, as he did, that if the general had but possessed an atom of his courage, all might have been averted. In view of this, posterity has forgiven him a disobedience to orders, which certainly occurred soon after. Putnam, with his Rangers, were stationed on a little island in Lake George, and intelligence was brought that a fatigue party, under Captain Little, was in danger of utter destruction by the French and Indians. Without a moment's hesitation, they dashed into the water and rushed to the rescue. As they passed the fort, the general peremptorily ordered them back to quarters. Putnam was seized with sudden deafness, and did not hear the order until after Captain Little's party had been rescued from the danger which threatened it. Disobedience to orders in the army is an awful crime, but, in consideration of the service rendered, no court-martial was held on the major.

There are so many kinds of bravery, that it not unfrequently happens that a perfectly courageous man may display weakness on some one point. He may be afraid of having a tooth pulled, or of crossing a stream in the dark, or of going up to the top of a high ladder. One of the most natural fears, even among the bravest of the brave, is the fear of fire. In 1757, the barracks of Fort Edward took fire, and would have extended to the magazine, which was only twelve feet distant, and contained 300 barrels of gunpowder, had it not been for Putnam's individual perseverance, bravery, and coolness. He took his post on the roof of the barracks, and threw water on the flames until roasted from his position. Colonel Haviland, who had command of the fort, urged him to desist from his perilous efforts, but he begged permission to remain and continue his labors. He was now standing between the magazine and the flames, the external planks of the former frequently taking fire. A moment's delay in extinguishing the flame, wherever it appeared, would have resulted in instant destruction. Every one knew this; but such was the force of good example, that not a man would desert his post at the bucket-line; even the colonel expressed a desire that they might all be blown up together. At length the fire was happily extinguished. Putnam had labored at it for nearly two hours; his face, his breast, his arms were terribly blistered, and when he drew off the mittens on his hands the flesh came away too, and left all the nerves exposed. It was many weeks before he was able to go out, after this heroic display of stoical courage.

During the reverses of Abercrombie at Ticonderoga, Putnam performed good service, but was, of course, unable to divert the unfortunate tendency of events. The weak point of the campaign was that green English officers, who knew nothing whatever of the Indian element in warfare, and were otherwise ignorant of the local precautions necessary to insure safety to an army—that these fine-feathered gentlemen were placed in command, not only of the European troops, which they might understand, but also of the American auxiliaries, which they could not. Had more reliance been placed on shrewd, cool officers like Putnam, the disasters would certainly have been fewer. We have no intention of following the events of this period, and shall therefore merely select those in which our hero was mainly interested.

One day, while Putnam, with five men, was lying in a boat near the Rapids by Fort Miller, he received a sudden warning that the Indians were upon him. Before he had time to escape, the savages fired upon the little party, and killed one of its number. There seemed scarcely a hope of retreat. On either side were the Indians, in front the Rapids, and thus what seemed to be certain death in every direction. Without a moment's hesitation, Putnam preferred risking the Rapids. Seizing the helm, he steered straight into the vortex of the foaming waters. The boat was whirled round like a chip on the surface of a whirlpool, but his steady hand kept it in the channel, and carried it past all impediments, until, like an arrow, it darted into the tranquil waters below. It is said that the Indians were so overcome by this exhibition of cool skill that they looked on it as something supernatural, and conceived it would be an affront to the Great Spirit to kill this favored mortal with powder and ball.

Up to this time we have had nothing but good luck to record of Major Putnam. On one of his reconnoitring expeditions, however, he was ambuscaded, and, after a fierce struggle, captured. While the two parties were still hotly contesting the ground, he was tied to a tree, and exposed to the cross-fire of friends and foes. At length he was untied by his captors, stripped of his clothing, laden with the packs of the wounded, tightly pinioned, and in this sad plight forced to march many miles, in the midst of triumphant enemies, to Ticonderoga, where he was examined by the French commander-in-chief, the Marquis of Montcalm. He was afterward removed to Montreal, and treated with great humanity and indulgence. Here, through the intercession of Colonel Schuyler, he soon obtained his release, in an exchange of prisoners which took place between the two armies.

In 1760 the English triumphs in Canada were almost perfected. Montreal was the only important post remaining in the hands of the French. To reduce this, General Murray was ordered to ascend the River St. Lawrence; Colonel Haviland, with the second corps, was directed to penetrate by the Isle au Noix; while 10,000 men under Amherst were to pass up the Mohawk, traverse Lake Ontario, and, by descending the St. Lawrence, unite with the other two divisions. To this latter corps was Putnam attached. In falling down the river, they came upon an unexpected obstruction in the shape of two armed vessels, and farther progress was for the moment impossible. Putnam was the first to volunteer to clear the way. With a thousand men and fifty boats he undertook to carry the vessels by boarding. At the appointed moment the flotilla started on its way. The victory, however, was bloodless. Dismayed by the force brought against them, the crews of the armed vessels compelled their commanders to haul down the colors. The next point of attack was the fort of Oswegatchie, situated on an island, and defended by a high abatis of black ash, projecting every where over the water. A mode of attack was devised by Putnam, and immediately put in operation. Each boat was surrounded with fascines, musket-proof, and a board, twenty feet long, fixed in the manner of a half draw-bridge, which was to be dropped on the pointed bush. The signal was given for the attack, but the sight of the strange machinery disconcerted the besieged, and they, like their marine compatriots, surrendered without a blow.

In the rupture between Spain and Great Britain in 1762, a formidable expedition against Havana was committed to the charge of Lord Albemarle. One of the contingents was a Connecticut regiment, one thousand strong, under the command of Putnam. The transports arrived in safety off the Queen of the Antilles, but a storm arose, and Putnam and five hundred of his party were wrecked upon a dangerous reef of rocks. By much industry and fatigue they reached the main land, where they made a fortified camp, and remained unmolested. Their presence was of infinite service in the subsequent reduction of Havana.

The general peace in Europe of 1763 put an end to these large struggles, but the Indians in America were still hostile. Putnam's great experience made him a very desirable officer against this savage foe, and, with the rank of colonel, he proceeded to the West, under General Bradstreet's command, and remained until the Indians had been brought to a state of subjection. Putnam's military career seemed now at an end. He had served his country gallantly and faithfully for ten years, and, laying his honors meekly on the national altar, returned to his homestead, and once more peacefully followed the plow.

The obnoxious Stamp Act was warmly opposed by Putnam. He was one of the most active in preventing the circulation of the objectionable paper. In 1766 the act was ungraciously repealed, and Putnam once more resumed his agricultural labors; but the agitation which had been provoked by the folly of the English government was not destined to die ingloriously. It was perfectly understood that, although the government had abandoned its position from outside pressure, it did not surrender what it conceived to be a right. These matters were warmly discussed in the various states, and still more hotly in the principal cities. Putnam made frequent visits to Boston, and was known as one in whom perfect confidence might be placed when the hour of trial should arrive. On the 19th of April, 1775, the news of the battle of Lexington was carried to Putnam as he was laboring in the field. He left his plow standing in the furrow, threw himself across one of the team, and, without a moment's delay, hurried to the scene of action, without even waiting to change his clothes. Two days later he attended a council of war at Cambridge, and throughout the struggle which now commenced, took an active command. At Bunker Hill the coolness and intrepidity of his action contributed in a large measure to the glory of the American cause. It is supposed, and with every show of reason, that he had entire command of the forces on this occasion.

The incidents of our glorious struggle have been so often rehearsed, and belong so essentially to history, that in a biography of this brief kind it would scarcely be desirable to repeat them. The great hero was Washington, and whom he honored we honor. From the first Putnam secured the respect and confidence of this great man, and was frequently complimented in General Orders. Not only did he bring invincible courage and patriotism to the cause of his country, but, what was almost of equal importance in those dark days, he possessed rare tact—the faculty of making insufficient means abundantly satisfactory. An illustration will suffice. Captain Macpherson, a Scotch officer of the seventeenth British regiment, had received, in the battle of Princeton, a severe wound, which every one thought would prove fatal. Putnam visited the wounded prisoner, procured surgical assistance, administered to his comforts, and solaced him in the apparent hour of death. Contrary to every prognostication, the captain recovered; but, prior to this, in the darkest hour of his suffering, he made a request to Putnam that a friend in the British army might be permitted to come and aid him in the preparation of his will. The general was involved in great perplexity. On the one hand, he was charitably anxious to gratify the dying prisoner; on the other, he was very unwilling that an officer from the enemy's camp should spy out his own weakness. His presence of mind and natural shrewdness helped him out of the difficulty in an extremely amusing way. A flag of truce was dispatched, with orders not to return with the captain's friend until after dark. "By the time of his arrival lights were displayed in all the apartments of the College Hall, and in all the vacant houses in the town; and the army, which then consisted of fifty effective men, were marched about with remarkable celerity, sometimes in close column, and sometimes in detachments, with unusual pomp and circumstance, around the quarters of the captain. It was subsequently ascertained, as we are assured by Colonel Humphreys, that the force of Putnam was computed by the framer of the will, on his return to the British camp, to consist, on the lowest estimate, of five thousand men." It is in emergencies of this kind that the native genius of a man displays itself. Decision and firmness of character were ever manifest in all that Putnam undertook to perform. We will give an instance where these qualities were displayed in a tragic manner. Edmund Palmer, a lieutenant in a Tory regiment, had been discovered in the American camp. To avert the fate of a spy, the commander of the British forces sent a flag of truce to Putnam, claiming the prisoner as a British officer, and intimating that his execution would be attended with serious consequences. Putnam returned the flag with the following characteristic and perfectly dramatic note:

"Head-quarters, 7th August, 1777.

"Edmund Palmer, an officer in the enemy's service, was taken as a spy lurking within our lines; he has been tried as a spy, condemned as a spy, and shall be executed as a spy, and the flag is ordered to depart immediately.

"Israel Putnam.

"P.S.—He has been accordingly executed."

The only reverse which Putnam ever met with, in his singularly eventful life, was at Fort Montgomery, which, owing to insufficient support, he was compelled to abandon to the enemy. The subsequent movements were not in accordance with the orders of the commander-in-chief, and Washington consequently expressed some dissatisfaction with Putnam. A Congressional inquiry was made into the matter, and, in deference to public clamor, he was, for a time, superseded in his command. This, however, did not dampen his ardor. He returned to Connecticut, raised new levies, and displayed all his old activity. About this time he was the hero of a well-known exploit. One day, while visiting his outposts at West Greenwich, he was surprised by Governor Tryon with a corps of fifteen hundred men. Putnam had only a hundred and fifty men and two pieces of artillery to defend himself against this overpowering force. With these, he took his station on the brow of a steep declivity. As the British advanced, they were received with a sharp fire from the artillery; but, perceiving the dragoons about to charge, Putnam ordered his men to retire to a swamp inaccessible to cavalry, while he himself forced his horse directly down the precipice. His pursuers, who were close upon him, were horror-stricken at the audacity of the thing, and paused breathlessly until he was out of danger. The declivity, from this circumstance, has since borne the name of Putnam's Hill.

During the campaign of 1779, which terminated General Putnam's military career, he commanded the Maryland line. Being stationed two miles below West Point, at Buttermilk Falls, he directed the principal part of his attention to strengthening the works of that important fortress. In December, when the American army went into winter-quarters at Morristown, New Jersey, he obtained leave of absence to visit his family for a few weeks. As he was journeying toward Hartford, on his way back to Morristown, his progress was arrested by an attack of paralysis, by which the use of his limbs on one side was lost. He was unwilling to admit the real character of the disease, and endeavored, by vigorous exercise, to throw off the torpidity. The effort was unavailing, and for the remainder of his eventful life he was an invalid. On the 17th of May, 1790, he was suddenly attacked by an inflammatory disease, and two days later died. His remains were borne to the grave with the usual ceremonies due to a distinguished military commander, and a feeling eulogy was pronounced on the occasion. He was consoled in the last few years of his life with the knowledge that the cause which he had espoused with such signal ardor and intrepidity had triumphed, and that he had been one of the humble instruments in the hands of a divine Providence to raise a down-trodden colony to the dignity and glory of a great nation.

JOHN PRIDEAUX.

The story of John Prideaux, a quaint fragment of early biography, affords at once an instructive lesson, and an amusing insight into an early period of English history. Prideaux was born on the 17th of December, 1578, at Stowford, near Plymouth, England. His father was in moderate circumstances, but, owing to the requirements of a large family, was unable to supply his sons with liberal educations. John, who was the fourth, was merely taught to read and write. In spite of this drawback, he was soon destined to enter on public life. The parish clerk of Ugborough, a village about five miles from Stowford, had died, and his office was still vacant. John Prideaux was gifted with a fine voice, and, in spite of his youth, determined on applying for the situation. There was another competitor in the field—an experienced man, who had canvassed the village in a thoroughly business-like way. The parishioners determined on giving the rivals a fair trial, and arranged that one of the competitors should give out the psalms in the morning, and the other in the afternoon, and that the place should be given to the candidate who was most approved by the congregation. The result was what might have been expected—experience carried the day; the parishioners decided in favor of Prideaux's rival. It was fortunate that it so happened. In later days he used to say, "If I could have been parish clerk of Ugborough, I never should have been Bishop of Worcester." But the disappointment was a trying one, and bruised his young heart. There was a kind old lady in the village who observed the earnestness of his sorrow, and sympathized with it. She comforted the poor young fellow, and told him that "God might design him for greater things, and therefore he ought not to lament having failed in his recent attempt." She did more than this; she placed him at the grammar-school, and maintained him there until he had acquired some knowledge of Latin and the higher branches of a solid education. A very kind and sensible gentlewoman was Mistress Fowell.

Prideaux's thirst for knowledge was now thoroughly aroused;

the country school could not supply his wants, and he determined to perfect his education at an English University. Accordingly, quitting parents, relatives, friends, and the scenes of his childhood, he set out for Oxford, performing the journey on foot, and trusting entirely to his good fortune for the result. The journey was a long and dismal one, and not without danger. He suffered many privations, but, in spite of these, reached Oxford in safety. At this renowned seat of learning he repaired to Exeter College, then largely patronized by gentlemen from the county of Devon. It is probable that he had some acquaintances there, or, at all events, some family friends, who would lend him a helping hand. He was an ingenuous lad, with engaging manners, and an open, frank way of looking people in the face; and then he was an enthusiast not easily repulsed. To some of these causes must be attributed his success; he obtained admission to the college. His situation at first was but an humble one, he being employed as an assistant in the kitchen and in other menial offices. There are many fine minds that would sink beneath the degrading drudgery of such a situation, but Prideaux conceived it to be no disgrace to begin on the lowest step of the ladder. He never complained, but, on the contrary, was so cheerful and happy that he obtained the good-will of every one. The consequence was, that in 1596 he was admitted a poor-scholar of Exeter College, and was placed under the tuition of Mr. William Helme, an able scholar, and Bachelor of Divinity. He now applied himself to study with a vigor which would have been fatal to a man with a less robust constitution. Night and day he pored over his books, and, being gifted with a remarkably tenacious memory, was soon able to master their contents. In less than three years he obtained his degree of Bachelor of Arts (1599); three years later, he was elected a probationer fellow of his college (1602). In the following year he obtained his master's degree, and soon after entered into holy orders. To the study of divinity he directed all his energies, and he became recognized as the best theologian in the college. His bachelor's degree in divinity was taken in 1611, his master's degree in the following year. This was, indeed, rapid promotion for a poor boy who had worked his way to learning through the pots and kettles of the kitchen; but a greater honor was in store for him; in 1612 he was elected Rector of Exeter College. Quaint old Anthony à Wood says, that "in the rectorship of his college he carried himself so winning and pleasing, by his gentle government and fatherly instruction, that it flourished more than any house in the University with scholars, as well of great as of mean birth; so also with many foreigners that came purposely to sit at his feet to gain instruction." In 1615 Prideaux succeeded to the professorship of divinity in the University, to which office are annexed a canonry of Christ Church, and the rectory of Ewelme in Oxfordshire. In the professional chair he was a strenuous assailant of the doctrines of Arminius and Socinus, which were at that time gaining ground. His lectures were remarkable for vigor and perspicuity. Prince, in his account of the worthies of Devon, characterizes the style of Prideaux as being "manly for the strength, maidenly for the modesty, and elegant for the phrase thereof." It was also said of him that "the heroic spirit of Jewel, Rainolds, and Hooper, as though they were united in him, seemed once more to triumph, and to threaten the hierarchy of Babylon with a fatal blow."

Prideaux held the professorship of Divinity for twenty-seven years, during which period he filled the dignified office of vice-chancellor five times. He was also domestic chaplain to Prince Henry, son of James I., and subsequently to King James himself, and Charles the First. These honors and preferments did not make him unmindful of his origin. He was uniformly compassionate to the poor, and to his parents affectionate and beneficent. The latter he delighted to surprise with unexpected visits, and by generous bounty to gladden their hearts, and cheer their path of life. In one of his visits to Devonshire for this purpose, as he passed through the parish of Ugborough, the church bell was tolling. On being told that it was for the funeral of an old woman who had been his godmother, he suspended his journey, accompanied the body to the grave, and delivered a suitable discourse upon the occasion. There is not much in an incident of this kind; but it shows a simple nature, and an estimable trait in an ecclesiastic, who might, under such circumstances, consult dignity rather than natural impulse. Though unfeignedly pious, Prideaux was of a cheerful disposition, and loved to exhibit a chaste and elegant wit, always gay, but never bitter. He was fond of manly sports, and was an excellent archer.

A man of so much distinction could not fail of preferment. On the 2d of November, 1641, he was nominated Bishop of Worcester, and in the following December was consecrated. The office was a dignified one, but it was beset with perils. A sense of duty rather than a love of power induced him to accept it. The tyranny of Laud, and the slavish doctrines taught by many of the prelates, had ulcerated the minds of the people, and made them loathe the mitre and all who wore it. Only eight days after the consecration of Prideaux, nearly one half of the English bishops were guilty of an act which, under all the circumstances, would seem to have been prompted by insanity, or by passion bordering on insanity. Misled by the intriguing Archbishop of York, eleven prelates signed with him that extraordinary protest, by which they took upon themselves to nullify all proceedings that might take place in Parliament during their absence. Public indignation was intense, and too bitter to be discriminate. Although Prideaux's name did not appear in the obnoxious document, he was doomed to share the odium it occasioned.

In those days there were many wise men who believed in the divine right of kings (as if there was any thing divine in brutal stupidity, tyranny, and wrong), and Prideaux was unhappily of the number. When the people took up arms against the sovereign, Prideaux endeavored to intrench himself behind prerogative, and to intimidate his foes by threats of excommunication. The torrent was too strong for such puny efforts. He was plundered, expelled, laid under sequestration, and at last reduced to such straits that he was fain to sell his valuable library and some fragments of property to provide for the wants of his family. "Having first, by indefatigable studies," says old Anthony, "digested his library into his mind, he was after forced again to devour all his books with his teeth, turning them, by a miraculous faith and patience, into bread for himself and his children." Prideaux explains the process with wonderful equanimity and humor. Being questioned about his health, he replied, "Never better in my life, only I have too great a stomach, for I have eaten that little plate which the sequestrators left me; I have eaten a great library of excellent books; I have eaten a great deal of linen, much of my brass, some of my pewter, and now I am come to eat iron, and what will come next I know not."

Prideaux survived his misfortunes for many years, and outlived the king for whom he had made so great a sacrifice. On the 20th of July, 1650, Prideaux departed this life, leaving to his offspring a "pious poverty, God's blessing, and a father's blessing." The event drew forth various eulogiums, and Cleveland, the poet, sang his praises in exalted verse. Prideaux was twice married, and had a large family. As a writer, he has left several works, principally in the Latin tongue, which evince great learning and clearness. In his habits he was devout, simple-minded, humble, and virtuous. He had a horror of any thing like pride, and, as a perpetual remembrancer of his humble origin, the coarse attire in which he walked from Stowford to Oxford was hung up in his wardrobe, by the side of his episcopal robes. He was emphatically a good man, and a remarkable instance of that strength of character which is the peculiar blessing of self-made men, and which, wherever and whenever manifest, rises superior to iron fortune and cruel circumstances.

ROGER WILLIAMS.

THE founder of religious toleration in the New World is justly esteemed a worthy of American history, and his name will endure so long as civilization shall have its records. Of the early history of this illustrious individual we know nothing, except that, whatever his birth and education, he had to fight his way in the world. In England, of which country he was a subject (having been born in Wales in the year 1599), the independence of his views, and the earnestness with which he inculcated them from the pulpit, soon raised him up an army of enemies and detractors. To escape these, he emigrated on the 1st of December, 1630, in the ship *Lion*, from the port of Bristol. After a tempestuous voyage of sixty-six days, he arrived at Boston on the 5th of February, 1631, where he was received by the Church with every manifestation of delight. Williams's reputation as a powerful and earnest preacher had preceded him, and the theocracy of Narraganset Bay looked to him as an instrument of might sent for their special good. There is no doubt but he was, although not in the way they intended.

It seems strange in these days to say that a man was "remarkable" for advocating entire freedom of conscience; yet such was the case with Roger Williams. The doctrine was new and particularly unpalatable in England. In Massachusetts it was equally offensive. He left the former country in consequence, but in the latter he was determined to fight it out. It will be seen in the sequel that the struggle was long and bitter, but triumphant. Society, as it then existed in Massachusetts, was completely under the dictation of the Church. The religious and the civil power were blended together, and the people, accustomed to it, and to a great extent preferring it, bent their necks or their knees, as occasion demanded. They did not think for themselves, but left that task to their pastors, believing that it was impossible to think rightly in the absence of clerkly lore. Then, if they neglected their duty, they submitted to the interposition of the magistrates, who made them do all that the pastors said they ought to do. In such a community Roger Williams was not destined to be long at peace. Very shortly after his arrival he removed to Salem, and, in opposition to the magistrates of Boston, became minister of the church there. As his opinions became known, the opposition became more intense and irksome. Notwithstanding some popularity in Salem, he found it desirable, for the sake of peace and quietness, to remove out of the jurisdiction of the court of Massachusetts Bay, and seek a secluded home in the colony of Plymouth. For this purpose he migrated in the autumn of 1631, and was cordially received by the Pilgrim fathers; but the court of Massachusetts pursued him, and tried very hard to frighten away his congregation with rumors of heresy. It is probable that this hostility was not without its result, for in August of 1633 we find Roger Williams returning to Salem, as if with the special object of bearding the lion in his den. His residence in Plymouth was principally remarkable for numerous excursions among the Indians, during which he studied their language, and obtained much moral power over many chiefs of tribes. "God was pleased to give me," he says, "a painful, patient spirit, to lodge with them in their filthy, smoky holes, even while I lived at Plymouth and Salem, to gain their tongue."

With his second sojourn in Salem Roger Williams's eventful history properly commences. The magistrates renewed their hostility, but, in spite of this, he succeeded in obtaining the pastorship of the church. One of his first acts was to call in question the expediency of a meeting of ministers, which had been established in the colony for the discussion of questions in theology, and for other similar purposes of mutual improvement. The magistrates saw in this the indications of a wavering orthodoxy, which might at any moment inquire into *their* expediency. Another offense was a pamphlet which Williams had written, but never published, "On the Nature of the Right claimed by the Monarchs of the several Nations of Christendom to dispose of the countries of Barbarous Tribes, by virtue of discovery." In this treatise, says Governor Winthrop, "among other things, he disputed their right to the land they possessed, and concluded that, claiming by the king's grant, they could have no title, nor otherwise, except they compounded with the natives." Notwithstanding the fact that this pamphlet was simply a manuscript document in his own desk, he was required to surrender it to the authorities, and, as they considered it dangerous and offensive, he was summoned to appear before the court and receive censure. Williams replied to the magistrates that his pamphlet had been written "only for the private satisfaction of the Governor of Plymouth," and, while disclaiming any intention of offending the authorities, adhered manfully to the opinions he had uttered, but sent the manuscript to be burned by the hangman, if they thought fit. This bold course appears to have mollified the authorities; "they found the matters not to be so evil as at first they seemed."

The fundamental point on which Williams differed from his contemporaries, and which was the immediate cause of the hostility of the court of Massachusetts, was that of liberty of conscience. He believed "that no human power had the right to intermeddle in matters of conscience; and that neither Church nor State, neither bishop, nor priest, nor king, may prescribe the smallest iota of religious faith." Living in a community where every thing was prescribed, this doctrine was singularly sweeping and heretical. It is not remarkable, therefore, that every new assertion of it was listened to by the authorities with horror and misgiving—a protest against things as they existed. His own church was satisfied, but even this was looked on with displeasure, as an evidence of malign influence already exerted. To increase the bad feeling, a spirit of jealousy had sprung up between Salem and Boston, and any unusual proceedings in the former found savage commentators in the latter. The result was that Williams had to appear constantly before the court on the most trivial charges. Eminent divines, with no stain of heterodoxy on their characters, were sent to convert the obdurate Williams; but he was unyielding, and they came back with more confirmed notions of his dangerousness. The exaggerations which were the natural result of these interviews were repelled by straightforward declarations from Williams, denying what he did not believe, and reiterating the faith which he held. He was unmerciful on the civil power. "It extends," he maintained, "only to the bodies, and goods, and outward estates of men;" concerning spiritual matters, "the civil magistrate may not intermeddle, even to stop a church from apostasy and heresy."

An opportunity soon occurred for venting the displeasure of the court not only against Williams, but against Salem. The people of the latter town preferred to the court a claim for a tract of land lying in Marblehead Neck; but the court, as a punishment for the contempt of authority the town had shown in settling Mr. Williams, refused to allow the claim. The injustice of this refusal excited the sturdy spirit of Williams. In conjunction with the Church, he wrote "letters of admonition unto all the churches, whereof any of the magistrates were members, that they might admonish the magistrates of their injustice." This direct appeal from the terrible decision of the court was too flagrant to be tolerated. The deputies of Salem were deprived of their seats until the letter had been satisfactorily explained, and ample apology made for its doctrines. The town of Salem, terrified by these proceedings, made the proper submission, but not before Williams had farther committed himself by urging them to renounce all communion with the other churches of the colony. Thus abandoned by his Church and his townsmen, he stood alone to face the fierce storm which was gathering. A committee was sent to Salem to deal with him and censure him; but he refused to be dealt with and censured, and expressed himself "ready to be bound, and banished, and even to die," but not to renounce his conscientious convictions. In the following July he was summoned to Boston to answer the charges brought against him at the General Court, which was then in session. The following were the charges: "First, that the magistrate ought not to punish the breach of the first table otherwise than in such cases as did disturb the civil peace. Secondly, that he ought not to tender an oath to an unregenerate man. Thirdly, that he ought not to pray with such, though wife, child, etc. Fourthly, that a man ought not to give thanks after sacrament, nor after meat." These charges were the subject of long and serious debate, which terminated in allowing him and the Church in Salem "time to consider these things till the next General Court, and then either to give satisfaction or to expect the sentence."

The next General Court met in October, 1635. Williams appeared in obedience to the summons, and stood manfully to his principles. Many of his old adherents deserted him now that the crisis had arrived. He stood alone, the majestic impersonification of Principle. The decision of the court was as follows: "Whereas, Mr. Roger Williams, one of the elders of the Church of Salem, hath broached and divulged divers new and dangerous opinions against the authority of magistrates, as also writ letters of defamation, both of the magistrates and churches here, and that before any conviction, and yet maintaineth the same without any retraction; it is therefore ordered that the said Mr. Williams shall depart out of this jurisdiction within six weeks now next ensuing, which if he neglect to perform, it shall be lawful for the governor and two of the magistrates to send him to some place out of this jurisdiction, not to return any more without license of the court." This unjust decree was endorsed by all the ministers save one; but, notwithstanding this clerical sanction, it caused much excitement, and the more moderate of the colonists viewed the act with abhorrence. It was complained soon afterward that people were "taken with an apprehension of his godliness;" that is to say, they began to look on him in the light of a martyr. This unexpected sympathy threw the court into new doubts. It was apprehended that many of his old communicants would withdraw with him, and thus, perhaps, found a new and rival colony. To prevent this, it was determined to ship the refractory clergyman to England, and so dispose of him for good. A fresh summons was served on him, demanding his presence once more before the court at Boston; but this he was unwilling or unable to respect. His health had given way under the manifold oppressions and persecutions to which he had been subjected. The magistrates were too eager to be thus bluffly foiled. A warrant was sent to Salem to apprehend him, and convey him on board an English vessel in the harbor. The officer to whom was intrusted the unpleasant task found Mrs. Williams and her family, but Roger Williams had departed. The cold winter wind howled over the dreary landscape where he wandered, and the falling flakes of snow obliterated all traces of his footsteps.

For days and days he wandered in the unbeaten tracks of the forest, across wild ridges of mountains, through treacherous morasses, over still more treacherous snow-banks. "I was severely tossed," says he, "for fourteen weeks, in a bitter winter season, not knowing what bread or bed did mean." Broken in health and spirits, pursued by well-grounded fears of apprehension, scented by wild beasts, can any thing more pathetic, more earnest be imagined than the picture of this true Christian patriot, toiling through the savage wilds, and sustaining himself with the one hope that he might yet succeed in removing the bandage from bigot eyes, and the one conviction that he was Right before God.

During his early residence at Plymouth he availed himself of many opportunities of cultivating a friendly feeling with the Indians, and even acquired some knowledge of their language. In his wanderings he reaped the advantage of these advances. He fell in with many tribes. "These ravens fed me in the wilderness," he says, and his life was doubtless preserved by their kindly hospitality. The famous chief Massasoit was more than kind. He received the toil-spent wanderer, overwhelmed him with attentions, and, when the spring came, gave him a tract of land on the Seekonk River, where "he pitched, and began to build and plant." When the news of his safety reached his Salem friends, several of them flocked to his side, anxious to share his exile, and to help establish an independent colony, where toleration should be more than an empty word. All bade fair to end happily, when suddenly Williams received a communication from the Governor of Plymouth, informing him that he was still within the bounds of the colony, and advising him to remove to the other side of the river. The advice was tendered in a friendly way, and Williams took it without hesitation. He abandoned the land he had commenced tilling, pulled down the house he had built, and, embarking in a rude Indian canoe, dropped down the stream in company with five companions. He passed round the headlands now known as Fox Point and Indian Point, up the harbor to the mouth of the Mooshanic River, and there landed. It was summer now, and the foliage looked bright and beautiful in the gay sunshine. The solitude of primeval nature was unbroken save by the chirruping of birds and the murmuring of a beautiful spring at which they refreshed themselves. Roger Williams felt that he had been guided to this delicious retreat by an all-wise Providence, and with a thankful heart he called the spot Providence, and struck the first stake of the "plantations of Providence." "Rhode Island," says Mr. Bonner, in his excellent "Child's History of the United States," "is a very small state, and looks quite insignificant on the map when compared with such great states as New York, Pennsylvania, and Ohio; but when I remember that Rhode Island was the first place in the world where liberty of conscience was established, I can not think of any country in which it is more glorious to have been born."

We have seen that Roger Williams attached no importance to the patents which kings were in the habit of granting, because he argued they had no right to grant what did not belong to them. He did not feel justified, however, in taking possession of the island on which he found himself without first obtaining permission from the rightful owners. He went, therefore, to the sachems of the country, and purchased the lands "lying upon the two fresh rivers called Mooshanic and Wanasquatucket." In consideration of former kindnesses, the Indians voluntarily ceded to him all the other land lying between the above-named rivers and the Pawtuxet. In order to raise the funds needed for this purpose, and for removing his wife and family to the new settlement, he had to mortgage his house and land in Salem. Little did he imagine how utterly unequal the bargain would soon become.

His ambition was to make the new settlement "a shelter for persons distressed for conscience." It was no part of his plan to assume any kind of authority over the settlers, or to take for his share more land than they had for theirs, although of right it all belonged to him. Those who came were located cheerfully, and not a penny demanded. Thus humanely and generously did this good man found the infant State of Rhode Island. As, however, some kind of obligation was needed from the many who now flocked to the settlement, the following instrument was drawn up, and adopted by each new resident: "We, whose names are here underwritten, being desirous to inhabit the town of Providence, do promise to submit ourselves, in active or passive obedience, to all such orders or agreements as shall be made for the public good of the body, in an orderly way, by the major consent of the present inhabitants, masters of families, incorporated together into a township, and such others whom they shall admit into the same, only in civil things." It was June, 1636, when Williams stepped on shore from his canoe; this simple compact endured for four years, without any special interpreters. In 1640 we find mention of a treasurer, but of no other officer. It was a complete little family party, with a glorious, genial, generous father at its head.

If Roger Williams ever bore resentment against the authorities of Massachusetts Bay, he soon forgot it. During the Pequot war, which ended in the extermination of the Pequot race, he exerted himself with remarkable bravery and ardor on their behalf, and subsequently he never missed an opportunity of proving how easily a good man may forget injury. But the authorities were not to be appeased. They saw that the disaffected of their own colony flew to Roger Williams's settlement as to a place of sanctuary; that they became good citizens there, and did as their conscience bade them, without bringing perdition on those around them. What was worse, they raised their voices against the bigotry and intolerance of the older colony, and loudly denounced every fresh act of injustice. A letter was even dictated, coming from Providence, which complained of the acts of the General Court and the prevailing spirit of the colony. The authorities became greatly incensed, and immediately passed an order that if any of the settlers of Providence should be found within the jurisdiction of Massachusetts, he should be brought before one of the magistrates, and, if he gave his sanction to the letter, he should be sent home, and forbidden to come again into the jurisdiction, on pain of imprisonment and farther censure. The effect of this unjust act was severely felt in Providence, but no revengeful spirit was aroused in the tranquil bosom of Roger Williams.

He was doomed, however, to be sorely perplexed, soon after, by a wild fellow named Gorton, who, after having been turned out of the Boston, Plymouth, and Rhode Island settlements, sought refuge at Providence. He was of course welcomed, but the simple restraints of the compact we have copied were insufficient for his turbulent spirit. Gorton had his adherents, who followed him in his various ejectments, and who soon got the little community into a dispute. It is said that the inhabitants of Providence became so incensed that they appealed to arms, and it was only by the personal intervention of Williams that a combat of the two parties was averted. The anger excited by this state of things did not soon subside. To end the dispute, the weaker party sent an appeal to Massachusetts for aid—contrary, of course, to the wish of Williams. It was refused, but the appeal suggested a new course of policy to the Massachusetts authority. This was none other than to assert, whenever the opportunity occurred, complete jurisdiction over the settlement of Providence.

The confederation of the colonies of New England for mutual protection took place in 1643. Plymouth, Massachusetts Bay, Connecticut, and New Haven were the parties to the union, Providence being entirely ignored. An application was subsequently made by this settlement, and by the sister one of Rhode Island, to be included in the compact, but it was sternly refused. The settlers on the plantations were thus thrown entirely on their own resources for protection as well as support. They continued in prosperity, however, and daily received new accessions to their strength. Their neighbors constantly taunted them with their exposed position, and insisted that they were even without any civil power. Finding themselves thus placed, they were induced at length to unite in seeking the favor and protection of the mother country. The mission was intrusted to Roger Williams, who, in the summer of 1643, set sail from New York for his native land. He was received cordially, especially by Sir Henry Vane, a member of the Privy Council, who was himself a famous advocate of freedom of conscience. Mainly through his exertions, Williams succeeded in getting a charter for the towns of Providence, Portsmouth, and Newport, entitled "The Incorporation of Providence Plantations, in the Narraganset Bay, in New England." The charter was dated March 14th, 1644, and gave to the inhabitants full power "to make and ordain such civil laws and constitutions as they, or the greatest part of them, shall by free consent agree unto." The charter distinctly recognized all that was claimed for the civil government by the founder of the colony, and had the additional virtue of not going farther than was actually needed. Having accomplished all that his most sanguine wishes led him to expect, he returned to America, and arrived at Boston on the 17th of September, 1644. He brought with him a conciliatory letter to the authorities, signed by some of the most eminent men in England; but it had no effect. The only concession they made was to allow him to pass through their territory unmolested. A far different reception awaited him in his own settlement. All the inhabitants turned out to meet him upon the road and bear him back in triumph.

Owing to fresh disturbances among the Indians, and other causes, a form of government under the new charter was not agreed upon until May, 1647. Roger Williams's disinterested love was again manifested. Instead of becoming the first president of the new colony, as of right he should hvae been, he accepted the subordinate office of assistant for the town of Providence. We do not find such modesty among public men in our days. One of the first acts of the new Assembly was to vote a sum of one hundred pounds to defray the expenses which Roger Williams had been put to in obtaining the charter from the English government. We are sorry to add that this sum was never paid in full. A code of laws was also adopted at the same meeting, similar in spirit to those of the mother country, but with this characteristic provision, that, "otherwise than what is herein forbidden, all men may walk as their consciences persuade them, every one in the fear of his God."

The sacrifices he had made for the public service, and the inability or unwillingness of the colonists to reimburse him, compelled Williams (who had a large family) to seek an honest living in some profitable mercantile way. The fur trade was then extensively carried on, and it occurred to him that, by establishing a trading-house, he might easily secure much of the Indian traffic. His popularity with the various tribes and knowledge of their language rendered him peculiarly fitted for this business. Accordingly, he withdrew from the town, and erected a trading-house. He was not disappointed in his expectations. The Indians were delighted to deal with a man so fair, honest, and straightforward. In a little while he established a remunerative business, which he says brought him in a hundred pounds a year profit. He was not destined long to enjoy this gleam of prosperity. A number of difficulties sprung up in the little colony, arising from the loose wording of the charter. Dissensions were rife, and ill-will grew up between man and man. The best disposed appealed to Roger

Williams for help; they prayed that he would once more go to England for them, and permanently settle all the points which caused this agitation. With a wife and a large family to support, and the recollection of former losses, he was at first naturally unwilling to undertake this mission; but when fresh and more earnest representations were made to him, he yielded. The colonists were too poor to pay his expenses, so he sold his trading-house, and once more sailed for England. Under the auspices of Sir Henry Vane, he was again triumphant. It needed time, however, to obtain all that was required, and for a poor man time is a very expensive luxury. In order, therefore, to support his wife and family at home, he obtained employment in London as a teacher of languages. During his sojourn he received a letter from the General Assembly of Providence, thanking him for his care and diligence, and expressing the opinion "that it might tend much to the weighing of men's minds, and subjecting of persons who have been refractory to yield themselves over as unto a settled government, if it might be the pleasure of the honorable state to invest, appoint, and empower himself to come over as governor of the colony for the space of one year." A request like this was so diametrically opposed to his principles, that Williams merely put the letter in his pocket. That was the last heard of it. In the summer of 1654 he returned to Providence, and was dismayed to find the colony still in a distracted state, and its people quarreling and fighting among themselves. A meeting of the town was soon after held, and subsequently of the commissioners of all the towns, which resulted in the reorganizing of the colony, and the adoption of measures for its future prosperity and happiness. At the first general election Roger Williams was chosen president of the colony. His administration lasted two years, and was marked by great liberality of sentiment and firmness of character. In such a strangely-mixed community, it was not remarkable that some vexatious spirits should try to abuse the freedom which they enjoyed, and convert it into an irresponsible license. They were soon aroused to a perception of what liberty of conscience meant. In a quaint letter, Roger Williams gave them an insight into the kind of authority that might be exercised over them. "There goes many a ship to sea," he wrote, "with many hundred souls in one ship, whose weal and woe is common, and is a true picture of a commonwealth, or a human combination or society. It hath fallen out, sometimes, that both Papists and Protestants, Jews and Turks, may be embarked in one ship; upon which supposal, I affirm that all the liberty of conscience that ever I pleaded for turns upon these two hinges: that none of the Papists, Protestants, Jews, or Turks be forced to come to the ship's prayers or worship, or compelled from their own particular prayers or worship, if they practice any. I further add, that I never denied that, notwithstanding this liberty, the commander of this ship ought to command the ship's course, yea, and also command that justice, peace, and sobriety may be kept and practiced, both among the seamen and all the passengers. If any of the seamen refuse to perform their service, or passengers to pay their freight; if any refuse to help, in person or purse, toward the common charges or defense; if any refuse to obey the common laws and orders of the ship concerning their common peace and preservation; if any shall mutiny and rise up against their commanders and officers; if any shall preach or write that there ought to be no commanders or officers, because all are equal in Christ, therefore no masters and officers, no laws nor orders, no corrections nor punishments—I say I never denied but in such cases, whatever is pretended, the commander or commanders may judge, resist, compel, and punish such transgressors, according to their deserts and merits. This, if seriously and honestly minded, may, if it so please the Father of Lights, let in some light to such as willingly shut not their eyes." In spite of this plain definition of what the authorities might do, a hot dispute arose between Roger Williams and an extremist of the name of Harris, who maintained that, according to his conscience, he "ought not to yield subjection to any human order among men." This strange being was afterward prosecuted, but with no result, the case being sent to England for adjudication. In the controversy which ensued, it is to be regretted that both Williams and Harris lost their tempers. That liberty of conscience was amply maintained, in the best sense of the word, was proved by the fact that the persecuted Quakers found a refuge in the colony, where they were amply protected, in spite of the remonstrances and threats of Massachusetts.

In May, 1658, Roger Williams retired from the office of president, with no desire to return to it. He was, however, frequently honored by civil appointments of trust and weight when great honesty and probity were needed; and in the new charter granted by Charles the Second in 1663, was appointed one of the assistants under the governor. This charter was the one for which he had made his second visit to England. He was unable to remain until it was completed, and his colleague, Mr. Clarke, had the honor of obtaining it from the king. "It was the first charter," says Mr. Gammell, "that ever bore the signature of a king, and was the astonishment of the age in which it was granted. Like that which preceded it, it secured the most perfect freedom in matters of conscience, and thus guaranteed the perpetual exercise of the great principles on which the colony was founded. It continued to be the fundamental law of Rhode Island for nearly a hundred and eighty years, protecting the rights and securing the happiness of a long succession of generations, and 'holding forth a lively experiment that a most flourishing civil state may stand, and best be maintained, with a full liberty in religious concernments.'" It was not supplanted until 1843.

In 1670 Williams was again chosen assistant, and also in 1677, but declined to be re-elected. He was now advanced in life, and needed repose. It was probably with the object of securing this that he declined the solicitations of his friends; but a man of his standing and popularity was not likely to be overlooked in or out of office. In 1672 he engaged in his celebrated Quaker controversy, endeavoring by argument to confute the peculiar doctrines of this sect. It is unnecessary to add that he failed in this effort; but it is well to remind the reader that, although he sheltered the Quakers when they needed shelter, he was by no means their friend, and frequently displayed more temper concerning them than we can account for by his antecedents. In the summer of 1675, the disastrous Indian crusade, headed by the famous King Philip, commenced. It was intended, by a confederation of all the tribes, to expel the whites from the country. The attempt was vigorous, and ended in the destruction of a vast amount of property, and the massacre of some five hundred of the colonists. At first Williams tried to exercise his wonted power over the savage minds of his enemies, but, failing in this, he girded on the sword, and commanded a train-band for the protection of the city. Unfortunately, it fell beneath the devastating hands of the Indians, and most of the public records were destroyed, thus obliterating much of the written testimony of this man's excellence.

The remaining years of Roger Williams's life were unmarked

by any event of historical importance, or, if such occurred, we are now without the record. It is probable that his exertions were directed mainly to the healing of old sores which still existed among the colonists, and that, like a benevolent sage, he acted the part of a public pacificator. At the time of his death he was in his eighty-fourth year, but the precise day when he departed this life is unknown. The only record of the event is found in a letter of the 10th of May, 1683, which mentions "that the Lord hath arrested by death our ancient and approved friend, Mr. Roger Williams, with divers others here."

Mr. Williams was the author of several literary works, mostly of a theological and controversial character. His style was not remarkable for elegance or clearness, but it possessed a rude pioneer strength which served all the purposes of more polished composition. As an ecclesiastic he has been accused, and not unjustly, of wavering in his profession of doctrinal faith; but this is not remarkable. His experience of extreme religious tenacity, as exhibited by the ecclesiastics of Boston, may have warned him against a similar course, and led him to doubts, and fears, and wanderings in search of the truth. One thing has never been doubted: he was a good and sincere Christian, indefatigable in his labors and unwearied in his diligence, and "one of the most disinterested men that ever lived—a most pious and heavenly-minded soul."*

* Callender.

WILLIAM HUTTON.

The subject of this memoir was a native of England, born at Derby on the 30th of September, 1723. His parents were in very humble circumstances, and belonged to the dissenting sect. Hutton says that they were remarkable for their steady love of peace and pudding; remarkable, also, for memory; not given much to receive, keep, or pay money; often sensible, always modest; the males inactive, the females distinguished for capacity. William was the most ordinary-looking child of the family, and his mother used to say that she was afraid she could not love him; but poverty—that awful test of human goodness—softened her heart, and she was true and kind to him as to the others. The family was sorely pressed at times, and more than once the poor woman sat with one infant on her knee and others nestled around her, on the cold floor, wailing for food, and when at length it arrived in scanty quantities, she surrendered her share to the more eager wants of her offspring. Time produced nothing but tatters and children.

A lad so pitiably circumstanced was not likely to receive much education. For a very short time he was sent to school, and underwent the discipline of a petty tyrant, who imagined that it was necessary to break a boy's head in order to get any thing into it. At the age of seven he had to earn his own living, and was accordingly apprenticed for seven years to a silk-mill. As he was too short to reach the engine, the superintendents elevated him on a pair of pattens, and on this false footing he remained until nature kindly supplied him with a few more inches.

In 1733, the family received a severe blow in the death of Mrs. Hutton. It was a fatal event for the children, who found themselves without a home, for their father took to drinking, and gave them but few of his thoughts. William did all that lay in his power, and struggled with his hard fate bravely and cheerily; but, in spite of his attentions, he had the wretchedness of seeing his little sister perish of want and neglect. In 1737 he quitted the silk-mill, of which he gives the following dismal picture: "I had to rise at five every morning during seven years; submit to the cane whenever convenient to the master; be the constant companion of the most rude and vulgar of the human race, never taught by nature, nor even wishing to be taught. A lad, let his mind be in what state it would, must be as impudent as they, or be hunted down." The following year he removed to the adjacent town of Nottingham, where he found a generous, friendly uncle, and a mean, sneaking aunt—the one seriously religious, the other seriously hypocritical. He also made the acquaintance of two of his uncle's apprentices, whom he describes, the one as a rogue, the other as a greater. Under the roof of this relative it was intended that he should pass seven years of his existence in learning the business of stocking-weaving, and probably would have done so but for an event which made him naturally enough dissatisfied with the treatment he received. On one occasion (it was holiday time) William was a little behind-hand with his work. His uncle noticed it, and reproved him with want of industry, giving him at the same time a task to be executed by a certain time. The day arrived, but the work was unfinished. "Could you have done the task I ordered?" asked the uncle. William, scorning to tell a falsehood, meekly replied, "I could." Instead of being pleased with this manly acknowledgment, his uncle flew into a violent rage, and fell on his nephew with a stick, repeating his blows until the lad thought he would be broken to pieces. The whole neighborhood was aroused by the clamor, and a double punishment was thereby inflicted upon the lad. The very next day a female acquaintance pointed to him derisively as the boy "who was licked last night." Stung to the quick by the publicity which had thus been given to his disgrace, he resolved on putting an end to it by flight. Concealing himself till the family were gone to meeting, he took two shillings from a glass which contained ten, and packed up his small stock of movables. His uncle having locked the door and taken the key with him, Hutton was compelled to scale an eight-feet wall to make good his escape.

He was now a boy of seventeen, not elegantly dressed, nearly five feet high, and rather Dutch-built in appearance. He had a long, narrow bag of brown leather, holding about a bushel, in which was neatly packed up a new suit of clothes; also a white linen bag, holding about half as much, containing a sixpenny loaf of coarse bread, a bit of butter wrapped in the leaves of an old copy-book, a new Bible worth three shillings, one shirt, a pair of stockings, a sun-dial, and his best wig, carefully folded and laid at the top, so that it might not be crushed. The ends of the two bags being tied together, he slung them over his left shoulder, while hanging to the button of the coat was his best hat. Thus heavily caparisoned, and with two shillings in pocket, he started on his pursuit of fortune. He carried neither a light heart nor a light load. "I considered myself," he says, "an outcast, an exuberance in the creation, a being now fitted to no purpose." He turned his steps toward his home, and from thence proceeded to Burton, at which place he disbursed the first penny from his scanty funds—not for refreshment, as one might suppose, but for the luxury of having some one to take care of his bags while he took a stroll in the town. In the evening of the same day he reached the vicinity of Lichfield. Hiding his bags under a hedge, he perambulated the city for two hours, and then returned to find a lodging for the night. Having been disappointed with respect to one barn, he went a short distance to look after another, and, imagining that his property would be safe, left it behind him. After an absence of ten minutes he returned, and, to his horror and dismay, discovered that his treasure had disappeared. Driven almost to madness by this disaster, he ran raving and lamenting about the fields, roads, and streets, asking every one he met if they had seen his bags. Midnight approached, and, disappointed and broken-hearted, he threw himself on a butcher's block to rest his weary limbs. In the morning he recommenced his search, but it was in vain. Possessing nothing now but the paltry remnants of his two shillings, he departed once more for the manufacturing towns, where he hoped and expected to obtain employ. In due time he arrived at Birmingham. There were but three stocking-makers in the place; to these Hutton instantly applied. The first was a Quaker, who refused to have any thing to say to him on the ground that he was an apprentice who had run away from his employ. The second gave him a penny to get rid of him. The third got rid of him without the penny. Dejected, weary, and hungry, he sat down on a door-step to rest himself and meditate on his hard fortune. While thus wretchedly musing, two men in aprons caught sight of his woeful face, and, taking compassion on his youth, invited him to a supper of bread and cheese and a pint of ale. Subsequently they procured him a bed in a neighboring tavern at an expense of three cents. It does not necessarily require a fortune to perform a kind and timely act of hospitality. From Birmingham Hutton proceeded to Coventry, and thence to Nuneaton and Hinckley. In the latter place he fell in with a townsman, who urged him, in the most earnest manner, to return to his uncle's. Weary of his misfortunes, Hutton was ready to accede to any proposition. He had discovered that running away was by no means a certain escape from present evils, and that it was better to endure some things than to hazard others.

A reconciliation was soon effected with his uncle, who probably felt that he had, in a moment of passion, treated his nephew with unnecessary harshness, and Hutton served the remaining term of his apprenticeship without any particular event which need be mentioned. During a part of this period he derived much benefit from the conversation and advice of an old gentleman named Webb who came to lodge with his uncle, and who seems to have taken a fancy to the young fellow. In his moments of leisure Hutton practiced music on an old harp which he had purchased for half a crown, and was so successful that he resolved to make a dulcimer, and borrowed one as a pattern. He was without timber or tools, or money to procure them; but, in spite of these trifling obstacles, succeeded. By pulling to pieces a large family trunk, converting the hammer-key and plyers of the stocking-frame into a hammer and pincers, using his pocket-knife as an edge-tool, and making the remaining prong of a broken fork serve as a sprig-awl and gimlet, he obtained all that was necessary for his purpose. The instrument he turned out was of such a superb kind that an enthusiastic baker's boy purchased it for the sum of sixteen shillings, with which Hutton bought a coat. The career of the dulcimer, however, was brought to an untimely end. Somehow or other the baker's apprentice could not induce it to discourse "excellent" or any other music, and one day was so enraged with what he considered the mere obstinacy of the instrument that he put it to an ignominious death by consuming it in his oven—a professional revenge which must have been grateful to his feelings.

At Christmas, 1744, the term of Hutton's apprenticeship expired. He had now served two terms of seven years each to two trades, upon neither of which, as he remarks, could he exist. He continued to work as a journeyman for his uncle, but the business did not interest him. He began to have an inclination for books, and to the extent of his scanty means purchased old volumes, the binding of which he repaired with much ingenuity, and the contents of which he devoured with eagerness. In his binding experiments he was encouraged by the bookseller from whom he bought his books, and his success in this business was the first step on the ladder of fortune. Before this was accomplished, he suffered, in common with thousands of others, severe privations. On one occasion, the products of the stocking-frame were at such a low ebb that he had to travel as far as Leicester to sell half a dozen pair of hose, and could find neither a purchaser nor an employer. As he stood before a gentleman to whom he offered his goods, he burst into tears to think that he should have served seven years to a trade at which he could not get bread.

In 1746 Hutton lost his uncle, who died from the bursting of a blood-vessel. His sister Catharine then took a house, and Hutton went to board with her. With her assistance, he added the business of book-binding to the rattling of the stocking-frame. The novelty of the combination secured him many customers, principally among those who were not particularly qualified to judge of the excellence of his work. He went on improving, however, and in a little time found that he needed better tools, especially for lettering. He wished also to open an account with some wholesale London house, so that he might in future purchase all his materials to the best advantage. His sister came to his assistance, and advanced a sum of fifteen or twenty dollars, with which the young enthusiast took his departure for the metropolis. He has left us a full account of this journey. The first day he walked fifty-one miles (he was, of course, too poor to ride), and, being unused to so much exercise, got his feet badly blistered; but he did not lose courage or time, and reached London on the third day. He put up at a tavern, and ordered a luxurious supper, consisting of a mutton-chop and a pint of porter; but, notwithstanding the expensiveness of the banquet, he was unable to touch it. Fatigue had deprived him of his appetite. He did not make another experiment of the same kind, but breakfasted the next morning at a wheelbarrow-stand in Smithfield. During the remainder of his stay his mode of living was economical. Sometimes he had a halfpenny worth of soup and another of bread; at other times, bread and cheese.

Having transacted all his business satisfactorily, he tramped back to Nottingham. Where to fix his residence with the best prospect of obtaining trade was now the question which engaged his attention. His choice fell upon Southwell, fourteen miles off, which he afterward described as "a town despicable as the road to it." Here he took a shop (1749), at the rent of twenty shillings a year, intending merely to keep it open on the market-days. His stock of books was slim, but it was the best in the place, and perhaps too good. During a very rainy winter, he set out at five every Saturday morning, carried a burden of from three pounds' weight to thirty, opened store at ten, starved in it all day upon bread, cheese, and ale, took from one to six shillings, shut up at four, and, by trudging through the solitary night and the deep roads for five hours more, arrived at Nottingham by nine, where he always found a mess of milk porridge by the fire, prepared by his kind sister.

By perseverance and frugality, his circumstances became so much better that in the following year he determined on removing to Birmingham, for which town, ever since his runaway visit, he had felt a strong predilection. In February, 1750, he journeyed thither, in order to see what opportunities were open to enterprise. He found that there were only three considerable booksellers in the place, and determined at once that he would take his humble chance to obtain a share of public patronage. On his journey home he met with an adventure, which we will recount in his own words. "Meaning to take Swithland on my return to Nottingham, to visit my two aunts, I was directed through Tamworth, where I spent one penny; then through a few villages, with blind roads, to Charnwood Forest, over which were five miles of uncultivated waste, without any road. To all this I was a stranger. Passing through a village in the dusk of the evening, I determined to stop at the next public house; but, to my surprise, I instantly found myself upon the forest. It began to rain; it was dark; I was in no road; nor was any dwelling near. I was among hills, rocks, and precipices, and so bewildered that I could not retreat. I considered my situation as desperate, and must confess I lost the fortitude of a man.

"I wandered slowly, though in the rain, for fear of destruction, and hallooed with all my powers, but met with no return. I was about two hours in this cruel state, when I thought the indistinct form of a roof appeared against the sky. My vociferations continued, but to no purpose. I concluded it must be a lonely barn; but, had it been the receptacle of ghosts, it would have been desirable. At length I heard the sound of a man's voice, which, though one of the most terrific, gave me pleasure. I continued advancing, perhaps thirty yards, using the soft persuasives of distress for admission, even under any roof, but could not prevail. The man replied that all his out-buildings had been destroyed by a mob of freeholders, as standing on the waste. He seemed to be six feet high, strong built, and, by the sound of his voice, upward of fifty.

"I could not, as my life was at stake, give up the contest, but thought, if I could once get under his roof, I should not be easily discharged. Though his manner was repelling as the rain, and his appearance horrid as the night, yet I would not part from him, but insensibly, at length, wormed myself in. I was now in a small room, dignified with the name of a house, totally dark except a glow of fire, which would barely have roasted a potato had it been deposited in the centre. In this dismal abode I heard two female voices—one that of an old aunt, the other of a young wife.

"We all sat close to this handful of a fire, as every one must who sat in the room. We soon became familiarized by conversation, and I found my host agreeable. He apologized for not having treated me with more civility; he pitied my case, but had not conveniences for accommodation. Hints were now given for retiring to rest. 'I will thank you,' said I, 'for something to eat; I have had nothing since morning, when I left Birmingham.' 'We should have asked you to eat, but we have nothing in the house.' 'I shall be satisfied with any thing.' 'We have no eatables whatever, except some pease-porridge, which is rather thin —only pease and water, and which we are ashamed to offer.' 'It will be acceptable to a hungry man.'

"He gave me to understand that he had buried a wife, by whom he had children grown up. Being inclined to marry again, he did not choose to venture upon a widow, for fear of marrying her debts; he therefore had married a girl thirty years younger than himself, by whom he had two small children, then in bed. This I considered as an excuse for misconduct.

"While supper was warming—for hot it could not be—a light was necessary; but, alas! the premises afforded no candle. To supply the place, a leaf was torn from a shattered book, twisted round, kindled, and shook in the hand to improve the blaze. By this momentary light, I perceived the aunt, who sat opposite, had a hare-shorn lip, which, in the action of eating, so affected me that I was obliged to give up my supper. By another lighted leaf we marched up to bed. I could perceive the whole premises consisted of two rooms, house and chamber. In the latter was one bed and a pair of bedsteads. The husband, wife, aunt, and two children occupied the first, and the bedstead, whose head butted against their bedside, was appropriated for me. But now another difficulty arose: there were no bed-clothes to cover me. Upon diligent inquiry, nothing could be procured but the wife's petticoat, and I could learn that she robbed her own bed to supply mine. I heard the rain patter upon the thatch during the night, and rejoiced it did not patter upon me.

"By the light of the next morning I had a view of all the family faces except the aunt's, which was covered with a slouched hat. The husband seemed to have been formed in one of nature's largest and coarsest moulds. His hands retained the accumulated filth of the last three months, garnished with half a dozen scabs, both perhaps the result of idleness. The wife was young, handsome, ragged, and good-natured.

"The whole household, I apprehend, could have cast a willing eye upon breakfast, but there seemed a small embarrassment in the expectants. The wife, however, went to her next neighbor's, about a mile, and in an hour returned with a jug of skimmed milk and a piece of a loaf, perhaps two pounds, both of which I have reason to believe were begged; for money, I believe, was as scarce as candles. Having no fire, we ate it cold, and with a relish.

"When I left the house, I saw the devastation made by the rioters, a horde of monsters I have since had reason to dread. My host went with me half a mile to bring me into something like a track, when I gave him a shake of the hand, a sixpence, and my sincere good wishes. We parted upon the most friendly terms. Though I seemingly received but little, yet a favor is great or small according to the need of the receiver. I had seen poverty in various shapes, but this was the most complete. There appeared, however, in that lowest degree, a considerable share of content. The man might have married a widow and her debts with safety, for no creditor durst have sued him. Neither need he have dreaded a jail, except from the loss of liberty, for he would have risen in point of luxury. I have also seen various degrees of idleness, but none surpassed this. Those wants can not merit pity which idleness might, but will not prevent."

In April Hutton commenced business in Birmingham, having rented half of a small store for the sum of one shilling per week. A stroke of luck placed him in possession of about two hundred weight of books, the refuse of a clergyman's library. This gentleman was benevolent and kind-hearted. He saw that Hutton was struggling with the world in an honorable way, and assisted him by letting him have the books at a nominal price, taking his note of hand as security even for this. The document was a curious one, and read as follows: "I promise to pay to Ambrose Rudsdall one pound seven shillings when I am able.—WILLIAM HUTTON." His business prospects at first were of a very dismal kind, and, although naturally of a cheerful temper, he could not help being depressed by them; but he never lost courage or neglected an opportunity. As the year progressed, his spirits rose; he became known as a steady, persevering young man, and people liked to patronize him. At its close he had saved about twenty pounds, the result of great industry and frugality. The following year some of his friends induced him to take a house in a better location. Hutton was at first frightened at the rent, which amounted to the dreadful sum of eight pounds, but was finally persuaded. The speculation turned out an advantageous one; his customers were more numerous and of a better class; so that, in the third year of his residence, he was able to boast that he had a smiling trade, to which he closely attended, and a happy set of acquaintances, whose society gave him pleasure. Under these circumstances, it was not remarkable that Hutton began to aspire to the comforts of a domestic circle of his own. He had made several attempts at housekeeping, but they all failed, owing to the indifference of domestics. Men's eyes get opened in this way, and it is astonishing how sharp they can look out for a wife. His first "courtings" were not eminently successful; but after a while a neighbor sent for one of his nieces, Miss Susan Cock, a pretty and amiable woman. At the outset she did not seem to like Hutton, nor was he attracted by her. In process of time, however, the coldness in both disappeared, and "by Christmas," he says, "our hearts had united without efforts on either side. Time had given numberless opportunities of observing each other's actions, and trying the tenor of conduct by the touchstone of prudence. Courtship is often a disguise. We had seen each other when disguise was useless." Forty-one years later he wrote as follows: "Three months before her death, when she was so afflicted with an asthma that she could neither walk, stand, sit, nor lie, but while on a chair, I was obliged to support her head, I told her that she had never approached me without diffusing a ray of pleasure over the mind, except whenever any little disagreement had happened between us. She replied, 'I can say more than that. You never appeared in my sight, even *in* anger, without the sight giving me pleasure.' I received the dear remark, as I now write it, with tears."

Having saved two hundred pounds, he embarked in the paper trade (in connection with his own business), and, being the only one in the town, he found it extremely lucrative. He followed it for forty years, and, according to his own admission, acquired an ample fortune. This he risked in the manufacture of the article; but the knavery of those around him occasioned him much loss, and the enterprise was abandoned. Prosperity continued to crown his efforts; he became richer and richer every day. Although strictly exact and economical, he was not in the slightest degree niggardly. He denied neither to himself or his family any comfort or amusement which they could enjoy without injury to their future welfare.

Being a man of influence in the community, he was, of course, selected for parochial and civic honors, and, like most honest men who undertake public offices for the first time, endeavored to bring about many reforms. These labors were not fruitful, and at length he retired from the contest in disgust, finding that it was impossible to stem the torrent of corruption. Previous to this he had frequently amused himself with writing verses, which occasionally found their way into the magazines; but it was not till 1780, when he was in his fifty-seventh year, that he thought of regularly appearing before the public in the character of an author. His first prose attempt was a History of Birmingham. It came out in 1782, was received favorably, and gained for the author the honor of being elected a member of the Scottish Antiquarian Society. Encouraged by success, Hutton continued his literary career, and between 1782 and 1808 produced thirteen other works, which issued from the press in the following order: Journey to London, 1784; The Court of Requests, 1787; The Hundred Court, 1788; History of Blackpool, 1788; Battle of Bosworth Field, 1789; History of Derby, 1790; The Barbers, a poem, 1793; Edgar and Elfrida, a poem, 1793; The Roman Wall, 1801; Remarks upon North Wales, 1801; Tour to Scarborough, 1803; Poems, chiefly tales, 1804; Trip to Coatham, 1808; and his "Life," a posthumous work, and the most excellent of all his productions. Many of his topographical and antiquarian works are remarkable for their exactness and research. They all display considerable ability in the writer, and a pleasant vein of original geniality. His poetical productions were principally remarkable for their kindly feeling; in other respects they are worthless.

The prosperous condition in which he found himself enabled him to pursue his career as an author with attention and ease. His fortune progressed steadily. He possessed a country house of his own building, kept horses, and finally set up a carriage, and solaced himself and family with visits to all places of interest. He possessed the happy faculty of enjoying to the full what he had earned, without launching into unnecessary extravagance. In 1791, however, a political storm arose, which for a time put an end to his tranquillity. It involved a general proscription of the Dissenters, to which sect Hutton belonged, and led to a series of mischievous and disgraceful riots. Mobs, of what kind soever, dislike rich men, and Hutton at once became an object of aversion, not only because he was rich, but because he was a Dissenter, and, as a commissioner of the Court of Requests, had been compelled to decide against many of the creatures who were now eager for his destruction. The result was as might be expected. They attacked his house, threw his furniture and extensive stock into the street, reduced the house to a mere skeleton, and made several attempts to set it on fire, which were fortunately frustrated. On the following day they went to his country house at Bennett's Hill, in the vicinity of the town, made three bonfires of the furniture, and then gave the building to the flames. Hutton was not a man to quietly submit to injustice. He made an effort to resist the depredations of the mob; but such was the consternation that prevailed among the respectable portion of the community that not a man could be got to stir in the matter. As his life was now more than ever in danger, he was prevailed upon to retire into the country for a time. He took lodgings at Sutton Coldfield; but in the evening his landlady was seized with a panic, and begged him to quit, that her abode might not be destroyed. He was compelled to proceed with his family to Tamworth, where they slept for the night, and then moved to Castle Bromwich, in order to be nearer Birmingham in case of danger. But even here he was pursued by the apprehensions of those around him. At night, some of the rioters having visited Castle Bromwich, the villagers were terrified, and advised him, for his safety's sake, to retreat to Stonnel. "I was avoided," he says, "as a pestilence. The waves of sorrow rolled over me, and beat me down with multiplied force; every one came heavier than the last. My children were distressed; my wife, through long affliction, was ready to quit my own arms for those of death, and I myself reduced to the sad necessity of humbly begging a draught of water at a cottage! What a reverse of situation! How thin the barriers between affluence and poverty! By the smiles of the inhabitants of Birmingham I acquired a fortune; by an astonishing defect in our police, I lost it. In the morning of the 15th I was a rich man; in the evening I was ruined. At ten at night, on the 17th, I might have been found leaning upon a milestone upon Sutton Coldfield road, without food, without a home, without money, and, what is the last resort of the wretched, without hope." Shortly after this the military were called out, and the disturbances came to an end. On his return to Birmingham he was warmly welcomed by his friends, among whom were sixteen members of the Established Church, who placed their houses at his disposal; a mark of consideration which he esteemed as a proof that he was not looked on as a party man. But the persecution of the Dissenters did not end with their temporary safety. The leaders of the mob were put on trial; but they were speedily released, and became more rampant than ever. Such was the prejudice which prevailed, that Hutton was actually unable to obtain a home for himself and family, and was obliged to board and lodge at a tavern. He commenced a suit for damages sustained in the riot, and, after much vexatious litigation and expense, obtained a verdict for about one third of the actual loss sustained. His expenses in the suit were nearly nine hundred pounds. Disgusted with this unfair treatment, he determined to retire from business (1793), and immediately resigned in favor of his son, amusing himself occasionally by assisting gratuitously in the management. The increasing infirmities of his wife also demanded more of his attention. He has left us a very touching memorandum of the way he passed his time. "My practice," says he, "had long been to rise about five, and relieve the nurse of the night by holding the head of my dear love in my hand, with the elbow resting on the knee. At eight I walked to business at Birmingham, where I staid till four, when I returned. I nursed her till eight, amused myself with literary pursuits till ten, and then went to rest." Early in 1796 Mrs. Hutton was released from her sufferings. Hutton was severely affected by the event, and to the day of his death cherished the warmest veneration for his unfortunate partner.

In his seventy-eighth year Hutton achieved a remarkable feat of pedestrianism. He had long had a desire to examine the old Roman Wall, which was erected to keep off the savage barbarians of the north, and portions of which still remain. His daughter was going on a tour, and he determined to accompany her as far as Penrith, and then explore the Wall, while she went on to the Lakes. She was to ride; but nothing could dissuade him from making all the journey on foot. From Penrith he pushed on, through Carlisle, to the Irish Sea, followed the line of wall to Wall's End, on the North Sea, and retraced it again to Carlisle, having twice crossed the kingdom in one week. The journey from and to Birmingham was six hundred and one miles, occupied thirty-five days, and was made under a burning July sun, when the ground was not cooled by a single drop of rain. He was so delighted with the journey, and performed it with such ease, that in the course of the following year he made excursions to the counties of Derby, Leicester, and Northampton; explored the beauties of Matlock, and wandered among the ruins of Fotheringay Castle. He describes the scenes and adventures of this trip with his usual pleasantness and geniality. The greatest wonder he met at Matlock, he says, was Phebe Brown. She was six feet six inches in height, thirty years of age, well proportioned, round-faced, and ruddy. "Her step is more manly than a man's, and can cover forty miles a day. Her common dress is a man's hat, coat, with a spencer over it, and men's shoes. As she is *un*married, I believe she is a stranger to the breeches. She can lift one hundred weight in each hand, and carry fourteen score; can sew, knit, cook, and spin, but hates them all, and every accompaniment to the female character, that of modesty excepted.

A gentleman, at the New Bath, had recently treated her rudely. 'She had a good mind to have knocked him down.' She assured me 'she never knew what fear was.' She gives no affront, but offers to fight any man who gives her one. If she never has fought, it is, perhaps, owing to the insulter having been a coward, for the man of courage would disdain to offer an insult to a female. Phebe has strong sense, an excellent judgment, says smart things, and supports an easy freedom in all companies. Her voice is more than masculine—it is deep-toned. With the wind in her favor, she can send it a mile. She has neither beard nor prominence of breast. She undertakes any kind of manual labor, as holding the plow, driving a team, thatching the barn, using the flail, etc.; but her chief avocation is breaking horses, for which she charges a guinea a week each. She always rides without a saddle, is thought to be the best judge of a horse or cow in the country, and is frequently employed to purchase for others at the neighboring fairs. She is fond of Milton, Pope, and Shakspeare; also of music; is self-taught, and performs on several instruments, as the flute, violin, harpsichord, and supports the bass-viol in Matlock church. She is a marks-*woman*, and carries the gun on her shoulder. She eats no beef and pork, and but little mutton. Her chief food is milk, which is also her drink, discarding wine, ale, and spirits."

For several years Hutton preserved the vigor of his mind and body. He was always employed, and never allowed either the one or the other to get rusty. At the age of eighty-four he underwent an operation for cancer; the wound healed up with rapidity, and a cure was effected. On his ninetieth birthday he walked ten miles, and to the last maintained his habit of pedestrianism. On the 20th of September, 1815, he sank into his last sleep without a struggle or a groan. A more perfect and estimable character is not to be found in the annals of biography.

Hutton's daughter described her father as a man of five feet six inches high, well made, strong, and active; a little inclined to corpulency, which did not diminish till within four or five months of his death. From this period he gradually became thin. His countenance was expressive of sense, resolution, and calmness, though, when irritated or animated, he had a very keen eye. Such was the happy disposition of his mind, and such the firm texture of his body, that ninety-two years had scarcely the power to alter his features or make a wrinkle in his face.

JOHN PAUL JONES.

John Paul Jones, more familiarly known as Paul Jones, a Scotchman by birth, was born on the 6th of July, 1747, at a little place called Kirkbean. His father was a gardener, and Paul followed the same calling for a few early years of his life. It may be well in this place to mention that his proper name was simply John Paul. Events which will be narrated hereafter caused him to assume the name of Jones, by which he is so widely known. Being of an adventurous and sanguine disposition, he was not long content with the humble sphere in which Nature had cast him. The sea was his escape. At the age of twelve he crossed the Frith to Whitehaven, and entered into articles of apprenticeship with Mr. Younger, a merchant in the American trade. Soon after, he made his first voyage in the *Friendship*, of Whitehaven, bound to the Rappahannock. He was a very studious and valuable apprentice, and the excellent qualities he manifested recommended him strongly to the house by whom he was engaged. All his spare time was devoted to the study of the profession he had selected, and the general cultivation of his mind. Before the term of apprenticeship had expired, the house failed, and in a very generous way surrendered his indentures, instead of assigning or transferring them to some one else. Paul, thrown on his own resources, looked around for employment, and in a little while succeeded in getting an appointment as third mate of a vessel bound on a slaving voyage. In this service he subsequently rose to the rank of chief mate; but, feeling disgust for the cruelties which it is feared are inevitable in the traffic, he relinquished it. In 1768, when returning from Jamaica to Scotland as a passenger, the master and mate of the brig were seized with sickness, and died of fever. In this extremity Paul assumed the command, and under his charge the vessel arrived safely in port. In return for this, the owners placed him on board the same vessel as master and supercargo for the next voyage to the West Indies. The voyage was successfully prosecuted, and the brig *John* (that was her name) started on a second voyage to the same regions. On the passage a difficulty arose between Paul and the carpenter of the ship, Mungo Maxwell by name, which resulted in the latter being tied up and flogged in the usual brutal style of the navy. The punishment was undoubtedly called for, but it was an unfortunate necessity. Maxwell left the ship, and soon after was seized with a fever, of which he died. There is no doubt now that the man owed his death entirely to the action of malignant disease, but at the time it was broadly asserted that the flogging had caused it, and in Scotland especially this cruel rumor was believed to the prejudice of Paul. The owners of the brig, however, gave him an honorable discharge when they dissolved partnership; but, in spite of this, it is probable that he experienced difficulty in getting a new ship.

In 1773 he went to Virginia, to arrange the affairs of a brother who had died there intestate and without children. He became possessed of the estate of this brother, and at once entered on the career of an agriculturist; but, from incumbrances on the farm or other causes, he found it extremely difficult to gain a living, and when the war of the Revolution broke out, was, according to his own account, in great penury. Although he had only resided in the country for two years, he espoused its cause from the first, and tendered his services to the government. On the 22d of December, 1775, he received a commission as lieutenant in the navy, and in this document his name first occurs as John Paul *Jones*,

Why he added the last name to his patronymic we can only surmise; he gives no reason himself. It is probable that he wished to efface some of the events of his early life for which he had become notorious, such, for instance, as the death of the carpenter, and a brief career on the Scottish coast as a smuggler. He might have felt that it was necessary for the preservation of discipline in any position he might acquire that these circumstances should be forgotten.

At the end of the first voyage Paul Jones was promoted to the command of the *Alfred*, but was afterward superseded on the 14th of January, 1777—probably on account of his being a foreigner. The Marine Committee, however, expressed regret that they had not a good ship vacant for him, and Congress expressed its satisfaction with his first cruise (in which he took several prizes, and inflicted serious injury on the enemy) by giving him, a few months later, the command of a new ship called the *Ranger*. On the 1st of November, 1777, he sailed from Portsmouth, bound for Nantes, in France. On the passage he made two prizes, in spite of a fleet of ten sail which gave him chase. He succeeded also in getting the American flag (which he was the first to hoist on an American ship) properly saluted by a foreign power. We copy his own account of this event. "I am happy in having it in my power to congratulate you on my having seen the American flag for the first time recognized in the fullest and completest manner by the flag of France. I was off their bay on the 13th instant, and sent my boat in the next day to know if the admiral would return my salute. He answered that he would return to me, as the senior American Continental officer in Europe, the same salute which he was authorized by his court to return to an admiral of Holland, or any other republic, which was four guns less than the salute given. I hesitated at this, for I had demanded gun for gun; therefore I anchored in the entrance of the bay, at a distance from the French fleet; but, after a very particular inquiry on the 14th, finding that he had really told the truth, I was induced to accept of his offer, the more so as it was, in fact, an acknowledgment of American independence. The wind being contrary and blowing hard, it was after sunset before the *Ranger* got near enough to salute La Motte Piquet with thirteen guns, which he returned with nine. However, to put the matter beyond a doubt, I did not suffer the *Independence* (a vessel of Jones's squadron) to salute till next morning, when I sent the admiral word that I would sail through his fleet in the brig, and would salute him in open day. He was accordingly pleased, and returned the compliment also with nine guns."

Paul Jones sailed from Nantes for the Irish and Scotch coasts. The course he had laid down for himself, and which proved so eminently successful, was to make sudden descents on unexpected spots, and, by striking a rapid succession of small blows, in this way to stupefy and confuse the enemy. One of the first places to which he paid some attention was the port of Whitehaven, where, it will be remembered, he had commenced his maritime career. It was his intention to set fire to all the shipping, and for this purpose he made a bold attempt with two boats and thirty-one men. He only succeeded in setting fire to one ship and in spiking a few guns. There was no fighting on either side. Jones's next attempt was to seize the person of the Earl of Stirling (in whose family he once lived), imagining that the possession of this nobleman's person might be useful when exchanges were made between the two countries. The earl being absent from home, he did not succeed in his base scheme; his men, however, plundered the house, Paul waiting outside, like an experienced burglar, while his men performed the dirty work. He became properly ashamed of this transaction, and, to his credit be it said, returned the plunder.

These incursions alarmed the enemy, and a ship of war called the *Drake* was sent in pursuit of Jones. A regular engagement took place between them, and was kept up obstinately at close quarters for more than an hour. At length the British vessel surrendered. Her captain and first lieutenant were killed, and no fewer than forty-two of the ship's company were found to have been killed or wounded, while Jones, on his side, merely lost one officer, one seaman, and six wounded. The prize was carried in safety to Brest, and the hero of the fight became a great lion. He was not without his troubles, however; money was scarce, and the men became dissatisfied. Jones, too, was ambitious and hasty; he wanted to get into a larger ship, and took every opportunity of magnifying his own importance, which was, of course, annoying to other officers. The lieutenant, in particular, was indignant, and his indignation aroused the resentment of Jones, who made all sorts of charges against him, demanded a court-martial, and did other intemperate things. The result was, that Jones's ship, the *Ranger*, was placed under charge of Lieutenant Simpson, and ordered back to America, and Jones himself was requested to remain in France, to be in readiness for some important operations which were about to be undertaken. For five months he remained in a state of inactivity, employing his time mostly in indefatigable correspondence with every one who was in the slightest degree likely to forward his interests. He was an excellent letter-writer, clear, forcible, and persuasive; but men in office are not easily moved by letters, even when they are written with the most masterly ability, and those of Jones's were without a result. One day, while fretting and fuming at the unmerited neglect with which he was treated by the French government—who, after having promised to furnish him with a vessel for the service of the American cause, displayed such unwillingness to do so—his eye fell on one of Poor Richard's proverbs. It was in Franklin's famous Pennsylvania Almanac, and was to this effect: "If you would have your business done, go; if not, send." It occurred to him instantly that if, instead of writing letters, he were to proceed to the French capital, and spend time in personally advocating his claims, a better and more immediate result might be obtained. Without any farther delay he hurried to Paris, and not an official in that large city could call a moment his own until Jones's claims had been listened to. He hunted them like rabbits; waited outside their holes, and pounced upon them the instant they put out their heads. No circumlocution-office could resist such direct and inveterate application. In a very few days Jones received a letter from the French minister, informing him that the ship *Duras*, of forty guns, was placed at his command. Paul Jones asked leave to change the name of the vessel, and, on obtaining it, rechristened the ship to the *Bon Homme Richard*, out of respect to Poor Richard's Almanac, which he imagined had first indicated the proper course to adopt to secure a result.

In his first cruise, Jones conceived some bold designs against the enemy—such, for instance, as the meditated attack on the town and harbor of Leith, in Scotland; but the squadron which was supposed to be under his command had a voice in the direction of affairs, and interposed many obstacles in the way of the daring commander. On the coast of Scotland, however, he came across the Baltic fleet of merchantmen, under the escort of English war vessels. An engagement immediately ensued. Jones engaged the frigate *Serapis*, and, after a terrific struggle of three and a half hours, captured her. So obstinate was the struggle, that the men on either vessel knew not which had struck until the American flag decided the question. Both ships were completely torn to pieces by the engagement, and the *Bon Homme Richard* leaked so fearfully that the next day she went down. Nothing but the determined bravery of Jones gave him this glorious victory, for the *Serapis* had more guns and threw more metal than the *Poor Richard*. In other respects she was more completely armed, could sail better, and was manned with a well-disciplined crew. To conquer such a vessel was sufficient to make any man famous. Paul Jones became at once the naval hero of the day, the terror of the seas. It was the principal achievement of his life, and was subsequently commemorated by Congress, who caused a medal to be struck in honor of the hero.

Without entering into great, and, to most readers, uninteresting details of private history, it would be impossible to follow the career of Paul Jones. He employed his time usefully in the service of the Commonwealth, his desires being far ahead of the limited means of the Congress, and his importunities, in consequence, extremely unpleasant. When the independence of the United States became duly recognized, Paul Jones looked abroad for a new field of action. He received an invitation to join the Russian fleet, with the rank of rear admiral, but was disappointed in obtaining command of the fleet. He served for some little time, but, becoming irritable and unduly vainglorious, he received permission to retire. To revenge this, he made efforts to change his flag—to go over to Russia's enemy, Sweden. Fortunately failing, he returned to Paris, where he remained for some time, prosecuting his claims for prize-money. Ill health, provoked by constant irritation, ensued, and on the 18th of July, 1792, he died, in comparative poverty and obscurity.

Paul Jones was a man of unquestionable talent and courage; he conducted all his operations with great boldness, and calculated their chances of success with extreme nicety. He was, however, of an unpleasant temper, easily irritated, and remarkably offensive to those beneath him. He was absurdly vain, not very truthful, and greedy of applause. From the first he appears to have entertained a great spite against Scotland, and he never returned to that country, where he was remembered with loathing and abhorrence. He had some relatives, however, with whom he corresponded, and also assisted pecuniarily. "The glaring defect of Paul Jones's character," says Mr. Mackenzie, in his Life, "and the foundation of many others, was his abounding vanity. This evinced itself in the stress which he laid on the honors he had received from kings and Congresses, and which, though not unmerited, were in no slight degree drawn forth by his own well-applied solicitation; in the multiplication of his busts and medals; and the constant recapitulation, with due exaggeration, of his various achievements. No hero, indeed, ever sounded his own trumpet more unremittingly or with a louder blast. This absorbing vanity led him to claim for himself the whole glory of his victories. In all his elaborate reports of his engagements—except, indeed, during his Russian campaign, where the slight passed upon his officers became a reflection on himself—he is the hero, and the sole hero of his own tale. The only occasion on which he commends any of his officers is in small notes at the foot of each of their certificates, appended to his charges against Landais, and where his object is to give force to their testimony. It may be said, in excuse, that this vanity of distinction, which was the cause of his injustice in restraining him from giving credit to others, was also the exciting motive of his actions, by so powerfully stimulating him to excel. Still, his unwillingness to commend others, and award to each of his followers his just meed of praise, was a very great fault. A commander can have no more sacred duty than that which he owes in this respect to those who, even in the humblest stations, contribute to his glory."

WILLIAM FALCONER.

THIS illustrious poet of the sea, a poet who possesses more fascination for the youthful mind than almost any other, was the son of a poor man at Edinburgh, Scotland, and was born about 1736 or 1737. His father was, at various times, a barber, a maker of wigs, and a grocer, but, in spite of these numerous professions, he remained poor, and could barely struggle against the wants of the world. There were several children in the family, but, melancholy to relate, they were all deaf and dumb with the exception of William. The latter was a lumpish, heavy-looking lad, very careless and dirty in his dress, and was commonly addressed by the mellifluous name of Bubly-hash Falconer. He received only a few weeks' schooling, and was then placed, reluctantly on his part, on board a merchant vessel at Leith. Subsequently he became second mate on a vessel employed in the Levant trade, and, while on a passage from Alexandria to Venice, was shipwrecked near Cape Colonne, on the coast of Greece. The exact date when this calamity happened is not known; only three of the crew survived, among whom was Falconer. The event made such a powerful impression on his mind, that he gave it poetic shape and utterance in his remarkable poem of "The Shipwreck."

In 1751 Falconer commenced his poetical career, although at that time a common sailor. He wrote an elegy, and a few miscellaneous poems, such as most young men compose, which appeared in the Gentleman's Magazine without creating any remarkable consternation in the literary world. In 1762 he published his poem of "The Shipwreck," dedicating it to the Duke of York, who, as an old salt, felt not a little proud of the work, coming as it did from an humble, untutored sailor. The poem attracted immediate attention, and was hugely commended in the Monthly Review. We quote a portion of the criticism: "The main subject of the poem is the loss of the ship Britannia, bound from Alexandria to Venice, which touched at the island of Candia, whence, proceeding on her voyage, she met with a violent storm that drove her on the coasts of Greece, where she suffered shipwreck near Cape Colonne, three only of the crew being left alive. The ship putting to sea from the port of Candia, the poet takes an opportunity of making several beautiful marine descriptions, such as the prospect of the shore, a shoal of dolphins, a water-spout, the method of taking an azimuth, and working the ship. In the second canto, the ship having cleared the land, the storm begins, and with it the consultation of the pilots and operations of the seamen, all which the poet has described with an amazing minuteness, and has found means to reduce the several technical terms of the marine into smooth and harmonious numbers. Homer has been admired by some for reducing a catalogue of ships into tolerably flowing verse, but who, except a poetical sailor, the nursling of Apollo, educated by Neptune, would ever have thought of versifying his own sea language? What other poet would ever have dreamed of reef-tackles, halliards, clew-garnets, buntlines, lashings, laniards, and fifty other terms equally obnoxious to the soft sing-song of modern poetasters?

"Many of his descriptions are not inferior to any thing in the Æneid, many passages in the third and fifth books of which our author has had in view. They have not suffered by his imitation, and his pilot appears to much greater advantage than the Palinurus of Virgil. Nor is the poet's talent confined to the description of inanimate scenes; he relates and bewails the untimely fate of his companions in the most animated and pathetic strains. The close of the master's address to the seamen, in the time of their greatest danger, is noble and philosophical. It is impossible to read the circumstantial account of the unfortunate end of the ship's crew without being deeply affected by the tale, and charmed with the manner of the relation." Poets in our days labor in vain for praise like this. We may well ask ourselves if it was entirely deserved. Falconer's poem had unquestionable merit, not the least of which was its novelty. It has taken its place among the classics of English literature; but to compare it with Virgil requires an effort of unscrupulous kindness not common in this degenerate age.

In 1763 Falconer was appointed purser of the Glory frigate of 32 guns. Soon after, he married a young lady of the name of Hicks, and lived with her in great harmony and happiness until the time of her death. When the Glory was laid up in ordinary,

Falconer employed himself in the compilation of a valuable marine dictionary (1769), and soon after adopted the profession of literature, with the usual conveniences—that is to say, a garret and debts. He struggled on, however, and at length was fortunate enough to receive a proposal from Mr. Murray, the bookseller, to join with him in taking Mr. Sandby's business, opposite St. Dunstan's Church, London. He did not accept this proposition, but the fact of its having been made shows that, at this time, he had at least one influential friend.

In 1769 a third edition of the "Shipwreck" was called for, but before its publication the author had been appointed purser of the *Aurora* frigate (probably weary of literature), bound for India, and on the 30th of September he took his departure. The vessel was never heard of more. It has been supposed that she perished by fire, but the more general opinion seems to be that she foundered in the Mozambique Channel. Burns alludes to the event with feeling. "Falconer," says he, "the unfortunate author of the 'Shipwreck,' which you so much admire, is no more. After weathering the dreadful catastrophe he so feelingly describes in his poem, and after weathering so many hard gales of fortune, he went to the bottom with the *Aurora* frigate." In person, Falconer was about five feet two inches in height, of a thin, light make, with hard features, and a weather-beaten complexion. His hair was brown, and he was marked with the small-pox. In his common address, it is said, he was blunt and forbidding, but quick and fluent in conversation. His observation was keen, and his judgments acute and severe. His natural temper was cheerful, and he used to amuse his companions, the seamen, with acrostics which he made on their favorite nymphs. He was a good and skillful seaman. As for education, he assured Governor Hunter that it was confined to reading, English, and arithmetic. In his voyages he had picked up a little colloquial knowledge of Italian and Spanish, and such other languages as are spoken on the shores of the Mediterranean. That he was esteemed by his messmates is shown in a passage of a little work called the "Journal of a Seaman," written in 1755, and published by Murray in 1815. "How often," says the author, "have I wished to have the associate of my youth, Bill Falconer, with me, to explore these beauties, and to read them in his sweet poetry. But alas! I parted with him in old England, never, perhaps, to meet more in this world. His may be a happier lot, led by a gentler star; he may pass through this busy scene with more ease and tranquillity than has been the fortune of his humble friend Penrose."

Falconer's reputation as a poet rests almost entirely on his poem of the "Shipwreck," and this, to be enjoyed, requires a young and ardent imagination, indifferent to faults of style and defects of measure, and intent merely on the stirring incidents of danger, which are depicted with unusual minuteness and force. The poem will always be popular, for the subject is one which possesses a never-failing interest. Considering the educational and social difficulties under which the author labored, it is a work of extraordinary power, and evinces poetic genius of a high and commanding order.

O

SIR HUMPHREY DAVY.

One of the many sons of science to whom the world is largely indebted, not only for philosophical disquisitions and great learning, but for practical and useful inventions of every-day utility, is the illustrious gentleman whose name is at the head of this article. He belongs in an eminent degree to our series. With very few advantages of birth and education, he rose to eminence mainly through his own exertions. We shall trace his history chiefly from the loving memorials of his brother, Dr. John Davy.

Sir Humphrey Davy was the eldest son of Robert and Grace Davy, and was born at Penzance, in Cornwall, on the 17th of December, 1778. He was a precocious child, and gave evidence of the possession of unusual faculties. When scarcely five years old he made rhymes, and recited them in the Christmas gambols, attired in some fanciful dress prepared for the occasion by a playful girl who was related to him. His disposition as a child was remarkably sweet and affectionate. His father followed the profession of a carver in wood, and, although not in affluent circumstances, was able to send his son to the grammar-school of Truro, where he acquired a rudimental education. At the age of seventeen he was apprenticed to an apothecary in Penzance, and, with none of the usual vacillation of youth, set about a complete course of study. The following memorandum, copied from a note-book of this year, will show that he was not afraid of hard work:

PLAN OF STUDY.

1. Theology, or Religion, } { Taught by Nature,
   Ethics, or Moral Virtues, } { " by Revelation.
2. Geography.
3. My Profession:
    1. Botany;
    2. Pharmacy;
    3. Nosology;
    4. Anatomy;
    5. Surgery;
    6. Chemistry.
4. Logic.
5. Language:
    1. English;
    2. French;
    3. Latin.
    4. Greek;
    5. Italian;
    6. Spanish;
    7. Hebrew.
6. Physics:
    1. The Doctrines and Properties of Natural Bodies;
    2. Of the Operations of Nature;
    3. Of the Doctrines of Fluids;
    4. Of the Properties of organized Matter;
    5. Of the Organization of Matter;
    6. Simple Astronomy.
7. Mechanics.
8. Rhetoric and Oratory.
9. History and Chronology.
10. Mathematics.

The study of chemistry, like that of mathematics, is irresistible to certain minds, and Davy soon found himself completely absorbed in its pursuit. The activity and suggestiveness of his mind outstripped all formula. He entered upon speculations and inquiries far in advance of the rudiments he was studying. These, in due time, assumed a practical guise in the shape of essays, and, being crude and imperfect, excited the ire of the reviewers. "These critics," he writes, "perhaps do not understand that these experiments were made when I had studied chemistry only four months, when I had never seen a single experiment executed, and when all my information was derived from Nicholson's Chemistry and Lavoisier's Elements."

The early experiments of this philosopher were performed in a small bed-room in Mr. Tomkins's house, with a laboratory consisting of vials, wine-glasses, tea-cups, tobacco-pipes, and earthen crucibles; his materials chiefly the mineral acids, the alkalies, and the other articles common to an apothecary's shop. He had no furnace, and, when he needed heat, was compelled to go into the kitchen, where you may rest assured the cook did not thank him for his devotion to science. Notwithstanding these drawbacks, he made rapid progress in the study of chemistry and the relative sciences, and before he had reached his twentieth year was remarkable for the exactness of his information on many learned subjects. He now left Penzance, having obtained the situation of superintendent of the Pneumatic Institution which had been established at Clifton for the purpose of trying the medicinal effects of various gases. Davy remained here for some time, and was quite enthusiastic about the prospects of curing disease by the use of various gases hitherto unknown to medicine. He describes his occupation as "useful to mankind; pursuits which promise me, at some future time, the honorable meed of the applause of enlightened men." This prophetic feeling of distinction was soon about to be realized. The Royal Institution had been founded a short time previously, after a plan of Count Rumford's, for the purpose of diffusing a knowledge of science and of its application to the common purposes of life, and of exciting a taste for science among the higher ranks. In consequence of the expected retirement of the professor of chemistry, a successor was sought for, and the choice fell upon Davy. The duties on which he entered were those of assistant lecturer on chemistry and director of the laboratory; but, according to the terms on which he accepted the situation, this was merely a temporary arrangement, and to last only until he should deem himself fit to fill the professor's chair. On the 31st of May, 1802, he was formally appointed to the office, and, notwithstanding his youth, immediately attracted the attention of the philosophical world. His lectures were eagerly attended by the distinguished in science, literature, and position. Compliments, invitations, and presents were showered upon him in abundance from all quarters; his society was courted by all, and all appeared proud of his acquaintance. His youth, his simplicity, his natural eloquence, his happy illustrations, and well-conducted experiments, were the introductions which gave him welcome every where. In 1803 Davy was elected a Fellow of the Royal Society, and for ten sessions delighted the institution and enriched its Transactions with his lectures. His scientific labors during this time may be divided into two portions, the earlier one terminating with his great discovery of the decomposition of the fixed alkalies, the result and reward of his electro-chemical researches; the latter in the re-establishment of the simple nature of chlorine.

During the first portion of the period, among a great variety of objects of research, his attention was more particularly directed to the following: First, the investigation of astringent vegetables, in connection with the art of tanning; secondly, the analysis of rocks and minerals, in connection with geology; thirdly, the comprehensive subject of agricultural chemistry; and, fourthly, galvanism, and electro-chemical science. In the year 1812, unsolicited by Davy, the prince regent conferred on him the honor of knighthood. It was intended, doubtless, as a mark of respect to a man of unusual genius, and was so accepted. In those days men of genius were flattered by such little trifles. In these later times they despise them. A few days after this event Davy married a charming widow, Mrs. Appreece by name. Honors were showered on him; this happiness he achieved.

It is unnecessary and uninteresting in the present day to recount the innumerable distinctions that were bestowed on Davy by the learned bodies of Europe; to say when he was appointed a corresponding member of this society, and an honorary member of that. It is sufficient for our purpose that he was accepted and received as a man of mark in the scientific world, and to hasten to what he accomplished to give him this distinction.

One of the fruits of his researches was the "safety-lamp," now familiar to every eye. The object which this simple instrument so happily accomplishes is the prevention of explosions of fire-damp in mines. From innumerable experiments, Davy found that this gas required to be mixed with a very large quantity of atmospheric air to produce an explosion; that it was the least readily combustible of all the inflammable gases, or required the highest temperature, being neither exploded nor fired by red-hot charcoal or red-hot iron; and, farther, that the heat it produced when inflamed was less than from any other inflammable gas, and, consequently, that the expansive effect from heat attending its explosion was also less. He found that on mixing one part of carbonic acid gas or fixed air with seven parts of an explosive mixture of fire-damp, or one part of azote with six parts, their power of exploding was destroyed. He found that in exploding a mixture in a glass tube of one fourth of an inch in diameter and a foot long, more than a second was required before the flame reached from one end to the other; and that in tubes of one seventh of an inch in diameter, explosive mixtures could not be fired when they opened into the atmosphere; and that metallic tubes prevented explosion better than glass tubes. These were the facts from which the discovery of the safety-lamp was made. In reasoning upon the various phenomena, it occurred to Davy that, as a considerable heat was required for the inflammation of the fire-damp, and as it produced, in burning, a comparatively small degree of heat, the effect of carbonic acid and azote, and of the surfaces of small tubes in preventing its explosion, depended upon their cooling powers, upon their lowering the temperature of the exploding mixture so much that it was no longer sufficient for its continuous inflammation. He says, "This idea, which was confirmed by various obvious considerations, led to an immediate result—the possibility of constructing a lamp in which the cooling powers of the azote or carbonic acid formed by the combustion, or the cooling power of the apertures through which the air entered and made its exit, should prevent the communication of explosion." The prosecution of this idea led to the invention of the safety-lamp—a cage of wire gauze, which actually made prisoner the flame of the fire-damp, and in its prison consumed it; and while it confined the dangerous explosive flame, it permitted air to pass and light to escape; and though, from the combustion of the fire-damp, the cage might become red hot, yet still it acted the part of a safety-lamp, and restrained the flaming element within its narrow bounds, simply by presenting a surface of network, the temperature of which, under ordinary circumstances, could not be raised sufficiently to explode the surrounding atmosphere of fire-damp, or to allow the flame within to pass unextinguished.

Another useful and valuable discovery was made by Davy, namely, a method of preserving the copper sheathing of ships from the corrosive action of salt water. The principle of protection was found to be perfect, but in its practical application some difficulties arose which Davy did not live to obviate, although he made some valuable suggestions toward that end. Many other useful and eminently practical discoveries were made by Davy, especially in the tanning business, which in those days was carried on with hereditary rather than chemical skill. The experimental character of his mind led him naturally into new fields of investigation, and it is but justice to say that whatever he approached he benefited. Few men possessed a more practical yet thoroughly refined taste than Davy. Philosophers not unfrequently lose themselves in the abstruseness of the subjects they investigate, but with him this was never the case. He was a man of the world; keenly observant; mindful of its wants, and anxious to lend all the force of his character and genius to the onward progress of civilization. He was of a contented and beautiful disposition, fond of innocent amusements, and especially delighted with the ever-varying aspects of nature. He had traveled much, and, at the time when death overtook him, was on the Continent, endeavoring to regain in genial climes the health he had lost by too close application. It was during this time that he recomposed his delightful little book on fly-fishing, called "Salmonia," a work which justly ranks next to old Izaak Walton's for variety of information and charming picturesqueness of detail. He was also engaged on another work called "The Last Days of a Philosopher," since given to the world. He was a voluminous writer, and it may be doubted if any modern philosopher has contributed more largely to the literature of science than he.

Sir Humphrey Davy died at Geneva on the 30th of May, 1829. He had only arrived in that city the day before, and having been attacked by apoplexy after he had gone to bed, expired at an early hour in the morning.

ROBERT DODSLEY.

"I KNEW Darteneuf well, for I was his footman." Such was the characteristic admission of the subject of this memoir, uttered to that severest of critics, Dr. Johnson, and at a time, too, when the name of Dodsley was a passport to much excellent society. An individual blessed with such strength of character presents many excellent traits worthy of imitation, and we give his biography as an essential element of self-made success.

Robert Dodsley was born in 1703 at Mansfield, in Nottinghamshire. Nothing is known of his parents, except that they were poor, and unable to give him more than an ordinary rudimental education. Early in life he became a male servant, or footman, in the service of the Honorable Mr. Lowther, and continued in that somewhat degrading employment for many years, wearing a livery, and exhibiting his calves in the most approved fashion of the day. He was steady and observant, and his natural abilities gave him some little distinction beyond that awarded to his station. Having made some attempts at versification, he found patrons who induced him to publish them, and exerted themselves to procure a handsome list of subscribers. The title of this work, which was published in 1732, was, "The Muse in Livery. A Collection of Poems. By R. Dodsley, Footman to a Person of Quality at Whitehall." The contents of the volume were not remarkable for poetic beauty or for exactness of measure, but, heralded in such a candid way, they attracted attention, and induced Dodsley to prepare another work for the press, called "The Toy Shop." This was a dramatic satire on the fashionable follies of the day, and had merit. Pope (to whom it was shown) expressed himself warmly in its favor, and exerted himself to get it brought out on the stage. In 1735 it was produced at Covent Garden Theatre, and at once achieved a signal success.

There was now a fair prospect for Dodsley in the literary world. Many men have adopted the profession of letters with much smaller capital. But, although a poet, he was of a practical turn of mind, and could see that commerce was better than literature in a pecuniary point of view. To combine the two was his ardent wish, and, with the profits of his play and other assistance, he determined to do so. With this object in view, he opened a bookseller's store in Pall Mall, London (1735), and by politeness and attention succeeded in making it a daily resort of the most eminent authors. Pope was his great literary patron, and his countenance was, of course, a powerful auxiliary. In a short time Dodsley became celebrated for the fairness of his dealings and the liberality with which he conducted his business, and soon had the most famous and most prosperous publishing house in the British metropolis. Among the works of sterling merit which in the early part of his career he ushered into the world, was Johnson's "London," the copyright of which he purchased after several other houses had declined to have any thing to do with it. Nor was his own pen idle. In 1737 he produced "The King and the Miller of Mansfield," a farce founded on a traditionary story of English history. It was acted at Drury Lane, and was quite as successful as his first effort. In the following year he wrote a sequel to this piece, called "Sir John Cockle at Court," and subsequently two other pieces, all of which have been forgotten, and need not be mentioned here. In 1748 he collected these productions into a volume with the unassuming title of "Trifles," adding to the number a pantomime on a new plan. He was fond of dramatic composition, and made it the vehicle for holding pleasant communion with the public. Beside his original compositions, Dodsley was engaged in planning and publishing many other works. It was he who suggested to Johnson the idea of an English Dictionary.

In 1750 Dodsley produced an original work, which was at once a source of profit and reputation to him. It was called "The Economy of Human Life," and professed to be a translation from an Indian manuscript by an ancient Brahmin. For some reason, into which it is unnecessary to grope, the work was universally ascribed to the Earl of Chesterfield. It had a considerable share of merit, and enjoyed a wide reputation, having been translated in France by several publishers. Indeed, its reputation was so great that many imitations followed its advent, one of which boldly assumed to be a second part by the author of the first. In 1754 Dodsley tried his skill in an elaborate poetical composition, the subject being Public Virtue. The public failed to display a proper interest in virtue, and Dodsley satirically remarked that it was not a subject to interest the age. In 1757 he published "Melpomene, or the Regions of Terror and Pity. An Ode." The poem contained some fine passages, and was successful. It is considered the best of his poems. In the following January he produced a tragedy called "Cleone," with applause. Bennet Langton relates that Dodsley one day began to read "Cleone" to Johnson, who displayed obvious signs of uneasiness. At the end of an act, however, he said, "Come, let's have some more; let's go into the slaughter-house again, Lanky. But I am afraid there is more blood than brains." Yet he afterward said, "When I heard you read it, I thought higher of its powers of language; when I read it myself, I was more sensible of its pathetic effect;" and then he paid it a high compliment. "Sir," said he, "if Otway had written this play, no other of his pieces would have been remembered." This anecdote gives us a good insight into the very unequal character of Dodsley's writing, leaving the reader uncertain whether to condemn or to praise, but finding justification for either extreme. "Cleone" was the last of his poetical effusions. Having acquired a handsome fortune, Dodsley retired from the active pursuit of business. A predisposition to gout was perhaps one of the reasons why he did so, for business was unquestionably pleasure with him. Of this disease he died on the 25th of September, 1764, in the 61st year of his age. He was buried in the Abbey Church of Durham, and the following just epitaph is inscribed on his tombstone:

"If you have any respect for uncommon industry and merit, regard this place, in which are deposited the remains of Mr. Robert Dodsley, who, as an author, raised himself much above what could have been expected from one in his rank of life, and without a learned education; and who, as a man, was scarce exceeded by any in integrity of heart, and purity of manners and conversation. He left this life for a better, September 25th, 1764, in the 61st year of his age."

ANTONIO CANOVA.

ANTONIO CANOVA, the most remarkable sculptor of modern times, whose works lend grace, beauty, and durability to the homes of the nineteenth century, was a native of Possagno, a village situated at the foot of the Venetian Alps, where he was born in 1757. He was descended from a family of sculptors, the arts descending from father to son in Italy like the titles of the privileged classes. His father had some little reputation, but young Antonio derived no advantage from it, for he was an orphan at the age of three years. A grandfather adopted the lonely boy, and gave him some instruction in the rudiments of art, employing him in the quarries and in the workshop of the old stonemason. His grandmother was most kind and affectionate, and neglected no opportunity of encouraging the lad. Not only for fame, but for fortune, she was desirous that her grandson should stride beyond the narrow limits of the stone-cutting room. At an early age he modeled in clay, and shaped little fragments of marble into easily-recognized objects. He was enthusiastic, and loved his adopted profession. Nothing afforded him so much delight as being left alone with a few tools and a piece of marble. They were all the companions he needed.

Progress was the necessity of such a disposition. So early as his ninth year young Canova could command the wages of a workman, and was a favorite even at that. His grandfather was proud of him, and, whenever any repairs were to be done to the neighboring palaces, took the youthful journeyman with him. His remarkable talents were not long in attracting notice. A Signor Falieri, a gentleman of cultivated tastes, interested himself in the lad, and volunteered to take him into his house in order that he might enjoy advantages of an education which his grandfather's humble means utterly denied him. A story has been told that Canova first attracted the attention of the Falieri family by modeling a lion in butter for that gentleman's table, but it is very questionable if this story has any actual foundation in truth.

After receiving some general instruction in the family of the Falieri, he was placed under Torretto, one of the best Venetian sculptors. He accompanied this distinguished artist to Venice, and remained under his tuition until the time of his death, which occurred two years later. By this event Canova was left without any guidance or restraint, at a moment, too, when both were most needed. His patron, Falieri, once more came to his assistance, and secured him admission into the studio of the sculptor Gio Ferrari, who was engaged at the time on a series of statues for the Casa Tiepolo at Carbonara. With this *maestro* Canova continued for about twelve months, and saw sufficient to convince him that the conventionalities of art were a restraint on genius, and impeded the natural suggestions of a poetic temperament. From these conventionalities he determined to cut loose, and explore the wide and ever-remunerative paths of nature. His first known works were two baskets of fruit, still to be seen on the first landing-place of the Farsetti Palace, now the Hotel della Gran Brettagna, at Venice. The performance did not give promise of that excellence which Canova afterward attained, but it was perhaps a step in the right direction.

An effort of a more ambitious kind was the group called Orpheus and Eurydice, part of which was completed, and the whole designed before his sixteenth year. This composition, executed in soft stone, was publicly exhibited in Venice on the occasion of the festival of the Ascension, and attracted considerable attention.

The following year he executed the same subject in marble, having obtained his first important commission for that group. Much of his time was still occupied with studies. He divided his day into three parts: the morning he devoted to study in the Academy or Galleries, the afternoon to the labor of the workshop, and the evening to the improvement of his mind in general knowledge. "I labored," he says in one of his letters, "for a mere pittance; but it was sufficient; it was the fruit of my own resolution, and, as I then flattered myself, the foretaste of more honorable rewards, for I never thought of wealth."

Having thus obtained some popularity, and being still a favorite with his old patron Faliero, he found ready employment on busts. He also modeled his group of "Dædalus and Icarus," a work which may be said to have laid the foundation of his future fame, and which was immediately beneficial, inasmuch as it induced his patron to insist that he should repair to Rome, and in that ample theatre of the arts extend his studies and his fame at the same time. In October of the year 1779 Canova reached the Eternal City, and enjoyed the delicious sensations which all devotees must experience in that vast emporium of plastic masterpieces. He received a cordial welcome from the artists of the day, and was warmly praised for his "Dædalus and Icarus" group, which he took with him as a specimen of what he could do. "On the first exhibition of this work," says his biographer, "he was surrounded by the most distinguished artists and critics then residing at Rome, who contemplated the group with silent astonishment, not daring to censure what, although at variance with the style then followed, commanded their admiration and revealed the brightest prospects. The embarrassment of the young artist was extreme, and he frequently spoke of it afterward as one of the most anxious moments of his life. From this state of anxiety he was, however, soon relieved by the almost unanimous approbation of the spectators. Even the critics praised—an effort which they are not willing to make in the cause of mediocrity. They saw in the production of the young man much simplicity, expression, and unaffected truth to nature. From that day Canova had a position among the highest. More than this, he received the kindly advice of the best critics and connoisseurs, and was able to detect errors in his own style which he was not too proud or too foolish to rectify."

The Venetian embassador at Rome became an admirer and patron of the sculptor. He placed at his command a block of fine marble, and suggested a subject for a group—Theseus, conqueror of the Minotaur. The work was conducted throughout in the palace of the embassador, and every kind of assistance was rendered to the artist. In this work Canova followed those true principles by which he had proposed to himself to be guided in his works—a composition by which a new path was opened to all productions of imitative art. The embassador, who watched the progress of the work with true art enthusiasm, obtained a cast of the head of Theseus as soon as it was ready, and displayed it to a party of artists and critics who were assembled in his house. He took the precaution not to inform them whence it came, and they uttered a profound opinion that it was of Grecian origin, varying, however, on some points of merit. Several thought they had seen the marble from which it had been taken, not being able to recollect exactly where it was. Delighted and flattered with the result of his experiment, the embassador led them into the studio of the artist, and placed them before the entire group. Their surprise was only exceeded by their admiration. They saw and acknowledged that a new era in art had commenced.

Important employment was now not difficult to obtain. He received a commission to execute the monument of Pope Clement the Fourteenth for the church of the SS. Apostoli in Rome. This fine work was exhibited in 1787, and established Canova's claim to the highest rank in his profession. Before it was completed, Canova had commenced Clement the Thirteenth's monument for St. Peter's, a splendid work of genius and executive skill. A story is told in Rome of Canova putting on a monk's dress and cowl, and in this disguise mixing with the crowd, to hear the criticisms that were made when the work was first exposed to public view.

Canova's powers of imagination were superb, and in works demanding their exercise he was unsurpassed. In the mere mechanical portions of his business he had many superiors. His busts were not considered remarkable. It is not strange, therefore, that he devoted himself to subjects requiring an exercise of the higher order of genius. To recapitulate the works which he produced in rapid succession would be tedious and unnecessary. Of statues and groups he executed forty; of busts, eleven; of monuments, sixteen; of bas reliefs (principally in models), fifteen. Many of these productions were of colossal proportions, and most of them of the size of life. To accomplish so much, Canova applied himself with unflagging industry to his vocation. In his habits he was regular and moderate. He rose early, and immediately proceeded to his studio, where he worked on his models for a time, and then proceeded with the chisel. In the mere manual labor of the sculptor Canova introduced some innovations, which account in a great measure for the multiplicity of his works. Up to this time it was customary for the artist to execute all his own work, from the rough hewing of the marble to the last touch of the chisel. Much valuable time was necessarily expended in the first operation without any commensurate result, for an ordinary stone-cutter was quite as capable of sawing off a piece of marble as Canova himself. It occurred to the latter, therefore, that, by making the models similar in size to the statues, he could employ a number of dexterous assistants, who would relieve him of all the mechanical drudgery of the business. He made the experiment, and succeeded. Every sculptor of the present day has his studio liberally supplied with assistants.

Canova traveled, when young, over part of Germany, and was twice in Paris. At his last visit, when sent there by the Roman government to superintend the removal of the works of art which had been seized by the French army, and which the allies had decided should be restored to Italy, he proceeded to England, chiefly for the purpose of seeing the Elgin marbles, of which he expressed the highest admiration. His reception in that country was extremely cordial, and was a subject of much pleasure to him. On his return to Rome he received a patent of nobility, and was created Marquis of Ischia. With a republican feeling remarkable as it was creditable, he never adopted this title, but to the last called himself Antonio Canova—a far preferable name than the Marquis of Ischia in many people's estimation. It is worthy of remark in this connection, that one of Canova's best works was executed for America. It was the sitting statue of Washington, in marble, executed for the United States, and forwarded to America in 1820.

In the month of May, 1822, Canova went to Naples to inspect some preparations for a colossal work, and returned to Rome with a tendency to disorder in his stomach, which was always badly affected by that climate. Not having entirely recovered from this attack, he determined on a visit to his native place, and on the 17th of September arrived at Possagno. Unfortunately, the journey was too severe for his constitution, and aggravated the complaint under which he labored. He was very ill on his arrival, but did not take to his bed, expecting relief from his native air and the waters of Recodro. All was unavailing. On the 4th of October Canova arrived at Venice, intending to stay there a few days; but, continuing to get gradually worse, he received the last offices of religion, and resigned himself to die with the utmost constancy and serenity, uttering only short sentences of a pious character to those who attended him. Approaching his end, he said to those who moistened his dying lips, "Good, very good; but it is in vain." His last words were, "Pure and lovely spirit." These he uttered several times just before he expired. He spoke no more; but his visage became, and continued for some time, highly radiant and expressive, as if his mind was absorbed in some sublime conception, creating powerful and unusual emotions in all around him.

Canova was a man of the most amiable and conciliatory manners, extremely friendly and gentle toward his fellow-artists, and encouraging and liberal toward the numerous students who filled his studio. To several of the latter, whose means were scanty, he gave pensions, to enable them to prosecute their studies. He also established out of his own purse a handsome premium for sculpture in the Academy of St. Luke at Rome, of which he was president. In personal appearance Canova was rather below the common stature, and toward the close of his life stooped as he walked. His features were strongly-marked, but well-formed, his nose aquiline, and his eyes deeply set and full of expression. The general expression of his countenance was genial and pleasing.

Concerning the merit of his works, a competent critic remarks that, in execution and the whole treatment of his marble, Canova was unrivaled; but those who judge of sculpture by the pure principles of Greek art (or, in other words, of nature, selected and exhibited in its finest and most approved forms), will discover in many of his works some affectation, both in the attitudes and expression, and a littleness in some of the details, which are not in accordance with the simplicity and breadth of style of the best productions of the ancients. Admitting this to be the case (particularly in some of his later performances), still his works evince so great a progress in art, and in many respects approach so much more nearly than those that had for a long period preceded them to the excellence of ancient sculpture, that Canova must be confessed to be one of the great regenerators of the art; and his name, as the restorer of a purer style of design, will always be held in honor by those who wish to see sculpture practiced upon true principles.

PHILIP VAYRINGE.

MECHANICAL genius of a high order is a gift so rare in the world, that the few men who have possessed it in an eminent degree are certainly worthy of remembrance. The subject of this sketch, although unknown in the present century, was in his day considered remarkable enough to merit the appellation of the Lotharingian Archimedes. Philip Vayringe was a native of Lorraine, born in 1684 at Nouilloupont, a small village which is situated in the department of the Meuse, between Longwy and Verdun. He was one of a large family, and at an early age experienced harsh treatment from a step-mother, which induced him to run away from home. It was his intention on this occasion (he was ten years old, and could scarcely spell his name correctly) to make a pilgrimage to Rome; but, before he got very far on his way, he met two of his schoolfellows, who prevailed on him to return to the paternal roof. Philip, however, became so enamored of the town of Metz, through which they passed, that he gave his companions the slip, and made up his mind to remain there. Strolling about the town, he was first attracted by the operations of a locksmith, who sat working at his bench near the open window. Observing the youth's curiosity, the artisan spoke to him, asked him some commonplace questions, and finally wound up by offering to take him into his employ at the liberal stipend of tenpence a month. Philip accepted the terms on condition that he should be allowed to try to make a lock. The permission was, of course, readily granted, and he succeeded so well that an addition was at once made to his wage. In six months he had become so familiar with the business that he found no difficulty in getting employment at three times the price paid him by his first master.

In the following winter he returned to Nouilloupont, residing this time with a brother-in-law, who was at once a gunsmith and edge-tool maker. Philip was, of course, useful in such a shop, but a circumstance soon occurred which diverted his attention from the fabrication of locks. A clock was brought in to be repaired, and its delicate mechanism filled Philip with admiration. It was only left in the shop for an hour and a half, but in this short time he had fixed all the parts in his mind, and knew exactly on what principle it worked. A few months afterward he made a successful copy of this clock, much to the astonishment of the simple villagers. He was now determined to be a clock-maker, and, with twenty-five shillings in his purse, started for Nancy, the capital of Lorraine. There was but one clock-maker in the place, and, as he had three sons, there was no opening for Philip. He was fortunate, however, in finding a friend in a Parisian master locksmith and worker in iron, who had come to Nancy to fabricate a highly-ornamental gate for the choir of the Benedictine church. This person having shown him his designs, Philip requested that he would teach him how to draw similar ones with a pen, and carry them into execution. His kind friend immediately offered to take him into his employ at a salary of ten shillings a month, and to give him all the instruction in his power. He was thus employed for twelve months. In the mean time, he did not forget the subject of horology. His employer possessed the unusual treasure of a watch, so valuable in those days that it was actually the first Philip had seen. Anxious to penetrate the mystery of its intricate workings, he begged permission to examine it. His request was complied with by his kind friend, who seemed to place implicit confidence in the ingenuity of the youth. Philip hurried home in triumph, and in no time had the watch to pieces, and discovered the object of all its movements, making drawings of those which he could not sufficiently remember. He succeeded in putting the fragments together again, and in restoring the watch to its owner in perfectly good condition. The result of his various investigations was an extremely ingenious clock, which he made in his leisure moments, and for which he had to fabricate tools. It was nine inches in height and six in width, and had four different movements: hours, quarters, striking, and chimes. The chimes played an air every hour, while the image of the Savior, followed by the twelve apostles, passed across a gallery. Nearly a year was spent in forming this complicated piece of mechanism, but it brought him much renown, and, better still, was indirectly the means of procuring him a very advantageous wife, a charming young orphan of fourteen (he was twenty-seven), with two thousand dollars in cash. They lived long and happily together, and did the state some service by bringing into the world no fewer than nineteen children.

About a year after his marriage he started in business on his own account. His shop was distinguished by a sign of his own invention, which, he tells us, was admired as a masterpiece. It was probably a piece of mechanism, but he has left us no description of its character or appearance. Having borrowed some tools, he immediately set about making a watch, similar to the one he had borrowed from his Parisian friend and employer. He accomplished his task successfully in eighteen days. Customers soon became numerous, but he found that a Parisian reputation was necessary, and he determined, therefore, to visit the capital of France. Furnished with letters of introduction to several of the most important watch-makers in the metropolis, he set out. Many men would have deemed a limited apprenticeship desirable under such circumstances, and Vayringe was of that opinion, but he limited the apprenticeship to one day; that is to say, he requested a person to whom he was recommended to allow him to work in his shop for a single day. He found out all he wanted in that time, and, having visited the shops of the most eminent watch-makers, purchased tools and materials, and amused himself with contemplating the wonders of Versailles, he returned to his home after a fortnight's absence.

The first thing he did on his return was to imitate the machinery he had seen in the workshops of Paris, adding many improvements of his own which were of obvious utility. His reputation was now established, and business pressed in upon him in the most satisfactory manner. With increased resources, he gave free rein to his invention, and indulged in the fabrication of many curious machines not actually useful or actually useless. Among other things, he endeavored, like all ingenious men of his time, to solve the problem of perpetual motion. While thus occupied, he succeeded in making many very simple movements, and, "among others, those of an eight-day clock with only three wheels, and which nevertheless struck the hours and half hours, and repeated them, and, besides, indicated the revolution and the various phases of the moon." He finished, also, a watch which repeated the hours and quarters, though it had merely the wheels of a common watch. He worked likewise at all sorts of mathematical instruments, both for engineers and geographers.

In 1720 Vayringe was appointed watch-maker and mechanist to Duke Leopold of Lorraine, and removed from Nancy to Luneville, the capital of that province. Here he occupied himself not only with clocks and watches, but with astronomical instruments, and several models of hydraulic machines, the simplicity and powerful action of which were much praised. One of the models, that of a machine to throw five jets of water to a height of sixty feet, was afterward carried into effect in the ducal gardens of Luneville. In the year 1721 Vayringe had occasion to visit the British metropolis on business for the duke, and became an inmate in the house of the celebrated Desaguliers. This accidental circumstance was of great advantage to him, and he improved the occasion with avidity. Desaguliers taught him geometry and algebra, and explained minutely the properties and management of all the instruments and machines by which he himself illustrated his annual courses of experimental philosophy. More than this, he caused a similar apparatus to be made for Vayringe. After a residence of thirteen months in London he was recalled to Luneville. The duke was so delighted with the instruments he brought with him, that he gave Vayringe instructions to complete the set by making what were necessary for the full illustration of a complete course of philosophy. In pursuance of this order, Vayringe produced a variety of works, one of the most curious of which was a planisphere, on the Copernican system, "above which," says he, "the planets, supported by steel wires, performed their courses, according to the calculations of the most celebrated astronomers." This was, in fact, a kind of orrery, an instrument which had been shown and explained to him by Desaguliers during his visit to the English capital, and which was then new to the world of science. The duke was so astonished by this masterpiece of ingenuity that he considered it to be a worthy present for the emperor, and Vayringe was accordingly dispatched with it to Vienna. The emperor was equally delighted, and he rewarded the maker with a massy gold medal and chain, and a purse containing two hundred ducats.

On his return to Luneville he found M. de Boifranc, architect of the King of France, who was anxious for him to proceed to Paris to superintend the construction of a steam-engine for a mine in Peru. When this important job was finished, he returned to Luneville, and employed himself in the manufacture of many curious philosophical machines, especially an orrery. In 1729, Duke Leopold, his patron, died, and for a time some of his most extensive works were discontinued. In the following year Leopold's successor remodeled the Academy of Luneville, and appointed Vayringe professor of experimental philosophy. His lectures immediately attracted much attention, and were, like Duval's in the same establishment, largely attended by foreigners. His popularity continued undiminished as long as the house of Lorraine held the government of its hereditary dominions; but in 1737, political arrangements between France and the emperor transferred the duchy to Stanislaus, and eventually to France, and in exchange gave to the duke the sovereignty of Tuscany. Despots think nothing of "swopping" whole generations of men. "I was," says Vayringe, "soon a witness to the evacuation of Lorraine. I saw her highness the Duchess Regent, and the two august princesses, her daughters, tear themselves from their palace, their faces bathed with tears, their hands raised toward heaven, and uttering cries expressive of the most violent grief. It would be utterly impossible to depict the consternation, the regrets, the sobs, and all the symptoms of despair to which the people gave way at the aspect of a scene which they considered as the last sigh of the country. It is almost inconceivable that hundreds of persons were not crushed under the wheels of the carriage, or trodden under the feet of the horses, in throwing themseves blindly as they did before the vehicles to retard their departure. While consternation, lamentations, horror, and confusion were reigning in Luneville, the inhabitants of the rural districts hurried in multitudes to the road by which the royal family was to pass, and, throwing themselves on their knees, stretched out their hands to them, and implored them not to abandon their people." Vayringe accompanied the duke to his future territories, although earnestly entreated to remain by the new sovereign of Lorraine. It was an unfortunate step for him. In Lorraine mechanical genius was appreciated and understood, but in Tuscany no one cared about such things. The Grand Duke did, indeed, continue his patronage to the artist, but his example was not followed by his court or his subjects. After a miserable sojourn of eight years in his new home, Vayringe wrote in the following melancholy vein: "I had figured to myself," he says, "that Tuscany having been, as it were, the cradle of genuine experimental philosophy, a taste for that science would have been preserved, as in the time of the Galileos, Torricellis, and the Academy del' Cimento, and that, consequently, the lectures which I had delivered at Luneville would be still more attractive at Florence." But his conjectures were erroneous; he found the young men addicted to gallantry, the ladies to coquetry, and every one to triviality, not unmixed with sensuality. He published a syllabus of all the experiments he had made in Lorraine, but the Florentine public paid no attention to it, and it fell dead. "It is true," he writes, "that my being a foreigner contributed in no small degree to this indifference. I was given to understand that Italy, in all ages, had possessed the privilege of teaching other nations, and was not at all accustomed to take lessons from them. It may with truth be said that this miserable prejudice, together with the spirit of trifling and parsimony of which I have spoken, are the rocks on which the Academy of Lorraine has been wrecked. Transferred to Tuscany at an immense expense, and having the same professors who had rendered it so flourishing, it has there been wholly deserted. The school of experimental philosophy, one of the most curious and complete in Europe, has shared the same fate, though the cost of the lectures which were given there was reduced to less than half the sum that was paid at Luneville. Thus the talent for mechanics which Providence has bestowed on me has become totally useless as far as regards the public, in consequence of the indifference of my new fellow-citizens, and the state of inaction in which they have left me to stagnate."

Circumstances of this depressing nature were too much for the sanguine temperament of an inventor, whose imagination, at the best of times, is too sensitive and warm. He became careless of himself, like all dissatisfied people, and felt disposed to brave all sorts of dangers. On one occasion he was indiscreet enough to expose himself to the deadly malaria of that pestiferous district called the Maremma. A slow fever was the result, which, after eighteen months' duration, ended in dropsy. He died under the effect of this latter disease on the 24th of March, 1746, and was buried in the Barnabite Church at Florence, where his monument may still be seen, erected by his friend Duval. "Probity, candor, and the most ingenuous simplicity," says Duval, "characterized his disposition, and they may be said to have beamed upon his countenance and in all his actions."

NATHANIEL BOWDITCH.

The subject of this sketch was the son of a cooper, and was born at Salem, Massachusetts, March 26th, 1773. At an early age he had the misfortune to lose his mother, to whom, like most men of eminence, he owed much that was good and beautiful in his nature. He was only ten years of age when this happened, and previous to it had attended school for a short time. It is related that, even at this early day, he displayed a remarkable aptitude for figures, and intuitively performed arithmetical feats far in advance of his studies.

When little more than ten years of age he was bound apprentice to Messrs. Ropes & Hodges, who were ship-chandlers, and while in their service always kept a slate and pencil by his side, so that, when not engaged in serving customers, he could pursue his favorite study. Every moment that he could call his own was devoted to the same object. He rose early, and went to bed late, so that, by thus economizing his time, he was able to make considerable progress in the mathematics. The labor which he cheerfully undertook to make himself master of the subject was prodigious. Most of his books he borrowed from the Salem Athenæum, and, in spite of dryness, copied them. The fruits of his diligence still exist in more than twenty folio and quarto volumes. He did not allow any thing to impede his progress. That he might read Newton's "Principia," he learned Latin, the tongue in which it is written, and so with the French language. With these two powerful auxiliaries, he translated the former elaborate work, and the extensive one of La Place.

In a few years Mr. Bowditch became known as an extremely accomplished man of science, and was employed with another gentleman to make a thorough survey of the town of Salem. After this (1795) he was induced to undertake a voyage to the East Indies, under Captain Prince. The vessel returned after a year's absence, and Bowditch was so satisfied with the voyage that he made a second, third, and fourth with the same captain. The leisure which this occupation afforded him was doubtless one of its charms, for he was able not only to prosecute his mathematical studies, but to perfect himself in several languages, the French especially, and Italian, Spanish, and Portuguese to a great extent. His method of learning a language was peculiar. He obtained a New Testament in the desired language, and, with the aid of a Dictionary, worked through it. At the time of his death he possessed New Testaments in no fewer than twenty-five languages, and Dictionaries of a still larger number. He was by no means stingy of his knowledge, but, knowing its advantage, tried to diffuse it. Among the sailors he was eminently popular, and made the ship a perfect school of learning. Slates and pencils were in great demand, and conversations like the following are recorded: "Well, Jack, what have you got?" "I've got the *sine.*" "That ain't right; *I* say it's the *cosine.*" According to Captain Prince, there were twelve men on board capable of working lunar observations for all practical purposes. Bowditch's habits at this time have been described very accurately by a companion. "His practice was to rise at a very early hour in the morning, and pursue his studies till breakfast; immediately after which he walked rapidly for about half an hour, and then went below to his studies till half past eleven o'clock, when he returned, and walked till the hour at which he commenced his meridian observations. Then came dinner, after which he was engaged in his studies till five o'clock; then he walked till tea-time, and after tea was at his studies till nine o'clock in the evening. From this hour till half past ten o'clock he appeared to have banished all thoughts of study, and while walking he would converse in the most lively manner, giving us useful information, intermixed with amusing anecdotes and hearty laughs, making the time delightful to the officers who walked with him, and who had to quicken their pace to accompany him. Whenever the heavenly bodies were in proper distance to get the longitude, night or day, he was sure to make his observations once, and frequently twice in every twenty-four hours, always preferring to make them by the moon and stars, on account of his eyes. He was often seen on deck at other times walking rapidly, and apparently in deep thought; and it was well understood by all on board that he was not to be disturbed, as we supposed he was solving some difficult problem; and when he darted below, the conclusion was that he had got the idea. If he were in the fore part of the ship when the idea came to him, he would actually run to the cabin, and his countenance would give the expression that he had found a prize."

The nicety of Bowditch's observations enabled him to detect many errors in the existing books on navigation, and especially one in which the year 1800 was set down as a leap-year. The immediate effect of this error, producing a difference of twenty-three miles in the reckoning, was to cause the loss of many vessels. The publisher of the work, hearing of Mr. Bowditch's corrections, applied to the young navigator for assistance, and at his suggestion the latter undertook the laborious task of revising all the tables. In this operation he discovered no fewer than ten thousand errors. Concerning some of these, Mr. Bowditch remarks that, although they would not seriously affect the result of any nautical calculation, yet, since most of the tables were useful on other occasions where great accuracy was needed, it was not useless to have them corrected. Such a fabulous number of blunders have not been common since Bowditch's day.

In 1802 Mr. Bowditch published his first edition of the "Practical Navigator," a work of inestimable value to the maritime world, and which is still used to a great extent in the French and English navies. It gave the author a wide-spread reputation, and was no doubt instrumental in directing his attention to the publication of other scientific works. In part payment for his "Navigator," Bowditch received a copy of La Place's splendid

Mécanique Céleste, a work with which our author's name became closely associated. About this time he abandoned the sea as a profession. He had a reputation to rest on, and had been honored by several learned societies. He was a member of the American Academy of Arts and Sciences, and just before his last voyage Harvard University conferred upon him the honorary degree of Master of Arts (1802).

Soon after the close of his seafaring life, Mr. Bowditch was chosen president of the Essex Fire and Marine Insurance Company, in which office he remained nearly twenty years. Mainly owing to his good and practical management, the shareholders were able to secure large dividends on their investments. "For this situation," says one of his biographers, "his affability, regular habits, sagacity, and strict integrity, no less than his great scientific attainments, remarkably fitted him. The duties he had to discharge were severe, and occupied most of his time, but his favorite studies were never neglected. He never went down to the office without a volume of mathematics in his pocket, and every moment that he was not engaged in business he pored over its contents. During his residence at Salem he contributed twenty-three papers to the several volumes of the Transactions of the American Academy of Arts and Sciences. Some of these were on mathematical subjects, but the majority were astronomical. On the preparation of these he expended an amount of labor which even an enthusiast may contemplate with wonder. On the subject of the orbit of the comet of 1811, the manuscript volume containing his calculations (still in existence) was filled with one hundred and forty-four pages of closely-written figures, probably exceeding a million in number. The article itself was but *twelve pages* in length. Mr. Bowditch was a contributor to the Monthly Anthology, the North American Review, Silliman's Journal, the Analyst and Mathematical Diary. He also wrote several articles for the American edition of Rees' Cyclopedia.

We have already referred to La Place's great work, *Mécanique Céleste.* Bowditch's admiration for this masterly production—describing the entire mechanism of the heavens on mathematical principles—was so complete that he determined on translating it, and accompanying it with a copious commentary. The varied accomplishments required for the latter task can only be understood by taking a comprehensive glance at the subjects treated by La Place. Some of them are as follows: The laws of equilibrium and motion; the law of universal gravitation, and the motions of the centres of gravity of the heavenly bodies; the figures of the heavenly bodies deduced theoretically, and then compared with the actual observations made of the figures of the earth and the planet Jupiter; the oscillations of the sea and the atmosphere; the motions of the heavenly bodies about their own centres of gravity; the theory of the planetary motions, and their inequalities and perturbations; the theory of comets; light, and the theory of astronomical refractions, etc., etc. The work was declared by Professor Playfair to be an example "solitary in the history of human knowledge, of a *theory entirely complete;* one that has not only accounted for all the phenomena that were known, but that has discovered many before unknown, which observation has since recognized. To translate a work of this kind, and to write a commentary on it, was a task of prodigious labor, and required powers and attainments of the highest order." Dr. Bowditch used to say, "Whenever I meet in La Place with the words 'Thus it plainly appears,' I am sure that hours, and perhaps days of hard study, will alone enable me to discover *how* it plainly appears."

It was the object of the translator to elucidate the difficult demonstrations by supplying the deficient steps, and carrying the processes still farther, if necessary; and to continue the work to the present time, so as to put the reader in full possession of all the recent "improvements and discoveries in mathematical science." He accomplished this truly Herculean task, and placed the great work before the public in a luminous and perfectly intelligible shape. On almost every page the notes exceeded the text; indeed, these have in themselves a value almost equal to the original matter. They are thoroughly critical, and examine the truth without any blind adherence to La Place's version of it. Some idea of the pains bestowed on the work may be formed from the fact that it was not published until twelve years after the translation was completed. It appeared at last—four quarto volumes of a thousand pages each; the fifth volume of the original work was never translated.

In 1823 Dr. Bowditch (he was made a doctor by Harvard University in 1816) accepted an engagement in Boston as actuary to the Massachusetts Hospital Life Insurance Company. On his departure from Salem he received a public demonstration of regard and admiration, and in his new home was selected for many offices of distinction and trust. He remained in Boston to the time of his death, which occurred on the 16th of March, 1838, in the sixty-fifth year of his age.

Dr. Bowditch was twice married, and left a widow, a devoted and admirable woman, who contributed in no small degree to the doctor's energy of purpose and ultimate fame. To her memory he dedicated the translation and commentary of La Place's great work.

The doctor was a diligent man, and eminently methodical. He was able to accomplish great tasks with ease, mainly owing to these qualifications. He was always careful of his health, and never neglected taking a due amount of physical exercise. Men of studious habits are too apt to overlook the requirements of the body in their eagerness to cultivate the mind. He was the recipient of many honors and degrees. In 1806 he was elected Professor of Mathematics in Harvard University; in 1818 he was requested by Mr. Jefferson to take the same office in the University of Virginia; in 1820 Mr. Calhoun offered him the vacant professorship of Mathematics at West Point. The American Philosophical Society admitted him as a member in 1809; the Connecticut Academy of Arts and Sciences in 1813; the Literary and Philosophical Society of New York in 1815; the Edinburgh Royal Society in 1818; and the Royal Irish Society in 1819. After the translation of La Place's work he was chosen a member of the Royal Astronomical Society of London, the Royal Academy of Palermo, and the Royal Academy of Berlin.

Dr. Bowditch left a very valuable library, which is still preserved unbroken, and placed at the disposal of the public by Dr. Bowditch's family in Boston.

VALENTINE JAMERAI DUVAL.

DUVAL, whose history is perhaps the most romantic of any in this volume, was born at the little village of Artonnay, in Champagne, some time in 1695. His parents were in an extreme state of poverty, and before he was ten years of age he had the misfortune to lose his father. To contribute in some small degree to the sustenance of his mother's family now became an object of the utmost importance. On a neighboring farm he obtained the privilege of looking after the turkeys, for which he obtained a small remuneration. It was not till he was fourteen that Duval had an opportunity of obtaining the faintest rudiments of an education. He then learned the alphabet. When he was fourteen he ceased to be a watcher of turkeys, the agricultural distress which prevailed rendering it necessary for the farmers to pursue a system of the strictest economy. To add to the troubles of the period (1709), a winter of unprecedented severity set in. Such was its arctic rigor that the courts of justice were closed, the sacramental offices were suspended, from the impossibility of keeping fluid the wine which was used, and numbers of even the strongest travelers were struck dead upon the high roads. In such a cruel winter the poor were exposed to the most frightful hardships, and even those whose circumstances were not actually indigent experienced many pressing wants. Young Duval was unwilling to become a burden on his poor mother at such a season, and, friendless and helpless, went forth in the bitter wind to procure shelter and food among the villages and hamlets of Champagne. For several days he continued his dreary way, nearly frozen and famished, when suddenly he was attacked by an excruciating pain in the head. It was with the greatest difficulty that he struggled to a small farm-house which he observed in the distance. Arrived there, he begged that he might be permitted to rest his limbs in an out-house. A female servant took compassion on him, and led him into a building where the sheep were kept. In the morning the farmer discovered the poor boy in a most deplorable condition. He was in a burning fever, and angry pustules had made their appearance on different parts of his body. The farmer knew the symptoms, and bluntly declared that Duval was laboring under an attack of small-pox, assuring him also, by way of consolation, that it would infallibly kill him. Although rough and uncultivated, he was a good-hearted man, and did more for the little patient than might have been expected, considering the fearful nature of the disease, and the alarm it is apt to occasion. He procured a bundle of rags, stripped off the boy's clothing, and wrapped him up in the rags like a mummy. Having done this, he took off several layers of dung from a heap, and in the warm place thus created made a purely agricultural bed, placed the patient on it, strewed chaff on him, covered him up to the neck with the layers which he had taken off, and then concluded by making the sign of the cross on the boy, whom he recomended to God and the saints, believing that it would be little else than a miracle if he escaped death.

Duval's biographer thinks that, rude as were the bed and the chamber where the youth lay, they were perhaps more beneficial to him than any he could have found in the farmer's humble abode. The fermenting of the dung and the breath of a flock of sheep diffused a warmth which he would not elsewhere have enjoyed, and which brought on a profuse perspiration. The virus of the disease was thrown out to the surface instead of being repelled into the vital parts. While he was lying helpless, he was exposed to one annoyance from his fellow-lodgers. The sheep would lick his face. He did his best, he says, to avoid these cruel caresses, less on his own account than in the fear that the poison with which he was covered might be hurtful to the poor sheep. He did not then know that the poison of the small-pox is reserved for the human family alone. He was exposed to other troubles even more dangerous. The place in which he was sheltered was overhung with large trees. Often in the dead of night he was aroused by loud reports as of cannon or thunder. When he inquired what had occasioned these strange sounds, he was informed that the intensity of the frost had rent many of the trees to the roots, and caused them to "go off" in the way mentioned, scattering huge fragments on the place where lay the poor boy. The crisis passed, he slowly recovered, receiving to the last all the little attentions which his kindly host could bestow on him. Inexpensive as was his food and lodging, they were more than the impoverished farmer could bear. When he had sufficiently recovered, he was reluctantly compelled to tell his guest that he could no longer support him. He, however, found him a temporary asylum by applying to the parish priest, and with this functionary Duval remained until the extreme severity of the weather had abated, and his health was completely restored. It was then hinted that he must provide for himself.

Past sufferings had taught him that one of the greatest calamities a poor man could encounter was cold. When he left the priest's house, he asked in what direction were warmer lands, and being told that to the east the sun exercised more power, he resolved to bend his course to the eastward. His ideas concerning the earth and the sun were of the most primitive kind; the former he believed to be a plane, bounded by the horizon and supporting the heavens; the latter, which he had always seen represented with a human face, was an animated and intelligent being, moving at a small distance from the ground, and dispensing light and heat. With these ideas in his mind, and with the most generous and appreciative feelings toward the sun, he took his departure in an easterly direction. He passed through districts stricken with famine and oppressed with the most horrible poverty—districts in which it was mockery to ask for charity, and which could yield nothing but herbs and roots for the hungered boy. When he reached the boiling springs of Bourbonne les Bains, the spectacle of hot water issuing from a cold earth so alarmed him that he seriously believed he was in the vicinity of the infernal regions, and fled the town with precipitation.

In the flourishing duchy of Lorraine, the scene changed as if by magic; the people were well clad, and of cheerful, healthy countenances; the houses were commodious and solidly built, and the soil was carefully tilled and richly productive. Charmed with these external indications of prosperity, and with the beauty of the country, Duval wished to stay in a land so genial and happy. He succeeded in obtaining a situation as a shepherd-boy, and for two years pursued that pastoral life. During the time he made the acquaintance of a hermit named Brother Palemon, who lived at the hermitage of La Rochelle. With this recluse Duval now took up his residence, assisting him in his rural labors, and making himself generally useful. Palemon was a kind-hearted, devout man, who respected God's gifts to man. In a very little time he discovered that Duval was blessed with a mind which craved knowledge and could digest it. He encouraged and assisted him, and placed him on the road to fame by imparting to him the rudiments of an education. At the end of twelve months Duval was forced to leave this worthy old man, the superiors of his order having sent another brother to reside with him in Duval's place. Palemon parted from the youth with regret, and gave him a letter of introduction to the hermits of St. Anne, whither he proceeded.

The hermits of St. Anne were four in number, aged men, of virtuous hearts and kind dispositions, indulgent to others, austere only to themselves. Their subsistence and the means of dispensing charity were derived from the cultivation of twelve acres of land, partly planted with fruit-trees, and from six cows. In the management of their farm it was thought that Duval might find some kind of employment, and he was not disappointed. His opportunities for obtaining knowledge were thus preserved. One of the hermits undertook to teach him to read, and from a book which he found in the hermitage he obtained a smattering of arithmetic. His chief employment was not intellectual, tending cattle in the woods, but it was favorable to the reflective disposition of Duval. From the earliest days astronomy has been indebted to shepherd-boys for much of its just interpretation. Duval's mind soon became deeply interested in the contemplation of the heavens. He had seen in almanacs that on such a day the sun would enter the sign of the Ram or the Bull, and imagining that there must be some clusters of stars resembling those animals, he began to look for them. He constructed a rude observatory in the forest on the top of the tallest oak he could find, but his untutored eyes gazed on the starry field without result. He was about to give up his astronomical inquiries in despair, when a lucky chance put him on the right road. He was fortunate enough to procure half a dozen maps of the constellations, the world, and the four quarters of the globe. With these he soon learned the relative places of the constellations; but, to render this knowledge useful, he had yet to find out a fixed point in the heavens to serve as a basis for his proceedings. He had heard it said that the polar star was the only star of our hemisphere which had no apparent motion; but where to find this star? His first plan was to pick out a star of the proper magnitude, and then bore a hole immediately opposite it to observe if it changed its position. He next hollowed out a piece of elder so as to make a tolerably straight tube, and, suspending this rude telescope to a branch of a tree, made observations through it until he discovered the exact position of the polar star. It was now easy for him, with the aid of his map, to become acquainted with all the principal stellar groups of the northern hemisphere. The immensity into which he thus penetrated filled him with awe and surprise to such an extent that for a time he was compelled to desist, lest his reason should be overthrown. From the study of the skies Duval turned to the study of the earth, and thus brought into use the remaining maps of his collection. He was a long time before he could understand the various lines and figures which are so important in works of this kind; but a friend loaned him an Introduction to Geography, and by the help of this guide, and perpetual reference to his maps, which he always took out with him, he made such rapid advances that "the knowledge of the globe became almost as familiar to him as that of the forest of St. Anne."

The appetite for knowledge was now thoroughly aroused. All his scanty means were devoted to the purchase of books, and he devised means to add to his available funds for this purpose. He set snares for the wild animals, and sold their skins to a furrier at Luneville, and he caught birds, which, he says, contributed to his instruction by the loss of their liberty. Hares, too, would occasionally come in his way, although they were not allowed to do so by law. In these hunting excursions he was often exposed to danger, and on one occasion a wild-cat fixed her teeth and talons so deeply in his head that it was with the greatest difficulty he could release himself and dispatch the brute. He did not regret the wounds, for the skin brought a good price. In a few months he amassed a small fortune of thirty or forty crowns, and with a joyful heart carried his treasure to Nancy to purchase books. Of their value he knew nothing, but he had confidence in human honesty, and, when he entered the shop, said to the bookseller, "You will have the goodness not to charge me too much, for I am very poor, and want to get all the books I can." There was only one bookseller in Nancy who did not cheat him; all the others took advantage of his simplicity. The honest tradesman supplied him on equitable terms, and even gave him credit for twenty shillings' worth of goods. When, in after years, Duval asked this worthy man why he was induced to place so much confidence in a stranger, he replied, "Your countenance and your love of study. I saw in your face that you would not deceive me." Honesty met with its reward, for Duval procured for this worthy man the appointment of bookseller to the Duke of Lorraine.

He had now a few books which he studied devoutly. An incident occurred which enabled him to greatly add to their number. Strolling in the forest one day, he observed some shining article lying on the ground. It proved to be a gold seal of curious workmanship, evidently dropped by accident. On the following Sunday he caused the priest at Luneville to announce publicly that this article was in his possession, so that the owner might apply for it. A few weeks afterward a gentleman on horseback came to the hermitage, and desired to speak with him. He was an Englishman, and bluntly stated that the seal was his. "Very good, sir," replied Duval; "but, before I give it up to you, I must request that you will blazon the arms which are engraved on it." The Englishman laughed at the idea of such a rough-looking customer knowing any thing of heraldry. Duval, who had made himself master of the science by reading one of Meneshier's works, coolly answered, "You may think what you please, but the ring does not go out of my possession until you have regularly described the coat of arms." The Englishman, whose name was Foster, put various questions to him, and, finding that the youth was well-informed, gave the correct heraldic description, and, of course, obtained the seal. Duval was rewarded with a couple of Louis d'or, and Foster was so much pleased with the lad, that, so long as he remained in Lorraine, he had him to breakfast on every holiday morning, made him a present of five shillings each time, and gave him much good counsel as to the choice of books and maps, and the method of studying to advantage. His library prospered exceedingly under these circumstances, and numbered nearly four hundred volumes, all of which were extensively thumbed. His devotion to study at length excited the alarm of one of the hermits, Father Anthony, who gravely exhorted him to renounce all human science, and content himself with the life of a devout recluse. Duval, of course, paid no attention to this advice, and Brother Anthony, interpreting his obstinacy by the blue light of superstition, began to suspect that his studies were of an extremely improper character, and determined to find out what they were. He took advantage of the youth's absence to enter his chamber, and the sight he beheld, papers scrawled with geometrical signs, and curious instruments glittering in the sunshine, confirmed him in all his worst suspicions. He was certain now that young Duval was on the high road to perdition, and in direct communication with the Prince of Darkness. Full of this idea, he hurried off to his confessor, and told such a frightful story that the confessor felt it a religious duty to visit the youth. When he discovered the true state of the case, he laughed at Brother Anthony, and encouraged the young man to persevere in his studies. Brother Anthony took the matter much to heart, and, like all ignorant men, felt incensed that things were taking place beneath his nose which he could not understand. His anger broke out at last, and he threatened Duval that he would take away his books and tear up his maps. The threat roused Duval, and he defied the brother. The hermit advanced toward him, apparently intending to give him a box on the ear. Still more enraged by this threatening gesture, Duval seized a fire-shovel, and brandished it over the head of the astonished hermit. He took to his heels, and Duval secured the door of his chamber, prepared for the worst. The clamor and excitement had drawn all the brothers to the garden, and there they stood beneath Duval's window waiting for a parley. Duval addressed the superior, who listened to him patiently, and then impartially blamed Brother Anthony for his blind zeal, and Duval for having allowed his irritated feelings to obtain the mastery. A capitulation was dictated by Duval, and agreed to by the brothers. He required an amnesty for his indecorous burst of rage, and to be allowed two hours daily for his studies, except at seed, harvest, and vintage times; in return for which he would willingly serve them during ten years, "with all imaginable zeal and affection," and expect nothing more for his services than food and clothing. These terms were acceded to, and on the following day Duval had the agreement regularly drawn up by a lawyer, and signed by all the contracting parties.

He was not destined to fulfill his portion of this contract. On the 13th of May, 1717, he was tending cattle in the forest, and beguiling the time with his favorite study of geography. While busily employed with his maps and books, a gentleman approached him, and inquired what he was doing. "I am studying geography, and finding out the shortest way to Quebec." "For what reason?" "That I may travel thither, and continue my studies in the University of that city, which, I am told, is well conducted." "But," replied the stranger, "what necessity is there for you to travel to the other end of the world, when there are Universities at hand which are equally good as that of Quebec?" In the midst of this dialogue they were joined by two youths, another gentleman, and a train of attendants. The youths were the Princes of Lorraine; the gentlemen were the Baron de Pfutschner and the Count de Vidampierre, the latter of whom was the person who had been talking to the rustic of St. Anne's. It reads like the scene of a play, but it was no fiction, as he soon found out. The baron volunteered to place Duval in the Jesuits' College, but this offer was rejected. In a few days he returned to say that the duke would take Duval under his protection, and furnish him with the means of pursuing his studies. This was, of course, too desirable an opportunity to be neglected. He closed with the offer, and was immediately conveyed to the court at Luneville, where his literary acquirements excited much curiosity. From Luneville he removed to Pont-à-Mousson, where he recommenced his untiring search for knowledge. Geography, history, and antiquities were his favorite subjects of inquiry, but he neglected nothing. Working on a methodical plan, and with judicious advisers to guide his steps, he added greatly to his stock of ideas. It is curious to note how strangely mingled with gross ignorance were his best accomplishments. Thus it is related that he was smitten with a violent passion for a beautiful female, which so tormented him that he ate a large quantity of hemlock to allay it, that being the nostrum recommended by St. Jerome as an antidote to love. He suffered severely from this act of imprudence, and, indeed, came near losing his life by it.

Toward the close of the year 1718 the Duke of Lorraine visited Paris, and in his suite was Duval. During his stay at this place the latter paid a visit to the Opera-house, and witnessed the representation of Quinault's opera of "Isis." The effect produced upon his mind by the music, scenery, and acting was so powerful, that for several days he could think of nothing else. Such wholeness and completeness seemed little else than magical, and the memory of it deprived him of the power of eating and sleeping. After leaving Paris he visited the Netherlands and Holland, returning to Luneville late in the following year. The duke now appointed him his librarian, but the post was one of honor rather than profit, for the duke was wretchedly poor. On the death of Leopold in 1729, his successor, Francis Stephen, made an addition of two hundred livres to Duval's stipend, and, what was even better, paid it punctually. Soon after he bestowed on him the appointment of professor of history, antiquities, and ancient and modern geography in the Academy of Luneville. It was with difficulty that Duval was induced to accept this appointment. He yielded at last, and set strenuously to work to make his lectures worthy of approbation, and with such decided success that in a little while he had so many private pupils that he could count on a clear annual gain of four thousand livres. Among his hearers was William Pitt, afterward Earl of Chatham, then a youth upon his travels, but who displayed such talents that his future greatness was more than once predicted by Duval.

Duval's simple habits enabled him to amass a considerable fortune out of his income, and the first use he made of it was to discharge what he considered a debt of gratitude. He rebuilt, in a handsome style, the hermitage of St. Anne, and added to it a chapel and an extensive piece of land. Part of this land he directed to be laid out as a nursery for fruit-trees of the best kind. For this benefit, the only return that he required was that the hermits should gratuitously supply the neighborhood for three leagues round with the produce of the nursery, and should go themselves to plant the trees whenever their assistance was wanted. During the remainder of his life he displayed the same interest in the hermitage, regarding it as the gateway through which he had passed to fortune and distinction.

In 1743, after many changes in the duchy of Lorraine, Duval was called to Vienna by the Grand-duke, husband of the celebrated Maria Theresa, and in the Austrian capital he spent nine months, returning, after that time, to Florence, where his old patrons now resided. Beneath the soft skies of Italy his time glided away happily, passed, for the most part, in studying, cultivating a small garden, and making occasional journeys to Rome and Naples. In the Eternal City all his old love of the antique revived, and he began to form a cabinet of ancient medals. In 1748 he received a summons from his royal master to take up his residence at

Vienna. Francis, then Emperor of Germany, was forming a cabinet of coins, and desired that Duval should take charge of it. The appointment was much to his liking, and he devoted himself to its duties with the greatest assiduity. The simplicity and natural independence of his character endeared him to the royal household; he was received as a friend, and had no irksome ceremonies imposed on him. The entire confidence of the emperor and empress was manifested in the following year by their offering him the honorable situation of sub-preceptor to the young Archduke Joseph. Duval, however, declined to accept it, on the ground that the immethodical manner in which he had pursued his own studies rendered him unfit for dictating a course to others. Duval persisted in his refusal to accept the post proffered to him, and his sincerity induced his patrons to withhold their entreaties without withdrawing any of their friendship. That the latter was genuine is illustrated in the following anecdote, which we hope is authentic: One day, a foreigner, who had a letter of introduction to Duval, was in vain attempting to find him in the labyrinth of the palace, when he was accosted by a person, who said, "Come with me, and I will show you the way." After many turnings and windings, the person opened the door, and called out, "Duval, I have brought somebody to see you." This obliging guide was the emperor. On another occasion the empress displayed an equal contempt of ceremonious forms. It was Carnival time, and there was to be a grand masked ball. The empress invited Duval to her apartment, and prevailed upon him to assume the garb of a Turkish dervis, having previously made a wager with the emperor that there would be a character at the ball whose incognito he could not penetrate. "Come, Duval," she said, gayly, "I hope you will at least dance a minuet with me." "I, your majesty!" exclaimed he; "in my native woods I never learned any thing more graceful than turning heels over head." The empress laughed heartily; they entered the ballroom, and, though the emperor did his best to discover who was the dervis, he lost his wager.

In 1752 Duval was forced to suspend his literary and antiquarian labors. Intense application had made serious inroads on his health, and his physicians advised a tour. He traveled through various parts of Germany and the Netherlands, and then visited Paris, where he met with a hospitable reception from all the literary characters of the day. On his return he passed through his native province of Champagne, and availed himself of many opportunities of showing a kindly remembrance. In Lorraine, also, he rebuilt the hermitage of St. Joseph de Messui, originally erected by the founder of St. Anne's, and which was now inhabited by the hermit who had first taught him the rudiments of reading and writing.

The remainder of his days were passed blamelessly amid books, medals, conversations, correspondences, and other kindred occupations. Duval was the author of various numismatic catalogues—works requiring an unusual amount of exact antiquarian knowledge; also of three volumes of letters and fragments, and two unpublished works—the one a treatise on medals, the other a philosophical romance. He remained in firm health until his eightieth year, when he was attacked with a painful disease which overthrew his hearty constitution, and brought him to the brink of the grave. He rallied for a while, but the shock proved too severe, and on the third of November, 1775, he died, in the eighty-first year of his age. By his will he left the interest of eleven thousand florins to be divided yearly, as a marriage portion, among three poor young girls of Vienna; a pension to a widow, with whom he had boarded; and annuities to his servant and a deserted child, whom the servant had found in the street and taken under his protection.

CHARLES DICKENS.

In the minds of a good many excellent critics this illustrious gentleman represents the genius of modern fiction. A structure of wonderful comprehensiveness and beauty is upheld on his brawny shoulders, and future generations, they say, will point to it as to the mighty ruins of the Parthenon, saying here is a guide and a study. A writer so curiously varied and fresh as Mr. Dickens provokes naturally a vast amount of exaggerated admiration. The most discreet find it difficult to assign him a place. He shoots out so strangely in every direction, and yet possesses such a wonderful power of concentration, that we are always liable to say too much or too little of his powers. One thing is certain, the world has produced but few men of Mr. Dickens's calibre. He belongs incontestably to the same order of genius as Shakspeare, Fielding, and Sir Walter Scott. It would not be utterly absurd to say that in some particulars he is superior to either of these illustrious officers of the legions of literature, nor would it be difficult to prove that in many things he is their inferior. The best established fact that can be mentioned, and one which bears its own significance, is that he has given a distinctive character to the age in which he wrote. It has been Mr. Dickens's pleasant task to originate a peculiar kind of fiction, and his good fortune to create the appetite for it. We say a peculiar kind of fiction because an analysis of his works displays the fact that he never touches the bad without making us grieve for its badness, never whispers the truth without making us glory in its triumph. With a sensibility which is almost divine he searches out the hidden springs of charity and refreshes us with their genial flow before we well know that we have been touched with the rod of the magician. No human creature ever was or ever will be so vile but good-will in some shape clings about his heart; whether it be for man, or beast, or inanimate thing, it is there, and Mr. Dickens, with his witty springes, his pathetic pitfalls, his eloquent lunges, his humorous shafts, is sure to take it captive, and once in his glowing embrace escape is impossible until what is good becomes better. The secret of Mr. Dickens's enormous popularity is to be found in this circumstance. We all think we are very good creatures, and Mr. Dickens makes us feel that we are becoming better. It is a pleasant thought, and travels from pole to pole of constituted society.

Mr. Charles Dickens is now (1858) in his forty-sixth year, having come into this world, which he has much comforted with his genial genius, on the 15th of February, 1812, at Landport, Portsmouth. His father was employed at the time in the naval establishment, and, when the war ceased, was rewarded with a pension, on which, like a sensible man, he retired. Being a person of considerable talent and education, he gravitated naturally to London, and soon after, feeling the lack of some kind of employment, and perhaps finding his half-pay insufficient for metropolitan life, obtained a situation to report the debates in Parliament for the "Chronicle," on the staff of which paper he continued for several years.

Concerning the early education of Mr. Charles Dickens we have no information. It was his father's wish that he should adopt the law as a profession, and it is said that the future novelist was actually articled to an attorney, but for how long he devoted his attention to Blackstone and Chitty we know not. From an early period his inclinations were to the press, and he set himself to the task of learning short-hand in order that he might the more readily obtain a footing in a newspaper office. Reporters were then neither so numerous or expert as they are now, and from the facility with which the senior Dickens had obtained a position on a first-class paper Mr. Charles Dickens augured hopefully of his own chances. He was self-taught in the art of short-hand writing. "I bought," he says, "an approved scheme of the noble art and mystery of stenography (which cost me ten and sixpence), and plunged into a sea of perplexity that brought me in a few weeks to the confines of distraction. The changes that were run upon dots, which in one position meant such a thing, and in another position something else entirely different; the wonderful vagaries that were played by circles; the unaccountable consequences that resulted from marks like flies' legs; the tremendous effects of a curve in the wrong place—not only troubled my waking hours, but reappeared before me in my sleep. When I had groped my way blindly through these difficulties, and had mastered the alphabet, which was an Egyptian temple in itself, there then appeared a procession of new horrors, called arbitrary characters—the most despotic characters I have ever known—who insisted, for instance, that a thing like the beginning of a cobweb meant expectation, that a pen-and-ink sky-rocket stood for disadvantageous. When I had fixed these wretches in my mind, I found that they had driven every thing else out of it; then beginning again, I forgot them; while I was picking them up I dropped the other fragments of the system—in short, it was almost heart-breaking."

But the triumph came, and in due time Dickens found himself with a note-book in his hand and a pocketful of pencils, as the representative of a paper called "The True Sun." It was not a very flourishing concern, and, at the first opportunity, Mr. Dickens transferred his services to the "Morning Chronicle," where the peculiar clearness and force of his reports were justly appreciated. Simply to convey other people's ideas to the reading public was not the destiny that Mr. Dickens had proposed to himself. He felt that he could do more, and that he had the gift to address the world's mind in his own person. Like most young writers who possess the power of observation he commenced his literary career with a series of sketches, afterward known as "Sketches by Boz." They were published in the evening edition of the "Chronicle," and at once attracted public attention. There was a breadth and vigor in the delineations, a heartiness and gusto, which was new to the reading classes. The sketches were filled with ridiculous ideas and many exaggerations leading to an excessively spasmodic and far-fetched kind of fun, but these drawbacks were not the defects of a common man, but rather the exuberant wild-growth of a fancy unusually alive to impressions of a humorous nature. In looking for characters, too, Dickens totally abandoned the perfumed boudoirs of the Minerva press, and went among the people—even vulgar people—and found truth, if not inspiration. A cry was at once raised that his tastes were vulgar, and it enjoyed a considerable popularity for some years. It is not heard very often now.

The exaggerated humor and local breadth of the sketches were such that their success was prodigious, and a publishing house—Chapman and Hall—waited on the young author and proposed a new literary serial to illustrate a collection of sporting prints designed by Mr. Seymour, an eminent pencil humorist. In this work it was intended to approach the novel form in a free and easy way, so that the literary interest of a tale might blend with the sporting unction of the illustrations without absorbing too much of their interest.

The suicide of Mr. Seymour left the author entirely to his own judgment, and the reader of the "Pickwick Papers" will not fail to notice the steady improvement which characterizes the work as it progresses. The early chapters abound in absurd situations, and the principal characters are little better than wild burlesque exaggerations. As we proceed, however, the actors stand forth more luminously, and the scenes change to the actual realities and places of life. The wonderful graphic power of the author begins to manifest itself, and we feel the pressure of his large humane hand, the pulsations of his big heart, and, we may add, the sting of his trenchant ridicule. A manner of writing so novel attracted universal attention, and the "Pickwick Papers" were in all hands. No recent work had created half so much of a sensation. Even now, when most of the jokes of the redoubtable Sam Weller have become thoroughly staled, the work retains much of its original attractiveness. A curious and remarkable fact connected with this first work of Mr. Dickens is that even in the wild and unconnected pages of "Pickwick" he aimed at an object, and directed his batteries against the Fleet Prison, which soon crumbled beneath the operation.

It was while the "Pickwick Papers" were in progress that Mr. Dickens took unto himself a wife. The lady was Miss Caroline Hogarth, daughter of Mr. George Hogarth, a celebrated musical writer and critic, and a man of mention in literary circles. Mr. Hogarth had been a lawyer in Edinburgh, and enjoyed the friendship of Sir Walter Scott, Lord Jeffrey, and other distinguished literary men. The lady is still Mrs. Dickens in name, but we regret to say no longer occupies the honored position of head of Mr. Dickens's household. An unhappy combination of circumstances has recently (1858) led to an estrangement between the couple, and they live apart, although not legally divorced. Rumors of a cruel character have been circulated to the disadvantage of Mr. Dickens—the world, as is usual in such cases, espousing the cause of the lady—but, if we may be permitted to judge of his actual feelings by the tone of the cards he has published on the subject, we certainly should not be tempted to regard the matter in a grave light, but rather to attribute the estrangement to one of those unhappy flights of humor which, even in households of long standing, are not unfrequent. The plea of incompatibility of temper, after twenty-five years of married life and a family of eight children, sounds strangely, and can mean, we hope, nothing of very frightful import. Publicity, in a case of this kind, is the thing most to be dreaded. Its direct tendency is to widen any unhappy breach that may exist, and to agglomerate round each extreme a party hostile to the other. As the most prominent writer of England, and a man whose genial philanthropy has made him conspicuous, Mr. Dickens is peculiarly exposed to the shafts of envy and malice. Few men have lived so long and done so much without exciting the uncharitableness of their contemporaries. It is not remarkable that, now the bare opportunity has arrived, the finger of scorn, however mean and dirty, is pointed at him. The grievance, it has been stated, is of long standing, but Mr. Dickens treats it with forbearance, and the least we can do is to imitate his example. Mrs. Dickens's sister is now the head of the author's household.

Mr. Dickens's second work was "Nicholas Nickleby," in which he made a ferocious attack on Yorkshire schools, and succeeded in bringing them into ill favor. These schools were generally situated in some remote county, and, by reason of their inaccessibility, were safe places of keeping for the poor helpless little creatures who were sent there. Heartless parents, who found their unloved ones too much in the way, sent them to these vile places, where they were taken care of with much less kindness than they would have received in the penitentiary as culprits. It frequently happened that they died beneath the treatment. Escaping this blessed relief, they served out their term of imprisonment, and with faculties benumbed with hardship, went their way into the world degraded and friendless. There are many such schools even in the present day, but their worst features were modified by the publicity excited by Mr. Dickens. The cruel meanness and indifference of parents and guardians are, we fear, beyond the curative reach of literature.

The novel materially increased the author's reputation, especially with the better class of readers. In its construction it is far superior to "Pickwick," and freer from comic exaggerations, although developing a wonderful range of individualities, and knowledge of character. The Yorkshire schoolmasters were greatly incensed at the character of Squeers, forgetting that their indignation stamped the veracity of the portrait. One individual, in particular, who happened to have but one eye, and resembled Squeers physically as well as mentally, even went so far as to threaten the author with an action at law. In "Nicholas Nickleby" we have the first of those amusing dashes at theatrical life which have so often delighted Mr. Dickens's readers. For the stage and its members Mr. Dickens has always had a warm regard, and of late years he has often appeared in public in company with other literary amateurs. It is conceded on all hands—and most cordially by those who are best able to form an opinion—that he is an actor of rare ability. Probably there are some worthy managers of the CRUMMLES kind who have a different opinion.

The first ambition of a successful novelist is to become the editor of a literary magazine. Creative minds of all kinds experience the same desire, and the cause is to be traced to that general facility which all active minds enjoy, and which leaves more to be said than can be compassed within the limits of a novel or of any one beaten track. The monthlies in those days were devoted to the big-wiggery of criticism, and were stilted and pompous to a degree. An awful sanctity prevailed in their columns, a fearful amount of correct vigor in their opinions, and more or less of respectable dullness in every thing they contained. They were not, as now, the vehicles of the best literature of the day, although their articles were certainly the best written. Learning rather than observation characterized their tone. They were sharp, brilliant, and witty, because it was considered low to be genial, humorous, and observant. A good number was that which most resembled a porcupine in the number and delicacy of its points. With the beadledom of such publications Mr. Dickens could have no sympathy. However much they might excite his respect, they could not win his admiration. Either he was too low or they were too high, and he determined that the public should decide. The experiment was made, and "Bentley's Miscellany," of which he became editor, obtained at once an immense circulation and a character and standing of its own which it has never lost. It was in this magazine that Mr. Dickens published "Oliver Twist," issuing it in monthly parts, with illustrations by George Cruickshank. No other work of the author deals so largely with the lower classes. The story is of the intensest kind, and, in an artistic point of view, it may be regarded as one of the author's best successes. "Never before," says a critic, "were so much dirt, vice, and depravity so completely exposed, and yet so cleanly trodden under foot. The author passes through a very pest-house without a breath of contagion."

After the completion of "Oliver Twist," Mr. Dickens gave up the editorship of "Bentley's Miscellany," discovering in all probability that the dry drudgery of the position was too much of a restraint on his creative powers. The reins passed into the hands of Mr. Harrison Ainsworth, who, in the effort to follow in the footsteps of Mr. Dickens, commenced the well-known story of "Jack Sheppard," a work in which vice became attractive. This work enjoyed a dreadful popularity for a few months. It was dramatized extensively. There was not a thief in London who did not find his way to the gallery of the theatre. The flash songs with which the thing abounds became the national music of Roguesville, and were yelled by men, women, and children. In a word, the scamps of London had a perfect orgie on this delectable production of Mr. Harrison Ainsworth's genius. In due time, however, public taste recovered its healthy action. "Jack Sheppard" was viewed in its proper light as an extremely vicious sensation novel, calculated to fling a halo round the gallows, and make every bold thief think that he was a hero. People began to notice how vastly different was Mr. Dickens's treatment of characters equally vile, how thoroughly different the argument which the work enforced. Mr. Ainsworth's "Jack Sheppard," which was intended to destroy Mr. Dickens on his own ground, simply contributed to the latter gentleman's reputation.

Although Mr. Dickens had discovered that a monthly form of periodical was not the thing for him, he was still anxious to place himself at the head of a serial of some sort. Not only would it form a convenient channel for much miscellaneous matter, but in the end it might prove a valuable property. We know now that in this effort he has succeeded, and that in "Household Words" he is surrounded by a set of writers who imitate his style so closely that if he does not actually write an article once in a month it is scarcely noticed; but it was only after three hard and persevering efforts that he succeeded in hitting the public taste. The circumstances attending the first we have already narrated. After resigning the editorship of "Bentley's," his second attempt was made on his own account. This was "Master Humphrey's Clock," which, in its original shape, was a weekly, and intended to contain short tales, essays, communications, etc. The plan was found to be obsolete, and after a few numbers Mr. Dickens commenced his exquisite story of the "Old Curiosity Shop," which, in a short time, absorbed the weekly issue, and left the public nothing to regret. On its conclusion, Mr. Dickens's first historical story of another period, "Barnaby Rudge," was commenced, a tale of astonishing power, which contributed in a large measure to the reputation of the author.

On its conclusion Mr. Dickens made that celebrated trip to America, which resulted in the publication of a volume of "Notes." He was received with great favor, and among all classes of people was fairly idolized. It is probable, even, that he was "bored" by the excessive generosity of his reception. Whatever the impression, he gave it honestly in his "Notes," and has stuck by it manfully to the present day, notwithstanding an immense loss of popularity in this country and also in Europe. It is useless and stupid to think that a man shall think our way simply because we feast him, and still more absurd to attribute mean and interested motives to him because we can account for his strictures in no other way. Much that is offensive in Mr. Dickens's book is merely so because it is placed in an absurd European light, not because it is untrue in the abstract. After all, however, it was a cruel shock to find that the man we approached with such confident love should turn round on us and utter, truly or not, so many harsh things. That he did so was an indication that he felt himself under a business necessity to write a book, and, perhaps, of making it as scandalous as possible. The piquant relish with which Miss Martineau's volume had been received some time before was yet new to the trade. There was room for something more of the same sort, and Mr. Dickens was indiscreet enough to supply the demand. The blemishes which destroy the interest of the book for an American reader are much to be regretted, for it contains passages of great beauty, and there are bits of graphic description, purely American, that have rarely been equaled.

Mr. Dickens made farther use of his American experience in the novel of "Martin Chuzzlewit," and contributed a good petard to the hoisting of the villainous land-swindles which were then much in vogue. This work belongs to what may be termed Mr. Dickens's second period, and deals in the minute delineation of character rather than the development of an intense plot. It enjoyed an immediate success, and was allowed on all hands to be the most elaborate and finished of the author's productions. The characters, or at least a part of them, have become household words. If we are told that such a man is a regular Pecksniff, we know all that we wish to know about him, and bestow our pity on the inevitable Tom Pinch who we are quite sure is in the neighborhood to be sponged on. Bailey Junior, and Sarah Gamp, with her invisible and immortal friend Mrs. Harris, Montague Tigg, Mrs. Todgers, and half a dozen others we might mention, are well-remembered acquaintances, whose names serve as easy symbols in every-day conversation.

While "Martin Chuzzlewit" was in progress the world was agreeably delighted by the announcement that Mr. Dickens had a Christmas book in the press. In due time the famous "Carol" made its appearance, and it is not too much to say that hundreds of thousands of hearts beat quicker to its lovely staves, and remembered with keener joy the festive duties of the Christian season.

The originality and brightness of the "Carol" secured for it an immediate popularity, which it has never lost. It is not going too far to say that of its sort it is the finest work in the English language, and while human nature exists it is difficult to see how such a work can be dimmed by time. An enormous edition was disposed of, and the profits were such as to enable Mr. Dickens to assume a better position with his publishers, or, rather, to change them entirely. One of the sacred privileges of genius is to be in debt, and we may remark, without committing an unpardonable act of bad taste, that Mr. Dickens is not without his little scandals in this matter. Few writers have probably derived so much directly from the public, but in cases of this kind any amount is almost sure to be insufficient. A popular favorite is to a great extent public property. He becomes the observed of all observers. His household is an object of curiosity, and, from the mere duties of hospitality, it becomes vastly inflated. Then it is notorious that men of sentiment and genial inspiration always incline to the profuse and liberal rather than the economical and discreet. Mr. Dickens maintains a large household, and his expenses are undoubtedly very great. Among his acquaintances may be numbered the highest in the land, and, although persons of this class do not demand extravagance, and, in point of fact, are often remarkable for their disregard of it, they lead necessarily to conditions of domestic plenty and luxury which are not easily imposed on the income of the literary man. In a theoretical point of view, Mr. Dickens seems to have had his eye directed to the main chance for many years, and in a letter to Lord Jeffrey, which has been made public, speaks of a certain provision or imbankment for his family, which the canny Scotchman says he is surprised to find "still so small." It was probably owing to the advice of this discreet friend that Mr. Dickens freed himself from the influence of his former publishers and made an arrangement with Messrs. Bradbury & Evans, who have since issued his works at a bare percentage on the actual cost of manufacture. All that can be made from their sale goes directly into the pocket of Mr. Dickens without any intermediate taxation. Still it is pretty generally understood that Mr. Dickens's income, although undoubtedly greater than that of the President of the United States, falls short of his outgoings. It is a matter with which the public has nothing whatever to do, and the scandal, like all other scandals, is simply impertinent. No man in literature, or in any thing else, has worked harder than Mr. Dickens. In mere quantity, he has produced more than an entire generation would have produced when reputations were easily achieved. If he goes a little beyond his capital, it is no one's business but his own.

The furore occasioned by the publication of the "Christmas Carol," and the pecuniary profit which resulted therefrom, led naturally to a repetition of the experiment on the following Christmas, when "The Chimes, a Goblin Story" made its appearance, accompanied by any quantity of Christmas books by other authors. It is doubtful if this work is in any way inferior to the "Carol," while in point of careful writing it far excels it. A very generous success rewarded the author, and induced him to continue the experiment of Christmas books for some years subsequently. The "Cricket on the Hearth," "The Battle of Life," and "The Haunted Man," made their appearance in regular succession, but their interest was not the same. The truth of the matter, we suspect, is that the "Carol" was a happy inspiration, while all the others were more or less of a task. There was also an attempt to improve on the design of the first work, which was superfluous, inasmuch as inspiration is an essence which does not submit to artistic distillation.

A disposition to ramble belongs naturally to the literary character. Mr. Dickens, although a family-man, does not neglect his little opportunities. When the vacation comes, and come it does even to the popular author, he packs his carpet-bag and flies away with the best of them. We have enjoyed the pleasant experience of his observation in many fugitive pieces, particularly since the establishment of "Household Words." In 1844 Mr. Dickens determined to take a stroll through Italy in a large and responsible manner. He staid there for a year, surrounded by his family, and living in a palace. It is probable that he would have remained longer but for a new speculation which engaged his thoughts. This was none other than the establishment of a daily newspaper to rival and perhaps extinguish "The Times." In due time the first issue made its appearance, and the "Daily News" became a reality among newspapers. Mr. Dickens was placed at the head of the literary department, and the weight of his name undoubtedly gave prestige to the undertaking. But starting a newspaper is a slow and laborious process. Its results are not more rapid than those of a new vineyard planted in uncertain soil. To succeed with any thing like moderate rapidity it is necessary to have a staff of men thoroughly broken in to the work, for newspaper writing and newspaper work are in themselves peculiar, and demand study and practice. Literary men are very apt to suppose that because they can write a good story they can necessarily dash off an editorial with infinite and almost contemptible ease. Nothing can be farther from the fact. The best newspaper writers are those whose imaginations never tempt them into the realms of fiction, men who can fix their mind on a fact with the absolute certainty of conquering it. Moreover, in the conduct of a public journal it is necessary to observe a rough sort of descrimination, without staring too sternly at absolute propriety, or making it apparent at every step that you have a side to keep up. There is a blunted conscientiousness about an experienced editor which is no less serviceable than curious. He says not only what is necessary to be said, but frequently what is absolutely unnecessary. His advances and his concessions, his liberalities and his meannesses are so metaphysically balanced that it is almost impossible for a literary man, or, indeed, any man given to exact thought, to understand their drift. The truth of the matter is that an editor when he becomes good ceases to be the champion of a bare principle. He yields to the pressure from without, simply giving to it a shape and complexion consonant with his education and mode of thought. Young writers, on the other hand, cling to their own ideas with a tenacity which, if it fails to excite admiration, is sure to create disgust. They work themselves into an ill-temper with a facility which is wonderful, and generally succeed in producing the same result in their readers.

All Mr. Dickens's roseate visions of journalistic life, if he ever had any, were soon knocked on the head. Good as the paper was, it failed to pay expenses, partly owing to the smallness of the price which was charged for it, and partly owing to the fact that a young newspaper always must pay too much for its whistle. It was determined to raise the price to three pence, but even this did not do. There was still a loss, and finally the price was made the same as the "London Times." This was not, we apprehend, a good way of competing with that powerful and well-conducted journal, but it was perhaps the best thing that could be done in London, where people are apt to look with suspicion on any thing that is cheap and new. Whatever the immediate result, we know now that the "Daily News" holds its own against the "Thunderer" with such marked ability that as an exponent of public opinion is second only to it. To return, then, to Mr. Dickens. In this paper, besides numerous "editorials," he published the series of communications known as "Pictures from Italy," the result of his sojourn in the sunny land. They are exceedingly light, and repay a hasty perusal, their greatest fault being, in point of fact, that they are too light even for the ephemeral columns of a newspaper. Considering that they came from the pen of Mr. Dickens, it is not saying too much to state plainly that they failed. This circumstance, combined with others of a pecuniary character, induced Mr. Dickens to relinquish the duties of the editor's chair. "The Pictures from Italy" were subsequently published in book form, but they failed to attract general attention.

And here we will take the liberty of mentioning a work by Mr. Dickens which is not so widely known as it deserves to be. It has never been added to his complete works, although in its way it is undoubtedly one of the completest of them all. In 1844 a little book was published called "The Evenings of a Working-man, being the occupation of his scanty leisure, by John Overs; with a preface relating to the author by Charles Dickens." The story of this little volume is touching enough. John Overs was a working-man, a carpenter, who devoted his evenings to literary composition. He wrote to Dickens to ask him to assist him in obtaining a publisher. A correspondence took place, and an interview in which Dickens endeavored to dissuade John Overs from placing too much expectation on literary renown or profit. "He wrote to me," says Mr. Dickens, "as manly and as straightforward, but, withal, as modest a letter as ever I read in my life. He explained to me how limited his ambition was, soaring no higher than the establishment of his wife in some light business and the better education of his children. He set before me the difference of his evening and holiday studies, such as they were, and his having no better resource than an ale-house or a skittle-ground." The book was published with an introduction by Mr. Dickens. It accomplished its object, but it was incapable of bringing health to the blanched cheek of the poor artisan. John Overs is no more, and his book is forgotten, but Dickens's gentleness to this smitten laborer is surely worthy of remembrance.

"Dombey and Son" was the next work which came from the pen of Mr. Dickens, appearing in the usual monthly form, and consuming something more than a year and a half in publication.

The critics were divided concerning the merits of this work. Portions of it, such, for instance, as the passages relating to little Paul Dombey, were universally extolled. On the whole, however, it was regarded as something of a failure. The story found its way to the stage, and in all parts of the world the name of Captain Cuttle is famous.

Perhaps Dickens himself had a feeling that "Dombey" was not quite up to the usual standard, and this consciousness, added to the fact that Mr. Thackeray had just made his mark in "Vanity Fair," led to a very careful revision of his subsequent work, "David Copperfield." This work is universally accepted as one of Mr. Dickens's best, and is rendered doubly interesting by the knowledge that it is, to an extent at least, an autobiography. The whole story is wonderfully human, and paints the struggles of life, brought down absolutely to the moment in which we live and breathe, with a vividness which fairly illuminates the brain and floods the heart. The struggles of the poor boy-hero, surrounded by flinty-hearted relatives, the sympathy which he excites in the bosom of lowly fisher-folk, the wonderfully earnest story of the poor seduced girl, and that loveliest of all lovely creations, the rough yet delicate loyalty of the old fisherman for his lost niece, are so far beyond the efforts of the modern writer of fiction that they take us into a new world of emotion, and create an enjoyment which it may honestly be said belongs only to the contemplation of virtue. In a merely artistic point of view, it is the best written of Mr. Dickens's productions, and displays a prodigious command of the pure narrative style, peculiarly enjoyable when the author is describing his own modest efforts in literature. There are characters in the work which again give significance to modern society. There are few of us who do not know a Micawber, a modified Uriah Heap, a child-wife, an Agnes, or some other of the innumerable groupings which give dramatic vigor to its plot.

In 1840 Mr. Dickens issued the first number of his celebrated periodical known as "Household Words." It is, as our readers are aware, a large weekly serial, entirely free from advertisements, and filled with original matter. Nearly all the most prominent of the young English writers have contributed to its columns, and several of the number have acquired a style which compares favorably with that of Mr. Dickens, especially Mr. Sala, a writer of very pleasant observation and great industry. It was in this publication that Mr. Dickens published his famous "Child's History of England," a work avowedly intended for children, but containing so many vivid pictures of grand English events that it fascinates the most cultivated minds. A vast number of articles on topics of the day and a novel called "Hard Times" have also appeared in its columns from the same prolific pen. The undertaking is understood to be a very profitable one, and Mr. Dickens devotes much of his time to its conduct. The miscellaneous association with men of letters which the editorship of a journal involves probably suggested to Mr. Dickens the idea of the "Guild of Literature and Art," which, in 1851, was projected under the joint auspices of himself and Sir Edward Lytton Bulwer. To assist in raising a fund for the objects of this charitable association, a series of amateur performances were given in London and elsewhere, the author of "The Caxtons" writing a new comedy for the occasion called "Not so bad as we seem."

Mr. Dickens's latest works are "Bleak House" and "Little Dorritt," both of which are of such recent origin that additional remarks are unnecessary. We may add in this place that Mr. Dickens is the author of a "Life of Grimaldi, the Clown," and of an opera and a farce. The first of these neglected children may sometimes be met with, but the others appear to be lost.

In personal appearance, says a writer in the "Biographical Magazine," Mr. Dickens is prepossessing; his figure small but well made, his look intelligent, and his eye peculiarly quick, vivid, and expressive. When he enters a room he appears to take a complete catalogue and estimate of the furniture and people at a glance. His powers of penetration are remarkable, and his facility of description we all know is equally extraordinary. In private Boz talks much or little, according to the sympathy he has with the company. His conversation is, as might be expected, easy, flowing, and genial; he hates argument, and never talks for effect. He excels in telling a story, which he does in general with humorous exaggerations. He is a great admirer of Tennyson's poetry and of Maclise's pictures. His house in Devonshire Terrace is adorned with pictures of the best living artists, and every corner shows the influence of taste and wealth. His library is extensive, and in the literature of his country, in which few are better read, very well selected. He is, or rather was, very active and fond of dancing, his favorite dance being Sir Roger de Coverly. He has also a remarkable passion (which is shared by Macaulay) for midnight wandering in a city's streets.

SIR THOMAS LAWRENCE.

This celebrated painter was born in 1769, and was the youngest of a family of sixteen children. His father, although a man of some cultivation, and originally educated to the law, was an innkeeper at Bristol (where Thomas was born), and made a miserable living. His success, indeed, was so very limited, that in a short time he abandoned business and repaired to Devizes. Mr. Lawrence was, in some respects, a very remarkable man. His mind always appears to have been occupied with matters out of his business, and not in it. One of his most remarkable passions was for poetry, which he not only wrote, but spouted with great gusto. He would sometimes walk into the parlor of his hotel, and insist that all the guests should leave off their affairs while he recited a poem for their better edification. Poetry, under certain conditions of life, is delightful, but, thrust down the unwilling throat in this abrupt manner, it loses all its charm, and becomes a serious bore. It is not at all remarkable that his customers deserted him for a more tranquil hostelry.

Thomas was a prodigy from his earliest years. He is thus described by an "eye-witness" in Barrington's Miscellanies (1781). After speaking of the early musical talent exhibited by the Earl of Mornington, he proceeds: "As I have mentioned so many other proofs of early genius in children, I can not here pass unnoticed Master Lawrence, son of an innkeeper at Devizes, in Wiltshire. This boy is now (1780) nearly ten years and a half old, but at the age of nine, without the most distant instruction from any one, he was capable of copying historical subjects in a masterly style, and also succeeded amazingly in compositions of his own, particularly that of Peter denying Christ. In about seven minutes he scarcely ever failed of drawing a strong likeness of any person present, which had generally much freedom and grace, if the subject permitted. He is likewise an excellent reader of blank verse, and will immediately convince any one that he both understands and feels the striking passages of Milton and Shakspeare." Mr. Lawrence was, of course, enormously proud of his youthful son, and never neglected an opportunity of bringing him out before his friends to recite a poem. At the age of six Thomas was sent to school, where, however, he only remained for a couple of years. This, with the exception of a few lessons in Latin and French which he received some time after, was all the schooling he ever received. His early proficiency in drawing belonged entirely to innate talent. So remarkable was it, that one gentleman of wealth volunteered to maintain him in Italy, if he would repair to that country to study. But one of his father's queer whims interfered with the operation of this plan. He was afraid that study in the schools would cramp and restrain the development of his son's native genius. He became so absurd on this subject that he would not even allow Thomas to take lessons from resident masters.

Mr. Lawrence failed in business in Devizes, as he had done in Bristol, and probably from the same cause. He now removed to Bath, a fashionable watering-place, where people who think they are sick drink very nasty water and believe they are well. The reputation of young Thomas had preceded him, and much curiosity was displayed to witness his productions. Mr. Lawrence saw that something profitable might be made out of this, and he was right. Thomas took portraits at a guinea apiece, and had so many sitters that he raised the price to a guinea and a half. He conducted this business with complete success for a period of six years, during that long time supporting his father and family by his unassisted labors. He is said to have worked regularly in painting portraits at least four hours a day. The rest of his time was devoted to studies and efforts to obtain mechanical excellence. Among his patrons were some who owned valuable pictures, and who readily gave the young artist permission to copy them. Among other copies which he executed at this time was one of the Transfiguration by Raphael. This was sent to the Society of Arts, but, owing to some informality, was inadmissible to the exhibition. The society, however, were so satisfied of its merits that they bestowed on the young artist their large silver palette and five guineas in cash.

During his stay in Bath he received some valuable lessons from Mr. Hoare, a crayon painter of exquisite taste, fancy, and feeling. Under the instruction of this gentleman he acquired considerable ability in the execution of crayon portraits. The extreme delicacy of his finish gave to his pictures a superior charm even at this early day, and he found no scarcity of sitters. His father took him on excursions to Oxford, Salisbury, and Weymouth, where he obtained ready occupation for his pencil, and finally he removed to London, imagining that, in a larger field, his son would have a better opportunity for exercising his abilities to advantage. It is probable, also, that Thomas's success with the Society of Arts had something to do with this determination. The resolution of this society is worthy of preservation. It is as follows: "Took into consideration the drawings of the Transfiguration, marked G., and opened the paper containing the name of the candidate, according to the directions of the society; and it appeared to the committee that the candidate was T. Lawrence, aged 13, 1783, in Alfred Street, Bath. The committee, having received satisfactory information that the production is entirely the work of the young man, resolved to recommend to the society to give the greater silver palette gilt and five guineas to Mr. T. Lawrence, as a token of the society's approbation of his abilities."

In London Thomas Lawrence pursued his profession with success. Besides portraits, he executed many drawings, which were finished with such exquisite lightness and grace that the smallest found a ready sale at half a guinea. Lawrence's first appearance as an exhibitor was at Somerset House in 1787, when he contributed seven pictures. The next year he removed into a fashionable neighborhood, and contributed six of his performances to the exhibition. The following year he sent no fewer than thirteen, and in 1790 twelve pictures. Among the latter were portraits of some of the most eminent personages in the land. In the catalogue of 1792 he is described as "Thomas Lawrence, a principal painter in ordinary to his majesty." The year previous he had been elected an associate of the Royal Academy.

Under ordinary circumstances he would now have been in easy circumstances, but his pecuniary affairs were far from affluent. The draughts made on his purse by his parents were frequent and deep. Thomas was only too glad to supply their wants, and toil for more, that they might share it.

On the death of Sir Joshua Reynolds in 1792, Mr. Lawrence had not completed his twenty-third year, but was the recipient of many honors which had been denied to others. The Dilettanti Society unanimously chose him to succeed Sir Joshua as their painter, although to effect this they were obliged to rescind a regulation (and a very stupid one) which prevented the admission to the society of any person who had not crossed the Alps. Mr. Lawrence's foot had never quitted the soil of England. The king, George the Third, also appointed him to succeed Sir Joshua Reynolds as his principal painter in ordinary.

Thus established as the popular portrait painter of the day, Lawrence experienced no scarcity of patrons. He gradually raised his prices as he advanced in fame, but the sitters came even in larger numbers. In 1802 his charge for three quarters size was thirty guineas; for a full length, sixty guineas; and for a whole length, one hundred and twenty guineas. In 1806 the three quarters rose to forty guineas, and the whole length to two hundred. In 1808 he raised the smallest size to eighty guineas, and the largest to three hundred and twenty guineas; and in 1810, when the death of Hoppner swept all rivalry out of the way, he increased the price of the heads to one hundred, and the full-lengths to four hundred guineas.

About this time he was suspected of serious love-making in a very high quarter, and a good deal of scandal was the consequence. For some time Lawrence had been a frequent guest at Montague House, Blackheath, the residence of the Princess of Wales; and as he continued his attentions after the portrait of that unfortunate lady was finished, his visits were ascribed to no proper motive. This was rigorously inquired into by the commissioners appointed to investigate the general conduct of her royal highness. Light of heart, and of a natural levity, which disregarded the smaller delicacies of her sex; deserted or driven away by one who had taken upon himself the office of protector, and with manners much more free than were common in England, this princess was exposed to insinuations which any other lady in the kingdom might have escaped. From all that was criminal, the charity or the justice of the commissioners of that day entirely freed her, and the conduct of the painter would have been forgotten, had not his own restlessness under the suspicion hurried him before a magistrate, to make oath that his visits arose from friendship, and were platonic and pure.

Sir Thomas Lawrence died very suddenly on the 7th of January, 1830. Four days previous he had been dining with some friends. After their departure, he felt so indisposed that he sent for his friend, Dr. Holland, who conceived his case so dangerous that he even sat up with him the whole night. No idea of danger had been previously entertained, nor any notion that he was worse than what is usually called poorly. On the evening before his death he was so much better that he received two of his friends, and entered into a pleasant and easy conversation on the subject of art and other matters. After a while the two friends left the sick man's chamber, and retired for a short time to an adjoining one. Presently they were alarmed by the servant's cries for assistance, and, on running into the room, to their horror they beheld Sir Thomas a corpse. The servant related that when he was called in his master's arm was bleeding (he had been bled at the commencement of the attack). He leaned back in his chair, seemed much oppressed, and exclaimed, "I am very ill; I must be dying!" These were the last words he uttered. A *post-mortem* examination revealed the fact that he died from very extensive ossification of the vessels of the heart. He was buried with great pomp in the Cathedral of St. Paul's, where lay the earthly remains of the preceding president of the Royal Academy, Sir Benjamin West.

Sir Thomas Lawrence was a remarkable instance of a perfect artist, entirely self taught. Painting was with him so natural a gift, that some of his earliest productions are marked by the same grace and finish that characterize his later works. An eminent writer says with great justice, "To become the most illustrious portrait painter of any age or country, somewhat more is required than the attributes, however essential, of a mere artist. A practiced mastership of the manual dexterities of his art, an exquisite perception of the beautiful, a mind delicately organized and enlightened by study, are not alone sufficient to form a Titian, a Vandyke, a Reynolds, or a Lawrence. In addition to those characteristics, it is indispensable that the tone and address of an individual destined to record upon his canvas all that is illustrious and beautiful in his time, should be such as to qualify him for habitual familiarity with the objects who seek favor with posterity through his interpretation—that he should live, and move, and have his being in that factitious atmosphere which has called into life the fair and fragile flowers whose beauty is destined to be immortalized by his touch. Instead of rising from the sordid trivialities of vulgar life to welcome some noble into his *studio*, before whose overpowering dignity his own greatness of conception sinks rebuked, the painter of princes should be the guest of princes—should learn to note the aspect of the vain beauty, not as when, discontented and shivering, she throws her listless length into a chair to be copied by the servile painter, but as when, with all her beauties radiant around her, with all the enchantments of her grace called into energy by the emulation and inspiring flattery of the ball-room, she expands into a brighter self. Nay, more than this, he should be permitted to follow his subjects into the gorgeous retreat of their luxurious homes, catching the air and negligent individuality of the statesman, pen in hand, beside his own disordered table, and the domestic loveliness of the young mother, who exchanges the diamond necklace for the twining arms of her beautiful children. It was to a participation in advantages such as these that the super-eminence of Sir Thomas Lawrence as a court painter might in a great measure be attributed. The airy grace, the exquisite high-breeding of his female portraits—the *tone*, in short, of his art, was but the tact of an elegant mind refined by high association."

WILLIAM GIFFORD.

William Gifford was born at Ashburton, Devonshire, England, April, 1756. His father was a wild, dissipated fellow, who neglected his wife and family for the fatal attractions of the ale-house. He was a plumber and glazier, and made some feeble attempts to teach his son the same profession, but he was too idle and dissolute even for this. He died finally of a decayed and ruined constitution, leaving a widow and two children, of whom William was the eldest. For a time Mrs. Gifford endeavored to carry on her husband's business for the sake of the family, but the effort was ruinous. Taking advantage of her ignorance, her two knavish journeymen wasted her property and embezzled her money. Overcome by anxiety and grief, she sank into the grave within twelve months of her unworthy husband.

The children were left completely destitute, for what few things were left in the house at Mrs. Gifford's decease were seized by the landlord. William was taken into the house of this individual, probably because he was useful, while his little brother was sent to the almshouse. Rumors began to circulate in the town that the landlord had more than overpaid himself by the property taken from the deceased widow, and, to hush these unpleasant rumors, he made a show of taking a great interest in William, and sent him to the grammar-school, where the boy made the most of his opportunities. But, at the end of three months, the old curmudgeon of a landlord began to grudge the expense and trouble of William's education, and determined that he would get rid of him. At first he tried to place him on a farm, but Gifford was physically unable to endure the laboriousness of this occupation. As he could read and cipher, his godfather next proposed to send him out to Newfoundland, to assist in a store-house. A Mr. Houldsworthy, of Dartmouth, was to fit him out and have his services. When, however, they met, the boy was ignominiously dismissed as "too small." Finally he obtained a berth on a small coasting vessel. In this situation Gifford remained for nearly twelve months, undergoing considerable hardship as a seaman, and in addition performing all the menial offices of the cabin. At length the knowledge of his situation became known in Ashburton, and became the scandal of the place. His godfather determined to recall him, and on Christmas-day, 1770, he ceased to be a sailor boy. Once more he was sent to school, and his diligence was again unexceptionable. In arithmetic, which was his "darling pursuit," he made such rapid progress that in a few months he was at the head of the school. On some occasions he was even called on to assist the teacher, and when this happened, he received a trifle as a reward. This circumstance suggested the idea of obtaining subsistence by becoming the master's regular assistant, and also by instructing a few evening scholars. He hoped that, if he could bring this to bear, he might ultimately succeed his former master, Mr. Hugh Smerdon, who was now so old and infirm that his tenure of office was not likely to last beyond three or four years. These ideas were put to flight by his godfather, Carlile, who informed him that he intended to bind him apprentice to a shoemaker. Shortly after the ceremony took place, and Gifford, burning with literary ambition, was consigned to the lapstone for six years. A business so distasteful failed, of course, to engage his attention, and he became the common drudge of the shoemaker's family. But his ambition was unaltered; he determined to make the most of every opportunity to add to his scanty stock of knowledge, so that, if fortune befriended him, he would be found ready. His opportunities were few, and the temper of his master unfavorable. He possessed but one book, a treatise on algebra, and this was unintelligible to him, owing to his ignorance of simple equations. A lucky chance enabled him to overcome the difficulty. His master's son had bought "Fenning's Introduction," which he secreted, so that no one but himself might peruse it. Gifford discovered its hiding-place, sat up several nights to study it, and had completely mastered its contents before its owner was aware that it had been used. He was now in a position to use his own book, if he could only procure pens, ink, and paper. What was to be done? He had no money and no credit. He beat out scraps of leather till they were smooth, and on these he wrote his problems with a blunted awl. He was assisted by his memory, which was so tenacious that he could multiply and divide by it to a great extent.

About this time he displayed some aptness in making rhymes,

generally little squibs on passing affairs. He says of them that "nothing on earth was more deplorable," but they served a very important purpose. They made him an object of sympathy; people liked to hear him repeat these effusions, and made little collections for him, so that, on great, appreciative occasions, the bard received as much as sixpence in an evening. To one who had long lived in the absolute want of money, such a resource seemed little less than a Peruvian mine. He furnished himself by degrees with paper, etc., and, what was of more importance, with books of geometry and of the higher branches of algebra, cautiously concealing the latter, lest they should excite the indignation of his employer. The necessity for this precaution was soon apparent. Gifford's master became dissatisfied with his apprentice, maintaining, not unjustly, perhaps, that he paid no attention to business. He was ordered to give up his papers, but this he refused to do. His refusal provoked summary measures; his garret was searched, his little hoard of books and papers was discovered and taken away, and he was sternly forbidden to study any longer. This was a severe blow, but it was followed by another which affected him much more distressingly. This was the death of Mr. Hugh Smerdon, and the filling up of the vacant place which he had aspired to, and which was the sole end and aim of all his ambition. Describing his feelings at this time, he says, "I look back on that part of my life which followed this event with little satisfaction; it was a period of gloom and savage unsociability. By degrees I sunk into a kind of corporeal torpor, or, if roused into activity by the spirit of youth, wasted the exertion in splenetic and vexatious tricks, which alienated the few acquaintances which compassion had yet left me. So I crept on in silent discontent, unfriended and unpitied, indignant of the present, careless of the future, an object at once of apprehension and dislike."

Brighter days were in store for him. A benevolent gentleman of Ashburton, named Cookesley, heard of the poor lad's story, and sent for him. "My little history was not untinctured with melancholy," says Gifford, "and I laid it fairly before him. His first care was to console; his second, which he cherished to the last moment of his existence, was to relieve and support me." This good old gentleman, who was a surgeon by profession, immediately conceived the idea of extricating Gifford from his forlorn position, and establishing him in a school, for which his tastes inclined him.

Being a man of limited fortune, he was unable to do all this himself, so he set on foot a subscription "for purchasing the remainder of the time of William Gifford, and for enabling him to perfect himself in writing and English grammar." It must be remembered that, although Gifford was expert at figures, and had penetrated the mysteries of mathematics, all the other elements of a solid education were wanting. A man who scratches on leather with an awl is not likely to know much about caligraphy.

The influence of good Mr. Cookesley was sufficient to secure the objects he had in view. Gifford was rescued from the drudgery of the shoemaker's stall, and placed under the tuition of the Reverend Thomas Smerdon. His spirits were buoyant, his hopes sanguine, and he applied himself to study with such determination and success, that when the funds for his support were exhausted, his patrons willingly renewed their contributions, that his education might be continued for another year. At the end of two years and two months Mr. Smerdon pronounced him fit for the University; and so extraordinary had been his progress, that his patrons abandoned the idea of putting him in a country school. They were of opinion that his extraordinary talents should be fully cultivated, and that for this purpose he should be sent to Oxford. Accordingly, in 1780, Gifford was removed to Exeter College. The proficiency he had already obtained in the mathematics was fully attested by one circumstance. He had been but a short time at Oxford before it was intimated to him that his farther attendance at the mathematical lectures was unnecessary, as he had carried himself as far in the science as the University required. He was consequently left more at leisure to devote himself to the classics and poetry, in which he soon distinguished himself. During his residence at Oxford he had the misfortune to lose his good friend, Mr. Cookesley. The event threw him into a state of despondency from which he found it difficult to rescue himself. A better and kinder man never lived. He had been more than a father to Gifford—had dragged him from the vulgar purlieus of an obscure trade, and had placed him on the high road to fortune and distinction.

During his residence at Oxford he made the acquaintance of a Mr. Peters, a gentleman who acquired reputation as an artist, and who subsequently became a clergyman. The acquaintance ripened into friendship, and when Mr. Peters left the University for the metropolis, a regular correspondence was maintained between the friends. At his desire, Gifford's letters were sent under cover to Lord Grosvenor. It chanced that in one instance Gifford forgot to direct the inclosed letter, and, naturally supposing that it was meant for himself, his lordship opened and read it. The contents surprised and interested the peer to such an extent that he desired to make the acquaintance of the writer. This was a happy stroke of luck for Gifford. He was introduced to his lordship, and was at once treated with the greatest consideration. In course of time he was appointed tutor to his lordship's son, one of the most amiable and accomplished young noblemen of the country, and with him made the tour of Europe.

In 1791 Gifford made his first appearance before the public in the character of author and critic. At that time the town was deluged with a sickly flood of sentimental poetry. Gifford attacked it in the Baviad, a free imitation of the first satire of Persius. His stinging sarcasm and ridicule proved fatal to the Della Cruscan school (as it was called); laughter took the place of admiration, and the puny lights of the age were extinguished. The lyrists destroyed, Gifford next turned his attention to the dramatists of the same class. In 1794 he published the Mæviad, an imitation of the tenth satire of the first book of Horace. The attack was equally valiant and praiseworthy, but it did not meet with the success which had attended his first onslaught. These two productions won for Gifford a high standing in the literary world, and it was at once awarded to him. In 1797 he became connected with a paper (political) called the "Anti-Jacobin, or Weekly Examiner," and contributed some of the best articles to that hot-headed sheet. Some of Gifford's personal criticisms were of the severest kind, especially when, in defending himself from the attacks of his numerous enemies, he believed he had the right on his side. Dr. Wolcot, better known as Peter Pindar, was one of the unfortunates who fell deservedly under his lash. Wolcot resolved to take personal vengeance, and proceeded to the publication office, where he found the object of his revenge. Having asked the gentleman if his name was Gifford, and having received an answer in the affirmative, he instantly aimed a blow at that head where the means of his disgrace and anguish had been conceived. Mr. Gifford, who was active in body as in mind, caught the blow on his hand, wrenched the stick from his assailant, gave him two smart strokes on the head, and was proceeding in the good work, when two gentlemen who unfortunately happened to be present interfered and prevented the farther execution of justice. Peter was now turned, bleeding and bellowing, into the street, where his clamorous complaint soon drew around him a crowd of hackney-coachmen and other lovers of fun, to whom he began to relate his melancholy story. Never was discomfort and disgrace so complete.

In 1802 Gifford published his long-expected translation of Juvenal, prefaced by an autobiographical sketch of his own early life. It was favorably received by the public, and still ranks as one of the best translations of the author. After a lapse of many years the translator added to his Juvenal a version of the Satires of Persius. In 1809 he became editor of the Quarterly Review, then started for the purpose of counteracting the influence of the Edinburgh Review. For fifteen years he fulfilled the arduous duties of this office with an ability which gave to the periodical a world-wide fame. He was entirely the man for the place. His ability was unquestionable; his politics confirmed and unswerving; his temper defiant, and his pen unscrupulous and savage. The most influential party leaders trembled at his word, and no literary reputation was secure until he had recognized it. There are few men in the world who can conscientiously say that they are free from prejudices, and Gifford was not of the number. Like all men who think for themselves, he had many private convictions, to which he gave expression as general principles. His prejudices, however, were honest ones; he was no mere hireling scribe; his pen could not be bought; he wrote as he thought, and always thought that he wrote rightly. "He disliked," says a friend, "incurring an obligation which might in any degree shackle the expression of his free opinion. Agreeably to this, he laid down a rule from which he never departed, that every writer in the Quarterly should receive so much, at least, per sheet. On one occasion, a gentleman holding office under government sent him an article, which, after undergoing some serious mutilations at his hands preparatory to being ushered into the world, was accepted; but the usual sum being sent to the author, he rejected it with disdain, conceiving it a high dishonor to be *paid* for any thing except his place. Gifford, in answer, informed him of the invariable rule of the Review; adding, that he could send the money to any charitable institution, or dispose of it in any manner he should direct, but that the money *must be paid.* The doughty official, convinced that the virtue of his article would force it into the Review at all events, stood firm to his refusal. Greatly to his dismay, the article was returned. He revenged himself by never sending another. Gifford maintained that the author's indignation was occasioned by the alterations he had made in the manuscript."

In addition to his various duties on the Review, he found time to prepare for the press several valuable editions of the old English dramatists, accompanying the letter-press with extensive notes and commentaries, and generally finding an opportunity to demolish some preceding editor. The popularity of his name made these editions salable, and led to a favorable pecuniary result. His circumstances were now highly prosperous. He enjoyed a pension of four hundred pounds a year from his former pupil, now Lord Grosvenor; was appointed to two sinecure offices under the government, bringing in about nine hundred pounds per annum; and his income from the Review, which, commencing at two hundred pounds a year, speedily rose to nine hundred. Being of economical habits, it is not surprising that he succeeded in accumulating a fortune of nearly twenty-five thousand pounds. In 1824 Gifford resigned the editorship of the Review; he would have done so at an earlier period if a proper successor could have been found. Infirmities had come heavily upon him; the sight of one eye was gone, and for many years he had been so oppressed by asthma as often to be deprived of the power of speech. Soon after relinquishing the editorship, a friend expressed a hope that he might recover and live several years; to which he replied, "Oh no; it has pleased God to grant me a much longer life than I had reason to expect, and I am thankful for it; but two years more is its utmost duration." His words were prophetic; only two years elapsed before he ceased to exist. During the latter months of his life his debility was so extreme that he was incapable of the slightest exertion. He expired calmly and without a struggle on the 31st of December, 1826. He was interred in Westminster Abbey. The bulk of his property he bequeathed to the Reverend Mr. Cookesley, the son of his early benefactor.

As a satirist, critic, and politician, Gifford was severe and unsparing, and belonging, as he did, to a party tenacious of power, had frequent occasions to indulge in the harshest comments; but in private life he was quiet, retiring, and amiable; he never forgot a kindness, and was an unalterable friend. In personal appearance he was remarkable, especially toward the close of his career, when, having lost an eye, a double intensity appeared to be imparted to the remaining one. He was short in stature; his hair of a remarkably handsome brown color, and as glossy and full at the time of his death as at any previous period. His head was of a very singular shape, being by no means high, if measured from the chin to the crown, but of unusual horizontal length from the forehead to the back of the head. His forehead projected at right angles from his face in a very remarkable manner. In his habits he was secluded and studious; not parsimonious, but economical, and disposed to lay one dollar on another.

BENJAMIN WEST.

Benjamin West, the earliest and most renowned of American painters, and an artist whose works command the attention of the world, was a native of Pennsylvania, and born in Chester County, near Springfield, in that state, on the 10th of October, 1738. His family were Quakers, and emigrated from England to America in 1699. Benjamin's father remained in England to be educated, and did not join his family until he had reached his fifteenth year.

At a very early age Benjamin gave evidence of art gifts. It is related that, in the month of June, 1745, when only seven years of age, he was left to take care of his little niece, who lay peacefully slumbering in a cradle by his side. The boy-artist sat watching her. Presently the baby smiled in its innocent sleep, and the supreme beauty of its arch tranquillity filled young Benjamin's breast with admiration. To give this expression, he seized a pen, and with red and black ink endeavored to transfer the beautiful picture to paper. When his mother returned she was surprised and delighted at the attempt, and, with the keen eye of affection, detected a portrait of the sleeping infant. At this time it is said that West had never seen a picture or an engraving, and most assuredly had never beheld any one attempting to copy the lineaments of nature. The latter part of the anecdote is probably reliable, but the first allegation may well be questioned. Soon after this occurrence Benjamin was sent to school. Pen and ink still constituted the objects of his amusement, and we may suppose that his school-books presented a highly pictorial appearance. From the Indians he learned the use of the red and yellow colors with which they painted their belts and ornaments, but before this epoch in his artist career he depended on the most sombre effects. The colors he used were principally charcoal and chalk, mixed with the juice of berries. With these colors, laid on with the hair of a cat, drawn through a goose-quill, when about nine years of age he drew on a sheet of paper the portraits of a neighboring family, in which the delineation of each individual was sufficiently accurate to be immediately recognized by his father when the picture was first shown to him. When about twelve years of age he performed a more difficult task, and drew a portrait of himself, with his hair hanging loosely about his shoulders. The knowledge which he had gained from the Indians extended his field of operations, and when he had obtained possession of a bit of indigo, which he coaxed out of his mother, he had the three primary colors to work with.

The atmosphere of a Quaker house is not very congenial to the development of art, but West's parents appear to have been liberal-minded, and worthily proud of their son. His little productions adorned their dwelling, and attracted the attention of their visitors. In this way the father of General Wayne became acquainted with the talents of the lad. He was so much pleased with the rough sketches he saw around him, that he asked the privilege of taking some of them home. The next day he saw young West, and presented him with six dollars—a magnificent sum to his fervid imagination. It was to this early reward that he attributed his subsequent artist career. Mr. Wayne was not the only admirer that the youthful artist possessed. A Mr. Pennington, of Philadelphia, who was related to the West family, paid a visit one day, and was astonished to find the apartments of the Quaker hung with drawings of birds and flowers, executed with native but untutored genius. To encourage the youth, he presented him with a box of colors and pencils. To these were added several pieces of canvas prepared for the easel, and six engravings by Greveling. Such a mine of treasure was beyond price to the young man. He could not sleep for thinking of it, and night and day nursed the gift with the most extreme fondness. Shortly after this he went on a visit to Philadelphia, and for the first time beheld the impressive spectacle of a noble stream teeming with magnificent shipping. It made a deep impression on his young imagination, and was the immediate cause of his first composition, a picturesque view of a river, with vessels floating on the surface, and cattle pasturing on its banks. Among the other wonders which he saw in the city was a picture by Williams, of Philadelphia, which astonished and delighted him. The perusal of the works of Fresnoy and Richardson did the rest. His future destiny was fixed in his own mind—he would become an artist.

Returning to Springfield with the reputation of a prodigy, he received many commissions to paint portraits, for which, as we have seen, he displayed great natural aptitude. A gunsmith of the name of William Henry, who was of a literary turn, suggested to him that he should engage himself on something more important than portraits, and gave him the subject of "Socrates' Death" as one worthy of illustration. West seized the idea, and produced his first historical picture. It attracted a good deal of attention, and led to the formation of many friendships which were afterward of great use to the young painter. Among these was that formed with Dr. Smith, provost of the college at Philadelphia, who was delighted to observe the efforts of the young artist, and offered to assist him in gaining an education, the want of which he now began to experience. The result led to Benjamin being transferred to the residence of his brother-in-law in Philadelphia.

At the age of sixteen, it was determined among the friends, after long deliberations, that Benjamin should be allowed to cultivate the art of painting. In Philadelphia he was able to pursue his studies with many advantages. He had free access to all the famous pictures of the city, and was, of course, hugely delighted and impressed with what he saw, especially with a Murillo in Governor Hamilton's collection. It was a St. Ignatius, and West copied it enthusiastically, before he even knew its author or appreciated its art value. His application at this time was so great that his health became impaired, and he was for a time stretched on a bed of sickness. The room in which he lay was darkened, and the only light that entered was through the cracks in the window-shutters. An anecdote is related of this time which illustrates in a forcible manner his keen powers of reasoning and observation. As he was lying in bed, partly recovered from a fever, he was surprised to see "the form of a white cow enter at one side of the roof, and, walking over the bed, gradually vanish at the other. The phenomenon surprised him exceedingly, and he feared that his mind was impaired by his disease, which his sister also suspected, when, on entering to inquire how he felt himself, he related to her what he had seen. She soon left the room, and informed her husband, who accompanied her back to the apartment; and as they were both standing near the bed, West repeated the story, exclaiming that he saw, at the very moment in which he was speaking, several little pigs running along the roof. This confirmed them in the apprehension of his delirium, and they sent for a physician; but his pulse was regular, the skin moist and cool, the thirst abated, and, indeed, every thing about the patient indicated convalescence. Still, the painter persisted in his story, and assured them that he then saw the figures of several of their mutual friends passing on the roof, over the bed, and that he even saw fowls picking, and the very stones of the street. All this seemed to them very extraordinary, for their eyes, not accustomed to the gloom of the chamber, could discover nothing; and the physician himself, in despite of the symptoms, began to suspect that the convalescent was really delirious. Prescribing, therefore, a composing mixture, he took his leave, requesting Mrs. Clarkson and her husband to come away and not disturb the patient. After they had retired the artist got up, determined to find out the cause of the strange apparitions which had so alarmed them all. In a short time he discovered a diagonal knot-hole in one of the window-shutters, and upon placing his hand over it, the visionary paintings on the roof disappeared. This confirmed him in an opinion that he began to form, that there must be some simple natural cause for what he had seen, and having thus ascertained the way in which it acted, he called his sister and her husband into the room, and explained it to them." He profited by this investigation; made a box with one of its sides perforated, and thus, without ever having heard of the invention, contrived a *camera obscura*.

At Philadelphia West obtained much employment as a portrait painter, and on the death of his mother, which occurred when he was about the age of eighteen, established himself in that profession, and by his skill and moderate prices (he used to charge twelve dollars) obtained a large number of patrons. Notwithstanding the hard work he performed in this way, he found time to execute an original work called "The trial of Susannah," and in this, as in the "Death of Socrates," the principal figures were carefully copied from living models. From Philadelphia West went to New York, still pursuing his profession with energy and success. During the eleven months he passed in the metropolis he painted another composition, entitled "A Student reading by Candle-light," and then, having sufficient means for the purpose, resolved to visit the classic shores of Italy. An opportunity soon occurred for taking ship to Leghorn, in company with a young gentleman, the son of a friend, who was going on the voyage for the benefit of his health. West was engaged on the portrait of Mr. Kelly, a merchant of New York, when he determined to sail from Philadelphia. He mentioned his plan to Mr. Kelly, who approved it, paid him for the picture, and gave him a letter to his agents in Philadelphia. West presented the letter, and was astonished to find that it contained an order for fifty guineas, "a present to aid in his equipment for Italy." We repeat this anecdote as an evidence of the good feeling and kindness which West received and undoubtedly deserved during his long career. West embarked in 1760, reached Leghorn in safety, and immediately proceeded to Rome, which he entered on the 10th of July, 1760. He never returned to America.

West was provided with excellent letters of introduction, and was at once introduced to Cardinal Albani, who, although nearly blind, was considered a great connoisseur. An anecdote is related of the first interview with this potentate, which we give for what it is worth. The cardinal passed his hand over the face of the young artist, in order to judge of his features. He was satisfied. "This young savage has good features, but what is his complexion? Is he black or white?" The English gentleman who introduced West replied that he was "very fair." "What!" cried the astonished cardinal, "as fair as I am?" The interrogation caused much merriment, the cardinal not being remarkable for his beauty in this respect. When it was found that the young man was neither black nor a savage, but fair, intelligent, and already an artist, he became the lion.

One of West's best advisers at this period was Mengs, a celebrated painter of the day. At his suggestion, he painted a portrait of Mr. Robinson, afterward Lord Grantham. Mengs found much to commend in the effort, accompanying his praise with some sensible advice. "You have already the mechanical part of your art," he said; "what I therefore recommend to you is, examine every thing worthy of attention here, making drawings of some half dozen of the best statues; then go to Florence, and study in the galleries; then proceed to Bologna, and study the works of the Caracci; afterward visit Parma, and examine attentively the pictures of Corregio; and then go to Venice, and view the productions of Tintoretto, Titian, and Paul Veronese. When you have made this tour, return to Rome, paint an historical picture, exhibit it publicly, and then the opinion which will be expressed of your talents will determine the line of art which you ought to follow." It was some time before Mr. West was in a position to follow this judicious advice; but, owing to the liberality of his friends in America, he was at length able to do so under the most gratifying circumstances. He visited Florence, Bologna, and Venice, and on his return to Rome declared that the Apollo of Belvidere "was the exact resemblance of a young Mohawk warrior," and that the hieroglyphics on the Egyptian obelisk were exactly similar to those which appear on the wampum belts of the Indians. The object of his mission to Italy being now accomplished, he began to make preparations for returning to America, but, previous to doing so, determined, in accordance with his father's wish, to visit England. Having passed through Savoy into France (where he found much to instruct him), Mr. West arrived in England on the 20th of August, 1763.

In England Mr. West found so much encouragement that, contrary to his first intention, he resolved to settle there. He became acquainted with Sir Joshua Reynolds, and Mr. Richard Wilson, the celebrated landscape painter. He was introduced by Dr. Markham (afterward Archbishop of York) to Dr. Johnson and Mr. Burke, in the latter of whom he recognized the features of the chief of the Benedictine monks at Parma, and afterward discovered that they were actually brothers. In 1765, Dr. Newton, Bishop of Bristol, engaged him to paint "the Parting of Hector and Andromache;" while for Dr. Johnson, then Bishop of Worcester, he undertook "the Return of the Prodigal Son." These commissions, and others which came to him, established his position as a historical painter. It was so far recognized that Lord Rockingham offered the rising artist an engagement of three thousand five hundred dollars a year if he would undertake to embellish his family mansion with pictures. Liberal as was this offer, West declined it, thinking, correctly enough, that his best patrons would be the public. Feeling easy in his mind concerning his future prospects, West consulted his heart on a matter which had engaged it for several years. Prior to his departure from America he had contracted a sincere affection for a young lady of the name of Shewell, and had paid his suit with such success that he was accepted. Now that the honors and riches of the world were at his command, he desired to make her his wife. At first it was his intention to undertake a voyage to America for the purpose of effecting the marriage, but this was prevented by a kind interposition of his father, who took the bride to England, where, on the 2d of September, 1765, she was wedded to the man of her choice.

Dr. Drummond, Archbishop of York, became one of West's most zealous patrons, and for him he painted the "Agrippina landing with the ashes of Germanicus." After hearing the passage of Tacitus in which is described all the circumstances of this mournful affair, and listening to the remarks of the prelate, our artist returned home, and composed a sketch for the picture, which was finished before going to bed. Next morning he carried it to the archbishop, who was both astonished and delighted to find his own ideas so forcibly endorsed by West. Perhaps for this reason he became doubly attached to our artist, and on the very first opportunity introduced him to the king, who graciously ordered a picture, "the Final Departure of Regulus from Rome," and read from Livy the passage which he wished illustrated. The friendship between the king and West, thus commenced, lasted for upward of forty years. He was frequently invited to spend the evening at Buckingham House, where he generally remained, conversing on the best means of promoting the study of the fine arts. It was in these conversations that the plan of the Royal Academy was first broached and discussed. An existing society, known as "the Society of Incorporated Artists," no longer answered the requirements of the time. Dissensions had occurred, and many of the most prominent members had withdrawn. The moment was propitious; the Royal Society was properly organized, Sir Joshua Reynolds elected president, and on the 10th of December, 1768, became an established institution of the country. At the first exhibition of the infant society West's "Regulus" was exhibited, and obtained much applause. The king's next commission was for "Hamilcar making his son Hannibal swear implacable enmity to the Romans." In the mean time Mr. West had finished one of his most celebrated pictures, namely, "the Death of Wolfe," a picture which has become world-wide in its reputation, but which created at the time a sensation even beyond its merits. This was owing to a daring innovation on the customs and usages of artists. Up to West's time it was usual in depicting modern heroic pieces to costume the characters in the flowing robes of the ancient Greek and Roman heroes. West dissented from this time-honored custom, and, in spite of remonstrances from very high authorities, painted the death of Wolfe in the dress of the actual persons. He thought he should gain far more in the life and truth of expression than he should lose in picturesqueness and grace. The result showed his sound judgment. Reynolds, who had opposed the innovation, acknowledged its force and manliness. "West has conquered; he has treated his subject as it ought to be treated; I retract my objections. I foresee that this picture will not only become one of the most popular, but will occasion a revolution in art." The picture *did* become one of the most popular, and *did* occasion a revolution in art, the good effects of which we observe to the present day.

It is unnecessary for the purposes of this sketch to dwell on each production of West's prolific pencil. He became firmly established in public favor, and each elaborate work which he produced received the instant attention of the art world. The king's admiration for the great artist was unbounded; and when he formed the design of erecting a magnificent oratory or private chapel at Windsor Castle, for the express purpose of illustrating the history of revealed religion, West was selected to fill the panels. "No subtle divine," says Mr. Cunningham, "ever labored more diligently on controversial texts than did our painter in evolving his pictures out of this grand and awful subject. He divided it into four dispensations—the Antediluvian, the Patriarchal, the

Mosaical, and the Prophetical. They contained, in all, thirty-six subjects, eighteen of which belonged to the Old Testament, the rest to the New. They were all sketched, and twenty-eight were executed, for which West received, in all, twenty-one thousand seven hundred and five pounds. A work so varied, so extensive, and so noble in its nature was never before undertaken by any painter."

On the death of Sir Joshua Reynolds, West was unanimously elected President of the Royal Academy, and continued in that honorable position to the time of his death. His first discourse was merely complimentary, but subsequently he delivered valuable dissertations on the principles of painting and sculpture, of embellishments and architecture; on the taste of the ancients; on the errors of the moderns, and on composition in general. He concluded one of these lectures in the following complimentary terms: "That our annual exhibitions, both as to number and taste, ingrafted on nature and the fruit of mental conception, are such, that all the combined efforts in art on the Continent of Europe in the same line have not been able to equal. To such attainments, were those in power but to bestow the crumbs from the national table to cherish the fine arts, we might pledge ourselves that the genius of Britain would in a few years dispute the prize with the proudest periods of Grecian or Italian art."

When George the Third became superannuated, West's income of a thousand pounds per year was suddenly stopped, and the pictures in the chapel of "revealed religion" discontinued. Having thus lost the royal patronage, the president determined to appeal to the public, and he did so with eminent success. Some of his best pictures were put on exhibition, and crowds of people went to see them. One of the most remarkable was the famous picture of "Christ healing the Sick," which was originally executed for the Philadelphia Hospital, but which was subsequently purchased by the British Institution for the sum of three thousand guineas. West parted with the picture "on condition that he should be allowed to make a copy, with alterations." In the copy which he transmitted to Philadelphia, he not only made alterations, but added an additional group. Its exhibition in the United States was attended with so much success that the committee were actually enabled to enlarge the hospital for the reception of no less than thirty additional patients.

The death of Mrs. West, which event occurred on the 10th of December, 1817, was a severe blow for the aged artist. His own health began to decline, and his hand had lost some of its power. He felt the blow severely, and never entirely recovered from its effects. Three years later (11th of March, 1820), he departed this life without any fixed complaint, his cheerfulness uneclipsed, his mental faculties unimpaired, and with a mind serene and benevolent. Mr. Galt enables us to enter into details concerning this event: "The last illness of Mr. West was slow and languishing. It was rather a general decay of nature than any specific malady; and he continued to enjoy his mental faculties in perfect distinctness upon all subjects as long as the powers of articulation could be exercised. To his merits as an artist and a man I may be deemed partial, nor do I wish to be thought otherwise. I have enjoyed his frankest confidence for many years, and received from his conversation the advantages of a more valuable species of instruction, relative to the arts, than books alone can supply to one who is not an artist. While I therefore admit that the partiality of friendship may tincture my opinion of his character, I am yet confident that the general truth of the estimate will be admitted by all who knew the man, or are capable to appreciate the merits of his works.

"In his deportment Mr. West was mild and considerate; his eye was keen, and his mind apt; but he was slow and methodical in his reflections, and the sedateness of his remarks must often, in his younger years, have seemed to strangers singularly at variance with the vivacity of his look. That vivacity, however, was not the result of any particular animation of temperament; it was rather the illuminations of his genius; for, when his features were studiously considered, they appeared to resemble those which we find associated with dignity of character in the best productions of art. As an artist, he will stand in the first rank; his name will be classed with those of Michael Angelo and Raffaelle; but he possessed little in common with either. As the former has been compared to Homer and the latter to Virgil, in Shakspeare we shall perhaps find the best likeness to the genius of Mr. West. He undoubtedly possessed but in a slight degree that energy and physical expression of character in which Michael Angelo excelled, and in a still less degree that serene sublimity which constitutes the charm of Raffaelle's great productions, but he was their equal in the fullness, the perspicuity, and the propriety of his compositions. In all his great works, the scene intended to be brought before the spectator is represented in such a manner that the imagination has nothing to supply. The incident, the time, and the place are there as we think they must have been; and it is this wonderful force of conception which renders the sketches of Mr. West so much more extraordinary than his finished pictures. In the finished pictures we naturally institute comparisons in coloring, and in beauty of figure, and in a thousand details which are never noticed in the sketches of this illustrious artist. But, although his powers of conception were so superior, equal in their excellence to Michael Angelo's energy or Raffaelle's grandeur, still, in the inferior departments of drawing and coloring he was one of the greatest artists of his age. It was not, however, till late in life that he executed any of those works in which he thought the splendor of the Venetian school might be judiciously imitated. At one time he intended to collect his works together, and to form a general exhibition of them all. Had he accomplished this, the greatness and versatility of his talents would have been established beyond all controversy; for unquestionably he was one of those great men whose genius can not be justly estimated by particular works, but only by a collective inspection of the variety, the extent, and the number of their productions."

Added to his unquestionable genius, West had diligence and enthusiasm. He was at once a patient and an expeditious worker. At the time of his death he left upward of four hundred paintings and sketches in oil, many of them of a large size, besides more than two hundred original drawings in his portfolio. It was calculated that, to exhibit all his productions, a gallery would be required of four hundred feet in length, fifty in breadth, and forty in height. West's pictures were sold after his death for upward of twenty-five thousand pounds. During his life he received large sums. From 1769 to 1779 he obtained £4126 for seventeen compositions, seven of which were historical, and the remainder family portraits. For the religious subjects £21,705 were paid. For eight subjects illustrative of the history of Edward the Third he received £6930, while for some miscellaneous works, executed for the same patron, he received £1426. These sums, which were received from the king alone, are exclusive of innumerable others of equal importance, and amount in all, including sale, to upward of three huudred thousand dollars. The proceeds of his brush during his residence in England could not have amounted to less than half a million of dollars.

West was a kind and considerate countryman to all the Americans he met in England, and felt genially toward the land of his birth, although the circumstances which had surrounded his life led him to look on the Revolutionary war with great pain. He had received nothing but kindness from the mother country. Some of his most distinguished pupils were Americans, and he never failed to render them all the assistance that lay in his power. When Trumbull was arrested during the war by order of the British government, West immediately waited upon the king, and made known to his majesty his pupil's character and purposes, and received the assurance that, at all events, the personal safety of the prisoner should be fully attended to. When Gilbert Stuart was in London, a young painter without resources, West not only afforded him direct pecuniary aid, but employed him in copying, and otherwise assisted him in his study of that branch of the art in which he afterward excelled his master. A few weeks after Allston's arrival in England he was introduced to Mr. West, and thus speaks of him in a letter: "Mr. West, to whom I was soon introduced, received me with the greatest kindness. I shall never forget his benevolent smile when he took me by the hand; it is still fresh in my memory, linked with the last of like kind which accompanied the last shake of his hand when I took a final leave of him in 1818. His gallery was open to me at all times, and his advice always ready and kindly given. If he had enemies, I doubt if he owed them to any other cause than his rare virtue, which, alas for human nature, is too often deemed cause sufficient."

Mr. West was buried with great pomp in St. Paul's Cathedral, beside the earthly remains of Sir Joshua Reynolds, Opie, and Barry. The pall was borne by noblemen, embassadors, and academicians; his two sons and grandson were chief mourners, and sixty coaches brought up the splendid procession.

JOHN FITCH.

The life-stories of men of genius are often sad, and filled with incidents of cruelty and neglect which after-generations can only deplore. There is none sadder, more truly pitiable, than that of John Fitch. He was a man of pre-eminent force of character; of native genius; of strength and originality. But these characteristics carried with them restlessness, impetuosity, dissatisfaction, querulousness, and defiance. Such a spirit baffled its own soarings, and, moth-like, rushed more madly to destruction at the first sensation of pain.

We have no intention in this paper to reopen the much-discussed question of "who was the first inventor of the steam vessel." In our article on Fulton we have dropped into the judicious track of most modern inquirers, and awarded to that illustrious man the honor of having first rendered steam navigation generally useful. On this point there can no longer be a doubt. But if the question of originality be mooted—if it be asked who was the most vigorous and original *inventor*, Fulton or Fitch, the answer would, we fancy, be in favor of Fitch. The former was a perfecter; he took the materials which already existed, and blended them with master hand. The latter was a creator; he shaped things in his own mind, and brought them forth rudely fashioned, but pregnant with undeveloped strength. It has happened in the world before, and will happen again, that the man who adapts receives more homage than he who invents. There is a common-sense reason why it should be so. The mass of mankind can not understand a theory; their instruction must be of a practical character. He who can impart this reaps the reward, even though it be merely an inculcation of the theory of his predecessor.

John Fitch, of whose sad life we purpose to give a brief sketch (compiled chiefly from his own manuscripts in the Franklin Library of Philadelphia), was born on the 21st of January, 1743, old style. His father was a farmer in good circumstances, but of an extremely harsh and parsimonious disposition. At four years of age John was sent to school, and, it is said, made some little progress in the usual branches of an English education. His father did not deem it necessary that he should be taught more than to read and write, and, when he had acquired these accomplishments, set him to work on the farm. But John was eager for knowledge, and greedily devoured all the books that lay in his way. When he was eleven years of age, he heard of a volume which he fancied would give him a knowledge of the whole world—this was Salmon's Geography. He repeatedly asked his father to get it for him to no purpose, but the latter consented to give him some headlands at the end of a field in which he might plant potatoes. Our hero was delighted with the prospect of earning the money for the coveted volume, and set to work with such assiduity that, when the season came round for disposing of his stock, he collected the enormous sum of ten shillings, and intrusted the same to a merchant who dealt in New York to procure him the book. He did so; but the book cost twelve shillings, and John had to run in debt two shillings, which he says gave him a great deal of uneasiness. He congratulated himself that he soon became the best geographer of the *world* that Connecticut could produce, according to Salmon, at that time.

Being of a "stunted" and weakly habit, which he attributed to the ill usage received from his father and brother, Fitch abandoned all idea of becoming an agriculturist. Salmon's Geography had given him a taste for travel, and he determined to go "down to the sea in ships." He made a couple of experiments in coasting-sloops; but the cruelties and hardships of the maritime profession discouraged him, and he abandoned it. His next experiment was in the clock-making business; but after two years' servitude, during which time he was principally employed in running errands, he left, almost entirely ignorant of the business. Fitch made another attempt to learn it with a brother of his former employer; but here, again, his wishes were frustrated. His employer was jealous of the secrets of the trade; worked in a distant part of the room; locked up his tools when he had finished, and forbade Fitch to meddle with them in any way. He was ill used in more ways than this. "Although I possessed a small appetite," he says, "I never was given sufficient to satisfy it, except on one occasion, when I managed to make a good hearty meal on potatoes. Being an inferior, I was helped last at the table; the females would then discourse upon gluttony, and my master, hastily devouring his own food, would immediately return thanks for that which himself and others ate, as well as for that which his apprentice did *not*." On leaving this curious specimen of humanity, he employed himself "in doing small brass-work," being unable to obtain employment as a journeyman watch and clock maker even with his very limited knowledge of those businesses. He pursued his new vocation with industry, and at the end of two years found himself the master of fifty pounds. A portion of this capital he embarked in the potash business, but was unsuccessful, owing, in a great measure, to the unfairness and incapacity of one of his partners. On the 29th of December, 1767, he entered into a matrimonial alliance with a Miss Lucy Roberts—a most unhappy match, their tempers being totally incompatible. A separation soon became inevitable, the bitterness of which was aggravated by the circumstance that Mrs. Fitch took with her a child whom he "loved as dear as himself."

After this event the subject of our sketch became a wanderer, and roamed from city to city in search of occupation. Unable to procure this in any familiar trade, he gave reins to his ingenuity, and became a button-maker, first at New Brunswick, and afterward at Trenton. He appears to have been tolerably successful. During the Revolutionary war he repaired the arms of the Continental army, became alternately the prisoner of the Indians and of the British, and was finally exchanged, and returned to the Atlantic towns.

In 1785 Fitch first turned his thoughts to the subject of steam, with the intention of using it as a propeller of ordinary carriages on common roads. He pursued this idea, according to his own account, for one week, gave it over as impracticable, and turned his attention to steam navigation. From that time to the day of his death he pursued the latter subject with unremitting assiduity. "The perplexities and embarrassments through which it has caused me to wade," he writes, "far exceed any thing that the common course of life ever presented to my view; and to reflect on the disproportion of a man of my abilities to such a task, I am to charge myself with having been deranged, and, had I not the most convincing proofs to the contrary, should most certainly suppose myself to have been *non compos mentis* at the time." The most remarkable evidence of the inventive genius of Fitch is found in the fact that the whole scheme of steam-travel by land and by water, and also of the steam-engine itself, originated in his own mind, and was worked out by the fiery process of independent genius. In Europe the steam-engine was simply known as an amusing plaything, for the philosophic youth, Watts, had not yet developed its latent powers, or bridled them for the use of man. It was therefore by no means remarkable that Fitch had not heard of the invention. He says himself, "I did not know there was a steam-engine on earth when I proposed to gain a force by steam, and I leave my first drafts and descriptions behind, that you may judge whether I am sincere or not. A short time after drawing my first draft for a boat, I was amazingly chagrined to find at Parson Irwin's, in Buck's County, a drawing of a steam-engine; but it had the effect to establish me in my other principles, as my doubts at that time lay in the engine only."

Men of capital are notorious for the distrust they exhibit toward inventors. They are too prone to look on them as mere visionaries—men who conceive wild ideas of what *ought* to be rather than what *can* be. It required time, patience, self-sacrifice, and heart-sickness to induce the possessors of wealth to listen to the schemes of a poor enthusiast like Fitch. In time, however, he succeeded in forming a small company for carrying out his plans. Dr. Thornton, who was a member of this company, has given in his "Account of the Origin of the Steam-boat" an interesting narrative of the manifold difficulties Fitch and his associates had to contend with, even after they had obtained a certain amount of protection from state privileges. "We worked incessantly at the boat to bring it to perfection, and under the disadvantages of never having seen a steam-engine on the principles contemplated, of not having a single engineer in our company or pay. We made engineers of common blacksmiths, and, after expending many thousand dollars, the boat did not exceed three miles an hour. Finding great unwillingness in many to proceed, I proposed to the company to give up to any one the one half of my shares who would, at his own expense, make a boat to go at the rate of eight miles an hour, in dead water, in eighteen months, or forfeit all the expenditures on failing; or I would engage with any others to accept these terms. Each relinquished one half of his shares, by making the forty shares eighty, and holding only as many of the new shares as he held of the old ones, and then subscribed as far as he thought proper to enter on the terms, by which many relinquished one half. I was among the number, and in less than twelve months we were ready for the experiment.

"The day was appointed, and the experiment made in the following manner: a mile was measured in Front (Water) Street, Philadelphia, and the bounds projected at right angles as exactly as could be to the wharf, where a flag was placed at each end, and also a stop-watch. The boat was ordered under way at dead water, or when the tide was found to be without movement; as the boat passed one flag, it struck, and at the same instant the watches were set off; as the boat reached the other flag, it was also struck, and the watches instantly stopped. Every precaution was taken before witnesses: the time was shown to all; the experiment declared to be fairly made, and the boat was found to go at the rate of *eight miles an hour*, or one mile in seven minutes and a half, on which the shares were signed over with great satisfaction by the rest of the company. It afterward went *eighty miles* in a day."

Notwithstanding the extremely satisfactory character of this experiment, the company became irritated at the continued outlays, and, in the end, obstinately refused to continue the project. We can paint to ourselves the anxiety and agony of Fitch as he observed the shareholders one by one withdrawing from the concern. The consciousness of truth was all that sustained him; he knew that he was *not* pursuing a chimera. In 1792, when the boat and his hopes appeared to be docked forever, he wrote a letter to Mr. Rittenhouse containing this memorable prophecy: "This, sir, will be the mode of crossing the Atlantic in time, whether I bring it to perfection or not." His enthusiasm on the subject never diminished for one moment. Steam was the constant theme of his discourse whenever he could prevail upon any one to listen to him. Upon one occasion he called on a smith who had worked at his boat, and, after dwelling some time upon his favorite topic, concluded with these words: "Well, gentlemen, although I shall not live to see the time, you will, when steamboats will be preferred to all other means of conveyance, and especially for passengers; and they will be particularly useful in navigating the River Mississippi." He then retired, when a person present observed, in a tone of deep sympathy, "*Poor fellow! what a pity he is crazy!*"

In the winter of 1792–1793, Fitch crossed the Atlantic on a

visit to France, whither he went warmly commended, and with strong hopes of success. He was cordially received by the government, and assistance was offered to him. His usual ill luck interposed, however. Throes of the approaching revolution distracted the attention of the ministers, and poor Fitch was laid aside for subjects of political importance. Dejected, and with scarcely a hope left, he crossed the Channel to London, and, without accomplishing any thing in that metropolis, soon afterward returned to his native land, so poor that he had, it is said, to work his way home as a common sailor. He landed in Boston in 1794 in utter destitution, and, but for the hospitality of a brother-in-law, might have perished from actual want. Three years later he made a journey to the West, to see after some grants of lands which had been made to him for services rendered to the State of Kentucky as a surveyor, a knowledge of which business Fitch imbibed while residing on his father's farm. These grants had been long neglected, and, as many settlements had been made on them, it was not without difficulty that he obtained possession of them. A number of suits had to be instituted, and the delays and uncertainties of the law contributed to his other vexations. He became irascible and eccentric, dressed himself in a peculiar way, and excited the observation of the passers-by. His health began to decline; he was easily irritated, and, when touched on the subject of steam navigation, expressed himself with a warmth which exposed him to the ridicule of the idle and unfeeling. "When excited by his theme," says Mr. Whittlesey, in his biography, "his power over language was great, his remarks powerful, eloquent, and convincing; but he asserted, and perhaps truly, that the generation in which he lived was incapable of comprehending his invention. His expectations were fixed upon posterity; and with an abiding confidence that the steam-boat would bless and astonish his successors, he reserved for them that fame which he was not disposed to ask, but to demand. It was with such sentiments that he inclosed the manuscripts and drawings presented to the Philadelphia Library, and left an injunction that they should not be opened until thirty years after his death."

He appears to have lost all hope from this time. Weary, and anxious for the rest which the grave could alone give, he abandoned himself to habits of obliviousness, fully conscious that they would soon lead him to "that bourne whence no traveler returns." In June, 1798, he executed his last will and testament, and in July following it was admitted to probate. His death was in one or other of the two months—*which* is not known. The landlord of the inn where he resided procured a cherry coffin for the remains of his unfortunate boarder, and, attended by a few friends, carried it to the church-yard of Bardstown. No monument, no headstone, no rough tablet carved by hands of affection marked the spot, and in a little while it was forgotten.

Fitch was a man of uncommon stature, being six feet two inches in height, erect and full in carriage, his head slightly bald, but not gray, his manner dignified, distant, and imposing. His countenance was pleasing, with an eye remarkably black and piercing. "To strangers his manners had never been prepossessing, but to men of intelligence, who could comprehend his projects, he proved a most interesting companion. As a friend, he was faithful and devoted while the friendship lasted, carrying his efforts in behalf of others beyond the line of worldly prudence."

Misfortune pursued Fitch even after death. A number of papers, drawings, etc., to which he referred as evidence of the originality and priority of his plans, were destroyed by fire, and the first model of his steam-boat, made in 1785, has been lost, so that his claims as an original inventor are always liable to be disputed, especially as the fire in the Patent Office destroyed many other proofs of his originality. Truly a more unfortunate man has never lived.

PATRICK HENRY.

When we take up the newspaper of a morning, and find the first page filled with a closely-printed speech of some aspiring orator, who does not, perhaps, much interest us, we are very apt to lay the sheet aside and say there is nothing in it, indifferent to the fact that a hundred years hence it will be prized as a document of inestimable value. The appetite for long speeches belongs to the past or to the future, and can only be aroused in the present day by events of vital importance to the Commonwealth, and then only by men of the highest intellectual capacity. The newspaper editor has to a terrible extent superseded the orator, and makes a paragraph where of old our grandfathers made a speech. Every thing is brief and rapid, to suit the rail-road speed of the age. Oratory in its pure state—that is to say, the spontaneous utterance of noble thoughts and magnificent images as the symbolical representatives of coarser things, is almost unknown to us. If a man wants to make a long speech now, he toils at it in the closet, builds it on the most raking and logical model, rivets it with sharp-pointed facts, and takes good care not to launch it on the stormy waters of debate before it is thoroughly sound and seaworthy. The newspapers print it at length in one column, and condense it in another, so that, like Webster's Dictionary, the student can either take it in bulk or in miniature. No arrangement could be more happy. The time-pressed merchant gets the points from the editorial summary, and the historian gets the substance in the verbatim report. What if a few people do go to sleep over the latter? Is there any thing more comfortable than being talked to sleep?

It was far different in the days of Patrick Henry—a great man, whose marvelous powers of oratory were exercised at a time when men's eyes gazed earnestly into the inspired face of the orator, and men's thirsty souls panted for words of patriotism. There were no newspapers then to cool down the enthusiasm of the oration by after-breakfast comments on it. People came from afar to hear it fresh from the speaker's lip, for that was the only fount at which it could be quaffed in its purity. They crowded the court-house in anticipation of the event. They endured the pressure of contending thousands, and considered themselves fortunate if they were rewarded with a glimpse of the orator, and caught a few of his glowing sentences. They were dragged out fainting to the open air, and were again newly stifled by eager crowds pressing around them to hear by repetition what could not otherwise be enjoyed. Every auditor, in fact, was a sort of newspaper, and circulated his report to the best of his ability. He was at once a man of influence and consideration. People stopped him at the street corner with courtesies to betray him into copiousness. If he came from the country, his return home was little else than a triumphal progress attended with all sorts of ovations and hospitalities.

And the orator, what was he? In the days of Patrick Henry he was *the* power. There were but few newspapers, and they were dry and unreliable. The orator supplied their place with liberality and the inspiration of life. His opinions, if they were not always in advance of the day, were tinctured, at least, with all the day could supply. He inculcated them with the earnestness of a prophet, and his personal influence was commensurate with the impression he was capable of making on his hearers. It can scarcely be estimated now. The many-tinted rays of individual opinion which are brought to bear on public topics, resulting from the habit of critical scrutiny and suspicion, detract from the individual light which the modern orator can throw on them, no matter how brightly it may shine. DEMOSTHENES and CICERO would find it difficult to preserve their reputation—at all events, their popularity, in these times. The newspapers would handle them with the dreadful weapons of common sense, and would batter their tropes and figures about their heads. But their speeches would be reported with marvelous accuracy, and the future historian could turn to them with the certainty of finding ample material for forming his own judgment of the merits of earlier criticism.

It is the absence of this invaluable record that we have most to regret in treating the life of Patrick Henry. We know by the influence he had on his times that he was one of the most extraordinary orators the world has ever produced, but unfortunately this knowledge is based entirely on tradition. We can not furnish an adequate specimen of his matchless eloquence. The few imperfect reports of his speeches that have been handed down to us are evidently wretched reflexes of the burning language the orator employed. We shall endeavor to use these to the best advantage, but the reader must never forget that they are entirely inadequate to the reputation of Patrick Henry. We can only judge of the eminence of that great man by the mighty influence he exercised on, and the concurrent testimony of his contemporaries. Jefferson, whose opinion is sufficient to endorse every tradition, says that "he was the greatest orator that ever lived," and "the person who, beyond all question, gave the first impulse to the movement which terminated in the Revolution;" sufficient, in all reason, to interest the American reader in the biography we are about to write.

PATRICK HENRY was the second son of John and Sarah Henry, and one of a family of nine children. He was born on the 29th of May, 1736, at the family seat called Studley, in Hanover County, Virginia. His father, John Henry, was a native of Aberdeen, Scotland, and emigrated to Virginia about the year 1730. He was followed, some years after, by his brother Patrick, a clergyman of the Church of England. Both brothers were remarkable for their loyalty to the king and his church. John Henry married the widow of Colonel Syme, a native of Hanover County, and daughter of the family of Winston, a lady remarkable for the ease and brilliancy of her conversational powers. Shortly after

Patrick Henry's birth the family removed to another seat in the same county, then called Mount Brilliant, now The Retreat. His parents were by no means wealthy, but they were comfortably situated, and by the exercise of economy could make both ends meet in a genteel way. They moved in the best society, and were on intimate terms with all the big guns of the colony. Patrick was sent to an "Oldfield" school, to keep him out of mischief, until he was ten years of age, and then, having acquired the elements of learning, was taken home to prosecute his studies under the care of his father. It was with the greatest difficulty that the rudiments of the Latin tongue were implanted in his mind, and with still greater difficulty that he mastered the crooked characters of the Greek alphabet, beyond which he never proceeded. He was a very idle scholar, and never put his heart in his studies. They were tasks to him in the severest sense of the word, and he flew from them with delight. The only study for which he seems to have had some kind of liking was the mathematics, in which he is said to have made considerable progress. It is certain, however, that for five years he made but feeble effort to cultivate his mind. When fourteen years old (1750), he accompanied his mother in a carriage to hear Samuel Davies preach, whose eloquence, it is said, made a deep impression on his mind. This orator was celebrated for his patriotic sermons, and it is more than probable that he first kindled the fire and afforded the model of Henry's elocution. Throughout his lifetime Henry declared that he always held Davies to be the greatest orator he had ever heard.

His personal appearance at this time is described as coarse, and his manners awkward, his dress neglected, and his faculties entirely obscured by habitual indolence. In mixed companies he contributed little or nothing to the conversation—a good sign, for it showed that he was modest. He preferred listening to the talk of others, and never failed to improve himself by it. He possessed, like all great men, a fine memory, and could easily recall what had been said by any speaker. One of his most favorite amusements was to analyze the characters of his friends, and observe in what respects they differed from each other. Patrick Henry's character at this time may be summed up in few words. He was a modest, observant man, fond of seeing every thing and of hearing every thing, but bashful, and afraid of thrusting himself forward. Unlike most young men, he was utterly indifferent to dress; a new coat had no charm in his eye; and at any time he would rather have had a new fish-line than a new pair of shoe-buckles. He was nearly six feet high, spare and raw-boned, with a slight stoop in the shoulders. His complexion was dark and sallow, and his general expression grave, thoughtful, and penetrating.

Such was Patrick Henry at the age of fifteen. Finding that he was not likely to make much progress in literary or professional pursuits, his father undertook to establish him in trade. It was a very common mistake in those days, and even in these, to suppose that a less amount of shrewdness was needed for the conduct of a business than for the pursuit of a profession. After a year's drilling in the counting-room of a neighboring merchant, Patrick and his brother William opened a small store. It is not easy to imagine a firm with less practicability at its disposal. The confinement soon began to annoy Patrick, and he relieved it as much as possible by making the store the gathering-place of all the gossips in the town. The class of people who patronized him were careless and often unprincipled, depending more on their power of persuasion than on their reputation for credit. Neither Patrick nor his brother were good at making bargains—indeed, the latter seems to have been more helplessly indolent and incapable than the former. In about a year the concern failed. William retired at once, while Patrick was employed for two or three years afterward in bringing it to a close. Considering the short time it had run, it required a great deal of winding up. All the future orator had gained by his first adventure in commerce was a knowledge of the violin and flute, which (impressed with the necessity of amusing himself) he had studied in business hours—rather expensive accomplishments, one would think.

At the age of eighteen he married a Miss Skelton, the daughter of a poor but honest farmer in the neighborhood. Young Henry was now, by the joint assistance of his father and father-in-law, started in life again. Trade having failed, it was determined to try agriculture. He was furnished with a small farm, and also one or two slaves to assist him in cultivating it. But it was of no use. His want of skill, his indolent habits, and his aversion to systematic labor of any kind, still pursued him. After an experiment of two years he sold off his farm at a sacrifice, and once more embarked every thing in merchandise. But, unfortunately, he had not forgotten his former method of conducting business. The flute and the violin were again called into requisition; all the idle politicians of the place gathered on the old spot; and occasionally the store would be shut up altogether, when his favorite sports in the open air called him forth. For the latter he always had the most passionate love, and, strange to say, preferred pursuing them alone. He would lie for hours beneath the shadow of a tree, watching with the calm earnestness of a sportsman for the expected bite, or, gun in hand, would wait in the same still manner for a chance shot at a passing deer. Whether it was a contemplative habit, or simply a lazy one, that made him like this kind of quiet sport, it is impossible to say. Under such manifold disadvantages, it is not remarkable that his second mercantile experiment turned out even more disastrous than his first. He was now thrown upon the world not only with a mass of debts upon his shoulders, but with a wife to support, and with relations who certainly could not be pleased with his conduct, or disposed to assist him again. It is probable that he felt the degradation to which a course of mere selfish indolence had reduced him. Idleness and its necessary associations had twice brought him to bankruptcy; and now, in his twenty-fourth year, he was absolutely without the means of making a living. It is from this crisis that he belongs to our biographies of "self-made men." He had sacrificed all the advantages of favorable birth and early associations, and had paid the penalty of wanton loss of time and indolence. Most men, under such circumstances, would have sunk beneath the load of ignominious misfortune; but Henry determined to bear up against it, and commence the world anew. Notwithstanding his ill luck in trade, he was undoubtedly a stronger man for the contests of the world now than at any former period of his life. He had gained that most expensive of all knowledge, the knowledge of mankind. He knew thoroughly the habits and feelings of those by whom he was surrounded, and could adapt his sail to the first wind which should blow him fortune. He had many friends too. They might shake their heads when his name was mentioned, and say that he was a good-for-naught, but for all that they were willing to help him along whenever the opportunity occurred for doing so, for they knew that he was no man's enemy but his own.

While he was engaged in his second mercantile experiment he cultivated a taste for reading, and studied attentively the geography, history, and political memorials of his native state, the historians of Greece and Rome, and, in particular, the English translation of Livy. The latter, indeed, was a kind of manual with him, and he never failed to read it at least once a year.

After his second failure, Henry was, as we have seen, entirely thrown on the world. His young wife returned to the house of her father, who was now the proprietor of a small hotel at Hanover Court-house. It is probable that Patrick accompanied her, and to this circumstance may be traced the oft-repeated assertion that he was, for a portion of his life, at least, a bar-tender. The biographers do not dwell on this event with proper attention. It was the cause, undoubtedly, of all his later career; for it was while in this humble station that he first came in contact with members of the legal profession who frequented the court-house, and thus, as it were, gained an insight into the mysteries of their vocation. There must have been small and great lawyers in those days as now, and Henry no doubt fancied that if he could not be the one, he might, at least, rival the shrewdness of the other. He therefore determined to embrace the legal profession without delay. He had several inducements. His father was on the bench; his father-in-law in a position to influence a considerable number of small clients, and he himself popular with the masses.

Henry's preparation for the new profession did not give promise of future excellence. He devoted to this study the ridiculously brief period of *six weeks*, and then presented himself to the examiners for license to practice. He met with some opposition, but, by the exercise of some tact and persuasion (for both of which he was remarkable), he succeeded in getting a license. For three years after this he devoted himself to the interests of the few clients who would trust their causes to his hands. He was thus able to make a scanty living, and for the first time to taste the sweet reward of honest industry. He was economical, and this important change in his habits induced many of his former friends to assert that he grew mean in his old age. The truth of the matter was simply that he had learned the value of money in the hard and bitter school of poverty.

The first cause that brought Henry prominently before the public, made him, at the same time, famous. This was none other than the celebrated Parsons' Cause. The Parsons' Cause was an action by the Reverend James Maury against the collector of taxes for Hanover County and his sureties, for the recovery of damages for the non-payment of a certain quantity of tobacco alleged to be due to him on account of his salary. The action sprung out of a warm controversy which had lately arisen between the clergy and the rate-payers of the colony. The Church of England was at this time the legal church establishment, and, by an early act of the Assembly, the salary of each minister was fixed at 16,000 pounds of tobacco; or if, for convenience, they preferred to have cash, they could take 16,000 twopences ($640)—twopence per pound being the ordinary price of tobacco. The clergy were in the habit of commuting the delivery of the article in kind for a money payment calculated on this standard. They had a right, however, by virtue of a statute of the colony, to demand payment in the article itself, if they felt so disposed. It was in view of this right that the Reverend Mr. Maury brought his action, and the reason why he was anxious to claim the right was simply this: the crop of tobacco had fallen short, and the price had greatly risen in consequence. The clergy claimed the advantage of this fluctuation in the market, and contended that the planters had no right to receive fifty or sixty shillings a hundred for their tobacco, while they paid their debts due in that article at the old price of sixteen shillings and eightpence. There was a side issue concerning the validity of an act of the Legislature, but it is unimportant for our purposes. The popular feeling was strongly in favor of the planters and against the clergy. It was on behalf of the former that Mr. Henry held his brief. The suit against the collector of the county was gained by the clergy before Mr. Henry had any thing to do with it, and the question now was merely as to the amount of damages. The leading counsel of the planters left Mr. Henry to argue the question at the next court, imagining, in all probability, that no farther victory was to be achieved worthy *his* steel. The case came on for trial on the 1st of December, 1763, before the County Court of Hanover, in which the father of Henry sat as presiding magistrate. The clergy appeared in full force, and the position of the young barrister became in the highest degree embarrassing, not only because he had to speak in open court before his father as presiding magistrate, but because he had to stretch his unfledged wings in an atmosphere already darkened by defeat. Among the clergy who came to hear the argument was the Rev. Patrick Henry, uncle to our orator, who had himself commenced a suit against the collector, and who was, therefore, peculiarly and pecuniarily interested in the result of the proceedings. The fact that Henry was not employed by his uncle is a sufficient proof that little was expected of him, even by those who knew him most intimately. On seeing his relative approach, Henry walked up to him, and expressed his regret at seeing his uncle there. "Why so?" inquired the uncle. "Because," replied Henry, "I fear that, as I have never yet spoken in public, I shall be too much overawed by your presence to do justice to my clients. Besides," he added, "I shall be under the necessity of saying some *hard things* of the clergy, which it may be unpleasant for you to hear." "As to *your* saying hard things of the clergy," said the old gentleman, good-naturedly, "I advise you to be cautious, as you will be more likely to injure your own cause than theirs. As to my leaving the ground, I fear, my boy, with such a cause to defend, my presence will do you but little harm or good. Since, however, you seem to think otherwise, and desire it of me so earnestly, you shall be gratified." He then entered his carriage and drove home.

The case came on. The opposing counsel behaved with the magnanimity of a man certain of gaining the day. He was full, fair, liberal, and eloquent. Now came Mr. Henry's turn. He rose from his seat with trepidation, and felt and looked thoroughly uncomfortable. It was with difficulty that he contrived to blunder through the exordium of his speech; but, when he had got thus far, a sudden change came over his whole appearance. His attitude, by degrees, became lofty and erect, his eye grew luminous, his hands swept the air with graceful curvings, and mentally and physically he seemed to expand with inspiration and divine force. Wirt says that "the people, whose countenances had fallen as he rose, had heard but a very few sentences before they began to look up; then to look at each other with surprise, as if doubting the evidence of their own senses; then, attracted by some strong gesture, struck by some majestic attitude, fascinated by the spell of his eye, the charm of his emphasis, and the varied and commanding expression of his countenance, they could look away no more. In less than twenty minutes they might be seen in every part of the house, on every bench, in every window, stooping forward from their stands in death-like silence, their features fixed in amazement and awe, all their senses listening and riveted upon the speaker, as if to catch the last strain of some heavenly visitant." Unfortunately, this remarkable speech is not preserved. That it was of marvelous power, and filled with strong appeals to the passions of the hearers, does not admit of a doubt. The jury were so moved by it that, disregarding the admitted rights of the plaintiff, they returned a verdict of *one penny damages.* A motion was made for a new trial, but the court overruled it. No sooner was the cause decided than the people seized the fortunate advocate, and carried him about on their shoulders, amid the wildest excitement and applause. We can only judge properly of this initial effort of the young orator by the effect it had on the public mind. This must, indeed, have been enormous. For years and years afterward the Virginians used to say of an eloquent man, "He is almost equal to Patrick Henry when he plead against the Parsons."

By a single bound Henry had thus reached a grand and enviable position in the public regard. He was looked on as the representative of popular rights, and became identified with the people. In those days, silly class-distinctions existed to a pernicious degree, and it was a triumph for the masses that they could claim such a man as Henry for their champion against their wealthy, aristocratic, and overbearing neighbors. As an orator, he could desire no greater distinction than to be the idol of the masses, from whom he knew full well all power must eventually come.

Henry found no difficulty in getting practice after his triumph in the Parsons' cause, and, in order to extend his field of operations, he removed to the County of Louisa. Here he resumed his professional labors, diversifying them occasionally by a hunting tour in the woods, but keeping steadily on the newly-discovered path to fortune. He was not free from occasional difficulties, and still had to struggle against want. But he had a hopeful and stout heart within, and did not despair of victory in the end. He had frequent cause to repent his early want of application, and was more than once humiliated by a consciousness that men far inferior to himself succeeded in gaining victories over him simply on account of technical knowledge, which he had neglected, but which they possessed. It was in addressing the jury that Henry shone to best advantage, and, consequently, it was on criminal days that he most distinguished himself. Judge Lyons, of Virginia, was accustomed to say that he could write a letter, or draw a declaration or plea at the bar with as much accuracy as he could in his office, under all circumstances, *except when Patrick rose to speak;* but that, whenever *he* rose, he was obliged to lay down his pen, and could not write another word until the speech was finished.

There was no event of importance to draw out the rare powers of our orator until the passage of the famous Stamp Act, in January, 1765. The object of this measure was, as every one knows, to raise a revenue by taxing the colonies, and the result of the policy which suggested it was the war of Independence. On the rumor that such a measure was in contemplation, the Virginia House of Burgesses prepared three remonstrances, to the king, to the House of Lords, and to the Commons of England, but they received no attention. The Stamp Act was ordered to go into effect in November, 1765. Henry was a member of the House of Burgesses, and had been elected to that honorable post to represent the people, who, to tell the truth, were somewhat oppressed by the "cold shade of aristocracy." At such a crisis he felt himself under the necessity of giving expression to the public indignation thus provoked by the tyranny of the British government. Consequently, he brought forward his celebrated resolutions on the Stamp Act. They were brief, plain, and earnest, and asserted that the General Assembly of the colony had the sole right and power to lay taxes and impositions upon the inhabitants, and that any attempt to vest such power in any person or persons whatsoever, other than the General Assembly aforesaid, had a manifest tendency to destroy British as well as American freedom. After a stormy debate, the resolutions were carried by a majority of one or two only. It was sufficient for the purpose. The great point of resistance to British taxation was established in the colonies, and it was this, as Henry remarks, "which brought on the war, and finally separated the two countries, and gave independence to ours." Of the speech made by Henry at this debate there is no satisfactory record. It was vehement and patriotic, beyond a doubt. A passage from the close has been often quoted, and, as it is thoroughly authenticated, may be given here. He dwelt upon the danger which tyrants suffer from the indignation their acts provoke. "Cæsar," said he, "had his Brutus, Charles the First his Cromwell, and George the Third—" Here the orator was interrupted by loud cries of "Treason! Treason!" He paused for a moment, and then continued with perfect calmness, "and George the Third may profit by their example. If this be treason, make the most of it."

This was Patrick Henry's first appearance as an orator on purely political topics. It is a rather singular circumstance, remarks Dr. Everett, in his very admirable memoir, that in this department, as in that of legal practice, no subsequent effort seems to have surpassed, or even quite equaled in immediate effect, the first. His speech in the Continental Congress soon after its organization called forth the strongest admiration. Many of his speeches in the Virginia Convention on the Federal Constitution were received with unbounded enthusiasm, and produced very extraordinary results. His argument in the British Debt case, which occupied three days, is analyzed at great length by Mr. Wirt, and dwelt upon as a sort of masterpiece; but, even at the present time, a Virginian who is requested to mention the leading titles of Henry's glory, appeals without hesitation to the speeches on the Stamp Act and the Parsons' cause. The peculiar circumstances attending each of these cases may have contributed something to give them their comparative importance; but, independently of any other cause, there is a certain freshness in the first efforts of a powerful mind which gives them an advantage over those of later years, that, on careful analysis, may appear, as works of science and art, fully equal, if not superior.

Although the British government repealed the Stamp Act on account of the opposition that had been raised to it in the colonies, it was soon apparent that the principles of that opposition were not in the slightest degree recognized, and that the British government still claimed the right of taxing the colonies. Duties were imposed upon various articles of general use—tea among others. A riot took place in Boston, and an armed demonstration was made by the troops. A quick succession of events of this character greatly excited the public mind. It would be wrong to say that the idea of total separation from the mother country was entertained by the mass of the people, but a growing dislike to the English government began to pave the way for it. Some few advanced minds—among the number Henry's—began to see that these things could only end in a vital struggle and independence.

The colonies were now in such a critical condition, especially the eastern ones, that it was considered necessary to call a general Congress, at which deputies should meet to discuss the state of public affairs, and determine on a unanimous course of action. On the 4th of September, 1774, the old Continental Congress met at Philadelphia. Among the deputies from Virginia were George Washington and Patrick Henry. We have again to lament the absence of any authentic record of the speeches made on this occasion. They are represented by Mr. Wirt, on the authority of those who heard them, as having been in the highest degree powerful and impressive. Henry, however, broke down in the *routine* work of the Congress. He was requested to draw up a petition to the king. He did so, but it was found so unsatisfactory that another one had to be prepared in its place. Judge Chase, of Maryland, who was a member of this Congress, on hearing the speeches of Henry and Lee, walked across the floor to the seat of his colleague, and said to him, in an under tone, "We may as well go home; we are not able to legislate with these men." But, after their talent for transacting the public affairs had been tested, the judge was heard to remark, "I find, after all, they are but men, and, in mere matters of business, but very common men."

On returning home from this Congress Mr. Henry was, of course, closely questioned by his friends as to the other members. He was asked, among other things, whom he thought the greatest man in Congress. "If you speak of eloquence," said Henry, "Mr. Rutledge, of South Carolina, is by far the greatest orator; but if you speak of solid information and sound judgment, Colonel Washington is unquestionably the greatest man on the floor."

On the 20th of March, 1775, a convention of Virginia delegates (the second) assembled at Richmond. Henry was, of course, among the number. Resolutions were introduced expressive of the sentiments of the colonies concerning certain matters, and ending with the hope of a speedy restoration of peace and good-will. Henry objected to these resolutions on the ground that they were too tame for the crisis. He introduced another series, which he conceived to be more to the point. The last resolution was as follows: "Resolved, therefore, that this colony be immediately put into a state of defense, and that a committee be raised to prepare a plan for embodying, arming, and disciplining such a number of men as may be sufficient for that purpose." The Convention was not prepared for such decided steps, and the resolutions were warmly opposed, even by men who were patriotic and keenly alive to the critical state of affairs. Mr. Henry took the ground that it was impossible to remain longer happily united to England, and in strengthening this position delivered one of the most famous speeches ever uttered by an American orator. "Mr. President," said he, "it is natural to man to indulge in the illusions of hope. We are apt to shut our eyes against a painful truth, and listen to the song of that siren till she transforms us into beasts. * * * * For my part, whatever anguish of spirit it may cost, I am willing to know the whole truth; to know the worst, and to provide for it. I have but one lamp by which my feet are guided, and that is the lamp of experience. I know of no way of judging of the future but by the past. * * * Let us not, I beseech you, sir, deceive ourselves longer. Sir, we have done every thing that could be done to avert the storm which is coming on. We have petitioned; we have remonstrated; we have supplicated; we have prostrated ourselves before the throne, and have implored its interposition to arrest the tyrannical hands of the ministry and Parliament. Our petitions have been slighted; our remonstrances have produced additional violence and insult; our supplications have been disregarded, and we have been spurned with contempt from the foot of the throne. In vain, after these things, may we indulge the fond hope of peace and reconciliation. *There is no longer any room for hope.* If we wish to be free—if we mean to preserve inviolate those inestimable privileges for which we have been so long contending—if we mean not basely to abandon the noble struggle in which we have been so long engaged, and which we have pledged ourselves never to abandon until the glorious object of our contest shall be obtained, we must fight! I repeat it, sir, we must fight! An appeal to arms, and to the God of Hosts, is all that is left us. * * * If we were base enough to desire it, it is now too late to retire from the contest. There is no retreat but in submission and slavery. Our chains are forged. Their clanking may be heard on the plains of Boston. The war is inevitable, and let it come! I repeat it, sir, let it come! It is vain, sir, to extenuate the matter. Gentlemen may cry peace ! peace ! but there is no peace. The war is actually begun. The next gale that sweeps from the north will bring to our ears the clash of resounding arms. Our brethren are already in the field. Why stand we here idle? What is it that gentlemen wish? What would they have? Is life so dear, or peace so sweet, as to be purchased at the price of chains and slavery? Forbid it, Almighty God! I know not what course others may take, but as for me, give me liberty or give me death!"

This soul-firing speech determined the character of the proceedings of the Convention. The resolutions were adopted, and a committee appointed to carry them into effect. Among other illustrious names on this committee were those of Washington and Jefferson.

The great national drama of the Revolution was now shortly to be enacted. The first collision occurred at Lexington on April the 18th, 1775, and was caused, it will be remembered, by an attempt, on the part of the British, to seize some military stores at Concord. Similar attempts were now made in Virginia, almost simultaneously with those in the East. The patriotism of Henry was about to be tested in the camp. A quantity of powder and arms were seized at Williamsburg, during the night, by the governor. Henry assembled an independent company, marched immediately to the scene of action, and demanded either restitution of, or payment for the powder seized. The king's receiver general thought it advisable to hand over a bill of exchange for £330. By this and by similar acts of prompt bravery, Patrick Henry rose rapidly in the estimation of the people as a military chieftain. He was elected colonel of the first regiment of troops, and commander-in-chief of all the forces raised or to be raised for the defense of the colony. He did not long retain his commission. In consequence of some jealous opposition, he resigned.

Things had now assumed such a threatening aspect that Lord Dunmore, the governor, thought it necessary for his own safety to desert the colony, which was, in consequence, left without a chief magistrate. In this emergency, a convention of delegates from the various counties of the state proceeded to draw up a plan of government. On the 15th May, 1776, Mr. Cary reported from a committee of the whole house, with a suitable preamble, two important resolutions, one of which instructed the delegates to the General Congress to propose to that body a *declaration that the united colonies were free and independent states*, while the other provided for the government of the new commonwealth of Virginia. In pursuance of the second resolution, Patrick Henry was elected the first republican governor of his native state. The same honor was reconferred on him in 1777, and also in 1778. He declined a re-election in 1779, from a belief that the Constitution did not allow him to serve four years in succession. During the second year of Henry's administration a disgraceful intrigue against Washington occurred, and an attempt was made to implicate him in it; but he behaved with such prompt and manly straightforwardness that the general was satisfied, as posterity is, that he had nothing to do with it.

During these years—and they were the gloomiest America had ever seen—the services of the patriot orator were devoted entirely to the good of his country. They were so keenly appreciated, that in 1784, six years after the close of his former term of service, Henry, being again eligible for office, was once more elected governor, and, at the termination of the official year, was re-elected. It was the desire of the Legislature that he should complete another three years' term, but, at the end of the second year, he declined. The truth of the matter was that his private affairs were in a somewhat embarrassed condition. The salary of governor was insufficient for the expenses of the office, and he had been compelled to contract debts which it was necessary he should pay. He concluded, therefore, to decline office, and once more to resume the practice of the law. In the mean time, he had been elected to the House of Assembly, whither we shall follow him.

More than once during his public career he had felt it his duty to propose or advocate measures in opposition to the popular sentiment of the times. Henry was a man who thought for himself on all great topics, and never, under any circumstances, surrendered his judgment to the keeping of others. The force of his judgment and the decision of his character were generally exercised to the advantage of the community, although he was sometimes led away by patriotic fears, which were, as time has proved, utterly unfounded. Immediately after the termination of the Revolutionary struggle he introduced a measure for the return of the British refugees. There was, of course, at this time a strong and natural prejudice against the misguided men who, if they had not actually opposed the American struggle, at all events had done nothing to forward it. Mr. Henry exerted all his influence and genius to remove this prejudice, and, on the grounds of humanity, justice, and policy, advocated the liberal plan of forgetting the past. In the same generous spirit he supported and carried, against a vigorous opposition, a proposal for removing the restraints on British commerce. "Why should we fetter commerce?" he asked: "a man in chains droops and bows to the earth; his spirits are broken; but let him twist the fetters from his legs, and he will stand upright. Fetter not commerce, sir; let her be free as air. She will range the whole creation, and return on the wings of the four winds of heaven to bless the land with plenty."

In 1786 Henry was sent by the Legislature as a delegate to the Convention for revising the Articles of Confederation among the States. In September, 1787, the Constitution was adopted with a proviso that the ratification of it by nine states should be sufficient for its final establishment. Conventions were at once held in all the states for the due consideration of the important document. The Virginia Convention met in Richmond on the 2d of June, 1788, and such men as Marshall, Madison, Monroe, and Henry were among those who formed it. Patrick Henry appeared in that assembly as the determined opponent of the Constitution. We know very well at this day that he was wrong, and that the fears he entertained for the stability of a government based on the new system have turned out altogether wrong. Fortunately, he found powerful opponents, especially in Mr. Madison, who on this occasion distinguished himself by calm good sense, instinctive sagacity, and vast information. Notwithstanding the "cloud-compelling" opposition of Mr. Henry, the Constitution was adopted, and he himself lived to regard it with much less fear than at first. There was nothing factious about Mr. Henry's opposition. The moment the Constitution was adopted as the law of the land, his opposition ceased.

Mr. Henry declined a re-election to the Virginia Legislature, and, although frequently solicited, never again took an active part in politics. In the fall of 1791 he was engaged in the British Debts case before the Circuit Court of the United States. For three days he proceeded with his argument, and such was the excitement that prevailed that it was found impossible to go on with the business of the State, the members of the Legislature being in the court listening to Henry, instead of attending to their own business in the House. When he finally sat down, says Mr. Wirt, the concourse rose with a general murmur of admiration; the scene resembled the breaking up and dispersion of a great theatrical assembly which had been enjoying, for the first time, the exhibition of some new and splendid drama.

In 1794, Mr. Henry, having acquired a competency, retired from professional life, loaded with honors and universal affection. In the bosom of his family he now hoped to pass the tranquil evening of his life; but in 1799, although somewhat feeble in health, he felt called upon to offer himself as a candidate for the Legislature on account of some important measures which had been introduced, called the Alien and Sedition Laws. He was elected by a large majority, but did not live to take his seat in the Assembly. On the 6th of June, 1799, he died of a disease under which he had been suffering for two years, leaving behind him a wife and nine children. He had been twice married, and at one time numbered fifteen children. No man was better fitted to enjoy the happiness of such a domestic circle. He was a loving husband, a kind father, and a brave, upright patriot and Christian, thoroughly imbued with religious feeling, and devout in all his aspirations. As an evidence of his religious sincerity, we may mention that, in 1790, he published at his own expense, and gratuitously circulated, an edition of Soame Jenyns's "View of the Internal Evidences of Christianity." Among his favorite works were Doddridge's "Rise and Progress of Religion in the Soul," and Butler's "Analogy of Religion, Natural and Revealed."

Patrick Henry has been called the greatest orator of the New World, and it is probable that he is fully entitled to that distinction. The immense influence of his oratory is amply substantiated, although the orations themselves have not been handed down to us in a way to explain this influence. There is no doubt that he owed much of his success to natural gifts of voice, appearance, and manner; indeed, all orators do. For the rest, he was a man of sincere convictions, with a rapid judgment, much earnestness, and a deep-seated sensibility. These attributes are the happiest that can belong to an orator, and, combined with sound common sense, never fail to achieve distinction. It must forever be regretted that the early years of this great man's life were wasted in the indolent pursuit of pleasure. Had he cultivated the faculties which the Almighty intrusted to his keeping, he would have lived in the imperishable literature of his country as well as in its political history. It is difficult to account for this early indolence, except on one theory. He was a man of wonderful organization, mental and physical. Nature had made him robust, active, and eager for the enjoyments of life. He was strong in body as in mind. It was in accordance with nature's plan, therefore, that the physical luxuriance of the man should unfold itself before the mental. Had he been weak or sickly, the case would have been different. The story of his early life affords no example worthy of imitation, but it shows at least that an observant mind is never actually idle. The happy faculty he possessed of seizing on the things of the moment, and bending them to his purpose as illustrations, was doubtless the result of quiet observation, pursued amid the excitement of the chase or the still expectation of the angle. A man who spends his life in books rarely possesses this talent. However this may be, there is no doubt that, so long as America shall have a history, the name of Patrick Henry will be inscribed on its tablets as the greatest natural orator of a century.

ELI WHITNEY.

In a gay little frame house of Westborough, Worcester County, Massachusetts, Eli Whitney, the inventor of the cotton-gin, was born on the 8th of December, 1765. His father was a respectable farmer. At a very early age Eli gave indications of unusual mechanical and constructive genius, and was able to handle the tools in the farm workshop with dexterity. When he was twelve years of age he distinguished himself by making a violin, which, it is said, produced good music, and was, of course, the wonder of the neighborhood. It obtained so wide a fame that he was afterward employed to repair violins, and had many nice jobs, which were always executed to the entire satisfaction of his customers. Whitney, like most ingenious boys, was fascinated by the perfect finish and admirable adaptability of the various parts of a watch. His fingers itched to take it to pieces and learn the secret of its usefulness; but his father, to whom it belonged, had very different wishes on the subject, and was apt to reward curiosity with punishment. For a long time Eli's inquisitive mind had to postpone its yearnings, but at length an opportunity presented itself. "One morning, observing that his father was going to meeting, and would leave at home the wonderful little machine, he immediately feigned illness as an apology for not going to church. As soon as the family were out of sight, he flew to the room where the watch hung, and, taking it down, he was so delighted with its motions that he took it all in pieces before he thought of the consequences of his rash deed; for his father was a stern parent, and punishment would have been the reward of his idle curiosity had the mischief been detected. He, however, put the work all so neatly together, that his father never discovered his audacity until he himself told him, many years afterward." Similar instances of ingenuity were of constant occurrence, and gave abundant indications of the natural bent of his mind.

When Whitney was fifteen or sixteen years of age, he determined to turn his tool-handiness to some account. He asked permission of his father to set up as a maker of nails, for which there was a great demand. His father consented, procured him a few simple tools, and left him to pursue his labors as best he could. For two winters he labored diligently at this arduous trade. His industry was unflagging. Nothing was permitted to interfere with the day's labor, and, when that was completed, he amused himself with making tools for his own use, and in doing little fancy jobs for the neighbors. In the summer months he did ordinary field-work on his father's farm. When the nail business began to fail, he directed his attention to the making of long pins for the fastening of ladies' bonnets, and also to the manufacture of walking-canes. Both these curious articles were turned out with such peculiar neatness that he had a complete command of the market.

Whitney's industry was from the first directed to the attainment of one coveted object. It was his ambition to win for himself a superior education, and to enjoy the advantages of a collegiate course of study. In 1789 he had so far made himself the master of circumstances as to be able to enter the freshman class at Yale College; three years later he had obtained his first degree, and immediately afterward he went into the world as a private teacher. In the family of General Greene, of Mulberry Grove, near Savannah, he was received with great kindness and consideration, and while in the enjoyment of their hospitality commenced the study of the law. Mrs. Greene, like most fashionable ladies of the time, amused her leisure with the elegant pastime of tambour-work. One day she complained that the frame or tambour was clumsily constructed, and tore the delicate threads of her work. Whitney's inventive faculties and his gallantry were immediately excited. In a few days he produced a new frame, on a totally different plan. It was found to work admirably, and Mrs. Greene never forgot the ingenuity of her young friend. Not long after, a conversation sprang up between some guests of the house on the usual topic of Southern talk, the cotton crop. A good many regrets were expressed that there was no way of cleaning the seed from the green seed-cotton, which prevented much profitable cultivation of the plant on lands unsuitable for rice. According to the then existing system, only one pound of the clean staple could be separated from the seed in a day. Mrs. Greene suggested that the subject should be proposed to Whitney, on the score that he could make any thing, and took an early opportunity to introduce the parties. At this time Whitney had never seen cotton-seed in his life, but, without a moment's delay, he turned his thoughts to the accomplishment of the object proposed. In Savannah he found it impossible to procure tools, and was under the necessity of making them for himself, and even then had to draw his own wire. In the effort to which he now devoted himself, he was warmly encouraged by an old college friend, Mr. Miller, and by Mrs. Greene. The gentleman possessed capital, and was so well satisfied with Whitney's plans, that he proposed to become a joint adventurer with him, and to bear the whole expense of maturing the invention until it should be patented. If the machine should succeed in its intended operations, the parties agreed "that the profits and advantages arising therefrom, as well as all privileges and emoluments to be derived from patenting, making, vending, and working the same, should be mutually and equally shared between them." This instrument bears date the 27th of May, 1793. Immediately afterward the firm of Miller and Whitney commenced operations.

The advantages which were to be derived by the cotton planters from Whitney's machine were too important to allow of its being constructed without exciting curiosity. The excitement became so intense that multitudes arrived from all quarters of the state to inspect the machine. Seeing how admirably it was calculated to assist them, their cupidity was excited, and some unprincipled wretches broke into the building and carried off the yet incomplete model. In order to prevent the recurrence of such a disgraceful act, Whitney repaired to Connecticut, where he knew he would be unmolested; but his idea had been already appropriated by the greedy ruffians who had broken into his house. Within three days of his departure, Mr. Miller wrote to him to say that there were two other claimants to the honor of the invention; and almost immediately afterward a new cotton-gin made its appearance, constructed in every important respect precisely like Whitney's. It was evident that his troubles were about to commence, and that, like all original inventors, he would have to be content with the empty honors of his genius. The demand for the machines, however, when he had commenced their manufacture, far exceeded Whitney's ability to make them. He was cramped for want of money. Thus the pirates had every inducement to bring in their spurious copies. The planter who had not a machine, felt it necessary to procure one, either from Whitney or some other source, simply as a measure of protection against his more fortunate neighbor. In March, 1795, in addition to these troubles, Whitney's manufactory in Connecticut, with all his stock of machines, his papers, and his implements and tools, was destroyed by fire. Such an untimely calamity reduced the concern to a state of bankruptcy. As though this were not enough to appease the cruel fates, intelligence was received from England condemning the cotton cleaned by machines, on the ground that the staple was greatly injured. There is no doubt that this decision was provoked in consequence of the imperfect operations of the rival machines. Indeed, many respectable factors made a special reservation in favor of Whitney's, but it was of little avail against the torrent of spurious ones which now deluged the South. "The extreme embarrassments," wrote Whitney at this time, "which have been for a long time accumulating upon me, are now become so great that it will be impossible for me to struggle against them many days longer. It has required my utmost exertions *to exist*, without making the least progress in our business. I have labored hard against the strong current of disappointment which has been threatening to carry us down the cataract, but I have labored with a shattered oar, and struggled in vain, unless some speedy relief is obtained. * * * * Life is but short at best, and six or seven years out of the midst of it is, to him who makes it, an immense sacrifice. My most unremitted attention has been devoted to our business. I have sacrificed to it other objects, from which, before this time, I might certainly have gained twenty or thirty thousand dollars. My whole prospects have been embarked in it, with the expectation that I should, before this time, have realized something from it."

Whitney's success now depended not only on the introduction of his own machines, but the extinction of all others, for the latter not only interfered with the sale of his own, but, what was of far greater importance, brought the machine-prepared staple into discredit with the English manufacturers. It was determined, therefore, to prosecute the violators of the patent rights. The first trial came off on the 11th of May, 1797. The tide of popular opinion appeared to be running in Miller & Whitney's favor; the judge was well-disposed toward them, and charged the jury pointedly in their favor. The jury retired to consider their verdict. In an hour they returned, and, to the consternation of every one, brought in a verdict against the plaintiffs. As if to add additional harshness to this unrighteous decision, the verdict was made general, so that no appeal could lie. "Thus, after four years of assiduous labor, fatigue, and difficulty," wrote Mr. Miller, "are we again set afloat by a new and most unexpected obstacle. Our hopes of success are now removed to a period still more distant than before, while our expenses are realized beyond all controversy." Efforts were made to obtain a new trial, and also to obtain a verdict on a fresh issue, but without success. It became evident that justice could not be obtained in Georgia, and in 1799 Mr. Miller wrote, "The prospect of making any thing by ginning in this state is at an end. Surreptitious gins are erected in every part of the country, and the jurymen at Augusta have come to an understanding among themselves that they will never give a cause in our favor, let the merits of the case be as they may." The only chance of protection was in an appeal to the Legislatures of the several states. It was determined to make a first effort with the State of South Carolina. Accordingly, in the winter session of 1801, Mr. Whitney proceeded to Columbia, and, after attending on the Legislature for a couple of weeks, was fortunate enough to dispose of the patent right for that state. The sum of fifty thousand dollars was fixed upon as the price, twenty thousand to be paid down, and the balance by yearly instalments of ten thousand dollars. Better times appeared to be ripening for the disappointed inventor. In December of the following year Mr. Whitney negotiated a sale of his patent right with the State of North Carolina. The Legislature laid a tax of two shillings and sixpence upon every saw employed in ginning cotton, to be continued for five years, and, after deducting the expenses of collection, the avails were faithfully handed over to the patentee. A similar negotiation was entered into with the State of Tennessee. In the midst of this apparent prosperity, and when every thing seemed to be tending to an equitable adjustment of difficulties, the State of South Carolina suddenly repudiated its obligations, refused to pay any more of the purchase-money, and commenced actions for the recovery of what had been paid. This unworthy meanness was basely imitated by Tennessee; but North Carolina, with manly liberality and righteousness, adhered to its contract, and even reaffirmed it, as if to make assurance doubly sure. In the following year South Carolina felt ashamed of its meanness, rescinded the act of repudiation, and paid some timely compliments to Mr. Whitney.

On the 7th of December, 1803, Mr. Miller, the faithful and devoted associate of Whitney, departed this life, leaving him alone, amid innumerable difficulties to contend with and embarrassments to surmount. The immediate pressure of the latter was in some measure mitigated by the steady receipts which now flowed in from North and South Carolina. But there was constant trouble in Georgia, and no end of vexatious lawsuits. It was so difficult to obtain a verdict on the merits of the patent that the latter had nearly expired before Judge Johnson gave his celebrated decision affirming the legal rights of the patentee. Long before this, Whitney had despaired of gaining any thing like competency from his invention, and began to entertain serious thoughts of turning his talents to some sure and lucrative business in which industry, frugality, and merit would meet with their just reward. On the 14th of January, 1798, he concluded a contract with the Secretary of the Treasury to supply the United States government with a large stock of arms, and, without more ado, proceeded to the erection of a suitable manufactory for the prosecution of the business of arms-making. The site selected was near the city of New Haven, and is now called Whitneyville. The machinery and tools for the manufacture were partly invented and wholly made by Whitney, and, under his eye, a number of inexperienced workmen were converted into skillful artisans. "Under the system of Mr. Whitney," says a writer in *Silliman's Journal*, to whom we, in common with all subsequent biographers, are largely indebted, "the several parts of the musket were carried along through the various processes of manufacture in lots of some hundreds or thousands of each. In their various stages of progress they were made to undergo successive operations by machinery, which not only vastly abridged the labor, but at the same time so fixed and determined their form and dimensions as to make comparatively little skill necessary in the manual operations. Such was the construction and arrangement of this machinery, that it could be worked by persons of little or no experience, and yet it performed the work with so much precision, that when, in the later stages of the process, the several parts of the musket came to be put together, they were as readily adapted to each other as if each had been made for its respective fellow. A lot of these parts passed through the hands of several different workmen successively (and in some cases several times returned, at intervals more or less remote, to the hands of the same workman), each performing upon them every time some single and simple operation by machinery or by hand until they were completed. Thus Mr. Whitney reduced a complex business, embracing many ramifications, almost to a mere succession of simple processes, and was thereby enabled to make a division of the labor among his workmen, on a principle that was not only more extensive, but also more philosophical than that pursued in the English method."

The muskets made by this process were not only cheaper, but better than any others in the market. So thoroughly satisfied was the government on this point, that they cheerfully entered into a second contract on the completion of the first. Mr. Whitney was not without opposition. Many of the old established gun-makers, who pursued the old routine, and supposed it impossible for any thing better to be contrived, competed with him, but brains told against capital in this instance, and Whitney enjoyed a well-earned reputation and put money in his purse.

In the year 1812 Mr. Whitney made application to Congress for a renewal of his patent for the cotton-gin. In a temperate and admirably-written memorial, he put forward all his claims to this slight consideration. It was of no avail. The very men who had been most benefited by the invention were those who opposed the inventor most virulently. They were successful; the extension was refused, and those who had so long robbed him illegally now did it with the protection of the law. In a letter to Mr. Fulton on this subject, Whitney says, "The difficulties with which I have had to contend have originated principally in the want of a disposition in mankind to do justice. My invention was new, and distinct from every other; it stood alone; it was not interwoven with any thing before known; and it can seldom happen that an invention or improvement is so strongly marked, and can be so clearly and specifically identified; and I have always believed that I should have had no difficulty in causing my rights to be respected, if it had been less valuable, and been used only by a small portion of the community. But the use of this machine being immensely profitable to almost every planter in the cotton districts, all were interested in trespassing upon the patent-right, and each kept the other in countenance. Demagogues made themselves popular by misrepresentation and unfounded clamors, both against the right, and against the law made for its protection. Hence there arose associations and combinations to oppose both. At one time, but few men in Georgia dared to come into court and testify to the most simple facts within their knowledge relative to the use of the machine. In one instance I had great difficulty in proving that the machine *had been used in Georgia, although, at the same moment, there were three separate sets of this machinery in motion within fifty yards of the building in which the court sat, and all so near that the rattling of the wheels was distinctly heard on the steps of the court-house.*"

Fortunately, his worldly prosperity did not now depend upon the uncertain privileges of letters patent and state rights. The new enterprise in which he was embarked proved, as we have hinted, eminently lucrative, and pointed out a clear road to affluence. His circumstances now being comparatively easy, he began to yearn for the social comforts of home—for the tranquil joys which nestle around the family hearth—for the solace, consolation, and gentle ministrations of a wife. In January of 1817 he gratified this ardent and amiable desire, and was wedded to Miss Henrietta F. Edwards, the youngest daughter of the Hon. Pierrepont Edwards, of the District Court of the State of Connecticut. His happiness was subsequently rendered complete by the addition of a son and three daughters to his domestic circle. Every thing seemed to promise a brilliant and gorgeous decline to a life too much spent in toil and trouble. But it was not to be. At the moment when the cup of happiness appeared to be brimming at his lips, it was dashed to the ground by the treacherous approaches of the fell destroyer. Disease in an aggravated and tedious form attacked him. He struggled against it with his accustomed firmness, but King Death's patent rights can not be set aside. After a long and painful illness, he died on the 8th of January, 1825.

His death occasioned a sensation of profound sadness to a large community, who knew and respected him not only for the material good he had done his country, but for the amiable qualities of his heart and mind. The citizens of New Haven paid every respect to the memory of the deceased, and caused a eulogy to be pronounced over his remains by President Day, of Yale College. A neat tomb has been erected over his grave, fashioned after the model of that of Scipio at Rome. It marks a spot that should be honored by every American who is jealous of his country's glory.

BENJAMIN FRANKLIN.

The life of this extraordinary man presents a solid instance of high eminence and national esteem achieved by the conscientious and timely nurture and exercise of temperate and healthy faculties. In the picture of his life there is nothing that attracts us by its glare and tinseled brilliancy. The coloring, if any thing, is cold and sombre; but there is clearness in the outline, and never-failing boldness and vigor in the filling up. We are astonished at the absence of every thing like mere effort for show. He never seems to say to himself, "This will look well;" but rather, "This is correct, and therefore beautiful." Biographers have experienced difficulty in doing full justice to the life of Franklin for the reason that he presents so many points of excellence, all glowing with quiet splendor. By one he is considered remarkable principally for his philosophical experiments and discoveries; by another, for his ingenuity and devotion as a diplomat; by a third, for his clear-headed organization of philanthropic societies; by a fourth, for his patriotism, and so on. Each separate advocate finds abundant materials for eulogizing the hero, but each and all do the hero an injustice, for it was not the possession of a single faculty that made Franklin remarkable, but the nice adjustment of many. Even Franklin himself fails to do justice to his life. His Autobiography is simply the story of a prudent man, who exalts the virtues generally, and adds economy and money-making to the list because he practices them. If our knowledge of Franklin were confined simply to this record, it would be very imperfect and unsatisfactory.

It must not be supposed that Franklin's character is one of such extreme complexity that it can not be understood by ordinary intelligences. On the contrary, its utter simplicity is what is apt to confuse; for a virtuous character presents more admirable phases than any other; and, in dwelling on any individual phase, we are likely to do injustice to the others. Franklin had what is called by phrenologists a well-balanced organization. Every faculty was largely formed and assiduously cultivated. He knew exactly his own strength, and, consequently, never failed of success in what he undertook. He armed himself with right—might he possessed—and never laid it down until he had gained the victory. His life is remarkable for two things, great ambition and great virtue. He determined to be famous and to be good. He succeeded in both.

Benjamin Franklin was the fifteenth child of a family of seventeen, and was born in Boston on the 17th January, 1706. His father, an English Nonconformist, emigrated to New England about the year 1682, for the sake of enjoying the free exercise of his religion. He was a tallow-chandler and soap-boiler by profession, and a man of considerable force of character. At eight years of age young Benjamin was put to the grammar-school, but continued there for a very brief period. It was his father's wish to devote him to the service of the Church; but, burdened with a numerous family, he was unable to bear the additional expenses of a fitting education for that important sphere, and therefore took him from the grammar-school, and gave him a commercial education in a private establishment kept by Mr. George Brownwell. At ten years of age he was able to help his father in the business of cutting wicks, filling moulds, etc., but, disliking the occupation, conceived the idea, common to all dissatisfied youth, of going to sea. In order to divert his mind from this project, his father took him round to various manufactories and workshops, in order that he might see the operations of the workmen, and thus fix on some profession that would be agreeable to his taste. The elder Franklin determined in favor of the cutler's trade, and endeavored to place Benjamin with a member of that craft; but the latter demanded too large a fee, and he was taken home again, with a gloomy prospect of the candle and chandlery business. At length it was resolved that Benjamin (who from his earliest days had displayed a strong bookish inclination) should be apprenticed to his brother James, a printer, who had just established himself in business (1717). According to the absurd custom of that day, he was bound for no less a period than nine years—that is to say, until he was twenty-one years of age. In a little time he made great progress in the business, and became a useful hand to his brother. What attached him most to the business was the additional facility with which he could now obtain books for reading. With these he would delight himself on every possible opportunity, often sitting up in his chamber the greater part of the night, in order that he might punctually return the book he had borrowed. In course of time, the activity of his mind began to display itself in various ways, such as discussing ethical topics with his companions, and building up verses on the popular events of the day. His father watched his progress with calm interest, and freely criticised what attempts at literary productions fell in his way, and, what was more extraordinary, even succeeded in convincing his son that they were not remarkable for elegance of expression, method, or perspicuity. To remedy these defects, the young man procured an odd volume of the *Spectator*, and endeavored to imitate the Addisonian style of writing. In order to increase his stock of words, he turned some of the articles into verse, and after a time, when he had pretty well forgotten the prose, turned them back again. The time he allotted for writing exercises and for reading was at night, or before work began in the morning, or on Sunday.

When about sixteen years of age he became a convert to the vegetarian doctrine, and refused to eat the flesh of any animal that had been slaughtered for food. He was a little annoyed by the members of his brother's family, with whom he boarded, on account of this sudden and somewhat remarkable conversion, and therefore determined to board himself. He proposed it to his brother, and agreed that, if the latter would give him weekly half the money he paid for his board, he would take care of himself. Of course, his brother acquiesced in such an economical arrangement, and Benjamin found that out of his small sum he could save at least half for the purchase of books. This was not the only economy, for, owing to the lightness of his repasts, they did not take him long to dispatch, and he had the greater part of the usual dinner-hour left to himself.

Franklin's brother was the proprietor of a newspaper, which he had started in 1720 or 1721, and which was the second newspaper in America. It was called the *New England Courant*, and the subject of this memoir assisted, of course, in doing the press-work and setting up the type. The contributors to this paper were principally among the private friends of Mr. James Franklin, and often came to the office to talk over the affairs of the colony, and listen to a little mutual admiration. Benjamin's ambition became excited, and he made up his mind to have a try at newspaper writing; but, doubting if his brother would publish a contribution if he knew it to be from his pen, he disguised his hand, and put the manuscript under the door of the printing-house. It was found in the morning, and placed in the hands of the writing friends who formed the literary tribunal of the establishment. They read it, commented on it in Benjamin's hearing, and he had the exquisite pleasure of finding that it met with their approbation, and that, in their different guesses at the author, none were named but men of some character for learning and ingenuity. He followed up this first attempt with many others, until he could keep his secret no longer, and so made it known. His brother treated him with a little more consideration after this, but mixed with it somewhat of jealousy. He was afraid his apprentice would get too vain, and forget that he had a master. A good deal of unhappiness resulted, and Ben, like the monkey in the story, received more kicks than halfpence for his exertions. His brother was very passionate, and often struck him without reasonable provocation. Ben began to yearn for some opportunity of shortening the term of his hardships, and soon found it in a very unexpected but agreeable manner. An article in the paper gave offense to the authorities, and the proprietor, Mr. James Franklin, was imprisoned for a month. In those days the liberty of the press was not so thoroughly understood as in the present, and, if an editor said an unpleasant thing, he stood a very good chance of paying the penalty of his temerity among the common felons of a jail. During his brother's confinement the management of the paper was placed in the hands of young Benjamin, and he gave the authorities some rubs on the subject of liberty of speech. When James was discharged from prison, his release was accompanied with an order that "he should no longer print the newspaper called the *New England Courant*." It was proposed to elude this order by printing the paper in the name of Benjamin Franklin, and, in order to avoid the censure of the Assembly, James consented that the latter's indentures should be canceled. This was accordingly done, and for some months all went well; but fresh differences took place between the two brothers, and a separation ensued. Ben sold his books, and with the proceeds started secretly for New York, where he arrived (October, 1723) without the least recommendation or knowledge of any person in the place. He was unable to gain employment, and therefore went on to Philadelphia, where he arrived hungry, sore-footed, and travel-soiled. His first visit was to the baker's, where he purchased three penny worth of bread, consisting of three great puffy rolls, one of which he placed under each arm, eating the other through the principal streets. A draught from the river completed his frugal meal. On his way he met many well-dressed persons, who all seemed to go in the same direction. Ben joined them, and thereby was led into the great meeting-house of the Quakers. He sat down among them, and, feeling drowsy, soon fell fast asleep, and continued so until the meeting broke up, when some one was kind enough to rouse him.

He was more successful in Philadelphia than he had been in New York, and, after a few days, obtained a situation as pressman to one Keimer, an individual who united the professions of printer and poet, and composed verses in type directly out of his head. By industry and frugality, Ben succeeded—as all young men must succeed—very well. No one knew of his whereabouts except a Boston crony who had assisted in his escape, and had kept the secret faithfully; nor did he desire that his brother, who had tried with some success to injure his reputation in other cities, *should* know of his retreat. But the difficulty of keeping a secret is proverbial, especially if you want to do so. An incident occurred which completely upset all Benjamin's plans for the future. A brother-in-law, Robert Holmes, master of a sloop that traded between Boston and Delaware, hearing of the young man, wrote a letter to him, mentioning the grief of his relations, and exhorting him to communicate with or return to them, and promising that every thing should be arranged in a satisfactory manner. Ben wrote an answer to this letter, thanking him for his advice, and stating his reasons for quitting Boston in such a full and convincing manner that he soon discovered the lad was not so much in the wrong as he had at first supposed. Sir William Keith, governor of the province, happened to see this letter, and was much struck with its force and clearness, and, seeing that the writer was a young man of promising parts, encouraged him, and said that, as the printers of Philadelphia were very poor ones, he would set him up there, and use all his influence to get him into business. In the mean time it was to be kept a secret, and our hero went on working for Keimer, who, you may rest assured, was not a little surprised to find one of his workmen on such amicable terms with the principal personage in the state. In 1724 Franklin returned to Boston. His unexpected appearance surprised the family; all, however, were very glad to give him welcome, except his brother, who eyed him from head to foot in a cold way, and went on with his work again. Ben was partly to blame for this, for he made a display of his worldly success by showing his money and his watch to the workmen, and thus irritated his brother, who said that he insulted him before his people —stupidly forgetting that the money and the watch were the results of industry and economy, and not of kindness in a new master.

Ben's father did not approve of the governor's plan of starting him in business on his own account, although he was, of course, agreeably flattered and impressed by the friendship of that gentleman. His principal fear was that the lad was too young and inexperienced in the ways of the world. But the governor was not discouraged, and on Ben's return to Philadelphia still insisted on his plan, and went so far as to promise to supply him with money to procure all necessary materials from England. He went even farther than this, and suggested that the lad should himself go to England and select all the things he required, and establish correspondences in the bookselling and stationary line. Accordingly, our hero prepared for the voyage, and waited anxiously for the letters of credit which the governor promised to give him.

For these letters he called at different times, but a future day was always named, and in this manner the days slipped away. Having taken leave of his friends, and exchanged promises with Miss Read, a young lady of Philadelphia, for whom he entertained tender sentiments, our hero quitted the city, and floated down to the anchorage at Newcastle. When he went to the governor's lodgings, the secretary came to him, and, with many expressions of regret, said that the governor was much engaged, but that he would send the necessary letters on board, and that they would be found all right, and many other things to the same effect. The governor's dispatches came on board sure enough, and Ben was happy in the belief that his letters were among them. The bags were opened in the English Channel, and he found six or seven with his name on them as under his care, and as one was directed to the king's printer, and another to a stationer, he thought all was right. He arrived in England on the 24th of December, 1724, and immediately waited on the stationer, and delivered what he supposed to be his letter from Governor Keith. "I don't know such a person," said he; but, opening the letter, "oh, this is from Riddlesden. I have lately found him to be a complete rascal, and I will have nothing to do with him, nor receive any letters from him." There was not a single letter from the governor, who, it seems, was a weak person, and made promises without the slightest idea of fulfilling them. Thus was Franklin thrown on the world once more, with nothing but habits of industry and economy to depend on. He lost no time in looking out for work, and immediately succeeded in obtaining a situation in a famous printing-office. From step to step he rose in the good esteem of his employers, making, also, many friends among the learned and curious. He remained in London for about eighteen months, and then thought of taking a journeyman tour through Europe with a companion printer; but this scheme was frustrated by a Mr. Denham, a gentleman who became acquainted with our hero on the voyage out, and who, from observation of his general habits and unquestionable ability, entertained a sincere respect for him. Mr. Denham was now about returning to America with a great quantity of goods for a store which he intended to open, and proposed to take Franklin with him as his clerk. He added, that, as soon as he should be acquainted with mercantile business, he would send him with a cargo of flour and breadstuffs to the West Indies, and procure him profitable commissions from other houses, and, if he managed well, would eventually establish him handsomely in business on his own account. The thing pleased Franklin, and he immediately closed with Mr. Denham. On the 23d of July, 1726, he set sail from Gravesend, and, after a voyage of nearly three months, arrived once more in Philadelphia. Keith was no longer governor, but our hero met him walking in the streets like an ordinary citizen. He seemed to be a little ashamed, and walked on without saying any thing. In the mean time, his old sweetheart, Miss Read, had despaired of the fidelity of her lover (who, very wrongly, neglected to answer her letters), and, by the advice of her friends, had married. It was not a happy union. Her husband turned out a dissolute fellow, and, after giving her much uneasiness, deserted her, and finally died in the West Indies. Mr. Denham opened a store in Water Street, and every thing went on in the most amicable way. Franklin respected and loved him, and he looked on our hero as a son. They might have gone on together very happily, but, unfortunately, in February, 1727, they were both taken ill. Franklin's distemper was a pleurisy. He suffered greatly, and gave up the point in his own mind, and says, in his Autobiography, that he was, at the time, rather disappointed when he found himself getting better, inasmuch as at some future time he would have all that unpleasant work to go through again. Mr. Denham was not so fortunate; he suffered a long time, and was at last carried to the grave. He remembered his *protégé* in his will, bequeathing him a small legacy as a mark of his respect. Once more Franklin was left to the wide world, not much richer, in a pecuniary point of view, than on former occasions, but with an increased wealth of reputation, and a better knowledge of the devious ways of life. Keimer, his old master, was still in business, and, to all appearance, flourishing. He had not forgotten his young workman, and tempted him with the offer of large wages to take the management of his printing-house. Franklin closed with him a little unwillingly, for he did not like the man, on account of his loose moral principles. Franklin soon perceived that Keimer's object in engaging him at liberal wages was simply that he might use him as an instructor for his other hands, most of whom were new to the trade. He went about his business very cheerfully, however, and made himself useful in every possible way; even contriving to cast new type—a process unknown in America at that time—to make the ink used in printing, and to engrave small things for ornaments. Notwithstanding his diligence, he soon found that his services became every day less important as the other hands improved, and Keimer began to grumble about the wages. At length a trifle snapped their connection. A great noise occurred in the court-house, and Franklin, curious to see what was the matter, popped his head out of the window to take a look. Keimer was in the street, and, seeing him, called out in a loud and angry voice, bidding him mind his business, and adding some reproachful words, rendered doubly nettling from their publicity. He afterward resumed the quarrel in the printing-office, until stopped by Franklin, who calmly took his hat and walked out of the room.

One of Keimer's hands was a young Welshman named Meredith, between whom and our hero had sprung up a spirit of fellowship. He sympathized with Franklin in his recent trouble, and advised him to set up for himself. Franklin objected that he had no money. "That can soon be remedied," he answered; "if you will take me for a partner, my father will supply us with all the money we want." It was soon arranged between them that they should try their fortunes together in the coming spring. In the mean time, a sort of conciliation was brought about by Keimer, who once more wanted Franklin's assistance, and the latter resumed work under his employ.

It was during this winter that our hero started the famous "Junto" club. It consisted of a number of young men, who met for mutual improvement. Franklin drew up the rules, and required that every member, in his turn, should produce one or more queries on any point of morals, politics, or natural philosophy, to be discussed by the company, and once in three months produce and read an essay of his own writing, on any subject he pleased. The club continued in existence for upward of forty years, and was the best school of philosophy, morality, and politics that then existed in the province. Among the members was the celebrated mathematician, Thomas Godfrey, inventor of what is now called Hadley's Quadrant, and very unjustly so called.

When Franklin & Meredith commenced in the following spring, they derived a good deal of benefit from the patronage of the club, every member of which exerted himself to procure patronage for the young firm. Dr. Baird, speaking of Franklin at this time, said, "The industry of that Franklin is superior to any thing I ever saw of the kind; I see him still at work when I go home from the club, and he is at work again before his neighbors are out of bed." This observable industry soon brought its reward; work flowed in steadily, and the wholesale houses were anxious to extend credit to the young firm. Franklin, whose passion for writing never deserted him, now began to think of starting a paper on his own account; but Keimer, who heard of the intention, forestalled it by issuing one himself. Our hero was of course vexed at this, and, to counteract the effect as much as possible, shrewdly commenced writing for an opposition paper. By this means the attention of the public was diverted to that paper, and Keimer's was burlesqued and ridiculed. After carrying it on for three quarters of a year, the latter was glad to dispose of it to Franklin (1729). It must not be supposed that our hero's career was altogether smooth. He had many difficulties to contend with, and especially with respect to his partner, Meredith, who, in addition to being a very indifferent workman, was also addicted to the vice of drunkenness. Besides this, Mr. Meredith's father, who was to have paid for the materials used in the business, was unable to advance more than one hundred pounds, leaving a hundred more still due to the merchants, who grew impatient, and commenced actions at law. Honesty and industry always have protectors, and Franklin found two friends who came to his rescue. Shortly afterward Meredith retired from the business, and Franklin was his own master. The frugality and perseverance with which he pursued it attracted the attention of every one. "In order to secure my credit and character as a tradesman," he says, "I took care to be not only in reality industrious and frugal, but to avoid the appearances of the contrary. I dressed plain, and was seen at no places of idle diversion. I never went out a fishing or shooting; a book, indeed, sometimes debauched me from my work, but that was seldom, was private, and gave no scandal; and, to show that I was not above my business, I sometimes brought home the paper I purchased at the stores through the streets on a wheelbarrow. Thus, being esteemed an industrious, thriving young man, and paying duly for what I bought, the merchants who imported stationery solicited my custom; others proposed supplying me with books, and I went on prosperously."

In September, 1730, Franklin (after an unsuccessful and somewhat mercenary flirtation with another young lady) married his former love, who was now a widow, and who proved a good and faithful helpmate. About this time, also, he put on foot his first project of a public library. Proposals were drawn up, and, by the help of his friends and the members of the "Junto," fifty subscribers were obtained. Afterward a charter was granted, and the company increased to one hundred subscribers. This was the parent of all the North American subscription libraries, now so numerous and highly esteemed. In 1732 Franklin commenced the publication of his famous Almanac, under the name of *Richard Saunders*. It was continued for twenty-five years, and commonly called *Poor Richard's Almanac*. The feature of this publication was the immense amount of practical wisdom it contained, conveyed mostly in the shape of proverbs. These proverbs, which contained the wisdom of many ages and nations, were afterward put into a connected form, and prefixed to the Almanac of 1757 as the harangue of a wise old man to the people attending an auction. The piece met with universal approbation, was copied into all the papers, and translated into many languages. The Almanac was a source of considerable wealth to the compiler. In 1733 Franklin began to study languages, and soon mastered the French, Italian, and Spanish. He was surprised to find, on looking over a Latin Testament, that he understood more of that language than he had imagined, and was therefore encouraged to undertake the study of it. In 1736 he received his first public promotion by being chosen clerk of the General Assembly, and was reappointed the following year, notwithstanding the powerful opposition of a member whose fortune, education, and talents gave him great influence in the House. Franklin, with his usual shrewdness, saw the propriety of conciliating this opponent, not by any servile advances, but by the establishment of some mutual feeling between them. Having heard that he possessed a certain scarce and curious book, our hero wrote a note to him, expressing a strong desire to peruse it, and requesting that he might be favored with the loan of it for a few days. The book was sent immediately, and Franklin returned it after a week with a polite note of thanks. The next time they met in the House they had something to talk about, and immediately afterward became great friends. In 1737 Franklin was appointed deputy postmaster-general at Philadelphia. He now began to turn his thoughts seriously to public affairs, and rapidly introduced a number of important municipal reforms, among which was a plan for better protecting and watching the property of the city, and the organization of a citizen fire company, the first ever established in America. During all this time his business was constantly augmenting, and his circumstances daily growing easier. In 1743 he drew up a plan for establishing an academy for the complete education of youth. A year later he succeeded in establishing the Philosophical Society, one of the best and oldest institutions in the country, and at the same time awakened the community to a proper knowledge of the defenseless state of the province, and induced the establishment of several militia companies and the erection of a battery. He was appointed to all sorts of city offices, and discharged the duties pertaining thereto with such ability that he had more offers for similar posts than he could well afford to attend to. So much respected and esteemed was he by his fellow-citizens, that it was said there was no such thing as carrying a public project through without his being concerned in it. In 1751, Dr. Thomas Bond, a particular friend of Franklin's, conceived the idea of establishing a hospital in Philadelphia for the reception and cure of poor sick people of every condition. Franklin threw himself into the scheme with ardor, and it was principally through his exertions that the first public hospital in Philadelphia was established.

Disputes and difficulties had long existed between the English proprietaries of the province and the inhabitants concerning certain exemptions which the former claimed, but which the latter would not concede. Every governor who came over from the Old Country, filled with notions of privilege and power, went back again with a flea in his ear, and in this way a constant feud was maintained between one portion of the government and the people. It was determined to bring this state of things to an end by petitioning the king in person, and it became necessary to appoint a fitting agent to convey the document to England, and otherwise look after the interests of the American people. The choice fell on Franklin, and once more he crossed the Atlantic, not as a journeyman printer in search of employ, but as the representative of a people who demanded their rights. He arrived in London, after a narrow escape from shipwreck, on the 27th of July, 1757.

Before we proceed farther with the narrative of Franklin's public career, it is necessary to refer at some length to another phase of his character. From the exactness of his observation and the force of his reasoning powers he was naturally a philosopher. It cost him very little trouble to find out the cause of things. The restlessness of his mind led him into irresistible trains of investigation, which inevitably resulted in truth. In 1746, Dr. Spence, a Scottish lecturer, arrived at Boston, and, having some electrical apparatus, performed many curious experiments. Although not well done, they were sufficient to inflame the curiosity of our hero, who immediately began to inquire into the nature and properties of electricity, and especially the source whence it came. After a number of experiments, conducted with great exactness and simplicity, Franklin constructed the general outlines of his theory. All bodies in nature, he considered, had a certain quantity of electricity, which might be diminished by part being given out to another body, or increased by receiving electricity from a cylinder. In the one case he regarded the body as negatively, in the other as positively electrified. In the one case it had less, in the other more than its natural quantity; in either case, therefore, supposing it to be composed of electricity and common matter, the usual equilibrium or balance between its two constituent ingredients was for the time upset or destroyed. Upon this theory Franklin constructed a system, which has been aptly described as one of the most beautiful generalizations in the whole compass of science. A brilliant discovery rewarded the philosopher for his hours of patient thought and investigation. It had long been surmised that electricity and the lightning of the heavens were one and the same fluid, but no one had succeeded in demonstrating that such was actually the fact. In a paper dated November 7, 1749, Franklin enumerates all the known points of resemblance between lightning and electricity. In the first place, he remarks, it is no wonder that the effects of the one should be so much greater than the other; for if two gun barrels, electrified, will strike at the distance of two inches, and make a loud report, at how great a distance will ten thousand acres of electrified cloud strike and give its fire, and how loud must be that crack? He then notices the crooked and waving course both of the flash of lightning and, in some cases, of the electric sparks; the tendency of lightning, like electricity, to take the readiest and best conductor; the fact that lightning, like electricity, dissolves metals, burns some bodies, rends others, strikes people blind, destroys animal life, reverses the poles of magnets, etc. From these obvious premises he concludes that the fluid is the same. But how to demonstrate this, so that no kind of keen skepticism could demolish the fact? At first he thought he might make a successful series of experiments from some high tower, such as the spire of a church, etc.; but there was no such thing at hand. It is true a large spire was in process of erection, but it might be months, years, before it was finished, and men on the eve of a great discovery are naturally impatient. Other means were to be discovered. The philosopher walked about, and measured the height of every projection in his mind's eye. None of them were tall enough to snatch the lightnings from the heavens and land them in safety at his feet; not even the trees, whose riven trunks spoke only of their fury. One day he was taking a thoughtful walk in his accustomed way, quietly watching every thing and turning it to philosophical account. His attention was directed to a little boy, who, with a face full of glee, watched the stately sweepings of a kite which he had sent up high into the sky. In a moment the idea struck him that here was the method of reaching the clouds in the quickest and most inexpensive manner. He went home and constructed a kite of silk, and with this simple apparatus awaited the next thunder-storm. It came, and, accompanied only by his son, Franklin repaired to the fields, raised the kite, and waited the result. This was in June, 1752. To the lower end of the string he fastened a key, and insulated it by attaching it to a post with silk threads. For some time no effect was perceptible. At length, however, just as Franklin was beginning to despair, he observed some loose ends of the hempen string rise and stand erect, indicating that they were under the influence of the electric fluid. He immediately applied his knuckles to the key, and, to his inexpressible joy, drew forth the well-known spark, and received the most welcome rap of the knuckles that any man ever received. As the rain came on, the kite and the cord became better conductors, and the key gave out copious streams of electricity. By this simple experiment, Franklin solved the great philosophical problem of the day, and gained a merited immortality. Eminently practical in every thing he did, his next endeavor was to render this discovery of some benefit to mankind. He was not long in doing so. Wherever you see a lightning conductor guarding the exposed angles of a dwelling, and arresting the fierce thrusts of the forked lightning, think of Franklin. He was the inventor of lightning conductors.

In course of time, the fame of these experiments reached Europe. Franklin was recognized as an eminent philosopher, and his papers were quickly translated into the European languages. Many learned degrees were conferred on him, and the Royal Society of London made amends for early neglect by voluntarily choosing him a member of their body; remitting all the customary fees, and furnishing him with their "Transactions" gratuitously. In 1753 they presented him with the gold medal of Sir Godfrey Copley, accompanied with a very handsome speech. Some years afterward, the University of St. Andrew's conferred upon him the degree of Doctor of Laws, and its example was followed by the Universities of Edinburgh and Oxford.

We have dwelt exclusively on Franklin's electrical experiments and discoveries, for it is on these that his fame principally rests; but, if our space permitted, we could dilate with equal pleasure on other phases of his philosophical career. We must, however, return to the memoir of his life, now entirely devoted to the public good, and will only add, in the words of Lord Brougham, that "his discoveries were made with hardly any apparatus at all; and if at any time he had been led to employ instruments of a somewhat less ordinary description, he never seemed satisfied until he had, as it were, afterward translated the process by resolving the problem with such simple machinery that you might say he had done it wholly unaided by apparatus."

Franklin's mission to London as the agent of the Assembly comprehended more than had been intrusted to any previous agency. It was one not only of reconciliation, but of remedy—to cure and to prevent. Innumerable difficulties were, of course, thrown in his way by the proprietaries, and for the first year little or nothing was done. The public mind, too, was distracted by the war on the Continent, and public men were querulous with the colonists for making a noise about their affairs at such a moment. Franklin found plenty to do, however. He vindicated his cause with his pen, and the journalist who ventured to attack him invariably got the worst of it. Several brisk fights took place, and any number of pamphlets were discharged by the disputants. It was not until 1760 that the business upon which he was sent to England was satisfactorily concluded. In the following summer he made a tour of Europe, and in August, 1762, arrived once more in Philadelphia. During his absence he had been chosen to represent the city in the Provincial Assembly, and on his appearance in the House they voted three thousand pounds to defray his expenses, and their thanks for his services on their behalf. "Franklin replied that he was thankful to the House for the very handsome and generous allowance they had been pleased to make him for his services, but that the approbation of the House was in his estimation far above every other kind of recompense."

It was not possible to effect any lasting sympathy between the English proprietors and the colonists. The governor appointed by the former was always too ready to lend himself to their interests, and to abuse the confidence and liberality of the Americans. After again experiencing the truth of this, the Pennsylvanians determined on their often-threatened appeal to the throne, praying the king to take the province out of the hands of the proprietaries, and assume its government. This course had been pursued by several other provinces, and always with decided advantage. Franklin warmly approved of the plan, and, in consequence, incurred the displeasure of the governmental members, and, mainly through their exertions, lost his seat in the House. But he was encouraged by the people, and in spite of all opposition, and to the intense chagrin of the governor, was appointed once more a commissioner to England to present the petition, and discharge all necessary duties relating thereto. "Under whatever circumstances this second mission was undertaken, it appears to have been a measure preordained of Heaven; and it will be forever remembered to the honor of Pennsylvania that the agent selected to assert and defend the rights of a single province at the court of Great Britain became the bold assertor of the rights of America in general, and, beholding the fetters that were forging for her, conceived the magnanimous thought of rending them asunder before they could be riveted."* On the 7th of November—less than a fortnight after his appointment—Franklin embarked at Chester

* Dr. William Smith.

for England. A cavalcade of three hundred of his friends attended him to the wharf, and took an affectionate farewell. The expenses of his agency were subscribed by the merchants of Philadelphia, to be reimbursed by the next Assembly. Franklin reached Portsmouth on the 9th of December, 1764, after a short passage of thirty days. He found the people of England more occupied with the affairs of America than usual, arising from the discussions on the Stamp Act in the newspapers and in the houses of Parliament, and the opposition which that measure had provoked in the colonies. He complained of the disposition of the people. "Every man in England," he said, "seems to consider himself as a piece of a sovereign over America, seems to jostle himself into the throne with the king, and talks of *our subjects in the colonies.*" Once more he took up the cudgels for his countrymen, and fought their battles in the newspapers. In the mean time, the object of his mission seemed to progress favorably, and there appeared to be every reason for supposing that the king would receive the petition. On the 22d of March, 1765, however, the famous Stamp Act was passed. Franklin had opposed it with all the force and ability he could command, but without avail. The English ministers were irritated with the independent tone of the colonists, and not disposed to listen to the cool reasoning of their representative. It is fortunate for us that they did not. The law became a dead letter; at the beginning of 1776 not a single stamp was to be found in America. Every schoolboy knows the history of this remarkable period, and it is not necessary to repeat it here. In England the opposition of the colonists caused great excitement, the ministry was dissolved, and a new one called into power. American affairs were the leading topics of parliamentary discussion. All sorts of plans were concocted for coaxing, conciliating, driving, or bullying the obstreperous colonists. The new ministry, conscious of the errors of its predecessor, brought in a measure for the repeal of the obnoxious act, and, after a long and stormy discussion, carried it; but it was too late to do any good. In the course of this struggle, Dr. Franklin was called before the committee of the whole house, to whom had been referred the petitions of the colonists, and other papers relating to the controversy. He was not unprepared for the call, and took good care to be well up in his answers. The account of the examination, which was extremely lengthy, and embraced a great variety of topics, was afterward published, and immediately became a document of great parliamentary importance. It gave a clear and comprehensive idea of the state and condition of America, and of the temper and feeling which prevailed there concerning the measure in question. The questions are put with subtlety and judgment, says a critic in the *Gentleman's Magazine* for 1767, and they are answered with such deep and familiar knowledge of the subject, such precision and perspicuity, such temper, and yet such spirit, as did honor to Dr. Franklin, and justified the general opinion of his character and abilities.

After the repeal of the Stamp Act, Franklin recruited his health by taking a tour in Germany and France. He was received cordially wherever he went, not only in the halls of learning, but in the courts of princes. On his return to England, public business crowded upon him. In 1768 he was appointed agent for Georgia; in 1769 he was chosen agent for New Jersey, and in 1770 Massachusetts paid him a similar compliment. His Pennsylvania agency still continued, and thus, at the ripe age of sixty-four, he had the agency of four colonies, in each of which circumstances of peculiar difficulty and embarrassment required the full exercise of his wisdom and prudence. Fresh difficulties were constantly occurring between the colonial governors and the people. Events were rapidly ripening for the coming struggle, and every arrival furnished material for the invective of statesmen and the spleen of party presses. Franklin's position in the British metropolis was by no means enviable. In a letter to a friend, he said, "I do not find I have gained any point in either country, except that of rendering myself suspected by my impartiality—in England of being too much an American, and in America of being too much an Englishman." The latter suspicion came to a sudden death when the events of the Revolutionary war rendered a decided position necessary. Indeed, it became weaker and weaker every year, and the displeasure of the British government (who persisted in looking on Franklin as the representative man of America, as indeed he was) proportionately increased. In 1774 he was dismissed from his office of postmaster general. It was intended as a measure of retaliation, but its effect was highly beneficial to Franklin's reputation. "It relieved him at once from his anomalous position as the holder of office under the British government, and removed the suspicion that his enemies entertained and encouraged that he was playing a double part."*

* Weld's Life of Franklin.

During his sojourn in England Franklin was overtaken by a heavy affliction; he received intelligence of the death of his wife, to whom he had been wedded forty-four years, and who, in all his successes, had been the constant object of his affectionate pride. The blow was a severe one for Franklin, and contributed in some measure to his additional sojourn in England, although the public duties with which he was charged rendered this to some extent necessary. The state of affairs in America entirely engrossed the public mind; debates in either House of Parliament were of daily occurrence, and the members who participated in them sought the assistance of Franklin, whose great experience and diplomatic sagacity were of invaluable service to his countrymen in tempering the zeal of their patriotism. The English ministers, however, proved intractable, and, after ten years of incessant effort, Franklin returned to Philadelphia (May, 1775), with bold and decided ideas as to the future policy of America. On the day after his arrival the Assembly of Pennsylvania elected him to the Continental Congress; also a member of the Committee of Safety. To the various duties of these important offices he devoted himself with earnestness, and throughout the great drama of Independence he was a principal actor. It is unnecessary to repeat the events of this period; they are a part of our common history, and must be studied separately.

On the 26th of September, 1776, Franklin was appointed a commissioner to join Silas Deane and Arthur Lee, already in Europe, and "transact the business of the United States at the court of France." He arrived in that country in December of the same year. The object of the mission was to obtain the moral and material aid of France for the struggling republic; and it was triumphantly gained. Money and munitions of war were loaned by the French monarch, and any quantity of volunteers offered their services to fight against their ancient foe, the English. In 1778, a formal treaty of commerce was signed between the American commissioners on the one part, and France on the other, and in March of the same year the commissioners were formally received by the French monarch as the representatives of an independent power. It is, of course, unjust to attribute the entire success of this mission to Franklin, but he, perhaps, more than any other individual member, contributed, by the popularity and known rectitude of his character, to its successful issue. On the dissolution of the commission, Franklin was appointed minister plenipotentiary, and in that capacity remained in France to perform a great variety of offices, divided, in the present day, among several representatives. His industry was truly marvelous, and equal to any emergency. Although far advanced in years, he displayed the liveliest mental activity, throwing himself into the topics of the day, scientific and political, with the fervor of youth. When the time arrived for coming to terms with Great Britain, he was appointed one of the United States commissioners to effect a treaty of peace between the two countries. A great deal of delicate skill had to be displayed in the construction of this treaty, for there were keen susceptibilities on both sides which might easily be wounded. The calmness, dignity, and wisdom of Franklin's bearing was of inestimable value. So excellently was the preliminary treaty drawn up, that on the 3d of September, 1783, it was signed as the definitive one. After thus happily assisting at the inauguration of peace, Franklin insisted on returning to his own country. He had been absent in France for nearly nine years, and felt that he could no longer resist the encroachments of age. On the 27th of July, 1785, he set sail from London, and on the 14th of September he arrived once more in Philadelphia, where he was received with every demonstration of popular love and respect. It was difficult for a man of Franklin's eminence to obtain the repose of private life. So long had he been accustomed to bear the weight of public duties, that he could not throw off the load without injury to himself. The remaining years of his life were destined to be passed in the public service and in the pursuit of scientific subjects. He was chosen (1787) a delegate to the Convention for adopting a Constitution for the United States, and was a working member of that body. During the last years of his life he continued to wield his pen with the force and clearness of youth, and never missed an opportunity of proving that he was yet hale and hearty in mind, if weak and feeble in body.

Dr. Franklin suffered severely from gout, to which was added a painful calculous disease. The two became so distressing and continuous that he was scarcely able to leave his bed for the last twelve months of his life. "About sixteen days before his death," writes Dr. Jones, who attended the philosopher in his last sickness, "he was seized with a feverish disposition, without any particular symptoms attending it till the third or fourth day, when he complained of a pain in his left breast, which increased until it became extremely acute, attended by a cough and laborious breathing. During this state, when the severity of his pains drew forth a groan of complaint, he would observe that he was afraid that he did not bear them as he ought; acknowledging his grateful sense of the many blessings he had received from the Supreme Being, who had raised him from small and low beginnings to such high rank and consideration among men, and made no doubt but that his present afflictions were kindly intended to wean him from a world in which he was no longer fit to act the part assigned him. In this frame of body and mind he continued until five days before his death, when the pain and difficulty of breathing entirely left him, and his family were flattering themselves with the hopes of his recovery; but an imposthume, which had formed in his lungs, suddenly burst, and discharged a quantity of matter, which he continued to throw up while he had power, but, as that failed, the organs of respiration became gradually oppressed, a calm, lethargic state succeeded, and on the 17th instant (April, 1790), about eleven o'clock at night, he quietly expired, closing a long and useful life of eighty-four years and three months." The funeral took place on the 21st of April, and his remains were placed, according to his request, at the side of those of his wife, in the northwest corner of Christ Church cemetery. No monument marks his resting-place, for he had by will prescribed a plain marble slab. When a young man of twenty-three years, he penned the following quaint epitaph:

The Body
of
BENJAMIN FRANKLIN
(Like the Cover of an old Book,
Its contents torn out,
and stripped of its lettering and gilding)
Lies here, food for worms.
But the work shall not be lost,
For it will, as he believed, appear once more
In a new and more elegant edition,
Revised and corrected
by
The Author.

ufacture three thousand a minute, and perform the work with much more satisfaction and completeness than by hand. He was cheated out of his right to the profit of this invention. It was the usual fate of an inventor.

At the age of twenty-five Mr. Evans married, and soon after entered into business with his brothers, who were millers. Here was a proper field for the exercise of his ingenuity, and he cultivated it in a way that has placed the milling fraternity under perpetual obligations to him. The improvements and inventions he applied were the elevator, the conveyor, the hopper-boy, the drill, and the descender, which five machines are variously applied in different mills according to their construction, so as to perform every necessary movement of the grain and meal from one part of the mill to the other, or from one machine to another, through all the various operations, from the time the grain is supplied from the farmer's wagon until it is converted into flour, ready for sending to all parts of the world. These improvements were labor-saving, and important in every respect. They required much time to perfect, and were, of course, received with opposition from interested sources. It was extremely difficult to introduce them. Mr. Evans dispatched his brother through the States of Pennsylvania, Delaware, Maryland, and Virginia, to offer his inventions gratis to the first in each county who would adopt them. Notwithstanding this remarkable inducement, he returned wholly unsuccessful, and without any favorable prospects for the future. The Brandywine millers, in particular, were especially hostile, and it was only after several mills had adopted the improvements that they held a consultation to inquire into its merits. The result of this meeting was conveyed to Mr. Evans in the following language—at least so Mr. Howe says, in his biographical sketch: "Oliver, we have had a meeting, and agreed that, if thou would furnish all the materials, and thy own boarding, and come thyself to set up the machinery in one of our mills, thee may come and try, and, if it answers a valuable purpose, we will pay thy bill; but if it does not answer, thee must take it all out again, and leave the mill just as thee finds it, at thy own expense." Those Brandywine millers were very obstinate and very blind up to the last moment, and gave no end of trouble to poor Evans, for they had the reputation of being excellent in their business, and hundreds of others were influenced by their decision. They were the

OLIVER EVANS.

Oliver Evans, who has been called the Watt of America, was born at Newport, Delaware, about the year 1755 or 1756. His parents were respectable farmers, and at the age of fourteen Oliver was placed as an apprentice to a wheelwright—an excellent and lucrative business. Having received but the simple rudiments of an education, Oliver was desirous of improving himself, and in the evenings, when his regular work was done, devoted himself attentively to study. His master, an illiterate man, observing the youth engaged in what he considered an unprofitable amusement, endeavored to put a stop to it by denying Oliver the use of candles. But the thirst for knowledge is not so easily snuffed out. Oliver collected the shavings he had made during the day, set them in a blaze, and continued his studies by their grateful light.

At this early period of his life young Evans gave evidence of the possession of active inventive faculties. He endeavored to find out a method of propelling carriages on common roads without the aid of horses or other animal power. All that had been written on the subject he perused carefully, studied the various experiments, and made himself master of the subject generally. The result was that he concluded it impracticable with the means then known to mechanics. During this time, however, he became acquainted with the powers of steam; he renewed his experiment, and with increased confidence in this force he declared unhesitatingly that he could accomplish his object. Of course, such a confident declaration, coming from so young a man, excited the ridicule of his hearers, and compelled him to abandon his scheme until a later day, when more age, if not more wisdom, would give weight and importance to his opinion.

Evans's ingenuity and aptness carried him much beyond the limits of his trade. When he was twenty-three or twenty-four years of age he was engaged in making card teeth by hand, that being the only way then known. Finding this process too slow, he set his wits to work and contrived a machine that would man-last to adopt the improvements, and paid the penalty of their tardiness by losing much of their pre-eminence.

Mr. Evans was successful in obtaining patents for his inventions, among which was a steam-carriage to run on common roads, but the latter was considered so visionary that he was unable to obtain a capitalist to join him in the speculation. In 1800 or 1801, Mr. Evans determined to construct a steam-carriage at his own expense. He set about doing so, and had to make many modifications and new appliances in the steam-engine necessary for this purpose. The result was an engine of a new construction, useful not only for this, but for other purposes. Struck with this circumstance, he conceived the possibility of obtaining a patent, and forthwith laid aside his carriage to perfect the engine. He constructed a model on a large scale, and expended every sixpence he possessed in bringing it to perfection. At the age of forty-eight he found himself without means, with a large family, and with nothing to fall back upon but the model of a steam-engine, which few could understand, and against which there was much prejudice, even among scientific men. He had staked every thing on this last cast. We will give the result in his own words. "I could break and grind three hundred bushels of plaster of Paris, or twelve tons, in twenty-four hours; and, to show its operations more fully to the public, I applied it to saw stone, on the side of Market Street, where the driving of twelve saws in heavy frames, sawing at the rate of one hundred feet of marble in twelve hours, made a great show, and excited much attention. I thought this was sufficient to convince the thousands of spectators of the utility of my discovery, but I frequently heard them inquire if the power could be applied to saw timber as well as stone, to grind grain, propel boats, etc., and, though I answered in the affirmative, they still doubted. I therefore determined to apply my engine to all new uses, to introduce it and them to the public. This experiment completely tested the correctness of my principles. The power of my engine rises in a geometrical proportion, while the consumption of fuel has only an arithmetical ratio, in such proportion that every time I added one fourth more to the consumption of the fuel, its powers were doubled, and that twice the quantity of fuel required to drive one saw would drive sixteen saws at least; for when I drove two saws, the consumption was eight bushels of coal in twelve hours, but when twelve saws were driven the consumption was not more than ten bushels; so that, the more we resist the steam, the greater is the effect of the engine. On these principles very light but powerful engines can be made, suitable for propelling boats and land-carriages, without the great encumbrance of their weight as mentioned in Latrobe's demonstration."

In 1804 Mr. Evans applied his engine successfully to the dredging apparatus employed on the Schuylkill, performing all the operations that were required of it, and propelling the vessel in the steam-boat fashion of the present day, except that the wheel was behind. Even this did not satisfy the skeptics. They persisted in looking on Evans's imperfect machine as the consummation of all that could be effected in that way, and abused it for its slowness and weight. The inventor silenced them by answering that he would make a carriage propelled by steam, for a wager of three thousand dollars, to run upon a level road against the swiftest horse that could be produced. This machine Evans named the Oructor Amphibolis, and Mr. Howe states that it was the first application in America of steam power to the propelling of land-carriages. In the same year Mr. Evans made a proposition to the Lancaster Turnpike Company to construct carriages on the same principle, but the company paid no attention to his request. He was absolutely without patronage and sympathy. Possessing as he did the secret of the high-pressure principle—a principle of universal application in the present day, and indispensable on rail-roads and rapid streams—he was treated with contempt and scorn as an idler and a visionary. How far this was the case will be seen from the following quotation from his writings, which speaks almost in the language of prophecy: "The time will come when people will travel in stages moved by steam-engines from one city to another, almost as fast as birds fly, fifteen or twenty miles an hour. Passing through the air with such velocity, changing the scene in such rapid succession, will be the most exhilarating exercise. A carriage (steam) will set out from Washington in the morning, the passengers will breakfast at Baltimore, dine at Philadelphia, and sup in New York the same day. To accomplish this, two sets of rail-ways will be laid, so nearly level as not in any way to deviate more than two degrees from a horizontal line, made of wood or iron, or smooth paths of broken stone or gravel, with a rail to guide the carriages, so that they may pass each other in different directions, and travel by night as well as by day. Engines will drive boats ten or twelve miles per hour, and there will be many hundred steam-boats running on the Mississippi."

Upward of thirteen years were required to introduce his mill inventions and improvements, and the expenses were so great that the fees received from the licenses were barely sufficient to cover them. But even this was too much for unfortunate Mr. Evans. When the advantages of his system became more fully recognized, the inducements to cheat were augmented. He appealed to the United States Circuit Court of Pennsylvania, but, through some informality in the patent, the decision was against him, and his mean enemies were at liberty for a time to rob him. In 1808, however, he petitioned Congress for a new patent, and was successful in obtaining it, and even in sustaining it against the interested opposition of a number of millers, who presented a memorial to Congress, saying "that the public had been grossly deceived in regard to Evans being the original inventor of his patented mill machines; for, so far from having invented *all*, he was not the original inventor of any of them."

The remainder of Evans's life was spent in useful devotion to the subjects of steam and mechanics. He succeeded in establishing an iron foundry and machine shop in Philadelphia, where he had ample opportunity for making experiments and executing his plans on a limited scale. There is no doubt that, had Evans been favored by circumstances, and by kindly patronage and support, he would have proved himself one of the most distinguished inventors of the age. His experiments on the subject of steam-boat navigation were made fifteen or twenty years before those of Fulton, and his high-pressure engine was the parent of all steam appliances on rail-road or river. As it was, the world treated him with neglect, and he died poor and broken-hearted, while men of less native genius, but more practical temperament, bore off the palm. Mr. Evans died on the 21st of April, 1819.

ROGER SHERMAN.

ROGER SHERMAN was born at Newton, Massachusetts, on the 19th of April, 1721. His ancestors came from Dedham, England, about the year 1635, and settled at Watertown, near the place of his nativity. The father of Roger Sherman was a respectable farmer, but his circumstances were too humble to allow him to give his son much of an education. Young Roger enjoyed all the limited advantages of the parish school, and at an early age was apprenticed to a shoemaker, whom he served faithfully for five or six years, and continued to follow the occupation for many years after. From his youth Roger Sherman was distinguished by an eager thirst for knowledge, and neither the limited means of his school nor the long hours of his daily toil interfered with his pursuit of knowledge. He was in the habit of sitting at his work with a book before him, devoting to study every moment that his eyes could leave the work on which he was engaged. In this way he gained a very commendable acquaintance with general science, the system of logic, geography, mathematics, the general principles of history, philosophy, theology, and particularly law and politics.

In 1741 his father died, leaving him the responsible head of a large family. This was a serious trust, but Roger, although only twenty years of age, felt the weight of the obligation, and discharged it with kindness and devotion. Toward his mother, who was spared to see her son eminent and honored, he manifested the most devoted attachment.

In 1743 Roger Sherman removed to the town of New Milford, where he commenced business as a shoemaker, but, as the speculation did not promise to be lucrative, he abandoned it, and went into trade with an elder brother, who resided in the same place. The undertaking was successful, and Sherman became a man of mark in the community. His knowledge of mathematics was now put to practical use. He was appointed county surveyor. In 1748 he also supplied the astronomical calculations for an almanac published in New York city, and continued to do so for several subsequent years.

In 1749 Roger Sherman married, and this event gave a new direction to his thoughts, and a new impetus to his aims. An anecdote is related of him at this time. A neighbor had become involved in difficulties, arising out of the settlement of a testamentary trust. He needed legal advice, and stated his case to Sherman, who, as we have already mentioned, made law one of his numerous studies. Sherman took down the heads of the case in writing, and was then desired to consult with a lawyer who resided in a neighboring town. He did so, and, while conversing with this gentleman, made frequent reference to his memorandum. As it was necessary to make an application, by way of petition, to the proper tribunal, the lawyer desired that Sherman's minutes might be left with him. Sherman reluctantly consented, telling him that they were merely jotted down for his own use. The lawyer read the document with surprise. He perceived that, with the addition of a few technicalities, it was equal to any petition which he himself could prepare, and, consequently, that none other was necessary. Upon this the legal gentleman made some inquiries concerning Sherman's avocations, and being told that he was a shoemaker by trade, urged him to abandon that business, and adopt a profession for which nature had evidently qualified him. The demands of a large family prevented his acting on this suggestion immediately, but it gave a direction to his future studies, and paved the way for the distinction which he afterward obtained. In 1754 he was qualified and admitted to the bar. His practical and sound judgment, combined with inflexible integrity, soon gave him a pre-eminence in his profession, and pointed him out as a fitting object for public trust. In 1755 he was appointed a justice of the peace for New Milford, and was also elected a member of the Colonial Assembly. Four years later he was appointed judge of the Court of Common Pleas for the county of Litchfield, and for two years discharged the duties of that office with distinguished ability. He then removed to New Haven, where he acted as treasurer of Yale College. In consideration of his attainments and studious habits, he received from that learned institution the honorary degree of Master of Arts. In the following year (1766) the colony elected him a member of the Upper House in the General Assembly of Connecticut. As the members of the Upper House held their meetings with closed doors, we have no record of his career in that body; but from the subsequent events of his life we may reasonably suppose that it was satisfactory. During the same year Mr. Sherman was also appointed judge of the Superior Court of Connecticut. The first office he retained for twenty-three years, the last for nineteen years. He would probably have held them much longer had not a law been passed rendering the two offices incompatible.

We have briefly recapitulated the offices of trust bestowed on Mr. Sherman prior to the Revolution, and may now turn to the latter, as the drama in which Mr. Sherman became one of the principal actors, and with which, to the end of time, his name will be associated. In August, 1774, Mr. Sherman was nominated delegate to the General Congress of the colonies. It was a period requiring great calmness, unusual sagacity, and unflinching patriotism; and when Roger Sherman took his seat in the first Continental Congress, every one knew, and acknowledged, that he brought these requisites with him, and would even there be the glory of his country. He soon became one of the most prominent men in the assembly, and was appointed to the most important committees, among which was one to concert a plan of military operations for the campaign of 1776; to prepare and digest a form of confederation, and to repair to head-quarters at New York, and examine into the state of the army. But what was more important than these was that, in connection with Franklin, Adams, Jefferson, and Livingston, he was one of the committee appointed to prepare the Declaration of Independence. This immortal document, as is well known, was written by Jefferson, and it is probable that Sherman's influence was principally exerted in carrying it through Congress; but that he was engaged at all argues the consideration in which he was held. John Adams says of him that he was "one of the soundest and strongest pillars of the Revolution." He was indefatigable in his labors, and considered nothing too minute for his special attention.

In 1784 Mr. Sherman was elected mayor of New Haven, an office which he held for the remainder of his life. Toward the close of the war he was appointed one of the committee to revise the laws of the state, and in 1787 received a similar appointment to form the Constitution of the United States. Among his manuscripts a paper has been found, containing a series of propositions prepared by him for the amendment of the old Articles of Confederation, the greater part of which are incorporated, in substance, in the new Constitution. In the debates in that convention Mr. Sherman bore an important part. In a letter to General Floyd, he expresses his opinion of the Constitution. "Perhaps a better Constitution could not be made upon mere speculation. If, upon experience, it should be found to be deficient, it provides an easy and peaceable mode of making amendments; but if the Constitution should be adopted, and the several states choose some of their wisest and best men, from time to time, to administer the government, I believe it will not want any amendment. I hope that kind Providence, which guarded these states through a dangerous and distressing war to peace and liberty, will still watch over them, and guide them in the way of safety."

Having exerted all his power to secure a proper form of government, Sherman's abilities were now called in demand to secure its adoption by his native state. There were many local objections and prejudices to overthrow—objections which, in some states, were nearly fatal. Mainly owing to Sherman's argument and influence, Connecticut adopted the Constitution. After its ratification, he was immediately elected a representative of the state in Congress. He served in this capacity for two years, and was then elected to the United States Senate (1791). He continued in the full discharge of his senatorial duties until death dragged him from the helm. Mr. Sherman died on the 23d of July, 1793, in the seventy-third year of his age.

Mr. Sherman was a man of strictly religious principles and instincts. He was a devout reader of the Bible, and it was his custom to purchase a copy of the Scriptures at the commencement of every session of Congress, to peruse it daily, and to present it to one of his children on his return. His temperament was of a high moral order, and healthy as his physical man. It was impossible to swerve him from the line of conscientious duty: integrity was the essence of his thoughts, and penetrated his smallest action. He was remarkable for common sense, and for taking a clear view of perplexed subjects which others scarcely dared to handle. "He was capable of deep and long investigation. While others, weary of a short attention to business, were relaxing themselves in thoughtless inattention or dissipation, he was employed in prosecuting the same business, either by revolving it in his mind, and ripening his own thought upon it, or in conferring with others." It was in this way that he accomplished so much, and did it so well. In person Mr. Sherman was considerably above the common height; his form was erect and well proportioned; his complexion fair, and his countenance manly and agreeable. His bearing was naturally modest, but, when matters of importance were discussed, he became unreserved, free, and communicative.

The following is the inscription on the tablet which is placed over his tomb:

In memory of
the Hon. ROGER SHERMAN, Esq.,
Mayor of the City of New Haven,
and Senator of the United States.
He was born at Newton, in Massachusetts,
April 19th, 1721,
and died in New Haven, July 23d, A.D. 1793,
aged LXXII.

Possessed of a strong, clear, penetrating mind,
and singular perseverance,
he became the self-taught scholar,
eminent for jurisprudence and policy.
He was nineteen years an assistant,
and twenty-three years a judge of the Superior Court,
in high reputation.

He was a delegate in the first Congress,
signed the glorious Act of Independence,
and many years displayed superior talents and ability
in the national Legislature.
He was a member of the General Convention,
approved the Federal Constitution,
and served his country with fidelity and honor
in the House of Representatives,
and in the Senate of the United States.
He was a man of approved integrity;
a cool, discriminating judge;
a prudent, sagacious politician;
a true, faithful, and firm patriot.
He ever adorned
the profession of Christianity
which he made in youth;
and, distinguished through life
for public usefulness,
died in the prospect of a blessed immortality.

ROBERT FULTON.

It seldom happens that a man of genius receives the full measure of homage to which he is entitled. He is apt to be ridiculed as a visionary, and persecuted as a plagiarist during his life, and forgotten after his death. These hard conditions seem to be the penalty which one man pays for overlapping his neighbor in intellectual greatness; a sort of iniquitous compensation which the rabble insists on establishing. If there is one man more than another who fortunately can not complain of this cruel injustice, it is Robert Fulton. Every American must experience a thrill of satisfaction in knowing that the greatest benefactor of his country lives also in its best recollection. The name of Fulton is truly "familiar in our mouths as household words." In every considerable city of the New World the streets are named after him; large and populous cities bear his honored name; across every Ocean, through every inlet, away to the remotest corners of the earth, richly-laden vessels, also named after him, plow their rapid way. It is not only their name, but their present perfection, that they owe to this worthy son of the land of freedom. Without his application and industry, without his early perception and steady pursuit of the useful ends of steam power, America might yet be, to a great extent, an impenetrable and unwieldy forest. All the vast resources of the great West, all the riches of the South, all the industrial resources of the North and East, would be limited and narrowed to circumscribed sections of our country, and distributed there at greatly enhanced prices. With the rapid and convenient transit of the steam-ship, every variety of produce is now conveyed to the nearest market, and circulated in material wealth to all corners of the land. Every stream, with a respectable depth of water, boasts of its own steam navigation. We have all heard of the captain who had a boat of such a buoyant character that he could run it any morning after a heavy dew. Exaggerations are always based on some truth, and even this gasconade hints at a perfection which really does exist. For this, and for all that pertains to the present advanced state of steam navigation, we are largely, if not entirely, indebted to Robert Fulton. It is just and proper that he should be held in high esteem by his countrymen, and it is creditable to the latter that they have not, like too many other nations, allowed the name of a great benefactor to sink into oblivion.

Robert Fulton was born at Little Britain, in Lancaster County, Pennsylvania, in the year 1765. His parents were in humble condition, and at the death of his father, which occurred when he was three years of age, he was left, with very little assistance, to cut for himself a path in the rough world. He possessed a native taste for art, and could use his pencil skillfully at a very early age. So much pleasure did he derive from the exercise of this talent, that he became ambitious to excel, with a view to adopting the profession of a painter. He made rapid progress, and, at the age of seventeen, proceeded to Philadelphia, where he established himself as a painter of portraits and landscapes. In a short time he was able to make more than a living; he could save, and, like a sensible, prudent man, provide for the emergencies of sickness or other accidents of life. Before he was twenty-one years of age he had accumulated a little capital sufficient for the purchase of a small farm in Washington County, Pennsylvania, in addition to comforting and supporting a widowed mother. It would be well if all young men of talent imitated Fulton's example. By industry and economy he placed a solid bar of comfort between himself and the exigencies of life, and to this, more than any thing else, we owe his subsequent devotion to mechanics. If he had simply dallied with the arts, he would have been a poor painter all his life; but he seized them with a vigorous hand, and moulded them to his purpose. When this was accomplished he breathed more freely, and began to yearn for greater perfection, and for communion with men who made art what it was—a noble, soul-inspiring vocation. At this time the great American painter, Benjamin West, was the ruling spirit of the art world, the centre around which all that was great and commanding in wealth and intellect revolved. He was the pet of the English aristocracy, and the Jupiter of the fraternity of English painters. Now that he was at ease, Fulton determined on making a pilgrimage to the temple of this art god. He was warmly welcomed by his countryman, and invited to become an inmate of his house. Such a cordial invitation was of inestimable value to the young artist, and he became not only the guest, but the pupil of the great master.

For several years Fulton pursued his studies with devotion and success. He made many valuable acquaintances, and, being a man of considerable information on mechanical subjects (for which he always had a strong regard), he drew around him the sympathies of a large number of distinguished amateurs, among whom may be numbered the Duke of Bridgewater and the Earl of Stanhope. The first-named nobleman was the first to introduce a perfect system of canal navigation into the United Kingdom, and, at the time Fulton made his acquaintance, was largely interested in similar important enterprises all over the country. Fulton had devoted some attention to the subject of canals, and was prepared to give well-digested opinions concerning the merits of the various systems then in agitation. The Duke of Bridgewater was so well pleased with his aptness in these respects, that he cordially recommended him to abandon the profession of painter, and take to that of civil engineer. Fulton acted on this advice, and shortly afterward we find him residing in Birmingham—the central workshop of England—engaged in the construction of those numerous canals which have since added so much to the extent and importance of that town.

Earl Stanhope was a man with a decided genius for mechanics. He devoted his time and his fortune to the prosecution of various experiments in connection with the newly-discovered powers of the steam-engine. One of his projects was to propel a vessel through the water with gigantic ducks' feet worked by machinery. He mentioned this plan to Fulton, but the latter objected to its practicability, and suggested other means whereby the desired object might be obtained, he thought, in a more easy and economical way. Earl Stanhope continued his experiments, and soon found that Fulton's objections were valid and fatal. A few years later Fulton applied the suggestions he had proffered to the nobleman, and succeeded in propelling satisfactorily the first steam-vessel that ever pressed its way through the waters.

Fulton threw himself into the subject of canal navigation with great enthusiasm; wrote a book concerning it, and took out a patent for some improvements which he conceived belonged to him, but which, in the end, turned out to be of no practical use. He made the acquaintance of Watt, and neglected no opportunity of improving himself in practical mechanics and machinery. After remaining for some time in Birmingham, he determined on visiting France. One of his reasons for this step was a desire to enter into negotiations with the French government for the sale of a marine missile, called a *torpedo*, which Fulton asserted would destroy the navy of an enemy with the greatest possible ease and expedition. Experiments were made in the Seine, but with little success. The French government declined to have any thing to do with Mr. Torpedo. Fulton then offered his invention to the English government, and afterward to the government of his own country. Extensive experiments were made, but the invention was again found wanting, and after a while died a natural death. It is fortunate for the world, perhaps, that it did. If it were capable of doing what Fulton said it would, he was criminally wrong in offering it to any other government than his own. Such an instrument of warfare should only be placed in the most righteous hands, and where it is likely to be used on the side of truth, justice, and human progress. Fulton's conduct in the matter shows that he had no moral sentiment on the subject, but merely looked out for the best market.

The Scriptures teach us that out of evil cometh good. It is probable that Fulton's efforts in the torpedo line greatly improved his mechanical dexterity, and, by bringing him in contact with water craft, directed his attention once more to the subject of marine locomotion. Many attempts were being made in all countries to invent a vessel which, with the aid of steam, should defy the winds and the tides, and move wherever the hand of man chose to direct it. Until Mr. Watt had invented his double-action condensing engine, there seemed no possibility of effecting this desirable object; but when that great improvement was introduced, it became apparent to Fulton that the moment had arrived for victoriously snatching the laurels from various competitors. There is now no doubt that he did so openly and fairly, although it has been the custom to assert that he stole some of them, at least, from other men, particularly Fitch and Rumsey. We have no space to devote to controversy, nor is it profitable to open up a question satisfactorily settled by eminent and conscientious authorities. All that Fulton claimed they have conceded to him. Others may have gone in the same direction that he did, and aimed for the same goal, but they did not take the same path, and consequently he got there first.

The improvement Fulton suggested to Earl Stanhope was simply to substitute a water-wheel for the propelling power instead of an imitation webbed foot. Experience soon proved the latter to be of no use, and Fulton was therefore additionally anxious to test the merits of his own scheme. He was fortunate in getting a partner who not only thoroughly understood the subject, but who unhesitatingly expressed his confidence in the success of the undertaking. The first experiments were made in France, where Mr. Fulton and Mr. Livingston were then living. They were measurably successful, and arrangements were entered into for the prosecution of the scheme in America. An application was at once made to the Legislature of the State of New York for the exclusive privilege of navigating its waters by steam. It was considered so impracticable that there was no opposition to the grant, the only condition being that a vessel should be propelled at the rate of *four miles an hour* within a certain prescribed period. The engines for Fulton's first boat were ordered from England, and arrived in America in 1806. The vessel was entirely finished in August, 1807, and a trial trip was immediately announced, invitations being sent to all the leading scientific, literary, and political men of the city. A more critical assemblage could scarcely be gathered together, or one more keenly disposed to ridicule failure. Many expressed a decided opinion that the whole affair was a mere catchpenny humbug; others shook their heads, as if *they* knew perfectly well what *could* be done in the way of steam navigation, and were certain that Fulton's was not the plan. All were unanimous on one point—that it was worse than throwing money away to speculate in such a wild and thriftless undertaking. When, however, the unshapely vessel was observed to move silently from her dock on the Jersey shore, and cleave her course through the foaming stream, the doubters began to have doubts about their doubts; the skeptics, to be skeptical of their skepticism; the lukewarm boiled over with excitement, and the indifferent became enthusiastic. The first turn of the big wheels effected a double revolution, in the water and in men's minds. Cries of acclamation arose from either shore, and the first steamship in the world—the *Clermont*—moved like a mighty conqueror amid shouts of wonder and admiration.

In a few days the *Clermont* started on her first long trip. This was to Albany, and concerning it Mr. Fulton wrote as follows: "My steam-boat voyage to Albany and back has turned out rather more favorable than I had calculated. The distance from New York to Albany is one hundred and fifty miles; I ran it up in thirty-two hours, and down in thirty. I had a light breeze against me the whole way, both going and coming, and the voyage has been performed wholly by the power of the steam-engine. I overtook many sloops and schooners beating to windward, and parted with them as if they had been at anchor. The power of propelling boats by steam is now fully proved. The morning I left New York there were not, perhaps, thirty persons in the city who believed that the boat would ever move one mile an hour, or be of the least utility; and while we were putting off from the wharf, which was crowded with spectators, I heard a number of sarcastic remarks. This is the way in which ignorant men compliment what they call philosophers and projectors. Having employed much time, money, and zeal in accomplishing this work, it gives me, as it will you, great pleasure to see it fully answer my expectations. It will give a cheap and quick conveyance to the merchandise on the Mississippi, Missouri, and other great rivers, which are now laying open their treasures to the enterprise of our countrymen; and although the prospect of personal emolument has been some inducement to me, yet I feel infinitely more pleasure in reflecting on the immense advantage that my country will derive from the invention."

The navigation of the Hudson by steam was now accepted as a fact, and the *Clermont* was regarded as such a public convenience that regular voyages were insisted on, and passengers at both ends were eager for the opportunity to travel in her. Fulton kept a sharp look-out for defects in the machinery, and never went a voyage without making extensive observations. In the winter the *Clermont* was remodeled and repaired; guards and housings for the wheels were added, and many other improvements, which tended largely to the comfort and expedition of the trip. Unfortunately, however, Mr. Livingston insisted on trying his hand at an invention, and popped into the boat a boiler which was, no doubt, very pretty in a theoretical point of view, but which, as Fulton predicted, turned out practically a complete failure. The *Clermont* lost popularity for a short time in consequence of this, but Fulton came to the rescue with a boiler of unquestionable capacity, and all went well again. A regular and rapidly-increasing intercourse was thus established by Fulton between Albany and New York. It became apparent that more boats would be needed, and that an amount of business far exceeding his expectations would shortly press on his hands. Nor was he without opposition. The skippers of the river entered into combinations against him, and some speculators started a rival boat, which was to be moved by a pendulum, but which, in the long run, had to be moved by steam and paddle-wheels exactly in the same way as Fulton's. As this was clearly an infringement of Livingston and Fulton's rights, they applied to the Court of Chancery for an injunction, which, however, was refused. On an appeal to the Court of Errors this decision of the chancellor was reversed, and the water privileges of the State of New York remained in the exclusive possession of Fulton and his associate. Several new boats were added to the line, and Fulton, although the possessor of large and valuable interests, found himself short of money by the incessant disbursements occasioned by the rapidly-increasing business of the line.

In the spring of 1808 Fulton crowned his triumphs with the happy wreath of matrimony. He was fortunate in the selection of an amiable and accomplished spouse, the niece of his friend Livingston. In her society ever afterward he enjoyed the calm tranquillity and happiness which the married state can alone afford. This wise step appears almost to have been indicated by a beneficent Providence, for immediately after his marriage he was assailed by all sorts of worldly troubles. People, when they found that steam navigation was no longer the idle vision of a dreamer, but a substantial fact, began to overlook the claims of the man who introduced it. They fulminated against the monopoly enjoyed by Fulton; grumbled at the accommodations afforded by his boats; complained that the fares were exorbitant; and, finally, maintained that Fulton was not entitled to exclusive privileges, because he was not the inventor of the system. The latter was, of course, jealous of his rights, and endeavored to protect them to the best of his ability. He came in contact with the State of New Jersey, the government of which had granted exclusive privileges to Fitch. The ferry communication was stopped, and more unpopularity was heaped upon our hero. In these days monopolies are looked on with proper distrust, and perhaps the people were not altogether wrong even then for complaining that the public interests were mortgaged to private individuals. But it must be remembered that the patent laws were in a very imperfect state, and that the only chance an inventor had of remunerating himself was by securing extensive state monopolies. No doubt there was a great deal to be said on both sides. If Fitch's invention had been less known, Fulton would perhaps have received more sympathy. But the long and valuable labors of that ingenious man undoubtedly gave him a claim on the public regard, and people thought that if any one was entitled to a monopoly, it was he, and not Fulton. The state settled the difficulty some time afterward by declaring the monopoly unconstitutional.

Fulton's partner endeavored to get a revision or reversal of the Jersey law, and when the day came on for trying the matter (January, 1815), the subject of this memoir appeared as a witness. The weather was severe, and the Hudson became unnavigable for steam-boats. Anxious to return to his family, Fulton exposed himself to the bitter blasts in a row-boat, which conveyed him to New York. Immediately on his return he was seized with a violent fit of illness. From this he partly recovered, but again committed an act of indiscretion by exposing himself at the Brooklyn Navy-yard. A relapse was the consequence. He became gradually worse, and his shattered system held out no hopes of recovery. His death shortly followed, on the 24th of February, 1815.

This calamity occasioned a sudden revulsion of public feeling. All petty oppositions and jealousies were forgotten, and the highest to the lowest in the land alike vied in paying tribute to the memory of a man who had at least shed lustre on the country of his birth.

Fulton was rather above the middle height; intelligent in countenance and conversation; attached to the home circle, in which he was pre-eminently fitted to shine; familiar with all the topics of the day; well bred and easy in his intercourse with friends, and polite, affable, and kindly to all. He never entirely abandoned the fine arts. Only a short time before his death he executed oil paintings of his family, and was pleased with the dexterity he still preserved. In closing this memoir, we can not do better than quote the just and dispassionate remarks of Dr. Renwick: "If we consider Fulton as an inventor, it may be difficult to say in what exact particular his merits consist. As the blow of the mallet, by which the mighty mass of a ship of the line is caused to start upon its ways, in the act of launching, is undistinguishable among the numerous strokes by which that mass is gradually raised, so the minute particulars in which his labors differ from former abortive attempts may almost escape research; but if we contemplate him in the light of a civil engineer, confidently building a finished and solid structure upon the incomplete foundation left by others, we must rank him among the first of his age, and place him, in the extent of his usefulness to mankind, as second to Watt alone."

SIR WILLIAM JONES.

THIS extraordinary linguist and Oriental scholar was born in London in the year 1746. When only three years of age he had the misfortune to lose his father, a distinguished mathematician and scholar, and was left entirely to the guidance of a fond mother. Being a woman of strong mind, she determined that her son should have a good education, and devoted all her time, energies, and means to the accomplishment of this object. The boy early displayed an acuteness uncommon in one of his age; and to his questionings the mother invariably replied, *Read, and you will know.* To this admonition the great scholar admitted that he was mainly indebted for his subsequent attainments. When only seven years of age young William was placed at the celebrated school at Harrow, being accompanied there by his mother, who took a small place in the village in order that she might minister to his wants, and direct his mind as far as lay in her power. Under the routine of the school his precocity disappeared, and for two years he was more remarkable for diligence than quickness. In his ninth year he met with an accident by which his thigh bone was broken.

He was unable to attend school for a year, but his mother availed herself of the opportunity to initiate him into the glorious field of English literature, and he became acquainted with some of the best poets. On returning to school he was put into the same class which he had left, but found, to his dismay, that he was far behind his old classmates. What contributed to his pain, even more than this knowledge, was the fact that even the master mistook his necessary retrogression for dullness or laziness, and threatened to punish him, the ferrule being considered an excellent stimulant to mental activity in those days. The threat had no effect on poor young Jones; but his pride was touched, and he made up his mind that he would overtake his classmates. By hard study, he accomplished his purpose and took his place at the head of the class, gained the prize offered in every department, and carried his proficiency much beyond what was required of boys in his form. In his twelfth year he entered the upper school, and soon after astonished teacher, scholars, and every body else by a remarkable display of memory. Theatrical representations took place among the scholars, and on one occasion it was determined to give Shakspeare's "Tempest." Unfortunately, there was not a copy to be had. To supply the deficiency, young Jones wrote it out from memory with sufficient correctness to enable the boys to act it with pleasure to themselves. About the same time he began the study of Greek, and prosecuted his Latin with more zeal than ever. He conquered many of the difficulties of Latin prosody before his teachers and schoolmates were aware that he had thought of the subject, and so with many other subjects. During the vacation he found time to perfect himself in French, and to study Italian and arithmetic. He also learned something of Arabic, and enough of Hebrew to enable him to read some of the Psalms in the original. He was now in his thirteenth year, and his inclination to study at this period was so earnest that it was thought proper to check it, lest it might injure his health. His attendance at school was therefore interdicted, and for a time he was prohibited all kind of study.

At the age of seventeen it was decided that he should go to one of the Universities, and in the spring of 1764 he was entered for University College, Oxford. It is characteristic of his elevated temperament that he was disappointed with the course of instruction provided here. He was astonished to find that he could not receive the assistance he anticipated, and that the professors and tutors were not prepared for giant strides. He conceived very bitter sentiments against the establishment, unmindful apparently of the fact that it was intended for the average capacities of students, and not for the unusual ones of young men like Jones. In later days he modified the hasty impression of his youth. A testimony to his scholarship was soon given by his being elected one of the four scholars on the foundation of Sir Simon Bennett. His love for Oriental literature began to manifest itself, and he commenced studying Arabic from a native of Aleppo whom he discovered in the streets of London and transported to Oxford. From this individual he obtained a fluent knowledge of the vulgar Arabic. He then studied Persian. Nor did he, in the mean time, neglect his old friends, the Greeks and Latins. The Greek poets and historians, and especially the writings of Plato, he carefully perused. With the Italian, Spanish, and Portuguese, he had become so familiar that he could read their best authors with ease. While following these multitudinous studies, he did not neglect the requirements of the body. He knew that a healthy mind could only be secured by a healthy body, and never neglected to take a systematic course of exercise in connection with his studies. In this way he was able to preserve a high tone of health, and, "with the fortune of a peasant, to give himself the education of a prince." Without these precautions it would have been impossible for a feeble constitution to resist the intense labor and application imposed on it.

In the summer of 1766 he was unexpectedly elected to a fellowship at Oxford. The appointment was very acceptable in many ways. In the first place, it was a recognition of his attainments, and, in the second, it furnished him with an income, with which he might, if he felt so disposed, pursue his studies to any extent he pleased, and remain within the classic precincts of the University city. He had felt the want of money so much previous to this event, that in the preceding year he had accepted an invitation to become the private tutor of Lord Althorpe (afterward Earl Spencer). In the family of this nobleman he passed some years, and appears to have been treated with kindness and consideration. In 1767 he accompanied his lordship on a tour of the Continent, and availed himself of the opportunity of learning German. On his return he devoted himself largely to the preparation of his "Commentaries on Asiatic Poetry"—a learned work which he had in progress—and also found time to learn the Chinese.

In 1768, the King of Denmark was on a visit to England, and brought with him an Eastern manuscript containing the life of Nadir Shah. This manuscript had puzzled the *savans* of the Continent, and he brought it to England, hoping that Jones would undertake to *translate it into French.* As might be expected, Mr. Jones declined; but the king pressed his request so earnestly that he was afraid of being misunderstood if he refused any longer. He performed the task, and in less than a year laid the work before his majesty—the work of a young man of twenty-four years of age, critically exact in two totally opposite languages.

During the performance of this very laborious undertaking, which, it is unnecessary to say, required the greatest concentration of his faculties, he was not unmindful of his invariable rule of preserving his physical health. At various times, when he was pursuing a study with more than ordinary devotion, he took lessons in horsemanship, fencing, etc., in order to utterly relax his mind at certain periods of the day. While applying himself to the King of Denmark's serious task, he found time to study music, a study which, be it observed, should belong more especially to literary men, relieving as it does the pressure of severer studies with one which is at once delicious and refreshing. He went into society, also, and made the acquaintance of many eminent men.

During the summer of 1769 he accompanied his pupil to Harrow, and left him there in charge of his old preceptors. During his temporary stay he completed a Persian grammar, and commenced a Persian dictionary. His mind, too, became seriously directed toward the truths of Christianity, and he resolved, for his own satisfaction, to peruse carefully the Scriptures in the original. The result was transcribed on the fly-leaf of his own Bible, and ran as follows: "I have carefully and regularly perused these Holy Scriptures, and am of opinion that the volume, independently of its divine origin, contains more sublimity, purer morality, more important history, and finer strains of eloquence, than can be collected from all other books, in whatever language they may have been written."

After his return from Harrow he determined to commence the study of the law, with the view of following it as a profession.

He did not at first think it necessary to forsake entirely his Oriental pursuits, nor would it have been possible for him to do so in a moment. Literature (especially that of Eastern countries) had become a part of his life. Still, he was capable of devoting himself with great assiduity to the study of jurisprudence. "I have just begun," he writes, "to contemplate the stately edifice of the laws of England, 'The gathered wisdom of a thousand years,' if you will allow me to parody a line of Pope. I do not see why the study of the law is called dry and unpleasant; and I very much suspect that it seems so to those only who would think any study unpleasant which requires great application of the mind and exertion of the memory. * * * I have opened two commonplace books, the one of the law, the other of oratory, which is surely too much neglected by our modern speakers. * * * But I must lay aside my studies for about six weeks, while I am printing my grammar, from which a good deal is expected, and which I must endeavor to make as perfect as a human work can be. When that is finished, I shall attend the Court of King's Bench very constantly."

Honors began to reward the industrious scholar. In 1772 Mr. Jones was elected Fellow of the Royal Society, and, two years later, published his Commentaries on Asiatic Poetry. They had been finished for some years, but he delayed the printing, in order to submit them to the criticism of scholars. They were written in Latin, and commanded the attention of *savans* throughout the world. In 1778 he published a translation of a part of the orations of Isæus. During all this period he pursued the study of the law with his usual avidity.

In 1780 he lost his mother, a calamity which fell heavily on him, but which was not unexpected. That estimable woman had lived to see her proudest hopes realized, and left the world with the conviction that her son would be, if he was not already, the most distinguished man of the century. The event seems to have awakened thoughts in the mind of Jones which had heretofore been crowded out by the hurry and excitement of continual study, namely, that there was a limit to his own life. The apprehension that he might die imperfect in some matters which afforded him great mortal interest nerved him with new determination. He now laid down a plan for his future studies. The memorandum is in his own handwriting, and reads as follows:

"*Resolved*, to learn no more *rudiments* of any kind, but to perfect myself in, first, twelve languages, as the *means* of acquiring accurate knowledge of the

I. History of, 1. Man; 2. Nature.

II. Arts: 1. Rhetoric; 2. Poetry; 3. Painting; 4. Music.

III. Sciences: 1. Law; 2. Mathematics; 3. Dialectics.

The twelve languages are Greek, Latin, Italian, French, Spanish, Portuguese, Hebrew, Arabic, Persian, Turkish, German, English. 1780."

In March, 1783, Mr. Jones was appointed Judge of the Supreme Court of Judicature at Fort William, in Bengal, and at the same time received the honor of knighthood. Being thus rendered entirely independent in his means (the appointment was for life), he gratified the warm ambition of his manhood, and married the beautiful and accomplished daughter of the Bishop of St. Asaph. Immediately after the nuptial tour he embarked for India, and bade farewell to the land of his birth, a land which he was destined never to see again. He was now in his thirty-seventh year, full of health and strength, and bounding with hope of future distinction and attainments. On the voyage he amused himself by drawing up a scheme of what he should do during his residency in India. The list is curious, and is headed

"*Objects of Inquiry during my residence in Asia:*

1. The Laws of the Hindoos and Mohammedans.
2. The History of the *Ancient* World.
3. Proofs and Illustrations of Scripture.
4. Traditions concerning the Deluge, etc.
5. Modern Politics and Geography of Hindostan.
6. Best mode of governing Bengal.
7. Arithmetic and Geometry, and mixed Sciences of the Asiatics.
8. Medicine, Chemistry, Surgery, and Anatomy of the Indians.
9. Natural productions of India.
10. Poetry, Rhetoric, and Morality of Asia.
11. Music of the Eastern Nations.
12. The Ski-King, or 300 Chinese Odes.
13. The best accounts of Thibet and Cashmir.

14. Trade, Manufactures, Agriculture, and Commerce of India.
15. Mogul Constitution, contained in the Defteri, Alemghiri, and Agein Acbari.
16. Mahratta Constitution.

To print and publish the *Gospel* of St. Luke in Arabic.
To publish Law Tracts in Persian or Arabic.
To print and publish the Psalms of David in Persian verse.
To compose, if God grant me life,

1. Elements of the Laws of England.
   MODEL: The Essay on Bailment—Aristotle.
2. The History of the American War.
   MODEL: Thucydides and Polybius.
3. Britain Discovered, an heroic Poem on the Constitution of England. Machinery. Hindoo Gods.
   MODEL: Homer.
4. Speeches, Political and Forensic.
   MODEL: Demosthenes.
5. Dialogues, Philosophical and Historical.
   MODEL: Plato.
6. Letters.
   MODEL: Demosthenes and Plato.

"12th July, 1783, *Crocodile* Frigate."

Sir William Jones reached Calcutta in safety, and immediately entered upon the discharge of his judicial duties. He was warmly received by all classes of the community, his reputation having preceded him. The highest expectations were formed of his administration, and his opening charge to the grand jury more than sustained the good opinion which prevailed. As soon as his judicial duties allowed him, he turned his attention to the objects above enumerated, and devised a plan of a society for carrying on researches in a more thorough way than could be expected from an individual. The presidency of this society was offered to Warren Hastings, who at that time was Governor General of India; but that celebrated man declined the honor, and Sir William Jones was elected to the office. He immediately commenced the study of the Sanscrit, both that he might better fulfill his duties as president, and still more that he might be able to judge more accurately and independently of the spirit of Hindoo law.

While at Calcutta, the attraction of his conversation drew around him so many friends that his hours of study were much encroached upon. He therefore chose a country residence, a few miles from the city, where he might receive less interruption and enjoy better health. The duties of the court, however, frequently called him to town, and his devotion was so great that, even when he felt his health declining, he refused to relax in his attendance. "How long my health will continue in this town," he writes to a friend, "with constant attendance in court every morning, and the irksome business of justice of peace in the afternoon, I can not foresee. If temperance and composure of mind will avail, I shall be well; but I would rather be a valetudinarian all my life than leave unexplored the Sanscrit mine which I have just opened." In another letter he gives us an insight into his occupations. "By rising before the sun, I allot an hour every day to Sanscrit, and am charmed with knowing so beautiful a sister of Latin and Greek." It was then his custom to walk to town, arriving there before the sun had gained much ascendency, and remaining until evening, when he walked home again. "It rarely happens," he says, "that favorite studies are closely connected with the strict discharge of our duty, as mine happily are: even in this cottage, I am assisting the court by studying the Arabic and Sanscrit, and have now rendered it an impossibility for the Mohammedan or Hindoo lawyers to impose upon us with erroneous opinions." It was one of his favorite projects to make a complete digest of Hindoo and Mohammedan laws, after the model of the Pandects of Justinian. The importance of this was evident from the fact that the Hindoo and Mohammedan laws were written, for the most part, in Sanscrit and Arabic. "My experience justifies me in declaring," he says, "that I could not, with an easy conscience, concur in a decision merely on the opinion of native lawyers in any cause in which they could have the remotest interest in misleading the court; nor, how vigilant soever we might be, would it be very difficult for them to mislead us; for a single obscure text, explained by themselves, might be quoted as express authority, though, perhaps, in the very book from which it was selected, it might be differently explained, or introduced only for the purpose of being exploded." In the execution of this great project he enlisted the sympathies and assistance of Lord Cornwallis, the new governor general, who placed all the facilities of the state at his disposal, and thus enabled Jones to select as his assistants the most learned natives of the district.

In the beginning of 1794 he published a translation of the ordinances of Menu, an extremely curious work, illustrating the manners and customs of a very ancient people, and their peculiar religious ceremonies, to which they have adhered down to the present time. During all this time Sir William enjoyed good health, and frequently boasted of having conquered the climate; but his lady suffered severely from the scorching heat, and became so much debilitated that Sir William was alarmed, and induced her to return to England. She took her departure in a sailing vessel, and bade farewell to a husband whom she was doomed never to see again. Four months later, and Sir William was attacked with what appeared to be the ague, arising, as he imagined, from indiscreet exposure to the night air. Medical assistance was called in, and the disease was pronounced to be inflammation of the liver—the scourge of British India. The symptoms became more aggravated, and, in spite of every attention, the patient sunk on the seventh day. Sir William was in the forty-seventh year of his age. Few men have died so universally respected. His amiable disposition, added to his great acquirements in almost every department of human knowledge, endeared him to all classes of people. There is no doubt that his zeal in the discharge of his duties ("I never was happy," he wrote, "till I was settled in India") predisposed his constitution to the attack which terminated his life. His acquaintance with the history, philosophy, laws, religion, science, and manners of nations, was most extensive and profound. As a linguist, he has scarcely, if ever, been surpassed; he had made himself acquainted with no fewer than twenty-eight different languages, and was studying the grammars of several of the Oriental dialects up to within a week of his lamented death. In accordance with a determination to which we have already referred, he perfected himself in Greek, Latin, Italian, French, Spanish, Portuguese, Hebrew, Arabic, Persian, Turkish, German, and English; made himself master of Sanscrit, and less completely of Hindostanee and Bengalee, and also of the dialects called the Tibetian, the Pâli, the Phalavi, and the Deri. The other languages which he studied more or less completely were the Chinese, Russian, Runic, Syriac, Ethiopic, Coptic, Dutch, Swedish, and Welsh.

It was by the observance of a few simple maxims that Sir William Jones was able to accomplish what he did. One of these was, never to neglect an opportunity of improvement; another was, that whatever had been attained was attainable by him, and that therefore the real or supposed difficulties of any pursuit formed no reason why he should not engage in it. "It was also," says Lord Teignmouth, "a fixed principle with him, from which he never voluntarily deviated, not to be deterred by any difficulties which were surmountable from prosecuting to a successful termination what he had once deliberately undertaken." Like all great workers, Jones was scrupulously methodical, and had a particular time for every occupation, thus avoiding interruption and confusion.

The best monument of his fame was raised by his widow, who published a splendid edition of his works in 6 vols. quarto, 1799, and also, at her own expense, placed a fine marble statue to his memory, executed by Flaxman, in the ante-chamber of University College, Oxford.

CAPTAIN JOHN SMITH.

THIS redoubtable hero was born at Willoughby, in Lincolnshire, in the year 1579. He was descended, he says in his autobiography, from the family of the ancient Smiths of Crudley, in Lancashire, on the father's side, and from the Rickards, of Great Heck, in Yorkshire, on the mother's. At an early age, his parents having died, he was placed under the care of guardians, but these unfaithful stewards ill-treated the youth, squandered his property, and otherwise behaved in a manner highly offensive to his sensitive nature. In those days, young people considered it an excellent plan to run away, if all things were not quite comfortable at home. There were no electric telegraphs, rail-roads, or steam-boats to dart after the truant and bring him back again. If he had a stout heart, a keen wit, or a sharp sword, it was probable that he would make a way for himself in the world, and so utterly escape from all his former grievances. Smith's disposition became known to his guardians, and, to punish it, they sent him as an apprentice to a merchant at Lynn. The drudgery of a counting-house was the last thing in the world that could suit his ardent nature. He gave it a very brief trial, and then, borrowing all the money he could (amounting to about ten shillings), he started for the Continent, in the company of Mr. Peregrine Bertz. He does not appear to have been a great favorite with this gentleman, and in a short time was dismissed from his train. Not in the slightest degree discouraged by this untoward event, young Smith determined to go in search of his own fortunes. He repaired, accordingly, to the Low Countries, where a plentiful dish of hard fighting was always supplied to the hungry visitor. Here he baptized his infant weapon, and performed prodigies of valor during four long but exciting years of warfare. At length, becoming weary of the struggle, he took his leave, and proceeded to Scotland, where, after a slight touch of shipwreck, he arrived in safety. The hospitality of the Scotch was lavished on the hero, but the court of King James entirely overlooked his existence. Slightly in disgust, therefore, he turned his back on the Scottish metropolis, and once more returned to Willoughby, in Lincolnshire. The good folks made a lion of him at first, and bored him with their invitations and attentions, "in which," he says, "he took small delight." To rid himself of these pests, he retired from the town, and established himself in an open field a good way from it. Here, beside a gay little rivulet, he built himself a pavilion of boughs, and, dispensing with all the luxuries of civilization, devoted himself to the study of war and morals. Concerning the latter he appeared to have somewhat loose notions. He looked upon the earth as a large domain, bestowed indifferently upon all Adam's children, who might, without blame, make use freely of what they found in their way. Practically applied, this theory resulted in a pastime which the law frowns at, under the name of poaching. In other words, he was in the habit of replenishing his scanty board with the prime venison and plump pheasants of his neighbors. He did not exactly do it himself. He had a worthy retainer who performed the important functions of the commissariat department, while the virtuous Smith improved himself in the pages of Machiavelli and Marcus Aurelius. The only amusement he took was on horseback, either hunting, or tilting with the lance, and acquiring a dexterity with that weapon for which he was afterward renowned. Such a character in a quiet agricultural district became necessarily an object of extreme curiosity. Every one talked about the chivalric hermit, and not a few fair damsels sighed for the possession of such a strange, fascinating knight, who seemed to live in a romance world of his own, with which this coarser firmament had no sort of connection. There were others, too, who became interested in his strange life, especially one—an Italian gentleman—of the name of Peodoro Polaloga, a superb horseman, and rider to the Earl of Lincoln. Smith derived so much satisfaction from this gentleman's society, that he was, after a time, persuaded to abandon his pavilion of boughs, and once more return to the world.

There is no doubt that peace was a very objectionable state of things to Smith, and that he infinitely preferred cutting throats wherever and whenever that relaxation could be enjoyed. At that time the Turks were ravaging Hungary, and pitching into the Christian armies with unusual ferocity. Smith, who, to use a vulgar expression, was spoiling for a fight, determined to join the Christians, and show the infidels what hard fighting really meant. With this object in view, he attired himself in great splendor, and conveyed himself and arms on board ship. The attractiveness of his appearance excited the cupidity of some of the rogues on board, who, seeing that he was as innocent as a child of all matters relating to the world, made up their minds to rob him. One of the band made approaches to Smith, pretending to be a nobleman of high degree, while three of his confederates were in attendance in the capacity of servants. A sort of intimacy sprung up between them; Smith divulged his plans for the future, and the man of birth condescendingly undertook to introduce him to a French duchess, "whose husband," he said, "was commander for the emperor in Hungary." The prospect of such desirable patronage was too much for our guileless hero. Gorgeous visions of splendid military success and advancement sprang from his fervid mind, and gave lustre to his manly eye. At length the vessel arrived in the roads of St.Valery-sur-Somme. Here the pretended nobleman undertook to convey Smith's baggage ashore, and, with the assistance of the captain, who was in league with the robbers, did so in the most effectual manner. It was landed with such safety that poor deluded Smith never saw it again. He was reduced to such straits by this misfortune, that he had to sell his cloak in order to proceed on his journey. One of the passengers on board—a soldier—did all he could to mitigate the annoyance, and even accompanied Smith to Mortain, where the robbers (who resorted to the profession as a kind of elegant diversion) resided. But in those days of tardy justice, the words of an injured foreigner were not listened to with eager attention. The villains escaped. With such funds as he could now command, our hero turned once more toward the sea-coast, and traveled from port to port, with the hope of finding a ship to convey him to his destination. It was not so easy in those days, and his slender means were soon exhausted; weariness, hunger, and heart-sickness overtook him; he dropped from exhaustion, and thought, as you or I would have done, of the gay, glad things at home, which he would never, never see again. Happily, a rich farmer found him as he lay by the road side, and bore him tenderly to his house, where he was properly cared for, and sent on his journey again with renewed vigor.

Shortly after this he came across one of the four villains who had robbed him, and a very quiet and earnest fight immediately ensued. It is to be hoped the poor wretch had said his prayers, for his black soul took flight that day through a convenient aperture made for the purpose by our hero. Smith now traveled through the western and southern provinces of France, visited the kingdoms of Bearne and Navarre, and at length arrived at Marseilles, where he embarked for Italy. The passengers being mostly bigoted Catholics, and Smith, on the other hand, being a tremendous Protestant, fierce disputes immediately ensued, and, when a terrific storm arose, all the black-coated priests declared that it was caused entirely by Smith's presence on board, and so, to put a stop to it, they threw him overboard. Fortunately, he had learned the art of swimming, and managed to buffet his way to the lonely shore of an uninhabited island, where, as good luck would have it, a vessel lay at anchor waiting for the storm to abate. The captain turned out to be a friend of some of Smith's acquaintances, and, when he heard his story, behaved in the most handsome manner. But the captain was afflicted with the moral looseness of the times, and erred on the side of piracy. During the voyage they came across several vessels which they fought and plundered in a perfectly systematic manner. Smith behaved with such gallantry that, when he reached the Roads of Antibes, he found himself the master of a good deal of ready cash—500 zechins, and of a box containing as many more—which, he observes rather brazenly, "God sent him." Feeling now completely at his ease, he made the tour of Italy, and, having gratified his curiosity in that land of romance, started on his way once more, and in due time joined the army of Ferdinand, Arch-duke of Austria, afterward Emperor of Germany. He soon distinguished himself by great personal bravery, and by the exercise of many ingenious military tactics, which caused him to be promoted to the rank of captain. But he appears never to have had what he considered a fair share of fighting, although he took an active part in all the battles, and perforated Paynim bodies with the heartiest of wills and the sharpest of weapons. To satisfy his appetite in this respect, he cheerfully accepted any private invitations to fight. On one occasion, a Turkish officer—desirous, as he said, of amusing the ladies—solicited some Christian officer, of equal rank, to engage with him in a passage of arms before Regal. Lots were cast, and Smith won the privilege. He mounted his war-horse with great glee, and, lance in hand, started for the ground. "The ramparts of Regal," he says, "were lined with ladies, while the Christian host stood in battalions on the plain, to observe the conduct of their own champion." The combat was of short duration. Smith rushed at the Osmanli, and pierced him through the head with his lance, and then descending, cut off the poor fellow's damaged member, and bore it in triumph to his camp. The Osmanlis were not satisfied with this. On the following day they sent a special challenge to Smith, staking the head, horse, and armor of another champion against his prowess. Smith was quite willing to accommodate the Osmanlis. They met, and at the first charge shivered their lances without doing any particular damage. Pistols were then drawn, and finally a hand-to-hand struggle ensued, both grappling fiercely on the ground. When Smith got up, he was the possessor of a bleeding head, a horse, and a suit of armor. Imagining that the Osmanlis might not yet be thoroughly happy in their mind, and anxious to accommodate them in every reasonable way, he now sent a challenge to Regal, expressing his willingness to restore the two heads he had in his possession, provided they would send some one who would make the number three, by adding that of the challenger. A redoubtable Osmanli, of the name of Bonamalgro (at least so Smith calls him), took up the gage thus thrown down, and promised to entertain Smith with pistol, battle-axe, and sword, but not with the lance, of which he appears to have had a wholesome distrust. They met with the proposed conveniences; pistols were discharged without effect, and they began chopping each other with their battle-axes. It was a tough fight, and at one moment, when Smith lost his weapon, appeared to be entirely in the hands of the Turk. A shout was raised from the ramparts of Regal, and in both armies Smith was looked upon as a lost hero. But dexterously avoiding the heavy blow aimed at his skull, and drawing his sword, he soon turned the tables on his adversary, and rolled him in the dust, with a fatal thrust through a vital part. For these brilliant exploits Smith was suitably honored by his comrades, and the general embraced him, and presented him with a horse superbly caparisoned, and a cimeter and belt worth three hundred ducats; he was promoted, also, to the rank of major. In acknowledgment of his services, the Duke of Transylvania gave him permission to wear three Turks' heads quartered on his shield, and swore ever after to bear them in his own colors. In addition to this, he bestowed on him his portrait set in gold, and a pension for life of 300 ducats per year. The coat of arms (with the motto, "Vincere est vivere") was afterward admitted, and recorded in the English College of Heralds.

The good fortune which had tarried with him such an unusual time now took wings. During one of the many engagements in which he had part, he was wounded, and lay stretched on the field of battle to all appearances a corpse. The ghouls who go over the battle-field at night to plunder the dead came across him in this situation, and perceiving, by the elegance and splendor of his armor, that he was a man of distinction, spared his life in the expectation of a heavy ransom. As this did not come, our wounded hero was sold for a slave, and, with many other captives, marched off to Adrianople. We have not space to follow his adventures while in this cruel position; suffice it that he succeeded in getting up a love affair with a lady of quality, for which he was removed to a distant settlement, and subjected to great indignities and hardships by his master, the lady's brother. He put a stop to these in a characteristic way, and made his escape into Southern Russia, on his way back to the field of battle. He was received with great hospitality, and made a sort of triumphal progress through Hungary and Bohemia, until he fell in with his distinguished patron, the Duke Sigismund, who generously bestowed on him 1500 ducats in gold, and a military diploma stating his rank and services. Smith now traveled through Germany, France, and Spain. He then crossed over into Morocco (where there was a little fighting going on), but, finding nothing worthy of his steel, embarked for his native land. On the voyage home the ship was attacked by two Spanish men-of-war, and a desperate fight took place, but it escaped in a very glorious manner, and our hero was once more permitted to tread the greensward of his fatherland.

It is probable that Captain John Smith was a great lion, and that for some time he did nothing but travel from one hospitable board to another. We have no record of his doings. Evidently he looked on the triumphs of peace as unworthy of chronicling. It is only when fresh adventures are afoot that he again appears prominently before the public. About the year 1604 every one was wild with the marvelous discoveries in the Western World. All the gay, roving spirits of the day were eager for an opportunity to cross the Atlantic and participate in the huge gold mines and diamond beds which were supposed to exist there. The mystery which shrouded that distant land was sufficient to captivate the imagination of Captain John Smith. The rest was accomplished by Captain Bartholomew Gosnold, whose acquaintance he had made, and who at this time was on the point of starting for Virginia with a large number of colonists. Smith threw himself into the enterprise with all his accustomed ardor, and any objections that were urged by capitalists to repeating an experiment already unsuccessfully attempted were demolished by his triumphant eloquence. At length every thing was arranged for starting. Letters patent were granted by the king, who, in order to cause as much confusion as his stupid brain could devise, and to exercise a little authority, inclosed a list of the names of the future governors of the colony in a box, the seals of which were not to be broken till the arrival of the whole party in Virginia. On the 19th of December, 1606, the vessel set sail, and, after many adventures and perilous delays, arrived at the mouth of Chesapeake Bay on the 26th of April, 1607. Upon the first land they made they bestowed, in honor of the Prince of Wales, the name of Cape Henry. Here thirty of the colonists disembarked, and, while amusing themselves with local explorations, were set upon by a party of five Indians, who inflicted dangerous wounds on two of their number, and taught them to proceed with greater caution.

King James's mysterious box was duly opened, and they learned that the council—invested with power to elect presidents for a year — was to consist of Bartholomew Gosnold, Captain John Smith, Edward Wingfield, Christopher Newport, John Ratcliffe, John Martin, and George Kendall. Affairs of importance were to be examined by a jury, but determined by the decision of a majority of the council, in which the president had two votes. On the 13th of May following the colonists fixed on a site for their city, and called it Jamestown. The members of the council were duly sworn, and Mr. Wingfield elected the first president. Although Smith was expressly mentioned in the royal charter as one of the council, he was excluded by the other members of that body. It is probable that his talents and popularity were viewed with distrust and jealousy. Whatever the cause, Smith considered it unworthy of notice. The stern work of raising a city in the forest now commenced. The industrial music of the hammer, the anvil, and the saw was heard from morning till night. Smith and Newport, with twenty others, were dispatched to discover the source of the river on the banks of which they had commenced building. They proceeded up the river six days, passing many native villages, until they arrived at the falls. Here they visited the renowned chief Powhatan, with whom they exchanged civilities and promises of friendship. Their farther progress being interrupted by the rapids, they put about and prepared to return home. The behavior of the natives was kind and hospitable until they had got within twenty miles of Jamestown: their conduct then began to excite suspicion. On returning to the colony the reason became apparent. An attack had been made on the town, and, owing to the defenseless state of the place, through the culpable negligence of Governor Wingfield, the natives had gained an advantage, and now evidently looked forward to the total extermination of the whites. Made wiser by experience, the governor now fortified the place, and, a few days after the return of Smith, the savages sued for peace.

The ships which had brought out the colonists soon weighed anchor, and sailed for home, leaving the little band to shift for themselves as best they could. The white streak of their wakes had scarcely disappeared from the waters when a terrible sickness broke out among the settlers, so that very few could walk or stand. Scarcity of provisions contributed largely to the sufferings of the poor creatures. The common food was scarcely fit for human beings to eat, and the rations were much too scanty. To add to their troubles and heighten the horrors of famine, it was discovered that the governor was a greedy hog, and had laid up stores of nice things for himself, while his poor companions were starving and rotting around him. One half of the colonists died in this miserable way, and the remainder, like sensible men, deposed the bad governor, and elected Captain John Ratcliffe in his stead. Nothing could be more desperate than the condition of the small garrison. Their provisions were exhausted; the fisheries yielded but a small and uncertain supply, and they were in momentary expectation of an attack from the hostile Indians in the vicinity. The latter apprehension, however, was soon removed, for the savages took pity on their wretchedness, and, instead of attacking, actually brought them liberal supplies of fruits, vegetables, and game. The new governor, however, did not turn out much better than his predecessor. He lacked the force of character and strength of judgment essential to such a crisis. Smith was pre-eminently endowed with these qualities, and it was but natural, therefore, that the harassed and desponding settlers should look to him as their only hope. He commenced setting things to rights with characteristic energy. By his own industry he stimulated the industry of others, and by pointing out what had to be done in a quiet, solicitous way, he got it done expeditiously and well. In a short time he had procured lodgings for every one but himself. The most knotty question to be solved was how to procure provisions sufficient to hold out until the harvesting time came round again. He determined to go on a trading excursion, and endeavor to procure a supply from the Indians. Accordingly, he fitted out the shallop, manned it with all the spare hands he could muster, and dropped down the river. The natives were well informed of the abject state of the settlement, and, when Smith spoke about barter, they only laughed at him, evidently rejoiced at the prospect of a speedy destruction of the whites. Smith was not the right kind of person to laugh at with impunity, and the moment he found that all fair means were of no avail, he changed his tactics. The word was given to fire, and then, suddenly running the boat ashore, the natives were so frightened and astonished that they scampered away in all directions. This was precisely what Smith wanted. Without a moment's delay, he marched straight into their village, and discovered plentiful heaps of corn. His companions wanted to help themselves without any kind of parleying, but Smith, who looked to the future as well as the present, would not consent to the pillage. Presently the Indians, to the number of sixty or seventy, painted all sorts of colors, and bearing in front their most redoubtable idol, returned to the spot, and boldly attacked the English. A discharge of musketry soon taught the poor wretches that their idol was of no avail against the white man's gunpowder. A number lay stretched upon the ground, and the remainder hastily retreated, leaving their false god behind them. Shortly afterward they sent a priest to treat with the victors for the restoration of the idol. Smith told them that, if six of the tribe would come unarmed, and aid him in loading his boat, he would not only restore to them their *okee*, or idol, but make them large presents besides of beads, copper, and hatchets. This was agreed to, and the natives soon returned, bringing with them venison, common fowls, turkeys, and bread.

The success of this first expedition led to several others, in all of which Smith's tact, decision, and firmness were eminent. But he labored for an improvident set of fellows, who were much too willing to depend on his trading voyages, rather than work for their own daily bread. Indeed, when we reflect on the many vexations that their idleness must have caused our hero, we are forced to admire the estimable generosity which actuated him in not only working, but exposing himself to danger for their maintenance. One would certainly think that such a capital fellow could have no enemies; but he had, and mean ones too. Foremost among these were Wingfield and Kendall, who had been living in disgrace, and watching the growth of Smith's popularity with jealous spite. They took advantage of his absence on one occasion to conspire with some disorderly malcontents and escape to England in the bark, which, by Smith's direction, had been fitted up for a trading voyage, to be undertaken the next year. They had already, in part, executed their design when Smith returned, for they were actually on board, and the pinnace was preparing to descend the stream. Smith brought them to in prompt style. He assembled his men on the beach, invited the deserters to return to their duty, and, when they refused, gave them a volley as a persuader. A brisk action ensued, and it was only when Kendall had fallen that the others surrendered.

It was Smith's misfortune shortly after this to fall into the hands of the Indians. They set upon him unexpectedly, and, before he had time to protect himself, wounded him in the thigh with an arrow. Notwithstanding this impediment, he made a gallant resistance, and would have escaped from their clutches but for another accident. In retreating with his face to the foe, he backed into a morass, and stuck fast up to the waist in peat. None of the Indians dared approach him, even in that helpless position, and it was only when he was half dead with cold and had thrown away his arms that they drew him out. He was, of course, conducted to the chief of the tribe, and, having been condemned to death, was tied to a tree for immediate execution. Without losing the slightest particle of his customary self-possession, he pulled out a small pocket compass which he happened to have with him, and presented the instrument to the chief, accompanied with a speech, which, as it might be his last, he did not strive to make particularly short. In return for this, the chief released him from the tree, but sent him a prisoner to one of the villages. He was to be reserved for a more epicurean death: they intended to get him into fine condition, and then eat him; at least so poor Smith imagined, from the profusion of food with which he was supplied. He was kept in suspense for a long time, but at last, when tolerably plump, they conducted him to the residence of the famed Powhatan, who received him with imposing ceremony, "seated on a kind of throne, elevated above the floor of a large hut, in the midst of which was a fire. He (Powhatan) was clothed with a robe of raccoon skins. Two young women, his daughters, sat one on his right and the other on his left, and on each side of the hut there were two rows of men in front, and the same number of women behind. When Smith was brought home, they all set up a great shout." Smith was indulged with another feast in the palace of this dusky monarch, but, considering the mysterious preparations that were going on, it is scarcely probable that he had a very hearty appetite. It became certain that his fate was now to be decided, and equally certain that the decision was against him. The fatal preliminaries were soon arranged. A couple of ominous-looking stones were brought in, and placed before Powhatan. Upon one of these unpleasant pillows Smith was compelled to lay his head. Rascally-looking chiefs then approached with heavy clubs raised in the air, ready to dash out his brains at the word of command. At this moment Pocahontas, the favorite daughter of the great chief, interceded for the prostrate prisoner, and begged piteously for his life. Finding that Powhatan was inexorable, she determined, with true Indian fortitude, to perish herself, rather than give up her point. She rushed to the stone, placed her own pretty head upon that of the prisoner, and told them that they should kill her before they touched him. Moved by this scene, Powhatan, her father, granted Smith his pardon, and shortly afterward agreed that he should be sent to Jamestown, provided he would give them two great guns and a grindstone by way of ransom. The chief was ready to bestow on him a large tract of country, and to regard him as his son, immediately on receipt of these valuable articles.

After this romantic incident Smith got on very well with the Indians, and was able to procure constant supplies of provisions. Pocahontas, his beautiful protectress, paid frequent visits to the settlement, and on several occasions, when little difficulties appeared to be growing up between the king and the settlers, her gentle intercession brushed away the angry clouds and restored quiet.

The hungry fellows of the colony had to be fed by hand, like so many ravens, and, as the ships from the Old Country did not come in with great regularity, they were often reduced to great straits. The subject of our memoir was their sole dependence. At the proper moment he fitted out the boat, and sailed away into the interior in search of provisions, never coming back empty-handed. In one of these expeditions he discovered the Bay of Chesapeake, and afterward explored it minutely, and constructed a map, which was wonderfully accurate, all things considered. Wherever he went he was respected and feared by the natives, but, on the other hand, the moment his back was turned, the colonists began scheming and quarreling, and making their wretched lives still more miserable. The only creditable thing they did, by way of atonement, was to elect Captain John Smith their president, in place of Ratcliffe, who, like his predecessor, turned out an idle, greedy fellow. But even this they afterward repented, for Smith, knowing that safety and abundance depended entirely on their own exertions, set them all to work, some to collect pitch, tar, and soap-ashes, and others to hew timber in the woods. They who were discontented, says the quaint historian, drowned the noise of every third blow by a curse, which induced the president to make a rule against swearing. Every man's oaths uttered during the day were to be counted, and for each offense he was to have a gallon of water poured down his sleeve. So effectual was this punishment, that scarcely a profane expression was heard in a week. Notwithstanding all his protestations, constant watchfulness had to be exercised toward Powhatan, who was treacherous, and disposed to be revenged on the whites whenever the opportunity occurred. The readiest way of doing this was to starve them out. Experience had taught him that they were improvident, and always in need of corn. He issued orders that none should be supplied. Every kind of persuasion was used in vain, until at length Captain Smith determined that he should be brought to reason in a summary way. Accordingly, with forty-six men in the pinnace and two barges, he set out to meet the wily chief. Every where they heard warnings of Powhatan's treachery, but they went on their way, and, when they came to his village, sent him a friendly message. He came in no pleasant mood; told them that they were uninvited; that his subjects had no corn, and that he could give only forty baskets of grain in exchange for forty swords. In the end, a collision took place between the English and the Indians. The latter endeavored to cut off the former by surprise, and were only prevented by the faithful conduct of the beautiful Pocahontas, who came and warned them of their danger. From Powhatan Smith proceeded to another Indian town, where the chief conceived a cunning plot to murder the party. Being in one of the native houses, Smith saw a great concourse of savages without, and their chief near the door, asking him to come forth and receive a present. Such an ambush was a trifle too playful for the keen military eye of Smith, and, instead of popping into it, he desired his companions to keep careful watch on all the entrances. Then, seizing his opportunity, he darted out, caught the old chief by the beard, leveled a pistol at his breast, and led him trembling into the midst of his assembled tribe. This daring act struck terror into the whole multitude. They gave up their leader's arms, and cast down their own; while Smith, still holding his captive by the hair, addressed him in a speech, half of conciliation, half of threats, which had the desired result, for a quantity of provisions were brought, and all parties returned to their homes in apparent amity.

We have not the space to follow Smith in all his bold adventures, although they are eminently interesting, and characterized by the noble bearing, courage, and disinterestedness of his chivalric nature. It must suffice that under his rule the colony became as prosperous as it was possible for it to become with such a strange population of worthless, ill-tempered, idle fellows. Quantities of tar, pitch, and soap ashes were collected; a successful experiment was made in the manufacture of glass; twenty new houses were built, with a more convenient church; and nets for fishing were manufactured. To defend themselves, the colonists also erected two or three wooden forts, or block-houses, and, to provide for the next year, planted nearly forty acres with vegetables and grain. Altogether the prospects were cheering to every one except the London speculators, who, not having received large cargoes of virgin gold or bags full of precious stones, were greatly dissatisfied with the way things had been managed. To such an extent did they carry their dissatisfaction, that in 1609 they obtained a new charter from the king, annulling the former one. Immediately afterward they dispatched nine ships, with 500 emigrants, to take possession of the colony, and regulate it according to the latest system of colonial wisdom. When the proper officers had arrived, Smith made preparations to return to England. The magnanimity of his character was illustrated in the cheerful assistance he rendered to his successors, many of whom were pigheaded and insolent, and very jealous of Smith's popularity. Those poor creatures who had worked and suffered in the colony were very sorry when they heard that their brave president was about to leave them, and they tried all they could to get him to stay; but Smith suffered severely from an accident he had met with, occasioned by the explosion of a bag of gunpowder, and felt sure that if he did not go back and get good medical advice he would infallibly die. So Captain John Smith, after a wonderfully active and wonderfully troubled career of more than two years, took his departure for the land of his fathers. Immediately afterward the colony sunk into a state of great confusion; "large parties were cut off by the savages; a division of authority produced entire disorganization; improvidence wasted the stores which had been accumulated, and the settlers fell into the last stage of abasement and misery. Within six months after the loss of their virtuous president, the number at Jamestown was not more than sixty, including women and children. They had to feed on roots, herbs, acorns, walnuts, and berries, with now and then a scanty supply of fish. They ate their starch, and at last even the skins of their horses. 'Nay, so great,' says the narrator, 'was our famine, that a salvage we slew and buried, the poorer sort took him up again and ate him, and so did divers one another, boyled and stewed with roots and herbs. And one among the rest did kill his wife, powdered her, and had eaten part of her before it was known, for which he was executed, as he well deserved. Now, whether she was better roasted, boyled, or carbonadoed, I know not; but of such a dish as powdered wife I never heard.'" Their miseries were fortunately terminated by the arrival of Sir Thomas Gates and Sir George Somers, with 150 men and a quantity of provisions.

We hear nothing of Captain John Smith for several years after his return to England. It is certain that he was much sought after by the lion-hunters, and that he became very famous for his strange adventures. It is also certain that some of the incidents of his strange life were worked into a dramatic form, and represented at the theatres, much to the annoyance of our hero. In 1614 we find him once more embarked for the New World, but not for Virginia. This time his enterprising spirit sought new laurels in the cold and barren ground of New England. There were two ships in the expedition, one commanded by himself, and the other by Captain Thomas Hunt. On the 30th of April they arrived at the coast of Maine, and immediately commenced looking for mines of gold. As they did not succeed in their search, they turned their attention to the next most improbable product of the country, and went about in boats to capture whales. Finally they abandoned both pursuits, and devoted their attention to the catching and curing of codfish. While the crew were thus employed, Captain Smith, with eight men in a small boat, surveyed and examined the whole coast from Penobscot to Cape Cod, trafficking with the Indians for furs, and twice fighting with them. He constructed a map of the country, and, after six months' absence, once more returned to England. In the following year our restless hero embarked once more for the Western World, but, when about a hundred and twenty leagues from port, he encountered a violent storm, which so shattered his vessel that he had to return and procure another one. On the 24th of June,

1615, he started once more in a small bark of sixty tons, manned by thirty men, and carrying with him sixteen settlers. Soon after his departure he was chased by an English pirate, but succeeded in getting away on friendly terms. Near Fayal he came across two French pirates. His crew were panic-stricken, and wanted him to surrender; but he scorned the idea, and told them that he would rather blow up the ship than yield while he had any powder left. So he blazed away with his four little guns, and contrived to make his escape. Near Flores he was chased, and, sad to say, overtaken by four French men-of-war. For some strange reason Smith was kidnapped, and kept on board the French frigate while she cruised about snapping up prizes. In the mean time the crew of his own vessel put about, and returned to the port whence they came. Smith had no opportunity of making his escape until one stormy night, while the vessel of his captors was lying at anchor in the harbor of Rochelle. When it was quite dark he dropped into a boat, and with the fragment of a handspike in place of oars, floated away on the fierce waters. A strong current carried him out to sea, and all night he was rocked about in one of the most fearful tempests that had been known on that coast for many years. A kind and watchful Providence surely shielded him on that sad night, for, when he was carried in by the morning tide, he discovered that the French ship from which he had escaped had been wrecked, and the captain and half the crew drowned; yet his poor little cockle-shell outlived the fury of the elements! On landing at Rochelle he lodged a complaint with the judge of the Admiralty, but without any satisfactory result. Shortly afterward he returned to England, and in 1616 published the narrative of his two voyages to New England, which he had written, in a great measure, while a prisoner on board the French vessel. Although he made many efforts to return to the country in which he was so deeply interested, and which owed all its prosperity to his presence, and all its misfortunes to his absence, he was never able to do so. As a speculation, the New World had been ruinous to the capitalists who embarked in it, and there was no disposition to risk more. The remainder of his life was therefore passed in England, but in what way we know not. Mr. Hillard, in his Memoir, says, "The death of Captain Smith occurred in 1631, at London, in the fifty-second year of his age. We know nothing of the circumstances which attended it, and we are equally ignorant of his domestic and personal history, with whom he was related and connected, where he resided, what was the amount of his fortune, what were his habits, tastes, personal appearance, manners, and conversation, and, in general, of those personal details which modest men commonly do not record about themselves. From the fact that he expended so much money in the great objects of his life, and particularly in the publication and distribution of his pamphlets, we may infer that he was independent in his circumstances, if not wealthy. For his labors and sacrifices he never received any pecuniary recompense. In a statement addressed to his majesty's commissioners for the reformation of Virginia, and written, probably, about 1624, he says that he has spent five years, and more than five hundred pounds, in the service of Virginia and New England; 'yet,' he adds, 'in neither of those countries have I one foot of land, nor the very house I builded, nor the ground I digged with my own hands, nor ever any content or satisfaction at all, and though I see ordinarily those two countries shared before me by them that neither have them, nor know them but by my descriptions.' "

JAMES BRINDLEY.

To this individual the world is indebted for one of its most valuable and economical means of internal communication. James Brindley, a self-made man, was the founder of canal navigation. The first undertaking of the kind was projected in 1759, under the patronage of the Duke of Bridgewater, and the subject of this memoir was the man by whose talents the scheme was carried into execution.

James Brindley was born in 1716 at Tunstead, or at Thornsett, in Derbyshire. His father was a spendthrift, who cared more for his own enjoyment than for the prosperity of his family. Consequently, Brindley was denied the advantages of an education, and at an early age had to obtain employment on the neighboring farms. When he was seventeen he apprenticed himself to a millwright, and soon displayed so much expertness that he was frequently left for whole weeks to execute works concerning which he had received no instruction from his master. His mechanical ingenuity was great, and when he experienced a difficulty, his inventive genius assisted him to get out of it. In every thing he undertook, he displayed so much ready skill that the millers considered it a favor to obtain his services in preference to those of his master.

In due time he set up for himself as a millwright, and by his ingenious inventions and contrivances acquired a widely-spread reputation, extending even to the metropolis. He was employed in the construction of the most complicated machinery, and seldom undertook a task of the kind without introducing some important improvements of his own.

From pursuits of this kind Brindley was called away to others of much greater importance. The Duke of Bridgewater was owner of an estate at Worsley, about seven miles from Manchester, beneath the soil of which were immense mines of coal, from which no profit accrued to him, because the cost of land-carriage was so heavy that it prevented the coal from being brought into the market. To remedy this evil, the duke obtained acts of Parliament (1758–9) enabling him to form a navigable canal from Worsley to Manchester. Brindley's reputation had reached the duke's ears, and he selected him as a fitting person to carry out his scheme. The enterprise was one of remarkable difficulty, and had to be prosecuted in the face of prejudice and sneers. To avoid the waste of water which the lockage would occasion, the canal was to be on a dead level, and, to effect this, tunnels must be perforated, enormous embankments raised, and an aqueduct of three arches thrown over the navigable river Irwell, at an elevation of little less than fifty feet. The audacity of this last idea—carrying water over water—exposed Brindley to so much ridicule, that for a moment he lost confidence in himself, and begged the duke to consult some other engineer, and convince himself that he was not insane. A learned man was accordingly sent for, and the matter proposed to him. He ridiculed the idea, and, when the height and dimensions were communicated to him, exclaimed, "I have often heard of castles in the air, but never before was shown where any of them were to be erected." Such a self-sufficient ignoramus was properly estimated by the duke; he disregarded his opinion, and directed Brindley to proceed. The Worsley canal was soon in successful operation; the impossible aqueduct was begun and completed in twelve months.

This triumphant demonstration was the making of Brindley as an engineer, and at no distant period turned the attention of the public to the subject of opening water communication with various parts of the kingdom. The Duke of Bridgewater immediately determined to continue his canal to the tideway of the Mersey, at

Runcorn, so as to connect Liverpool and Manchester by water in a thoroughly practical way. The distance to be accomplished was thirty miles, and there were two rivers and many deep and wide valleys to be crossed, the one by aqueducts, the other by broad and lofty embankments. Notwithstanding these obstacles, the undertaking was completed in five years. There were but ten locks on the whole line, and these were constructed on such easy principles that they could be worked with little or no delay. The next in order to the Bridgewater canals was that which the proprietors designed to call the Trent and Mersey Canal, but to which Brindley gave the name of the Grand Trunk, because he was convinced that many branches would be extended from it, as was subsequently the case. This work was ninety-three miles in length, united the ports of Hull and Liverpool, and required seventy-six locks, three aqueducts, and five tunnels to carry it through the route. Here was an opportunity for the display of the highest engineering skill, and Brindley availed himself of it with avidity. An eminence called Harecastle Hill was considered the great obstacle of the line. Brindley made up his mind that it should be tunneled, and, notwithstanding innumerable difficulties, arising from the nature of the soil, succeeded in boring the hill at the distance of seventy yards from the surface. The tunnel is more than a mile and a half long.

Now that the entire practicability of canal navigation had been fully established, Brindley found himself overwhelmed with business. His enthusiasm led him to undertake more than he could well attend to without encroaching on his constitution. He was destined to fall a martyr to the cause in which he was engaged. For some years previous to his death he suffered constantly from intermittent fever, aggravated, of course, by frequent exposure to moist, unwholesome atmospheres. His system became completely worn out, and on the 27th of September, 1772, he died, in the fifty-sixth year of his age.

The character of Brindley was quiet, modest, and unassuming. Devoted entirely to his occupations, and accustomed to find every resource within himself, he did not cultivate society, or feel much at home in it. His appearance was rather against him than otherwise, being boorish and provincial; but his conversation is described as pleasing, and strongly colored with the warm imagination of a man who would not see an impossibility. During the latter years of his life, his whole soul was absorbed in speculations respecting canals; he meditated on them not only by day, but dreamed of them by night. Most of his schemes were remarkable for their vastness and practicability, but, in common with other ingenious men, he had his wild dreams of the impracticable. To this order belonged his scheme for uniting Ireland to England by means of a navigable canal. He had such faith in aqueducts that he believed even the sea might be spanned by them. A funny circumstance is recorded concerning the fixity of his ideas on these subjects. While he was under examination before a committee of the House of Commons, he spoke so slightingly of rivers that a member asked him for what purpose he supposed them to have been created. "To feed navigable canals," replied Brindley. Once, and but once in his life, he saw a play. It happened while he was in London, and for several days afterward he complained that it had confused his ideas and unfitted him for business. So strong and disagreeable was the effect produced, that he declared nothing on earth should ever induce him to see another play.

When any extraordinary difficulty occurred to Mr. Brindley in the execution of his works, having little or no assistance from books, or the labors of other men, his resources lay within himself. In order, therefore, to be quiet and uninterrupted while he was in search of the necessary expedients, he generally retired to his bed; and he has been known to lie there one, two, or three days, till he had attained the object in view. He would then get up, and execute his design without any drawing or model. Indeed, it never was his custom to make either, unless he was obliged to do it to satisfy his employers. His memory was so remarkable, that he often declared he could remember and execute all the parts of the most complex machine, provided he had time, in his survey of it, to settle in his mind the several departments, and their relations to each other. His method of calculating the powers of any machine invented by him was peculiar to himself. He worked the question for some time in his head, and then put down the results in figures. After this, taking it up again in this stage, he worked it further in his mind for a certain time, and set down the results as before. In the same way he still proceeded, making use of figures only at stated periods of the question. Yet the ultimate result was generally true, though the road he traveled in search of it was unknown to any one but himself; and perhaps it would not have been in his power to have shown it to another.

THOMAS HOLCROFT

was the son of a shoemaker, and was born in London on the 10th of December, 1745. The paternal Holcroft was, in many respects, a remarkable character. He possessed a passion for making experiments in all sorts of businesses; he dealt in greens and oysters as well as shoes, and, finding that this was not sufficient, he added the undignified calling of horse-dealer. For this latter business he conceived a strong affection, which manifested itself in an ardent desire to teach Master Thomas to ride. When the latter was very young, his father discarded his petticoats, and placed him in pantaloons, in order that he might straddle a horse in the proper way. One accomplishment led to another. The elder Holcroft conceived a fresh notion that his son was a great musical genius, and immediately placed him under the tuition of a violin player. What progress he made in the instrument is unknown, but he says himself that at the age of seven he had wholly forgotten all he had learned.

About this time a change took place in his father's circumstances, and he left London in great embarrassment. The family removed to Berkshire, where Thomas obtained a small amount of schooling. This was the most remarkable era in his life, and he notes it with enthusiasm. He made such rapid progress, and gave such extraordinary evidence of a remarkable memory, that his father was completely astonished, and made him a show-child. He imposed heavy tasks on him too, and set him eleven chapters of the Bible to learn every day. A neighboring farmer caught the youth with his Bible in his hand, and asked him if he could read already. Holcroft answered yes, began at the place where the book was open, read fluently, and afterward told him that, if he pleased, he should hear the tenth chapter of Nehemiah. At this the farmer seemed still more amazed, and, wishing to be convinced, bade him read. After listening till he found he could really pronounce the uncouth Hebrew names so much better and more easily than he supposed to be within the power of so young a child, he patted his head, gave him a penny, and said he was an uncommon boy. "It would be hard to say," writes Holcroft, "whether his praise or his gift was the most flattering to me."

After a short residence in Berkshire, Holcroft's family led a wandering sort of life, and eventually settled once more in London, in very straitened circumstances. So poor were they, indeed, that Mrs. Holcroft had to turn peddler, and vended pins, needles, tape, etc., through the streets, accompanied by her son, who trotted after her. Notwithstanding these exertions, it seemed impossible to make a living in the metropolis, and the family started on a peddling tour through the provinces. They came at length to a village which Holcroft thought remarkably clean, and which Mr. Holcroft pronounced to be the handsomest in the kingdom. "We must have been very poor at this time," says the author, "for it was here that I was sent one day by myself to beg from house to house. Young as I was, I had considerable readiness in making out a story, and on this day my little inventive faculties shone forth with much brilliancy. I told one story at one house, and another at another, and continued to vary my tale just as the suggestions arose. The consequence was, I moved the good people exceedingly. One called me a poor fatherless child; another exclaimed, 'What a pity! I had so much sense;' a third patted me on the head, and prayed God to bless me, that I might make a good man. The result of this expedition was that I brought away as much as I could carry to the place of rendezvous appointed by my parents. There I astonished them by again reciting the false tales I had so readily invented. My father seemed greatly alarmed, and, fearing that I was in danger of growing up a liar and a vagrant, declared I should never go on such errands again." It was fortunate for Holcroft that he had such a father. Indeed, this parent, although eccentric in the extreme, and of decidedly vagrant habits, was a good man, and at all times and in all places made his son repeat his prayers and catechism morning and night, and on Sundays read the prayer-book and Bible. He was fond of exercising his son's memory. On one occasion, a copy of the celebrated ballad, "Chevy Chase," came into his possession. "Well, Tom, can you get that song by heart?" he asked. The boy replied yes, and was then promised a bribe of a halfpenny if he committed it in three days. The task was performed (like many others of a similar kind), and Tom became a wealthy man in his own estimation.

The next business in which we find Mr. Holcroft was that of carrier. He procured two or three asses, and Tom was set to drive them from place to place. In this employment he suffered many hardships and privations. The bad nourishment he met with, the cold and wretched manner in which he was clothed, and the excessive weariness he endured in following the animals day after day, and being obliged to drive creatures perhaps still more weary than himself, were miseries much too great for his little heart, and filled it with sorrows which he remembered poignantly years and years afterward. At times he had to travel great distances on foot, and in one instance walked thirty miles. When near the end of this wearisome journey, his little legs refused to carry him farther, and a kind countryman picked him up and carried him to his destination.

When he was about twelve years of age he obtained a situation as stable-boy at Newmarket, and entered on what he calls "a new existence." Being new to the trade, a good many tricks were played off on him. "I do not recollect one half of the tricks that are played off upon new-comers," he writes, "but that with which they begin, if I do not mistake, is to persuade their victim that the first thing necessary for a well-trained stable-boy is to borrow as many vests as he can, and in the morning, after he has dressed and fed his horse, to put them all on, take a race of two or three miles, return home, strip himself stark naked, and immediately be covered up in a warm dunghill, which is the method, they assure him, which the grooms take when they sweat themselves down to ride a race. Should the poor fellow follow these directions, they conclude the joke with pails full of cold water, which stand ready for the purpose of cooling off. Another of their diversions used to be that of hunting the owl. To hunt the owl is to persuade a booby that there is an owl found at roost in a corner of the farm; that a ladder must be placed against a hole, through which, when the persons shall be pleased to hoot and hunt him, as they call it, he must necessarily fly, as the door is shut, and every other outlet closed; that the boy selected to catch the owl must mount the ladder on the outside, and the purblind animal, they say, will fly directly into his hat. The poor candidate for sport mounts to his place, thoughtless of any thing but fun. The chaps within, laughing and shouting, pretend to drive the ill-starred bird nearer and nearer to the hole, when all at once they discharge the contents of pails and tubs upon the devoted head of the expecting owl-catcher, who is generally precipitated in fright and terror from the ladder into some soft, but not very agreeable preparation below." Against these traps for the unwary young Holcroft received timely warning, and averted their dire effects. He remained in this employment for upward of three years. The life of a stable-boy in a sporting town is not calculated to develop any latent literary ability that he may happen to possess, but young Holcroft found time to read a few books. Swift and Addison afforded him much delight, and books of piety, if the author were but inspired with zeal, fixed his attention wherever he met with them. John Bunyan he ranked among the most divine authors he had ever read. He contrived to improve his education too, and out of his scanty income (four pounds a year) paid five shillings a quarter for singing lessons, and five shillings a quarter for instruction in arithmetic. The former he practiced in a hayloft, the latter he studied with an old nail and the back of the stable door.

In the mean time Mr. Holcroft had established himself in London, and was once more at work in his cobbler's stall. Tom made up his mind to abandon stable-life and repair to the metropolis. He despised his companions for the grossness of their ideas, and the total absence of every pursuit in which the mind had any share. The little knowledge he possessed exposed him to their ridicule: this he could avoid in the quiet shop of his father. He carried out his idea; arrived in London, learned his father's business, and became an expert workman. He could command the highest wages, but did not become rich. Every penny he could spare was spent in the purchase of books, and a great deal of time was consumed in mastering their contents.

In 1765 Mr. Holcroft married, and soon after opened a school for teaching children to read in Liverpool. Not being successful in this undertaking, he abandoned it, and returned to London. Once more he resumed the shoemaking business; but its sedentary nature injured his health, and brought on a return of his old enemy, asthma, a complaint with which he had been troubled from youth. He was compelled to quit the bench, and seek other and more congenial employment. With this object in view, he repeated his Liverpool experiment and opened a school, but with no better luck. After living three months on potatoes and buttermilk, and having only one scholar, he discontinued his labors. About this time he commenced his literary career. A few essays from his pen found their way into the Evening Post, and the editor paid him for them at the rate of five shillings a column; not a large remuneration, but grateful to the feelings and welcome to the pocket of the young author. His means were now at their lowest ebb, and he was compelled to take a situation in the family of Granville Sharpe. He did not retain this long, for his habits were not the habits of a servant. Thrown out of employment, and reduced to a state of the extremest poverty, he was on the point of embarking for British India as a common soldier in the ranks of the Indian army, when a friend persuaded him to join a band of strolling players. With this company he traversed Ireland, where he first appeared on the stage, and every part of England. His success was not extraordinary, and, as a general thing, he received more censure than praise; but, for want of better employment, he continued in the profession for seven or eight years, suffering much misery, and at times almost reduced to a state of starvation. Only one advantage accrued from his connection with the players: he was able to prosecute a successful course of reading, and make himself extensively acquainted with English literature. What was of immediate advantage to him was the acquaintance he succeeded in forming with Garrick, the famous actor, and Mrs. Siddons. With such associations, his thoughts naturally took one direction. He became ambitious to write for the stage. Some early compositions, of little merit, were favorably received, and he persevered. A farce, called the "Crisis," achieved a decided success, and from this time he continued to apply himself unceasingly to literary pursuits. He became eminent as a dramatist, and wrote extensively for the booksellers. In the interest of the latter he went to France, and made several translations of works which he selected for the purpose. His knowledge of the French language and of German, howsoever picked up, was perfect. Among the important works which he translated were the writings of Frederick the Great, in twelve large volumes, and the curious and entertaining works of Lavater, the celebrated physiognomist of Germany. His contributions to the stage were numerous, and one work in particular, "The Road to Ruin," carried his fame to all corners of the world where the English language was spoken. It is a favorite with American audiences to the present day, and is a commendable work in every respect.

During his stay in France Mr. Holcroft imbibed much of the liberalism of the day, and when he returned to England became an active reformer. He wrote much for the people, and contributed largely to the alarm of the government—an alarm which resulted in the suspension of the *Habeas Corpus* Act (1794). Informations were filed against Holcroft and eleven of his associates, and they were seized and committed to the Tower to await their trial on a charge of high treason. In October the trials came on at the Old Bailey. The day had arrived when the great question whether the people were to have any share in the government, even to speak against its abuse or in favor of its reform, was to be decided. Thomas Hardy, a celebrated English democrat, was the first placed in the dock. Mr. Erskine was his counsel, and for seven hours he harangued the jury with matchless eloquence. "I claim no merit with the prisoner for my zeal," he said, in his peroration; "it proceeds from a selfish principle inherent in the human heart. I am counsel, gentlemen, for myself. In every word I utter, I feel that I am pleading for the safety of my own life, for the lives of my children after me, for the happiness of my country, and for the universal condition of civil society throughout the world." Excitement was at its height, and the crown yielded. The prisoners were ordered to be set at liberty; "the acclamations of the Old Bailey reverberated from the farthest shores of Scotland, and a whole people felt the enthusiastic transports of recovered freedom." Holcroft continued his efforts in the cause of constitutional reform without farther molestation.

The remainder of Holcroft's life was passed in arduous literary labor. He visited Hamburg and Paris, where he made researches in various departments of letters. In the latter capital he remained about two years, and subsequently published an elaborate work concerning it, which enjoys a high position in literature. He was methodical and industrious, and accomplished great tasks with ease and completeness. His mental activity was extraordinary—so excessive, at times, that it interfered with his general health; but his intellect remained unimpaired to the last, and he died in March, 1804, in his sixty-ninth year. The life of Thomas Holcroft is calculated (we quote his own words) "to excite an ardent emulation in the breasts of youthful readers, by showing them how difficulties may be endured, how they may be overcome, and how they may at last contribute, as a school of instruction, to bring forth hidden talent."

ROBERT BLOOMFIELD,

who has been described as the "most spiritual shoemaker that ever handled an awl," was born in the county of Suffolk, England, in the year of freedom, 1776. His parents were in extremely poor circumstances, and at an early age his father died. To provide the means of support for herself and children, Mrs. Bloomfield opened a small school in the village, and it was under her roof that Robert gained most of the knowledge he possessed. For a few months he went to an academy of a better kind, but a single quarter was probably the extent of his course.

When Robert was eleven years of age he went to live with his uncle, Mr. Austin, a reputable farmer, who treated him kindly, but paid him no wages. His mother supplied him with clothes so long as she was able, but was at length compelled to look to two elder sons, who were shoemakers in London, to assist her. She accordingly wrote to them upon the subject, and it was at length resolved that Robert should go to London, where one brother promised to initiate him into the mysteries of St. Crispin, and the other to clothe and support him until he was able to gain his own living. The mother was pleased with this arrangement, and made a pilgrimage to great smoky London in order to place her darling boy in the custody of his elder brothers. She charged them, as they valued a mother's blessing, to set good examples for him, and "never to forget that he had lost his father."

The brothers were in humble circumstances, and lodged and labored in a little garret, which served them for every purpose. "As we were all single men lodgers at a shilling per week, our beds were coarse, and all things far from being clean and snug, like what Robert had been accustomed to at home. Robert was our man to fetch all things to hand. At noon he brought our dinners from the cook-shop, and any one of our fellow-workmen that wanted to have any thing brought in would send Robert, and assist in his work, and teach him, as a recompense for his trouble. Every day, when the boy from the public house came for the pewter pots, and to learn what porter was wanted, he always brought the yesterday's newspaper. The reading of this newspaper we had been used to take by turns, but, after Robert came, he mostly read for us, because his time was of the least value." The task was an agreeable one, but not unattended with difficulty. The little fellow tumbled across words which he had never read before, and which bothered him immensely. His brother George took compassion on his perplexity, and bought a Dictionary, for which he paid the enormous sum of fourpence. Robert soon became master of its contents, and was able to read the newspaper without impediment. He was considered so good that the workmen got books for him to read to them. "I, at this time," says George Bloomfield, "read the *London Magazine*, and in that work about two sheets were set apart for a review. Robert seemed always eager to read this review. Here he could see what the literary men were doing, and learn how to judge of the merits of the works which came out, and I observed that he always looked at the Poet's Corner. One day he repeated a long song which he had composed to an old tune. I was much surprised that he should make such smooth verses, so I persuaded him to try whether the editor of our paper would give them a place in the Poet's Corner. He succeeded, and they were printed." After this success he contributed a number of pieces to the same magazine, and felt all the exaltation which a young author may be expected to experience under such circumstances. His mind seemed to act with redoubled activity, and his powers increased with every fresh effort, as the true literary mind is sure to do.

Shortly after this Robert changed his lodgings, and was thrown into the society of a man of the name of Kay, who, being a reader himself, possessed several books, among which were "The Seasons," "Paradise Lost," and some novels. The first was Robert's especial delight, and he perused and reperused it until he had it nearly by heart. It was to this work that he was indebted for his idea of the "Farmer's Boy," a poem to which Bloomfield owes his reputation. In his eighteenth year he paid a visit to his native place, and the tutored eye of the poet discovered new beauties in the scenes which had surrounded him from youth, and which came back to him with a freshness and vigor indescribable. He returned to London, and subsided for a while into his usual occupations. He made an arrangement with the landlord of his brothers, who was also a shoemaker, and became his apprentice. Not only did he apply himself diligently to the duties of his station, but with some enthusiasm. He became an excellent workman, and worked hard for many years. His amusements were reading, music, and the composition of verses.

Being now in a position to marry, he selected an appropriate helpmate and removed to Coleman Street, where, in the garret, he followed his trade, as one among many journeymen. There, amid the din of hammers and voices, the noise and confusion of thoughtless men, the jokes and sneers of the illiterate, Robert Bloomfield composed his great poem, the "Farmer's Boy." Having no facilities for writing, he composed and remembered about six hundred lines before he put a single word to paper. At length the manuscript was finished, and the author, palpitating with anxiety, commenced his tour of the publishers, but no one would undertake its publication. The obscurity of the author and the length of the poem alike contributed to this result. The editor of the "Monthly Magazine" gives the following account of Robert's visit to his office: "He brought his poem to our office, and, though his unpolished appearance, his coarse handwriting, and wretched orthography afforded no prospect that his production could be printed, yet he found attention by his repeated calls, and by the humility of his expectations, which were limited to half a dozen copies of the Magazine. At length, on his name being mentioned where a literary gentleman, particularly conversant in rural economy, happened to be present, the poem was finally examined, and its general aspect excited the risibility of that gentleman in so pointed a manner, that Bloomfield was called into the room, and exhorted not to waste his time and neglect his employment in making vain attempts, and particularly in treading on ground which Thomson had sanctified. His earnestness and confidence, however, led the editor to advise him to consult his countryman, Mr. Capel Lofft, to whom he gave him a letter of introduction. On his departure, the gentleman present warmly complimented the editor on the sound advice which he had given the poor fellow, and it was naturally conceived that an industrious man was thereby likely to be saved from a ruinous infatuation."

Undismayed by this cold treatment, Bloomfield hurried off with his manuscript to Mr. Lofft. That gentleman took the trouble of examining the poem, and did not throw it down with disgust when he came to a badly-spelled word (stumbling-blocks of a very frequent kind in Bloomfield's manuscript). Mr. Lofft declared the poem to be eminently worthy of publication, and exerted himself in procuring a publisher so successfully, that Messrs. Vernor and Hood purchased the manuscript for fifty pounds. Bloomfield was astonished. He had offered it to the Monthly Magazine for five or six copies of that cheerful publication. The poem made its appearance in due time, and achieved an immediate success. Several editions were issued in rapid succession, and in a short time upward of twenty-five thousand copies were disposed of. The publishers behaved generously to the author (considering that he had no farther claim upon them), and presented him with a check for £200. In addition to this, he received much kindness from persons in position. The Duke of Grafton presented him with a life annuity of a shilling a day, and obtained for him a situation in a government office; but ill health compelled him to relinquish it, and return to an avocation to which his constitution had become better accustomed. Subsequently he made an unsuccessful effort to establish himself in the bookselling business. By this failure he lost the little money he had accumulated, and was reduced to poverty. Continued ill health added to his distress, and for many long years he dragged out a sickly existence, "as miserable," says Professor Wilson, "as the existence of a good man can be made by the narrowest circumstances." After much bodily suffering, aggravated by the causes we have mentioned, Robert Bloomfield died on the 19th of August, 1823, at the age of fifty-seven years. He left a widow and four children, and debts to the amount of £200, which sum was raised by the exertions of his benevolent friends and admirers, among whom was the poet-laureate Southey.

The works of Bloomfield are pervaded with the most amiable and benevolent feeling. In his descriptions he is simple, natural, and pathetic. He is always alive to the pure suggestions of nature, and his sentiments are lofty, virtuous, and healthful, without being strained and spasmodic. English literature is indebted to him for one of the finest poems illustrative of English rural life. The merit of the "Farmer's Boy" has been recognized and endorsed by the literary world in the most ample manner. It has been published and republished in every form, and maintains its position to the present day. An edition was published in Germany the year following its first appearance in London. At Paris, a translation, entitled "Le Valet du Fermier," was made by Etienne Allard; one was made into Italian; and in 1805, an extremely curious edition in Latin was published in London, with the title "'Agricolæ Puer, poema Roberti Bloomfield celeberrimum, in versus Latinos, redditum,' auctore Gulielmo Clubbe, LL.D." Bloomfield's subsequent publications fully maintained the reputation achieved by his first. In his "Rural Tales, Ballads, and Songs," his "Good Tidings, or News from the Farm," his "Wild Flowers," and his "Banks of the Wye," will be found exquisite touches of poetic beauty.

SIR RICHARD ARKWRIGHT.

THREE quarters of a century ago, a man was splendidly dressed if he displayed a linen shirt, and a woman felt proud of her neat ankles if she could show them in spotless cotton hose. Woolen habiliments were the order of the day. The nimble fingers of the domestic circle fabricated all that was needful for the adornment of the person. In the long winter nights, the humming of the spinning-wheel was heard in every cottage home, and tales of love were whispered to its music, and mighty meshes were thrown around gallant hearts. In those days, the possession of a town-bought skirt or coat was evidence of wealth, and the happy owner became the object of public curiosity. Critical damsels examined the weft and the woof with exact eyes, and failed not, on the first opportunity, to imitate their excellence. England was celebrated then as now for her manufactures. Her woolen goods were sent to all parts of the world, and were marvels of neatness and durability. In 1764, the total value of exported English cotton goods was little beyond two hundred thousand pounds, while that of woolen was more than ten times the amount. In the present day the case is precisely and wonderfully reversed. The woolen manufactures have sunk down to comparative unimportance, and the cotton manufactures have become the staple of the kingdom, employing directly and indirectly millions of men, women, and children, and yielding an enormous revenue to the country.

Richard Arkwright, the subject of this memoir, was the illustrious and memorable instrument that effected this great and astonishing change, and gave to his country an importance which it is scarcely possible it would have obtained but for his genius.

Toward the end of the seventeenth century the demand for cotton goods began to increase, and, owing to the difficulty of production, far exceeded the supply. The English cottons in those days had only the weft of cotton, the warp or longitudinal threads of the cloth being of linen. No one dreamed of making the latter of cotton, because, by hand-labor, it was impossible to make the thread strong enough for the purpose. Notwithstanding these drawbacks, the demand for cotton goods kept on steadily increasing. It was natural, therefore, that the manufacturers should endeavor to find out a means whereby a greater supply could be obtained with less difficulty and labor, and, consequently, at a less expense. Machinery was, of course, thought of, and many ingenious men set their wits to work to discover a way to spin several threads at one and the same time, instead of slowly twisting a thread. About the year 1764, Mr. Hargreaves, a native of Blackburn, in Lancashire, succeeded in producing a machine — since called the spinning-jenny—whereby the object desired could be effected. For this piece of ingenuity Hargreaves was rewarded by a mob, who broke into his house and destroyed his machine. The outrage was repeated several times, but in the end the spinning-jenny gained the day. So far one of the principal obstacles of the manufacture was removed; but Hargreaves's invention, although highly valuable, was still insufficient. It could not give to the warp the hardness and firmness which it required, and which Arkwright succeeded in effecting. It is necessary to mention these things before proceeding with our memoir.

Richard Arkwright was the son of poor parents, and the youngest of a family of thirteen. He was born on the 23d of December, 1732, at Preston, in Lancashire, England. The indigent circumstances of his parents rendered it impossible for them to bestow on their son even a simple education. It was not until late in life that he learned to read and write. He was brought up to the humble profession of barber, and established himself at Bolton. It is probable that he followed this vocation for many years. The class of customers he had was not likely to enrich him in a very rapid manner. It is said that he occupied an underground cellar, and put up a sign at the entrance, on which was inscribed, "Come to the subterraneous barber; he shaves for a penny." This invitation was so attractive in those days that his customers became numerous, and the other barbers of the place found that to compete with Arkwright they must reduce their prices to his standard. Arkwright was not to be outdone. He made another reduction, and startled the town with the promise of "a clean shave for a halfpenny." In the year 1760–61 he gave up his cellar, and became an itinerant dealer in hair. Wigs were then generally worn, and the immense quantity of hair which was required for them was collected by men who devoted themselves to the business, and traveled from place to place. This enterprise turned out a very profitable one, and in a few years he succeeded in collecting a little property. It was something more than good fortune that enabled him to do so. He had succeeded in making a new chemical hair dye, and, by using it adroitly, was able to please all his customers, and supply all demands. Arkwright experienced no scarcity of peculiar colors.

Arkwright had a strong bent for mechanics; and, now that he had a little leisure time and sufficient money, he devoted himself to mechanical experiments. They were, unfortunately, directed to a fallacious point—the discovery of perpetual motion—and made such inroads into his funds that in a short time, although a burgess of Preston, he was reduced to a state of poverty. His wife, impatient at what she conceived to be a wanton waste of time and money, seized some of his models and destroyed them, hoping thus to remove forever the cause of their privations. She committed a fatal error. Arkwright could never excuse or forgive such a wanton piece of cruelty, and shortly afterward separated from her in consequence of it.

In 1767 Arkwright became acquainted at Warrington with a man named Kay, a clockmaker, who assisted our hero in constructing some portions of his perpetual motion machinery, and afterward in making parts of other machines to which Arkwright's attention was at this time directed. His connection with Kay turned out very unfortunate, and for a time had an injurious effect on his reputation. Kay, many years after, having been dismissed from Arkwright's employment, abused his employer in a merciless manner, and even went so far as to state, in a court of law, that his so-called inventions were only plagiarisms on inventions made by a man named Highs.

After many mortifications and difficulties, Arkwright completed his first cotton machine, but, being without money, he was still at a loss how to bring it into use. He determined on making an effort in his native town, Preston. To Preston, therefore, he repaired, and his machine was fitted up in the parlor of the grammar school-house. To bring forward a labor-saving machine in a town where every man, woman, and child lived by the exercise of manual labor, was a dangerous experiment. The fate of poor Hargreaves was before Arkwright, and, as the indignation of the mob began to find expression, he wisely determined on packing up his machine, and carrying it to some less dangerous locality. In company with Kay, our hero removed to Nottingham. He was here fortunate enough to secure the co-operation of men of capital, who were shrewd enough to see the manifold advantages of his invention. A partnership was entered into between Need, Strutt, and Arkwright, and in 1769 the latter obtained for his invention the expensive protection of letters patent. In later years he obtained several other patents, and it will be well to explain here for what they were obtained. The machinery which they protected consisted of various parts, his second specification enumerating no fewer than ten different contrivances. The most important of these was a device for drawing out the cotton from a coarse thread to one perfectly fine and hard, thus rendering it fit for warp as well as weft. Nothing could be more beautiful or more effective than this contrivance, which, with an additional provision for giving the proper twist to the thread, constitutes what is called the water-frame or throstle. Arkwright claimed this as his own invention, admitting, with regard to some of the other parts, that he was rather the improver than the inventor. The original spinning machine for coarse thread—called the spinning-jenny—he acknowledged to be the invention of Hargreaves, but the water-frame or throstle, and all the other ingenious combinations whereby mechanical spinning was perfected and rendered infallible, belonged to him, and he felt justified in obtaining patents for them. Any one who has been in a cotton factory, and observed the marvelous precision with which the delicately-elaborated machinery performs its various functions, can understand what kind of application, energy, talent, and genius were needed to bring it to its present perfection. It was not the inspiration of a moment, but the application of years that triumphed over the roughness of mechanical motion. Even after he had succeeded in forming his partnership with Messrs. Need and Strutt, his success was far from being secured. For a long time the speculation was unprofitable and disheartening. He tells us himself that it did not begin to pay till it had been persevered in for five years, and had swallowed up a capital of more than twelve thousand pounds.

The first spinning machine on Arkwright's plan was erected at Nottingham, and was worked by horse-power. This being found insufficient, water was resorted to; and in 1771, a factory on a far larger scale than the first was built on the River Derwent, at Cromford, near Wirksworth, in Derbyshire; from this circumstance the machine received its name of the water-frame and the thread-water-twist. Now commenced Arkwright's persecutions. While there was nothing to be snatched from him, people were glad enough to give him the hand of fellowship; but so soon as the halfpenny barber raised himself above the commonest chin, every one was ready to aim a blow at him. The easiest way of doing this was to assail the originality of his contrivances, and to assert they were all more or less plagiarized from others. The Lancashire cotton manufacturers were, of course, anxious to overthrow Arkwright, and to dispose of a powerful rival. They refused to buy his materials, although confessedly the best in the market, and by a series of petty but vexatious oppositions, did every thing in their power to make Arkwright and his associates unpopular with the trade, with the public, and with the working community. In 1779 this spitefulness bore fruits. The mob rose in arms against machinery, and prowled about the manufacturing districts, destroying all they could find. A large mill built by Arkwright at Birkacre, near Chorley, was destroyed by a mob, in the presence of a powerful body of police and military, without any of the civil authorities requiring their interference to prevent the outrage. The inmates defended the mill as long as they were able, and on the first day drove the rioters back, with the loss of two men killed and eight wounded. It was not till the latter returned with greatly increased numbers that they accomplished their purpose. Nor was this the only blow he suffered. Manufacturers who used his machines, and paid for the privilege with a very ill grace, refused to do so any longer, on the old pretext that the inventions were not his. To put a stop to this, Arkwright, in 1781, brought actions against the pirates. They defended themselves on the plea that the specification of the inventions was obscure and unintelligible, and consequently that the patent was void. No attempt was made to show that the inventions were not original. Their plea was valid in law, and, much to the disgust of all right-minded people, Arkwright lost the day. At first he thought of making an appeal to Parliament; but, after preparing a case, which he submitted to the public, he abandoned this intention, but in 1785 brought another action against the infringers of his patent, and succeeded in getting a verdict. The cotton-spinners, who had been profiting by Arkwright's genius without giving him any thing in return, were greatly incensed. They formed powerful combinations against what they were pleased to call Arkwright's monopoly, and finally commenced proceedings against the patentee to try the validity of his patent. They asserted that the patent was a great inconvenience to the public; that when the patent was granted the invention was not a new one; that the invention was not Arkwright's, and that the specification was imperfect. The trial lasted from nine o'clock in the morning until half past twelve at night, and many witnesses were examined—among others, Kay, who said all he could to injure his former employer. Principally on the evidence of this man, the jury returned a verdict annihilating the patent, which Arkwright tried in vain to set aside. Thus, after years and years of steady application and thought, he found himself thrown on the mercy of his enemies, destitute of every kind of legal protection, and surrounded by men who were all too ready to thrust their hands into his pockets and his reputation, and leave him to perish, ruined and broken-hearted. But his enemies were doomed to grievous disappointment. Arkwright was made of stuff which did not shrink with the spiteful sprinklings of cold water. Goaded by injustice, he turned round on his enemies, and astonished them by an opposition which soon carried every thing before it. In a short time his partnership with Need and Strutt came to an end, and the mill at Cromford passed into his own hands. He connected himself with other manufactories, and soon obtained such a control of the trade that prices were fixed by him, and controlled all the other cotton-spinners. "The most marked traits in the character of Arkwright," says Mr. Baines, "were his wonderful ardor, energy, and perseverance. He commonly labored in his multifarious concerns from five in the morning till nine at night; and when considerably more than fifty years of age, feeling that the defects of his education placed him under great difficulty and inconvenience in conducting his correspondence and in the general management of his business, he encroached upon his sleep in order to gain an hour each day to learn English grammar, and another hour to improve his writing and orthography. He was a severe economist of time, and, that he might not waste a moment, he generally traveled with four horses, and at a very rapid speed. His concerns in Derbyshire, Lancashire, and Scotland were so extensive and numerous as to show at once his astonishing power of transacting business, and his all-grasping spirit. In many of these he had partners, but he generally managed in such a way that, whoever lost, he himself was a gainer. So unbounded was his confidence in the success of his machinery, and in the national wealth to be produced by it, that he would make light of discussions on taxation, and say that *he* would pay the national debt. His speculative schemes were vast and daring; he contemplated entering into the most extensive mercantile transactions, and buying up all the cotton in the world, in order to make an enormous profit by the monopoly."

A man of such strength of character requires but little protection. When once he has found the path to fortune, he is sure to pursue it to the temple of the goddess. He was able to face all opposition, and to reap a rich reward for his ingenuity, in spite of the illiberality of the laws which refused him protection. In 1786 he was appointed high sheriff of Derbyshire, and for delivering an address to the king, suggested by the escape of that individual from assassination, received the trumpery honor of knighthood, and became Sir Richard Arkwright. He did not long enjoy the distinction which had thus fallen on him by chance. For many years he had suffered from that terrible malady, asthma. The sedentary life which this demands, aggravated by incessant application to business, brought on a complication of disorders, of which he died on the 3d of August, 1792, in the sixtieth year of his age. The fortune he left behind is said to have amounted to the sum of half a million sterling. Whatever may have been the objections raised to his inventions during his lifetime, it is now universally conceded that Arkwright succeeded in establishing the cotton manufactures in England, and in benefiting millions of human beings by giving them the means of honest employment. He also secured to his country its most important branch of commerce by giving it machinery whereby it could excel other countries in production, excellence, and cheapness. "No man," justly observes Mr. M'Culloch, "ever better deserved his good fortune, or has a stronger claim on the respect and gratitude of posterity. His inventions have opened a new and boundless field of employment; and while they have conferred infinitely more benefit on his native country than she could have derived from the absolute dominion of Mexico and Peru, they have been universally productive of wealth and enjoyments."

HENRY KIRKE WHITE.

It is seldom that the life of a poet affords so unalloyed a pleasure as that furnished by the subject of this sketch. The pleasure is in the total absence of vice which it presents, and not in the career of the individual, for that was brief and unhappy. A more chaste and admirable man never lived.

Henry Kirke White was the son of a butcher, and was born at Nottingham, England, on the 21st of March, 1785. From his earliest days he displayed the susceptibilities of a poetic temperament, and was passionately fond of reading. "I could fancy," said his eldest sister, "I see him in his little chair, with a large book upon his knee, and my mother calling 'Henry, my love, come to dinner,' which was repeated so often without being regarded that she was obliged to change the tone of her voice before she could rouse him." At the age of six he was placed under the care of the Rev. John Blanchard, who kept the best school in Nottingham, where he learned writing, arithmetic, and French, and he continued there for several years. He was, even in those early days, a remarkable child. It is said that, when about seven, he was accustomed to go secretly into his father's kitchen, and teach the servant to read and write; and, to encourage her, he composed a tale of a Swiss emigrant, which he gave her. In his eleventh year he wrote a separate theme for each of the twelve or fourteen boys in his class, and the excellence of the various pieces obtained his master's applause.

Notwithstanding these indications of intellectual superiority, Henry's father insisted that he should be brought up to the butchering business. Even while he was at school, one day in every week, and his leisure hours on the others, were employed in carrying meat to his father's customers. Fortunately, his mother was not enamored of her husband's business, and, seeing the natural inclinations of her son, determined that they should not be utterly thwarted by a life which could not fail to be repulsive to his instincts. The alternative which she selected was scarcely better than the evil. Young Henry was placed at a stocking-loom, with the view of bringing him up to the hosiery business. His parents were still too poor to think of giving him a profession. It may be easily imagined that this new business failed to interest his imagination or satisfy his taste. He could not bear the idea, he says, of spending some years of his life in shining and folding up stockings. He poured his complaints into the willing ear of his mother; he wanted, he said, something to occupy his brain, and he should be wretched if he continued longer at this trade, or, indeed, in any thing except one of the learned professions. In an "Address to Contemplation," which he wrote at this time, he describes his feelings:

> "Why along
> The dusky track of commerce should I toil,
> When, with an easy competence content,
> I can alone be happy where, with thee,
> I may enjoy the loveliness of Nature,
> And loose the wings of fancy? Thus alone
> Can I partake the happiness of earth;
> And to be happy here is man's chief end,
> For to be happy he must needs be good."

He continued his remonstrances so earnestly, and importuned so incessantly, that his parents at length obtained his release from the hosier's loom, and placed him in the office of Messrs. Coldham & Enfield, town clerk and attorneys of Nottingham, some time in

May, 1799, he being in his fifteenth year at the time. These gentlemen required a premium, and, as his parents were too poor to pay the sum required, it was agreed that he should serve two years before his articles commenced. A few months after this arrangement had been entered into, Kirke White wrote to his brother in London, saying, "It is now nearly four months since I entered into Mr. Coldham's office, and it is with pleasure I can assure you that I never yet found any thing disagreeable, but, on the contrary, every thing I do seems a pleasure to me, and for a very obvious reason—it is a business which I like, a business which I chose above all others; and I have two good-tempered, easy masters, but who will, nevertheless, see that their business is done in a neat and proper manner." "A man that understands the law is sure to have business; and in case I have no thoughts—in case, that is, that I do not aspire to hold the honorable place of a barrister, I shall feel sure of gaining a genteel livelihood at the business to which I am articled." In his spare moments at home and at the office he devoted his attention to Latin, and in ten months was able to read Horace with tolerable facility, and had even made some progress in Greek. Mr. Southey, in his admirable memoir of Kirke White, gives an astounding account of his mental application. Though living with his family, he nearly estranged himself from their society. At meals, and during the evenings, a book was constantly in his hands; and as he refused to sup with them, to prevent any loss of time, his meal was sent to him in his little apartment. Law, Greek, Latin, Italian, Spanish, and Portuguese, chemistry, astronomy, electricity, drawing, music, and mechanics, by turns engaged his attention, and, though his acquirements in some of these studies were very superficial, his proficiency in many of them was far from contemptible. His papers on law evince so much industry, that, had that subject alone occupied his leisure hours, his diligence would have been commendable. He was a tolerable Italian scholar, and in the classics he afterward attained reputation; but of the sciences, and of Spanish and Portuguese, his knowledge was not, it may be inferred, very great. His ear for music was good, and, although he did not give much attention to the art, he could play pleasingly on the piano. It is said that he composed the base as he went on, which probably means that, like a good many other performers, he could do more with one hand than the other.

A man never devotes himself to intense study without a worthy object. White was determined to break loose from the fetters of iron fate, and to be the architect of his own fortunes in some high sphere of human usefulness. We have seen, in his letter to his brother, that he already aimed at forensic distinction, as being preferable to the drudgery of the attorney's office. He regarded the law as a pursuit which might end in riches, but he had another which he hoped would terminate in honor. The Muses had been his companions from earliest childhood, and he wooed them now with the devotion of a serious, intelligent lover. The literary society of his native town was not extensive, but it made up for the paucity of its members by the dignity with which they comported themselves. They formed a learned association, and excluded all rash enthusiasts from the privilege of membership. Several times was White refused admission within the charmed realms; but at length the Fates were propitious, and he was appointed to the "Chair of Literature." White took his revenge by delivering an inauguration address of two hours and three quarters in length.

A magazine, called the "Monthly Preceptor," was shortly afterward established, which proposed prize themes for young persons. Kirke White tried his hand with success, and carried off several of the prizes. After this he contributed to other periodicals.

It was, as we have said, his hope to become a barrister or advocate, and for this purpose he improved every opportunity. But a constitutional deafness now began to manifest itself, and sorrowfully he had to admit to his own conscience that the impediment was fatal to his hopes of distinction. From conscientious motives, his thoughts were instantly turned toward the Church. His literary companions were all more or less inclined to Deism, and this fact led to inquiries which terminated in full conviction of religious truth. It is instructive, says Sir Harris Nicolas, in his sketch, to learn to what circumstances such a person as Kirke White was indebted for the knowledge "which causes not to err." This information occurs in a letter from him to a Mr. Booth in August, 1801; and it also fixes the date of the happy change that influenced every thought and every action of his future life, which gave the energy of virtue to his exertions, soothed the asperities of a temper naturally impetuous and irritable, and enabled him, at a period when manhood was full of hope and promise, to view the approaches of death with the calmness of a philosopher and the resignation of a saint. After thanking Mr. Booth for the present of Jones's work on the Trinity, he thus describes his religious impressions previous to its perusal, and the effect it produced: "Religious polemics, indeed, have seldom formed a part of my studies; though, whenever I happened accidentally to turn my thoughts to the subject of the Protestant doctrine of the Godhead, and compared it with Arian and Socinian, many doubts interfered, and I even began to think that the more nicely the subject was investigated, the more perplexed it would appear, and was on the point of forming a resolution to go to heaven in my own way, without meddling or involving myself in the inextricable labyrinth of controversial dispute, when I received and perused this excellent treatise, which finally cleared up the mists which my ignorance had conjured around me, and clearly pointed out the real truth." From this moment he devoted himself entirely to the services of religion, and determined to enter the ministry, if that happy promotion could be achieved. His friends were, of course, opposed to any change in his profession, believing, as they had every reason to believe, that he would attain distinction in the law. But he was deaf to their remonstrances, and firm in his resolution to dedicate the rest of his life to the Church. The first thing that was absolutely necessary was to procure means to proceed to the University. For this purpose he ventured on the hazardous experiment of preparing a volume of poems for the press, the sale of which, he hoped, would place him in the possession of funds. Like all young authors of that time, he needed a patron or patroness to whom the book might be dedicated. He applied to the Countess of Derby, who declined on the ground that she never accepted a compliment of that character. Her ladyship probably looked on literature as a low, vulgar thing, beneath her consideration. He then addressed the Duchess of Devonshire, and a letter, with the manuscript, was left at her house. After a number of disheartening delays the required permission was granted, and the book came out in 1803. It is curious to know that, although a copy was transmitted to the duchess, she paid no attention to it, and neither rewarded the author with its price in kindness or money. The author was naturally nervous about his first production, and sent imploring letters to the Reviewers, depreciating his own effort, and bespeaking a little kindliness. It is unnecessary to add that this step was ill-judged and useless. It is no part of a Reviewer's duty to consult the feelings, be they modest or otherwise, of an author. The Monthly Review pitched into the young poet, and selected some of the worst lines to strengthen its position that the book did not justify any sanguine expectations. White was sorely distressed by this article, and writing to a friend said, "I am at present under afflictions and contentions of spirit heavier than I ever yet experienced. I think at times I am mad, and destitute of religion; my pride is not yet subdued; the unfavorable review (the 'Monthly') of my unhappy work has cut deeper than you could have thought, not in a literary point of view, but as it affects my respectability. It represents me actually as a beggar, going about gathering money to put myself at college, when my book is worthless, and this with every appearance of candor. They have been sadly misinformed respecting me; this Review goes before me wherever I turn my steps; it haunts me incessantly, and I am persuaded it is an instrument in the hands of Satan to drive me to distraction. I must leave Nottingham. If the answer of the Elland Society be unfavorable, I purpose writing to the Marquis of Wellesley, to offer myself as a student at the academy he has instituted at Fort William, in Bengal, and at the proper age to take orders there. The missionaries at that place have done wonders already; and I should, I hope, be a valuable laborer in the vineyard. If the marquis take no notice of my application, or do not accede to my proposal, I shall place myself in some other way of making a meet preparation for the holy office, either in the Calvinistic Academy, or in one of the Scotch universities, where I shall be able to live at scarcely any expense." The criticism referred to was unjust as it was ungenerous, and elicited from Mr. Southey, the poet, an encouraging letter, expressing his opinion of the merits of the book, and giving him some kind and timely advice. With the approbation of a man so distinguished, White thought no more of the Reviewer. "I dare not say all I feel respecting your opinion of my little volume," he wrote in reply. "The extreme acrimony with which the Monthly Review (of all others the most important) treated me, threw me into a state of stupefaction. I regarded all that had passed as a dream, and I thought I had been deluding myself into an idea of possessing poetic genius, when, in fact, I had only the longing, without the afflatus. I mustered resolution enough, however, to write spiritedly to them; their answer, in the ensuing number, was a tacit acknowledgment that they had been somewhat too unsparing in their correction. It was a poor attempt to salve over a wound wantonly and ungenerously inflicted. Still I was damped, because I knew the work was very respectable, and therefore could not, I concluded, give a criticism grossly deficient in equity, the more especially as I knew of no sort of inducement to extraordinary severity. Your letter, however, has revived me, and I do again venture to hope that I may still produce something which will survive me. With regard to your advice and offers of assistance, I will not attempt, because I am unable, to thank you for them. To-morrow morning I depart for Cambridge; and I have considerable hopes that, as I do not enter into the University with any sinister or interested views, but sincerely desire to perform the duties of an affectionate and vigilant pastor, and become more useful to mankind—I therefore have hopes, I say, that I shall find means of support in the University; if I do not, I shall certainly act in pursuance of your recommendations, and shall, without hesitation, avail myself of your offers of service and of your directions. In a short time this will be determined, and when it is, I shall take the liberty of writing to you at Keswick, to make you acquainted with the result."

By the united efforts of his friends, White was presented with a sizarship at St. John's College, Cambridge. On the 10th of April, 1804, he expressed his gratification at this event in the following devout strain: "Most fervently do I return thanks to God for this providential opening: it has breathed new animation into me, and my breast expands with the prospect of becoming the minister of Christ where I most desired it, but where I almost feared all probability of success was nearly at an end. * * * I return thanks to God for keeping me so long in suspense, for I know it has been beneficial to my soul, and I feel a considerable trust that the way is now about to be made clear, and that my doubts and fears on this head will in due time be removed." As a preparation for the college course, White placed himself with a private tutor for a year, and, while under that gentleman's care, he studied with such indiscreet fervor that fears were excited not for his health only, but for his intellect. On a former occasion he had brought on a severe attack of illness in the same way, and a similar penalty awaited him now. "I fear," he wrote, "my good genius, who was wont to visit me with nightly visions in woods and brakes, and by the river's marge, is now dying of a fen ague, and I shall thus, probably, emerge from my retreat, not a hair-brained son of imagination, but a sedate, black-lettered bookworm, with a head like an etymologicon magnum." He recovered after a while, and applied himself with great assiduity to the study of theology. In October, 1805, Kirke White became a resident member of St. John's College, Cambridge, and was soon distinguished for his classical knowledge; but it was at a fearful sacrifice. By neglecting to provide for the healthful requirements of the body, he had so enfeebled it that the seeds of disease took easy root, and now, while on the threshold of fame, he found his footsteps totter and his mind grow numb. He was told that the only chance of prolonging his life was to fly to a milder climate, and abandon study altogether. Such advice was not likely to be valued by one who looked on fame as dearer than existence, and was willing to perish so long as he perished at the wheel. He continued his pursuits unintimidated by the warnings of his friends. During the first term he became a candidate for one of the University scholarships, but the increased exertion he underwent was attended by results that obliged him to retire from the contest. "At this moment," says his biographer, "the general college examination approached, and thinking that, if he failed, his hopes would be blasted forever, he taxed his energies to the utmost, during the fortnight which intervened, to meet the trial. He became so sick in consequence that he was considered unable to go to the hall to be examined. His tutor, Mr. Catton, touched by the tears of his pupil, urged him to use stimulants during the six days of the examination. He did so, and was pronounced the first man of his year. Soon after this event he went to London for relaxation, was received cordially in literary circles, and returned to Cambridge in improved health. Unwarned by the past, he plunged into his old habits of study, and, as a necessary consequence, had a relapse. In a letter to a friend he describes his condition: "I have had a recurrence of my old complaint within this last four or five days, which has quite unnerved me for every thing. The state of my health is really miserable.

I am well and lively in the morning, and overwhelmed with nervous horrors in the evening. I do not know how to proceed with regard to my studies. A very slight overstretch of the mind in the daytime occasions me not only a sleepless night, but a night of gloom and horror. The systole and diastole of my heart seem to be playing at ball—the stake my life. I can only say the game is not yet decided; I allude to the violence of the palpitation. I am going to mount the Gog-Magog Hills this morning in quest of a good night's sleep. The Gog-Magog Hills for my body, and the Bible for my mind, are my only medicines. I am sorry to say that neither are quite adequate." He rallied again, but seems to have been aware that his end was not far distant, and determined to spend the next vacation at Nottingham. In April he proceeded to that town, and on the 7th wrote a very melancholy account of himself: "It seems determined upon by my mother that I can not be spared, since the time of my stay is so very short, and my health so very uncertain. The people here can scarcely be persuaded that any thing ails me, so well do I look; but occasional depressions, especially after any thing has occurred to occasion uneasiness, still harass me. My mind is of a very peculiar cast. I began to think too early; and the indulgence of certain trains of thought, and too free an exercise of the imagination, have superinduced a morbid kind of sensibility, which is to the mind what excessive irritability is to the body. Some circumstances occurred on my arrival at Nottingham which gave me just cause for inquietude and anxiety; the consequences were insomnia, and a relapse into causeless dejections. It is my business now to curb these irrational and immoderate affections, and, by accustoming myself to sober thought and cool reasoning, to restrain these freaks and vagaries of the fancy. When I am well I can not help entertaining a sort of contempt for the weakness of mind which marks my indispositions. Titus when well, and Titus when ill, are two distinct persons. The man when in health despises the man when ill for his weakness, and the latter envies the former for his felicity." On his return to college his prospects seemed to brighten in every thing save health. He was again pronounced first at the great examination; he was one of the three best theme-writers, whose merits were so nearly equal that the examiners could not decide between them; and he was a prizeman both in the mathematical and logical or general examination, and in Latin composition. His college offered him a private tutor free of expense, and Mr. Catton obtained exhibitions for him to the value of sixty-one pounds per annum, by which he was enabled to give up the pecuniary assistance he had received from his friends. The highest honors of the University were within his grasp, but it was ordained that death should stay his hand. In July he was seized with an attack which threatened his life, but from this he recovered. In September he went to London on a visit to his brother, but returned to college in a few weeks, in a state that precluded all chance of prolonging his existence. Toward the middle of the month (October, 1806), a friend informed his brother of his actual state. He hastened to him, but when he arrived he was delirious, and, although reason returned for a short time, he sunk into a low state, and on Sunday, the 19th, quietly expired. He was in his twenty-second year at the time of the unhappy event.

In whatever light, says Sir Harris Nicolas, the character of this unhappy youth be contemplated, it is full of instruction. His talents were unusually precocious, and their variety was as astonishing as their extent. Besides the poetical pieces which have given his name a lasting interest to English literature, and his scholastic attainments, his ability was manifested in various other ways. His style was remarkable for its clearness and elegance, and his correspondence and prose pieces show extensive information. To great genius and capacity he united the rarest and more important gifts of sound judgment and common sense. It is usually the misfortune of genius to invest ordinary objects with a meretricious coloring that perverts their forms and purposes, to make its possessor imagine that it exempts him from attending to those strict rules of moral conduct to which others are bound to adhere, and to render him neglectful of the sacred assurance that "to whom much is given from him will much be required." Nature, in Kirke White's case, appears, on the contrary, to have determined that she would, in one instance at least, prove that high intellectual attainments are strictly compatible with every social and moral virtue. At a very early period of his life religion became the predominant feeling of his mind, and she imparted her sober and chastened effects to all his thoughts and actions. The cherished object of every member of his family, he repaid their affection by the most anxious solicitude for their welfare, offering his advice on spiritual affairs with impressive earnestness, and indicating, in every letter of his voluminous correspondence, the greatest consideration for their feelings and happiness. For the last six years he deemed himself marked out for the service of his Maker—not like the member of a convent, whose duties consist only in prayer, but in the exercise of that philanthropy and practical benevolence which ought to adorn every parish priest. To qualify himself properly for the holy office, he subjected his mind to the severest discipline; and his letters display a rational piety and an enlightened view of religious obligations which is even superior to the fervor of his poetical pieces.

Kirke White's sacred poetry is extensively known, and, being the best of its kind, will preserve a place in English literature. Its great merits are the feeling and natural pathos with which the author writes. He speaks directly from his heart so simply that all who have hearts must be touched. His command of language is copious, but he lacks imagination and metaphorical color. He is pathetic, plaintive, and agreeable, and recalls associations which most people have experienced and like to have recalled. That he touched a tuneful chord in the human breast is evidenced by the fact that his works have gone through many hundred editions, and are, perhaps, better read than any contemporary poet.

Kirke White was buried in the church of "All Saints," Cambridge, and a tablet was erected to his memory by Mr. Francis Boot, of Boston, a liberal-minded American gentleman. The tablet has a medallion by Chantrey, and an inscription by Professor Smyth, of which the following is a copy:

"Warm'd with fond hope and learning's sacred flame,
To Granta's bowers the youthful poet came;
Unconquer'd powers the immortal mind display'd,
But, worn with anxious thought, the frame decay'd:
Pale o'er his lamp, and in his cell retired,
The martyr-student faded and expired.
Oh! genius, taste, and piety sincere,
Too early lost 'midst studies too severe!
Foremost to mourn was generous Southey seen;
He told the tale, and show'd what White had been:
Nor told in vain; for o'er the Atlantic wave
A wanderer came, and sought the poet's grave;
On yon lone stone he saw his lonely name,
And raised this fond memorial to his fame."

JAMES WATT.

James Watt, the world's most illustrious mechanic, was born at Greenock, Scotland, on the 19th of January, 1736. His father enjoyed a good social position, and was held in high esteem by his fellow-townsmen, having been appointed one of the magistrates of the town. The subject of our memoir received the rudiments of his education in his native place, the delicacy of his health prohibiting a resort to other and more distant academies. The natural studiousness of his disposition was perhaps increased by this weakliness. Reading supplied the place of rougher and less serviceable exercises. So tenacious was his memory, that at a very early age he was well informed on many subjects of a scientific character, especially those branches which were connected more or less with mechanics. Except that he was a quiet, amiable, studious youth, we know nothing of any particular importance concerning the early years of his life. At the age of eighteen he was sent to London to be apprenticed to a maker of mathematical instruments, but, in little more than a year, the feebleness of his health compelled him to abandon this profession and return to his home. He appears to have had a liking for the business, however, and probably practiced it until he felt that he knew enough to start for himself. This he did at Glasgow in 1757, and was appointed mathematical instrument maker to the college. He retained this situation for many years, and was able greatly to improve himself in every department of knowledge. One of his principal occupations was the repairing of the scientific apparatus of the college. The dexterity with which he did this, and the amount of knowledge he possessed on most mechanical subjects, brought him into friendly contact with the various professors. They met in his little room, and discussed subjects of natural philosophy, and no doubt theorized largely on all the leading topics of the day. One of young Watt's most frequent visitors was Mr. (afterward Dr.) Robison, who at that time was speculating on the possibility of applying steam as a motive power to wheel carriages. Watt had himself made some experiments on the elasticity of steam, assured that vast forces were yet to be secured from it. The steam-engine was then but slightly known, and, owing to its many imperfections, still more slightly used. Some recent improvements made by Newcomen only served to indicate what might be accomplished. While the two friends were discussing the matter, a model was sent in to be repaired by the professor of natural philosophy. On examination, it proved to be a miniature copy of Newcomen's improved engine. This treasure was eagerly examined by Watt, and criticised with technical exactitude. In a very little while he discovered the reason why the model would not work, and at the same time saw that, however admirably it might perform its functions, it was still an imperfect machine. With the view of remedying its defects, he commenced an extensive series of experiments. The boiler and the generation of steam were the first objects of his attention. He was soon rewarded with many valuable discoveries. The rapidity with which water evaporates, he found, depended on certain causes which were before unknown to him. He also ascertained the quantity of coals necessary for the evaporation of any given quantity of water; the heat at which water boils under various pressures, and many other particulars of a similar kind, many of which had never before been determined. When he had disposed of these questions, he turned his attention to the cylinder, which he declared to be radically defective. In Newcomen's engine, it had to be cooled after every stroke of the piston, in order to condense the waste steam. This was effected in an ingenious way, by the injection of a small jet of cold water *into* the cylinder, but it occasioned a great waste of power and an extravagant expenditure of fuel. If, argued Watt, the cylinder, instead of being thus cooled for every stroke of the piston, could be kept permanently hot, a fourth part of the heat which had been hitherto applied would be found sufficient. The question now was how this desirable object could be accomplished. It was his constant theme, walking, sleeping, dreaming. All the faculties of his suggestive mind were directed to the solution of the great and important problem. After brooding over it for some time, he abandoned the idea of getting rid of the waste steam in the vessel where it had been used; he could discover no possible way of doing so in a complete and thorough manner. The next question was how to dispose of it. At last it occurred to him that it might be possible to draw it off into another vessel, and so got rid of without inconvenience. This happy idea was the first step toward the vast improvements which he afterward made. In the course of one or two days, according to his own account, he had all the apparatus arranged in his own mind. The plan was extremely simple, and on that account more practicable and valuable. He proposed to establish a communication by an open pipe between the cylinder and another vessel, the consequence of which evidently would be, that when the steam was admitted into the former, it would flow into the latter, so as to fill it also. If, then, the portion in this latter vessel only should be subjected to a condensing process by being brought into contact with cold water, or any other convenient means, what would follow? Why, a vacuum would be produced, into which more steam would immediately rush from the cylinder; that likewise would be condensed, and so the process would go on till all the steam had left the cylinder. In this way, the main cylinder would be kept nearly at an equal temperature. When these views were tested by experiment, the result was found to answer Watt's most sanguine expectations. A great saving of fuel and a vast increase of power were effected. But the genius of the inventor had many serious obstacles to overcome. One of these was the difficulty of making the cylinder airtight. In the old engines, this was effected by covering the top with water, the dripping down of which into the space below, where it merely assisted condensation, was of little importance, but, now that the condensation was carried on in a separate vessel, it became highly necessary to prevent any thing entering the cylinder except the virgin steam. The admission of air tended to cool the cylinder, especially in the lower parts, while Watt's great object was to keep it dry and warm, and at an equal temperature throughout. It must be remembered, also, that at this time the top of the cylinder was entirely open; a column of steam thrust up the piston, and the weight of the atmosphere thrust it down again. It now occurred to Mr. Watt that the proper way to effect the object he had in view was to completely close the cylinder, leaving only room for the piston-rod to work up and down. The hole necessary for this purpose was padded with hemp and saturated with oil, so that the natural adhesion of atmospheric air to the piston-rod was wiped away in its descent downward. The next thing was to provide a compensating power for the atmospheric air, whose downward pressure had hitherto been essential to the action of the engine. This he accomplished by introducing a column of steam in the top of the cylinder, so that when the piston had been pressed up by the column from below, it was pressed down again by the column from above, and thus maintained the regularity of its motions by a *double-acting* steam power. Some minor improvements were afterward added, but what we have described were the radical features of Mr. Watt's first and great reform. The strength, precision, velocity, and controllability of the steam-engine were by these great inventions rendered of practical benefit to the human race. It came into his hands a toy; it left them a mighty instrument of beneficent Progress.

The subsequent improvements made by Watt were equally valuable and astonishing. Like a mighty lion-tamer, he seemed to delight in exhibiting the docility of the brute force he had subdued. "In the present perfect state of the engine," says Dr. Arnott, in his Elements of Physics, "it appears a thing almost endowed with intelligence. It regulates with perfect accuracy and uniformity the *number of its strokes* in a given time, *counting*, or *recording* them, moreover, to tell how much work it has done, as a clock records the beats of its pendulum. It regulates the *quantity of steam* admitted to work; the *briskness of the fire;* the *supply of water* to the boiler; the *supply of coals* to the fire; it *opens and shuts its valves* with absolute precision as to time and manner;

it *oils its joints;* it *takes out any air* which may accidentally enter into parts which should be vacuous; and, when any thing goes wrong which it can not of itself rectify, it *warns its attendants* by ringing a bell. Yet, with all these talents and qualities, and even when exerting the power of six hundred horses, it is obedient to the hand of a child. Its aliment is coal, wood, charcoal, or other combustible; it consumes none while idle; it never tires, and wants no sleep; it is not subject to malady when originally well made, and only refuses to work when worn out with old age; it is equally active in all climates, and will do work of any kind; it is a water-pumper, a miner, a sailor, a cotton-spinner, a weaver, a blacksmith, a miller, etc., etc.; and a small engine in the character of a *steam pony* may be seen dragging after it on a railroad a hundred tons of merchandise, or a regiment of soldiers, with greater speed than that of our fleetest coaches. It is the king of machines, and a permanent realization of the genii of Eastern fable, whose supernatural powers were occasionally at the command of man."

Watt did not escape the usual experience of inventors, or what Mr. Wilkins Micawber playfully describes as "the pressure of pecuniary liabilities." His own means were limited, and, in order to prosecute many of his experiments, he had to obtain the assistance of friends. If Dr. Roebuck was one of these, he certainly was a very greedy friend, for he made advances on the hard conditions that two thirds of the profits should be made over to him. Watt's first patent was obtained on these terms (1769). An engine was immediately afterward erected at the doctor's works. It was found to answer tolerably well, but various alterations were needed, and, consequently, a fresh advance of funds was necessary. However willing Dr. Roebuck may have been to assist Watt on the two-thirds principle, he was now unable to do so. He found himself involved in his business, and completely incapable of making farther advances. For nearly five years Watt abandoned the prosecution of his various plans, and sought a living by pursuing the profession of civil engineer. He seems to have waited in expectation of Dr. Roebuck's coming prosperity; but, finding that this was rather a slow process, he resolved to close with a proposal which had been made to him through his friend, Dr. Small, of Birmingham, that he should remove to that town, and enter into partnership with the eminent hardware manufacturer, Mr. Bolton, of the Soho Works. In a short time an arrangement was made with Dr. Roebuck, and Watt took his departure for what was destined to be the scene of all his future triumphs. The new firm of Bolton & Watt commenced the manufacture of steam-engines in the year 1775, and immediately erected a specimen machine on their premises, to which they invited the attention of all persons interested in, or likely to be benefited by the patent. "They then proposed to erect similar engines wherever required, on the very liberal principle of receiving, as payment for each, only one third of the saving in fuel which it should effect, as compared with one of the old construction." Small as this compensation appeared to be, it soon amounted to an enormous revenue, and at last excited the cupidity of other manufacturers, who tried to infringe the patents (of which Watt & Bolton had several), and, of course, to evade payment to the patentees. Six or seven years were spent in litigation, during which time all sorts of attempts were made to snatch the laurels from Watt's brow, but without avail. In 1799, a unanimous decision of all the judges of the Court of King's Bench established the validity of his claims, and thus disposed of opposition forever.

Watt's inventive genius found occupation in many other ways beside the perfecting of the steam-engine. An apparatus for copying letters, now in common use; a method of heating houses by steam; a new composition for the purposes of sculpture, having the transparency and nearly the hardness of marble; a machine for multiplying copies of busts and other works in carving and statuary, are enumerated among his minor inventions.

In 1800 Mr. Watt withdrew from business, and, although constantly in feeble health, enjoyed nineteen years of domestic felicity in the bosom of his family. He died on the 25th of August, 1819, highly respected by all who knew him, and honored to the present day as one of England's greatest benefactors. During his career he received frequent testimonials of esteem from the learned societies of Europe. In 1784 he was elected a fellow of the Royal Society of Edinburgh; in 1785, a member of the Royal Society of London; in 1787, a corresponding member of the Batavian Society; in 1806 he received from Glasgow the degree of Doctor of Laws; and in 1808 he was elected, first, a corresponding member, and afterward an associate of the Institution of France.

Mr. Watt was in the strictest sense a cultivated man. There was hardly a physical science or an art with which he was not pretty intimately acquainted. He was familiar with several modern languages, and well read in literature. "Perhaps no individual in his age," says Mr. Jeffrey, "possessed so much, and such varied and exact information; had read so much, or remembered what he had read so accurately and well. He had infinite quickness of apprehension, a prodigious memory, and a certain rectifying and methodizing power of understanding, which extracted something precious out of all that was presented to it. His stores of miscellaneous knowledge were immense, and yet less astonishing than the command he had at all times over them. It seemed as if every subject that was casually started in conversation had been that which he had been last occupied in studying and exhausting, such was the copiousness, the precision, and the admirable clearness of the information which he poured out upon it without effort or hesitation. Nor was this promptitude and compass of knowledge confined in any degree to the studies connected with his ordinary pursuits. That he should have been minutely and extensively skilled in chemistry and the arts, and in most of the branches of physical science, might, perhaps, have been conjectured; but it could not have been inferred from his usual occupations, and probably is not generally known, that he was curiously learned in many branches of antiquity, metaphysics, medicine, and etymology, and perfectly at home in all the details of architecture, music, and law."

WILLIAM COBBETT.

One of the most remarkable self-made men that England can boast is William Cobbett, the subject of the present sketch. From the author's own voluminous writings we are able to gather most of the materials of his eventful life, especially from that entertaining work, the *Life of Peter Porcupine*. It is unfortunate, however, that Mr. Cobbett never thought it worth while to dwell minutely on the early incidents of his life, and our information on that interesting era is necessarily imperfect and broken. We will endeavor to string together what we can in the author's own words.

William Cobbett was born in the town of Farnham, Surrey, England, in the spring of the year 1762. His father was a small tenant farmer, of very limited education and humble means, but he was considered learned for a man in his rank of life. He understood land-surveying well, and was often chosen to draw the plans of disputed territory, and, being honest, industrious, and frugal, was a man of consideration among his neighbors.

William says that he does not remember the time when he did not earn his own living. His first occupation was driving the small birds from the turnip-seed, and the rooks from the peas. His next employment was weeding wheat, and leading a single horse at harrowing barley. Hoeing peas followed, and thence he arrived at the honor of joining the reapers in the harvest, driving the team, and holding the plow. All the family were strong and laborious, and the father used to boast that he had four sons, the eldest of whom was but fifteen years old, who did as much work as any three men in the parish of Farnham. William says that he had some faint recollection of going to school to an old woman, who, he fancies, did not succeed in the arduous undertaking of teaching him his alphabet. In the winter evenings, however, his father taught him to read and write, and gave him some instruction in arithmetic and grammar.

From his infancy Cobbett displayed great fondness for rural occupations, which he describes as "healthy, rational, and heart-cheering pursuits, in which every day presents something new, in which the spirits are never suffered to flag, and in which industry, skill, and care are sure to meet with their due reward;" to which he adds, "I have never, for any eight months together, during my whole life, been without a garden." Under the influence of this healthful passion, he left home at the age of eleven with the determination of seeing Kew Gardens, of which he had heard so much that he could not rest. He describes the incident admirably. "At eleven years of age my employment was clipping of box edgings and weeding beds of flowers in the garden of the Bishop of Winchester at the Castle of Farnham. I had always been fond of beautiful flowers, and a gardener, who had just come from the king's gardens at Kew, gave such a description of them as made me instantly resolve to work in these gardens. The next morning, without saying a word to any one, off I set, with no clothes except those upon my back, and with thirteen halfpence in my pocket. I found that I must go to Richmond, and I accordingly went from place to place, inquiring my way thither. A long day—it was in June—brought me to Richmond in the afternoon. Two pennyworth of bread and cheese, and a pennyworth of small beer which I had on the road, and a halfpenny which I had lost somehow or other, left threepence in my pocket. With this for my whole fortune, I was trudging through Richmond in my blue smock frock, and my red gaiters tied under my knees, when, staring about me, my eye fell upon a little book in a bookseller's window, on the outside of which was written, 'Tale of a Tub; price *3d.*' The title was so odd that my curiosity was excited. I had the threepence, but then I could have no supper. In I went and got the little book, which I was so impatient to read that I got over into a field at the upper corner of Kew Garden, where there stood a haystack. On the shady side of this I sat down to read. The book was so different from any thing that I had read before—it was something so new to my mind, that, though I could not at all understand some of it, it delighted me beyond description, and it produced what I have always considered a birth of intellect. I read on till it was dark, without any thought of supper or bed. When I could see no longer, I put my little book in my pocket, and tumbled down by the side of the stack, where I slept till the birds in Kew Gardens awaked me in the morning, when off I started to Kew, reading my little book. The singularity of my dress, the simplicity of my manner, my confident and lively air, and, doubtless, his own compassion besides, induced the gardener, who was a Scotchman, to give me victuals, find me a lodging, and set me to work." It is not known how long he remained at Kew. We lose sight of him until 1782, when, having gone to visit a relation who lived in the neighborhood of Portsmouth, he first beheld the sea. Every young lad falls in love with that element, and Cobbett was no exception to the rule. He saw the English fleet riding at anchor, and his heart expanded with national pride. The next morning he walked down to the beach, got into a boat, and in a few minutes was on board the *Pegasus* man-of-war. Here he endeavored to enlist in the naval service, but without success. The captain advised him to go home, but he was not so easily dissuaded. He made an attempt to get his name enrolled in another vessel, but here again the captain advised him to go home. Very reluctantly he did so; but his peace of mind was gone. He dreamed of the sea, and of traveling round the world. Farnham—even England—became too small for him. He determined to escape. Accordingly, on the 6th of May, 1783, he sallied forth to seek adventures. "I was dressed in my holiday clothes, in order to accompany two or three lasses to Guildford Fair. They were to assemble at a house about three miles from my home, where I was to attend them; but, unfortunately for me, I had to cross the London turnpike-road. The stage-coach had just turned the summit of a hill, and was rattling down toward me at a merry rate. The notion of going to London never entered my mind till this very moment, yet the step was completely determined on before the coach came to the spot where I stood. Up I got, and was in London about nine o'clock in the evening. It was by mere accident that I had money enough to defray the expenses of this day. Being rigged out for the fair, I had three or four crown and half crown pieces (which most certainly I did not intend to spend), besides a few shillings and halfpence. This, my little all, which I had been years in amassing, melted away like snow before the sun when touched by the fingers of the innkeepers and their waiters. In short, when I arrived at Ludgate Hill, and had paid my fare, I had but about half a crown in my pocket." Fortunately, he had succeeded in making the acquaintance of a passenger—a hop merchant from Southwark—who knew his father, and who was disposed to lend a helping hand to the young man. He invited him to his house, which he told him he might look upon as his home till something turned up. In the mean time he wrote to his father, advising him of what had taken place. The latter desired Cobbett to return immediately, but a mistaken sense of false delicacy prevented his doing so. At length a situation as copying clerk in a lawyer's office was obtained for him, and for nearly a year he went through the wretched drudgery of that occupation—the only portion of his life, he says, which was "totally unattended with pleasure." It is not easy to escape from a lawyer's office into a higher sphere of usefulness, and to this circumstance we may perhaps attribute Cobbett's lengthened experiment in the gloom and wretchedness of the law. One fine spring morning in 1784, while strolling through St. James's Park, to cheer himself "with the sight of the trees, the grass, and the water," he read an advertisement inviting all loyal young men to serve their country, and reap honor and riches in that patriotic undertaking. Any life was welcome to Cobbett, provided it did not revolve on the high stool of an attorney's office. Without troubling himself about inquiries, he took the king's shilling, and became a private in the 54th regiment. He remained about a year at Chatham, during which time he learned his duties thoroughly, and occupied his leisure in reading and study. He says that during this year he learned more than he had ever done before. Whatever books came in his way (and he subscribed to a circulating library) he read with avidity, but, it is to be feared, with little profit. Knowledge is not gained by skimming over the gilded surface of novels, dramas, poems, etc. One branch of knowledge, however, he searched to the bottom—the grammar of his mother tongue. Cobbett procured a copy of Lowth's Grammar, and applied himself to the study of it with unceasing assiduity. It was a considerable time before he could comprehend all that he read, but the light shone in upon him at last. "The pains I took," he says, "can not be described. I wrote the whole grammar out two or three times. I got it by heart. I repeated it every morning and every evening, and when on guard. I imposed on myself the task of saying it all over once every time I was posted sentinel. To this exercise of my memory I ascribe the retentiousness of which I have since found it capable; and to the success with which it was attended, I ascribe the perseverance that has led to the acquirement of the little learning of which I am master."

A few months after his enlistment, the detachment to which he belonged sailed for Halifax, Nova Scotia, previous to which he had been promoted to the rank of corporal. From Nova Scotia he proceeded with his regiment to St. John's and New Brunswick. By the end of his third year in the army he was promoted to the rank of sergeant major over the heads of thirty sergeants—no slight compliment to his abilities and attention. He refers to this period of his life: "Before my promotion a clerk was wanted to make out the morning report of the regiment. I rendered the clerk unnecessary; and, long before any other man was dressed for the parade, my work for the morning was all done, and I myself was on the parade, walking, in fine weather, perhaps for an hour. My custom was thus: to get up, in summer, at daylight, and in winter at four o'clock; shave, dress, even to the putting on my sword-belt over my shoulder, and having my sword lying on the table before me ready to hang by my side. Then I ate a bit of cheese, or pork and bread. Then I prepared my report, which was filled up as fast as the companies brought me in the materials. After this I had an hour or two to read before the time came for my duty out of doors, unless when the regiment or part of it went to exercise in the morning."

While at New Brunswick Cobbett made the acquaintance of his future wife. She was then but thirteen years of age, and his attention was directed to her by seeing her, one frosty morning at daybreak, scouring out the washing-tub before her father's door. "That's the girl for me," said Cobbett to his companions. "From the day that I first spoke to her, I never had a thought of her ever being the wife of any other man more than I had a thought of her being transformed into a chest of drawers; and I formed my resolution at once to marry her as soon as we could get permission, and to get out of the army as soon as I could; so that this matter was at once settled as firmly as if written in the book of Fate." About six months after arriving at this determination the object of his affection left for England; and "now it was," says Cobbett, "that I acted a part becoming a real and sensible lover. I was aware that when she got to that gay place, Woolwich (her father was in the artillery), the house of her father and mother, necessarily visited by numerous persons not the most select, might become unpleasant to her, and I did not like, besides, that she should continue to work hard. I had saved 150 guineas, the earnings of my early hours in writing for the paymaster, the quarter-master, and others, in addition to the savings of my own pay. I sent her all my money before she sailed, and wrote to her to beg of her, if she found her home uncomfortable, to hire a lodging with respectable people; and, at any rate, not to spare the money by any means, but to buy herself good clothes, and to live without hard work until I arrived in England."

Owing to a difficulty with Spain, Cobbett was unable to get his discharge for four years. At the end of that time he landed at Portsmouth, and immediately set out in search of his lady-love. He found her working very hard in a private family as a servant-of-all-work. As soon as the greetings were over (that is to say, over for a moment or two), the dear little girl ran to her box and produced the 150 guineas untouched. In a few months they were man and wife, and ten years later he wrote that to "her gentleness, prudence, and fortitude I owe whatever I enjoy of pleasure, of fortune, or of reputation." Immediately after the honeymoon (March, 1792) he made a trip to France, where he remained for six months. It was his intention to have staid longer, but the events of the Revolution were hurrying on, and Cobbett thought it would be most prudent to leave the country. From Havre de Grace he embarked for America, and landed at New York in October, 1792.

It is not very clear what was his intention in coming to America. His finances were at a low ebb, and he knew very little about trade. He had, however, a letter of recommendation from the American embassador at the Hague to Mr. Jefferson, at that time Secretary of State, and may, perhaps, have looked on this as a golden key to fortune. He forwarded the document to Mr. Jefferson, who, in reply, told him that public offices were so few in America, and of so little value, as to offer no resource to talent. As it was now absolutely necessary to do something for a living, Cobbett determined to try his hand at teaching, and accordingly took up his abode in Philadelphia, with the intention of offering his services to Frenchmen as a teacher of English. We are not informed of his success, but he refers occasionally to his pupils, which indicates that he was not wholly without patronage.

In 1794 Cobbett commenced his career of author. He was in his thirty-third year, excessively patriotic, and a thorough-going Tory in every respect. The event which induced him to seize the pen was the arrival of Dr. Priestley in the United States. A pamphlet attacking that gentleman, and entitled *Observations on the Emigration of Doctor Joseph Priestley*, by Peter Porcupine, was his first effusion. He first offered this production to Mr. Carey, of Philadelphia. "Mr. Carey received me," says Cobbett, "as booksellers generally receive authors (I mean authors whom they get little by). He looked at the title from top to bottom, and then at me from head to foot. 'No, *my lad*,' says he, 'I don't think it will suit.'" He then went to Mr. Bradford, who agreed to publish it, and divide the profits, which, we are informed with great exactness, amounted to one shilling and seven pence half-penny currency, or eleven pence three farthings sterling! The pamphlet attracted attention, however, and the vigorous style of the author was in demand. During the next two years he wrote several pamphlets, obtaining for them the following prices: *Observations* (before referred to), 20 cents; *Bone to Gnaw, Part I.*, 125 dollars; *Kick for a Bite*, 20 dollars; *Bone to Gnaw, Part II.*, 40 dollars; *Plain English*, 100 dollars; *New Year's Gift*, 100 dollars; *Prospect*, 18 dollars. Total, 403 dollars, 20 cents.

Encouraged by the success of these publications, Cobbett determined to reap all the benefit which might accrue from his pen, and in the spring of 1796 commenced business in Philadelphia as a bookseller. Up to this time the secrecy of his *nomme de plume* had been preserved, and he was known simply as Peter Porcupine. He had hosts of enemies, but, so long as he preserved his incognito, their indignation was of little avail; but when he announced his intention to open a shop, and sell his own pamphlets as his own productions, his best friends became alarmed. But he did so, and took a store of such magnificent proportions, that a local paper declared on the spot that he was a British spy, and "Billy Pitt's agent." Soon after he had opened his establishment he commenced a daily newspaper called *Porcupine's Gazette*, which he continued for some years at the expense of French republicanism and American democracy, both of which he ridiculed with the fiercest sarcasm. Writing as he did with the most scrupulous disregard to private feelings, it is nothing but natural that he exposed himself to prosecutions from all quarters. Two libel suits were brought against him, one at the instance of the Spanish minister, which was lost, and one at the instance of Dr. Rush, of Philadelphia. The latter gentleman succeeded in obtaining a verdict of $5000 against Cobbett, which sum was subscribed by his admirers in a few days. But the verdict rankled in Cobbett's mind, and he remembered it in his parting address to America. This document is curious, and was published on the 1st of June, 1800, when he sailed from New York for England. Addressing the people of the United States, he says, "You will doubtless be astonished that, after having had such a smack of the sweets of liberty, I should think of rising thus abruptly from the feast; but this astonishment will cease when you consider that, under a general term, things diametrically opposite in their natures are frequently included, and that flavors are not more various than tastes. Thus, for instance, nourishment of every species is called food, and we all like food; but, while one is partial to roast beef and plum pudding, another is distractedly fond of flummery and mush. So it is with respect to liberty, of which, out of its infinite variety of sorts, yours, unfortunately, happens to be the sort which I do not like. * * * To my friends, who are also the real friends of America, I wish that peace and happiness which virtue ought to insure, but which I greatly fear they will not find; and as to my enemies, I can wish them no severer scourge than that which they are preparing for themselves and their country. With this I depart for my native land, where neither the moth of democracy nor the rust of federalism doth corrupt, and where thieves do not with impunity break through and steal $5000 at a time." With Cobbett's feelings, the best thing he could do was to go back to England. He was evidently unfit for America.

Immediately on his arrival in England he paid a visit to the place of his birth. His ideas had been expanded by his visit to America, and he wrote as follows: "The trees, the hedges, even the parks and woods seemed so *small!* It made me laugh to hear little gutters that I could jump over called *rivers*. The Thames was a *creek*. But when, in about a month after my arrival in London, I went to Farnham, the place of my birth, what was my surprise! Every thing was become so pitifully *small!* I had to cross, in my post-chaise, the long and dreary heath of Bagshot; then, at the end of it, to mount a hill called Hungry Hill; and from that hill I knew that I should look down into the beautiful and fertile vale of Farnham. My heart fluttered with impatience, mixed with a sort of fear, to see all the scenes of my childhood, for I had learned before the death of my father and mother. There is a hill not far from the town called Crooksbury Hill, which rises up out of a flat in the form of a cone, and is planted with Scotch fir-trees. Here I used to take the eggs and young ones of crows and magpies. This hill was a famous object in the neighborhood. It served as the superlative degree of height. 'As high as Crooksbury Hill' meant, with us, the utmost degree of height. Therefore the first object that my eyes sought was this hill. I could not believe my eyes. Literally speaking, I for a moment thought the famous hill removed, and a little heap put in its place; for I had seen in New Brunswick a single rock, or hill of solid rock, ten times as big, and four or five times as high!" Shortly after the conclusion of this tour, the first number of the *Porcupine* made its appearance (October, 1800), but, although perfectly fierce, it did not attract much attention, and in the following year amalgamated with another daily paper called the *True Briton*, soon after which event Mr. Cobbett ceased to have any connection with it. He then commenced the business of bookselling in connection with a partner of the name of Morgan, at the sign of the "Crown and Mitre," Pall Mall.

The first number of the *Weekly Political Register*, a periodical from which Cobbett derives most of his fame, appeared in January, 1802, and from that time to the year 1835, when he died, that "faithful record of his delightful egotism, his extreme opinionativeness, his matchless invective against all public offenders, and his numberless schemes for putting public affairs in perfect order, was kept up to the last with unabated vigor by the marvelous force of his single pen." For the first two or three years he tried to make the *Register* what it purported to be—a complete record of political intelligence; but the dry labor and routine of this scheme did not become pleasant by custom, and he soon perceived that the public cared more for what he wrote and thought than what he registered. So he wrote more and compiled less. The result was a complete success, and the *Register* obtained a circulation of 4000 copies, notwithstanding its high price of twenty cents a number. At first he espoused the Tory side, but, after some experience, he professed himself disgusted with that party, and advocated popular reforms. He wrote with amazing facility, and yet with strength, grace, and poetic warmth. In his style, says a popular writer, he has been compared to Swift, to Defoe, and sometimes to Franklin; nor would it be difficult to find many passages in the *Register* bearing no small resemblance to each of these writers. But, with much of the circumstantial, graphic narration-talent of Defoe, the charming simplicity and homely wisdom of Franklin, the idiomatic terseness and humor of Swift, there is an abounding heartiness and a garrulity in most of his writings which stamps them with a special charm, for which we might search in vain through most political writers.

Cobbett's leaning to the popular party became very decided in 1804, and his attacks on Mr. Pitt correspondingly severe. He had a happy faculty of nicknaming his opponents, and of speaking of them generally in a way that was far from pleasant. The members of the government, now the special objects of his attack, hated and feared him. No opportunity of crushing his power was allowed to pass unimproved. In 1804 he was convicted for libel, on the ground that he had published articles tending to bring the Earl of Hardwick, Lord Lieutenant of Ireland, and several Irish officials, into contempt. He was sentenced to pay a fine of £500. Two days after, Mr. Plunkett, Attorney General for Ireland, brought an action against him, laying the damages at £10,000. The jury returned a verdict against Cobbett, and he had to pay another five hundred pounds. These prosecutions were intended to silence Cobbett, but they had precisely the opposite effect, and his merciless blows fell thick and heavy on the ministerial shoulders. In 1809 he made some very severe remarks on the flogging of five soldiers belonging to a militia regiment then stationed at Ely, under a guard of the German Legion. The attorney general commenced a prosecution, and on the 15th of June, 1810, Cobbett was again found guilty. This time the ministers were determined to crush him: he was sentenced to be imprisoned in Newgate for two years, to pay a fine of £1000, and, at the expiration of the two years, to give security for his good behavior for seven years, himself in £3000, and two securities at £1000 each. In the *Register* of the 14th of July, 1810 (four days after sentence had been passed), he says: "After having published seventeen volumes of this work, embracing the period of eight years and a half, during which time I have written with my own hand nearly two thousand articles upon various subjects, without having, except in one single instance, incurred even the threats of the law, I begin the eighteenth volume in a prison. In this respect, however, I only share the lot of many men who have inhabited this prison before me; nor have I the smallest doubt that I shall be enabled to follow the example of those men. On the triumphing, the boundless joy, the feasting and shouting of the peculators or public robbers, and of all those, whether profligate or hypocritical villains, of whom I have been the scourge, I look with contempt, knowing very well, feeling in my heart that my situation, even at this time, is infinitely preferable to theirs; and as to the future, I can reasonably promise myself days of peace and happiness, while continual dread must haunt their guilty minds, while every stir and every sound must make them quake for fear. *Their* day is yet to come!" Mr. Cobbett neither forgot nor forgave this imprisonment; it became the topic of his life, and whenever he wanted an illustration of the blackest tyranny, he referred to it with savage pleasure. Coming as it did at a moment when he was at the height of his political popularity, and when he was surrounded by all the comforts of a happy home in the country, it is not remarkable that he felt with double acuteness the injustice of which he was the victim. But while in prison, he never allowed his spirits to sink; that would have been a triumph for his enemies. He continued his regular avocations, wrote from week to week to his readers in the *Register*, and carried on his farm by letter also. He had so much writing to execute that he found it absolutely necessary to have one or two of his children with him. For the use of a part of the keeper's house he had to pay the enormous rent of "twelve guineas a week."

On his liberation in 1812, a public dinner was given to Mr. Cobbett, at which the celebrated Sir Francis Burdett presided, and from this moment he was looked upon as a martyr in the public cause. He applied himself to the interests of his adherents with his usual enthusiasm; but the fines he had to pay, added to the fleecing sustained while in prison, and the unavoidable neglect of his interests during two years, placed him in a position of much embarrassment. He struggled against pecuniary difficulties of the most oppressive kind; but the fall in the price of agricultural-produce which followed the termination of the American war, added to circumstances of a purely political nature, thoroughly alarmed him, and induced him to fly to America (1817). The ostensible cause of his leaving England was his fear of again being sent to jail. According to his representation, ministers, in bringing forward the Six Acts Bill for suppressing freedom of discussion, had mainly in view the *Weekly Register*, which had been reduced to four cents some months previously, and had attained a weekly circulation of 50,000. From his farewell address, it would seem that he was under the influence of a panic, in which pecuniary and political considerations seem to have had an equal share. He was clearly of opinion that England was going to ruin, and, with less patriotism than we might have expected, he made up his mind to desert her.

Accordingly, he removed to America, and for two years and a half wrote his *Registers* on this side the Atlantic. To indulge his rural habits, he took a farm at Hyde Park, Long Island, where, in May, 1819, he suffered a severe loss, his house and the greater part of his farming stock being consumed by fire. Five months after this event he made up his mind to return to England, and in November arrived at Liverpool, bearing with him the bones of Thomas Paine, for whose genius he had suddenly conceived a singular regard, based, it is said, on his opposition to the funding system, which Cobbett detested. Soon after his arrival in the English metropolis he started a daily paper, called *Cobbett's Evening Post*, which run a rapid career of two months, and then died. At the end of that time he resolved to apply himself exclusively to the *Register*. In 1820 he made his first attempt to enter Parliament, but was defeated. In 1826 he repeated the experiment, with no better success. In April, 1830, he issued an address, the impudent egotism of which is remarkable, recommending that a subscription should be opened in every county in England for the purpose of purchasing for him an estate sufficient for the qualification of two members—himself and another whom he should nominate to work within him. The sum required was £10,000; the sum subscribed was £27 *2s.*

In 1831 Mr. Cobbett was again tried for libel. In this case it was alleged that an article he had written, called "The Rural War," was calculated to excite agricultural laborers to acts of sedition, insurrection, and arson. Cobbett defended himself in person, and delivered an able speech of six hours and a half. The attorney general then replied, and, after Lord Tenterden had summed up, the jury retired at five minutes past six o'clock. No verdict was given during the night, and at a little before nine in the morning the jury stated that they could not agree; upon which they were discharged, and Cobbett was set at liberty. A remarkably narrow escape.

The first general election after the passage of the Reform Bill saw Mr. Cobbett elected to the English House of Parliament as representative for the borough of Oldham. He polled a very large vote, and headed his opponent by four to one. On the 31st of January, 1833, he delivered his maiden speech, which produced no small amount of merriment by the homely colloquial style in which it was couched. Subsequently the members tried to interrupt him by calling out "Question! question!" and "Divide! divide!" but Mr. Cobbett convinced the house that the task of crying him down was a hopeless one. He was allowed to have his talk in his own way; but it soon became evident even to his warmest admirers that he was not destined to shine to advantage in the House of Commons. Nor was the change of habits necessary to his duties agreeable to him. At all times overworked, he had maintained his health by the observance of the most regular and healthful habits. Night-work in the confined atmosphere of the house made ruinous encroachments on his constitution, and laid the foundation of the illness which finally carried him off. However, Mr. Cobbett was re-elected for Oldham in 1834, and resumed his duties in spite of a severe inflammatory attack from which he was suffering. A motion was brought on for the repeal of the malt tax, and Mr. Cobbett attempted to speak in favor of it, but, owing to inflammation of the throat, he could not make himself heard. He remained to vote on the occasion, thereby increasing the complaint. A similar instance occurred soon after, and Cobbett saw the necessity of attending to himself. He repaired to his farm near Farnham, and in a few weeks appeared to be on the high road to health; but he calculated too much on his own strength, and was imprudent enough to take tea in the open air. A violent relapse was the consequence, and he lingered for a week, during which he recovered so far as to talk pleasantly and jovially of his various occupations. On the day previous to his death he could not rest in the house, but insisted on being carried round the farm. It was the last strong impulse of his hardy nature. About four o'clock on the following morning (18th of June, 1835), William Cobbett expired, aged seventy-four years. "On the 27th of June the funeral took place from Normandy farm. The procession was attended by Mr. Fielden, M. P., Mr. O'Connell, and several other members of Parliament. By the time it had reached Farnham, it was swelled by thousands of laborers in their smock frocks and straw hats, who followed the procession to the churchyard, where the mortal remains of England's greatest self-taught prose writer were deposited beside those of his humble ancestors."

The best of Mr. Cobbett's works have been largely reprinted in the United States, and it is almost unnecessary to speak of their excellence. He was a most voluminous writer, and the strongest partisan politician that ever lived. Pervading all his productions is a delightful aroma of country life, intensified by scraps of personal adventure, related in a vein so genial, forcible, and truthful, that it is doubtful if any thing superior can be found in English literature. Cobbett was an author by instinct. He knew little of what is called art, and even scorned that little; but no one can read his best productions without feeling that the essence of art, truthfulness, is there. As a reformer, he was, perhaps, the most influential man that ever lived, although the inconsistencies into which he frequently threw himself detracted from his power, and induced even his friends to doubt every thing except his integrity.

"On the subject of the intellectual character of this remarkable man," says a writer in the *English Cyclopædia*, "there is already a more general agreement of opinion than might have been expected, considering the vehement partisanship of the greater portion of what he has written. His mind was one of extraordinary native vigor, but, apparently, not well fitted by original endowment, any more than by acquirement, for speculations of the highest kind. Cobbett's power lay in wielding more effectively, perhaps, than they were ever wielded before, those weapons of controversy which tell upon what, in the literal acceptation of the words, may be called the common sense of mankind; that is, those feelings and capacities which nearly all men possess, in contradistinction to those of a more refined and exquisite character, which belong to a comparatively small number. To these higher feelings and powers he has nothing to say; they, and all things that they delight in, are uniformly treated by him with a scorn, real or affected, more frank and reckless, certainly, in its expression than they have met with from any other great writer. He cares for nothing but what is cared for by the multitude, and by the multitude, too, only of his own day, and, it may be even said, of his own country. Shakspeare, the British Museum, antiquity, posterity, America, France, Germany, are, one and all, either wholly indifferent to him, or the objects of his bitter contempt. But in his proper line he is matchless. When he has a subject that suits him, he handles it, not so much with the artificial skill of an accomplished writer, as with the perfect and inimitable natural art with which a dog picks a bone. There are many things that other men can do which he can not attempt; but this he can do, as none but himself can or ever could do it."

AMOS WHITTEMORE.

AMOS WHITTEMORE, the inventor of the card machine, was born at Cambridge, Massachusetts, April 19th, 1759. His father was a small farmer, whose means were limited, but whose industry enabled him to rear a large family in a creditable manner, and give to his children the rudiments of an English education.

Of the early life of Amos we know but little, and for that little are indebted to Mr. Howe. He was engaged in the usual avocations of the farm, rendering what small assistance lay in his power to his father. At an early age he manifested a considerable aptitude for mechanical pursuits, and a talent for science. These tastes induced him to select the business of a gunsmith as the one which he could follow with most pleasure to himself. During his apprenticeship he applied himself diligently to his new trade, and made many ingenious inventions and useful implements for perfecting his work. Long before the term of his apprenticeship had expired he was an excellent workman; so good, indeed, that his master declared he was unable to give him any farther instruction, and advised him to commence business for himself.

For several years subsequent to this period he pursued a variety of occupations with more or less success, and finally became interested with his brother and five others in the manufacture of cotton and wool cards. The firm was called Giles, Richards & Co., and supplied nearly all the cards then used in the country. Amos's knowledge of mechanics and his extreme ingenuity pointed him out as a fitting superintendent of the machine department.

Up to this time the manufacture of cotton and wool cards was conducted almost entirely by hand, and was necessarily imperfect and expensive. Whittemore immediately perceived that here was a field for the exercise of his inventive faculties. The immense value of a machine so constructed as to be able, by its own independent action, to hold the sheet of leather, pierce the holes, draw the wire from the reel, and shape and stick it in its proper place, was apparent to every one. From his brother he received every kind of encouragement, and at once proceeded to experiments, in the pursuit of which he was so indefatigable that his health was seriously impaired. He slept on wool cards, dreamed of wool cards, lived and breathed in wool cards. Such application could not be without result. After some failures, which only served to stimulate his invention, he produced a machine which was able to draw the wire from the reel, cut and shape it, pierce the holes in the leather, and even place the staples firmly in the sheet; but it was necessary to bend the wire after it was placed; without this, all was in vain. The difficulty was one which baffled him in every direction. He tried to surmount it in a thousand ways, but it seemed useless, and he abandoned himself to despair. The machine he had created lay before him like a beautiful corpse, perfect in every respect, but lacking the breath of life. He was plunged into the greatest despondency and gloom, and night or day could find but little rest for his troubled mind. Exhausted by this state of nervous excitement, he sunk into a slumber one evening. A strange vision visited him. He awoke with a perfect scheme for the accomplishment of his object. It had come to him in a dream, but it was reality in the morning, and before breakfast he was able to announce to his brother and friends the completion of his machine. Whittemore dwelt with much satisfaction on this dream in after years.

The machine, when completed, was a masterpiece of beautiful mechanism. In 1797, a patent right was granted to the inventor and his associates for the term of fourteen years. To procure the same protection in England, Whittemore sailed for that country in the spring of 1799, and returned the following year without having obtained any satisfaction. Numerous offers were made to Whittemore either to purchase the right or a share in the profits of the invention, but for some cause Whittemore did not come to terms. The consequence was that he derived no benefit from that country.

On his return, Whittemore and his brother entered into a copartnership with a man of capital, and commenced the manufacture of the improved machinery in a limited way. Before this firm had got properly into operation, the patent right was nearly expired. Considerable apprehension was felt; but Whittemore visited Washington with a full-sized machine as a model, and so charmed the members with its perfection, that by a unanimous vote the patent was extended for a further term of fourteen years. Immediately after this, efforts were made to establish a company with a sufficient capital to carry on the manufacture with energy. In 1812 an act was obtained incorporating the "New York Manufacturing Company." The capital was $800,000, of which nearly a half was to be employed in the manufacture of cotton and wool cards, and building the necessary machinery and factories. One of the first acts of the company was to purchase the patent right and entire stock and machinery of Whittemore for the sum of one hundred and fifty thousand dollars. The time was favorable to the operations of the company. A war raged between England and America; commerce was entirely interrupted, and the necessity of supplying ourselves with what was needed caused manufactories of cotton and woolen stuffs especially to spring up as if by magic. There was such a demand for hand-cards that the company was soon busily and profitably employed.

Exactly the reverse of this was the case when, in 1815, peace was proclaimed. An enormous influx of foreign goods glutted the market, and threw the native manufacturer entirely out of the field. The raw material was again in demand, and scarcely a pound of cotton or wool remained at home. Private individuals found it impossible to struggle against the reverse; corporations, much more unwieldy and thriftless, sunk hopelessly beneath the reaction. In 1818, after waiting three years for an improved state of things, the company proposed and effected a sale of its entire manufacturing property to Messrs. Samuel and Timothy Whittemore, the former a brother, the latter a son of the inventor. The first named person almost immediately relinquished his interest, and Whittemore became the sole proprietor. He conducted the business with varied success until within a few years. The "New York Manufacturing Company" invested its funds in the banking business, and continues its operations to the present day under the name and title of the "Phœnix Bank." The patent expired in 1825, and the machines were thereafter made by any one who chose to apply himself to the business. As an evidence of the perfection of the machine which Whittemore invented, it may be interesting to know that no important alteration has taken place in its construction, but that it remains essentially the same to the present day.

Whittemore purchased a comfortable estate in the town of West Cambridge, and resided there in the quiet pursuit of astronomical science to the time of his death, which occurred in 1828, in the sixty-ninth year of his age, leaving a widow and several children to lament his loss. "To his family," says his biographer, "he was an example of one who lived a pure and blameless life, and, though he left but an inconsiderable fortune, they inherited a far brighter treasure in an unsullied reputation." Whittemore was of a bland and conciliating disposition, even in temper, and in manners strikingly meditative, conversing but little, and often seen in profound mental cogitation.

CAPTAIN JAMES COOK.

JAMES COOK, the celebrated circumnavigator, was the son of peasants, and came into the world in the year 1728. His father was in the humblest circumstances, and gained a scanty living by working as day laborer on the small farms of his native county, Yorkshire, England. James assisted his father until his thirteenth year, when a change to circumstances rather more prosperous than what had before existed enabled him to attend school, and acquire some knowledge of reading, writing, and arithmetic. A few years later he was apprenticed to a shopkeeper in a small fishing town a few miles from Whitby, and here he acquired his first appetite for the sea. It is probable that he was not very useful in the mercantile way, for, when there was an opportunity of shipping off his apprentice, his master willingly gave up his indentures. Cook now entered on his seafaring career in the humble capacity of cabin-boy. The *Freelove* was the vessel in which he embarked, and she was engaged principally in the coal trade. In time Cook became a foremast man, and was considered so skillful and well-informed that the owners promoted him to the rank of mate. He was not popular with his fellow-seamen, who considered him taciturn and morose, while, in reality, he was merely retiring. Every opportunity he had he devoted to the acquiring of knowledge. Cook remained in this service until his twenty-seventh year. War had then broken out between France and England, and there was consequently a demand for seamen. Cook entered the navy, and his steady conduct and seaman-like qualities again served him. He was promoted to the quarter-deck by a master's warrant from the Admiralty, dated May 10th, 1759, Cook then being in his thirty-first year. His first appointment was to the *Mercury*, in which vessel he assisted at the reduction of Quebec under General Wolfe. In the dangerous navigation of the St. Lawrence Mr. Cook's talents were called into active operation. The buoys in that river had all been removed by the French at the first appearance of the English fleet, and it became vitally necessary that a survey should be made of the channels, and correct soundings obtained, to enable the ships to keep clear of the many dangers which beset that stream. By the recommendation of his commander, this onerous duty was intrusted to Mr. Cook, who cheerfully undertook it in a barge belonging to a seventy-four. He had to conduct many of his operations by night, on account of the watchfulness of the enemy, and one night he experienced a narrow escape; his boat was boarded by Indians in the pay of the French, and carried off in triumph, Cook and his companions barely escaping with their lives. The fleet, thanks to Cook's skill, reached its destination in safety.

On his return from Quebec, Mr. Cook was appointed master of the *Northumberland*, under Lord Colville, who was stationed as commodore at Halifax. Here he remained during the winter, improving his leisure with studies which would better enable him to pursue his profession with honor and distinction. He was determined to become thoroughly master of the art of navigation, and, with this object in view, he made himself master of Euclid's Elements of Plane Geometry, and proceeded thence to the higher branches of mathematical study, including nautical astronomy. By this course he was able to take astronomical observations, to calculate a ship's progress, and to ascertain the degree of latitude and longitude at any given spot on the ocean. Mixing as he did with men of education and refinement, he acquired also an urbane and courteous bearing, which conciliated all classes of people, and which certainly contributed largely to his future success in life.

In 1762 Mr. Cook returned to England, and married an estimable lady of the name of Batts. In the following year he was appointed to survey the whole coast of Newfoundland, which task he performed with his usual promptitude and skill. After this he made another trip under his old commander, Sir Hugh Palliser, a gentleman who was a true friend. Cook had now published several charts, and had made numerous observations. These matters brought him into correspondence with members of the Royal Society, and some of his papers were published in their Transactions. In this way he became known and recognized in the scientific world, and on his thirty-fourth birth-day could claim the friendship of many of the most eminent men in England.

At this time the project of a voyage of discovery for various scientific purposes was largely discussed. The principal object of the expedition was to observe a transit of the planet Venus over the face of the sun, which could only be done somewhere in the Pacific or Southern Ocean. The transit, according to the best calculations, was to happen in June, 1769. The Royal Society, as the representative of the scientific world, applied to the king to fit out an expedition suitable to take the observations, and the king complied with the request. The command was offered to Cook, and was so much to his mind that in a very short time he was ready for sea. He received the commission of a lieutenant from the king, and the *Endeavor*, of 370 tons, was placed at his disposal. She was provisioned for eighteen months, armed with twelve carriage-guns and twelve swivels, and manned with a complement of eighty-four seamen. A number of scientific gentlemen, with every requisite apparatus, accompanied the expedition, many of them doing so at their own cost. On the 26th of August, 1768, the expedition set sail from Plymouth Sound. On the 11th of April, after many delays, they came in sight of Otaheite, and two days after anchored in Port Royal (Matavai), where the scientific gentlemen landed, and made preparations for taking their observations. The natives were friendly, and Cook endeavored to keep them so by drawing up a code of regulations by which communication and traffic were to be carried on in an equitable way. But the savages were not accustomed to treaties of this kind, and in a few days violated it. A big fellow fell in love with the bright musket which a sentinel carried, and dexterously snatched it from his hands. The marines were ordered to fire, and the thief was shot dead. This was the first lesson that Cook taught the Otaheitans; the second related to his own crew. A butcher became too familiar with the wife of a native chief, and attempted to take liberties with her. Cook ordered the fellow to be flogged publicly. At the first stroke of the lash the natives prayed that the man might be forgiven; but Cook was inexorable. He did not wish them to imagine that he threatened a thing without intending to fulfill it.

Shortly after this the scientific gentlemen were thrown into a state of the greatest alarm and consternation. The quadrant, an instrument on which every thing depended, was nowhere to be found. Diligent search and the offer of a reward were without effect. It became evident that it had been pilfered by a native, and this proved to be the case. Fortunately, however, it was recovered by Sir Joseph Banks before it had suffered any damage. The time for observing the transit now approached, and on the morning of the 3d of June satisfactory observations were made. Their enterprise was consequently crowned with success. The only annoyance now experienced was from the thievish habits of the natives. Cook was unwilling to fire upon them, but every day it became more apparent that something had to be done. On one occasion he seized all their fishing canoes, partly laden; and though, from motives of humanity, he gave up the fish, yet he detained the vessels, under a hope that several articles which had been pilfered would be restored; but in this he was mistaken. Mr. Cook and Mr. Banks (afterward Sir Joseph) explored the island, the latter gentleman planting seeds of watermelons, oranges, lemons, limes, and other plants and trees, which he had collected for the purpose, some of which now grow in rich perfection. On the 13th of July the ship weighed anchor, having on board a principal native of the name of Tupia, and a boy of thirteen, both of whom asked permission to accompany the ship to England. After quitting Otaheite, the *Endeavor* visited a group of islands, which, in consequence of their contiguity, Cook named the Society Islands. The expedition was generally well received by the natives, except at Ulictea, where the natives displayed so much hostility that Cook deemed it best not to force a landing, and proceeded on his way to the southward, in search of a supposed continent. On the 6th of October land was discovered, which proved to be a part of New Zealand. Here again the natives were hostile, and made the most warlike demonstrations. Tupia acted as the interpreter, and entreated them to put confidence in the English; but this they declined to do. A conflict was the inevitable result, in which some of the New Zealanders were killed, and three boys taken prisoners, who were treated with much kindness. As the place afforded nothing that the voyagers wanted, Mr. Cook named it Poverty Bay, and when the ship was about to sail on its course, released the three boys, who, it was hoped, would create a favorable impression in the minds of the natives by the account of the kind treatment they had received. The experiment appeared to be successful; some of the Indians came off to the ship, but it was almost impossible to keep friends with them for more than an hour or two at a time. Armed parties in large canoes assembled, and paddled off to the *Endeavor* as if to trade, but in reality to plunder, and they performed the latter operation with such coolness that in several instances it was absolutely necessary to fire on them. On one occasion they stole Tupia's boy Tayeto, the lad being the only trifle which happened to be lying about. They were, of course, compelled to relinquish their prey, but blood had to be shed before they consented to do so. While standing along the coast, the *Enterprise* narrowly escaped being wrecked on the rocks that lay some distance from the land; and again, on the 5th of December, while turning out of the Bay of Islands. In the latter instance the ship drifted so close to the shore that, notwithstanding the incessant roar of the breakers, they could hear the voices of the natives on the beach. The pinnace was got out to tow the vessel's head round, but none expected to escape destruction. Fortunately, a breeze sprung up at the right moment, and the ship got clear. About an hour afterward, just as the man heaving the lead sung out "seventeen fathoms," she struck on a hidden rock; there was scarcely time for confusion before she was washed off by the swell and carried into deep water.

On the 14th of January, 1770, the expedition anchored in Queen Charlotte's Sound to refit the ship and make necessary repairs. They found a good supply of fresh water, and took plenty of fish, but of inhabitants they saw but few. In one of their rambles they discovered an Indian family, and had ocular demonstration of cannibalism. The natives were friendly and hospitable. After a month's stay in these pleasant quarters, they proceeded to explore three or four islands in the locality, giving names to capes, headlands, rocks, etc. On the 19th of April they came in sight of New Holland (New South Wales, as it is now called), and anchored in Botany Bay on the 28th, where they landed. Two or three Indians on the shore objected to the latter ceremony, and made a gallant opposition with their lances; but a few shots so astonished their uncultivated ears that they did not recover a tolerable presence of mind until the expedition was out of sight. The voyagers left beads and trinkets in the huts of the natives, but without any conciliatory result. They persisted in being profoundly unconscious of the presence of strangers. In the Bay they caught a fish called a string-ray, which, after the entrails were taken out, weighed 336 pounds. Cook continued his explorations in New South Wales with great energy, but on the 10th of June the voyage was nearly brought to an end by the *Enterprise* striking on a coral reef and remaining there for forty-eight hours. She was at length got off, after having thrown every thing overboard which could in the slightest degree lighten her weight. The danger, however, was not removed, for she had a large hole in her bottom, and made water rapidly. When they got into harbor the bottom was overhauled, and a large piece of rock was discovered sticking firmly in the hole. If it had fallen out the vessel would undoubtedly have gone to the bottom. As it was, many valuable specimens collected by the scientific gentlemen, and placed in the hold for security, were utterly destroyed.

After touching at a number of other islands, at the Cape of Good Hope, and at St. Helena, the *Enterprise* returned home in safety on the 10th of June. The success of the expedition was so complete and satisfactory that Mr. Cook was promoted to the rank of commander, and became a great lion in the English metropolis, where, being an agreeable man, he made the most of his adventures.

Cook's second voyage round the world was undertaken for the purpose of exploring Australia, which was then supposed to be a southern continent of great magnitude. The king was again the patron, and two stout ships were purchased—the *Resolution*, of 462 tons, commanded by Captain Cook, with a complement of 112 persons, and the *Adventure*, of 336 tons, commanded by Tobias Furneaux, with a crew, including officers, of 81 souls. The vessels were supplied with every thing that experience, philanthropy, or science could suggest, and a full staff of scientific men were also engaged. Cook's instructions were "to circumnavigate the whole globe in high southern latitudes, making traverses, from time to time, into every part of the Pacific Ocean that had not undergone previous investigation, and to use his best endeavors to resolve the much-agitated question of a southern continent." The vessels quitted Plymouth on the 13th of July, 1772, and after touching at Madeira for wine, and at the Cape de Verds for water, crossed the line with a brisk southwest wind, and anchored in Table Bay, Cape of Good Hope, on the 30th of October. From this point they shaped their course for Cape Circumcision, but, owing to the severity of the weather, and the great quantities of floe ice and icebergs which they encountered, they failed to find that point, and did not see land for 117 days, having in that time traversed 3660 leagues, and reached New Zealand. The vessels unfortunately parted company, and did not meet again until the Resolution reached Queen Charlotte's Sound. Subsequently they parted again, and did not meet until their return to England. Singular enough, they arrived within a day of each other.

Cook did his best to cultivate the good opinion of the New Zealanders, and on parting left them a male and female goat, and a boar and two sows. From Queen Charlotte's Sound they directed their course to Otaheite, and on the 17th of August anchored in Oaiti-piha Bay. The natives were perfectly friendly, and crowded on board with fruits, vegetables, etc., to trade for nails and beads. Shirts were bestowed on the most important chiefs, which enormously exaggerated their dignity. Unfortunately, however, their thieving propensities had not subsided, and Cook had to turn them out of the ship and frighten them with musketry in order to put them on their guard. At Matavai Bay they found themselves popular. The natives had remembered their former voyage, and crowded the decks with eagerness and curiosity. Cook went to see Otoo, the reigning chief or prince, and describes him as a fine, well-made man, six feet high, and about thirty years of age. He was not remarkable for bravery, for, being invited to visit the ship, he declined on the ground "that he was frightened of the guns." From Matavai Bay the ship proceeded to Owharre. The chief remembered Cook with much kindliness, and brought the presents he had received on the former voyage to show that he treasured them. A number of compliments passed between the parties, but they did not avert an outrage. Without any provocation, a man assailed Captain Cook with a club at the landing-place; and Mr. Sparrman, who had gone into the woods to botanize, was set upon, beaten, and stripped. The Indians generally expressed their indignation, and the king was so much affected that he wept aloud, and insisted on placing himself entirely in the hands of the British until the culprits were found. He was taken on board the Resolution as a hostage, and dined with Captain Cook, but nothing was heard of Mr. Sparrman's personal effects, with the exception of his hanger, which was restored. When the king was landed by Captain Cook in great state, the joy of the people knew no bounds. They made a serviceable demonstration by loading two boats with hogs and fruits, and sending them to their English friend.

The voyagers quitted this part of the world on the 17th, and sailed to the westward. By the 1st of October they had reached Middleburg, and were welcomed in the most cordial manner by the natives. Barter commenced, but the people on shore seemed more anxious to give than to receive, and threw into the boats whole bales of cloth without asking or waiting for any thing in return. After leaving some garden-seeds and other useful things, the ship proceeded to Amsterdam, where they met with a similar reception. The island was found to be in an admirable state of cultivation, and the fertility unexceptionable. Captain Cook paid a visit to the head chief, who was seated, and seemed to be in an idiotic state of self-complacent dignity. He did not pay the slightest attention to the captain or any one in the party. Perhaps he was selected by the people to be their king on account of these very qualities, for, as a rule, the natives were found to be intelligent and lively—the women especially so. Most of them had lost one or both of their little fingers, but no reason could be gathered for the cause of this amputation.

The voyage was renewed on the 7th of October, and after calling at several places, the ship hauled up in November at Queen Charlotte's Sound for repairs. It was here discovered that much of the bread had been destroyed by the salt water that had entered the hold during their accident. On the 26th Cook took leave of New Zealand, with his ship's company in good health and spirits. They were now bound on finding the southern continent or islands in high latitudes, and knew that they had to encounter many hardships and dangers before they could again see land. They were not long before they fell in with large fields of ice, and in latitude 67° 5′ they were nearly blocked up, and on the 22d of December attained the highest latitude they could venture (lat. 67° 31′, long. 142° 54′ west), but could discover no indications of the proximity of land. After traversing the ocean in a southerly direction as far as it was prudent to go, the scientific men gave it as their opinion that ice surrounded the pole, without any intervening land, and advised the captain therefore to turn the vessel northward, and look for the island of Juan Fernandez. About this time Captain Cook was seized with a violent and dangerous disease, which required all the skill of the doctors to conquer. On partially recovering, it became absolutely necessary that he should receive some fresh nourishment, his stomach being too weak to bear the ordinary salted provisions. Gastronomically considered, the only fresh meat on board was the unhappy little dog of Mr. Forster. Ponto had to suffer. An agreeable broth was made from his remains, and on this and a few tender bits the captain gained strength. On the 11th of March they came in sight of Easter Island, where they remained but a short time, owing to the insecurity of the harbor and the scarcity of food and fuel. Early in April they reached the Marquesas, where they found a plentiful supply of fresh meats, yams, fruits, and plantains. These provisions were never more welcome, for the ship's company had now been on salt victuals for fourteen weeks. Owing to the great care and cleanliness of the captain, however, there had been no sickness on board. From the Marquesas they proceeded to their old anchorage ground at Matavai Bay, where they found the king and the chiefs more warmly disposed than ever. The Otaheitans got up a grand naval review for the edification of their visitors. No fewer than 160 of the largest and handsomest double canoes were assembled, fully manned with chiefs and warriors in their most terrific costumes, who appeared upon the fighting stages with their clubs and other instruments of warfare ready for action. Besides these large vessels, there were 170 smaller double canoes, each having a mast and sail, and a sort of hut or cabin on the deck. Captain Cook calculated that the number of men embarked on them could not be fewer than 7760, most of them armed with clubs, pikes, barbed spikes, bows and arrows, and slings for throwing large stones. The demonstration was quite imposing, and astonished the English, who did not give the Otaheitans credit for such extensive resources. While staying in this hospitable bay a romantic incident occurred. One of the seamen fell desperately in love with an Indian girl, and made up his mind that he would marry her. With this honorable object in view, he contrived to make his escape from the ship, and gained the woods, where it was his intention to stay until the expedition had sailed. The natives were not unfriendly to the project, but Captain Cook interfered in time to prevent its fulfillment.

Leaving these friendly islands, the voyagers cruised about, discovered a number of smaller ones, named them, and finally reached Queen Charlotte's Sound, New Zealand, where, after refitting, they departed for the western entrance of the Straits of Magellan, in order to coast along the south side of Terra del Fuego, round Cape Horn to the Straits of Le Maire. On the 17th of December they reached the first-mentioned desolate region, and after coasting as far as 60° south, the course was altered to look for Bouvet's Land; but, though they reached the spot where it was laid down on the charts, and sailed over and over it, yet no such place could be discovered, and after two day's search more to the southward, Cook came to the conclusion that Bouvet had mistaken ice for land. He now steered for the Cape of Good Hope, and home. After an absence of three years and eighteen days, the expedition reached Portsmouth in safety, having in that time sailed 20,000 leagues, in all sorts of climates and all sorts of weather. So admirable were Cook's arrangements for preserving the health of his people, and so strict was he in enforcing them, that only one man was lost by sickness during the entire voyage.

The king once more expressed his satisfaction by making Cook a post-captain, and three days later a captaincy in Greenwich Hospital was conferred upon him, to afford an honorable and competent retirement from active service. On the 29th of February, 1776, he was elected a member of the Royal Society, and soon after was honored with the gold medal, accompanied with a eulogium from the lips of Sir John Pringle, who performed the ceremony of presentation. It was on the conclusion of this voyage that Cook made his first appearance in the character of author. The account of the voyage was written by Cook himself, and manifests decided ability.

Cook's third and last voyage was undertaken for the purpose of discovering a supposed northwest passage from the Atlantic to the Pacific Oceans. Numerous expeditions had been sent out for this purpose at various times, but they had all failed. It was resolved by the Admiralty to make one other trial, under the auspices of the successful circumnavigator. Accordingly, on the 10th of February, 1776, he was appointed to the command in his old and trusty ship, the *Resolution*, and Captain Clerke, in the *Discovery*, was ordered to accompany him. Cook's instructions were to proceed direct to the Pacific Ocean, and thence to try the passage by way of Behring's Straits; and as it was necessary that the islands in the Southern Ocean should be revisited, cattle and sheep, with other animals, and all kinds of seeds, were shipped for the advantage of the inhabitants.

The *Resolution* sailed on the 12th of July, 1776 (the *Discovery* was to follow), having on board a native of the Sandwich Islands to act as interpreter. Nothing of importance occurred on the outward voyage, and on the 12th of February, 1777, Cook arrived at Queen Charlotte's Sound, New Zealand, where he anchored. He found the natives suspiciously sly, and no amount of persuasion could induce them to venture on board. They had reason for their uneasiness. On the last voyage, the *Adventure* had visited this place, and ten of her crew had been killed in an unpremeditated skirmish. They apprehended chastisement, and thought it best to be on the alert. It was not convenient for Cook to add to any ill feeling that might exist, so he said nothing about the massacre, but tried to conciliate. From the Sound the ship proceeded to some of the South Sea Islands, where they obtained a plentiful supply of provisions, but were greatly annoyed by the thievish propensities of the natives. To check this, Cook hit upon a new device. He seized the culprit and shaved his head, thus making him an object of ridicule to his countrymen, and enabling the English to keep their eyes on him. At Tongataboo generous hospitality was shown to them, and the king invited Cook to reside with him in his house. Here he made a distribution of animals among the chiefs, explaining their uses, and how to preserve them. A horse and mare, a bull and cow, several sheep and turkeys were thus given away. But, in spite of this kindly reciprocity, thieving still went on. Cook became incensed, and determined that he would put a stop to it at any risk. Two kids and two turkey-cocks were abstracted from the stores. The captain seized three canoes, put a guard over the chiefs, and insisted that not only the kids and turkeys should be restored, but also every thing that had been taken away since their arrival. Much of the plunder was returned. But the chiefs, who were friendly, probably felt themselves insulted.

After remaining nearly three months in these hospitable but unprincipled regions, Cook took his departure for Otaheite, and thence for Matavai Bay, where he presented King Otoo with the remainder of his live-stock, among which were a horse and mare. To show the natives the use of the latter animals, Captains Cook and Clerke rode about the island on horseback, much to the astonishment of the simple people. More civilized people have sometimes been astonished when they saw, for the first time, Mr. Jack Tar astride a horse. The wonder of the natives never abated. At Huaheine a thief occasioned the voyagers much trouble. He was a determined rascal, and shaving his head and beard, and cutting off his ears, had no moral effect on him. He persisted in his evil ways, and defied public opinion. At Ulictea several desertions took place, the deserters being sheltered by the Indians. Both Captain Clerke and Captain Cook went in pursuit of the fugitives, but without success. The latter therefore ordered the chief's son, daughter, and son-in-law to be seized, and held as hostages until the deserters were given up. The remedy was effectual, and in a few days an exchange was effected. This severe policy of Cook was intended to save the spilling of innocent blood; but it produced much indignation among the savages, who felt that it was an outrage to seize the highest persons in their land for every trivial offense. Even at this early day schemes were afoot to assassinate Cook and Clerke.

On the 2d of January the ships resumed their voyage northward. They passed several islands, the inhabitants of which, though at an immense distance from Otaheite, spoke the same language. Those who came on board displayed the utmost astonishment at every thing they saw, and it was evident that they had never seen a ship before. They resembled the South Sea Islanders in another unpleasant respect—they were passionately addicted to stealing. To a group of these islands Captain Cook gave the name of the Sandwich Islands. New Albion was made on the 7th of March, the ships then being in latitude 44° 33′ north, and, after sailing along it till the 29th, they came to anchor in a small cove lying in latitude 49° 29′ north. A brisk trade commenced with the natives, who appeared to be well acquainted with the value of iron, and were eager to get it in exchange for skins, etc., rough and manufactured into garments. But the most extraordinary articles which they offered in trade were human skulls, and hands not quite stripped of the flesh, and which had the appearance of having been recently on the fire. Thieving was practiced in a dexterous and educated manner, but the natives were strict in being paid for every thing they supplied to the ships, with which rule Cook was happy to comply. This inlet was named King George's Sound, but it was afterward ascertained that the natives called it Nootka Sound, by which name it is more commonly known. From this point they exercised the greatest watchfulness, hoping to find an outlet into the Atlantic Ocean, but, as every one knows, without success. Cook was able, however, to ascertain the relative positions of the two continents, Asia and America, whose extremities he observed. He explored the coasts in Behring's Straits, where they found some Russian traders. The ships then quitted the harbor of Samganoodah, and sailed for the Sandwich Islands, Captain Cook intending to await the season there, and then return to Kamtschatka. In latitude 20° 55′ they discovered the island of Mowee, and a few days later fell in with another, which the natives called Owhyhee, the extent of which was so great that the voyagers were nearly seven weeks sailing round it and examining the coast. The inhabitants were extremely pleasant, and appeared to be entirely free from suspicion. Their canoes flocked around the ships in hundreds, and came well laden too, but the gentlemen were light fingered, and had but little fear of gunpowder. Captain Cook had an interview with Terreeoboo, king of the islands, in which great formality was observed on both sides, followed by an exchange of presents and an exchange of names. The natives were extremely deferential to Cook, displaying almost an amount of adoration. A society of priests (native) furnished the ships with a plentiful supply of hogs and vegetables, without requiring any return. On the day previous to their departure the king sent them an immense quantity of cloth, many boat-loads of vegetables, and a whole herd of hogs. The ships then sailed, but on the following day encountered such a severe storm that they had to put back in order to repair damages. They anchored at the old spot, and for a time things went on pleasantly; but a theft took place, and the seamen, becoming enraged at losing every trifling article they possessed, had an affray with the natives. It was not a trifling article in this instance, however, being, in fact, no smaller than the cutter of the ship Discovery. The boats of both vessels were immediately sent in search of her, and Captain Cook went on shore to arrange matters in a determined spirit. The robbery was of the most audacious kind, and certainly merited punishment, but it is questionable if Cook's policy (considering the kindness he had so lately experienced) was the best that could have been devised.

We have, in our sketch of the life of Ledyard, given the substance of what follows. Ledyard, it will be remembered, was a member of the expedition, and an acute observer of all that took place. There are, however, some slight variations in the two accounts, and we continue our narrative so that they may be compared by the curious.

Cook left the *Resolution* about seven o'clock, attended by the lieutenant of marines, a sergeant, a corporal, and seven private men. The pinnace's crew were likewise armed, and under the command of Mr. Roberts; the launch was also ordered to assist his own boat. On landing there was not the slightest symptom of hostility; crowds gathered around the Englishmen, and were kept in order by the chiefs, who seemed desirous that every thing should proceed in an orderly and pleasant manner. Captain Cook proceeded to the king's house, and requested that he would go on board the *Resolution*, intending, of course, to keep him as a hostage. The king, individually, offered but few objections, but his people evidently understood the manœuvre, and quietly commenced arming themselves with spears, clubs, and daggers, and protecting themselves with the thick mats which they usually donned in time of war like armor. While affairs were in this state, a canoe arrived from the opposite side of the bay, and announced that one of the native chiefs had been killed by a shot from the *Discovery's* boat. Indignant excitement now agitated the crowd; the women retired, and the men openly uttered threats. Cook, perceiving the threatening aspect that things had assumed, ordered Lieutenant Middleton to march his marines down to the boats, to which the islanders offered no objection. He then escorted the king, attended by his wife, two sons, and several chiefs. One of the sons had already entered the pinnace, expecting his father to follow, when the king's wife entreated him not to leave the shore, or he would be put to death. Matters were now hurrying to a crisis. A chief, with a dagger concealed under his cloak, was observed watching Cook, and the lieutenant of marines wanted to fire at him, but this the captain would not permit. The chief gained new courage by this hesitation, and closed on them, and the officer struck him with his firelock. Another native interfered, and grasped the sergeant's musket, and was compelled to let it go by a blow from the lieutenant. Cook, seeing that it was useless to attempt to force the king off, was about to give orders to re-embark, when a man flung a stone at him, which he returned by discharging small shot from the barrels of his piece. The man, being scarcely hurt, brandished his spear as if about to hurl it at the captain, who at once knocked him down, but refrained from using ball. He then addressed the crowd, and endeavored to restore peace, but while so engaged a man was observed behind a double canoe in the act of darting a spear at the captain. Seeing that his life was really in danger, Cook fired, but killed the wrong man. The sergeant of marines, however, instantly brought down the offender with his musket. For a moment the islanders seemed to lose some of their impetuosity, but the crowds that had gathered behind pressed on those who were the immediate spectators of what had occurred, and, what was even more fatal, poured in a volley of stones. The marines, without waiting for orders, returned the compliment with a general discharge of musketry, which was directly succeeded by a brisk fire from the boats. Cook was surprised and vexed at this accidental turn of affairs, and waved his hand to the boats to desist, and come on shore to embark the marines. The pinnace unhesitatingly obeyed; but the lieutenant in the launch, instead of pulling in to the assistance of his commander, rowed farther off, at the very moment when his services were most required. The marines crowded into the pinnace with precipitation and confusion, and were so jammed together that they were unable to protect themselves. Those who were on shore kept up the fire, but the moment their pieces were discharged the islanders rushed upon them, and forced the party into the water, where four of them were killed and the lieutenant wounded. When this occurred, Cook was standing alone on a rock near the shore. Seeing, however, that it was now clearly a matter of escape, he hurried toward the pinnace, holding his left arm round the back of his head to shield it from stones, and carrying his musket in his right hand. A remarkably agile warrior, a relation of the king's, was seen to follow him, and, before his object could be frustrated, sprang forward upon the captain, and struck him a heavy blow on the back of his head, and then turned and fled. Cook staggered a few paces, dropped his musket, and fell on his hands and one knee. Before he could recover himself, another islander rushed forward, and with an iron dagger stabbed him in the neck. He sunk into the water, and was immediately set upon by a number of savages, who tried to keep him down, but he succeeded in getting his head up. The pinnace was within half a dozen yards of him, and he cast an imploring look as if for assistance. The islanders forced him down again in a deeper place, but his great muscular strength enabled him to recover himself and cling to the rock. He was not there for more than a moment, when a brutal savage dealt him a heavy blow with a club, and he fell down lifeless. The Indians then hauled his corpse upon the rock, and ferociously stabbed it all over, handing the dagger from one to another, in order that all might participate in the sweet revenge. The body was left some time upon the rock, and the islanders gave way, as though afraid of the act they had committed; but there was no attempt to recover it by the ship's crew, and it was subsequently cut up, together with the bodies of the marines, and the parts distributed among the chiefs. The mutilated fragments were afterward restored, and committed to the deep, with all the honors due to the rank of the deceased. Thus ingloriously perished one of England's greatest navigators, "whose services to science have never been surpassed by any man belonging to his profession." It may almost be said, says Mr. Robert Chambers, that he fell a victim to his humanity; for if, instead of retreating before his barbarous pursuers with a view to spare their lives, he had turned revengefully upon them, his fate might have been very different.

The command of the *Resolution* devolved on Captain Clerke, and Mr. Gore acted as commander of the *Discovery*. After making some further explorations among the Sandwich Islands, the vessels visited Kamtschatka and Behring's Straits. There it was found impossible to accomplish the objects of the expedition, and it returned southward. Another misfortune befell the voyagers. On the 22d of August, 1779, Captain Clerke died of consumption. The ships visited Kamtschatka once more, and then returned by way of China, arriving in England on the 4th of October, 1780, after an absence of four years, two months, and twenty-two days.

When it became known in England that Captain Cook had perished, all classes of people expressed their sympathy and deep sorrow. The king granted a pension of £200 per annum to his widow, and £25 per annum to each of her children; the Royal Society had a gold medal struck in commemoration of his services, and at home and abroad honors were scattered on his memory. That Cook was justly entitled to these testimonials is beyond a doubt, not only for the good he did his country, but for his own individual merit. It would be difficult to find a more brilliant instance of purely self-made greatness. Starting in life under circumstances of the most depressing nature, he succeeded solely by the force of industry in acquiring accomplishments which gave him the foremost place among the scientific men of his age. From the obscure condition of a foremast man on a collier he rose to be the greatest discoverer of modern times. A recapitulation of what he accomplished may appropriately close this sketch. He discovered New Caledonia and Norfolk Island, New Georgia, and the Sandwich and many smaller islands in the Pacific; surveyed the Society Islands, the Friendly Islands, and the New Hebrides; determined the insularity of New Zealand; circumnavigated the globe in a high southern latitude, so as to decide that no continent existed north of a certain parallel; explored the then unknown eastern coasts of New Holland for two thousand miles; determined the proximity of Asia to America, which the discoverer of Behring's Straits did not perceive; and, wherever he went, brought strange people into communication with the civilized world, through the wide gates of commerce and mutual interest.

The rock where Captain Cook fell is an object of curiosity in Hawaii to the present day. The natives point it out with sorrow, and show the stump of a cocoanut-tree, where they say he expired. The upper part of this tree has been carried to England, and is preserved in the museum of Greenwich Hospital. On the remaining stump, which has been carefully capped with copper, is the following inscription:

Near this spot
fell
CAPTAIN JAMES COOK, R. N.,
the
renowned circumnavigator
who
discovered these islands,
A.D. 1778.

GEORGE STEPHENSON.

THE most remarkable social results of the nineteenth century in America, in Europe, and in other parts of the world less open to the ever-operating influences of civilization, have been obtained by the introduction of steam, and especially of its young, rapid, and vigorous creation, the locomotive engine. In a brief space of time, so brief that it seems like a dream, vast continents and strange peoples have been banded together into one social union, depending on each other for the necessaries of life, and sharing with fraternal pleasure its courtesies and hospitable cheer. Local animosities and petty jealousies have disappeared like the ugly hobgoblin of old story, and in their place stalwart manhood confronts the time with open brow and genial smile. Truth travels from land to land with the speed of lightning, and the most remote corners of the habitable globe are no longer strangers to its beneficence. It has ceased to dwell at the bottom of a well, cold and passive, as of old. In our days it leads a pretty fast life, hurrying from place to place at a speed of thirty or forty miles an hour, and never resting.

Great efforts were required to accomplish this desirable result, and men and nations have strained themselves to bring it to a happy issue. The capital which has been created and expended in the formation of railroads is of marvelous magnitude. Within a little period of thirty years more money has been spent in this single undertaking than had been used in all the commercial speculations of a century. In Great Britain alone (1855) not less than fourteen hundred million dollars have been sunk in the construction of 8297 miles of road. In America a smaller sum has sufficed for the construction of much more extensive works—not less than 26,000 miles of railroad being now in active operation. Not only do we possess the longest railroads in the world, but the cheapest. Practically, too, we have given them a new use Instead of merely facilitating travel between existing communities, as in Europe, they are to us the best of pioneers. Their sturdy limbs tread the way through the surly forest and the slumbering valleys. Thousands follow in the path trodden with such vigor, and a prosperous commonwealth ensues, adding vitality and new wealth to our exuberant national being.

The founder, and, to a great extent, the inventor of the present system of locomotion, was George Stephenson, a very humble person for one half of his life, but for the rest recognized as a benefactor of his age, and the coequal of Watt, Fulton, Arkwright, and Brindley. Mr. Stephenson was born on the 9th of June, 1781, in a tenement house occupied by colliers, and located in the little village of Wylam, Durham, England. He was the second of a family of six children, all of whom were dependent on the exertions of the father, Robert Stephenson, familiarly called "Old Bob," a hard-working and thrifty man, who was fireman to a shaft engine at a salary of twelve shillings a week.

The collier folk of the north of England are pre-eminently a migrating race. They have to follow the coal, and only wait until it is all "won" before they shift their quarters to some new pit. The Stephensons removed to Dewley Burn before George had reached his eighth year, and it was in this cold and cheerless place that the boy obtained his first employment. He was too young to find work in the colliery, but too big to remain idle. A widow woman, who had some cows and some turnips that needed attention, made him an offer, which he at once accepted. He became a kind of smoky shepherd at the magnificent salary of two-pence per day.

Brought up among steam-engines, it was natural that he should regard them with extreme admiration, and that he should look forward to the day when, like his father, he would enjoy the extreme happiness of making the fire blaze beneath their hissing boilers. This was his ambition, and it was bold, considering the depressing circumstances by which he was surrounded. For the present he fed his hope with the childlike amusement of making mud engines, fitted up with steam-pipes from hemlock stems, and he built little wheels for obtaining imaginary power from the neighboring streams. These things clearly indicated the bent of his mind. He never for a moment, even in his play, lost sight of his determination to become an engine-man.

It was some years before he could take the first step in this direction. At length, however, his father undertook to engage him as assistant fireman at the Denley pit. This was a most encouraging promotion, and gave him great satisfaction. But he was still a very little fellow for the employment, and was dreadfully afraid that he would be considered too young by the owner. Whenever this magnate made his rounds, therefore, George cleared out of the way, and remained out of sight until his back was turned. For assisting his father he received a shilling a day; but, magnificent as was this remuneration, it was not the great charm of his engagement. This lay in the fact that the first step toward the point of his ambition was accomplished. If a man of modest abilities and ordinary perseverance sets his mind on accomplishing a scheme of life, it is generally his own fault if he does not succeed. Stephenson was aware of this fact, and became, in consequence, habitually painstaking and steady. He neglected no opportunity of making himself thoroughly familiar with the duties of the engine-room. He studied the machinery night and day, until he knew the use of every part. A kind of personal intimacy sprang up between him and the engine, which, in the end, was certainly mutually advantageous. At the age of fifteen he became fireman, and shortly after was appointed engine-man to a colliery. "I am now a made man for life," he cried, triumphantly.

George Stephenson quickly gained the reputation of being a good mechanic, and a workman of uncommon penetration and forethought. He was now in his eighteenth year, very steady and reliable, and possessed of excellent practical information concerning machinery, but in other respects completely uneducated.

He had never attended a school, and was unable to read and write. His time was laboriously occupied with the duties of his calling for at least twelve hours of the day; after that, he was still to be found in the engine-room, taking to pieces and cleaning his pet engine. At other times he took recreation in manly sports, and improved his native strength. He was remarkably active and dexterous, and could bid defiance to all his associates in feats of strength. At one time he could raise sixty stone's weight from the ground.

He began to feel that the want of an education was a serious bar to his future progress, and determined, with that decision of character for which he was remarkable, to remedy the deficiency as far as in him lay the power. Big as he was, he went to the village school, and commenced his A B C like a little child. He made good progress, and before he had reached his nineteenth birth-day he enjoyed the happiness of signing his own name in a bold, legible hand. Subsequently he studied arithmetic, mathematics, practical and experimental philosophy, mechanics, and similar subjects, with marked success. He had a fine memory, and an understanding easily impressed. Moreover, he was simple and modest, and never ashamed of acknowledging his ignorance.

When he was twenty years of age he became brakesman at the Black Callerton Colliery, and received the best wages paid to men of his class. Being of a thrifty turn, and in love with a pretty village lass, he sought to increase his earnings by extra work. As this could not be obtained at the colliery, he contrived to obtain a knowledge of shoemaking, and patched up the boots and shoes of his fellow-workmen, to say nothing of the slippers of his sweetheart, which he repaired in the most skillful manner. He became quite expert in this business, and from its exercise managed to save enough money to furnish a home for the future bride.

He was much too steady for some of the men at the colliery, and one bully, who felt personally insulted by any thing which bore the semblance of respectability, insulted Stephenson, and invited him to a combat. To the surprise of every one, he accepted the challenge. The bully immediately abandoned his work and went into training. Stephenson said nothing, but, on the day of battle, coolly walked down from his work, pulled off his coat, rolled up his sleeves, and went to work at the head of his opponent as if it were a part of his contract with the owners of the colliery. The combatants pummeled each other for some time, but the bully was powerless beneath the plucky might of Stephenson. He was glad to cry for quarter, and sneak away, a better and a blacker man. It was Stephenson's first and last battle.

In 1802, Stephenson removed to Willington Quay, near Newcastle-on-Tyne, and was married to the young and estimable woman whose shoes he had soled on a former occasion. Here he pursued his old steady course, working, studying, and mending shoes. Owing to an accidental insight into the mysteries of clock-making, he was able to add a new profession to his other employments. He became a famous clock doctor. All the wheezy old timepieces of the place were sent to him, and some of his cures were said to be remarkable.

After remaining three years in Willington he removed to Killingworth (1804), one of the scenes of his subsequent triumphs. Here he was overtaken by a severe calamity, the death of his wife. The depression which this event produced induced him to accept an offer to work an engine in Scotland, whither he proceeded. After nearly a year's absence he returned to Killingworth, where his only child, a little boy (Robert Stephenson, the eminent engineer), was being nursed. He had saved upward of twenty-eight pounds in Scotland, and the arrival of this little fund was most timely. He rescued his father from pecuniary difficulties brought about by a very dreadful accident, and with the balance procured a substitute for the militia, in which service he had been drawn. The mining districts were greatly depressed at this time, and it was with difficulty that even an industrious man like Stephenson could procure a sufficiency of work. He allowed no means to go untried. He did all that was to be done at the colliery; repaired and made boots and shoes; cleaned and doctored clocks and watches, and even, it is said, cut out clothes for the pitmen's wives. He was stimulated to unusual exertion by the determination to provide an education for his son, who was now advancing to an age when he might receive the rudiments.

A man like Stephenson, who took a pride in understanding the practical construction of the machines under his control, had, of course, many opportunities for displaying his ingenuity; but the first really important case in which his skill was severely put to the test was in remedying the defects of an engine which had defied all the talent of the best engineers of the neighborhood, and of the maker himself. Stephenson found out the difficulty and remedied it. For this he received ten pounds' remuneration, and, what was more important to him, the appointment of engine-man to the colliery. In addition, he acquired the reputation of being the best engine doctor in the northern country, which unquestionably he was.

Stephenson's promotion (in 1812) to the rank of engine-wright was a source of great rejoicing to him. He was now, in a measure, relieved from the daily routine of manual labor, although, in reality, his duties were much heavier than before. All the engines and machinery of the colliery were placed under his control, and he was allowed to modify and alter them as he thought best. He introduced many improvements, both in the machinery of the shaft, and in the iron tram-ways, or railroads leading from it. He had devoted a good deal of attention to the subject of railroads, and was perfectly familiar with all the experiments that had been made to introduce the locomotive. Their huge and cumbrous wheels, cogs, screws, pistons, and levers had been tried in the haulage of wagons; but the speed accomplished was so tedious, and the wear and tear so disastrous, that they were in most cases abandoned. Stephenson, however, was not slow to perceive the immense advantages which would result from the use of a power so enormous as that promised by the locomotive, provided it could be brought into proper subjection, and already he began to perceive how this might be accomplished.

Setting himself down to the systematic study of the subject, he soon ascertained the cause of failure in preceding models, and declared that he could make an engine much better than any that existed. To accomplish this Mr. Stephenson now applied himself. He was warmly encouraged by the owners of the colliery in which he worked, and in which his ingenuity had been so often tested. Lord Ravensworth (one of the proprietors) advanced the necessary funds for the work, and, in remembrance of this, Stephenson called his first engine "My Lord."

The engine, after much labor and anxiety, and frequent alterations of parts, was at length completed, having been about ten months in hand. It was first placed upon the Killingworth Railroad on the 25th of July, 1814, and its powers were tried on the same day. On an ascending gradient of 1 in 450, the engine succeeded in drawing after it eight loaded carriages of thirty tons weight at about four miles an hour; and for some time after it continued regularly at work. Stephenson justified his boast, and really had produced the most successful working engine yet constructed. Still, it was very defective, and did not give promise of economical advantages over horse-power. The speed attained was little better than a horse's walk, and it was found difficult to increase it, owing to the slow combustion of fuel. He now directed all his energies to this subject, and in a short time added the steam-blast to his engine. The experiment was no sooner made than the locomotive's power became doubled. He introduced many other improvements, and in 1815 built his second locomotive, combining all the results of his discoveries and improvements. For this he obtained a patent. Its advantages over any other machine are thus described: simple and direct communication between the cylinder and the wheels rolling upon the rails; joint adhesion of all the wheels, attained by the use of horizontal connecting rods; and, finally, a beautiful method of exciting the combustion of the fuel by employing the waste steam, which had formerly been allowed uselessly to escape into the air. Although many improvements in detail were afterward introduced in the locomotive by Mr. Stephenson himself, as well as by his equally distinguished son, it is perhaps not too much to say that this engine, as a mechanical contrivance, contained the germ of all that has since been effected. It may, in fact, be regarded as the type of the present locomotive engine.

Many years elapsed before this important discovery (for so it may be termed) excited even the curiosity of the scientific. Stephenson was but a humble, self-taught mechanic at a colliery, and no one thought it worth while to pay any attention to him. Professional engineers wrapped themselves in the dignity of their calling, and refused to have any thing to say to an upstart who pretended to do more than they could.

In the mean time, Stephenson directed his attention to another subject. The loss of life from the explosion of fire-damp in the mines was frequent and disastrous. To prevent this, he proposed to invent a safety-lamp which would not ignite the dangerous gas, and yet be sufficient for the purposes of the miners. He did not know that Sir Humphrey Davy, the most eminent chemist in the country, was engaged on a similar subject, and with opportunities of investigating it that were utterly denied to the poor engine-wright. Trusting to his practical knowledge of what was wanted, he went to work, and, at the risk of his own life, made experiments which resulted in a safety-lamp used to the present day, and entirely effective. Although wrought out on purely mechanical principles by the inventor, it is philosophically the same as Davy's. Its similarity, indeed, led to a controversy, which was conducted with the usual ferocity of such discussions. Stephenson, however, was presented with a testimonial and a purse of one thousand guineas for the public benefit he had conferred on the mining community. This sum he subsequently invested in establishing his extensive works at Newcastle.

Railroads, up to this period, were confined exclusively to the mining districts, and there their use was restricted to the haulage of coals. The application of steam for the conveyance of passengers was not even dreamed of. Professed engineers endeavored to find out how a steam carriage could be constructed to run on the ordinary turnpike roads, and many ingenious contrivances were made and patented; but they all proved to be of no practical utility. From the first, Stephenson declared that the thing was impossible, and maintained that the only correct plan was to construct iron tramways as nearly flat as possible, and to use locomotives. He declared his conviction, moreover, that in a few years communication would be maintained entirely by these means.

His remarks were listened to with the usual indifference; men went on wasting money on steam carriages for the common roads; and Stephenson bided his time, in full confidence that it would yet come. For ten years he was, perhaps, the only man in the kingdom who took any sustained interest in locomotives.

Stephenson's reputation was purely local, but it was of service to him. A number of gentlemen, mostly Quakers, contemplated building a railroad, to be worked with horse-power, from the town of Darlington to the town of Stockton, on the River Tees. Foremost among these was a very enterprising and wealthy gentleman named Pease. To this gentleman Stephenson presented himself. The plans being still in a very unsettled state, Mr. Pease was glad to have the opportunity of gathering from him the results of his experience, but was a little startled when his visitor declared his preference for the locomotive over horse-power. "Come over to Killingworth," he said, "and see what my 'Blucher' can do. Seeing is believing, sir." Mr. Pease went, and was not only astonished, but convinced that Stephenson was right. Still, it was a bold idea, and his coadjutors were not prepared for it; so the Stockton and Darlington Railroad was constructed for the conveyance of goods by means of horses, inclined planes, and stationary engines. A clause, however, was inserted in the act, enabling the projectors, if they felt disposed, to use locomotives, and Mr. Pease promised that Stephenson (who had been appointed engineer of the road at a salary of £300 per annum) should have a fair trial.

The Stockton and Darlington Railroad (the first complete railroad in the world) was opened for traffic on the 27th of September, 1825, and one of Stephenson's engines was tried. It was attached to a train consisting of six wagons loaded with coals and flour; after these was the passenger coach, filled with the directors and their friends, and then twenty-one wagons, fitted up with temporary seats for passengers; and lastly came six wagon-loads of coals, making, in all, a train of thirty-eight vehicles. "The signal being given," says a local chronicler, "the engine started off with this immense train of carriages, and such was its velocity that, in some parts, the speed was frequently twelve miles an hour; and at that time the number of passengers was counted to be 450, which, together with the coals, merchandise, and carriages, would amount to nearly 90 tons." A large passenger traffic immediately sprang up, and was, of course, a source of unexpected profit. Three of Stephenson's engines were from the first employed, but, in spite of their acknowledged superiority, it was some years before locomotives were used uniformly in preference to other power. Mr. Pease's confidence in Stephenson was unbounded, and he became a partner in the locomotive works which subsequently were started in Newcastle.

With the successful issue of the Stockton and Darlington project the practicability of railroads became an established fact, and other schemes were immediately set on foot. The most important of these was the Liverpool and Manchester Railroad. The bill for constructing this line was opposed with great violence by the canal proprietors, whose monopoly it destroyed, and for a time their opposition was successful; but finally the bill was granted. Mr. Stephenson was engaged as the engineer of the line, and had to undergo the ordeal of an examination before a committee of the House of Commons. Referring to this matter many years after, he says, "The directors of the undertaking thought ten miles an hour would be a maximum speed for the locomotive engine, and I pledged myself to attain that speed. I said I had no doubt that the locomotive might be made to go much faster, but we had better be moderate at the beginning. The directors said I was quite right; for if, when they went to Parliament, I talked of going at a greater rate than ten miles an hour, I should put a cross on the concern! It was not an easy task for me to keep the engine down to ten miles an hour, but it must be done, and I did my best. I had to place myself in the most unpleasant of all positions, the witness-box of a parliamentary committee. I was not long in it, I assure you, before I began to wish for a hole to creep out at. I could not find words to satisfy the committee or myself, or even to make them understand my meaning. Some said, 'He's a foreigner.' 'No,' others replied, 'he's mad.' But I put up with every rebuff, and went on with my plans, determined not to be put down."

It was by no means certain that locomotives would be used, although so much trouble had been gone through to obtain parliamentary permission for the purpose. The majority of the stockholders were still in favor of stationary engines and horse-power, and were disposed to look on locomotives as costly experiments. Stephenson exerted himself to remove this erroneous impression, and succeeded in getting permission to use an engine in the construction of the works, which were of a gigantic kind, and entirely beyond any thing which had ever been attempted in England. This locomotive was found to be of great service in drawing the wagons full of marl from the two great cuttings. The directors became a little softened, and listened to Stephenson's protestations with greater respect. At length they determined to offer a prize of £500 for the best locomotive engine which, on a certain day, should be produced, and perform certain conditions in the most satisfactory manner. The conditions were these:

1. The engine must effectually consume its own smoke.

2. The engine, if of six tons' weight, must be able to draw after it, day by day, twenty tons' weight (including the tender and water-tank), at ten miles an hour, with a pressure of steam on the boiler not exceeding fifty pounds to the square inch.

3. The boiler must have two safety-valves, neither of which must be fastened down, and one of them be completely out of the control of the engine-man.

4. The engine and boiler must be supported on springs, and rest on six wheels, the height of the whole not exceeding fifteen feet to the top of the chimney.

5. The engine, with water, must not weigh more than six tons, but an engine of less weight would be preferred, on its drawing a proportionate load behind it: if of only four and a half tons, then it might be put on only four wheels. The company to be at liberty to test the boiler, etc., by a pressure of one hundred and fifty pounds to the square inch.

6. A mercurial gauge must be affixed to the machine, showing the steam pressure above forty-five pounds per square inch.

7. The engine must be delivered complete and ready for trial at the Liverpool end of the railway not later than the 1st of October, 1829.

8. The price of the engine must not exceed £550.

On the day appointed for the competition, the following engines were entered for the prize:

1. Messrs. Braithwaite & Ericsson's "Novelty."
2. Mr. Timothy Hackworth's "Sanspareil."
3. Mr. Robert Stephenson's "Rocket."
4. Mr. Burstall's "Perseverance."

The ground on which the engines were to be tried was a level piece of railroad on the new line near Rainhill, about two miles in length. Each engine was to make twenty trips, or equal to a journey of seventy miles, in the course of the day, and the average rate of traveling was not to be under ten miles an hour. The trial was appointed to take place on the 6th of October, 1829—a day which deserves to be historical, so great were its results.

Mr. Stephenson's engine was the first to be in readiness, and it immediately entered upon the contest. The engine was taken to the extremity of the stage, the fire-box was filled with coke, the fire lighted, and the steam raised until it lifted the safety-valve, loaded to a pressure of fifty pounds to the square inch. This proceeding occupied fifty-seven minutes. The engine then started on its journey, dragging after it about thirteen tons' weight in wagons, and made the first ten trips backward and forward along the two miles of road, running the thirty-five miles, including stoppages, in an hour and forty-eight minutes. The second ten trips were in like manner performed in two hours and three minutes. The maximum velocity attained by the "Rocket" during the trial trip was twenty-nine miles an hour, or about three times the speed that one of the judges of the competition declared to be the limit of possibility. The entire performance excited the greatest astonishment among the assembled spectators; the directors felt confident that their enterprise was now on the eve of success, and George Stephenson rejoiced to think that, in spite of all false prophets and fickle counselors, his locomotive system was safe.

The other engines were tried, but were so much inferior to Stephenson's that the prize of £500 was unanimously awarded to him. The public were so well satisfied with the experiment that the shares of the company immediately went up ten per cent. When the line was opened in September, 1830, other engines made by Mr. Stephenson far eclipsed the performances of the "Rocket." The "Northumbrian" engine conveyed the wounded body of a gentleman who had met with an accident a distance of fifteen miles in twenty-five minutes, or at the rate of thirty-six miles an hour. This incredible speed burst upon the world with all the effect of a new and unlooked-for phenomenon.

Stephenson's career was fairly commenced. From 1825 to 1847 he was recognized as the first railroad engineer of his country. Orders for locomotives came in from all parts of the world, and his workshops were crowded with busy artisans. Personally, his services were in great demand, and every company who obtained a bill tried to give it importance by getting Stephenson's name on it. But, with the exception of three or four principal lines entirely constructed by him, he did not lend himself to any new schemes. He had as much to attend to as he could undertake. He had accomplished the object of his life, and felt disposed to relax from his severe exertions. Before arriving at this conclusion, he paid a visit to France, Belgium, and Spain, and was extensively honored in those countries. His visit to Spain was extremely hurried, and occasioned a sickness from which he never entirely recovered. His constitution, so strong and hardy, became sensitive to disease. He contracted an intermittent fever, and was carried off, after a few days' sickness, on the 12th of August, 1848, in the sixty-seventh year of his age.

Mr. Stephenson, in the latter years of his life, was greatly assisted by his son Robert, and it is almost impossible to separate the works of one from the other. At the present day Mr. Robert Stephenson is probably the most eminent engineer in the world.

Mr. George Stephenson was a remarkable instance of the strength of purpose which is so often found in self-made men. He would never admit that he possessed more genius than others, but he was proud of his perseverance, and to this inestimable quality he attributed all his success in life. It is, indeed, the keystone of all human greatness, and when supported by sobriety and conscientiousness, never fails in achieving distinction. In the present instance, we behold a man struggling with the direst poverty, yet fiercely grasping one grand idea, with the intention of making it his own, sooner or later. From this intention he never swerved. By patient labor he made himself master of all the knowledge that was immediately essential to his purpose. He gradually conquered the mechanism of the steam-engine, so that, when opportunity offered, he was enabled to improve it, and to make it work when even its own maker was baffled. He practically studied hydraulics in the same plodding way, when acting as plug-man; and when all the local pump-doctors at Killingworth were in despair, he stepped in and successfully applied the knowledge which he had so laboriously gained. The battle which he fought for the locomotive would have discouraged most other men, but it only served to bring into prominence his sterling qualities. "I have fought," he said, "for the locomotive single-handed for nearly twenty years, having no engineer to help me until I had raised engineers under my own care." He persevered and he conquered.

In his deportment Mr. Stephenson was simple, modest, and unassuming, but always manly. "When a humble workman," says his biographer, "he had carefully preserved his self-respect. His companions looked up to him, and his example was worth even more, to many of them, than books or schools. His devoted love of knowledge made his poverty respectable, and adorned his humble calling. When he rose to a more elevated station, and associated with men of the highest position and influence in Britain, he took his place among them with perfect self-possession. They wondered at the quiet ease and simple dignity of his deportment, and men in the best ranks of life have said of him that 'he was one of nature's gentlemen.' "

The remains of George Stephenson were interred in Trinity Church, Chesterfield, where a simple but expressive monument has been erected to his memory.

THE END.

CURTIS'S HISTORY

OF THE

CONSTITUTION.

HISTORY OF THE ORIGIN, FORMATION, AND ADOPTION OF THE CONSTITUTION OF THE UNITED STATES. By GEORGE TICKNOR CURTIS. Complete in 2 vols. 8vo, Muslin, $4 00; Law Sheep, $5 00; Half Calf, $6 00.

A book so thorough as this in the comprehension of its subject, so impartial in the summing up of its judgments, so well considered in its method, and so truthful in its matter, may safely challenge the most exhaustive criticism. The Constitutional History of our country has not before been made the subject of a special treatise. We may congratulate ourselves that an author has been found so capable to do full justice to it; for that the work will take its rank among the received text-books of our political literature will be questioned by no one who has given it a careful perusal.—*National Intelligencer.*

We know of no person who is better qualified (now that the late Daniel Webster is no more), to undertake this important history.—*Boston Journal.*

It will take its place among the classics of American literature.—*Boston Courier.*

The author has given years to the preliminary studies, and nothing has escaped him in the patient and conscientious researches to which he has devoted so ample a portion of time. Indeed, the work has been so thoroughly performed that it will never need to be done over again; for the sources have been exhausted, and the materials put together with so much judgment and artistic skill that taste and the sense of completeness are entirely satisfied.—*N. Y. Daily Times.*

A most important and valuable contribution to the historical and political literature of the United States. All publicists and students of public law will be grateful to Mr. Curtis for the diligence and assiduity with which he has wrought out the great mine of diplomatic lore in which the foundations of the American Constitution are laid, and for the light he has thrown on his wide and arduous subject.—*London Morning Chronicle.*

To trace the history of the formation of the Constitution, and explain the circumstances of the time and country out of which its various provisions grew, is a task worthy of the highest talent. To have performed that task in a satisfactory manner is an achievement with which an honorable ambition may well be gratified. We can honestly say that in our opinion Mr. Curtis has fairly won this distinction.—*N. Y. Courier and Enquirer.*

We have seen no history which surpasses it in the essential qualities of a standard work destined to hold a permanent place in the impartial judgment of future generations.—*Boston Traveler.*

Should the second volume sustain the character of the first, we hazard nothing in claiming for the entire publication the character of a standard work. It will furnish the only sure guide to the interpretation of the Constitution, by unfolding historically the wants it was intended to supply, and the evils which it was intended to remedy.—*Boston Daily Advertiser.*

This volume is an important contribution to our constitutional and historical literature. * * * Every true friend of the Constitution will gladly welcome it. The author has presented a narrative clear and interesting. It evinces careful research, skillful handling of material, lucid statement, and a desire to write in a tone and manner worthy of the great theme.—*Boston Post.*

Published by HARPER & BROTHERS,
Franklin Square, New York.

*** HARPER & BROTHERS will send the above Work by Mail, postage paid (for any distance in the United States under 3000 miles), on receipt of the Money.

Harper's Catalogue.

A New Descriptive Catalogue of Harper & Brothers' Publications, with an Index and Classified Table of Contents, is now ready for Distribution, and may be obtained gratuitously on application to the Publishers personally, or by letter inclosing Six Cents in Postage Stamps.

The attention of gentlemen, in town or country, designing to form Libraries or enrich their Literary Collections, is respectfully invited to this Catalogue, which will be found to comprise a large proportion of the standard and most esteemed works in English Literature—COMPREHENDING MORE THAN TWO THOUSAND VOLUMES—which are offered, in most instances, at less than one half the cost of similar productions in England.

To Librarians and others connected with Colleges, Schools, &c., who may not have access to a reliable guide in forming the true estimate of literary productions, it is believed this Catalogue will prove especially valuable as a manual of reference.

To prevent disappointment, it is suggested that, whenever books can not be obtained through any bookseller or local agent, applications with remittance should be addressed direct to the Publishers, which will be promptly attended to.

A Superb Work.

THE POETS

OF THE

NINETEENTH CENTURY.

Selected and Edited by the Rev. ROBERT ARIS WILLMOTT. With English and American Additions, arranged by EVERT A. DUYCKINCK, Editor of "Cyclopedia of American Literature." Comprising Selections from the greatest Authors of the Age. Superbly Illustrated by 132 Engravings from Designs by the most Eminent Artists. In elegant Small 4to form, printed on Superfine Tinted Paper, richly bound in extra Cloth beveled, gilt edges, $5 00; Half Calf, $5 00; Full Turkey Morocco, $7 50.

By far the most beautiful gift-book of the year. Its covers are gleaming with purple and gold; its typography is delicate, on hot-pressed, cream-colored paper, and its many engravings, by the first artists in England and America, are exquisitely engraved and worked. It has a value beyond mere beauty, however, for the taste which has guided two accomplished minds in the selection of pieces has produced a collection of some of the finest poetry of the age. Mr. Willmott has labored with judgment and poetical feeling among the poets of the old country, and Mr. Duyckinck has been equally zealous and fortunate among those of America. The result, therefore, is a volume of sufficient permanent value, despite its delicate beauty, to take a place in the library as well as on the drawing-room table.—*The Press* (Phila.).

It is as handsome as it is good.—*Boston Post.*

"Here let the lover of splendid books pause content. Luxury of paper, type, and illustration, skill, taste, and art could not surpass this volume; and when this dress is the clothing of the gems of literature, the most exquisite thoughts of modern poetry, certainly the book-hunter may be satisfied with it. For a gift, in this season of gifts, for a never-wearying ornament of the drawing-room table —a never-failing source of entertainment to lovers of the beautiful in poetry or in art—a never-ceasing subject of conversation—and an unfailing suggester of pleasant thought and pleasant talk, this book has no rival."

A library of permanent value and delight.—*Boston Courier.*

We never saw a prettier book than this to lay on a drawing-room table.—*London Times.*

Published by HARPER & BROTHERS,
Franklin Square, N. Y.

☞ HARPER & BROTHERS will send the above work by Mail, postage paid, to any part of the United States, on receipt of the Money.

By William C. Prime.

Boat Life in Egypt & Nubia.

Boat Life in Egypt and Nubia. By WILLIAM C. PRIME, Author of "The Old House by the River," "Later Years," &c. Illustrations. 12mo, Muslin, $1 25.

Tent Life in the Holy Land.

By WILLIAM C. PRIME, Author of "The Old House by the River," "Later Years," &c. Illustrations. 12mo, Muslin, $1 25.

The Old House by the River.

By WILLIAM C. PRIME, Author of the "Owl Creek Letters." 12mo, Muslin, 75 cents.

Later Years.

By WILLIAM C. PRIME, Author of "The Old House by the River." 12mo, Muslin, $1 00.

ATKINSON'S SIBERIA.

ORIENTAL AND WESTERN SIBERIA: A Narrative of Seven Years' Explorations and Adventures in Siberia, Mongolia, the Kirghis Steppes, Chinese Tartary, and part of Central Asia. By THOMAS WITLAM ATKINSON. With a Map and numerous Spirited Illustrations from Drawings by the Author. 8vo (Uniform with Dr. Livingstone's South Africa), Muslin, $3 00; Half Calf, $4 00.

Mr. Atkinson's sketches were made by express permission of the late Emperor of Russia during seven years' hunting, sketching, and traveling in the plains and mountains of Oriental and Western Siberia, Mongolia, the Kirghis Steppes, Chinese Tartary, and Central Asia. Perhaps no English artist was ever before admitted into this enchanted land of history, or provided with the talisman and amulet of a general passport; and well has Mr. Atkinson availed himself of the privilege. Mr. Atkinson's encampments lead us away into forests, gorges of mountains, where the thunder shakes the ground and the lightning strikes, like God's sword-blade, among the trees—where the Tartars cower in their felt hut, and the tea-drinkers grow silent round the red logs. Rivers to swim, torrents to pass, became trifles to this adventurous traveler, who has brought us records of places never, perhaps, before visited; for no Englishman has been there—no Russian traveler has written of them.—*London Athenæum.*

A book of travels which, in value and sterling interest, must take rank as a landmark in geographical literature. Mr. Atkinson has traveled where it is believed no European has been before. He has seen nature in the wildest, sublimest, and also the most beautiful aspects the Old World can present. These he has depicted by pen and pencil: he has done both well. Many a fireside will rejoice in the determination which converted an artist into an author. Mr. Atkinson is a thorough Englishman, brave and accomplished, a lover of adventure and sport of every kind. He knows enough of mineralogy, geology, and botany to impart a scientific interest to his descriptions and drawings; possessing a keen sense of humor, he tells many a racy story. The sportsman and the lover of adventure, whether by flood or field, will find ample stores in the stirring tales of his interesting travels.—*London Daily News.*

"Mr. T. W. Atkinson, an artist of extraordinary merit, in pursuit of the picturesque, has ventured into regions where, probably, no European foot save his, has ever trodden. Mr. Atkinson's travels embrace Oriental and Western Siberia, Mongolia, Daouria, the Kirghis Steppes, Chinese Tartary, and portions of Central Asia, and occupied him for the space of seven years—time which he has turned to admirable account. It argues no slight devotion to Art to have undertaken the task of giving to civilized Europe a transcript of what is at once most beautiful and most wonderful in nature, in countries so remote, so difficult of access, and, in many instances, so dangerous to the traveler. The public may really feel grateful to Mr. Atkinson for thus widely extending our knowledge of this hitherto unknown but most interesting part of the globe."

It is a valuable addition to the literature of travel, and a famous contribution also to the list of show books. Mr. Atkinson's book is most readable. The geographer finds in it notice of ground heretofore left undescribed—the ethologist, geologist, and botanist find notes and pictures, too, of which they know the value—the sportsman's taste is gratified by chronicles of sport—the lover of adventure will find a number of perils and escapes to hang over, and the lover of a frank, good-humored way of speech will find the book a pleasant one in every page. Seven years of wandering, thirty-nine thousand five hundred miles of moving to and fro in a wild and almost unknown country should yield a book worth reading, and they do.—*London Examiner.*

Published by HARPER & BROTHERS,
Franklin Square, New York.

☞ HARPER & BROTHERS will send the above Work by Mail, postage paid, to any part of the United States, on receipt of the Money.

"A Grand Book—an Honor to America."

THE

PHYSICAL GEOGRAPHY

OF

THE SEA.

By Lieut. M. F. MAURY, U. S. N.

With Wood-cuts and Charts. New Edition. Enlarged and Improved. 8vo, Muslin, $1 50.

Notices of the Press.

Lieutenant Maury, in his fascinating book.—*Blackwood's Magazine.*

We err greatly if Lieut. Maury's book will not hereafter be classed with the works of the great men who have taken the lead in extending and improving knowledge and art; his book displays, in a remarkable degree, like the "advancement of learning" and the natural history of Buffon, profound research and magnificent imagination.—*London Illustrated News.*

We have not met for a long period with a book which is at once so minute and profound in research, and so plain, manly, and eloquent in expression. * * * At almost every page there are proofs that Lieut. Maury is as pious as he is learned. * * * This is but one passage of a book which will make a sensation not like that or equal to that made by "Uncle Tom's Cabin," but a durable and expanding impression in the general mind, and hereafter Lieut. Maury will be remembered among the great scientific men of the age, and the benefactors of mankind.—*London Economist.*

We have scarcely ever met with a work that has given us more instruction and pleasure. Under the author's clear and familiar treatment, the Ocean no longer seems a mere mass of waters, unvaried except by storms and tides; it becomes a living thing, as it were, an immense vital organ, composed of a wonderful congeries of powers, and performing a wonderful part in the natural economy of our terraqueous globe. Its currents and drifts, the temperature of its different parts, the depths of its several basins, its contents, the mountains, table lands, and profound valleys that occupy its bottom, its action on the atmosphere and the counteraction, its processes of evaporization, the courses of winds bearing its vapors to the regions where they are precipitated in rain or snow, the great maritime routes across its expanse, and how they are determined by oceanic and atmospherical phenomena—all are set forth in a plain, vivid, and very impressive manner.—*Universalist Quarterly Review.*

A grand book, an honor to America.—*Presbyterian Quarterly Review.*

Whoever may wish a perfect treat among the novelties of science, will find it in the "Physical Geography of the Sea."—*Methodist Quarterly Review.*

Pre-eminently popular and practical. Some of the theories of this ingenious book have already brought thousands, or even millions of dollars into the hands of commerce. As a contribution to science, and, above all, to popular and practical knowledge, hardly enough praise can be uttered.—*N. Y. Daily Times.*

Lieut. Maury's eulogy will be found, like that of the discoverer of the compass, in the practice of every future navigator, and his discoveries will kindle a pride in generations to come of his countrymen, akin to that we feel in the achievements of science of Franklin and Fulton.—*Journal of Commerce.*

Published by HARPER & BROTHERS,
Franklin Square, New York.

*** Harper & Brothers will send the above Work by Mail, postage paid (for any distance in the United States under 3000 miles), on receipt of $1 50.

DR. LIVINGSTONE'S TRAVELS.

Missionary Travels and Researches in South Africa; including a Sketch of Sixteen Years' Residence in the Interior of Africa, and a Journey from the Cape of Good Hope to Loando on the West Coast; thence across the Continent, down the River Zambesi, to the Eastern Ocean. By DAVID LIVINGSTONE, LL.D., D.C.L. Two Maps by ARROWSMITH, a Portrait on Steel, and numerous Illustrations. New Edition, with Copious Index. One Volume, 8vo, Price $3 00.

NOTICE.

Messrs. HARPER & BROTHERS take this opportunity of cautioning the public against several spurious publications, which, by artful advertisements, are made to appear as though emanating from Dr. Livingstone. They are authorised to say that Dr. Livingstone repudiates them entirely, and wishes it to be generally known that the present work is the *only authentic narrative of his Adventures and Travels in Africa.*

A book which, before it has been ten days in the hands of the public, will have been perused by perhaps 30,000 readers—a book second only to Lord Macaulay's History of England in the inordinate extent of its circulation. No wonder—it addresses itself to large and numerous classes—the great religious world, the commercial world, the scientific.—*Literary Gazette.*

The book is one of the most captivating description; in style simple, clear, and graphic, and in matter such as no other living traveler's experience could afford. From the beginning to the end of the volume there is not a page that does not compel the attention, not a page that does not offer something novel. It is a wonder-book all through.—*N. Y. Courier and Enquirer.*

This remarkable narrative, distinguished throughout by the modesty characteristic of true merit. Clear, concise, unaffected, and fluent, it charms the reader, and bears him along irresistibly, securing his attention from first to last.—*N. Y. Commercial Advertiser.*

At once scientific, literary, and religious, it deserves to be read and studied by all classes.—*Boston Post.*

A new chapter in the history of the world.—*Boston Leader.*

Since the days of Mandeville, Marco Polo, and Captain Cooke, no one person has traversed a more extended theatre of travel, or added more to the great discoveries of the world than Dr. Livingstone. The work combines the dignity of scientific research with thrilling narratives of personal adventure.—*Richmond Enquirer.*

The African Columbus has broken the egg, and let the world into his secret. What he has achieved, and endured, and conquered; the witchcraft which, for sixteen years, he has used against a vertical sun and a malign climate—how he has run the gauntlet of carnivores and pachyderms, and ophidia—how he has lived on roots, and locusts, and frogs, and moistened his mouth only with rain or river water—how he has striven with thirst and fever, with the loss of letters and the absence of intelligent companionship—how he has sounded unknown lakes, broken through thorny jungles, navigated unknown rivers, opened to light a world teeming with floral, animal, and mineral wonders—obtaining ingress for science, for commerce, for religion—and leading after him, as the special spoils of his expedition, a throng of colored indigeni, drawn along by no other fetters save of love and admiration. So runs the story of his book—a book not so much of travel and adventure as, in its purport and spacious relation, a veritable poem. —*Athenæum.*

The book will be sought for and read with more eagerness than a romance.—*N. Y. Observer.*

Published by HARPER & BROTHERS,
Franklin Square, New York.

*** HARPER & BROTHERS will send the above Work by Mail, postage paid (for any distance in the United States under 3000 miles), on receipt of Three Dollars.

"**The most magnificent contribution of the present century to the cause of geographical knowledge.**"

DR. BARTH'S NORTH AND CENTRAL AFRICA.

Travels and Discoveries in North and Central Africa. Being a Journal of an Expedition undertaken under the Auspices of H.B.M's Government in the Years 1849–1855. By Henry Barth, Ph.D., D.C.L., Fellow of the Royal Geographical and Asiatic Societies, &c., &c. Profusely and elegantly illustrated. Complete in 3 vols. 8vo, Muslin, $2 50 a Volume; Half Calf, $10 50 a set.

Dr. Barth's wonderful travels approach the Equator from the North as nearly as Dr. Livingstone's from the South, and thus show to future travelers the field which still remains open for exploration and research.—Vol. III., completing the work, is in the press, and will be published shortly.

The researches of Dr. Barth are of the highest interest. Few men have existed so qualified, both by intellectual ability and a vigorous bodily constitution, for the perilous part of an African discoverer as Dr. Barth.—*London Times, Sept.* 8, 1857.

It richly merits all the commendation bestowed upon it by "the leading journal of Europe."—*Corr. National Intelligencer.*

Every chapter presents matter of more original interest than an ordinary volume of travels.—*London Leader.*

For extent and variety of subjects, the volumes before us greatly surpass every other work on African travel with which it has been our fortune to meet.—*London Athenæum.*

Dr. Barth is the model of an explorer—patient, persevering, and resolute.—*London Spectator.*

No one who wishes to know Africa can afford to dispense with this work.—*Boston Traveler.*

A most wonderful record.—*Poughkeepsie Democrat.*

It is the most magnificent contribution of the present century to the cause of geographical knowledge.—*N. Y. Evangelist.*

The most important contribution to Geographical Science that has been made in our time. Thousands of readers in our country will be anxious to get posession of this treasure of knowledge.—*N. Y. Observer.*

One of the most important works of the kind which has appeared for an age.—*Lutheran Observer.*

It can not fail to find its way into the libraries of most scholars.—*Lynchburg Virginian.*

The personal details give the work great interest.—*Philadelphia Press.*

Dr. Barth's work is a magnificent contribution to geographical and ethnographical science.—*N. Y. Independent.*

Your curiosity is awakened, step by step, as with diminished resources he works his way through fanatical and rapacious tribes, ready in resources and never desponding, and buoyed up by the unconquerable desire to surpass his predecessors in the thoroughness and in the range of his discoveries.—*Albion.*

Among the most wonderful achievements of modern times.—*Western Christian Advocate.*

A most valuable contribution to the standard literature of the world.—*Troy Times.*

Published by HARPER & BROTHERS,
Franklin Square, New York.

*** Harper & Brothers will send the above Work by Mail, postage paid (for any distance in the United States under 3000 miles), on receipt of the Money.

HISTORY

OF THE

UNITED STATES OF AMERICA.

By RICHARD HILDRETH.

First Series.—From the First Settlement of the Country to the Adoption of the Federal Constitution. 3 vols. 8vo, Muslin, $6 00; Sheep, $6 75; Half Calf, $7 50.

Second Series.—From the Adoption of the Federal Constitution to the End of the Sixteenth Congress. 3 vols. 8vo, Muslin, $6 00; Sheep, $6 75; Half Calf, $7 50.

The first attempt at a complete history of the United States. The reader who desires to inform himself in all the particulars, military or political, of the American Revolution, will find that they have been scrupulously collected for him by Mr. Hildreth.—*London Athenæum.*

It has condensed into consecutive narrative the substance of hundreds of volumes.—*London Literary Gazette.*

The history of the Revolution is clearly and succinctly told.—*N. A. Review.*

Mr. Hildreth's sources of information have evidently been ample and various, and intelligently examined, his materials arranged with a just idea of their importance in the story, while his judgments are well considered, unbiassed, and reliable. His style is clear, forcible, and sententious.—*Christian Register.*

Mr. Hildreth is a very concise, vigorous, and impartial writer. His entire history is very accurate and interesting, and well worthy a place in every American library.—*Louisville Journal.*

He is laborious, conscientious, and accurate. As a methodical and very full narrative, its value is undoubted.—*New Orleans Bee.*

The calmness and ability with which he has presented his narrative will give his work rank among the standard histories of the country.—*Watchman and Observer.*

* * We have, therefore, read his book with distrust. But we are bound in candor to say that it seems to us valuable and very fair. Mr. Hildreth has confined himself to, as far as possible, a dispassionate collection of facts from the documents he has consulted and copied, and his work fills a void that has sensibly been felt in private libraries. As a documentary history of the United States, we are free to commend it.—*N. Y. Freeman's Journal.*

Mr. Hildreth has rendered an essential and permanent service.—*Providence Daily Journal.*

The volumes will be regarded as indispensable—it will take its place as a standard work. The author's style is dignified, perspicuous, and vivacious.—*Church Review.*

The work is very complete. The marginal dates, the two indexes, and running heads at the tops of the pages, render it very convenient for reference, points which scholars will find all important for utility.—*Newark Sentinel of Freedom.*

HILDRETH'S HISTORY OF THE UNITED STATES.

Written with candor, brevity, fidelity to facts, and simplicity of style and manner, and forms a welcome addition to the library of the nation.—*Prot. Churchman.*

Mr. Hildreth is a bold and copious writer. His work is valuable for the immense amount of material it embodies.—*De Bow's Review of the Southern and Western States.*

We may safely commend Mr. Hildreth's work as written in an excellent style, and containing a vast amount of valuable information.—*Albany Argus.*

His style is vigorously simple. It has the virtue of perspicuity. — *Zion's Herald.*

We value it on account of its impartiality. We have found nothing to indicate the least desire on the part of the author to exalt or debase any man or any party. His very patriotism, though high-principled and sincere, is sober and discriminate, and appears to be held in strong check by the controlling recollection that he is writing for posterity, and that if the facts which he publishes will not honor his country and his countrymen, fulsome adulation will not add to their glory.—*N. Y. Commercial Advertiser.*

We are confident that when the merits of this history come to be known and appreciated, it will be extensively regarded as decidedly superior to any thing that before existed on American history, and as a valuable contribution to American authorship. These stately volumes will be an ornament to any library, and no intelligent American can afford to be without the work. We have nobly patronized the great English history of the age, let us not fail to appreciate and patronize an American history so respectable and valuable as this certainly is.—*Biblical Repository (Bibliotheca Sacra).*

This work professes only to deal in *facts;* it is a book of *records;* it puts together clearly, consecutively, and, we believe, with strict impartiality, the events of American history. The work indicates patient, honest, and careful research, systematic arrangement, and lucid exposition.—*Home Journal.*

To exhibit the progress of the country from infancy to maturity; to show the actual state of the people, the real character of their laws and institutions, and the true designs of their leading men, at different periods, and to relate a sound, unvarnished tale of our early history, has been his design; and we are free to acknowledge that it has been executed with marked ability and triumphant success. Every lover of impartial history will accord to Mr. Hildreth his due meed of praise for the able and honest manner in which he has given the true history of the United States.—*Pennsylvanian.*

This work is full of detail, bears marks of care and research, and is written under the guidance of clear sight and good judgment rather than of theory, philosophical or historical, or of prejudice of any sort whatever. We trust that it will be widely read.—*N. Y. Courier and Enquirer.*

We pronounce it unsurpassed as a full, clear, and truthful history of our country so far. We rejoice that a work so important to our nation has been so ably performed.—*Literary American.*

Interesting, valuable, and very attractive. It is written in a style eminently clear and attractive, and presents the remarkable history which it records in a form of great simplicity and with graphic force. There is in it no attempt to palliate what is wrong, or to conceal what is true. It is a life-like and reliable history of the most remarkable series of events in the annals of the world.—*N. Y. Journal of Commerce.*

It is a valuable acquisition to American literature.—*Baltimore American.*

The history of our country with a scrupulous regard to truth.—*Buffalo Courier.*

We believe this to be a truthful, judicious, and valuable history, worthy of general acceptation.—*Philadelphia North American.*

The first complete history of our country.—*Chronotype.*

Published by HARPER & BROTHERS,
Franklin Square, New York.

*** HARPER & BROTHERS will send the above Work by Mail, postage paid (for any distance in the United States under 3000 miles), on receipt of the Money.

INSTRUCTION AND ENTERTAINMENT FOR THE YOUNG.

Books Adapted to Family, School, Town, District, and Sunday-School Libraries.

BY JACOB AND JOHN S. C. ABBOTT.

Abbotts' Illustrated Histories.

A Series of Volumes by JACOB and JOHN S. C. ABBOTT, containing severally full accounts of the lives, characters, and exploits of the most distinguished Sovereigns, Potentates, and Rulers that have been chiefly renowned among mankind, in the various ages of the world, from the earliest periods to the present day.

The Volumes of this Series are printed and bound uniformly, and are adorned with richly illuminated Title-pages and numerous Engravings. 16mo, Muslin, 60 cents per Volume; Muslin, gilt edges, 75 cents per Volume; Library Sheep, 75 cents per Volume. The Volumes may be obtained separately.

Cyrus the Great.	Alfred the Great.
Darius the Great.	William the Conqueror.
Xerxes.	Mary Queen of Scots.
Alexander the Great.	Queen Elizabeth.
Romulus.	Charles I.
Hannibal.	Charles II.
Pyrrhus.	Josephine.
Julius Cæsar.	Maria Antoinette.
Cleopatra.	Madame Roland.
Nero.	Hernando Cortez.

The narratives are succint and comprehensive, and are strictly faithful to the truth, so far as it can now be ascertained. They are written in a very plain and simple style, but are not *juvenile* in their character, nor intended exclusively for the young. The volumes are sufficiently large to allow each history to comprise all the leading facts in the life of the personage who is the subject of it, and thus to communicate all the information in respect to him which is necessary for the purposes of the general reader.

The several volumes of the series follow each other, in the main, in regular historical order, and each one continues the general narrative of history down to the period at which the next volume takes up the story; so that the whole series will, when completed, present to the reader a connected line of general history from the present age back to the remotest times. Thus the whole series constitutes a very complete and valuable treasury of historical knowledge, while yet each volume, consisting as it does of a single distinct and entertaining narrative, has all the interest, for the reader, of a tale.

Such being the design and character of the works, they would seem to be specially adapted, no tonly for family reading, but also for district, town, school, and Sunday-school Libraries, as well as for text-books in literary seminaries.

The volumes already issued have had a wide circulation in all parts of the country—more than two hundred thousand volumes having been already sold. The plan of the series, and the manner in which the design has been carried out by the authors in the execution of it, have been highly commended by the press in all parts of the country, and many individual parents have spoken of the books as exerting a very powerful influence in awakening a taste for instructive reading among their children, and a love for the acquisition of useful knowledge.

The whole series has been introduced into the school libraries of several of the largest and most influential states.

They have, moreover, been republished in England in many different forms, and have had a wide circulation in that country.

LOSSING'S PICTORIAL FIELD-BOOK

Of the Revolution; or, Illustrations, by Pen and Pencil, of the History, Biography, Scenery, Relics, and Traditions of the War for Independence. 2 vols. Royal 8vo, Muslin, $8 00; Sheep, $9 00; Half Calf, $10 00; Full Morocco, $15 00.

A new and carefully revised edition of this magnificent work is just completed in two imperial octavo volumes of equal size, containing 1500 pages and 1100 engravings. As the plan, scope, and beauty of the work were originally developed, eminent literary men, and the leading presses of the United States and Great Britain, pronounced it one of the most valuable historical productions ever issued.

The preparation of this work occupied the author more than four years, during which he traveled nearly ten thousand miles in order to visit the prominent scenes of revolutionary history, gather up local traditions, and explore records and histories. In the use of his pencil he was governed by the determination to withhold nothing of importance or interest. Being himself both artist and writer, he has been able to combine the materials he had collected in both departments into a work possessing perfect unity of purpose and execution.

The object of the author in arranging his plan was to reproduce the history of the American Revolution in such an attractive manner, as to entice the youth of his country to read the wonderful story, study its philosophy and teachings, and to become familiar with the founders of our Republic and the value of their labors. In this he has been eminently successful; for the young read the pages of the "Field-Book" with the same avidity as those of a romance; while the abundant stores of information, and the careful manner in which it has been arranged and set forth, render it no less attractive to the general reader and the ripe scholar of more mature years.

Explanatory notes are profusely given upon every page in the volume, and also a brief biographical sketch of every man distinguished in the events of the Revolution, the history of whose life is known.

A Supplement of forty pages contains a history of the *Naval Operations of the Revolution*; of the *Diplomacy*; of the *Confederation* and *Federal Constitution*; the *Prisons* and *Prison Ships of New York*; *Lives of the Signers of the Declaration of Independence*, and other matters of curious interest to the historical student.

A new and very elaborate analytical index has been prepared, to which we call special attention. It embraces eighty-five closely printed pages, and possesses rare value for every student of our revolutionary history. It is in itself a complete synopsis of the history and biography of that period, and will be found exceedingly useful for reference by every reader.

As a whole, the work contains all the essential facts of the early history of our Republic, which are scattered through scores of volumes often inaccessible to the great mass of readers. The illustrations make the whole subject of the American Revolution so clear to the reader that, on rising from its perusal, he feels thoroughly acquainted, not only with the history, but with every important locality made memorable by the events of the war for Independence, and it forms a complete Guide-Book to the tourist seeking for fields consecrated by patriotism, which lie scattered over our broad land. Nothing has been spared to make it complete, reliable, and eminently useful to all classes of citizens. Upward of THIRTY-FIVE THOUSAND DOLLARS were expended in the publication of the first edition. The exquisite wood-cuts, engraved under the immediate supervision of the author, from his own drawings, in the highest style of the art, required the greatest care in printing. To this end the efforts of the publishers have been directed, and we take great pleasure in presenting these volumes as the best specimen of typography ever issued from the American press.

The publication of the work having been commenced in numbers before its preparation was completed, the volumes of the first edition were made quite unequal in size. That defect has been remedied, and the work is now presented in two volumes of equal size, containing about 780 pages each.

www.ingramcontent.com/pod-product-compliance
Lightning Source LLC
LaVergne TN
LVHW021107110826
845150LV00001B/190

* 9 7 8 1 4 2 5 5 6 4 6 7 4 *